GLEIM®

2022 EDITION

CIA REVIEW

PART 3: BUSINESS KNOWLEDGE FOR INTERNAL AUDITING

by

Irvin N. Gleim, Ph.D., CPA, CIA, CMA, CFM

Aligned with the 2019 CIA exam reorganization

Gleim Publications, Inc.
PO Box 12848
Gainesville, Florida 32604
(800) 874-5346
(352) 375-0772
www.gleim.com/cia
CIA@gleim.com

For updates to the first printing of the 2022 edition of *CIA Review: Part 3*

Go To: www.gleim.com/updates

Or: Email update@gleim.com with **CIA 3 2022-1** in the subject line. You will receive our current update as a reply.

Updates are available until the next edition is published.

ISSN: 2638-8243

ISBN: 978-1-61854-453-7 *CIA Review: Part 1*
ISBN: 978-1-61854-454-4 *CIA Review: Part 2*
ISBN: 978-1-61854-455-1 *CIA Review: Part 3*
ISBN: 978-1-61854-357-8 *CIA Exam Guide: A System for Success*

This edition is copyright © 2021 by Gleim Publications, Inc. Portions of this manuscript are taken from previous editions copyright © 1981-2020 by Gleim Publications, Inc.

First Printing: June 2021

ALL RIGHTS RESERVED. No part of this material may be reproduced in any form whatsoever without express written permission from Gleim Publications, Inc. Reward is offered for information exposing violators. Contact copyright@gleim.com.

ACKNOWLEDGMENTS FOR PART 3

The author is grateful for permission to reproduce the following materials copyrighted by The Institute of Internal Auditors: Certified Internal Auditor Examination Questions and Suggested Solutions (copyright © 1980-2020), excerpts from *Sawyer's Internal Auditing* (5th, 6th, and 7th editions), parts of the 2021 *Certification Candidate Handbook*, and the International Professional Practices Framework.

CIA® is a Registered Trademark of The Institute of Internal Auditors, Inc. All rights reserved.

Environmental Statement -- This book is printed on recycled paper sourced from suppliers certified using sustainable forestry management processes and is produced either TCF (Totally Chlorine-Free) or ECF (Elementally Chlorine-Free).

The publications and online services of Gleim Publications and Gleim Internet are designed to provide accurate and authoritative information with regard to the subject matter covered. They are sold with the understanding that Gleim Publications and Gleim Internet, and their respective licensors, are not engaged in rendering legal, accounting, tax, or other professional advice or services. If legal advice or other expert assistance is required, the services of a competent professional person should be sought.

You assume all responsibilities and obligations with respect to the selection of the particular publication or online services to achieve your intended results. You assume all responsibilities and obligations with respect to any decisions or advice made or given as a result of the use or application of your selected publication or online services or any content retrieved therefrom, including those to any third party, for the content, accuracy, and review of such results.

The events, persons, and locations depicted in this book are fictional and not intended to portray, resemble, or represent any actual events or places, or persons, living or dead. Any such resemblance or similarity is entirely coincidental.

ABOUT THE AUTHOR

Irvin N. Gleim is Professor Emeritus in the Fisher School of Accounting at the University of Florida and is a member of the American Accounting Association, Academy of Legal Studies in Business, American Institute of Certified Public Accountants, Association of Government Accountants, Florida Institute of Certified Public Accountants, The Institute of Internal Auditors, and the Institute of Management Accountants. He has had articles published in the *Journal of Accountancy*, *The Accounting Review*, and the *American Business Law Journal* and is author/coauthor of numerous accounting books, aviation books, and CPE courses.

REVIEWERS AND CONTRIBUTORS

Garrett W. Gleim, CPA, CGMA, leads production of the Gleim CPA, CMA, CIA, and EA exam review systems. He is a member of the American Institute of Certified Public Accountants and the Florida Institute of Certified Public Accountants and holds a Bachelor of Science in Economics with a Concentration in Accounting from The Wharton School, University of Pennsylvania. Mr. Gleim is coauthor of numerous accounting and aviation books and the inventor of multiple patents with educational applications. He is also an avid pilot who holds a commercial pilot rating and is a certified flight instructor. In addition, as an active supporter of the local business community, Mr. Gleim serves as an advisor to several start-ups.

Grady M. Irwin, J.D., is a graduate of the University of Florida College of Law, and he has taught in the University of Florida College of Business. Mr. Irwin provided substantial editorial assistance throughout the project.

Lung-Chih Lin, M.S. Acc., received a Master of Science in Accountancy with a concentration in Data Analytics from the University of Illinois at Urbana-Champaign. Mr. Lin provided substantial editorial assistance throughout the project.

Joseph Mauriello, CIA, CISA, CPA, CFE, CMA, CFSA, CRMA, is a Senior Lecturer as well as the Director of the Center for Internal Auditing Excellence at the University of Texas at Dallas. He is also active in his local chapter of The IIA and currently holds the title of Past President. Professor Mauriello is the lead CIA Gleim Instruct lecturer and provided substantial editorial assistance throughout the project.

Mark S. Modas, M.S.T., CPA, holds a Bachelor of Arts in Accounting from Florida Atlantic University and a Master of Science in Taxation from Nova Southeastern University. Prior to joining Gleim, he worked in internal auditing, accounting and financial reporting, and corporate tax compliance in the public and private sectors. Mr. Modas provided substantial editorial assistance throughout the project.

Yiqian Zhao, M.Acc., CIA, CPA, CFE, CISA, received a Bachelor of Science in Accounting from Missouri State University, a bachelor's degree in International Business Administration from Liaoning Normal University, and a Master of Accounting degree from the University of Florida. Ms. Zhao provided substantial editorial assistance throughout the project.

A PERSONAL THANKS

This manual would not have been possible without the extraordinary effort and dedication of Jacob Bennett, Julie Cutlip, Ethan Good, Doug Green, Fernanda Martinez, Bree Rodriguez, Veronica Rodriguez, Teresa Soard, Justin Stephenson, Joanne Strong, Elmer Tucker, Candace Van Doren, and Ryan Van Tress, who typed the entire manuscript and all revisions and drafted and laid out the diagrams, illustrations, and cover for this book.

The author also appreciates the production and editorial assistance of Brianna Barnett, Sirene Dagher, Michaela Giampaolo, Jessica Hatker, Katie Larson, Bryce Owen, Shane Rapp, Michael Tamayo, and Alyssa Thomas.

The author also appreciates the critical reading assistance of Amanda Allen, Ali Band, Adrianna Cuevas, Kimberly Haft, Melissa Leonard, Nicola Martens, Tom Murphy, Maris Silvestri, and Chun Nam Wo.

The author also appreciates the video production expertise of Nancy Boyd, Gary Brook, Philip Brubaker, Matthew Church, Andrew Johnson, and Michaela Wallace, who helped produce and edit our Gleim Instruct Video Series.

Finally, we appreciate the encouragement, support, and tolerance of our families throughout this project.

Returns of books purchased from bookstores and other resellers should be made to the respective bookstore or reseller. For more information regarding the Gleim Return Policy, please contact our offices at (800) 874-5346 or visit www.gleim.com/returnpolicy.

TABLE OF CONTENTS

	Page
Detailed Table of Contents	vi
Preface	viii
Preparing for and Taking the CIA Exam	1
Study Unit 1. Strategic Management and Planning	9
Study Unit 2. Organizational Behavior and Performance Measures	39
Study Unit 3. Leadership, Organizational Structure, and Business Processes	69
Study Unit 4. Project Management and Contracts	119
Study Unit 5. Workstations, Databases, and Applications	149
Study Unit 6. IT Infrastructure	181
Study Unit 7. IT Framework and Data Analytics	209
Study Unit 8. Information Security and Disaster Recovery	245
Study Unit 9. Concepts and Underlying Principles of Financial Accounting	279
Study Unit 10. Advanced Financial Accounting Concepts and Analysis	329
Study Unit 11. Current Assets Management	371
Study Unit 12. Capital Structure and Budget, Basic Taxation, and Transfer Pricing	397
Study Unit 13. Managerial Accounting: General Concepts	435
Study Unit 14. Managerial Accounting: Costing Systems and Decision Making	467
Appendix A: The IIA CIA Exam Syllabus and Cross-References	505
Appendix B: The IIA Examination Bibliography	509
Appendix C: Sample Financial Statements	511
Appendix D: Glossary of Accounting Terms U.S. to British vs. British to U.S.	515
Index	517

DETAILED TABLE OF CONTENTS

	Page
Study Unit 1. Strategic Management and Planning	
1.1. Strategic Management and Planning	9
1.2. Globalization	19
Study Unit 2. Organizational Behavior and Performance Measures	
2.1. Organizational Theory	40
2.2. Motivation -- Need-Based Theories and Rewards	44
2.3. Motivation -- Process-Based Theories, Behavior, Job Design, and Other	48
2.4. Organizational Politics and Group Dynamics	51
2.5. Performance Measures -- Costs of Quality	57
2.6. Performance Measures -- Balanced Scorecard	58
Study Unit 3. Leadership, Organizational Structure, and Business Processes	
3.1. Leadership	69
3.2. Organizational Structure	81
3.3. Business Process -- Human Resources and Outsourcing	95
3.4. Business Process -- Pricing and the Supply Chain	101
3.5. Business Process -- Procurement	105
Study Unit 4. Project Management and Contracts	
4.1. Project Management -- Concepts	119
4.2. Project Management -- Techniques	128
4.3. Change Management	133
4.4. Contracts	134
4.5. Classification of Contracts	138
Study Unit 5. Workstations, Databases, and Applications	
5.1. Workstations and Databases	149
5.2. Application Development and Maintenance	163
Study Unit 6. IT Infrastructure	
6.1. Functional Areas of IT Operations	182
6.2. Web Infrastructure	184
6.3. IT System Communications and Software Licensing	188
6.4. Systems that Support Routine Processes	197
Study Unit 7. IT Framework and Data Analytics	
7.1. IT Control Frameworks and International Organization for Standardization (ISO) Framework	209
7.2. Aspects of Automated Information Processing	223
7.3. IT Controls	225
7.4. Data Analytics	230
Study Unit 8. Information Security and Disaster Recovery	
8.1. Information Security and Cybersecurity Related Policies and Controls	246
8.2. Authentication, Authorization, and Encryption	252
8.3. Information Protection	254
8.4. Contingency Planning and Disaster Recovery	265
Study Unit 9. Concepts and Underlying Principles of Financial Accounting	
9.1. Concepts of Financial Accounting	280
9.2. Financial Statements	283
9.3. The Accrual Basis of Accounting	290
9.4. The Accounting Process	293
9.5. Cash, Accounts Receivable, and Inventory	296
9.6. Property, Plant, and Equipment and Intangible Assets	301
9.7. Accounts Payable, Accrued Expenses, and Deposits and Other Advances	305
9.8. The Time Value of Money	309
9.9. Bonds	311
9.10. Pensions	314
9.11. Leases and Contingencies	316

Detailed Table of Contents

	Page
Study Unit 10. Advanced Financial Accounting Concepts and Analysis	
10.1. Risk and Return	330
10.2. Derivatives	333
10.3. Foreign Currency Transactions	337
10.4. Business Combinations and Consolidated Financial Statements	340
10.5. Corporate Equity Accounts and Partnerships	344
10.6. Financial Statement Analysis -- Liquidity Ratios	346
10.7. Financial Statement Analysis -- Activity Ratios	349
10.8. Financial Statement Analysis -- Solvency Ratios and Leverage	354
10.9. Financial Statement Analysis -- ROI and Profitability	356
10.10. Financial Statement Analysis -- Corporate Valuation and Common-Size Financial Statements Ratios	359
Study Unit 11. Current Assets Management	
11.1. Working Capital and Cash Management	371
11.2. Receivables Management	375
11.3. Managing Inventory Costs and Quantities	378
11.4. Inventory Management Methods	380
11.5. Inventory Systems	384
Study Unit 12. Capital Structure and Budget, Basic Taxation, and Transfer Pricing	
12.1. Corporate Capital Structure -- Debt Financing	397
12.2. Corporate Capital Structure -- Equity Financing	400
12.3. Corporate Capital Structure -- Cost of Capital	404
12.4. Capital Budgeting	408
12.5. Short-Term Financing	414
12.6. Methods of Taxation	418
12.7. Transfer Pricing	422
Study Unit 13. Managerial Accounting: General Concepts	
13.1. Cost Management Terminology	435
13.2. Budget Systems	437
13.3. Budget Methods	446
13.4. Cost-Volume-Profit (CVP) Analysis and Cost-Benefit Analysis	449
13.5. Responsibility Accounting	456
Study Unit 14. Managerial Accounting: Costing Systems and Decision Making	
14.1. Cost Behavior and Relevant Range	468
14.2. Activity-Based Costing	471
14.3. Process Costing	477
14.4. Absorption (Full) vs. Variable (Direct) Costing	483
14.5. Relevant Costs and Decision Making	487

PREFACE

In 1980, I set out with one mission: to help **you** prepare to pass the CIA exam. For over 40 years, our goal has been to provide an affordable, effective, and easy-to-use study program. While the delivery and technology have changed and are always evolving, our mission and the core learning techniques that we have perfected over decades remain the same. Our course

1. Explains how to optimize your score through learning strategies and exam-taking techniques.
2. Outlines all of the subject matter tested on Part 3 in 14 easy-to-use study units, including all relevant authoritative pronouncements.
3. Presents multiple-choice questions from past CIA examinations to prepare you for the types of questions you will find on your CIA exams.
    a. In our book, our answer explanations are presented to the immediate right of each multiple-choice question for your convenience. Use a piece of paper to cover our detailed explanations as you answer the question and then review all answer choices to learn why the correct one is correct and why the other choices are incorrect.
    b. You also should practice answering these questions through our online platform so you are comfortable answering questions online like you will do on test day. Our adaptive course will focus and target your weak areas.
4. Contains The IIA Glossary, The IIA Examination Bibliography, and a cross-reference between The IIA CIA Exam Syllabus and the Gleim CIA materials.

The outline format, the spacing, and the question-and-answer formats in this book are designed to facilitate readability, learning, understanding, and success on the CIA exam. Our most successful candidates use the Gleim Premium CIA Review System*, which includes our innovative SmartAdapt technology, first-of-their-kind Gleim Instruct video lectures, the Gleim Access Until You Pass guarantee, and comprehensive exam-emulating test questions. Candidates' success is based on the Gleim system of teaching not only the topics tested, but also what you can expect on exam day. Using Gleim, you will feel confident and in control when you sit for the exam.

We want your feedback immediately after the exam upon receipt of your exam scores. The CIA exam is nondisclosed, and you must maintain the confidentiality and agree not to divulge the nature or content of any CIA question or answer under any circumstances. We ask only for information about our materials, i.e., the topics that need to be added, expanded, etc.

Please go to www.gleim.com/feedbackCIA3 to share your suggestions on how we can improve this edition.

Good Luck on the Exam,

Irvin N. Gleim

June 2021

*Visit www.gleimcia.com or call (800) 874-5346 to order.

ACCOUNTING TITLES FROM GLEIM PUBLICATIONS

CIA Review:

- Part 1: Essentials of Internal Auditing
- Part 2: Practice of Internal Auditing
- Part 3: Business Knowledge for Internal Auditing

CMA Review:

- Part 1: Financial Planning, Performance, and Analytics
- Part 2: Strategic Financial Management

CPA Review:

- Auditing & Attestation (AUD)
- Business Environment & Concepts (BEC)
- Financial Accounting & Reporting (FAR)
- Regulation (REG)

EA Review:

- Part 1: Individuals
- Part 2: Businesses
- Part 3: Representation, Practices and Procedures

Exam Questions and Explanations (EQE) Series:

- Auditing & Systems
- Business Law & Legal Studies
- Cost/Managerial Accounting
- Federal Tax
- Financial Accounting

Gleim Publications also publishes aviation training materials. Go to www.GleimAviation.com for a complete listing of our aviation titles.

PREPARING FOR AND TAKING THE CIA EXAM

Read the CIA Exam Guide: A System for Success	1
Overview of the CIA Examination	1
Subject Matter for Part 3	2
Which Pronouncements Are Tested?	2
Nondisclosed Exam	2
The IIA's Requirements for CIA Designations	3
Eligibility Period	3
Maintaining Your CIA Designation	3
Gleim CIA Review with SmartAdapt	4
Gleim Knowledge Transfer Outlines	5
Time-Budgeting and Question-Answering Techniques for the Exam	6
Learning from Your Mistakes	7
How to Be in Control while Taking the Exam	7
If You Have Questions about Gleim Materials	8
Feedback	8

READ THE *CIA EXAM GUIDE: A SYSTEM FOR SUCCESS*

Access the free Gleim *CIA Exam Guide* at www.gleim.com/passCIA and reference it as needed throughout your studying process to obtain a deeper understanding of the CIA exam. This booklet is your system for success.

OVERVIEW OF THE CIA EXAMINATION

The total exam is 6.5 hours of testing (including 5 minutes per part for a survey). It is divided into three parts, as follows:

CIA Exam (3-Part)

Part	Title	Exam Length	Number of Questions
1	Essentials of Internal Auditing	2.5 hrs	125 multiple-choice
2	Practice of Internal Auditing	2 hrs	100 multiple-choice
3	Business Knowledge for Internal Auditing	2 hrs	100 multiple-choice

All CIA questions are multiple-choice. The exam is offered continually throughout the year. The CIA exam is computerized to facilitate easier and more convenient testing. Pearson VUE, the testing company that The IIA contracts to proctor the exams, has hundreds of testing centers worldwide. The online components of Gleim CIA Review provide exact exam emulations of the Pearson VUE computer screens and procedures so you feel comfortable at the testing center on exam day.

SUBJECT MATTER FOR PART 3

Below, we have provided The IIA's abbreviated CIA Exam Syllabus for Part 3. This syllabus is for the revised CIA exam offered since January 1, 2019. The percentage coverage of each topic is indicated to its right. We adjust the content of our materials to any changes in The IIA's CIA Exam Syllabus.

Part 3: Business Knowledge for Internal Auditing

I. Business Acumen	35%
II. Information Security	25%
III. Information Technology	20%
IV. Financial Management	20%

At the time of print, exams for the revised syllabus are currently available in Arabic, Simplified Chinese, Traditional Chinese, English, French, German, Japanese, Korean, Polish, Portuguese, Russian, Spanish, Thai, and Turkish. Candidates taking the exam in these languages should use this 2022 edition of Gleim CIA Review.

Appendix A contains the CIA Exam Syllabus in its entirety as well as cross-references to the subunits in our text where topics are covered. Remember that we have studied the syllabus in developing our CIA Review materials. Accordingly, you do not need to spend time with Appendix A. Rather, it should give you confidence that Gleim CIA Review is the best and most comprehensive review course available to help you PASS the CIA exam.

WHICH PRONOUNCEMENTS ARE TESTED?

New pronouncements are eligible to be tested on the CIA exam beginning 6 months after a pronouncement's effective date. Rest assured that Gleim updates our materials as appropriate when any new standard is testable and will only cover what candidates need for the current CIA exam.

NONDISCLOSED EXAM

As part of The IIA's nondisclosure policy and to prove each candidate's willingness to adhere to this policy, a Nondisclosure Agreement and General Terms of Use must be accepted by each candidate before each part is taken. This statement is reproduced here to remind all CIA candidates about The IIA's strict policy of nondisclosure, which Gleim consistently supports and upholds.

I agree to comply with and be bound by The IIA's rules, including this nondisclosure agreement and general terms of use.

I understand that The IIA's exam is confidential and secure, protected by civil and criminal laws of the United States and elsewhere. This exam is confidential and is protected by copyright law.

I have not accessed live questions that might appear on my exam. I agree not to discuss the content of the exam with anyone.

I will not record, copy, disclose, publish, or reproduce any exam questions or answers, in whole or in part, in any form or by any means before, during, or after I take an exam, including orally; in writing; in any internet chat room, message board, or forum; by SMS or text; or otherwise.

I have read, understand, and agree to the terms and conditions set forth in The IIA's Certification Candidate Handbook, including fees, policies, and score invalidations for misconduct, irregularities, or breaches of The IIA's Code of Ethics.

I agree that The IIA has the right to withhold or invalidate any exam score when, in The IIA's judgment, there is a good faith basis to question the validity of a score for any reason, and I will forfeit my exam fee.

I understand that if I do not agree to this nondisclosure agreement and these conditions, I will not be permitted to take the exam, and I will forfeit my exam fee.

THE IIA'S REQUIREMENTS FOR CIA DESIGNATIONS

The CIA designation is granted only by The IIA. Candidates must complete the following steps to become a CIA®:

1. Complete the appropriate certification application form and register for the part(s) you are going to take. Check the CIA blog at www.gleim.com/CIAApply for more information on the application and registration process. The CIA Review course provides a useful checklist to help you keep track of your progress and organize what you need for exam day.
2. Pass all three parts of the CIA exam within 3 years of application approval (4 years if approved before September 1, 2019).
3. Fulfill or expect to fulfill the education and experience requirements (see the free Gleim *CIA Exam Guide*).
4. Provide a character reference proving you are of good moral character.
5. Comply with The IIA's Code of Ethics.

ELIGIBILITY PERIOD

Credits for parts passed can be retained as long as the requirements are fulfilled. Candidates accepted into the certification program **on or after September 1, 2019,** must complete the program certification process within **3 years** of application approval. Candidates should note that this time period begins with application approval and not when they pass the first part. If a candidate has not completed the certification process within 3 years, all fees and previously passed exam parts will be forfeited.

NOTE: Candidates who received application approval **before September 1, 2019,** have **4 years** to complete the certification process. If a candidate approved into the program before September 1, 2019, does not complete the certification process within 4 years, all fees and previously passed exam parts will be forfeited.

Eligibility Extension: Candidates who have not successfully completed their exam(s), or who have been accepted into the program but have not taken their exam(s), have the opportunity to extend their program eligibility by 12 months. To take advantage of The IIA's one-time Certification Candidate Program Extension, candidates must pay a set fee per applicant and apply through the Candidate Management System.

Transition Information: Candidates who passed one or two parts of the exam prior to 2019 and still need to pass one or two parts will not lose credit for the part(s) already passed. Credit for any part(s) passed in the pre-2019 version of the exam remains valid for the 4-year eligibility window that begins with the application date.

MAINTAINING YOUR CIA DESIGNATION

After certification, CIAs are required to maintain and update their knowledge and skills. Practicing CIAs must complete and report 40 hours of Continuing Professional Education (CPE)–including 2 hours of ethics training–every year. The reporting deadline is December 31. Complete your CPE Reporting Form through the online Certification Candidate Management System. Processing fees vary based on location, membership status, and the method you use to report. Contact Gleim for all of your CPE needs at www.gleim.com/cpe.

GLEIM CIA REVIEW WITH SMARTADAPT

Gleim Premium CIA Review features the most comprehensive coverage of exam content and employs the most efficient learning techniques to help you study smarter and most effectively. The Gleim CIA Review System is powered by SmartAdapt technology, an innovative platform that continually zeros in on areas you should focus on when you move through the following steps for optimized CIA review:

Step 1:

Complete a Diagnostic Quiz. As you work through this quiz, you will get immediate feedback on your answer choices. This allows you to learn as you study the detailed answer explanations. Your quiz results set a baseline that our SmartAdapt technology will use to create a custom learning track.

Step 2:

Solidify your knowledge by studying the suggested Knowledge Transfer Outline(s) or watching the suggested Gleim Instruct video(s).

Step 3:

Focus on weak areas and perfect your question-answering techniques by taking the adaptive quizzes that SmartAdapt directs you to.

Final Review:

After completing all study units, take the first Exam Rehearsal, a full-length mock exam. Then, SmartAdapt will guide you through a Final Review based on your results. Finally, a few days before your exam date, take the second Exam Rehearsal. SmartAdapt will tell you when you are ready to pass with confidence.

To facilitate your studies, the Gleim Premium CIA Review System uses the most comprehensive test bank of exam-quality CIA questions on the market. Our system's content and presentation are the most realistic representation of the whole exam environment so you feel completely at ease on test day.

GLEIM KNOWLEDGE TRANSFER OUTLINES

This edition of the Gleim CIA Review books has the following features to make studying easier:

1. **Examples:** We use illustrative examples, set off in shaded, bordered boxes, to make the concepts more relatable.

EXAMPLE 4-4	Implied Contract
Kelly makes an appointment with a hairdresser. Kelly keeps the appointment and permits the hairdresser to cut her hair. Kelly has promised through her actions to pay for the haircut. A court infers from Kelly's conduct that an implied contract was formed and a duty to pay was understood and agreed to.	

2. **Gleim Success Tips:** These tips supplement the core exam material by suggesting how certain topics might be presented on the exam or how you should prepare for an issue.

An organization's strategic planning process flows from an understanding of its mission, its businesses and their markets, and the appropriate competitive strategy for each business.

3. **Stop and Review:** These reminders at the end of every subunit prompt you to practice with related multiple-choice questions so that you can solidify your understanding of the material before moving on to the next topic.

You have completed the outline for this subunit.
Study multiple-choice questions 1 through 10 beginning on page 29.

4. **Backgrounds:** In certain instances, we have provided historical background or supplemental information. This information is intended to illuminate the topic under discussion and is set off in bordered boxes with shaded headings. This material does not need to be memorized for the exam.

BACKGROUND 6-2	ERP
Because ERP software is costly and complex, it is usually installed only by the largest enterprises, although mid-size organizations are increasingly likely to buy ERP software. Major ERP packages include SAP ERP Central Component from SAP SE and Oracle e-Business Suite, PeopleSoft, and JD Edwards EnterpriseOne, all from Oracle Corp.	

TIME-BUDGETING AND QUESTION-ANSWERING TECHNIQUES FOR THE EXAM

Having a solid multiple-choice answering technique will help you maximize your score on each part of the CIA exam. Remember, knowing how to take the exam and how to answer individual questions is as important as studying/reviewing the subject matter tested on the exam. Competency in both will reduce your stress and the number of surprises you experience on exam day.

1. **Budget your time so you can finish before time expires.**
   - Spend about 1 minute per question. This would result in completing 100 questions in 100 minutes to give you 20 minutes to review your answers and questions that you have marked.

2. **Answer the questions in consecutive order.**
   - Do **not** agonize over any one item or question. Stay within your time budget.
   - Never leave a multiple-choice question (MCQ) unanswered. Your score is based on the number of correct responses. You will not be penalized for answering incorrectly. If you are unsure about a question,
     - Make an educated guess,
     - Mark it for review at the bottom of the screen, and
     - Return to it before you submit your exam as time allows.

3. **Ignore the answer choices so that they will not affect your precise reading of the question.**
   - Only one answer option is best. In the MCQs, four answer choices are presented, and you know one of them is correct. The remaining choices are distractors and are meant to appear correct at first glance. *They are called distractors for a reason.* Eliminate them as quickly as you can.
   - In computational items, the distractors are carefully calculated to be the result of common mistakes. Be careful and double-check your computations if time permits.

4. **Read the question carefully to discover exactly what is being asked.**
   - Focusing on what is required allows you to
     - Reject extraneous information
     - Concentrate on relevant facts
     - Proceed directly to determining the best answer
   - Be careful! The requirement may be an **exception** that features a negative word.

5. **Decide the correct answer before looking at the answer choices.**

6. **Read the answer choices, paying attention to small details.**
   - Even if an answer choice appears to be correct, do not skip the remaining answer choices. Each choice requires consideration because you are looking for the best answer provided.
   - Tip: Treat each answer choice like a true/false question as you analyze it.

7. **Click on the best answer.**
   - You have a 25% chance of answering the question correctly by guessing blindly, but you can improve your odds with an educated guess.
   - For many MCQs, you can eliminate two answer choices with minimal effort and increase your educated guess to a 50/50 proposition.
     - Rule out answers that you think are incorrect.
     - Speculate what The IIA is looking for and/or why the question is being asked.
     - Select the best answer or guess between equally appealing answers. Your first guess is usually the most intuitive.

LEARNING FROM YOUR MISTAKES

Learning from questions you answer incorrectly is very important. Each question you answer incorrectly is an **opportunity** to avoid missing actual test questions on your CIA exam. Thus, you should carefully study the answer explanations provided until you understand why the original answer you chose is wrong, as well as why the correct answer indicated is correct. This study technique is clearly the difference between passing and failing for many CIA candidates.

Also, you **must** determine why you answered questions incorrectly and learn how to avoid the same error in the future. Reasons for missing questions include

1. Misreading the requirement (stem)
2. Not understanding what is required
3. Making a math error
4. Applying the wrong rule or concept
5. Being distracted by one or more of the answers
6. Incorrectly eliminating answers from consideration
7. Not having any knowledge of the topic tested
8. Employing bad intuition when guessing

It is also important to verify that you answered correctly for the right reasons. Otherwise, if the material is tested on the CIA exam in a different manner, you may not answer it correctly.

HOW TO BE IN CONTROL WHILE TAKING THE EXAM

You have to be in control to be successful during exam preparation and execution. Control can also contribute greatly to your personal and other professional goals. Control is a process whereby you

1. Develop expectations, standards, budgets, and plans
2. Undertake activity, production, study, and learning
3. Measure the activity, production, output, and knowledge
4. Compare actual activity with expected and budgeted activity
5. Modify the activity, behavior, or study to better achieve the desired outcome
6. Revise expectations and standards in light of actual experience
7. Continue the process or restart the process in the future

Exercising control will ultimately develop the confidence you need to outperform most other CIA candidates and PASS the CIA exam! Obtain our *CIA Exam Guide* for a more detailed discussion of control and other exam tactics.

IF YOU HAVE QUESTIONS ABOUT GLEIM MATERIALS

Gleim has an efficient and effective way for candidates who have purchased the Premium CIA Review System to submit an inquiry and receive a response regarding Gleim materials directly through their course. This system also allows you to view your Q&A session in your Gleim Personal Classroom.

Questions regarding the **information in this introduction and/or the *CIA Exam Guide* (study suggestions, studying plans, exam specifics)** should be emailed to personalcounselor@gleim.com.

Questions concerning **orders, prices, shipments, or payments** should be sent via email to customerservice@gleim.com and will be promptly handled by our competent and courteous customer service staff.

For **technical support**, you may use our automated technical support service at www.gleim.com/support, email us at support@gleim.com, or call us at (800) 874-5346.

FEEDBACK

Please fill out our online feedback form (www.gleim.com/feedbackCIA3) immediately after you take the CIA exam so we can adapt to changes in the exam. Our approach has been approved by The IIA.

GLEIM CIA REVIEW

Gleim CIA has trained more CIAs than any other review course.

See why it is the #1 CIA Prep Course!

Not only were the Gleim course materials a great aid in helping me to pass sections 1-3, but the Gleim team was also amazing to work with. From the purchase of my materials and throughout studying, the folks at Gleim were supportive and encouraging. They provided great tips for success and followed up with me regularly to help keep me on target. Great materials and a really great group of folks! Could not have asked for a better experience! 5 Stars.

Whitney Greene, CIA

GLEIMCIA.COM   800.874.5346

STUDY UNIT ONE
STRATEGIC MANAGEMENT AND PLANNING

(20 pages of outline)

1.1	Strategic Management and Planning	9
1.2	Globalization	19

This study unit is the first of five covering **Domain I: Business Acumen** from The IIA's CIA Exam Syllabus. (Data Analytics, the final topic area of this domain, is covered in Study Unit 7.) This domain makes up 35% of Part 3 of the CIA exam and is tested at the **basic** and **proficient** cognitive levels. Refer to the complete syllabus located in Appendix A to view the relevant sections covered in Study Unit 1.

SUCCESS TIP

An organization's strategic planning process flows from an understanding of its mission, its businesses and their markets, and the appropriate competitive strategy for each business.

1.1 STRATEGIC MANAGEMENT AND PLANNING

1. A **strategy** is a plan to

    a. Allocate resources and actions to succeed in the entity's competitive environment,
    b. Obtain a competitive advantage, and
    c. Attain its highest level goals.

2. **Strategic management** is the set of decisions and activities needed to create strategies and implement them effectively.

3. **Planning** generally involves setting goals and specifying the means to be used. Plans must be established at each level of a complex organization.

    a. At the strategic level, a **mission** statement is drafted (generally by the board of directors) to explain the organization's purposes and values. It is also the ultimate basis for the goals and plans at each level of the organization and for stating the organization's primary competitive scopes. These scopes may extend to

        1) Industries,
        2) Products and services,
        3) Applications,
        4) Core competencies,
        5) Market segments,
        6) Degree of vertical integration, and
        7) Geographic markets.

    b. Businesses should be defined in market terms, that is, in terms of needs and customer groups. Moreover, a distinction should be made between a target market definition and a strategic market definition.

        1) For example, a target market for a railroad might be freight hauling, but a strategic market might be transportation of any goods and people.

c. A business also may be defined with respect to customer groups and their needs and the technology required to satisfy those needs.

d. A large firm has multiple businesses. Thus, the concept of the strategic business unit (SBU) is useful for strategic planning by large firms.

   1) An SBU is a business (or a group) for which separate planning is possible. It also has its own competitors and a manager who engages in strategic planning and is responsible for the major determinants of profit.

4. **Implementation**

   a. Strategic plans must be passed down the organizational structure through development of plans at each lower level. This process is most likely to succeed if

      1) The structure is compatible with strategic planning,
      2) Personnel have the necessary abilities,
      3) The organizational culture is favorable or can be changed, and
      4) Controls exist to facilitate implementation.

5. **Controls**

   a. Strategic controls should be established to monitor progress, isolate problems, identify invalid assumptions, and take prompt corrective action.

      1) As plans are executed at each organizational level, control measurements are made to determine whether objectives have been achieved. Thus, objectives flow down the organizational hierarchy, and control measures flow up.

      2) One category of strategic control measures relates to external effectiveness.

         a) At the business-unit level, performance in the marketplace (market share, etc.) is measured.
         b) At the business-operating-system level, customer satisfaction and flexibility are measured.
         c) At the departmental or work-center level, quality and delivery are measured.

      3) A second category of strategic control measures relates to internal efficiency.

         a) At the business-unit level, financial results are measured.
         b) At the business-operating-system level, flexibility (both an external effectiveness and internal efficiency issue) is measured.
         c) At the departmental or work-center level, cycle time (time to change raw materials into a finished product) and waste are measured.

      4) Senior managers broadly define **strategic** goals and plans for the entire organization.

   b. Middle managers develop **tactical** goals and plans needed to achieve strategic goals.

      1) Tactical plans are shorter-term and more detailed than strategic plans.

   c. Lower managers and supervisors develop **operational** goals and plans to achieve the strategic and tactical goals and plans.

      1) Operational plans are short-term, detailed, and measurable at the departmental or lower levels.

6. **Organizational planning** has the following phases:
    a. **Plan development** includes drafting a mission statement setting strategic goals and an overall plan.
    b. **Translation** of the plan at the tactical level includes
        1) Establishing objectives and plans.
        2) **Strategy mapping** of the objectives and plans to strategic goals.
        3) Contingency planning.
        4) Building **scenarios** to anticipate what might occur rather than merely reacting to what has already occurred.
        5) Appointing teams to engage in **boundary spanning** activities to connect the organization to its external environment.
            a) **Business intelligence** uses such tools as **big data analytics** to discover patterns, trends, and relationships. These tools rely on advanced software to search vast amounts of internal and external information.
            b) **Competitive intelligence** activities are directed towards rivals.
    c. **Operational planning and execution** require choosing performance targets that are
        1) Specific,
        2) Measurable,
        3) Challenging but reasonably attainable,
        4) Time limited, and
        5) Related to the entity's key performance indicators.
    d. Operational planning and execution also involve the following when attempting to meet performance targets:
        1) **Management by objectives (MBO)** is a systematic, cooperative method by which employees and managers
            a) Set goals at all levels,
            b) Establish action plans,
            c) Review progress,
            d) Take corrective action, and
            e) Evaluate final performance.
                i) A modification of MBO is **management by means (MBM)**. It addresses not only measurable goals, but also how they are achieved. The principle is that meeting expectations by inappropriate means is self-defeating.
        2) **Crisis planning** anticipates and prepares for disastrous events, e.g., a major labor strike or natural disaster.
            a) **Crisis prevention** consists of steps to avoid, or detect signs of, a crisis. A key element is creating strong relationships with stakeholders (e.g., customers, suppliers, and employees).
            b) **Crisis preparation** entails
                i) Assembling a crisis management team,
                ii) Developing a crisis management plan, and
                iii) Establishing emergency communications media.
        3) **Stretch goals** extend so far beyond the normal, incremental range of goal-setting that they can be attained only by paradigm-shifting innovation. But such goals must not be unreasonable if employees are to be inspired, not discouraged.

7. **Strategic management** seeks to obtain a **competitive advantage** that differentiates the organization and allows it to be successful in its environment. A competitive advantage has four aspects.
    a. Strategies should be developed that target specific **customers** whose needs can be met by the organization.
    b. The organization must be able to take advantage of **core competencies**, the things it does better than its competitors.
    c. Strategic management is facilitated when managers think synergistically. **Synergy** exists when a combination of formerly separate elements has a greater effect than the sum of their individual effects.
        1) **Market** synergy results when products or services have positive complementary effects. An example in the entertainment industry is a distributor's acquisition of content providers.
        2) **Cost** synergy reduces costs. It occurs in many ways, for example, in the recycling of by-products or in the design, production, marketing, and sales of a line of products by the same enterprise.
        3) **Technological** synergy is the transfer of technology among applications. For example, technology developed for military purposes often has civilian uses.
        4) **Management** synergy also involves knowledge transfer. For example, a firm may hire a manager with skills that it lacks.
    d. Providing **value** to the customers is crucial to an effective strategy.

8. **Operations Strategies**
    a. An operations strategy is reflected in a long-term plan for using resources to reach strategic objectives. The following are five operations strategies:
        1) A **cost** strategy is successful when the enterprise is the low-cost producer. However,
            a) The product (e.g., a commodity) tends to be undifferentiated in these cases.
                i) A product is undifferentiated when competitors sell essentially the same thing, such as the same kind of grain.
            b) The market is often very large.
            c) The competition tends to be intense because of the possibility of high-volume sales.
        2) A **quality** strategy involves competition based on product quality or process quality.
            a) Product quality relates to design, for example, the difference between a luxury car and a subcompact car.
            b) Process quality is the degree of freedom from defects.
        3) A **delivery** strategy may permit an enterprise to charge a higher price when the product is consistently delivered rapidly and on time. An example firm is UPS.
        4) A **flexibility** strategy involves offering many different products or an ability to shift rapidly from one product line to another.
            a) An example firm is a publisher that can write, edit, print, and distribute a book within days to exploit the public's short-term interest in a sensational event.
        5) A **service** strategy seeks to gain a competitive advantage and maximize customer value by providing services, especially post-purchase services, such as warranties on automobiles and home appliances.

9. **SWOT analysis** facilitates development of an overall strategy as a basis for planning to achieve the organization's mission. This process considers organizational strengths and weaknesses (a capability profile) and their interactions with environmental opportunities and threats.

   a. **Strengths and weaknesses** (the internal environment) usually are identified by considering the firm's capabilities and resources. What the firm does particularly well or has in greater abundance are its core competencies.

      1) **Core competencies** are the source of competitive advantages that in turn are the basis for an overall strategy.

   b. **Opportunities and threats** (the external environment) are identified by considering

      1) Macroenvironmental factors such as economic, demographic, political, legal, social, cultural, and technical factors and

      2) Microenvironmental factors such as suppliers, customers, distributors, competitors, and other competitive factors in the industry.

   c. For example, speed in reacting to environmental changes or introducing new products is an important competitive advantage. To achieve it, the organization may have to reengineer its processes.

10. **Competitive strategies** influence a firm's relative position in its industry (although choice of industry substantially determines profitability).

    a. Michael E. Porter's generic strategies model treats each competitive advantage as either a **cost** advantage (e.g., low cost) or a **differentiation** advantage (e.g., a unique product).

       1) The firm's advantages should be used within its **competitive scope** (target) to achieve its objectives. This scope may be **broad** (e.g., industry-wide) or **narrow** (e.g., a market segment).

       2) Using the variables of competitive advantage (cost or differentiation) and competitive scope (broad or narrow), four **generic** strategies may be implemented.

	Competitive Advantage	
Competitive Scope	Low Cost	Unique Product
Broad (Industry-wide)	Cost Leadership Strategy	Differentiation Strategy
Narrow (Market segment)	Focused Strategy: Cost	Focused Strategy: Differentiation

Figure 1-1

b. **Cost leadership** seeks competitive advantage through lower costs. It has a broad scope. Such a firm can earn higher profits than its competitors at the industry average price or charge a lower price to increase market share.

1) For example, a cost advantage may result from

    a) Vertical integration (acquisition of suppliers, wholesalers, or retailers)
    b) Exclusive access to low-cost materials
    c) Economies of scale (decline of average cost of output as output increases)
    d) Outsourcing

2) A cost leader usually has low profit margins, high sales, and a large market share. Such a firm

    a) Has efficient supply and distribution channels
    b) Is capable of large capital investment
    c) Has strengths in product design and process engineering if it is a manufacturer
    d) Closely supervises its labor force
    e) Is highly structured

3) Risks include

    a) Advances in technology or imitation by competitors.
    b) Adoption by many firms of a narrow cost focus strategy in their market segments.
    c) Failure to consider product and marketing changes. For example, the cost advantage must outweigh the differentiation advantages of others.

c. **Differentiation** seeks to provide a unique product or service. It has a broad scope. Such a firm may earn higher profits if consumers are willing to pay a higher price. But the price difference must exceed the additional cost of the differentiated product or service.

1) Successful differentiation creates a buyer belief that few, if any, substitutes are available. Thus, the firm may be able to pass supplier cost increases to buyers.

    a) Uniqueness may be based on, for example, massive promotion, excellence of design, superior service, technical leadership, or brand identification.

2) Typical strengths of successful broad-scope differentiators are

    a) Close cooperation of effective R&D and a strong marketing function
    b) Creative product development
    c) A reputation for quality or technical leadership
    d) A long tradition
    e) Effective coordination with suppliers and distributors
    f) An ability to apply the expertise of other enterprises
    g) An ability to attract skilled or creative people

3) Risks of differentiation strategy include
   a) Maturing of the industry with successful imitation by competitors
   b) Changes in consumer taste or lower demand for a differentiating factor
   c) Adoption by many firms of a narrow differentiation focus in their market segments
   d) A decrease in brand loyalty as lower-cost competitors improve quality

d. **Cost focus** seeks lower costs but with a narrow scope (e.g., a regional market or specialized product line). The reason is that the narrower market can be better served because the firm knows it well.
   1) Firms that successfully adopt a cost-focus strategy achieve strong customer loyalty. Their strengths and attributes are similar to those of cost leaders.
   2) Risks of a cost focus strategy include
      a) Lower purchasing volume and weakness relative to suppliers
      b) The advantage of a narrow scope offset by the cost advantage of broad scope competitors
      c) More narrowly focused competitors serving their niches better
      d) Changes in the narrow market
      e) A broad-scope competitor changing its product or service to compete effectively in the narrow market

e. **Focused differentiation** seeks to provide a unique product or service but with a narrow scope.
   1) The analysis of these firms is similar to that for cost-focus firms.

11. The **growth-share matrix** is a means of analyzing a **portfolio** of investments in strategic business units (SBUs).
    a. This approach supports
       1) Resource allocation,
       2) New business startups and acquisitions,
       3) Downsizing, and
       4) Divestitures.

b. The Boston Consulting Group's model for portfolio strategy has two variables.

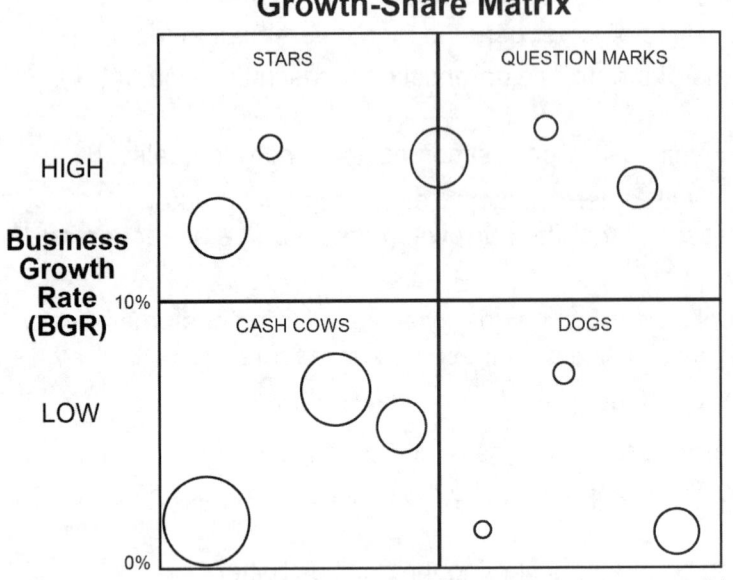

Figure 1-2

1) The **business growth rate (BGR)** (also referred to as market growth rate) is on the vertical axis. It relates to
   a) The maturity and attractiveness of the market and
   b) The relative need for cash to finance expansion.
2) **Market share (MS)** is on the horizontal axis.
3) The MS reflects an SBU's position in the market segment relative to competitors.

4) SBUs are represented in the quadrants by circles. A circle is proportional to the SBU's position in the entity's portfolio.

   a) **Dogs** (low MS, low BGR) are weak competitors in low-growth markets. They are candidates for disposal. Net cash flow is modest.
   b) **Question marks** (low MS, high BGR) are weak competitors that need cash infusions from cash cows. A question mark may become a star or a dog depending on whether MS increases significantly.
   c) **Cash cows** (high MS, low BGR) are strong competitors and cash generators. A cash cow ordinarily enjoys high profit margins and economies of scale. The SBU's excess cash can be used for investments in other SBUs. But marketing and R&D expenses should not necessarily be reduced significantly.
   d) **Stars** (high MS, high BGR) are strong competitors in high growth markets. Such an SBU is profitable but needs large amounts of cash for expansion, R&D, and meeting competitors' attacks.

5) Each SBU should have objectives, a strategy should be formulated to achieve those objectives, and a budget should be allocated.

   a) A **hold** strategy is used for strong cash cows.
   b) A **build** strategy is necessary for a question mark with potential to be a star.
   c) A **harvest** strategy maximizes short-term net cash inflow. Harvesting means zero-budgeting R&D, reducing marketing costs, not replacing facilities, etc. This strategy is used for weak cash cows and possibly question marks and dogs.

d) A **divest** strategy is normally used for question marks and dogs that reduce the firm's profitability. The proceeds of sale or liquidation are then invested more favorably.

　　i) A harvest strategy may undermine a future divestiture by decreasing the fair value of the SBU.

12. **Structural Analysis of Industries**

    a. An economy consists of sectors, industries, and segments.

    b. Examples of **sectors** are the healthcare sector or the transportation sector of the economy. Within each sector are multiple industries. An industry is a group of firms that provide products or services meeting the same fundamental customer needs.

    　　1) Thus, the transportation sector has an automobile industry, an airline industry, and a passenger rail industry. Each provides its own way of moving people from one place to another.

    　　2) A market **segment** is a set of customers with specific characteristics, needs, and wants.

    　　　　a) Thus, the automobile industry serves one market segment with sedans, another with sport utility vehicles, another with minivans, etc.

    　　　　　　i) Segments consist of customers, not firms.
    　　　　　　ii) One firm in an industry may attempt to serve multiple segments.

    c. Michael E. Porter has developed a model of the structure of industries and competition. It includes an analysis of the five competitive forces that determine long-term profitability as measured by long-term return on investment.

    d. A supplier may seek to limit buyers' power by choosing those with the least ability to bargain or switch to other suppliers. However, a preferable response is to make offers that are difficult to reject.

13. **Combination Strategies**

    a. According to Porter, using a combination of generic strategies may leave the firm stuck in the middle, that is, unable to create or sustain a competitive advantage. The danger is that attempting to follow more than one generic strategy will prevent the firm from achieving a competitive advantage.

    　　1) Thus, pursuit of, for example, both cost leadership and differentiation may interfere with reaching either goal. Furthermore, even if the firm could succeed by following multiple generic strategies, the result might be an ambiguous public image.

    　　2) A firm that pursues multiple generic strategies may be more likely to succeed if it creates a separate strategic business unit to implement each strategy.

    　　　　a) However, some writers argue that following a single strategy may not serve the needs of customers who want the best combination of product attributes, e.g., price, service, and quality.

    　　3) A firm also may need to adapt as a result of the changes that occur as the firm, its products or services, and the industry proceed through their life cycles.

    　　　　a) For example, an appropriate and successful focus strategy may need to be changed to a cost-leadership strategy as the firm matures.

14. **Competitive Strategies and Porter's Five Forces**
    a. Porter's generic strategies are responses to the five competitive forces.
        1) **Rivalry among Established Firms**
            a) Cost leadership permits a firm to compete by charging lower prices.
            b) Differentiation strengthens brand loyalty.
            c) Focus strategies provide superior attention to customer needs, whether for quality, price, or other product attributes.
        2) **Threat of New Entrants**
            a) Cost leadership permits a firm to reduce prices as a barrier to potential entrants.
            b) Differentiation creates uniqueness and brand loyalty that are barriers to new entrants.
            c) Focus strategies develop core competencies in a narrow market that potential entrants may not be able to match.
        3) **Threat of Substitutes**
            a) Cost leadership may result in low prices that substitutes cannot match.
            b) Differentiation may create unique product (service) attributes not found in substitutes.
            c) Focus strategies develop core competencies or unique product attributes that may protect against substitutes and new entrants.
        4) **Bargaining Power of Customers**
            a) Cost leadership may enable a firm to remain profitable while charging the lower prices required by strong buyers.
            b) Differentiation may reduce the power of strong buyers because of the uniqueness of the product and the resulting lack of close substitutes.
            c) Focus strategies also may reduce buyers' ability to negotiate in a narrow market. Substitutes may not be able to compete on price, quality, etc.
        5) **Bargaining Power of Suppliers**
            a) Cost leadership provides protection from strong suppliers.
            b) Differentiation may permit a firm to increase its price in response to suppliers' price increases.
            c) Focus strategies must allow for the superior bargaining power of suppliers when sellers operate in a narrow, low-volume market. For example, focused differentiation may permit the firm to pass along suppliers' price increases.

15. **Firm Orientations**
    a. Product-centered firms focus primarily on the product.
    b. Competitor-centered firms mainly base moves on competitors' actions and reactions.
    c. Customer-centered firms focus on customer developments and delivering value to customers.
    d. Market-centered firms watch both customers and competitors.
        1) Finding the balance between customers and competitors is the most effective orientation in today's market.

You have completed the outline for this subunit.
Study multiple-choice questions 1 through 10 beginning on page 29.

STOP & REVIEW

1.2 GLOBALIZATION

In the 2000s, globalization of the world's economic system accelerated. Besides such technical issues as exchange rates and tax differences, internal auditors also must be aware of the social, cultural, psychological, and other aspects of global business. They affect marketing, human resource management, and many other commercial activities and will be tested on the CIA exam.

SUCCESS TIP

1. **Overview**
    a. Globalization is the degree to which ideas, information, data, investment, and trade cross national borders.
        1) It is driven by the digital revolution that facilitates international commerce by providing capabilities that did not exist a relatively few years ago.
        2) It is also driven by
            a) The growth of China as an economic power,
            b) The emergence of other economic powers (e.g., India and Brazil),
            c) The expansion of the European Union, and
            d) The creation of other regional free trade zones.
        3) Accordingly, international economic activity effectively transcends national borders.

b. The unavoidable extent of globalization requires managers to have a **global mindset**. It is defined by Daft and Marcic (*Understanding Management*, 10th edition) as the "ability to appreciate and influence individuals, groups, organizations, and systems that represent different social, cultural, political, institutional, intellectual, and psychological characteristics."

   1) The **cognitive** element is the ability to understand cultural differences and adjust to global changes.
   2) The **social** element is the ability to develop relationships with people from different cultures.
   3) The **psychological** element is the ability to enjoy diverse modes of thought and behavior and cope with uncertainty.
   4) Among the activities that refine a global mindset are an emphasis on curiosity about other cultures and international affairs, including, but not limited to, business.
      a) Managers also may want to
         i) Establish relationships through social media and other means with people in other countries and cultures,
         ii) Travel and study abroad, and
         iii) Learn a foreign language.

2. **Other National Economies**

   a. **China** has the world's largest population and second largest economy and is the prime target of international investment. Its rapidly growing middle class makes it a large, if not the largest, market for many goods and services.

      1) The size and potential of the Chinese market must be considered by firms operating globally. But regulation and other government policies and the difficulties of dealing with state-owned enterprises are obstacles to doing business profitably.
         a) Other potential issues include
            i) Required technology transfer by foreign firms operating in China,
            ii) Problems in receiving prompt payment,
            iii) Culture differences that affect relationships,
            iv) The emergence of Chinese competitors in many industries, and
            v) Alleged currency manipulation.

   b. **India** has the world's second largest population, most of whom speak English. Thus, many companies have outsourced services there.

      1) India is a source of scientific and technological expertise as evidenced by its growth in software production, precision engineering, and pharmaceuticals.

3. **Multinationals**

   a. Multinational corporations (MNCs) also are known as global, stateless, or transnational. These entities have become numerous and powerful, some with revenues equivalent to the gross domestic products of countries.

      1) An MNC usually receives at least 25% of its sales from sources outside its home country. An MNC
         a) Is an integrated international business with affiliates that closely cooperate. Resources (e.g., employees, investments, and technology) may be transferred globally.
            i) Moreover, materials may be obtained and manufacturing may occur in the most profitable locations.

- b) Has central governance that makes strategic decisions and provides organizational integration to achieve its profit and other objectives.
- c) Generally has senior management with a global approach that treats the world as a single market.

2) But some MNCs are not **geocentric**, that is, truly internationally oriented and absorbing the best that various cultures offer, including managerial talent.

- a) **Ethnocentric** MNCs identify with the home country.
- b) **Polycentric** MNCs emphasize host country markets, and control is primarily local.

b. The operations of MNCs and free trade agreements have resulted in a globalization backlash.

1) Populations in many countries believe that free trade benefits others more than themselves.

- a) The counterargument is that, if governments and business leaders can prevent abuses, free trade and globalization ultimately
  - i) Lower prices,
  - ii) Expand markets and employment, and
  - iii) Increase profits.

c. A concept adopted by some MNCs is **serving the bottom of the pyramid (BOP)**. The BOP consists of the billions of people with the lowest per-capita incomes. This market is relatively untapped because products often are

1) Too costly,
2) Unsuitable for the needs of such customers, or
3) Not accessible.

- a) Various MNCs are seeking ways to design and market products to the BOP.

4. **Foreign Market Entry Strategies**

a. Foreign Markets

1) Attractiveness of a foreign market is a function of such factors as geography, income, climate, population, the product, and the unmet needs of the market.

- a) Entry into a market abroad may be based on many factors, for example, psychic proximity. Thus, a first-time venture abroad might be in a market with a related culture, language, or laws.

2) The internationalization process is of crucial interest to nations that wish to encourage local firms to grow and to operate globally. It involves the following:

- a) Lack of regular exports;
- b) Export via independent agents to a few markets, with later expansion to more countries;
- c) Creation of sales subsidiaries in larger markets; and
- d) Establishment of plants in foreign countries.

b. **Global outsourcing (offshoring)** is the use of cheaper resources (e.g., labor or materials) in other countries.

1) Given the decreased cost of information technology, outsourcing is no longer limited to lower-level work but may extend to, for example, software design and medical services.

c. Methods of expanding into international markets include the following:

1) **Licensing** gives firms in foreign countries the right to produce or market products or services within a geographical area for a fee.

   a) Licensing a process, patent, trade secret, etc., is a way to enter a foreign market with little immediate risk. However,

      i) The licensor may have insufficient control over the licensee's operations,
      ii) The licensor loses profits if the arrangement succeeds, and
      iii) The licensee ultimately may become a competitor.

2) **Exporting** is the sale of goods manufactured in one country and then sold in other countries.

   a) Indirect export requires lower investment than direct export and is less risky because of the intermediaries' expertise.

3) An **indirect export strategy** operates through intermediaries, such as

   a) Home-country merchants who buy and resell the product,
   b) Home-country agents who negotiate transactions with foreign buyers for a commission,
   c) Cooperatives that represent groups of sellers, and
   d) Export-management firms that receive fees for administering the firm's export efforts.

4) **Direct investment** has many advantages and risks.

   a) The advantages include

      i) Cheaper materials or labor,
      ii) Receipt of investment incentives from the host government,
      iii) A strong relationship with interested parties in the host country,
      iv) Control of the investment,
      v) A better image in the host country, and
      vi) Market access when domestic content rules are in effect.

   b) Direct investment is risky because of

      i) Exposure to currency fluctuations,
      ii) Expropriation,
      iii) Potentially high exit barriers, and
      iv) Restraints on sending profits out of the country.

5) In a **local storage and sale arrangement**, products manufactured in one country are then shipped to a marketing facility located in another country.

6) **Local component assembly** involves shipping individual parts from one country to an assembly facility in a second country. They are then turned into a salable product and sold in the second country or exported to other countries.

7) In **multiple or joint ventures**, several firms, even competitors, work together to create products that are sold under one or more brand names in different countries. They share responsibility, ownership, costs, and profits.

d. Unlike licensing, direct export, or outsourcing, **direct investment** provides control over and management of the productive assets.

1) In a **joint venture**, two or more firms, possibly competitors, work together to create products, build a plant, or establish a distribution network. They share responsibility, ownership, costs, risks, and profits.

   a) Some firms have established **alliance networks**. These are sets of partnerships with different partners that may extend across international borders.

      i) A partnership may be the least costly and risky foreign market entry strategy.

2) Direct acquisition of 100% of a **foreign affiliate** may be advantageous because of the expertise of local managers and the reductions of distribution channel, transportation, and storage costs.

e. A **greenfield venture** is a subsidiary in a foreign country that is not based on any existing business.

1) The benefits are (a) complete control of every aspect of the venture from the beginning and (b) potentially high profits.

2) The drawbacks may include lack of familiarity with the (a) culture, (b) language, (c) market, (d) labor conditions, (e) availability of local expertise, (f) legal issues, and (g) political and regulatory obstacles.

5. **The Global Environment**

a. Management of operations in more than one country addresses the same functions as in the domestic environment: (1) planning, (2) organizing, (3) leading, and (4) controlling.

b. **Economic** issues include the degrees of development and interconnection.

1) Countries may be classified as developing or developed. The usual statistical distinction is **per-capita income** (Gross domestic product or services ÷ Population).

2) Countries also may be classified based on **competitiveness**. The relevant factors are those promoting **productivity**, such as

   a) Government policies,
   b) Financial markets,
   c) The size of the national market,
   d) Key institutions, and
   e) Infrastructure, which includes

      i) The transportation network (e.g., roads, seaports, and airports),
      ii) The communications network (e.g., cell phone and telephone service and Internet connectivity), and
      iii) Utilities.

3) The ripple effects of financial and other crises in one part of the world, e.g., the severe recession in the U.S. in 2007-2008, demonstrate the interdependence of the participants in the global economy.

   a) A key aspect of interconnection is that many products contain parts and materials from international suppliers. Moreover, supplies of labor also may depend on global outreach.

c. **Political and legal** issues are complex in the international environment because of substantial statutory and regulatory differences from country to country.

1) For example, these differences extend to
   a) Taxation,
   b) Financial regulation,
   c) Labor law,
   d) Consumer protection, and
   e) Intellectual property rights.

2) International firms also must cope with different **political** systems. Governments may exercise greater oversight of, or even be hostile to, international firms.

   a) **Political risk** is the risk of economic loss from politically motivated actions of governments. For example, a host government may favor local firms and entrenched bureaucracies.
   b) **Political instability** is reflected in
      i) Changes in governments, whether or not peaceful;
      ii) Violent acts such as riots; and
      iii) Outright war.

d. **Social and cultural** differences may be even more difficult to resolve than economic, legal, and political issues, but they are crucial.

1) **Management** is the coordination in a common venture of the efforts of people with certain social and cultural values that vary from country to country.

2) **Culture** is the distinct set of values, beliefs, and symbols that guide patterns of behavior in a group. In international business, misunderstanding and conflict occur because people from different cultures have fundamentally different assumptions, values, etc.

   a) For example, American business people often are viewed as especially **ethnocentric**. This is the belief, common in all countries, that one's own group is superior.
      i) An individual can overcome ethnocentricity by understanding and appreciating the social and cultural values in other countries.

3) Psychologist Geert Hofstede researched national value systems in numerous countries where IBM employees worked.

   a) The result was identification of five distinct **dimensions of cultural differences**.
      i) **Power distance** is the degree of acceptance of unequal distribution of power in an organization. High means acceptance of inequality. Low means an expectation of equality.
      ii) The **individualism-collectivism** dimension addresses whether (a) individuals help each other and the organization protects its members in return for their loyalty (high) or (b) the individual must meet his or her own security needs (low).
      iii) The **masculinity versus femininity** dimension is the balance of (a) traditionally masculine traits (the centrality of work, aggressiveness, acquisitiveness, and performance) (high) and (b) traditionally feminine traits (the centrality of cooperation, relationships, group decisions, and quality of life) (low).

iv) **Uncertainty avoidance** relates to the extent of the threat posed by (a) ambiguous circumstances, (b) the significance of rules, and (c) the pressure for conformity. High means support for beliefs promising certainty and conformity. Low means tolerance for unpredictability and lack of structure.

v) **Long-term orientation** is the importance to society of traditions and values. It includes (a) perseverance, (b) thrift, (c) ordering relationships by status, and (d) having a sense of shame.

- **Short-term orientation** includes (1) reciprocating social obligations, (2) respect for tradition, (3) protecting one's "face," and (4) personal steadiness and stability.

b) The Global Leadership and Organizational Behavior Effectiveness (GLOBE) project has identified dimensions additional to Hofstede's.

i) **Assertiveness** values toughness and competitiveness (high) over tenderness and concern for others (low).

ii) **Future orientation** is the degree to which planning is emphasized over near-term results and immediate gratification.

iii) **Gender differentiation** is high when men have preferred social, political, and economic status. It is low when women have higher status and participate more meaningfully in decisions.

iv) **Performance orientation** is high when performance is strongly emphasized and excellence is rewarded. It is low when loyalty, affiliation, and background are stressed.

v) **Humane orientation** is high when qualities such as fairness, generosity, and kindness are cherished. It is low when self-sufficiency, self-improvement, and personal gratification are dominant attitudes.

4) **Communication** varies because of the distinction between high-context and low-context cultures.

a) In **high-context** cultures (e.g., Japanese, Chinese, Arabic, and Korean), much meaning is transmitted by nonverbal cues and situational circumstances.

i) Thus, a person's status in a firm, rank in society, and reputation convey the primary message.

ii) Moreover, investing time in relationship-building to establish trust and the welfare and harmony of the group are valued.

b) In **low-context** cultures (e.g., in northern European and North American countries), primary meanings are transmitted by words. For example, precise written contracts are highly valued in a low-context culture.

i) The emphasis of communication is on information exchange, transactions are more significant than relationships, and individuality is stressed more than the welfare of the group.

5) **Cultural intelligence (CQ)** has been defined as the ability to observe, reason about, interpret, and respond to culturally unfamiliar situations.

a) The elements of CQ are

i) Cognitive understanding,
ii) Emotional (relating to people), and
iii) Physical (changing speech, gestures, and behavior).

e. **Economic integration** is the joining of the markets from two or more countries into a free-trade zone. Examples of economic blocs of trading nations are the European Union and the North American Free Trade Agreement (NAFTA). Generally, a bloc provides trading incentives to members and discriminates against nonmembers.

1) The **European Union (EU)** is an economic and political association of European countries. The **euro** has replaced the currencies of the majority of EU members. Currently, the EU has 27 members. It provides

   a) A **single market for goods and services** without any economic barriers
   b) Free movement of people across borders

2) Under the **General Agreement on Tariffs and Trade (GATT)**, the signatory countries agreed to

   a) Equal treatment of all members,
   b) Multilateral negotiations to reduce tariffs, and
   c) The abolition of import quotas.

3) The GATT has been replaced by the **World Trade Organization (WTO)**. The WTO Agreement is a permanent set of commitments by most of the world's countries designed to prohibit trade discrimination among members and between imported and domestic products.

   a) Most of the rules of GATT are still applicable to trade in goods.
   b) The WTO provides for a multilateral **dispute settlement** apparatus.

4) The **North American Free Trade Agreement (NAFTA)** essentially provides for free trade among the U.S., Canada, and Mexico. NAFTA arranged for the gradual phasing-out over a period of 15 years of tariffs on almost all products sold among the three countries.

   a) Unlike the EU, NAFTA did not create a new set of administrative bodies to oversee the trading activities of the three members. It simply removed barriers to trade.

5) The **theory** of free trade zones is that

   a) They benefit consumers by lowering prices and
   b) Manufacturers and workers gain from expanded markets for the items each country produces most efficiently.

6. **Strategies for Global Marketing Organization**

   a. Four broad strategies are generally recognized:

   1) A **multinational (transnational) strategy** adopts a portfolio approach. Its emphasis is on national markets because the need for global integration is not strong, and the driving forces of localization (cultural, commercial, and technical) predominate.

      a) The product is customized for each market and therefore incurs higher production costs.
      b) This strategy is most effective given large differences between countries.
      c) Also, exchange rate risk is reduced when conducting business in this manner.
      d) Transnational firms lack a national identity, but they rely on a decentralized structure for management and decision making.

         i) They tend to be more aware of local customs and market forces because they take much more of their input from a local or regional management team.

2) A **global strategy** regards the world as one market. Among its determinants are ambition, positioning, and organization.
   a) The product is essentially the same in all countries with some adaptions.
   b) Faster product development and lower production costs are typical.
   c) The disadvantage of this strategy is the complexity of integration and coordination needed to keep operations running smoothly.
   d) Global firms are primarily managed from one central country. Even though their products may be sold throughout the world, their headquarters and most of their policy decisions are set from a central base of operations.
      i) Global firms plan, operate, and coordinate their activities worldwide. Thus, a global firm secures cost or product differentiation advantages not available to domestic firms.
3) In an **international strategy,** the value chain is controlled and marketed from the organization's home country, but products are sold globally.
   a) The product is essentially the same in all countries.
   b) Decision making is centralized with the home country.
   c) This strategy allows for strong control of operations with less coordination from host countries.
   d) The disadvantage of this strategy is that the value chain in a host country is not developed.
4) A **multilocal** or **multidomestic strategy** uses subsidiaries in the host countries to control operations.
   a) The product is adapted for each country.
   b) Decision making is usually left to the subsidiaries.
   c) This strategy allows for customization for local markets and the use of local resources. Also, less coordination is required by decision makers in the home country.
   d) The disadvantage of this strategy is higher costs and lower economies of scale.

b. Two compromise strategies adopt elements of the broad strategies.
   1) A **glocal strategy** seeks the benefits of localization (flexibility, proximity, and adaptability) and global integration.
      a) Successful telecommunications firms are examples of balancing these elements of localization and global integration.
      b) Local responsiveness is indicated when local product tastes and preferences, regulations, and barriers are significant.
      c) Global integration is indicated when demand is homogeneous and economies of productive scale are large.
   2) A **regional strategy** combines elements of multinational, international, and multilocal strategies. The goal of this strategy is to create regional products and a regional value chain.

7. **Steps to Brand Globally**
    a. The following steps should be taken to minimize the risks of expanding into foreign markets and to maximize growth potential:
        1) A firm must understand how diverse markets connect to form a global branding landscape. Individual countries vary in their historical acceptance of products and services.
            a) However, firms also may capitalize on similarities that are found in certain areas and regions.
        2) Branding and brand building must be a process. New markets must be developed where none previously existed.
            a) Thus, global firms must build awareness of the product and then create sources of brand equity.
        3) Establishing a marketing infrastructure is crucial. To create a successful marketing structure, the firm either must merge with the local marketing channels or create a completely new method of distribution.
        4) Integrated marketing communications should be developed. Markets must be approached with a broad range of messages, and sole reliance on advertising should be avoided.
            a) Other marketing communications include merchandising, promotions, and sponsorship.
        5) The firm may create branding partnerships. Global firms often form alliances with local distribution channels to increase their profitability while decreasing their marketing costs.
        6) The firm should determine the ratio of standardization and customization. Products that can be sold virtually unchanged throughout several markets provide a greater profit opportunity for a global firm.
            a) However, cultural differences may require extensive customization to appeal to markets in different countries.
        7) The firm should determine the balance of local and global control. Local managers may understand the wants and needs of their market, but the global firm still must retain control of certain elements of the marketing process and strategy.
        8) The firm should establish local guidelines so that local sales and profit goals are met.
        9) The firm should create a global brand equity tracking system. This equity system is a set of research processes that provide the marketers with pertinent information.
            a) The marketers can use this tracking system to create both long- and short-term strategies for expanding product sales and reach.
        10) The firm should maximize brand elements. Large global firms can achieve much greater expansion rates when the brand elements are successfully employed at the launch of a product or service.

STOP & REVIEW

You have completed the outline for this subunit.
Study multiple-choice questions 11 through 24 beginning on page 33.

QUESTIONS

1.1 Strategic Management and Planning

1. Which of the following is **least** likely to be an example of synergy?

A. A shopping mall with several businesses providing different products and performing different services.
B. A car dealership providing warranties on automobile parts to maximize customer value.
C. A manufacturing company hiring a new manager with technological experience lacking in the company.
D. Military Humvees being converted into sports utility vehicles for sale to civilians.

Answer (B) is correct.
REQUIRED: The least likely example of synergy.
DISCUSSION: Synergy occurs when the combination of formerly separate elements has a greater effect than the sum of their individual effects. However, a car dealership's provision of warranties reflects an operational strategy designed to provide post-purchase services to gain a competitive advantage and maximize customer value. It does not reflect the complementary sharing of resources, technology, or competencies. In contrast, synergy arises from selling a line of cars that share some components or a brand identification.
Answer (A) is incorrect. A shopping mall with several businesses providing different products and performing different services is an example of market synergy. **Answer (C) is incorrect.** Hiring a manager with needed skills is an example of management synergy. **Answer (D) is incorrect.** Conversion of Humvees to SUVs is an example of technological synergy.

2. Which of the following is a market-oriented definition of a business versus a product-oriented definition of a business?

A. Making air conditioners and furnaces.
B. Supplying energy.
C. Producing movies.
D. Selling men's shirts and pants.

Answer (B) is correct.
REQUIRED: The market-oriented business definition.
DISCUSSION: Businesses should be defined in market terms, that is, in terms of needs and customer groups. Moreover, a distinction should be made between a target market definition and a strategic market definition. For example, a target market for a railroad might be freight hauling, but a strategic market might be transportation of any goods and people. Accordingly, stating that a business supplies energy is a market-oriented definition as opposed to the product-oriented definition. Moreover, it is also a strategic market definition.

3. Which one of the following is a social trend affecting the organization?

A. Changes in labor markets.
B. Tougher legislation to protect the environment.
C. Rising inflation.
D. Replacements for steel in cars and appliances.

Answer (A) is correct.
REQUIRED: The social trend that affects organizations.
DISCUSSION: Social trends, such as changes in labor markets, reflect social, cultural, and demographic factors in the organization's macroenvironment that may constitute opportunities or threats (identified in a SWOT analysis). The attributes of people (age, education, income, ethnicity, family status, etc.) and their beliefs, attitudes, and values shape and are shaped by social trends that in turn affect the organization. Thus, changes in the characteristics, sources, locations, and costs of labor resources supplied (a basic factor of production) have great effects on an organization's strategic position.
Answer (B) is incorrect. Tougher legislation to protect the environment is a political trend. **Answer (C) is incorrect.** Rising inflation is an economic trend. **Answer (D) is incorrect.** Replacements for steel in cars and appliances represent a technological trend.

4. Which of the following best describes a cost synergy?

A. Recycling of by-products.
B. Selling one product strengthens sales of another product.
C. Transferring knowledge to new uses.
D. Acquiring new management skills.

Answer (A) is correct.
REQUIRED: The best description of a cost synergy.
DISCUSSION: Cost synergy results in cost reduction. It occurs in many ways, for example, in recycling of by-products or in the design, production, marketing, and sales of a line of products by the same enterprise.
Answer (B) is incorrect. Selling one product strengthens sales of another product is an example of market synergy. **Answer (C) is incorrect.** Transferring knowledge to new uses is an example of technological synergy. **Answer (D) is incorrect.** Acquiring new management skills is an example of management synergy.

5. According to Michael E. Porter's generic strategies model, a firm that successfully adopts a differentiation strategy is most likely to

A. Tend to disregard cost control.
B. Risk overlooking product changes.
C. Closely supervise its labor force.
D. Be able to pass supplier cost increases on to its customers.

Answer (D) is correct.
REQUIRED: The true statement about a firm that successfully adopts a differentiation strategy.
DISCUSSION: Differentiation is the generic strategy of a firm that seeks competitive advantage through providing a unique product or service. This strategy has a broad competitive scope. A successful differentiation strategy creates a consumer perception that few, if any, substitutes are available. Thus, a firm that adopts this strategy may have the additional advantage of being able to pass supplier cost increases to buyers.
Answer (A) is incorrect. A differentiation strategy does not signify a disregard for cost control, but simply a greater emphasis on creating a perception of the uniqueness of the product or service. **Answer (B) is incorrect.** A firm with a cost leadership strategy risks overlooking product changes. **Answer (C) is incorrect.** A firm with a cost leadership strategy is more likely to closely supervise its labor force.

6. A strategic business unit (SBU) has a high relative market share (RMS) and a low business growth rate (BGR). According to the growth-share matrix for competitive analysis created by the Boston Consulting Group, the SBU is a

A. Star.
B. Question mark.
C. Cash cow.
D. Dog.

Answer (C) is correct.
REQUIRED: The characterization by the growth-share matrix of an SBU.
DISCUSSION: The annual BGR reflects the maturity and attractiveness of the market and the relative need for cash to finance expansion. The RMS reflects an SBU's competitive position in the market segment. A high RMS signifies that the SBU has a strong competitive position. Cash cows have high RMS and low BGR. They are strong competitors and cash generators in low-growth markets.
Answer (A) is incorrect. Stars have both high RMS and high BGR because they are strong competitors in high-growth markets. **Answer (B) is incorrect.** Question marks are weak competitors in high-growth markets, meaning they have a low RMS and a high BGR. **Answer (D) is incorrect.** Dogs have both low RMS and low BGR, meaning they are weak competitors in low-growth markets.

7. Business strategies may be characterized by their effects on operations. The distinction between a compact car and a luxury car reflects which operational strategy?

A. Cost.
B. Flexibility.
C. Service.
D. Quality.

Answer (D) is correct.
REQUIRED: The operational strategy reflecting the distinction between a compact car and a luxury car.
DISCUSSION: A quality strategy involves competition based on product quality or process quality. Product quality relates to design, for example, the difference between a luxury car and a subcompact car. Process quality concerns the degree of freedom from defects.
Answer (A) is incorrect. A cost strategy is successful when the enterprise is the low-cost producer. However, the product (e.g., a commodity) tends to be undifferentiated in these cases, the market is often very large, and the competition tends to be intense because of the possibility of high-volume sales. **Answer (B) is incorrect.** A flexibility strategy entails offering many different products. This strategy also may reflect an ability to shift rapidly from one product line to another. An example firm is a publisher that can write, edit, print and distribute a book within days to exploit the public's short-term interest in a sensational event. **Answer (C) is incorrect.** A service strategy seeks to gain a competitive advantage and maximize customer value by providing services, especially post-purchase services such as warranties on automobiles and home appliances.

8. What operations strategy is most likely to be adopted when the product sold by an organization is a commodity and the market is very large?

A. Flexibility strategy.
B. Quality strategy.
C. Service strategy.
D. Cost strategy.

Answer (D) is correct.
REQUIRED: The strategy most likely to be adopted when the product sold by an organization is a commodity and the market is very large.
DISCUSSION: An operations strategy formulates a long-term plan for using resources to reach strategic objectives. A cost strategy is successful when the enterprise is the low-cost producer. However, the product (e.g., a commodity) tends to be undifferentiated in these cases, the market is often very large, and the competition tends to be intense because of the possibility of high-volume sales.
Answer (A) is incorrect. A flexibility strategy involves offering many different products. **Answer (B) is incorrect.** A quality strategy involves competition based on product quality or process quality. **Answer (C) is incorrect.** Service is not an issue in a sale of commodities.

9. Which of the following steps in the strategic planning process should be completed first?

A. Translate objectives into goals.
B. Determine actions to achieve goals.
C. Develop performance measures.
D. Create a mission statement.

Answer (D) is correct.
REQUIRED: The first step in strategic planning.
DISCUSSION: A mission statement is a formal, written document that defines an organization's ultimate purposes in society in general terms. After a situational analysis is performed, the entity develops a group of strategies for achieving the mission.
Answer (A) is incorrect. A subsequent step is to translate longer-range objectives into shorter-range objectives. However, the terms "objectives" and "goals" are defined differently by different authors. For example, "goals" might be longer-range than "objectives." **Answer (B) is incorrect.** Determining the specific actions to achieve objectives (goals) follows defining the mission. **Answer (C) is incorrect.** An organization does not develop performance measures before defining its mission.

10. In accordance with Michael E. Porter's generic strategies model, a firm with a broad competitive scope that has high sales volume, low margins, and efficient supply and distribution channels will most likely choose a

A. Cost leadership strategy.
B. Cost focus strategy.
C. Differentiation strategy.
D. Focused differentiation strategy.

Answer (A) is correct.
REQUIRED: The generic strategy most likely to be chosen by a firm with a broad competitive scope, high sales, low margins, and efficient supply and distribution channels.
DISCUSSION: Cost leadership is the generic strategy of a firm that seeks competitive advantage through lower costs. It has a broad competitive scope. Such a firm can earn higher profits than its competitors at the industry average price or charge a lower price to increase market share. The typical firm that follows a cost leadership strategy has low profit margins, a high volume of sales, and a substantial market share. Such a firm has efficient supply and distribution channels, is capable of large capital investment, has strengths in product design and process engineering, if it is a manufacturer, and closely supervises its labor force.
Answer (B) is incorrect. A cost focus strategy has a narrow competitive scope. **Answer (C) is incorrect.** Differentiation is the generic strategy favored by firms that seek competitive advantage through providing a unique product or service and that have a broad competitive scope. **Answer (D) is incorrect.** Focused differentiation is the generic strategy favored by firms that seek competitive advantage through providing a unique product and that have a narrow competitive scope, e.g., a regional market or a specialized product line.

1.2 Globalization

11. An advantage of a direct investment strategy when entering a foreign market is

- A. Reduction in the capital at risk.
- B. Shared control and responsibility.
- C. Assurance of access when the foreign country imposes domestic content rules.
- D. Avoidance of interaction with the local bureaucracy.

Answer (C) is correct.
REQUIRED: The advantage of direct investment.
DISCUSSION: Direct investment has many advantages: (1) cheaper materials or labor, (2) receipt of investment incentives from the host government, (3) a strong relationship with interested parties in the host country, (4) control of the investment, (5) a better image in the host country, and (6) market access when domestic content rules are in effect. However, direct investment is risky because of exposure to currency fluctuations, expropriation, potentially high exit barriers, and restraints on sending profits out of the country.
Answer (A) is incorrect. Direct investment maximizes capital at risk. **Answer (B) is incorrect.** Direct investment avoids shared control and responsibility. **Answer (D) is incorrect.** Direct investment means a closer relationship with governmental entities in the host country.

12. A global firm

- A. Has achieved economies of scale in the firm's domestic market.
- B. Plans, operates, and coordinates business globally.
- C. Relies on indirect export.
- D. Tends to rely more on one product market.

Answer (B) is correct.
REQUIRED: The nature of a global firm.
DISCUSSION: Global firms plan, operate, and coordinate their activities worldwide. Thus, a global firm secures cost or product differentiation advantages not available to domestic firms.
Answer (A) is incorrect. One reason to go abroad is that economies of scale are so great that they cannot be achieved in a domestic market. **Answer (C) is incorrect.** Global firms do not rely only on indirect export. They rely on direct export, which is potentially more profitable. **Answer (D) is incorrect.** A global firm may be a small firm that sells one product or class of products, or it may be a large firm with a multiproduct line.

13. Developing brand equity in a foreign market may be desirable but is subject to considerable risk. A global firm launching a new product in a new market most likely should

- A. Initially place most of the firm's emphasis on advertising geared to the local culture.
- B. Fully decentralize control of the marketing process.
- C. Avoid creating partnerships with local distribution channels to avoid dilution of the brand.
- D. Balance standardization and customization of the product.

Answer (D) is correct.
REQUIRED: The most likely step taken by a global firm launching a new product in a new market.
DISCUSSION: The firm should determine the ratio of standardization and customization. Products that can be sold virtually unchanged throughout several markets provide a greater profit opportunity for a global firm. However, cultural differences may require extensive customization to appeal to markets in different countries.
Answer (A) is incorrect. Integrated marketing communications should be developed. Markets must be approached with a broad range of messages. Sole reliance on advertising should be avoided. Other marketing communications include merchandising, promotions, and sponsorship. **Answer (B) is incorrect.** The firm should determine the ratio of local to global control. Local managers may understand the wants and needs of their market, but the global firm must still retain control of certain elements of the marketing process and strategy. **Answer (C) is incorrect.** The firm may create branding partnerships. Global firms often form alliances with local distribution channels to increase their profitability while decreasing their marketing costs.

14. The **least** risky method of entering a market in a foreign country is by

- A. Indirect exports.
- B. Licensing.
- C. Direct exports.
- D. Direct investments.

Answer (A) is correct.
REQUIRED: The least risky method of entering a market in a foreign country.
DISCUSSION: An indirect export strategy operates through intermediaries, such as home-country merchants who buy and resell the product, home-country agents who negotiate transactions with foreign buyers for a commission, cooperatives that represent groups of sellers, and export-management firms that receive fees for administering the firm's export efforts. Indirect export requires lower investment than direct export and is less risky because of the intermediaries' expertise.
Answer (B) is incorrect. Licensing a process, patent, trade secret, etc., is a way to gain a foothold in a foreign market with little immediate risk. However, the licensor may have insufficient control over the licensee's operations, profits are lost if the arrangement succeeds, and the licensee ultimately may become a competitor.
Answer (C) is incorrect. Direct export involves higher risk and investment but may yield higher returns.
Answer (D) is incorrect. Direct investment has many advantages: (1) cheaper materials or labor, (2) receipt of investment incentives from the host government, (3) a strong relationship with interested parties in the host country, (4) control of the investment, (5) a better image in the host country, and (6) market access when domestic contest rules are in effect. However, direct investment is risky because of exposure to currency fluctuations, expropriation, potentially high exit barriers, and restraints on sending profits out of the country.

15. Garrison Woodproducts and Mathis Woodproducts are the two largest wood product competitors in the United States. However, these two companies work together to produce woodproducts for Europe under the name of United Woodproducts. What method are Garrison and Mathis using to expand into global markets?

- A. Exporting.
- B. Licensing.
- C. Joint venture.
- D. Local component assembly.

Answer (C) is correct.
REQUIRED: The method used to expand into global markets.
DISCUSSION: In multiple or joint ventures, several firms, even competitors, work together to create products that are sold under one or more brand names in different countries. They share responsibility, ownership, costs, and profits.
Answer (A) is incorrect. Exporting is the sale in other countries of goods manufactured in one country. The facts in this question do not indicate an exporting arrangement. **Answer (B) is incorrect.** Licensing gives firms in foreign countries the right to produce or market products or services within a geographical area for a fee. The facts in this question do not indicate a licensing arrangement. **Answer (D) is incorrect.** Local component assembly involves shipping individual parts from one country to an assembly facility in a second country. They are then turned into a salable product and sold in the country or exported to other countries. The facts in this question do not indicate a local component assembly method.

16. Which strategy for a global marketing organization is based on a portfolio of national markets?

A. Creation of a division to manage international marketing.
B. A multinational strategy.
C. A glocal strategy.
D. Creation of an export department.

Answer (B) is correct.
REQUIRED: The global organization strategy based on a portfolio of national markets.
DISCUSSION: International marketing efforts take three basic forms: creation of an export department, creation of a division to manage international marketing, or global organization. The third form encompasses genuinely worldwide functions, e.g., manufacturing, marketing, finance, and logistics. Thus, worldwide operations are the organization's focus, not merely that of a department or division of a national firm. A global organization may follow a multinational, global, or glocal strategy. A multinational strategy adopts a portfolio approach. Its emphasis is on national markets because the need for global integration is not strong. The product is customized for each market and therefore incurs higher production costs. Decision making is primarily local with a minimum of central control. This strategy is most effective given large differences between countries. Also, exchange rate risk is reduced when conducting business in this manner.
Answer (A) is incorrect. Export departments and international divisions are organizational arrangements that precede the firm's evolution into a global organization. **Answer (C) is incorrect.** Glocal strategy balances local responsiveness and global integration. **Answer (D) is incorrect.** Export departments and international divisions are organizational arrangements that precede the firm's evolution into a global organization.

17. Which of the following is correct regarding the impacts of a global strategy on an organization?

	Slower Product Development	Higher Production Costs	Global Firms Managed through One Central Country
A.	Yes	Yes	Yes
B.	No	No	No
C.	No	No	Yes
D.	No	Yes	No

Answer (C) is correct.
REQUIRED: The effects of a global strategy.
DISCUSSION: A global strategy regards the world as one market. In a global strategy, faster product development and lower production costs are typical. Additionally, global firms are primarily managed from one central country, even though their products may be sold throughout the world.
Answer (A) is incorrect. A global strategy does not result in slower product development or higher production costs. **Answer (B) is incorrect.** A global strategy does result in global firms being managed through a central country. **Answer (D) is incorrect.** A global strategy does not result in higher production costs.

18. In a regional strategy, an organization has which of the following goals?

A. To combine the elements of multinational and international, but not multilocal, strategies.
B. To create a universal product and value chain that serves the needs of all countries in which the firm operates.
C. To combine the various operating segments of the organization based on the region in which they operate.
D. To create regional products and a regional value chain.

Answer (D) is correct.
REQUIRED: The goals of a regional strategy.
DISCUSSION: The goal of a regional strategy is to create regional products and a regional value chain.
Answer (A) is incorrect. Although a regional strategy combines elements of multinational, international, and multilocal strategies, it is not the goal of the organization undertaking such a strategy. **Answer (B) is incorrect.** In a regional strategy, the goal is not to create a single product or value chain. **Answer (C) is incorrect.** This is not a goal of a strategy for global marketing organizations.

19. Which of the following strategies combines elements of multinational, international, and multilocal strategies?

A. Multidomestic strategy.
B. Transnational strategy.
C. All-encompassing strategy.
D. Regional strategy.

Answer (D) is correct.
REQUIRED: The strategy combining elements of multinational, international, and multilocal strategies.
DISCUSSION: A regional strategy combines elements of multinational, international, and multilocal strategies. The goal of this strategy is to create regional products and a regional value chain.
Answer (A) is incorrect. A multidomestic strategy is another name for the multilocal strategy, which is a component of the regional strategy. **Answer (B) is incorrect.** A transnational strategy is another name for a multinational strategy, which is a component of the regional strategy. **Answer (C) is incorrect.** "All-encompassing strategy" is not a meaningful term in this context.

20. The disadvantage of a multilocal or multidomestic strategy is that the company

A. Uses subsidiaries in the home country to control operations.
B. Adapts the product for the global market but not for each country.
C. Makes decisions at a centralized location in the home country.
D. Incurs higher costs and lower economies of scale.

Answer (D) is correct.
REQUIRED: The disadvantages of a multilocal or multidomestic strategy.
DISCUSSION: A multilocal strategy has the disadvantage of increasing costs and decreasing economies of scale.
Answer (A) is incorrect. In a multilocal strategy, the organization uses subsidiaries in the host countries, not the home country, to control operations. **Answer (B) is incorrect.** In a multilocal strategy, the organization adapts the product for each country. **Answer (C) is incorrect.** A multilocal strategy typically leaves decisions to be made by the subsidiaries of the organization.

21. Davian Wood Products produces customized products for each country it operates in. As a result, it can be said that

A. Davian is using a multinational strategy and is saving production costs.
B. Davian is using a global strategy and is incurring higher production costs.
C. Davian is using an international strategy, resulting in centralized decision making.
D. Davian is using a multinational strategy and incurring higher production costs.

Answer (D) is correct.
REQUIRED: The type of strategy described.
DISCUSSION: A multinational strategy adopts a portfolio approach. Under this approach, the product is customized for each market, and higher production costs are incurred.
Answer (A) is incorrect. While a multinational strategy involves customizing products, higher (not lower) production costs are usually incurred. Answer (B) is incorrect. A global strategy regards the world as one market. The product is essentially the same in all countries, and lower production costs are typical. Answer (C) is incorrect. Under an international strategy, the product is essentially the same in all countries.

22. A firm wishing to sell its well-known brand of men's clothing in a certain foreign country redesigned the products because of the greater average size of consumers in that country. However, the firm retained the same basic advertising campaign. This firm has adopted which adaptation strategy?

A. Straight extension.
B. Product adaptation.
C. Forward invention.
D. Backward invention.

Answer (B) is correct.
REQUIRED: The adaptation strategy followed.
DISCUSSION: Using a product adaptation strategy, a firm makes changes to the product for each market but not its promotion. This strategy may reduce profit potential but also may provide a marketing advantage by considering local wants and needs.
Answer (A) is incorrect. The product was adapted. Answer (C) is incorrect. No new product was created. Answer (D) is incorrect. No older product was reintroduced.

23. Bulez Widgets, Inc., operates globally and has been praised for its ability to understand the needs and wants of the local market while retaining global control of certain elements of the marketing process and strategy. Bulez is

A. Establishing local guidelines so that local sales and profit goals are met.
B. Maintaining a good ratio of standardization and customization.
C. Maintaining a good ratio of local to global control.
D. None of the answers are correct.

Answer (C) is correct.
REQUIRED: The strategy used to brand globally.
DISCUSSION: Bulez is maintaining a good ratio of local to global control. Local managers may understand the wants and needs of their market, but the global firm must still retain control of certain elements of the marketing process and strategy.
Answer (A) is incorrect. Bulez is maintaining a good ratio of local to global control, not establishing local guidelines. Answer (B) is incorrect. A firm should determine a ratio of standardization and customization. Products that can be sold virtually unchanged throughout several markets provide a greater profit opportunity for a global firm. Answer (D) is incorrect. Bulez is maintaining a good ratio of local to global control.

24. Which method of expanding into international markets is most likely the riskiest?

A. A local storage and sale arrangement.
B. Local component assembly.
C. Direct investment.
D. Joint venture.

Answer (C) is correct.
REQUIRED: The method of expanding into international markets that is most likely the riskiest.
DISCUSSION: Direct investment has many advantages: (1) cheaper materials or labor, (2) receipt of investment incentives from the host government, (3) a strong relationship with interested parties in the host country, (4) control of the investment, (5) a better image in the host country, and (6) market access when domestic contest rules are in effect. However, direct investment is risky because of exposure to currency fluctuations, expropriation, potentially high exit barriers, and restraints on sending profits out of the country.
Answer (A) is incorrect. In a local storage and sale arrangement, products manufactured in one country are then shipped to a marketing facility located in another country. It is less risky than direct investment. **Answer (B) is incorrect.** Local component assembly involves shipping individual parts from one country to an assembly facility in a second country. They are then turned into a salable product and sold in the second country or exported to other countries. It is less risky than direct investment. **Answer (D) is incorrect.** In multiple or joint ventures, several firms, even competitors, work together to create products that are sold under one or more brand names in different countries. They share responsibility, ownership, costs, and profits.

Access the **Gleim CIA Premium Review System** featuring our SmartAdapt technology from your Gleim Personal Classroom to continue your studies. You will experience a personalized study environment with exam-emulating multiple-choice questions.

STUDY UNIT TWO
ORGANIZATIONAL BEHAVIOR AND PERFORMANCE MEASURES

(22 pages of outline)

2.1	Organizational Theory	40
2.2	Motivation -- Need-Based Theories and Rewards	44
2.3	Motivation -- Process-Based Theories, Behavior, Job Design, and Other	48
2.4	Organizational Politics and Group Dynamics	51
2.5	Performance Measures -- Costs of Quality	57
2.6	Performance Measures -- Balanced Scorecard	58

This study unit is the second of five covering **Domain I: Business Acumen** from The IIA's CIA Exam Syllabus. (Data Analytics, the final topic area of this domain, is covered in Study Unit 7.) This domain makes up 35% of Part 3 of the CIA exam and is tested at the **basic** and **proficient** cognitive levels. Refer to the complete syllabus located in Appendix A to view the relevant sections covered in Study Unit 2.

2.1 ORGANIZATIONAL THEORY

1. **Overview**

    a. According to Daft (*Understanding Management*, 10th ed.), an **organization** is a "social entity that is goal directed and deliberately structured." The four elements of an organization have been defined as follows:

        1) Coordination of effort in a cooperative social arrangement
        2) A common objective or purpose
        3) Division of labor (efficient work specialization)
        4) A hierarchy of authority

            a) **Authority** is the legitimate right to direct, and to expect performance from, other people to achieve the organization's goals. Those people are accountable to their superiors in the hierarchy.

    b. The test of an organization is its **performance**, for example, its effectiveness and productivity.

        1) In the narrow sense, **effectiveness** is achievement of goals by providing value to customers over time. It should be contrasted with **efficiency**, the ratio of output to input. In the broad sense, an organization must achieve its goals efficiently to be considered effective.

        2) Economists define **productivity** as the ratio of real output to a unit of input.

            a) For example, in a retail store, a critical output is revenue per square foot. Productivity of floor space, a limited resource, therefore should be analyzed.

            b) Increased productivity is the goal of every organization because it improves the measures of performance, such as profit.

        3) Depending on certain factors, the existence of **competition** may result in increased or decreased productivity.

            a) For example, competition between groups whose tasks are independent will result in increased productivity. But, competition between groups whose tasks are interdependent will result in decreased productivity.

    c. Continued profitability and growth are the obvious effectiveness criteria for businesses. However, society's expectations expressed through laws and regulations (e.g., antitrust, securities regulation, labor law, worker safety, environmental protection, pension security, antidiscrimination, consumer protection) provide many other criteria.

        1) The weighting of these criteria is difficult for all businesses.

    d. The definition of organizational effectiveness includes a time dimension. Thus, an organization needs to be effective beyond the near future. It should be effective and efficient, grow, be profitable, satisfy society's and its stakeholders' expectations, learn, adapt, develop, and survive over a period of years.

        1) The organization needs to meet expectations of society, owners, employees, customers, and creditors in the near term (about 1 year).

        2) It must adapt to change and develop its capacities in the intermediate term (about 2-4 years).

        3) It must survive in an uncertain environment full of threats and opportunities in the long term (about 5 years or more).

e. Organizational decline (inflexibility and loss of effectiveness and efficiency) may lead to downsizing, merger, reorganization, or liquidation. It results from decreased demand, resource limitations, or mismanagement.

  1) Management complacency is one of the main causes of organizational decline. The following are its characteristics:

     a) A lack of innovation
     b) Faulty perception of markets and competition
     c) Failure to observe or properly appraise the initial warnings of decline
     d) Not focusing on daily objectives

  2) Downsizing results from organizational decline, changes in the business cycle, or business combinations. The objectives are cost reduction, improved efficiency, and higher profits.

     a) These purposes often are not achieved. Many organizations follow cycles of hiring, firing, and rehiring that do not yield the expected benefits to offset the harm to terminated employees, the loss of morale of the survivors, and the damage to communities.
     b) Downsizing also tends to have a disproportionate effect on women and minorities, who tend to be the last hired and first fired.
     c) The more enlightened view is that employees are not readily disposable commodities but valuable resources who should be terminated only as a last resort. This view seeks alternatives to involuntary termination.

f. **Organizational charts** represent the formal organizational structure in two dimensions: vertical hierarchy and horizontal specialization. They often resemble a pyramid, with the chief executive on top and the operating workforce on the bottom.

  1) Lines show reporting relationships, lines of authority, and task groupings. An organizational chart also depicts promotional or career tracks and illustrates the span of control and the number of organizational levels.
  2) A shortcoming is that organizational charts do not show informal relationships, e.g., communication, influence, power, or friendship.
  3) Recent trends in management, including increased **span of control** and decreased hierarchy, have resulted in flatter organizational charts.

2. **Theories of Organizing**

  a. The **classical perspective** was a logical, scientific approach that evolved during the Industrial Revolution of the 19th and early 20th centuries. It addressed the **labor productivity** issues resulting from the need to manage large numbers of workers in factories.

     1) One approach was **scientific management**. It emphasized the production process and ways to make it more efficient. It was a systematic, quantitative approach based on the design of specific jobs that did not consider the social environment and individuals' needs. The following are the principles of scientific management:

        a) Scientific analysis of work to determine standard methods, e.g., time and motion study
        b) Scientific selection, training, and development of workers
        c) Planning the activities of workers
        d) Offering compensation for higher output to improve productivity

2) The **administrative principles** approach separated administration from technical, commercial, financial, and accounting operations.

   a) The following functions of management are the basis for the classification of a manager's activities:

      i) Planning
      ii) Organizing
      iii) Commanding
      iv) Coordinating
      v) Controlling

   b) Certain other administrative principles remain relevant.

      i) **Unity of command** requires each subordinate to have only one superior (but a superior may have as many subordinates as allowed by the span of control).
      ii) **Division of work** (specialization) improves the amount and quality of work for a given level of effort.
      iii) **Unity of direction** results when one manager is responsible for similar work activities.
      iv) The **scalar chain** of authority from the top to the bottom of the entity should include all employees.

3) A **bureaucracy** is the ultimate classical organization. It is founded on efficient military principles, including merit-based personnel decisions.

   a) A bureaucracy has the following characteristics:

      i) Division of labor
      ii) A hierarchy of clearly defined authority and responsibility (unity of objective)
      iii) Written rules to promote consistent organizational behavior that apply consistently to everyone
      iv) Separation of ownership (e.g., shareholders) and management
      v) Administrative acts and decisions are documented (e.g., minutes of meetings)
      vi) Employees are hired and promoted based on qualifications (e.g., education and certifications)

   b) Every large organization has a bureaucracy. Accordingly, managers should be aware of the symptoms of an inefficient and otherwise dysfunctional bureaucracy, such as ignoring the needs of customers and employees, pointless rules, and boring jobs.

b. The **humanistic perspective** considers individual, social, and group needs and behaviors.

   1) Early researchers emphasized the significance of (a) **superordinate** (common) goals to reduce conflict, (b) not treating organizations and people as machines, and (c) empowerment of employees.

      a) The humanistic perspective resulted in the insight that the **informal** organization (e.g., social groups and informal networks) benefits the formal organization if well managed.

      b) Another insight was that effective management may depend on employees' willing **acceptance of authority**.

   2) The **human relations** view is that productivity increases when employees' needs are met.

   3) The **human resources** approach is that job design should allow employees to reach their potential. Thus, it also relates to theories of motivation. (These concepts are covered in Subunit 2.2.)

   4) **Behavioral sciences** researchers use tools from many disciplines (e.g., psychology and sociology) to understand employee behavior in an organization.

      a) **Organizational development (OD)** evolved from behavioral sciences research. It is covered in Study Unit 4, Subunit 3.

c. The **contingency perspective** is that design of organizations depends on contingencies that can be discovered and studied. But no methods apply to all organizations.

   1) Because solutions are situationally determined, the key is finding the relevant factors in the organization's environment.

   2) Moreover, the greater the environmental uncertainty, the more adaptive the organization must be.

   3) Contingency design determines the structure that suits the environmental (state) uncertainty faced by the organization. Environmental uncertainty is a function of, among other things, the following:

      a) Stability of demand for the organization's goods or services
      b) Reliability of supply
      c) Rate of technological change
      d) Socioeconomic and political pressures

   4) However, the contingency perspective does not assume that every situation is unique. Rather, it applies similar responses to common problems.

STOP & REVIEW

You have completed the outline for this subunit.
Study multiple-choice questions 1 through 4 beginning on page 60.

2.2 MOTIVATION -- NEED-BASED THEORIES AND REWARDS

1. This subunit presents theories of motivation and describes how job design and rewards affect motivation.

2. **Motivation** is the set of internal and external forces that stimulate enthusiasm to persist in a course of action.

   a. The ideal management action motivates subordinates by structuring situations and requiring behaviors that satisfy the needs of subordinates and the organization.

3. **Rewards**

   a. **Extrinsic rewards** are received from others. They range from money to praise.

      1) Social rewards normally include acknowledgment of employee achievement through actions, such as solicitation of advice.

      2) Token rewards are normally nonrecurring. They show appreciation for the role of the employee. Examples are stock options, early time off with pay, or a paid vacation trip.

      3) Extrinsic threats and punishments use fear to motivate. An example is charging overweight employees more for health insurance.

         a) This practice is based on **loss aversion**, the tendency to respond more to a loss than a possible gain (e.g., a monetary reward for weight loss).

   b. **Intrinsic rewards** are the internal satisfactions that result from certain actions. Examples are enjoyable work and accomplishment of fulfilling tasks.

      1) Intrinsic anxieties and self-doubts may be exploited by managers, for example, the fear of unemployment during a recession.

   c. According to **equity theory**, employee motivation is affected significantly by relative as well as absolute rewards. An employee compares the ratio of what (s)he receives from a job (outcomes such as pay or recognition) to what (s)he gives to the job (inputs such as effort, experience, ability, or education) with the ratios of relevant others.

      1) If the ratios are equal, equity exists. If they are unequal, inequity exists, and the employee will be motivated to eliminate the inequity.

         a) Responses may be to alter (1) inputs to the job, (2) the outcomes (e.g., asking for a raise), or (3) the perceptions (e.g., by inflating job status).

         b) An extreme response is to leave the job.

4. **Need-Based Theories of Motivation**

   a. According to **Abraham Maslow**, human needs are a hierarchy, from lowest to highest. Lower-level needs must be satisfied before higher-level needs can influence (motivate) the individual.

      1) Maslow's **hierarchy of needs** is listed below, from lowest to highest:

         a) **Physiological needs** are the basic requirements for sustaining human life, such as water, food, shelter, and sleep. Until these needs are satisfied to the degree needed to maintain life, higher-level needs will not be motivators.

         b) **Security or safety needs** include protection from physical or emotional harm, the loss of a job, and other threats.

         c) **Affiliation or acceptance needs** are the needs of people as social beings for love, affection, friendship, and belonging.

         d) **Esteem** is the need to be valued by both one's self and others. These needs are satisfied by power, prestige, status, and self-confidence.

         e) **Self-actualization** is the highest need in the hierarchy. It is the need to realize one's own potential for growth and continued development.

            i) Thus, the job itself is an intrinsic motivation; no extrinsic motivation (such as rewards or reinforcements) is needed. Intrinsic motivation provides the worker with psychological utility.

      2) Research supports the assertion that biological needs must be satisfied before other needs become motivators. However, the strict order of the hierarchy may not always apply in other cases.

         a) Physiological and safety needs tend to decrease in importance for fully employed people. Needs for acceptance, esteem, and self-actualization tend to increase.

         b) Higher-level needs, esteem and self-actualization, are variable in their motivational effects, depending upon the individual.

      3) Maslow's hierarchy does not apply equally to all situations. It is dependent on the social, cultural, and psychological backgrounds of the people involved.

         a) People of different cultures respond differently.

         b) Professional workers, skilled workers, and unskilled workers react differently.

         c) Other social, ethnic, and cultural factors make people react differently.

         d) The hierarchy is not a smooth, step-by-step path. It is a complicated and interdependent set of relationships.

            i) However, the tendency to move upward as lower needs are satisfied does exist.

b. **ERG theory** is a simplified version of Maslow's hierarchy of needs.
   1) The classifications are the following:
      a) Existence (physical needs)
      b) Relatedness (satisfying relationships)
      c) Growth (needs for development of human potential)
   2) The **frustration** of not fulfilling a higher-level need (e.g., growth) may result in **regression** to a lower level (e.g., earning more money).
   3) Organizations increasingly are finding ways to motivate employees by a better balance of personal life and work.
      a) One method is a **flexible job schedule**. An extreme example is the elimination of a schedule and considering only work results.

c. Frederick Herzberg's **two-factor theory of motivation** is based on satisfaction. The following two classes of motivational factors exist in the job situation:
   1) Dissatisfiers (maintenance or hygiene factors) are found in the job context.
      a) Their presence will not especially motivate people, but their absence will lead to diminished performance. They include the following:
         i) Organizational policy and administration
         ii) Supervision
         iii) Working conditions
         iv) Interpersonal relations
         v) Salary and status
         vi) Job security
   2) Satisfiers (motivational factors) relate to job content.
      a) Their absence will not diminish performance, but their addition or availability will motivate employees. They include the following:
         i) Achievement
         ii) Recognition
         iii) Challenging work
         iv) Advancement
         v) Growth in the job
         vi) Responsibility
   3) Satisfaction and dissatisfaction are on a continuum. In the middle is the point at which an employee experiences neither job satisfaction nor dissatisfaction.
      a) At this point, (s)he is not dissatisfied with the job context but also is not positively motivated.
      b) If Herzberg is correct, job content should be improved through the use of job enrichment strategies.
      c) Some jobs obviously do not contain many motivators, but other jobs have the potential for more motivators than are being fully used by management. For example,
         i) Routine, low-status work, such as mail sorting, has few motivators.
         ii) A company that may be paying above the industry average (maintenance factor) also could increase satisfaction by openly acknowledging sales or other efforts by initiating a salesperson of the week recognition program.

d. Douglas McGregor's **Theory X and Theory Y** are models that define the extremes of managers' opinions on employee conduct. They permit a manager to evaluate his or her own tendencies.

1) Theory X is the perspective of the autocratic manager.

   a) Most people dislike work.
   b) Most people must be controlled and threatened to induce them to make an adequate effort to achieve organizational objectives.
   c) Most people want to be directed, lack ambition, and primarily seek security.

2) Theory Y is the extreme opposite of Theory X. The permissive manager assumes the following:

   a) Physical and mental effort in work is as natural as recreation or rest.
   b) Control and threats are not the only means of motivating individuals to make an adequate effort to achieve organizational objectives. Employees will be self-directed and self-controlled if they believe the objectives are worthy.
   c) Commitment to objectives is proportional to the rewards of accomplishment.
   d) Most people can learn to seek responsibility.
   e) The human ability to use imagination and creativity to solve problems is common.
   f) In modern industrial life, the intellectual ability of most people is not fully realized.

3) McGregor did not suggest that Theory Y was the only correct managerial behavior. He suggested these theories as starting points from which a manager can examine his or her own views about human nature.

e. According to the **acquired needs theory**, some needs are learned, not inherent.

1) The need for **achievement** is satisfied by high performance and skill in completing difficult assignments. But achievers are attracted to moderate (not high) risk. They also tend to be entrepreneurs.

2) The need for **affiliation** is satisfied by personal relationships and conflict avoidance. Affiliators tend to succeed as coordinators of business functions.

3) The need for **power** is the desire for influence or control, responsibility, and authority over subordinates. Power seekers often become chief executives.

STOP & REVIEW

You have completed the outline for this subunit.
Study multiple-choice questions 5 through 8 beginning on page 62.

2.3 MOTIVATION -- PROCESS-BASED THEORIES, BEHAVIOR, JOB DESIGN, AND OTHER

1. **Process-Based Theories of Motivation**
    a. According to **goal-setting theory** developed by Edwin Locke and Gary Latham, specific, difficult goals to which the employee is committed provide the best motivation tool.
        1) Performance improves when goals are (a) specific rather than general, (b) difficult rather than easy, and (c) accepted by employees rather than imposed by others.
            a) Goals therefore should be participative (self-set).
        2) Furthermore, specific feedback, especially self-generated feedback, also improves performance compared with lack of feedback.
        3) Goals serve as motivators because they (a) focus on specific results, (b) require continuous effort to achieve (persistence), and (c) are incentives for developing strategies and action plans.
    b. Victor Vroom's **expectancy theory** is based on the thought process that involves (1) subjective expectations of rewards, (2) beliefs as to what is valuable, and (3) expectations of receiving these rewards if effort is exerted.
        1) Thus, expectancy theory addresses individualized (a) motivations and (b) perceptions of the probability of success.
        2) High effort expended, ability, and accurate role assessment lead to high performance. That is, putting appropriate effort into the right task and having the right amount of ability to do it lead to high performance and an expectation of desirable outcomes.
            a) **E→P** expectancy is high if an individual perceives that (s)he has the ability, experience, resources, and opportunity to perform. But if it is low, motivation also is low.
            b) **P→O** expectancy is high if an individual perceives that performance leads to desirable outcomes (rewards). But if it is low, motivation also is low.
            c) **Valence** is the value an individual assigns to outcomes. Motivation varies directly with valence.
            d) Insufficient ability impedes performance despite effort.
            e) Executing a task that is not desired or is improperly performed according to role definition impedes performance despite effort or ability.
        3) **Expectancy** results from past experiences. It measures the strength of belief (the probability assessments) that a particular act will be followed by a specific outcome.
            a) Management is more able to control the expectancy factor than the individual perception of valence because expectations are based on experience.
                i) A consistent management policy reinforces employee expectations.
        4) Performance leads to rewards.
            a) Individuals evaluate rewards on the basis of the fairness of their treatment compared with others in similar jobs.
            b) If unfairness exists, individuals react, usually negatively.
        5) Perception of the equity of rewards leads to satisfaction.
            a) The level of satisfaction or dissatisfaction feeds back into the next cycle's estimates of reward values, individual abilities, and role perceptions.

2. **Behavior Modification**
    a. Behavior modification is based on reinforcement theory. According to the **law of effect**, positive reinforcement of a behavior tends to result in its repetition. Lack of positive reinforcement has the opposite effect.
        1) **Reinforcement** is something that results in repetition or inhibition of a behavior.
    b. The following are types of reinforcement methods:
        1) **Positive reinforcement** is providing a reward for desired behavior. The reward may be financial or nonfinancial (e.g., praise or attention).
        2) **Avoidance learning** (also known as negative reinforcement) is the removal of a negative effect of prior behavior. The avoidance of unpleasant consequences (e.g., criticism by a supervisor) increases the probability that the new and preferable behavior will be repeated.
        3) **Punishment** imposes a negative consequence (e.g., loss of pay, suspension, or firing) for unacceptable behavior. It decreases the probability that the behavior will recur.
        4) **Extinction** withholds a reward (e.g., praise or an increase in pay). The theory is that a behavior that is not positively reinforced eventually ceases.
    c. **Social learning theory** is based on the idea that observation of the behavior of others may be motivational.
        1) **Vicarious (observational) learning** is the result of seeing that desired behaviors are rewarded.
            a) For example, a trainee may be mentored by someone who models the desired behavior and teaches the necessary skills.

3. **Job Design**
    a. Job design links tasks to particular jobs using motivational research to increase productivity and employee satisfaction.
    b. One approach is to adapt people to jobs. For example, **job rotation** is a change in boring, highly specialized jobs. It also may have such benefits as cross-functional training.
    c. Another job design method is to adapt the jobs to the people performing them.
        1) **Job enlargement** is primarily intended to reduce boredom in repetitive or fast-paced jobs through the assignment of a variety of simple tasks as part of one job. Such jobs are horizontally loaded.
        2) **Job enrichment** structures the job so that each worker participates in planning and controlling. The purpose is satisfaction of social and ego needs and avoidance of routine work.
            a) Job enrichment should improve motivation by vertically loading the job, that is, increasing its complexity, challenge, and opportunities (e.g., for growth, recognition, and achievement).
            b) According to the **job characteristics model** described by Hackman and Oldham, jobs are enriched by improving the following **core job dimensions**:
                i) Skill variety, or the diversity of talents required
                ii) Task identity, or completion of an entire work product
                iii) Task significance, or the effect on other people
                iv) Autonomy, or level of discretion over how work is done
                v) Feedback, or receipt of information about performance
            c) Enrichment should produce three **critical psychological states**:
                i) Meaningfulness (first three core job dimensions)
                ii) Responsibility for work outcomes (autonomy)
                iii) Knowledge of actual work outcomes (feedback)
            d) The critical psychological states should produce high motivation, performance, and satisfaction; low turnover; and low absenteeism.
                i) However, worker satisfaction does not necessarily lead to improved performance. It is more likely that a productive worker is a happy worker.
                ii) The job characteristics model is most effective for people with a strong need for personal challenge and achievement.
            e) **Employee growth-need strength** is the last building block of the job characteristics model.
                i) People have distinct needs for growth and development.

You have completed the outline for this subunit.
Study multiple-choice questions 9 through 11 beginning on page 63.

2.4 ORGANIZATIONAL POLITICS AND GROUP DYNAMICS

1. **Organizational Politics**

    a. Organizational politics (impression management) is acting in self-interest given actual or perceived opposition in the workplace.

    b. Managers must understand organizational politics (1) as a matter of self-interest and (2) its negative effects on morale, the effectiveness of needed change, and ethical behavior.

2. **Behaviors**

    a. Self-interested behaviors are not based solely on competence or diligence or the results of good fortune.

    b. Positive political behaviors include coalition building, networking, and seeking mentors.

    c. Negative political behaviors include sabotage, threats, taking credit for others' work or ideas, and building revolutionary coalitions.

    1) Negative political behavior is considered by some managers to include **whistleblowing**. It is the reporting to internal or external parties (e.g., internal auditors, a compliance officer, government bodies, the media, or private watchdog groups) of entity conduct asserted to be wrongful.

        a) Some managers believe whistleblowing to be an act of revenge that is disloyal to the organization. Moreover, some whistleblowers may have personal financial motives.

        b) However, the prevailing view is that whistleblowing is a net social good. Revealing unethical behavior may be the only way to end misconduct that has substantial negative effects on the public interest.

        c) Thus, many governments have enacted whistleblower protection statutes. These laws prohibit retaliation against insiders who appropriately disclose wrongdoing.

        d) Some statutes even provide financial incentives. For example, in the U.S., a statute may allow employees of the government or of contractors to receive a percentage of any recovery of fraudulent payments made under defense contracts, provision of healthcare, etc.

3. **Organizational Culture**

    a. The organizational culture may encourage politics by creating unreasonable obstacles to group and individual advancement.

    b. The following perceptions about organizational politics are widely held:

    1) Political behavior increases as managers rise in the hierarchy.
    2) The frequency of political behavior increases as the organization grows.
    3) Line managers are less political than staff managers.
    4) Marketing managers are the most political, and production managers are the least.
    5) Reorganization results in more political behavior than other changes.
    6) Political behavior helps career advancement.
    7) Political behavior may be beneficial to the organization by promoting ideas, building teams, enhancing communication, and improving morale.
    8) Political behavior may have a negative effect on the organization by distracting managers from focusing on entity objectives.

4. **Political Tactics**

    a. The following are common political tactics:

    1) **Posturing** is an attempt to make a good impression, for example, by taking credit for others' work or seeking to stay ahead of a rival (one-upmanship).

    2) **Empire building** is an attempt to control greater resources. Thus, a manager with a larger budget may believe that (s)he is in a safer position and is more influential.

    3) **Making the supervisor look good** is an effort to impress the person who controls one's career path.

    4) **Collecting and using social favors** is a tactic used by someone who views favors as the currency of advancement, not as unselfish acts. Such a manager may help another to look good or not to look bad, for example, by concealing a mistake.

    5) **Creating power and loyalty cliques** is a tactic based on the premise that a cohesive group has more power than an individual.

    6) **Engaging in destructive competition** includes such behaviors as gossip, lying, and sabotage.

5. **Limiting Politics**

    a. Organizational politics may reduce productivity. To avoid this result, the organization should

    1) Create an open, trusting environment;

    2) Focus on performance;

    3) Discourage senior managers from modeling political behavior for other managers;

    4) Use work and career planning to make individual objectives consistent with organizational objectives; and

    5) Rotate jobs to develop a broader perspective and understanding of the problems of others.

6. **Group Dynamics**

    a. Group dynamics should be addressed in correlation with organizational politics.

    b. Management should improve the social capital of the organization by enhancing the relationships of the groups within its structure.

    1) A group consists of at least two individuals who interact freely, recognize themselves as group members (common identity), and agree on the reason for the group (common purpose).

7. **Formal Groups**

    a. Formal groups are work groups (designated as committees, teams, etc.) within the organization assembled to perform a productive activity.

    1) Individuals are assigned to formal groups based on their qualifications and the organization's purposes.

    2) Formal groups have explicitly designated leaders.

    3) Membership in formal groups is relatively more permanent than in informal groups.

    4) Formal groups are more structured than informal groups.

8. **Informal Groups**

    a. People seek association and group acceptance and tend to form informal as well as formal groups. Effective managers accept and take advantage of the informal organization.

        1) Informal groups are created within organizations because of the following:

            a) Authority relationships not definable on an organizational chart
            b) Unwritten rules of conduct
            c) Group preferences

        2) The following are characteristics of informal groups:

            a) Development primarily to satisfy esteem needs (friendship)
            b) Membership of most employees, including managers
            c) Conformity of most members to group pressures
            d) Small and often very complex

                i) They develop their own leaders, satisfy the needs of members, and usually result from the frequent work interaction among individuals.

        3) Favorable effects of informal groups include the following:

            a) Reducing tension and encouraging production
            b) Improving coordination and reducing supervision required
            c) Assistance in problem solving
            d) Providing another (often faster) channel of communication

                i) The grapevine is the informal communication system in every organization. Computer networks have strengthened the grapevine.

            e) Providing social satisfactions that supplement job satisfaction

        4) The following are examples of potentially unfavorable effects:

            a) Circumventing managerial actions
            b) Reducing production (slowdowns caused by social interactions)
            c) Dissension in the formal organization
            d) Spreading rumors and distorting information
            e) Adding to the cost of doing business
            f) Forming subgroups that hinder group cohesiveness
            g) Adoption of group norms contrary to the objectives of the organization
            h) Developing dominant members

9. **Group Commitment**
    a. Commitment to a group depends on its attractiveness and cohesiveness.
    b. **Attractiveness** is a favorable view from the outside.
    c. **Cohesiveness** is the tendency of members to adhere to the group and unite against outside pressures.
    d. Group attractiveness and cohesiveness are increased by the following:
        1) Its prestige and status
        2) Cooperation among the members
        3) Substantial member interaction
        4) Small size of the group
        5) Similarity of members
        6) Good public image
        7) Common external threat
    e. Group attractiveness and cohesiveness are decreased by the following:
        1) Its unpleasant demands on members
        2) Disagreements about activities and procedures
        3) Bad experiences with the group
        4) Conflict between the group's demands and those of other activities
        5) Its bad public image
        6) The possibility of joining other groups

10. **Roles and Norms**
    a. A role is the behavior expected of a person in a specific position. Everyone is expected to have different roles.
        1) The term also refers to actual behavior.
        2) Different people in the same position should behave similarly.
        3) Role conflict occurs when a person has two or more conflicting roles.
            a) Role models may help individuals resolve role conflicts.
        4) Roles may be formally defined in job descriptions and procedures manuals.
    b. Norms are general standards of conduct and have a broader effect than roles. Groups are guided by self-set norms of performance and behavior.
        1) Norms vary from culture to culture and most often are unwritten.
        2) The following are the functions of norms:
            a) Protect the group (survival)
            b) Better define role behavior and expectations
            c) Safeguard members from embarrassment (self-image)
            d) Reinforce the group's values and common identity
        3) Enforcement of norms in the positive sense follows from attention, recognition, and acceptance (social reinforcement).
            a) Enforcement of norms in the negative sense may be by ridicule or criticism. The ultimate punishment is rejection.

11. **Conformity**
    a. Conformity is compliance with roles and norms.
    b. The benefit of conformity is predictability of behavior, e.g., performance of assigned tasks. The cost may be illegal, unethical, or incompetent conduct.
    c. One danger of cohesive groups is **groupthink**. It is the tendency of individuals committed to the group to ignore input that varies from the group opinion.
        1) The following are symptoms of groupthink:
            a) Over-optimism
            b) Assumed morality of the preferred action
            c) Intolerance of dissent
            d) An urgent search for unanimity
        2) The following are ways of avoiding groupthink:
            a) Being aware of its dangers
            b) Encouraging members to think critically
            c) Seeking outside opinions
            d) Expressly assigning a member of the group to advocate contrary positions
            e) Expressly considering the consequences of different actions
            f) Not using a group to approve a decision without discussion or dissent
        3) Cooperative (constructive) conflict is a means of avoiding groupthink.
        4) Groupthink in formal groups (e.g., committees) can inhibit creative thinking and innovative viewpoints.

12. **Group-Aided Decision Making**
    a. Group-aided decision making and problem solving have the following advantages:
        1) The group has greater knowledge and experience than an individual
        2) Lateral thinking allows the group to explore diverse views
        3) Participants have a better understanding of the reasons for actions
        4) Active participants tend to accept the result
        5) Group involvement provides training for the less experienced members
    b. The following are the disadvantages of group-aided decision making:
        1) The social pressure to conform may inhibit creativity.
        2) The group may be dominated by a few aggressive members.
        3) The decision or solution may be a product of political dealing (logrolling).
        4) Secondary concerns, e.g., competing with a rival, may distract the group.
        5) The process may suffer from groupthink.
        6) Groups tend to take longer than individuals.

c. **Group decision making** differs from group-aided decision making.

   1) Groups submerge individual identity and accountability and conceal the link between individual effort and outcome. Thus, greater acceptance of risk results because accountability is dispersed.

      a) **Groupshift** is the difference between an individual's probable decision when the individual is alone and when the individual is in a group.

d. The following are methods that may be applied to improve creativity:

   1) **Attribute listing** is applied primarily to improve a tangible object. It lists the parts and essential features of the object and systematically analyzes modifications.

   2) **Brainstorming** is an unstructured, nonjudgmental group approach that relies on spontaneous contribution of ideas. It breaks down broad problems into their essentials.

      a) Brainstorming generates a large number of ideas and overcomes the pressure to conform while the group is identifying options.

      b) Brainstorming has no predictable effect on the group's commitment to the solution.

   3) **Creative leap** formulates an ideal solution and then works back to a feasible one.

   4) The **scientific method** systematically (a) states a problem, (b) collects data by observation and experimentation, and (c) formulates and tests hypotheses.

   5) The **Edisonian** approach is a trial-and-error method. It should usually not be applied unless other approaches have been unsuccessful.

   6) **Free association** generates ideas by reporting the first thought to come to mind in response to a stimulus, for example, a symbol or analogy pertaining to a product for which an advertising slogan is sought. The objective is to express the content of consciousness without censorship or control.

   7) **Lateral thinking** explores different approaches to an issue. These alternatives increase the probability of a solution.

STOP & REVIEW

You have completed the outline for this subunit.
Study multiple-choice questions 12 through 16 beginning on page 64.

2.5 PERFORMANCE MEASURES -- COSTS OF QUALITY

1. Performance measures – Financial vs. Nonfinancial measures

    a. **Financial** performance measures are derived from financial accounting data stated in monetary units. Various financial performance measures are described in Study Unit 10.

    b. **Nonfinancial** performance measures are not standardized and may have any appropriate form.

    1) **Product quality** measures include but are not limited to returns and allowances and the number and types of customer complaints.

    2) **Manufacturing** measures include but are not limited to

    a) Throughput time (the time required to convert materials into finished goods),
    b) The ratio of equipment setup time to total production time, and
    c) The ratio of reworked units to completed units.

    3) The **balanced scorecard** includes other nonfinancial measures. It is covered in Subunit 2.6.

2. The costs of quality must be assessed in terms of relative costs and benefits. Thus, an organization should attempt to optimize its total cost of quality.

    a. Moreover, nonquantitative factors also must be considered. For example, an emphasis on quality improves competitiveness, enhances employee expertise, and generates goodwill.

3. **Conformance costs** include costs of prevention and costs of appraisal, which are financial measures of internal performance.

    a. **Prevention** attempts to avoid defective output. These costs include

    1) Preventive maintenance,
    2) Employee training,
    3) Review of equipment design, and
    4) Evaluation of suppliers.

    b. **Appraisal** includes such activities as statistical quality control programs, inspection, and testing.

4. **Nonconformance costs** include internal failure costs (a financial measure of internal performance) and external failure costs (a financial measure of customer satisfaction).

    a. **Internal failure costs** occur when defective products are detected before shipment and additional costs are incurred on defective products. Examples are scrap, rework, tooling changes, and downtime.

    b. **External failure costs**, e.g., warranty costs, product liability costs, and loss of customer goodwill, result when problems occur after shipment.

    1) Environmental costs also are external failure costs, e.g., fines for nonadherence to environmental law and loss of customer goodwill.

STOP & REVIEW

You have completed the outline for this subunit.
Study multiple-choice questions 17 and 18 on page 66.

2.6 PERFORMANCE MEASURES -- BALANCED SCORECARD

1. **Critical Success Factors (CSFs)**

    a. The balanced scorecard is a management control approach that connects CSFs with measures of performance.

    b. The balanced scorecard also is a goal congruence tool that informs managers about the factors that senior management believes to be important.

       1) CSFs are specific measures that may be (a) financial or nonfinancial, (b) internal or external, and (c) short-term or long-term.

       2) The balanced scorecard facilitates best practice analysis. **Best practices** are methods of performing a function that are superior to all other known methods.

    c. CSFs are vital to competitive advantage.

2. **Measures**

    a. Specific measures for each CSF should be relevant to the success of the firm and reliably stated.

       1) Thus, the balanced scorecard varies with the strategy adopted by the firm.

    b. The scorecard should include **lagging** indicators (such as output and financial measures) and **leading** indicators (such as many types of nonfinancial measures, e.g., customer satisfaction, returns, and repeat customers).

       1) The latter should be used only if they are predictors of ultimate financial performance.

    c. The scorecard should permit a determination of whether certain objectives are being achieved at the expense of others.

       1) For example, reduced spending on customer service may improve short-term financial results at a significant cost that is revealed by a long-term decline in customer satisfaction measures.

3. **Possible CSFs and Measures**

    a. A typical balanced scorecard classifies objectives into one of four perspectives:

       1) The **financial performance** perspective addresses current and long-term results.

Possible CSF	Possible Measure
Sales	New product sales
Fair value of stock	Price-earnings ratio
Profitability	Return on investment, EVA
Liquidity	Quick ratio, current ratio, net working capital

2) The **customer service** perspective includes customer retention, customers' opinions about the firm, and their level of satisfaction.

CSF	Financial Measure	Nonfinancial Measure
Customer satisfaction	Trends in monetary amounts of returns	Market share
Dealer and distributor relationships	Trends in monetary amounts of discounts taken	Lead time
Marketing and selling performance	Trends in monetary amounts of sales	Market research results
Prompt delivery	Trends in delivery expenses	On-time delivery rate
Quality	Monetary amounts of defects	Rate of defects

3) The **internal business processes** perspective emphasizes production and other operational measures.

CSF	Financial Measure	Nonfinancial Measure
Quality	Scrap costs	Rate of scrap and rework
Productivity	Change in company revenue/ change in company costs	Units produced per machine hour
Flexibility of response to changing conditions	Cost to repurpose machine for new use	Time to repurpose machine for new use
Operating readiness	Set-up costs	Downtime
Safety	Monetary amount of injury claims	Number and type of injury claims

4) The **learning and growth** perspective relates to resource management and innovation.

CSF	Financial Measure	Nonfinancial Measure
Development of new products	R&D costs	Number of new patents applied for
Promptness of product introduction	Lost revenue (from slow introduction of new products to market)	Length of time to bring a product to market
Human resource development	Recruiting costs	Personnel turnover
Morale	Orientation and team-building costs	Personnel complaints
Competence of workers	Training or retraining costs	Hours of training

4. **Example Balanced Scorecard**

OBJECTIVES	PERFORMANCE MEASURES	TARGETS	OUTCOMES	CORRECTIVE INITIATIVES
PERSPECTIVE: Financial Performance					
Increase sales	Gross revenues	Increase 15%	Increase 3%	• Expand into new markets • Improve same-store sales
PERSPECTIVE: Customer Service					
Reduce returns	Number of returns	Decrease 10%	Decrease 2%	• Reduce number of defects • Determine customer needs prior to sale
PERSPECTIVE: Internal Business Processes					
Reduce scrap	Costs of scrap	Decrease 5%	Increase 4%	• Improve employee training • Seek higher quality materials
PERSPECTIVE: Learning and Growth					
Reduce personnel turnover	Length of time employed	Increase 50%	Increase 10%	• Improve hiring practices • Reevaluate compensation plan

STOP & REVIEW

You have completed the outline for this subunit.
Study multiple-choice questions 19 through 21 beginning on page 66.

QUESTIONS

2.1 Organizational Theory

1. Organizational charts often represent the formal structure of an organization. Often the organizational chart represents a pyramid with the chief executive on the top and the operating workforce on the bottom. Which of the following would **not** be included in a typical organizational chart?

   A. The span of control and the number of organizational levels.
   B. Communication channels.
   C. Promotional or career tracks.
   D. Informal influence or friendships.

Answer (D) is correct.
   REQUIRED: The limitations of organizational charts.
   DISCUSSION: Organizational charts often show the formal relationships between employers and employees. However, a shortcoming of organizational charts is that they do not show informal relationships between the upper and lower levels of the corporate hierarchy.
   Answer (A) is incorrect. The span of control and the number of organizational levels is demonstrated by the pyramid. The chief executive at the top has the greatest control over the organization and then the levels of the pyramid show the number of organizational levels. **Answer (B) is incorrect.** The communication channels are often up the pyramid and are shown on the organizational chart. **Answer (C) is incorrect.** The higher levels of the pyramid are the levels that employees can be promoted to.

2. Which of the following concepts is **not** consistent with the classical perspective on management?

A. Each subordinate should only have one superior.
B. Superiors may have as many subordinates as possible within the superior's span of control.
C. Employees may choose not to follow orders.
D. The hierarchy of authority should be precisely defined.

Answer (C) is correct.
REQUIRED: The concept not a characteristic of the classical perspective.
DISCUSSION: The humanistic perspective approached management by considering individual, social, and group needs and behaviors. One insight was that effective management may depend on employees' willing acceptance of authority. It is based on the acknowledgment that workers have free will and may decide not to follow orders.
Answer (A) is incorrect. The unity of command principle states that each subordinate should only have one superior in order to prevent confusion and frustration. **Answer (B) is incorrect.** The unity of command principle states that a superior can have as many subordinates as (s)he can reasonably manage. **Answer (D) is incorrect.** The unity of objective principle requires that the hierarchy of authority should be precisely defined to pursue common objectives.

3. Which of the following is true with regard to the contingency perspective to solving problems within an organization?

A. The organization's environment plays the largest role in finding situationally determined answers.
B. The organization may be less adaptive when the environment is more uncertain.
C. The organization should search for a solution that can be used in all cases.
D. The contingency approach is a scientific management perspective.

Answer (A) is correct.
REQUIRED: The true statement regarding the contingency approach to solving problems within an organization.
DISCUSSION: The contingency approach is that solutions are situationally determined. The key is finding the relevant factors in the organization's environment.
Answer (B) is incorrect. The organization should be more adaptive when the environment is uncertain. **Answer (C) is incorrect.** No single design format fits all organizations and situations. **Answer (D) is incorrect.** The contingency approach searches for the solution appropriate to the organization's circumstances.

4. Although bureaucracy is often perceived negatively by the public, bureaucracy is a feature of nearly every large company. Which of the following is a sign that a bureaucracy is dysfunctional?

A. A diversity of jobs.
B. Rules that obscure responsibility.
C. A large number of rules necessary for day to day operations.
D. Obedience to authority.

Answer (B) is correct.
REQUIRED: The symptoms of a dysfunctional bureaucracy.
DISCUSSION: A sign that a bureaucracy is dysfunctional is the development of rules that are meaningless or that obscure accountability. A lack of accountability shows that the bureaucracy is ineffective at identifying the source problems and creating solutions to solve the problems.
Answer (A) is incorrect. A diversity of jobs prevents employees from becoming bored with routine and unchallenging tasks. **Answer (C) is incorrect.** Many bureaucracies have rules to guide day-to-day operations. If the rules have a purpose, they do not create a dysfunctional environment. **Answer (D) is incorrect.** Obedience to authority is required for a corporation's operations to run smoothly. However, obedience at all costs is a sign that the bureaucracy is dysfunctional.

2.2 Motivation -- Need-Based Theories and Rewards

5. Frederick Herzberg postulated a two-factor theory of human behavior that included satisfiers and dissatisfiers. Which of the following is a dissatisfier?

  A. Promotion to another position.
  B. Salary.
  C. Challenging work.
  D. Responsibility.

Answer (B) is correct.
REQUIRED: The item that is a dissatisfier.
DISCUSSION: Frederick Herzberg's two-factor theory of human behavior postulates that there are two classes of factors in the job situation. Maintenance of hygiene factors (dissatisfiers) are those the presence of which will not especially motivate people but the absence of which will diminish performance. These factors are extrinsic to the work itself. They include supervision, working conditions, interpersonal relations, salary, and status. Motivational factors (satisfiers) are those the absence of which will not diminish performance but the addition or availability of which will motivate employees. Intrinsic to the work itself, these include achievement, recognition, challenging work, advancement, growth in the job, and responsibility.
  Answer (A) is incorrect. Recognition and achievement are satisfiers. **Answer (C) is incorrect.** Challenging work is a satisfier. **Answer (D) is incorrect.** Responsibility is a satisfier.

6. An employee with a good background and years of experience earns a salary at the top of his or her range. Under the company's compensation program, the employee must earn a promotion in order to increase his or her salary above the usual annual increase. Which of the following is most likely to be an effect on the employee's behavior?

  A. The employee may refuse new duties or tasks.
  B. The employee may become less productive.
  C. The employee may not be motivated to improve performance.
  D. The employee may seek a position with another company.

Answer (D) is correct.
REQUIRED: The effect on the employee's behavior of the limitation on possible rewards.
DISCUSSION: When an employee can earn a desired salary increase only through a promotion, (s)he is likely to be motivated to perform better. If this does not result in a promotion, (s)he will probably look for another job.

7. A Theory X manager most likely believes that employees

  A. Require little supervision.
  B. Are creative and imaginative.
  C. Need direction and security.
  D. Solve problems outside their immediate control.

Answer (C) is correct.
REQUIRED: The characteristic of a Theory X manager attributes to employees.
DISCUSSION: In the 1960s, Douglas McGregor developed two theories to describe the extremes of managers' views of human nature. Theory X is a negative view of people and the way they interact with the organization. Theory X assumes that people dislike work, must be threatened with punishment to work toward organizational objectives, require close supervision, avoid responsibility, and crave security.

8. Motivation is

A. The extent to which goal-specific performance is recognized by supervisors.
B. The extent to which individuals have the authority to make decisions.
C. The extent of the attempt to accomplish a specific goal.
D. The set of forces that stimulate enthusiasm and persistence.

Answer (D) is correct.
REQUIRED: The definition of motivation.
DISCUSSION: Motivation is the set of internal and external forces that stimulate enthusiasm to persist in a course of action. The ideal management action motivates subordinates by structuring situations and requiring behaviors that satisfy the needs of subordinates and the organization.
Answer (A) is incorrect. Recognition of goal-specific performance is characteristic of a reward system.
Answer (B) is incorrect. Autonomy is the extent to which individuals have the authority to make decisions.
Answer (C) is incorrect. Goal congruence is the sharing of goals by supervisors and subordinates.

2.3 Motivation -- Process-Based Theories, Behavior, Job Design, and Other

9. Two managers were discussing the merits of goal setting to improve employee performance. One manager felt that specific goals should not be established and that, to provide for flexibility, only generalized goals should be used. The other manager felt that specific, difficult goals produce the best results. As the discussion continued, other methods of goal setting were identified. Select the best method for setting goals.

A. The manager should provide generalized goals.
B. The manager should select specific, difficult goals.
C. The employee should develop generalized goals and obtain management concurrence.
D. The employee should develop specific, difficult goals and obtain management concurrence.

Answer (D) is correct.
REQUIRED: The best method for setting goals.
DISCUSSION: According to Edwin Locke's goal-setting theory, specific, difficult goals to which the employee is committed provide the best motivation tool. Performance improves when goals are specific rather than general, difficult rather than easy, and participative (self-set) rather than imposed by others. Feedback, especially self-generated feedback, also improves performance compared with lack of feedback. Commitment to goals, that is, a determination not to reduce or abandon them, and self-efficacy, that is, a belief in one's ability to accomplish the task, are additional qualities that result in better performance.
Answer (A) is incorrect. Specific, difficult goals provide more motivation than generalized goals.
Answer (B) is incorrect. Employee involvement in goal setting provides better assurance that employees will be committed to the goals. **Answer (C) is incorrect.** Specific, difficult goals provide more motivation than generalized goals.

10. Job enrichment is a motivational approach used by management that

A. Emphasizes the need for close supervision.
B. Is based on Maslow's analysis of survival needs.
C. Is based on Herzberg's analysis of factors extrinsic to the work.
D. Applies the principle of worker participation.

Answer (D) is correct.
REQUIRED: The true statement about job enrichment.
DISCUSSION: Job enrichment increases the scope of boring, repetitive tasks by using more of the employee's skills and allowing the employee more power to make decisions concerning the job, such as order of tasks, etc. Thus, it encourages worker participation in decisions previously made by management.
Answer (A) is incorrect. Job enrichment is based on the assumption that employees who have qualitatively improved jobs need less supervision. **Answer (B) is incorrect.** Survival needs are at the bottom of Maslow's hierarchy. Job enrichment seeks to meet the higher-level needs (affiliation, esteem, self-actualization). **Answer (C) is incorrect.** The intrinsic factors (challenge, growth, responsibility, etc.) are relevant to job enrichment.

11. Which of the following is **not** an example of positive reinforcement of behavior?

A. Paying a bonus to employees who had no absences for any 4-week period.
B. Giving written warnings to employees after only every other absence.
C. Assigning a mentor to each employee who exhibits a desire to develop leadership skills.
D. Having a lottery every month where 10% of the employees with no absences receive a US $200 bonus.

Answer (B) is correct.
REQUIRED: The action not an example of positive reinforcement.
DISCUSSION: Positive reinforcement encourages a desired behavior by following it with the presentation of a reward. But punishment discourages an undesired behavior by following it with a negative consequence. Although every undesirable behavior should be punished, this is not always possible. Thus, even though written warnings are given to employees only after every other absence, the action is considered punishment, not positive reinforcement.
Answer (A) is incorrect. Paying a bonus is a positive reinforcement. Answer (C) is incorrect. Assigning a mentor is a positive reinforcement. Answer (D) is incorrect. Holding a lottery is an intermittent positive reinforcement.

2.4 Organizational Politics and Group Dynamics

12. Which of the following tactics may employees use when feeling that their individual power is insignificant?

A. Employees may engage in posturing by taking credit for the work of a coworker.
B. Employees may engage in destructive competition by spreading false rumors.
C. Employees may engage in creating power and loyalty cliques with other coworkers.
D. Employees may attempt to conceal errors made by a supervisor in order to aid their own future advancement within the corporation.

Answer (C) is correct.
REQUIRED: The tactics employees engage in when they feel a cohesive group has more power than an individual.
DISCUSSION: Employees will often form groups when they feel their collective bargaining power is greater than the power of an individual.
Answer (A) is incorrect. Posturing is the attempt to make a good impression and is often used when an individual feels his or her power is adequate. Answer (B) is incorrect. Engaging in destructive competition does not reveal that an individual feels his or her power is insignificant. Answer (D) is incorrect. Concealing errors by an employee demonstrates that (s)he feels his or her power is great enough to hide errors and not get caught.

13. Which of the following is **not** true with regard to informal groups?

A. Members of the group are susceptible to group pressure.
B. The groups develop primarily to satisfy esteem needs.
C. Almost all employees and managers are members of an informal group.
D. Informal groups tend to be small and have simple relationships.

Answer (D) is correct.
REQUIRED: The false statement regarding informal groups.
DISCUSSION: Informal groups tend to be small and are often very complex. They develop their own leaders and usually result from the frequent interaction among individuals in the course of their work.
Answer (A) is incorrect. Group pressure is often a major characteristic of informal groups, and the pressure is often hard to resist because members seek acceptance from the group. Answer (B) is incorrect. Informal groups often form to establish friendships, which satisfy esteem needs. Answer (C) is incorrect. Almost everyone in an organization forms some type of friendship or other informal relationship with others in the organization.

14. Groupthink is

A. The tendency to conform and ignore relevant individual input that is at variance with the majority opinion.
B. The guidance of groups based upon self-set standards of performance and behavior.
C. The members of a group developing a solution to a problem after all the relevant information has been considered.
D. A way of brainstorming ideas to address an issue presented to a group by management.

Answer (A) is correct.
REQUIRED: The definition of groupthink.
DISCUSSION: Research into cohesive groups has revealed the prevalence of groupthink. Groupthink is conformity to a group's opinion despite information that it may be incorrect.
Answer (B) is incorrect. Norms are defined as the guidance of groups based upon self-set standards of performance and behavior. **Answer (C) is incorrect.** Considering all relevant information avoids the problem of groupthink. The group addresses issues that may change its opinion. **Answer (D) is incorrect.** Groupthink is not a way of developing ideas to address an issue. Groupthink is using the ideas of the group to address an issue, regardless of outside information.

15. The prevailing view of whistleblowing (i.e., reporting unethical or illegal conduct to internal or external parties) is that it is

A. An act of revenge.
B. Negative political behavior.
C. A net social good.
D. Financially motivated.

Answer (C) is correct.
REQUIRED: The prevailing view of whistleblowing.
DISCUSSION: The prevailing view is that whistleblowing is a net social good. Revealing unethical behavior may be the only way to end misconduct that has substantial negative effects on the public interest.
Answer (A) is incorrect. While some managers believe whistleblowing to be an act of revenge that is disloyal to the organization, it is not the prevailing view of whistleblowing. **Answer (B) is incorrect.** While some managers consider whistleblowing to be negative political behavior, it is not the prevailing view of whistleblowing. **Answer (D) is incorrect.** While some whistleblowers may have personal financial motives, it is not the prevailing view of whistleblowing.

16. A healthcare employee filed a complaint against his employer for failure to follow OSHA guidelines for safe patient handling. The behavior of the employee would be considered

A. Whistleblowing.
B. Positive political behavior.
C. Illegal.
D. Impression management.

Answer (A) is correct.
REQUIRED: The term that describes the behavior of the employee.
DISCUSSION: Whistleblowing is the reporting of entity misconduct to internal or external parties. The healthcare employee filed a complaint against his employer (either internally or externally) regarding unsafe practices or misconduct.
Answer (B) is incorrect. Positive political behaviors include coalition building, networking, and seeking mentors. **Answer (C) is incorrect.** Exposure of wrongdoing or illegal behavior is protected by many governments. These protection statutes prohibit retaliation against insiders who appropriately disclose wrongdoing. **Answer (D) is incorrect.** Impression management (organizational politics) is acting in self-interest given actual or perceived opposition in the workplace.

2.5 Performance Measures -- Costs of Quality

17. The cost of statistical quality control in a product quality cost system is categorized as a(n)

- A. Internal failure cost.
- B. Training cost.
- C. External failure cost.
- D. Appraisal cost.

Answer (D) is correct.
REQUIRED: The cost category that includes statistical quality control.
DISCUSSION: The four categories of quality costs are (1) prevention, (2) appraisal, (3) internal failure, and (4) external failure (lost opportunity). Appraisal costs include quality control programs, inspection, and testing. However, some authorities regard statistical quality and process control as preventive activities. They not only detect faulty work but also allow for adjustment of processes to avoid future defects.
Answer (A) is incorrect. Internal failure costs are incurred after poor quality has been found before shipment. Statistical quality control is designed to detect quality problems. **Answer (B) is incorrect.** Statistical quality control is not a training cost. **Answer (C) is incorrect.** External failure costs are incurred after the product has been shipped, including the costs associated with (1) warranties, (2) product liability, and (3) loss of customer goodwill.

18. Which of the following quality costs are nonconformance costs?

- A. Systems development costs.
- B. Costs of inspecting in-process items.
- C. Environmental costs.
- D. Costs of quality circles.

Answer (C) is correct.
REQUIRED: The nonconformance costs.
DISCUSSION: Nonconformance costs include internal and external failure costs. External failure costs include environmental costs, e.g., fines for violations of environmental laws and loss of customer goodwill.
Answer (A) is incorrect. Systems development costs are prevention (conformance) costs. **Answer (B) is incorrect.** Costs of inspecting in-process items are appraisal (conformance) costs. **Answer (D) is incorrect.** Costs of quality circles are prevention (conformance) costs.

2.6 Performance Measures -- Balanced Scorecard

19. Which of the following balanced scorecard perspectives examines a company's success in targeted market segments?

- A. Financial.
- B. Customer.
- C. Internal business process.
- D. Learning and growth.

Answer (B) is correct.
REQUIRED: The balanced scorecard perspective that examines success in targeted market segments.
DISCUSSION: Any critical success factor that addresses some aspect of the target market is included in the customer service perspective.
Answer (A) is incorrect. Typical success factors in the financial perspective of a balanced scorecard address matters such as sales, fair value of the firm's stock, profits, and liquidity. **Answer (C) is incorrect.** The internal business process perspective would not be the appropriate place to address market share. **Answer (D) is incorrect.** The learning and growth perspective would not be the appropriate place to address market share.

20. Under the balanced scorecard concept, employee satisfaction and retention are measures used under which of the following perspectives?

A. Customer.
B. Internal business.
C. Learning and growth.
D. Financial.

Answer (C) is correct.
REQUIRED: The perspective under which employee satisfaction and retention are measured on a balanced scorecard.
DISCUSSION: The level of employee satisfaction and retention directly relates to the learning and growth perspective.
Answer (A) is incorrect. Employee satisfaction and retention does not relate to the customer perspective. **Answer (B) is incorrect.** Employee satisfaction and retention does not relate to the internal business perspective. **Answer (D) is incorrect.** Employee satisfaction and retention does not relate to the financial perspective.

21. Which of the following is one of the four perspectives of a balanced scorecard?

A. Just in time.
B. Innovation.
C. Benchmarking.
D. Activity-based costing.

Answer (B) is correct.
REQUIRED: The perspective of a balanced scorecard.
DISCUSSION: The balanced scorecard is an accounting report that connects the firm's critical success factors determined in a strategic analysis with measures of its performance. The critical success factors (and appropriate measures thereof) are assigned to four perspectives on the business: financial, customer, internal business processes, and learning and growth. Innovation is a facet of the learning and growth perspective.
Answer (A) is incorrect. Just in time is a method for managing inventory. **Answer (C) is incorrect.** Benchmarking is a tool used in quality management. It involves analysis and measurement of key outputs against those of the best organizations. **Answer (D) is incorrect.** Activity-based costing is a method used to allocate costs to products.

Access the **Gleim CIA Premium Review System** featuring our SmartAdapt technology from your Gleim Personal Classroom to continue your studies. You will experience a personalized study environment with exam-emulating multiple-choice questions.

STUDY UNIT THREE
LEADERSHIP, ORGANIZATIONAL STRUCTURE, AND BUSINESS PROCESSES

(40 pages of outline)

3.1	Leadership	69
3.2	Organizational Structure	81
3.3	Business Process -- Human Resources and Outsourcing	95
3.4	Business Process -- Pricing and the Supply Chain	101
3.5	Business Process -- Procurement	105

This study unit is the third of five covering **Domain I: Business Acumen** from The IIA's CIA Exam Syllabus. (Data Analytics, the final topic area of this domain, is covered in Study Unit 7.) This domain makes up 35% of Part 3 of the CIA exam and is tested at the **basic** and **proficient** cognitive levels. Refer to the complete syllabus located in Appendix A to view the relevant sections covered in Study Unit 3.

SUCCESS TIP: Leadership, influence tactics, and the exercise of power are intangible qualities that substantially (if not decisively) affect organizational success. An internal auditor therefore must be aware of their effects on governance, risk management, and control processes.

3.1 LEADERSHIP

1. **Management and Leadership**

    a. **Management** is distinct from leadership. It is defined by Daft (*Understanding Management*, 10th ed.) as achieving organizational goals effectively and efficiently by planning, organizing, leading, and controlling.

    1) **Leadership** is defined by Daft as "the ability to influence people toward the attainment of goals." Accordingly, the essence of effective leadership is interaction with people.

    b. Management and leadership are essential to organizational success. But they require different qualities and skills and have different emphases.

    1) Management emphasizes the stability, reliability, and efficiency of the organization. It provides a rational basis for the exercise of leadership.

    2) Leadership's emphasis is on the people in the organization. It should provide them with a purpose and a vision for change given the uncertainties in a rapidly evolving organizational environment.

2. **Leader Traits**
   a. Research suggests that the following traits may correlate with leader effectiveness:
      1) Intelligence, knowledge, judgment, and decisiveness
      2) Drive to excel, persistence in goal attainment, and conscientiousness
      3) Aspiration to lead, self-confidence, honesty, and optimism tempered by reality
      4) Energy and stamina
      5) Education and social mobility
   b. The **emotional intelligence** of leaders (e.g., their interpersonal skills, judgment, tact, and ability to inspire cooperation) also contributes to leader effectiveness.
      1) These abilities can be learned, especially when a person understands that immaturity, erratic behavior, and uncontrolled negative emotions have a bad effect on the workplace.
   c. Effective leaders refine their **strengths**. These are talents that have developed through application of learning and skills.
      1) Having certain traits matters less than identifying and using the strengths that result in effective leader performance.
3. **Influence** is the effect of actions on not only the behaviors but also the attitudes and values of others.
   a. Influence in the work environment is an attempt to change the behavior of superiors, peers, or lower-level employees. Influence may be exerted in many ways, including the use of power and the exercise of leadership.
   b. The following are generic influence tactics:
      1) **Rational persuasion** is the use of facts and reason to convince others. This tactic is most likely to succeed when the leader has high credibility, for example, because (s)he is respected or has expertise.
      2) **Coalition tactics** (development of allies) involve the creation of networks of individuals who will assist in achievement of goals. This approach includes
         a) Understanding the needs of potential allies,
         b) Explaining the leader's positions, and
         c) Consulting about decisions or problems.
      3) **Upward appeals** (to higher authority) seek the support of more senior management. But inspiring trust because of a leader's honesty and expertise results in greater influence than simply exerting formal authority.
      4) **Exchange tactics** are based on doing favors for others to receive favors in return.
      5) **Ingratiating tactics** include generating goodwill and positive impressions. Being fair, considerate, respectful, trusting, and generous with praise helps a leader to be liked by those (s)he wants to influence.
      6) **Direct requests** that are clear and explicit may succeed simply because
         a) No preferable alternative is available or
         b) Other possibilities are unclear.
      7) **Consultation** permits the other person(s) to participate in the decision or change.
      8) **Inspirational appeals** are based on emotions, values, or ideals.
      9) **Pressure tactics** involve intimidation, threats, and demands.
   c. In general, leaders are perceived to be more effective when they apply multiple influence tactics. Moreover, some prefer to use softer or harder approaches.

4. **Power** is the potential to influence the behavior of others. **Authority** is the right to manage others. It differs from power, which is the ability to accomplish something. A manager may have one without the other.

   a. **Hard** power is based primarily on a leader's authority derived from a **position** in the organization. **Soft** power is based primarily on relationships and personal traits.

      1) The following are types of position-based **hard power**:

         a) **Legitimate power** is closely associated with formal authority. Employees tend to accept the need to follow the direction of a manager with formal authority. But they tend not to obey completely someone who relies solely on legitimate authority.

            i) Moreover, managers may not have the right to direct (exert formal authority over) some people whom they need to influence.

         b) **Coercive power** is based on the fear or threat of punishment.

         c) **Control of rewards** includes the power to determine pay raises and promotions (formal rewards) or provide praise and attention (informal rewards).

      2) The following are types of personal **soft power**:

         a) **Expert power** is conferred by clearly superior skill or knowledge. It need not be held by a leader.

         b) **Referent power** results from the leader's personal traits or employees' identification with the leader. The negative aspect of referent power is that the individuals who have it often abuse it.

   b. Power is not always associated with a specific position or individual. Furthermore, leaders and nonleaders may access the following power sources:

      1) **Personal effort**, e.g., exceptional initiative, hard work, willingness to do what others do not, and a focus on learning, may be a pathway to power.

      2) A **network of relationships** provides access to information about events in the organization or industry that is not widely known.

      3) Access to, and control over, **information** confers power. Access and control depend in part on a person's status in the managerial hierarchy.

   c. **Modern management theory** emphasizes employee empowerment. The question is not whether employees should be empowered but the circumstances in which it should occur.

      1) Individuals need to be honest, trustworthy, unselfish, and skilled.

      2) Empowerment is not the same as lack of control. Appropriate oversight is necessary.

      3) Employees should have adequate training, relevant information, and other necessary tools.

      4) Employees should participate fully in making important decisions.

      5) Employees should be fairly compensated.

      6) Managers who appropriately surrender power by empowering employees actually gain power. They have an increased ability to achieve desired results.

5. **Leader Behavior**
    a. Behavior-oriented researchers have examined leader behavior to determine whether leaders conduct themselves in certain ways. Among the significant leadership research topics are task-oriented behavior and people-oriented behavior.
        1) **Authoritarian or autocratic (task-oriented)**
            a) The manager does not share authority and responsibility. (S)he dictates all decisions to employees, so communication is downward with little employee input.
            b) Tasks are clearly defined.
            c) Authoritarian leaders rely on threats and punishment and do not trust employees.
            d) Such leadership can sometimes be the most effective, such as when the time to make a decision is limited or when employees do not respond to any other leadership style.
        2) **Democratic (people-oriented)**
            a) The leader delegates substantial authority.
            b) Employees participate in defining and assigning tasks, and communication is actively upward as well as downward. Thus, employees are more committed.
        3) **Laissez faire (people-oriented)**
            a) Employees in a group are given the authority and responsibility to make their own decisions.
            b) Communication is mostly horizontal.
            c) This style works best when employees show personal initiative, but the group also may be ineffective without the leader's guidance.
    b. According to an early model developed at **Ohio State University**, the initiation of structure (task orientation) and consideration (people orientation) by the leader are two behavior patterns that are consistently found in the study of leadership.
        1) This grid model defines the x axis as **initiating structure**. It measures the accomplishment of tasks (production).
        2) The y axis is defined as **consideration.** It measures the personal relationship (trust, respect, etc.) between the leader and the subordinate. Thus, it assesses how people-centered the leader is.

3) The following are the leadership styles in the Ohio State model based on the quadrants of the grid:

	Low Structure	High Structure
High Consideration	High consideration and low structure	High structure and high consideration
Low Consideration	Low consideration and low structure	High structure and low consideration

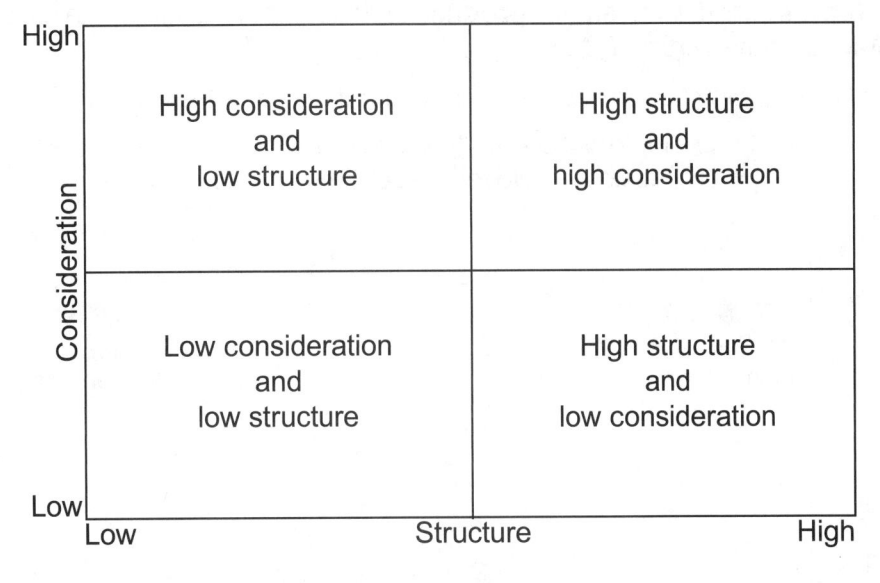

Figure 3-1

a) High consideration and low structure result from an emphasis on satisfying employee needs.

b) High structure and high consideration reflect a strong emphasis on both task accomplishment and satisfying employee needs.

c) Low consideration and low structure indicate a passive leader.

d) High structure and low consideration result from a primary focus on task accomplishment.

c. Early research at the **University of Michigan** concluded that the most effective leaders were **employee-centered**. They set high goals and manifested supportive behavior.

1) **Job-centered** leaders were less effective. They stressed cost-control, efficiency, and adherence to schedules, not goal attainment and employee needs.

d. The leadership grid developed by **Robert Blake** and **Anne McCanse** is a trademarked classification scheme. It was adapted from earlier work (the managerial grid) by Blake and **Jane Mouton**. Concern for **production** is on the horizontal (x) axis, and concern for **people** is on the vertical (y) axis.

   1) Concern for production emphasizes output, cost control, and profit.
   2) Concern for people emphasizes friendship, aiding employees in accomplishing tasks, and addressing employee issues (e.g., compensation).

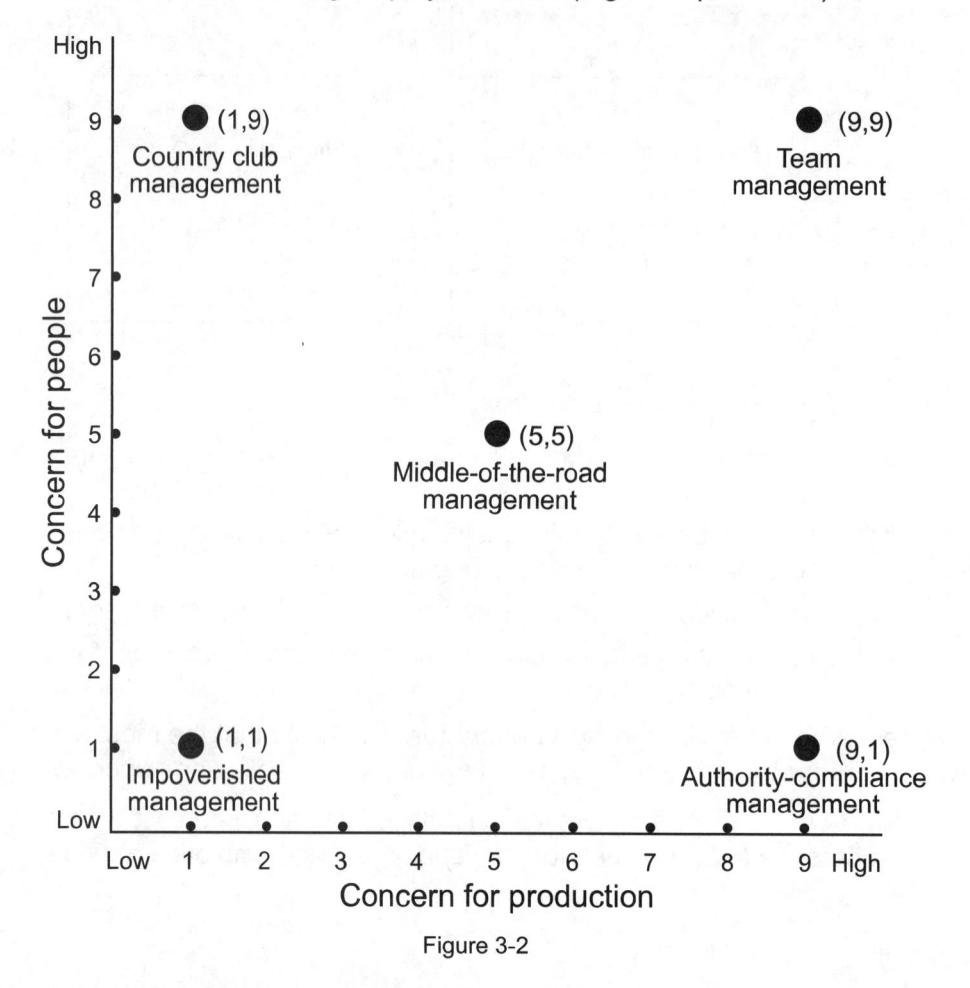

[Figure 3-2: Leadership grid showing Concern for people (y-axis, Low to High, 1-9) vs. Concern for production (x-axis, Low to High, 1-9). Points plotted: (1,9) Country club management; (9,9) Team management; (5,5) Middle-of-the-road management; (1,1) Impoverished management; (9,1) Authority-compliance management.]

   3) Each axis has a scale of 1 to 9. Thus, the primary styles are the following:
      a) **Impoverished management** has little regard for production or people. The manager's main concern is to remain employed.
      b) **Country club management** gives primary attention to human relationships and a friendly work atmosphere.
      c) **Authority-compliance management** has a primary concern for operating efficiency.
      d) **Middle-of-the-road management** balances adequate performance and satisfactory morale.
      e) **Team management** has great concern for production and people, trust, teamwork, and commitment. Blake and his associates assert that this management style is best. It produces the best operating results, health outcomes, and conflict resolutions.

6. **Contingency Theories**

    a. The assumption of contingency (situational) theories of leadership is that the appropriate leadership style depends on the situation. The emphasis is on flexibility because no one style is best in every situation.

    b. According to Fred E. **Fiedler's contingency theory**, people become leaders because of personality attributes, various situational factors, and the interaction between the leaders and the situation.

        1) Fiedler assumed that a leadership style is difficult to alter. Thus, the style should be matched with the situation in which it is most likely to be effective.

            a) The same person might not become an effective leader in different circumstances because of failure to interact successfully with that situation.

        2) Whether a leadership style is favorable for a leader depends on the following factors in Fiedler's model:

            a) **Position power** is based on the formal authority structure. It is the degree to which the position held enables a leader to evaluate, reward, punish, or promote group members.

                i) It is independent of other sources of power, such as personality or expertise.

            b) **Task structure** is how clearly and carefully members' responsibilities for various tasks are defined. Quality of performance is more easily controlled when tasks are clearly defined.

            c) **Leader-member relations** reflect the extent to which group members like, trust, and are willing to follow a leader.

        3) Leaders tend to be **task**-motivated or **relationship**-motivated.

            a) The task-motivated style is most effective when the situation is very favorable or very unfavorable.

                i) The situation is very **favorable** when the leader's position of power is high, tasks are well defined, and leader-member relations are good. The situation is very **unfavorable** when the reverse is true.

                ii) In a favorable situation, a leader has little need to address relationship issues and should therefore concentrate on the work. In an unfavorable situation, the leader must emphasize close supervision.

            b) The relationship-motivated style is most effective in **moderately favorable** situations that have a combination of favorable and unfavorable factors.

        4) The most effective leadership style depends upon the degree to which the three dimensions are present in a situation.

        5) An organization should identify leadership situations and managers' leadership styles and design the job to suit the manager if necessary.

c. According to the **situational leadership** theory developed by **Hersey and Blanchard**, the appropriate style depends on the **followers' maturity**.

   1) **Willingness** (confidence, commitment, and motivation) and **ability** (knowledge, experience, and skill) are the components of maturity. These qualities determine followers' readiness to be responsible for directing their behavior.

   2) The dimensions of the four styles of leadership described in the model are task and people needs.

      a) **Selling** (high focus on task and people needs). A selling leadership style explains decisions and provides opportunity for clarification. Followers are confident and moderately ready but lack ability.

      b) **Telling** (high focus on task, low focus on people needs). This style provides specific instructions and closely supervises performance. Followers are low in confidence, ability, and readiness.

      c) **Participating** (low focus on task, high focus on people needs). This style encourages sharing of ideas and develops followers' confidence and ability. Followers have high readiness but low confidence.

      d) **Delegative** (low focus on task and people needs). This style transfers responsibility for decisions and implementation. Followers have very high readiness, including ability and confidence.

   3) Accordingly, a leader should determine the readiness of followers and choose the style appropriate to the circumstances.

d. **Situational** variables may be in the form of organizational, task, or group circumstances that substitute for or neutralize task- or people-oriented leadership. A **substitute** eliminates the need for instructions from a leader. A **neutralizer** reduces or prevents leader behavior.

   1) The presence of a substitute or neutralizer allows use of the leadership style suitable to the work group. For example, if a task-oriented style is unnecessary, the leader may concentrate on people needs.

   2) The following **substitute** for task- and people-oriented styles because the group has little need for structure, direction, or consideration:

      a) Group professionalism and experience

      b) Strong group cohesion, e.g., substantial interaction and cooperation to unite against external pressure

   3) The following **neutralize** task- and people-oriented styles because the leader's ability to provide effective direction and consideration is impaired:

      a) Physical distance from subordinates

      b) Lack of organizationally-derived position power (legitimate, coercive, and reward power)

4) The following **substitute for or neutralize** one of the styles but not both:
   a) Organizational inflexibility (neutralizes the task-oriented style)
   b) Highly formalized organizational procedures and rules (substitutes for task-oriented style)
   c) Very structured task (substitutes for task-oriented style)
   d) Automatic feedback for task performance (substitutes for task-oriented style)
   e) Training or experience of the group (substitutes for task-oriented style)
   f) Inherently satisfying task (substitutes for people-oriented style)

e. **Path-goal theory** emphasizes motivation. It combines the research on initiating structure and consideration with expectancy theory.

   1) Leaders should motivate employees by clarifying employees' understanding of work goals, the relationship of achievement of those goals with rewards that matter to employees, and how the goals may be achieved.
   2) A leadership style should be chosen that complements but does not duplicate the factors in the environment and is consistent with employees' characteristics.
      a) The **directive** leader lets employees know what is expected of them, schedules work to be done, and gives specific guidance on how to accomplish tasks.
         i) A directive style is most effective when the employees are externally controlled (i.e., not directly managed), tasks are ambiguous or stressful, and substantial conflict exists in the work group.
         ii) Unknowledgeable or incompetent employees are best led using the directive style.
      b) The **supportive** leader is friendly and shows concern for the needs of the employees.
         i) The supportive style is best when tasks are highly structured and the authority relationships are clear and bureaucratic.
         ii) This approach depends on people who want to work, grow, and achieve.
         iii) The supportive style may be best when tasks are unsatisfying.
      c) The **participative** leader consults with employees and considers their suggestions before making a decision.
         i) The participative style is most useful when employees believe they control their own destinies, that is, when they have an internal locus of control. Such individuals may be resentful if they are not consulted.
      d) The **achievement-oriented** leader is a facilitator who sets challenging goals and expects employees to perform at their highest level.
         i) Achievement-oriented leadership is appropriate when tasks are nonrepetitive and ambiguous and employee competence is high.
   3) In contrast with Fiedler's approach, path-goal theorists believe that managers are able to adapt their styles to the situation.

7. A **transformational leader** is a change agent who combines task orientation and people orientation. This kind of leader can inspire employees to achieve more than they thought possible.

    a. Transformational leadership emphasizes the following:

        1) Vision of a better but difficult to attain future
        2) Development of followers' belief in their own ability and creativity
        3) Challenging traditional assumptions
        4) Empowerment of workers
        5) Innovation and dramatic change

    b. A **charismatic leader** has many qualities of a transformational leader. The key difference is that followers tend to have a primary belief in the person of the leader.

        1) Moreover, some charismatic leaders lack **humility**, which is an absence of ego, a tendency to self-effacement, and an intense determination to do what is best in the long run for the organization and its people.

            a) Thus, charismatic leaders who lack humility and are egocentric, self-serving, and exploitive may have negative effects on the group.

    c. A **transactional leader** is an effective manager who is task- and people-oriented. (S)he also is committed to (1) efficient operations and increased productivity and (2) the organization's norms and values.

        1) Unlike transformational leaders, transactional leaders seek not to change the future but to maintain the normal flow of operations.

8. **Mentoring** is systematic development of leadership by providing career counseling and social nurturing. It requires intensive tutoring, coaching, and guidance.

    a. Some organizations have formal mentoring programs that assign mentors to junior employees. However, some research indicates that a mentoring arrangement that occurs informally and voluntarily may have better results.

    b. Mentoring serves career and psychosocial functions.

        1) Career functions include sponsorship, visibility, coaching, protection, and assigning challenges.
        2) Psychosocial functions include role modeling, acceptance, confirmation, counseling, and friendship.
        3) Mentoring can be helpful in any working environment, even a negative one.

SU 3: Leadership, Organizational Structure, and Business Processes

9. **Modern Approaches**
   a. According to **Jim Collins**, **Level 5 leadership** is needed for an organization to progress from good to great. The following is the Level 5 hierarchy:
      1) **Level 1. Capable individuals** provide their abilities and experience.
      2) **Level 2. Contributing team members** work well as individuals and in groups.
      3) **Level 3. Competent management** of team members and assets achieves defined objectives.
      4) **Level 4.** An **effective leader** promotes high standards and commitment to a vision.
      5) **Level 5.** An **executive** "builds excellence through dedication and humility."
         a) At Level 5, an executive
            i) Is without personal ambition,
            ii) Champions organizational values far beyond financial success,
            iii) Deflects credit to others, and
            iv) Encourages development of leadership in all parts of the organization.
   b. **Servant leadership** is based on a concept described by **Robert Greenleaf**.
      1) It involves service to (a) others (e.g., helping employees meet their needs and achieve their objectives), (b) the broader society, and (c) the higher purposes of the organization.
      2) Servant leaders transfer (a) credit for organizational success, (b) recognition, and (c) power.
         a) They also may be philanthropists. Thus, they may prosper in not-for-profit organizations.
   c. **Authentic leadership** is practiced by those who (1) are genuinely self-aware, (2) behave in accordance with (and actively support) the highest ethical precepts, and (3) inspire trust and commitment in others because of their authenticity and candor. They also (1) encourage collaboration and a diversity of views and (2) help others become leaders.
      1) The following are elements of authentic leadership:
         a) **Passionate** devotion by the leader to a **purpose** that inspires followers
         b) **Values** grounded in a personal belief system consistently followed by the leader that help to create trust
         c) The ability to make difficult decisions without abandoning **compassion**
         d) Having positive long-term **relationships**, including choosing good associates and facilitating the personal and professional growth of others
         e) **Self-discipline** that avoids excessive or inappropriate risks to the organization or others, together with a willingness to admit mistakes
   d. **Interactive leadership** has similarities to other modern approaches. It is based on consensus and collaboration. Influence therefore results from relationships, not position power.
      1) The interactive style is most commonly adopted by female leaders. But men also may be effective interactive leaders.
      2) Research indicates that female leaders perform better than males regarding motivation, relationship building, and developing others.
         a) These qualities, which relate to authenticity and humility, are important in many 21st century organizations.

10. **Followership**
    a. Organizations need effective followers as well as effective leaders. Moreover, some of their sought-after qualities are the same.
        1) Leaders who understand the desirable qualities of followers may be able to help them to be effective.
    b. **Robert E. Kelley** developed a model of **follower styles** based on two dimensions:
        1) Critical thinking
            a) Independent, **critical** thinkers are aware of the effects of behaviors and decisions of their leaders and others in the organization, including themselves. They can provide constructive feedback and creative solutions.
            b) Dependent, **uncritical** thinkers simply follow instructions without consideration of alternatives and the effects on the organization.
        2) Acting/participation
            a) An **active** follower is not constrained by the definition of the job. (S)he (1) is involved in appropriate aspects of the organization, (2) takes ownership, and (3) seeks decisions by superiors about relevant matters.
            b) A **passive** follower (1) requires constant oversight, (2) does not seek responsibility, and (3) makes only the required effort.
    c. The following are the five follower styles:
        1) The **alienated follower** is an independent, critical thinker who is passive. The individual has the ability to be effective but avoids participation in the organization because of past disappointments.
        2) A **conformist** is an organizational participant who avoids conflict and is subject to groupthink. One reason for such conformity may be an authoritarian culture that imposes rigid rules.
        3) A **pragmatic survivor** adopts the follower style that avoids risk and maximizes personal benefit in a specific situation, e.g., when the organization is in crisis.
        4) A **passive follower** may be an employee who is discouraged from engaging in positive behaviors by a micromanaging superior.
        5) An **effective follower** is at the favorable end of each dimension. (S)he is (a) self-managed, (b) self-aware, and (c) committed to organizational success. (S)he also accepts appropriate risk and conflict in pursuit of higher goals.

STOP & REVIEW

You have completed the outline for this subunit.
Study multiple-choice questions 1 through 6 beginning on page 109.

3.2 ORGANIZATIONAL STRUCTURE

1. Daft (*Understanding Management*, 10th ed.) includes the following elements in a **vertical** organizational structure:

    a. Tasks of individuals and organizational subunits (e.g., departments)

    b. Reporting relationships in terms of authority, decision making, span of control, and hierarchical levels

    c. Designed coordination among employees and subunits

2. According to Henry Mintzberg, an organization has five basic parts. The organizational structure results from which part is dominant.

    a. The five parts of an organization are the following:

        1) Operating core (workers who perform the basic tasks related to production)
        2) Strategic apex (top managers)
        3) Middle line (managers who connect the core to the apex)
        4) Technostructure (analysts who achieve a certain standardization)
        5) Support staff (indirect support services)

    b. The following are the five organizational structures:

        1) A **simple structure** (entrepreneurial), such as that of a small retailer, has low complexity and formality, and authority is centralized. Its simplicity usually precludes significant inefficiency in the use of resources.

            a) The strategic apex is the dominant component.

        2) A **machine bureaucracy**, such as the military, is a complex, formal, and centralized organization that (a) performs highly routine tasks, (b) groups activities into functional departments, (c) has a strict chain of command, and (d) distinguishes between line and staff relationships.

            a) The technostructure dominates.

        3) A **professional bureaucracy** (e.g., a university or library) is a complex and formal but decentralized organization in which highly trained specialists have great autonomy. Duplication of functions is minimized. For example, a university has only one history department.

            a) The operating core dominates.

        4) A **divisional structure**, such as an industrial conglomerate, is essentially a self-contained organization. Hence, it must perform all or most of the functions of the overall organization of which it is a part. It has substantial duplication of functions compared with more centralized structures.

            a) The middle line dominates.

        5) An **adhocracy** (an organic structure), such as that of a small software developer, has low complexity, formality, and centralization. Vertical differentiation is low, and horizontal differentiation is high. The emphasis is on flexibility and response.

            a) Support staff dominates.

3. **New Structures**

    a. These emerging organizational structures tend to be flatter (fewer layers), make more use of teams, and create entrepreneurial units.

    b. An **hourglass** organization has the following three layers:

        1) The strategic layer determines the mission of the organization and ensures that it is successful.

        2) A few middle managers coordinate a variety of lower-level, cross-functional activities. These managers are generalists, not specialists, and they do not simply transfer operating information. Computer systems can instantly transfer such information directly to the top layer.

        3) Empowered technical specialists are most often self-supervised. They lack promotion possibilities but are motivated by

            a) Lateral transfers,
            b) Challenging work,
            c) Training in new skills, and
            d) Pay-for-performance plans.

    c. A **cluster** organization is in essence a group of teams. Workers are multiskilled and move among teams as needed. Communication and group skills are vital, requiring special training and team-building exercises. Pay is for knowledge.

    d. A **network** organization consists of relatively independent firms.

        1) A network is based on coordination through adaptation. It is a long-term, strategic relationship based on implicit contracts. A network allows member firms to gain a competitive advantage against competitors outside the network.

            a) A network is an ultimate expression of outsourcing, which involves obtaining goods or services from outside sources that could be acquired internally.

                i) For example, a firm may choose to outsource its computer processing or legal work, and a manufacturer may buy rather than make components.

        2) A network may be viewed as a group of activities involving suppliers and customers that add value. Each activity may be performed internally at an internal cost or subcontracted at an external cost.

            a) When an activity is subcontracted, a transaction cost is incurred.
            b) A restriction on a network is that the sum of external costs and transaction costs must be less than internal costs.
            c) The difference between a network and a normal market is that transaction costs in the market are low enough for any player.

    e. **Virtual** organizations are flexible networks of value-adding subcontractors who communicate using the Internet and telecommunicating technology.

        1) The emphasis is on speed and constant, if not too rapid, change.
        2) Constant learning is essential.
        3) Cross-functional teams are emphasized.
        4) Stress is high.

4. The organizational structure reflects **work specialization** (division of labor). Separating tasks into individual jobs increases efficiency.

   a. But excessive specialization (e.g., one task per employee) may limit coordination and impair employee morale.

5. The **chain of command** is a set of authority, responsibility, and reporting relationships.

   a. The **scalar chain** of authority from the top to the bottom of the entity should include all employees.

   b. **Unity of command** requires each subordinate to have only one superior (but a superior may have as many subordinates as allowed by the span of control).

   c. **Authority** is the legitimate right to direct (issue orders), and to expect performance from, other people to achieve the organization's goals. Those people are accountable to their superiors in the hierarchy.

      1) Authority includes the power to make decisions and allocate resources.
      2) Authority attaches to positions, not individuals, and flows down the hierarchy.
      3) According to the **acceptance** theory, a manager's authority depends on subordinates' choice to comply with direction.
      4) **Responsibility** is a duty to perform. Authority should suffice for the responsibility assigned.
      5) **Accountability** is the duty to report to a superior in the chain of command and to justify the performance (outcomes) achieved.
      6) **Delegation** involves determining expected results and assigning tasks and responsibilities. It also requires the transfer of authority to perform tasks.

         a) The benefits of delegation are time savings for the delegator, training and development of lower-level managers, and improved morale.
         b) The supervisor's expectations should be clear.

            i) The employee should also be involved in determining how to reach the desired outcome, thereby increasing both acceptance and understanding of the assignment.

   d. Managers of line activities have **line authority**. They are directly responsible for the primary functions, products, or services of the organization. Staff members provide technical expertise. They have limited **staff authority**.

      1) Staff activities are advisory. They are necessary to the organization but secondary to line functions.

6. The **span of management (span of control)** is a basic structural design principle. It is the number of subordinates reporting directly to a manager.
    a. The modern trend is to broaden the span of control and possibly to reduce hierarchical levels to promote delegation.
        1) The effect should be to have more routine decisions made at lower levels. Benefits include
            a) Allowing senior managers more time to address strategic matters and
            b) Developing the abilities of lower-level managers.
    b. The optimal span of control tends to **widen** in the following situations:
        1) Subordinates' jobs are similar, procedures are standardized, and the work is routine.
        2) Managers and subordinates are in the same physical location.
        3) Well-trained subordinates do not need close supervision.
        4) External activities (e.g., coordination with other subunits) require minimal time.
        5) The manager's style encourages a wide span.
        6) The manager has effective staff assistance.
    c. The optimal span of control **narrows** in the following situations:
        1) The work becomes more complex.
        2) The frequency and intensity of required supervision increase.
        3) The time needed for coordination with other supervisors increases.
        4) The time needed for planning increases.
    d. Span of control influences the number of levels.
        1) **Flat structures** have relatively few levels from top to bottom. They have wide spans of control.
            a) Flat structures provide fast information flow from top to bottom of the organization, increased employee satisfaction, and a high degree of coordination and cooperation.
            b) Disadvantages of reduced supervision are poorer employee training and behavioral problems.
        2) **Tall structures** have many levels between top and bottom. They have relatively narrow spans of control.
            a) Tall structures are faster and more effective at problem resolution than flat structures. They increase frequency of interaction between superior and employee and impose greater order.
            b) Disadvantages of too little delegation of authority are slow decision making, excessive supervision, greater administrative costs, and lack of initiative.
        3) Studies do not indicate great advantages for either flat or tall structures.

e. A senior manager's optimal span of control varies with situational factors.

1) Someone overseeing a reorganization may need a wider span to understand the changes in the entity and whether they are being implemented effectively.
2) A wider span also may be desired by a new manager who wants to understand the business and evaluate personnel.
3) A manager who must devote significant time to relationships with external parties (e.g., regulators or customers) may need a smaller span of control.

7. **Size-Structure Relationship**

    a. As an organization increases in size, its structure tends to become more formal. More policies and procedures are necessary to coordinate the increased number of employees, and more managers must be hired.

    1) The relationship of size and structure, however, is linear only within a certain range. For example, adding 100 employees to a company with 100 employees is likely to cause significant structural change. Adding the same number to a workforce of 10,000 is likely to have little structural effect.

8. **Unity of Command**

    a. This principle is emphasized in **traditional** organizations, e.g., the military. The authority and responsibility of the parties should be clearly defined, and every subordinate should report only to one superior.
    b. As organizations grow, unity of command becomes more important.

9. **Line and Staff Design**

    a. The traditional approach views line activities as those directly responsible for the primary function, product, or service of the organization. Staff members provide supporting technical expertise.
    b. Production is a line activity. Moreover, sales (marketing) and finance may be line activities.
    c. Staff activities are advisory activities that are necessary to the organization but secondary to the line functions.

    1) **Personal staff** are individuals assigned to a given manager.
    2) **Specialized staff** are functions that serve the whole organization.

    d. A line-and-staff design helps to preserve unity of command.

10. **Authority**
    a. The **behavioral** approach to line and staff relationships regards informal authority as a limit on formal chains of command.
        1) Advice offered by senior staff members may be similar to a command. They have access to senior management and can exercise more informal authority than a junior line manager.
    b. The difficult issue in a line-staff relationship is how to ensure adoption of specialized staff advice without undermining line authority. The resolution of this issue depends on whether a staff group's authority is advisory, concurrent, complete in a specialized area, or a form of control.
        1) **Advisory.** A staff group with advisory authority can offer only suggestions, prepare plans for consideration by line managers, and evaluate organizational performance.
            a) A staff member often has an area of technical expertise, such as law, industrial labor relations, operations research, or personnel.
            b) The staff member's goal is the approval (or rejection) of a complete recommended solution, but a line manager may want a quick fix to a problem rather than a complete solution.
            c) Consultation with line personnel is essential.
            d) The line manager is not required to use the staff's services.
        2) **Concurrent.** A staff group may have concurrent authority. Line management must persuade experts in specified areas to agree to an action or decision.
        3) **Complete in an area.** A staff group may be given complete authority in a specialized area, and its specialized activities are separated from line management.
            a) The line manager must use the staff services.
            b) Examples include information systems, purchasing, and personnel.
        4) **Control.** A staff group occasionally may be given control authority. Thus, line authority may be superseded by that of the specialist staff designated by higher levels of management to make certain decisions in the area of staff expertise.
            a) Control staff authority appears to violate the principle of unity of command. However, no violation occurs when members of the control staff act as agents for the higher-level line manager who delegated authority.
            b) For example, quality-control inspectors have the authority to reject marginal products. But, because this authority is exercised on behalf of the manufacturing manager, the chain of command actually remains intact.

11. Functional Authority

a. A hybrid of the control authority relationship of line and staff is functional authority. This kind of design is common in organic organizations.

b. An individual is given functional authority outside the chain of command for certain specified activities. The individual may be either a line or a staff manager who is a specialist in a particular field.

   1) For example, the vice president in charge of sales may be given functional authority over manufacturing executives in scheduling customer orders, packaging, or making service parts available.

c. Functional authority may be created for numerous reasons when a line manager is not the person best suited to oversee a given activity.

   1) For example, the vice president for industrial labor relations may have functional authority over the production manager for the purpose of negotiating a new labor contract, though no line relationship exists at other times.

d. Functional specialists have the authority to determine the appropriate standards in their own fields of specialization and to enforce those standards.

   1) For example, the chief engineer of an airline may have the authority to remove airplanes from service, overriding the vice president for operations.

12. Line and Staff Conflicts

a. Line and staff conflicts are inevitable given the differences in their backgrounds and activities. These individuals tend to have different training and education, perspectives on the organization, career and other objectives, and temperaments.

   1) Operating executives with line authority often see a high potential for harm in staff activity. A staff member with vaguely defined authority from a chief executive may effectively undermine line managers.

   2) Staff members normally are not responsible for the success of a line department. If an implemented suggestion fails, line managers tend to blame the suggestion and staff blame the implementation.

   3) Setting staff members apart from line responsibilities gives them the time and environment in which to think. However, this separation also can lead to thinking in a vacuum and suggestions by staff that are inappropriate or not feasible.

   4) Excessive staff activity may violate the principle of unity of command.

b. Line-staff conflicts may be minimized by

   1) Clearly defining areas of activity and authority.

   2) Sharply defining the nature and place of line managers and staff.

   3) Stressing the systems approach to all employees, whether line or staff, to encourage them to work together toward organizational goals.

   4) Reducing areas of possible conflict, e.g., keeping functional authority to a minimum and providing feedback to staff of line's reaction to proposals.

   5) Using the concept of completed staff work when possible. Thus, recommendations should be complete enough to make yes-or-no responses from line managers possible. Advice should be clear and complete.

13. **System Theory**
    a. Every position and task must contribute to achievement of organizational objectives.
        1) Distinctions between producers and helpers are irrelevant.
    b. The changing nature of work environments from predominantly production to predominantly service makes assignment of responsibility more difficult.
        1) For example, at a hotel with the objective of customer satisfaction, who is line and who is staff?
14. The degree of **centralization or decentralization** in an organization depends on the appropriate focus of decision making given situational factors. Accordingly, the lower the level of the hierarchy where significant decisions are made, the more decentralized the entity.
    a. The following are costs of decentralization:
        1) Dysfunctional decision making due to disagreements regarding overall goals and subgoals of the individual decision makers
        2) Decreased understanding of the overall goals of the organization
        3) Increased costs of developing the information system
    b. The following support greater decentralization:
        1) Improved decisions, because they are made by the most knowledgeable people
        2) Faster adjustments to the entity's external environment, especially if uncertainty is high and change is rapid
        3) Better use of the abilities of human resources
        4) Reducing the pressure on senior managers
        5) Positive influence on morale
    c. The following support greater centralization:
        1) More effective control
        2) Reduced costs through resource sharing
        3) A need to reduce duplication of effort
        4) Elimination of unsuccessful or inessential operations to increase the entity's focus, including greater accountability by senior managers
        5) An existential threat (e.g., bankruptcy) to the organization
    d. **Strategic Business Units (SBUs)**
        1) Establishment of SBUs is a means of decentralization used by large corporations seeking the entrepreneurial advantages of smaller entities.
        2) An SBU in principle is permitted by its parent to function as an independent business, including development of its own strategic plans. A true SBU
            a) Is not merely a supplier of the parent, but serves its own markets
            b) Encounters competition
            c) Is a profit center
            d) Makes all important decisions about its business although it may share resources with the parent

15. **Departmentation** is a structural format intended to promote coordination required as a result of work specialization (division of labor).

    a. Departmentation groups positions into significant subsystems (e.g., departments) and defines their relationships within the chain of command for the organization as a whole.

    b. Departmentation by **vertical function** also is called U-form or unitary structure. It is a means of organizing according to the **resources** (employees, buildings, equipment, etc.) required for a broad task (e.g., a function such as HR, manufacturing, or finance).

       1) In this vertical format, the grouping by common function extends throughout the entity. Moreover, each function has an organization-wide reach.

       2) **Advantages.** Functional departments tend to be efficient and provide economies of scale. They also allow for specialization and unified control by senior managers.

       3) **Disadvantages.** Communication among, and coordination of, departments may be difficult.

          a) Also, the entity may not act promptly if approvals by management at the apex of the hierarchy are needed. Accordingly, innovation and rapid adaptation to changes in the business environment may be impaired.

    c. **Divisional** structure also is called M-form or multidivisional (decentralized) structure. It is a means of organizing by kinds of **output** (e.g., products or product lines, service to customers or one customer, a business, or a project). Product departmentation is also appropriate for organizations that produce multiple lines of products (use of profit centers).

       1) Each division generally is autonomous and has its own functional departments necessary for its output. It has the personnel and other resources to operate independently.

       2) The divisional format is less centralized than the functional format. Conflicts among functions are addressed at the divisional level, not at the top of the hierarchy.

       3) The divisional structure also may be based on **geographic** locations (sections of a country, countries, or regions of the world).

          a) An **advantage** is the ability to sell products and services designed for local conditions and to market them in culturally appropriate ways.

          b) Another kind of divisional structure is based on **customer** groups.

       4) Functions in a self-contained division tend to coordinate effectively because of their proximity at one location. But coordination of the activities of independent divisions may be difficult.

       5) The connection of divisions to their business environments gives them the flexibility to react quickly to events. These entities also are more likely to be focused on customer needs.

       6) A **disadvantage** of a divisional structure is the inefficiency and cost of resource (functional) duplication. Another problem is that a division's smaller functional departments may provide less training and expertise.

d. In a **matrix structure**, the reporting relationships of an entity are in a grid or matrix. This structure allows authority to flow both vertically and horizontally, thereby combining functional and divisional formats. This structure violates the principle of unity of command.

   1) Thus, employees have **dual reporting** relationships, generally to a functional manager and a divisional manager.
   2) For example, an organization may have vertical authority exercised by functional departments (e.g., production, marketing, R&D, and accounting) and horizontal authority exercised by divisions (e.g., product, product line, or geographic entity).
      a) The employees who report to two managers at the same time are **two-boss** employees.
      b) A **matrix boss** is in charge of either the vertical or horizontal dimension of the matrix.
      c) The **top leader** supervises both chains of command (e.g., functional and product). Consequently, (s)he must address unresolved disputes between the two chains of command.
   3) The **advantages** of matrix structure include the following:
      a) Resources can be used more efficiently.
      b) Information flows better.
      c) Employees' motivation and commitment are enhanced.
      d) Management can respond to changing market and technical requirements rapidly.
   4) The **disadvantages** of matrix structure include the following:
      a) Confusion may occur because people may not recognize which manager to report to.
      b) Power struggles ensue when managers seek greater authority.
      c) Excessive overhead is incurred because greater management costs result from a dual chain of command.
      d) Strong relationship skills are necessary when two-boss employees encounter conflicting demands.

e. A **team** is a group to whom authority and responsibility have been delegated. The objective is to enhance organizational creativity, flexibility, and responsiveness.

   1) A group consists of two or more people who interact to accomplish a goal. All teams are groups, but not all groups are teams. A team differs from a group because team leadership often rotates, and team members are accountable to each other.
   2) A **cross-functional team** includes members who have different expertise. A research-and-development team is an example of a team that is typically cross functional in that many skills are needed to identify and create a new product.
      a) A cross-functional team enables horizontal coordination within a divisional or functional format.
      b) Team members generally report to their functions and to the team.

3) A **permanent team** is assembled from all functions of the organization and operates essentially as a department. The stress is on horizontal communication of information and coordination.

4) In a **team-based structure**, the entire entity consists of horizontal teams. Their activities are coordinated and include interaction with customers.

5) **Advantages.** Teams potentially include more cooperation, more rapid response resulting from prompt decision making, and improved employee attitudes and motivation.

6) **Disadvantages.** Team structure may include conflicting loyalties resulting from dual reporting, slower coordination because of the time spent in meetings, and excessive decentralization.

f. A **virtual network** is an ultimate expression of horizontal coordination through **outsourcing**, the transfer of a business function to an outside provider with special expertise.

1) A virtual network is an entity that outsources most of its significant functions to entities that perform them more efficiently. Coordination is from a small central organization.

    a) This structure is possible because electronic technology (e.g., the Internet and networked computers) facilitates collaboration with external parties.

    b) The network is a lean entity that minimizes overhead. The size of its staff and its holdings of property, plant, and equipment are far less than those of a comparable traditional organization.

    c) **Advantage.** The flexibility to change the network's components and respond quickly when its needs change. Another advantage is that the network can seek resources, including expertise, worldwide.

        i) This international reach allows it to control costs and quality and charge competitive prices.

    d) **Disadvantage.** The loss of the customary means of control. Managers must rely on contractual agreements, electronic communication, and negotiation with self-interested business partners.

        i) Moreover, customers may be lost if those partners' performance does not meet expectations.

        ii) The nature of a network also diminishes employees' loyalty because of the threat of outsourcing.

16. **Horizontal coordination** is management of activities by means other than the chain of command.

    a. According to Daft (*Understanding Management*, 10th ed.), coordination is "adjusting and synchronizing the diverse activities among different individuals and departments." It is necessary in any organizational structure.

        1) **Collaboration** also is necessary when different individuals and departments must work together to achieve a common goal.

    b. Effective horizontal coordination is required to react quickly when environmental change accelerates. One structural response is creation of **cross-functional** teams as mentioned on page 90.

        1) A **task force** is a group assembled temporarily to share information and address a problem affecting two or more departments of the entity.

        2) A **project manager** is an outsider who coordinates the work of two or more departments on a specified project.

        3) **Relational coordination** is a high degree and frequency of information sharing beyond boundaries within the organizational structure. It requires development of collaborative relationships based on common goals and respect to solve problems.

            a) Relational coordination is part of organizational culture rather than the organizational structure. It is facilitated by skills training, less rigid work rules, benefits based on team achievement, and even physical proximity of employees.

17. **Structural determinants** may be external or internal. Another issue is the extent of the need for formal vertical structure or horizontal structure that facilitates collaboration and communication.

    a. **External** contingencies include the business environment, strategies, and goals.

        1) Management should devise a structure that is consistent with **strategies**. Examples are Michael E. Porter's broad scope generic strategies: differentiation and cost leadership.

            a) Differentiation of products and services usually requires effective R&D and creative product development.

            b) Cost leadership requires internal efficiencies.

        2) A **mechanistic** structure most likely is adopted in a stable environment in which cost efficiency predominates. It is favored by the classical school of management. It is characterized by a centralized vertical structure, top-down decision making, and an emphasis on rules and procedures.

            a) In a very stable environment, an entity's strategic goal most likely is efficient cost leadership. Thus, a vertical functional structure is usually chosen.

            b) A less mechanistic structure may be consistent with strategic goals. An entity may prefer a structure with cross-functional teams and project managers.

3) An **organic** structure most likely is adopted in an uncertain environment in which flexibility and creativity are most valued. It is characterized by a decentralized horizontal structure with more decisions made at lower levels.

   a) In a very uncertain environment, an entity's strategic goal most likely is innovative differentiation. A horizontal team structure then provides the needed flexibility for rapid response.

   b) A less organic structure may be consistent with strategic goals. An entity may prefer a divisional structure with an emphasis on products and customers. But it is less flexible and responsive than a horizontal team structure.

4) Structure is a function of the following:

   a) **Size.** Larger organizations tend to be mechanistic because greater formalization is needed. Strategies also change as size changes. A growing organization often expands activities within its industry.

      i) For example, manufacturers might be unit producers (units or small batches), mass producers (large batches), or process producers (continuous processing).

         - Mass production is most effective if the organization has a mechanistic structure with moderate vertical differentiation, high horizontal differentiation, and high formalization.

      ii) Vertical differentiation is the depth of the hierarchy. More levels mean more complexity.

      iii) Horizontal differentiation is the extent to which tasks require special skills and knowledge. Greater diversity makes communication and coordination more difficult.

   b) **Technology.** An organic structure may be best for coping with nonroutine technology because formalization is low.

   c) **Environment.** In general, the more stable the environment, the more mechanistic the organization. A mechanistic structure also is appropriate when the environment has little capacity for growth.

      i) Dynamic environments require an organic structure because of their unpredictability.

         - Moreover, a complex environment (e.g., one with numerous and constantly changing competitors) also requires the flexibility and adaptability of an organic structure.

      ii) Uncertainty is a general, not a specific, environmental factor. The uncertainty in the environment depends on its

         - Capacity (the degree of growth an environment can support),
         - Volatility (the relative instability in the environment), and
         - Complexity (the amount of heterogeneity and concentration in the environment).

   d) **Formalization.** The extent to which job performance is standardized by job descriptions and clear procedures that define how tasks are to be accomplished.

      i) Low formalization enhances worker discretion.

b. **Internal** contingencies primarily relate to technology and its effects on production. Manufacturers and service entities apply different technologies.

1) According to Joan Woodward, the following are the broad categories of **manufacturing** technology:

    a) **Single-unit** (e.g., a ship) or **small-batch** (e.g., customized machinery) production consists of a unique product(s) made to the customer's specification. Individuals are significantly involved in the process.

    b) **Mass production** (e.g., of motor vehicles) results in large-volume output of standardized items. The technology is machine-oriented, and inventories are maintained for sale as demanded by customers.

    c) **Continuous process production** (e.g., oil refining) is automated. Individuals monitor the nonstop activity and repair machinery as needed but do not perform the productive work.

2) The categories of manufacturing vary in **technological complexity**, the extent to which machines replace individuals. Complexity ranges from low (small-batch), medium (mass), and high (continuous).

3) The categories of manufacturing also vary regarding the preferable structure.

    a) **Small-batch production** should have an organic structure. It has low centralization and a high ratio of direct to indirect labor. Moreover, it requires relatively few senior administrators.

    b) **Mass production** should have a mechanistic structure. It has high centralization and a large supervisor span of control. It also has a higher ratio of senior administrators than small-batch production.

    c) **Continuous process production** should have an organic structure. It has low centralization, a low senior administrator ratio, and the lowest ratio of direct to indirect labor.

4) **Service-oriented organizations** (e.g., auditors, financial institutions, and colleges) and even the service departments of large manufacturing companies (e.g., internal auditing or marketing) use service technology.

    a) This technology has the following basic characteristics:

        i) Services rendered are intangible and not inventoriable.

        ii) Service providers have direct contact with their customers. Thus, consumption occurs at the same time as production.

    b) A service entity (e.g., many financial institutions and franchised businesses) tends to be decentralized to achieve proximity to customers. It also emphasizes flexible horizontal communication and information sharing to assist customer service.

STOP & REVIEW

You have completed the outline for this subunit.
Study multiple-choice questions 7 through 11 beginning on page 111.

3.3 BUSINESS PROCESS -- HUMAN RESOURCES AND OUTSOURCING

1. **Overview**

    a. Managing human resources means acquiring, retaining, and developing employees in accordance with the strategy and structure of the organization.

    1) The human resource strategy is a systems approach that treats employees as human capital, that is, as intangible assets whose full potential should be developed.

    2) The human resources function is responsible for (a) recruitment and selection, (b) evaluation of performance, and (c) training and development.

    b. A people-centered human resource strategy improves employee retention and profits by adopting the following practices:

    1) A job security policy
    2) Stringent hiring procedures
    3) Employee empowerment (e.g., use of self-managed teams)
    4) Basing compensation on performance
    5) Comprehensive training
    6) Reduction of status differences
    7) Information sharing

    c. Human resource planning forecasts future employment requirements. It includes the hiring, training, and monitoring of employees.

    1) Planning includes scanning the external environment to understand the area's labor supply, workforce composition, and work patterns.

    2) Companies must forecast future employee needs to ensure adequate resources when needed. Labor resources are not always as mobile as raw materials.

    3) A human resource audit evaluates compliance with laws and regulations, determines whether operations are efficient, and considers the company's recruitment and salary and benefit programs.

    4) Human resource or human asset accounting attempts to measure the value, and the changes in value, of the organization's investment in human capital.

2. **Designing the Job**

    a. Job analysis involves (1) interviewing superior employees about the way they accomplish their tasks, (2) analyzing work flows, and (3) studying the methods used to achieve work-unit objectives.

    b. A **job description**, based on job analysis, should list basic duties. For higher-level positions, reporting relationships also may be included.

    1) For example, for an accounting clerk, the job description may include

        a) Preparing payroll checks,
        b) Maintaining inventory ledgers, and
        c) Preparing invoices.

    c. **Job specifications**, based on the job description, should list the abilities needed for a job, e.g., education, experience, physical characteristics, and personal characteristics.

3. **Recruitment**
    a. Many countries prohibit employment discrimination with regard to any employment action, for example, hiring, training, compensation, retention, or promotion. Prohibited bases of discrimination may be race, color, religion, sex, national origin, age, or disability.
    b. Using temporary or part-time workers gives management the flexibility to adjust quickly to changing market conditions.

4. **Selection**
    a. The criteria for employee selection are the job specifications developed from each job description.
        1) All requirements, including selection tests, must be based on their relationship to the ability to perform successfully in a specific job.
        2) Employee information preferably should be verified.
    b. The selection process includes the following:
        1) Preparation by developing job descriptions and job specifications
        2) Writing and reviewing interview questions for fairness and legality
        3) Organizing by defining the roles and methods of interviewers
        4) Collecting information from applicants
        5) Evaluating
        6) Meeting to discuss information about applicants
        7) Deciding whether to offer employment
    c. Interviewing is the usual selection method. Interviews range from unstructured to structured.
        1) In an **unstructured interview**, questions are not prearranged. They are asked spontaneously and vary among candidates. Also, the responses are not evaluated in any consistent manner. Accordingly, the unstructured interview is subject to cultural and other biases.
        2) In a **structured interview**, all candidates are asked the same questions, and their responses are assessed based on job-specific criteria using a predetermined scorecard. Bias is minimized, so the structured interview is more effective.
    d. Testing applicants for jobs with quantifiable output (e.g., jobs requiring clerical skills or manual dexterity) is easier than testing for positions with a less tangible work product (e.g., public relations director or human resource manager).
        1) All tests must be validated in each organization and for minority and nonminority groups before they can be predictive of successful performance.
        2) Tests must be given to all applicants for the same job category.

5. **Training and Development**

    a. Training consists of organizational programs to prepare employees to perform currently assigned tasks.

       1) On-the-job training, for example, by job rotation, apprenticeships, and mentoring arrangements, is usually less costly than off-the-job training. However, it may disrupt the workplace and result in increased errors. It is suited to acquisition of technical skills.

       2) Off-the-job training is provided, for example, in classroom lectures, film study, and simulations. It develops problem solving and interpersonal abilities and teaches complex skills.

       3) Computer-based training is expected to become more common.

    b. Development programs prepare people to perform future tasks and learn new skills.

       1) The focus is mostly on development of human relations skills. Management coaching and mentoring enhance development.

    c. Training and development programs succeed when the greatest retention (learning) of skills and knowledge is transferred to the job. The following is a model for learning:

       1) Establishing objectives (goal setting)
       2) Modeling the skills or making a meaningful presentation of facts
       3) Practicing the skills
       4) Obtaining feedback

    d. Evaluation and appraisal help identify individual strengths and weaknesses. Also, jobs and markets change, leading to a need for workers with different skills. Organizations thrive when workers value lifelong learning.

       1) Viewing performance evaluation as a training and developmental process can foster a culture in which evaluation is sought.

       2) A training-needs assessment should determine (a) what training is relevant to employees' jobs, (b) what training will improve performance, and (c) whether training will make a difference.

          a) It also should (1) distinguish training needs from organizational problems and (2) link improved job performance with the organization's objectives.

       3) Self-assessment normally yields shorter-term training benefits and may relate more to personal career goals than strategic business needs. Thus, self-assessment often is only a supplement to other approaches.

6. **Performance Evaluation**

    a. Reasons

        1) Evaluations are important to employees, the employer, and the organization.
        2) Evaluations provide an opportunity for growth and may prevent disputes.
        3) Evaluations tend to focus on who did the job, how it was done, or what was done.

    b. Types

        1) Behavior-oriented evaluation rewards the behavior desired by management. Behavior control examines work processes rather than work output.
        2) Goal-oriented evaluation measures how well the employee attained objectives.
        3) Trait-oriented evaluation tends to reward what the supervisor thinks of the employee.
        4) Employee-oriented evaluation focuses on who did the job.

    c. Purposes

        1) Performance criteria identify job-related abilities.
        2) Performance objectives direct employees toward achieving objectives without constant supervision.
        3) Performance outcomes promote employee satisfaction by acknowledging when jobs are completed and done well.
        4) Evaluation distinguishes effective from ineffective job performance.
        5) The organization develops employee strengths and identifies weaknesses.
        6) Evaluation sets compensation.

            a) But separating performance evaluations from compensation decisions may be beneficial. An advantage is that more emphasis is on long-term objectives and other rewards, such as feelings of achievement and the recognition of superiors.
            b) Another advantage is that the employee's good performance can be separated from the bad performance.
            c) A disadvantage is that the employee may not be motivated immediately by a good appraisal because of the delay of any monetary reward.

                i) The evaluation also may not be taken seriously by the employee if compensation is not correlated with performance.

        7) Evaluation identifies promotable employees.

            a) Internal promotions motivate employees and are less difficult and expensive than external hiring.
            b) Many firms hire external candidates because they have a different perspective on the organization's problems and may have more up-to-date training or education.

SU 3: Leadership, Organizational Structure, and Business Processes

7. **Major Types of Appraisals**

    a. Management by Objectives (MBO)

      1) Supervisors and subordinates mutually establish objectives. A rating is based on achievement of the objectives.

    b. Behaviorally Anchored Rating Scales (BARS)

      1) BARS describe good and bad performance. They are developed through job analysis for a number of specific job-related behaviors.

    c. Check-the-Box

      1) This method provides a list of categories for rating performance for the supervisor to check off. The following are examples:

        a) Graphic scale, consisting of a list of job duties and a scale to grade them, e.g., 1 = Excellent, etc.
        b) A checklist of statements relating to job performance.

    d. Comparative Methods

      1) These involve comparing an employee's performance with the work of others. Comparative methods include

        a) Ranking all employees from highest to lowest. This method can lend itself to bias on the part of the evaluator.
        b) Ranking an employee against other employee(s) (paired comparison).

    e. Narrative Method

      1) This approach includes essays and critical incidents (specific inferior or superior performance). Both require large amounts of time.
      2) Field reviews require human resources personnel to prepare the evaluation for each employee based on the supervisor's input.

    f. 360° Performance Appraisal

      1) This method uses a multirater model for employee assessment. It provides anonymous feedback by peers, customers, supervisors, and subordinates.
      2) Appraisal is subjective and may be affected by popularity.
      3) Evaluations do not include copies of job descriptions or performance goals.

8. **Business Process Outsourcing**

    a. Business process outsourcing is the transfer of some of an organization's business processes to an outside provider to improve service quality while achieving

      1) Cost savings,
      2) Operating effectiveness, or
      3) Operating efficiency.

    b. Such processes as human resources, payroll, and information services may not be core competencies of some organizations. To streamline operations and reduce costs, they outsource processes.

      1) By contracting with outside service providers who specialize in these functions, the organization also may avoid the problem of knowledge loss when key employees leave.

9. **Management Responsibilities**

    a. Management still is responsible for ensuring that an adequate system of internal control exists over processes performed by an external service provider.

    b. Practices for effective risk management and control of outsourced business processes include the following:

        1) Document the outsourced process and indicate which key controls have been outsourced
        2) Ensure that the effectiveness of the outsourced process is monitored
        3) Obtain assurance that the internal controls embedded in the outsourced process are operating effectively, either through internal audits or an external review
        4) Periodically reevaluate whether the business case for outsourcing the process remains valid

10. **Advantages and Disadvantages**

    a. **Advantages** of outsourcing include the following:

        1) Access to expertise
        2) Superior service quality
        3) Avoidance of changes in the organization's infrastructure
        4) Cost predictability
        5) Use of human and financial capital
        6) Avoidance of fixed costs

    b. The potential **disadvantages** include the following:

        1) Inflexibility of the relationship
        2) Loss of core knowledge
        3) Loss of control over the outsourced function
        4) Unexpected costs
        5) Vulnerability of important information
        6) Need for contract management
        7) Dependence on a single vendor

You have completed the outline for this subunit.
Study multiple-choice questions 12 through 16 beginning on page 113.

STOP & REVIEW

3.4 BUSINESS PROCESS -- PRICING AND THE SUPPLY CHAIN

1. **Pricing**
    a. A seller uses pricing strategy to identify the optimal prices for its products.
    b. **Pricing objectives** direct the pricing process. They include the following:
        1) Profit maximization
        2) Quality leadership
            a) Sellers set prices to signal the market that their products are of high quality.
        3) Quantity maximization
            a) Sellers establish prices to maximize unit sales. These entities usually intend to take advantage of economies of scale.
        4) Survival
            a) Sellers need to set prices to cover essential costs.
    c. General pricing strategies
        1) **Nonprice competition** is a differentiation strategy used to attract customers. Price does not provide a competitive advantage for these entities.
        2) A **competitive pricing** strategy is used by a seller for which price is a competitive advantage. Prices are based on the prices in the market or the prices of major competitors.
    d. Pricing strategies for new products
        1) A **skimming** strategy sets an initial high price and then slowly lowers the price to make the product available to a wider market.
        2) A **penetration pricing** strategy sets a low price to increase sales and market share. This strategy generates greater sales and establishes the new product in the market more quickly.
    e. Alternative pricing strategies
        1) **Cost-oriented pricing** is widely used. It includes cost-plus pricing and markup pricing.
            a) Using **cost-plus pricing**, sellers add a projected gross margin to the costs of producing the product.
                i) A similar concept is **markup pricing**, which adds a projected percentage to the retailer's invoice price to determine the final selling price.
            b) Using **breakeven analysis**, sellers can determine the minimum price needed to recover costs at a certain level of production.
                i) This approach is commonly combined with a **target rate of return**.
                ii) A detailed outline of breakeven analysis is in Study Unit 13.
        2) **Demand-oriented pricing** focuses on how customers' demand for a product changes at various price levels.
            a) **Price elasticity of demand** is used to measure the responsiveness of the quantity demanded of a product to a change in its price.

$$\text{Price elasticity of demand} = \frac{\text{Change in quantity} \div \text{Quantity}}{\text{Change in price} \div \text{Price}}$$

        3) **Value-based pricing** sets prices equal to the value of the benefits the products provide to customers.

2. **The Supply Chain**

    a. The supply chain consists of flows from sources of (1) materials, (2) components, (3) finished goods, (4) services, or (5) information through intermediaries to ultimate consumers.

    1) These flows and the related activities may occur across the functions in an organization's value chain (R&D, design, production, marketing, distribution, and customer service). They also may occur across separate organizations.

    2) The activities in the supply chain, wherever they occur, should be integrated and coordinated for optimal cost management.

Example of a Supply Chain

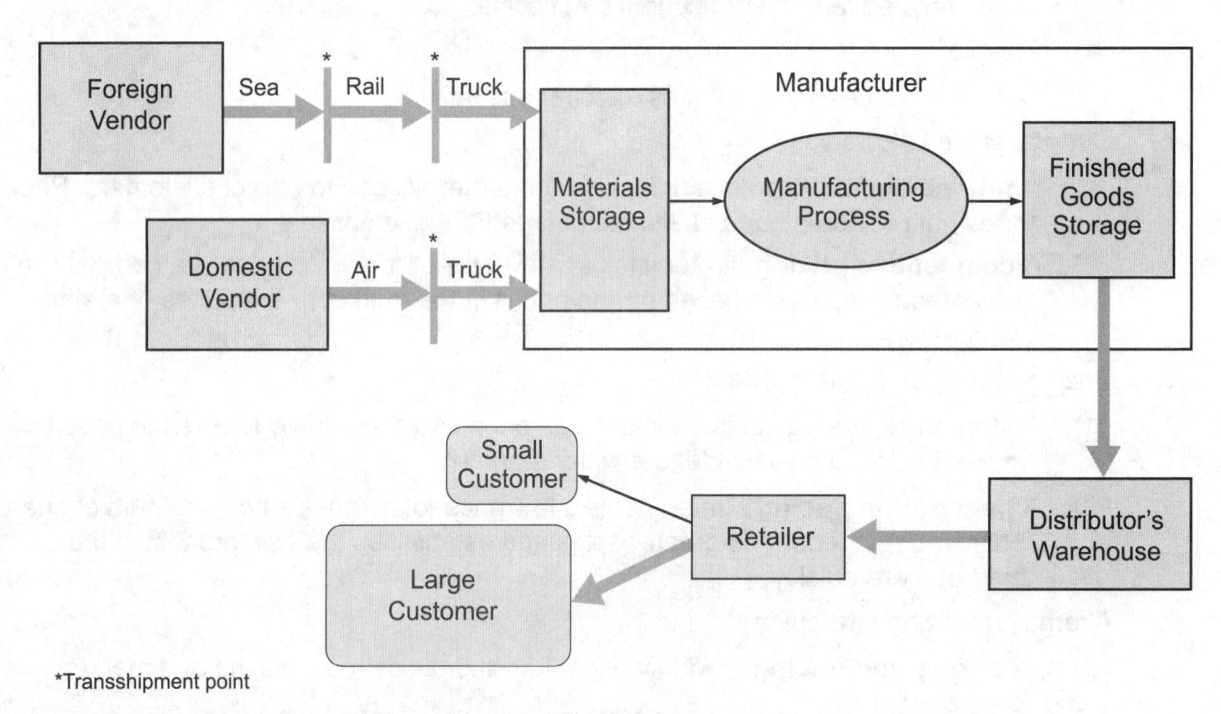

*Transshipment point

Figure 3-3

3. **Supply Chain Coordination**

    a. For a supply chain to be successful, the most important goal for all organizations involved is to establish bonds of trust. This facilitates the sharing of information and coordination.

    b. Sharing of information and coordination among the organizations in the supply chain can avoid the **bullwhip or whiplash** effect on inventories. This phenomenon begins when retailers face uncertain demand from consumers caused by randomness in buying habits.

    1) However, the **variability** of retailers' orders to manufacturers is affected by factors in addition to consumer demand. In turn, manufacturers' orders to suppliers may reflect a still greater variability because those orders depend on factors in addition to retailer demand.

2) This cascade of demand variability throughout the supply chain may be caused by the following:

   a) Difficulties of predicting demand and derived demand at each link in the supply chain
   b) The need to purchase or manufacture goods in cost-efficient batches
   c) Changes in price that may encourage purchases in anticipation of future increases
   d) Shortages that may lead to rationing by suppliers or manufacturers and hoarding by manufacturers or retailers

c. Sharing of information about sales, inventory, pricing, advertising campaigns, and sales forecasts by all functions and organizations in the supply chain moderates demand uncertainty for all parties. The following are desired results:

   1) Minimization of inventories held by suppliers, manufacturers, and retailers
   2) Avoidance of stockouts
   3) Fewer rush orders
   4) Production as needed by retailers

d. The following are examples of difficulties in supply-chain inventory management:

   1) Incompatibility of the information systems of the parties
   2) Refusal of some parties to share information, possibly because of security concerns
   3) Devoting insufficient resources to the task
   4) Fear that others will not meet their obligations

4. **Distribution**

   a. Distribution is the transfer of goods (and, in other contexts, services and information) from producers to customers or from distribution centers to merchandisers. Thus, distribution manages outflows, and purchasing manages inflows.

   b. Among the interrelated issues involved in distribution are selection of

   1) Distribution channels,
   2) Inventory placement,
   3) Means of transportation,
   4) Shipment schedules,
   5) Routes, and
   6) Carriers.

5. **Distribution Channel**

   a. A distribution channel is a series of interdependent marketing institutions that facilitate the transfer of a product from producer to ultimate consumer or industrial user. A distribution channel creates place, time, and possession utility by bringing sellers and buyers together.

   1) For example, in Figure 3-3, the intermediaries in the distribution channel are the distributor's warehouse and retailer.

b. The following are intermediaries (also called middlemen) between sellers and buyers:
1) Merchant **middlemen** buy the goods outright and necessarily take title to them. They include merchant wholesalers (often called distributors or jobbers) and most retailers.
2) An **agent** represents a principal in negotiating purchases, sales, or both, but does not take title to the goods.
3) A **broker** serves as a go-between. Unlike an agent, a broker ordinarily does not maintain a relationship with a particular buyer or seller. A broker also does not assume title risks. An example is a travel agency.
4) A **consignee** merely sells the consignor's goods for a fee. Title remains with the consignor until the goods are sold and title passes to the buyer.
5) Facilitating **intermediaries** are persons or entities outside the channel that perform some services (inventory control, financial services, risk management, information services, promotions) more effectively and efficiently than the channel members.

c. The efficiencies gained by introducing intermediaries into a distribution channel can be calculated mathematically.
1) For instance, if a certain channel has three producers that serve the same three customers, the number of contacts is nine (three producers × three customers). If a distributor begins serving this channel, the number of contacts is reduced to six (three products + three customers).

6. **Channel Structures**
a. The channel structure describes the relationship between the entities that make up the distribution system.
b. **Conventional distribution systems** consist of one or more independent producers, wholesalers, and retailers, each of which is a separate profit-maximizing business.
1) The profit objective of each independent channel member may result in actions that are not profit maximizing for the system as a whole.
2) The system offers no means for defining roles and controlling channel conflict.
c. In **vertical distribution systems**, producers, wholesalers, and retailers act as a unified system.
1) Channel conflict is managed through common ownership, contractual relationships, or administration by one or a few dominant channel members.
2) Conflict is between levels, e.g., when a manufacturer tries to enforce resale price agreements with dealers.
d. **Horizontal distribution systems** consist of two or more entities at one level of the channel working together to exploit new opportunities, such as the introduction of ATMs in supermarkets.
1) The joint nature of horizontal distribution efforts is the tool for managing channel conflict.
2) Conflict occurs at the same level, e.g., when service standards vary.
e. In a **multichannel system**, a single entity sets up two or more channels to reach one or more customer segments. Because such a system is managed by a single firm, channel conflicts can be evaluated and managed internally.
1) Conflict is between channels, e.g., when the manufacturer's stores compete with other retailers.

SU 3: Leadership, Organizational Structure, and Business Processes

7. **Inventory Placement**
   a. Forward placement puts inventory close to final customers at a distribution center (warehouse), wholesaler, or retailer. This option minimizes transportation costs and delivery times.
      1) Forward placement is typical for certain consumer goods and services that are usually low-priced and widely available. Consumers buy them often and with a minimum of comparison and effort.
         a) Examples are soap and newspapers.
         b) Producers of such goods ordinarily use intensive distribution to sell their products through a large number of retail or wholesale units, such as grocery stores.
   b. Backward placement involves keeping inventory at the factory or, in the extreme case, maintaining no inventory at all (i.e., building to order). This option is indicated when products are customized or when regional demand fluctuates unpredictably.
   c. Scheduling movements of freight balances purchasing, production, customer response times, shipping costs, and selection of routes and carriers.

STOP & REVIEW

You have completed the outline for this subunit.
Study multiple-choice questions 17 through 20 beginning on page 115.

3.5 BUSINESS PROCESS -- PROCUREMENT

1. **Management's Responsibility**
   a. Management is responsible for establishing the controls over the procurement process to ensure the following:
      1) Proper authorization of the purchase
      2) Ordering the proper quality and quantity of goods on a timely basis
      3) Acceptance only of goods that have been ordered
      4) Receipt of proper terms and prices from the vendor
      5) Payment only for those goods and services that were ordered, received, and properly invoiced
      6) Payment on a timely basis (e.g., to take advantage of cash discounts)

2. **The Auditor's Responsibility**
   a. The auditor is required to obtain an understanding of the entity and its environment, including its internal control, to assess the risks of material misstatement and to design further audit procedures. For this purpose, the auditor performs risk assessment procedures.
   b. The plan for further audit procedures reflects (1) the auditor's decision whether to test the operating effectiveness of controls over the purchases-payables-cash disbursement cycle and (2) the nature, timing, and extent of substantive procedures.

3. **Organizational Structure**

    a. The ideal structure segregates duties and responsibilities as follows:

        1) Authorization of the transaction

        2) Recording of the transaction

        3) Custody over the assets (e.g., inventory and cash disbursements) associated with the transaction

    b. However, cost-benefit considerations may affect the organizational structure, and complete segregation may not be feasible. Compensating controls are likely to be established when the segregation of duties is not maintained. Typical **compensating controls** may include

        1) More supervision or
        2) Owner involvement in the process.

4. **Responsibilities of Personnel**

    a. Personnel and department responsibilities in the procurement process include the following:

        1) **Inventory Control** provides authorization for the purchase of goods and performs an accountability function (e.g., Inventory Control is responsible for maintaining perpetual records for inventory quantities and costs).

        2) **Purchasing Agent** issues purchase orders for required goods.

        3) **Receiving** department accepts goods for approved purchases, counts and inspects the goods, and prepares the receiving report.

        4) **Inventory Warehouse** provides physical control over the goods.

        5) **Accounts Payable** (vouchers payable) assembles the proper documentation to support a payment voucher (and disbursement) and records the account payable.

        6) **Cash Disbursements** evaluates the documentation to support a payment voucher and signs and mails the check. This department cancels the documentation to prevent duplicate payment.

        7) **General Ledger** maintains the accounts payable control account and other related general ledger accounts.

5. **The Document Flow**

    a. The organizational chart presented on the next page displays the reporting responsibilities of each function.

        1) To simplify the presentation, the flowchart does not show the disposition, e.g., the filing of documents, or other supplemental procedures.

        2) Some text is added to the flowchart to facilitate understanding of the flow.

        3) The flowchart begins at the point labeled **START**.

        4) Copies of documents are numbered so they may be referenced through the system.

SU 3: Leadership, Organizational Structure, and Business Processes

Procurement Process Flowchart

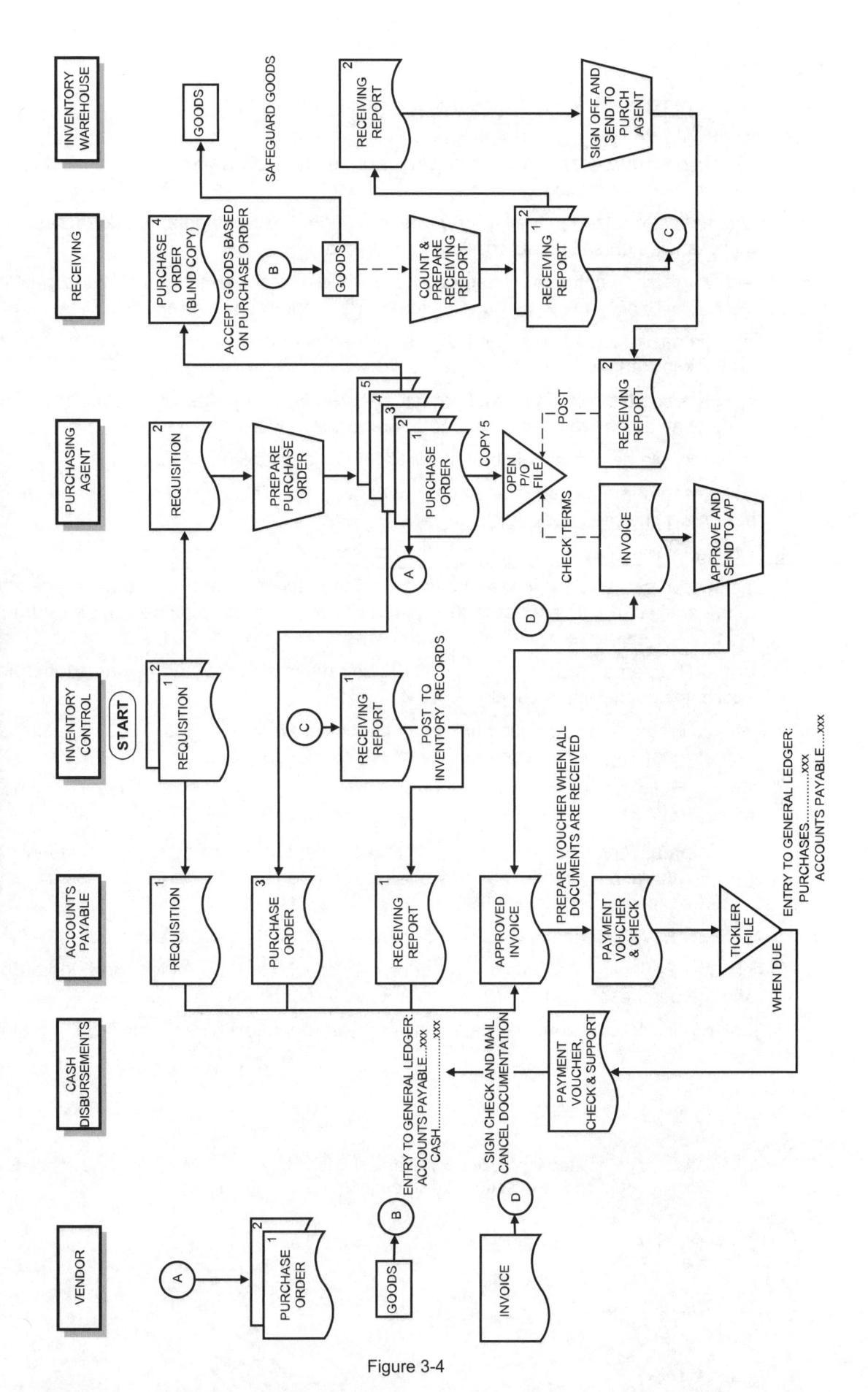

Figure 3-4

6. **Controls Implemented**

    a. The segregation of duties for the transaction is as follows: authorization, recording, and custody of assets.
    b. Requisitions, purchase orders, receiving reports, payment vouchers, and checks are prenumbered and accounted for.
    c. Purchases are based only on proper authorizations. Receiving should not accept merchandise unless an approved purchase order is on hand.
    d. Receiving's copy of the purchase order omits the quantity so that employees must count the goods to determine the quantity to record on the receiving report.
    e. The Purchasing Agent compares prices and terms from the vendor invoice with requested and acknowledged terms from the vendor.
    f. Vouchers and the related journal entries are prepared only when goods are received that have been authorized, ordered, and appropriately invoiced.
    g. The tickler file permits timely payments to realize available cash discounts.
    h. Cash Disbursements ascertains that proper support exists for the voucher and check before signing the check.
    i. Two signatures may be required for checks larger than a preset limit.
    j. Cash Disbursements, which reports to the CFO, mails the checks so that no one internal to the entity can gain access to the signed checks, and unused checks are returned to the CFO or the treasury department.
    k. Cash Disbursements cancels payment documents to prevent their use as support for duplicate vouchers and checks.
    l. Periodic reconciliation of the vouchers in the tickler file with Accounts Payable ensures proper recording in the accounts payable control account.
    m. Periodic counts of inventory, independently reconciled with perpetual records, provide assurance that physical controls over inventory are effective.

        1) Internal verification of inventory is independent if performed by an individual who is not responsible for custody of assets or the authorization and recording of transactions.

    n. Accounts Payable examines the vendor invoice for mathematical errors.
    o. Accounts Payable compares the vendor's invoice with the receiving report, the requisition, and the purchase order to ensure that a valid transaction occurred.
    p. Bank reconciliation should not be reviewed by someone with responsibility for custody of assets.

STOP & REVIEW

You have completed the outline for this subunit.
Study multiple-choice questions 21 through 23 beginning on page 116.

QUESTIONS

3.1 Leadership

1. A manager can use power and authority to accomplish objectives. The relationship between these two important concepts is best explained as follows:

A. Power is the right to do things, while authority is the ability to do things.
B. Authority is the right to do things, while power is the ability to do things.
C. Power and authority are both required to accomplish a task.
D. Power and authority are simply two words that describe the same concept -- how to get things done in organizations.

Answer (B) is correct.
REQUIRED: The relationship between power and authority.
DISCUSSION: Authority is the officially sanctioned privilege to direct others. A clear hierarchy of authority enhances coordination and accountability. Power is the ability to marshal organizational resources to obtain results. A manager may have both authority and power or have one without the other.
Answer (A) is incorrect. Authority is the right to do things, and power is the ability to do things. **Answer (C) is incorrect.** A manager may accomplish a task without having formal authority. **Answer (D) is incorrect.** Authority is the right to do things, and power is the ability to do things.

2. A leader who is able to gain compliance from a group based solely on personal attraction is said to have

A. Reward power.
B. Coercive power.
C. Referent power.
D. Legitimate power.

Answer (C) is correct.
REQUIRED: The type of power held by a leader who uses personal attraction to gain compliance from a group.
DISCUSSION: Referent power is based on identification of subordinates with a superior. Thus, personal magnetism (charisma) may be a basis for influencing others to comply with a manager's directives.
Answer (A) is incorrect. Reward power is based on a person's ability to grant benefits. **Answer (B) is incorrect.** Coercive power is rooted in the fear or threat of punishment. **Answer (D) is incorrect.** Legitimate power is the leader's right to expect cooperation from others.

3. A company's decisions are made solely by one person, who is the CEO and major shareholder. Which of the following powers is this person **least** likely to have?

A. Coercive power.
B. Legitimate power.
C. Referent power.
D. Reward power.

Answer (C) is correct.
REQUIRED: The power that the sole decision maker is least likely to have.
DISCUSSION: A person who is the head of a company may exert influence through five types of power. Referent power is the capacity of the individual's personality and style to cause others to identify with or like him or her. Thus, it is the one type of power not necessarily held by a CEO and major shareholder. This person has the ability to reward others and apply pressure. (S)he also has the right to expect cooperation.
Answer (A) is incorrect. Coercive power is based on the fear or threat of punishment. **Answer (B) is incorrect.** Legitimate power is the leader's right to expect cooperation from others. **Answer (D) is incorrect.** Reward power is the individual's ability to influence others through their expectation that good behavior will be rewarded.

4. Which of the following is a true statement about generic influence tactics?

A. Exchange tactics involve appealing to emotions, values, or ordeals.
B. Ingratiating tactics attempt to raise the other person's self-esteem prior to a request.
C. Coalition tactics try to convince others by reliance on a detailed plan, supporting evidence, and reason.
D. Pressure tactics are based on the formal or informal support of higher management.

Answer (B) is correct.
REQUIRED: The true statement about generic influence tactics.
DISCUSSION: Management literature describes generic influence tactics that may be upward, lateral, or downward. As noted by researchers, ingratiating tactics attempt to raise the other person's self-esteem prior to a request.
Answer (A) is incorrect. Exchange tactics are based on doing favors for others to receive favors in return. **Answer (C) is incorrect.** Coalition tactics seek the aid of others to persuade someone to agree. **Answer (D) is incorrect.** Upward appeals to higher authority seek the support of more senior management, whereas pressure tactics involve intimidation, threats, and demands.

5. The director of internal auditing for a large company has established an excellent reputation because of her strong professional credentials and tactful but firm handling of auditor-auditee relationships. With regard to auditees, she must rely upon what sources of power?

A. Expert and coercive.
B. Referent and reward.
C. Referent and expert.
D. Legitimate and coercive.

Answer (C) is correct.
REQUIRED: The sources of power relied on by a particular manager.
DISCUSSION: The internal audit director has neither formal (legitimate or position) power over auditees nor the power to coerce (punish) or reward them. Rather, her ability to exert power (influence others) must derive from her specialized ability and knowledge and the force of her personal qualities.

6. Power is synonymous with leadership. Simply put, it is the ability to influence other people. The sources of power are various. For example, the kind of power arising from the strength of the leader's personality is known as

A. Coercive power.
B. Legitimate power.
C. Expert power.
D. Referent power.

Answer (D) is correct.
REQUIRED: The kind of power resulting from the strength of the leader's personality.
DISCUSSION: Power may be classified as reward power (the leader controls resources), coercive power (the leader may punish the subordinate), legitimate power (the leader has the right to lead), referent power (the leader has fame, charisma, etc.), and expert power (the leader has specialized ability or knowledge).
Answer (A) is incorrect. Coercive power is based on the fear or threat of punishment. **Answer (B) is incorrect.** Legitimate power is the leader's right to expect cooperation from others. **Answer (C) is incorrect.** Expert power is conferred by clearly superior skill or knowledge.

3.2 Organizational Structure

7. Which of the following factors is **least** likely to affect a manager's optimal span of control?

A. Frequency of supervisor-subordinate contact.
B. The manager's willingness to delegate authority.
C. The manager's training and communication skills.
D. Number of people in the organization.

Answer (D) is correct.
REQUIRED: The factor least likely to affect a manager's direct span of control.
DISCUSSION: The optimal span of control is the number of subordinates a manager can effectively supervise. It is a function of many situational factors. However, the total number of people in an organization has no bearing on the optimal span of control of a particular manager.
Answer (A) is incorrect. Managers who can contact subordinates frequently are able to control more people than those who have relatively infrequent contact with subordinates. **Answer (B) is incorrect.** Managers who delegate authority have more time to control the subordinates who report to them. These individuals can therefore supervise more people than managers who prefer not to delegate authority. **Answer (C) is incorrect.** Managers who have received effective training and are skillful communicators are equipped to control more individuals than managers who are untrained or have deficient communication skills.

8. A claimed advantage of decentralizing is

A. Concentration of authority.
B. Manager development.
C. Elimination of duplication of effort.
D. Elimination of inessential operations.

Answer (B) is correct.
REQUIRED: The advantage of decentralizing an organization.
DISCUSSION: When an organization changes from a centralized to a decentralized structure, top management is delegating more authority to middle and lower levels. Thus, managers at these lower levels are usually hired and developed more rigorously than under the centralized structure.
Answer (A) is incorrect. Authority is more concentrated in centralized management structures. **Answer (C) is incorrect.** Some effort will inevitably be duplicated under decentralization, of which departmentation is a moderate form. **Answer (D) is incorrect.** Elimination of unsuccessful or inessential operations to increase the entity's focus is supportive of greater centralization.

9. Which of the following is a disadvantage of a flat organizational structure?

A. Employees are not encouraged to be creative.
B. The input of fresh ideas from outside the organization is limited because employee turnover is low.
C. Managers spend too much time training individuals and not enough time supervising.
D. Employees may not be performing work tasks properly.

Answer (D) is correct.
REQUIRED: The disadvantage of a flat organizational structure.
DISCUSSION: A flat organizational structure concentrates decision-making authority at one level. Tasks and performance objectives may be unclear to employees because of a lack of supervision.
Answer (A) is incorrect. The lack of supervision increases employee flexibility. **Answer (B) is incorrect.** The number of management levels limits the opportunity for advancement, which may cause high employee turnover. **Answer (C) is incorrect.** The lack of supervision decreases employee training.

10. Which of the following elements of an organization requires people to be accountable to superiors?

A. Coordination of effort.
B. Division of labor.
C. Common goal or purpose.
D. Hierarchy of authority.

Answer (D) is correct.
REQUIRED: The element requiring people to be accountable to their superiors.
DISCUSSION: A hierarchy of authority requires people to be accountable to their superiors in the hierarchy.
Answer (A) is incorrect. Coordination of effort involves cooperation in the social environment of the organization. **Answer (B) is incorrect.** Division of labor ensures efficient specialization of employees. **Answer (C) is incorrect.** A common goal or purpose is relevant to the employees and employer achieving a common objective.

11. Which of the following is a benefit of decentralization?

A. The head of the company is aware of and can influence all decisions before they are made.
B. The company is operated as one unit.
C. Specialists for a particular product have no authority but advise the company's top management.
D. Decisions are made on a more timely basis.

Answer (D) is correct.
REQUIRED: The benefit of decentralization.
DISCUSSION: Decentralization is the extent to which decision-making power is delegated within an entity. When approval from upper-level management is not required, lower-level managers can make more timely decisions because they are closer to the necessary sources of information.
Answer (A) is incorrect. The head of the company being aware of and being able to influence all decisions before they are made typifies a highly centralized entity. **Answer (B) is incorrect.** Operating the company as one unit typifies a highly centralized entity. **Answer (C) is incorrect.** Decentralization would give these specialists more authority.

3.3 Business Process -- Human Resources and Outsourcing

12. Performance appraisal systems might use any of three different approaches: (1) who did the job, (2) how the job was done, or (3) what was accomplished. Which approach is used by a system that places the focus on how the job was done?

A. Behavior-oriented.
B. Goal-oriented.
C. Trait-oriented.
D. Employee-oriented.

Answer (A) is correct.
REQUIRED: The approach used in a performance appraisal system that emphasizes how the job was done.
DISCUSSION: Behavior-oriented performance evaluation rewards the behavior that is desired by management. Behavior control involves examining work processes rather than work output.
Answer (B) is incorrect. The goal-oriented approach measures how well the employee attained the objectives or goals set by management. **Answer (C) is incorrect.** A trait-oriented approach tends to reward what the supervisor thinks of the employee rather than the job the employee did. **Answer (D) is incorrect.** An employee-oriented approach would focus on who did the job.

13. A manager discovers by chance that a newly hired employee has strong beliefs that are very different from the manager's and from those of most of the other employees. The manager's best course of action would be to

A. Facilitate the reassignment of the new hire as quickly as possible before this situation becomes disruptive.
B. Ask the rest of the team for their reaction and act according to the group consensus.
C. Take no action unless the new hire's behavior is likely to cause harm to the organization.
D. Try to counsel the new hire into more reasonable beliefs.

Answer (C) is correct.
REQUIRED: The manager's best course of action when a new employee has strong beliefs that are very different from the manager's beliefs.
DISCUSSION: The only legitimate grounds on which the supervisor may take action is the employee's behavior. Personal beliefs, such as those on religious and political matters, cannot be the basis of personnel actions. Discrimination on the basis of personal beliefs could expose the organization to legal action.

14. When faced with the problem of filling a newly created or recently vacated executive position, organizations must decide whether to promote from within or hire an outsider. One of the disadvantages of promoting from within is that

A. Internal promotions can have a negative motivational effect on the employees of the firm.
B. Internal promotions are more expensive to the organization than hiring an outsider.
C. It is difficult to identify proven performers among internal candidates.
D. Hiring an insider leads to the possibility of social inbreeding within the firm.

Answer (D) is correct.
REQUIRED: The disadvantage of promoting from within.
DISCUSSION: Hiring an internal candidate can lead to social inbreeding. Many firms look to external candidates for certain jobs because they bring a fresh perspective to the organization's problems and may have more up-to-date training or education.
Answer (A) is incorrect. Internal promotions usually lead to increased motivation among employees. **Answer (B) is incorrect.** Internal promotions are less expensive. The firm can avoid the expenses associated with an executive search and certain training costs. **Answer (C) is incorrect.** It is more difficult to identify proven performers from among outside candidates than internal candidates.

15. Evaluating performance is **not** done to

A. Determine the amount of nondiscriminatory benefits that each employee deserves.
B. Assess the available human resources of the firm.
C. Motivate the employees.
D. Determine which employees deserve salary increases.

Answer (A) is correct.
REQUIRED: The statement that is not a purpose of performance evaluations.
DISCUSSION: Evaluations reinforce accomplishments, help in assessing employee strengths and weaknesses, provide motivation, assist in employee development, permit the organization to assess its human resource needs, and serve as a basis for wage increases. Nondiscriminatory benefits are given to everyone in the organization in equal amounts, regardless of title, pay, or achievement of objectives.
Answer (B) is incorrect. Performance evaluation is done to assess the available human resources of the firm. **Answer (C) is incorrect.** Performance evaluation is done to motivate the employees. **Answer (D) is incorrect.** Performance evaluation is done to determine which employees deserve salary increases.

16. In some organizations, internal audit functions are outsourced. Management in a large organization should recognize that the external auditor may have an advantage, compared with the internal auditor, because of the external auditor's

A. Familiarity with the organization. Its annual audits provide an in-depth knowledge of the organization.
B. Size. It can hire experienced, knowledgeable, and certified staff.
C. Size. It is able to offer continuous availability of staff unaffected by other priorities.
D. Structure. It may more easily accommodate engagement requirements in distant locations.

Answer (D) is correct.
REQUIRED: The advantage of outsourcing internal audit functions.
DISCUSSION: Large organizations that are geographically dispersed may find outsourcing internal audit functions to external auditors to be effective. A major public accounting firm ordinarily has operations that are national or worldwide in scope.
Answer (A) is incorrect. The internal auditors are likely to be more familiar with the organization than the external auditors, given the continuous nature of their responsibilities. **Answer (B) is incorrect.** The internal auditor also can hire experienced, knowledgeable, and certified staff. **Answer (C) is incorrect.** The internal auditor is more likely to be continuously available. The external auditor has responsibilities to many other clients.

3.4 Business Process -- Pricing and the Supply Chain

17. The airlines have been leaders in the use of technology. Customers can make reservations either with an airline or through a travel agency. In this situation, a travel agency is classified as which type of distribution channel?

A. An intermediary.
B. A jobber.
C. A distributor.
D. A facilitating agent.

Answer (A) is correct.
REQUIRED: The type of distribution channel of which a travel agency is an example.
DISCUSSION: Marketing intermediaries assist companies in promoting, selling, and distributing their goods and services to ultimate consumers. For example, travel agents access an airline's computerized reservation system and make reservations for their customers without ever taking title to the ticket.
Answer (B) is incorrect. Jobbers buy from manufacturers, then resell the products. **Answer (C) is incorrect.** Distributors, or wholesalers, usually have selective or exclusive distribution rights. **Answer (D) is incorrect.** Facilitating agents assist in functions other than buying, selling, or transferring title.

18. An organization must manage its flows of materials, components, finished goods, services, or information through intermediaries to ultimate consumers. These flows may occur across the functions in an organization's

A. Supply chain.
B. Value chain.
C. Full-function chain.
D. Integrated chain.

Answer (B) is correct.
REQUIRED: The organizational arrangement in which flows of materials, components, goods, services, or information may occur.
DISCUSSION: The supply chain consists of flows from sources of (1) materials, (2) components, (3) finished goods, (4) services, or (5) information through intermediaries to ultimate consumers. These flows and the related activities may occur across the functions in an organization's value chain (R&D, design, production, marketing, distribution, and customer service). These flows and the related activities also may occur across separate organizations.
Answer (A) is incorrect. The supply chain consists of the flows that may occur across the functions in an organization's value chain or separate organizations. **Answer (C) is incorrect.** The phrase "full-function chain" is not a technical term. **Answer (D) is incorrect.** The phrase "integrated chain" is not a technical term.

19. A desired result of the sharing of information by all functions and organizations in the supply chain is

A. Fewer rush orders.
B. Maximization of inventories held by suppliers, manufacturers, and retailers.
C. Stockouts.
D. Incompatibility of the information systems of the parties.

Answer (A) is correct.
REQUIRED: The desired result from sharing information by all functions and organizations in the supply chain.
DISCUSSION: Sharing information about sales, inventory, pricing, advertising campaigns, and sales forecasts by all functions and organizations in the supply chain moderates demand uncertainty for all parties. The desired results are (1) minimization of inventories held by suppliers, manufacturers, and retailers; (2) avoidance of stockouts; (3) fewer rush orders; and (4) production as needed by retailers.
Answer (B) is incorrect. Minimization of inventories held by all parties in the supply chain is a desired result of sharing information. **Answer (C) is incorrect.** Avoidance of stockouts is a desired result of sharing information. **Answer (D) is incorrect.** Incompatibility of the information systems of the parties is a difficulty faced by supply-chain management, not a desired result of sharing information.

20. Which of the following is **not** a component of physical distribution?

A. Transportation.
B. Pricing.
C. Location of retail outlets.
D. Warehousing.

Answer (B) is correct.
REQUIRED: The factor not a component of physical distribution.
DISCUSSION: Physical distribution (market logistics) involves planning, implementing, and controlling the movement of materials and final goods to meet customer needs while earning a profit. Physical distribution systems coordinate suppliers, purchasing agents, marketers, channels, and customers. They include warehousing, transportation, and retail outlets.
Answer (A) is incorrect. A physical distribution system includes transportation. **Answer (C) is incorrect.** A physical distribution system includes the location of retail outlets. **Answer (D) is incorrect.** A physical distribution system includes warehousing.

3.5 Business Process -- Procurement

21. In a well-designed internal control system, the same employee may be permitted to

A. Mail signed checks and also cancel supporting documents.
B. Prepare receiving reports and also approve purchase orders.
C. Approve vouchers for payment and also have access to unused purchase orders.
D. Mail signed checks and also prepare bank reconciliations.

Answer (A) is correct.
REQUIRED: The functions the same employee may be permitted to perform in a well-designed control system.
DISCUSSION: The cash disbursements department has an asset custody function. Consequently, this department is responsible for signing checks after verification of their accuracy by reference to the supporting documents. The supporting documents should then be canceled and the checks mailed. Cancellation prevents the documentation from being used to support duplicate payments. Moreover, having the party who signs the checks place them in the mail reduces the risk that they will be altered or diverted.
Answer (B) is incorrect. The receiving department should not know how many units have been ordered. **Answer (C) is incorrect.** Accounts payable is responsible for approving vouchers, and purchasing is the only department with access to the purchase orders. The same employee should not approve the purchase and approve payment. **Answer (D) is incorrect.** The bank reconciliation is performed by someone with no asset custody function.

22. Which of the following internal control activities is **not** usually performed in the vouchers payable department?

A. Matching the vendor's invoice with the related receiving report.

B. Approving vouchers for payment by having an authorized employee sign the vouchers.

C. Indicating the asset and expense accounts to be debited.

D. Accounting for unused prenumbered purchase orders and receiving reports.

Answer (D) is correct.
REQUIRED: The control not usually performed in the vouchers payable department.
DISCUSSION: Employees in the vouchers payable department should have no responsibilities related to purchasing or receiving goods. The purchasing department accounts for unused prenumbered purchase orders. The receiving department accounts for unused prenumbered receiving reports.
Answer (A) is incorrect. Matching the vendor's invoice with the related receiving report, purchase requisition, and purchase order is a function of the vouchers payable department. **Answer (B) is incorrect.** Signing of vouchers by an authorized employee to signify that information has been verified is a function of the vouchers payable department. **Answer (C) is incorrect.** Indicating the affected accounts on the voucher is a function of the vouchers payable department.

23. During the audit of a construction contract, it was discovered that the contractor was being paid for each ton of dirt removed. The contract called for payment based on cubic yards removed. Which internal control might have prevented this error?

A. Comparison of invoices with purchase orders or contracts.

B. Comparison of invoices with receiving reports.

C. Comparison of actual costs with budgeted costs.

D. Extension checks of invoice amounts.

Answer (A) is correct.
REQUIRED: The internal control that might have prevented use of an incorrect measure of work done.
DISCUSSION: The contractor's invoice would have stated a unit of measure different from that in the contract. Thus, a comparison of the invoice with the original contract would have disclosed the error.
Answer (B) is incorrect. The dirt removed would not have been received by the company; hence, no receiving reports would have existed. **Answer (C) is incorrect.** This comparison would not have directly detected the specific reason for a variance. However, the cost comparison would have detected the variance and prompted an investigation of its cause. **Answer (D) is incorrect.** The problem was not a mathematical error but an erroneous basis for payment.

Access the **Gleim CIA Premium Review System** featuring our SmartAdapt technology from your Gleim Personal Classroom to continue your studies. You will experience a personalized study environment with exam-emulating multiple-choice questions.

118 *Notes*

STUDY UNIT FOUR
PROJECT MANAGEMENT AND CONTRACTS

(21 pages of outline)

4.1	Project Management -- Concepts	119
4.2	Project Management -- Techniques	128
4.3	Change Management	133
4.4	Contracts	134
4.5	Classification of Contracts	138

This study unit is the fourth of five covering **Domain I: Business Acumen** from The IIA's CIA Exam Syllabus. (Data Analytics, the final topic area of this domain, is covered in Study Unit 7.) This domain makes up 35% of Part 3 of the CIA exam and is tested at the **basic** and **proficient** cognitive levels. Refer to the complete syllabus located in Appendix A to view the relevant sections covered in Study Unit 4.

4.1 PROJECT MANAGEMENT -- CONCEPTS

1. This section is based on the **American National Standards Institute (ANSI)** standard for project management. The standard describes but does **not** require the processes generally recognized to be good practice for most projects most of the time.

   NOTE: The concepts in this subunit do not suffice for compliance with the ANSI standard.

   a. A **process** is a sequential set of activities intended to produce a result so that at least one input is acted on to generate at least one output.

2. A **project** is temporary because it has a specific beginning and end, but it may have a long duration. A project often involves a cross-functional team and working outside customary organizational lines.

   a. It is also intended to have a unique result (e.g., a tangible or intangible product or service).
   b. Projects may be as diverse as building a ship, designing a software application, or producing a movie.
   c. **Project management** applies knowledge, skills, and techniques to activities that meet its requirements. It involves the following:
      1) Identifying requirements
      2) Attending to the communication and other needs and expectations of **stakeholders**
         a) Stakeholders are individuals, groups, and organizations that are affected by or affect the project.
      3) Resource management
      4) Coping with such constraints as project scope and scheduling, cost, quality, and risk
   d. The risk of an unsuccessful project can be analyzed in terms of four components:
      1) Ensuring that resources are adequate
      2) Maintaining scope by avoiding the temptation to continue adding functions to a new system or process
      3) Controlling cost
      4) Providing deliverables

3. A project may be part of a **program**, that is, a set of related projects and program activities managed together to obtain the benefits of synergy.

    a. A **portfolio** is a set of projects, programs, and operations, coordinated to achieve strategic goals.

4. **Governance** of a project may relate to the following:

    a. Oversight of the work
    b. Adherence to standards (legal and otherwise) and policies, such as those set at the organizational governance level (e.g., a board)
    c. Defining roles, responsibility, and authority
    d. Decisions about risk (e.g., escalation to a higher level), approval of project changes (e.g., in plans), and resources
    e. Monitoring performance, including review at the end of a project stage or phase
    f. A framework that addresses the foregoing matters, including those beyond the project manager's authority

5. A project should realize an opportunity consistent with an entity's strategic goals.

    a. A **business case** for the project is a feasibility study prepared prior to the project to document its objectives, investments, and success criteria.

        1) The sponsor ordinarily is accountable for the business case document.

            a) A **sponsor** of a project, program, or portfolio provides resources and support and is responsible for enabling success.

    b. Examples of strategic considerations are market demand, social needs, legal requirements, technology improvements, and forecasted problems.

    c. A **benefits management plan** is prepared prior to the project. It states how and when benefits will be delivered and the measurement methods. The following are possible elements of the plan:

        1) Targeted benefits (tangible or intangible business value)
        2) Alignment of benefits with the entity's strategy
        3) Phase benefits over the plan's timeframe (short- or long-term or ongoing)

            a) A **phase** is a set of related activities that end with completion of a deliverable(s).

                i) A **deliverable** is a unique and verifiable result (e.g., a product or the ability to perform a service) required to be achieved at the end of a process, phase, or project.

            b) For example, a project might have such phases as feasibility study, design, prototyping, and testing.
            c) Phases may be repetitive, in sequence, or overlapping.

        4) Benefits owner (person or group that reports realized benefits)
        5) Benefits metrics (measures, direct or indirect, of benefits realized)
        6) Risks

6. The **project life cycle** is the set of phases of a project.
   a. At the **control point** (also called a phase gate, phase review, or control gate), the project's **charter** (formal authorization by the initiator or sponsor) and **business documents** (e.g., business case and benefits management plan prepared before project initiation) are reviewed to compare performance with the project management plan.
      1) The result is the project's change, cancellation, or continuation.
   b. Regardless of the nature of a project, it has the following **generic phases**:
      1) Start
      2) Organization and preparation
      3) Doing the work
      4) Closure
   c. Risk and stakeholders' ability to influence the final result without a material effect on cost and scheduling are highest at the start.
      1) Risk declines as decisions are made and deliverables are accepted. But costs of changes significantly increase.
7. **Stakeholders** may be internal or external.
   a. Examples of **internal** stakeholders are the sponsor, resource manager, program manager, and team members.
   b. Examples of **external** stakeholders are suppliers, customers, end users, shareholders, and regulators.
   c. Stakeholders may be individuals or entities in a spectrum from survey participants to full sponsors providing financial and political support.
      1) Project success depends on engaging stakeholders and effectively managing their expectations.
8. A **project manager** leads the team responsible for achieving project objectives and stakeholder satisfaction.
   a. Reporting responsibilities depend on the organization's unique structure and project governance. For example, a manager may not have line authority over some team members.
   b. The manager should have the necessary specific skills and general management expertise. Among other things, the manager also should have certain other qualities:
      1) Knowledge of project management and the business environment
      2) Skills required to lead the team, coordinate work, and collaborate with stakeholders
      3) Ability to manage the project scope, schedules, budgets, resources, risks, plans, and reports
      4) Interpersonal skills (motivating, managing conflict, communicating, etc.), leadership, and strong ethics

9. The following 10 **project management knowledge areas** are sets of processes required for most projects most of the time:
   a. **Integration** processes define, combine, and coordinate the processes and activities within the process groups described in item 10. beginning below.
   b. **Scope** processes limit the work only to that needed to complete the project successfully.
   c. **Scheduling** processes involve timely completion.
   d. **Cost** processes (e.g., estimating, budgeting, funding, and controlling) should keep the project within the budget.
   e. **Quality** processes reflect the entity's policy for project and product quality. They apply to planning, management, and controlling project and product quality to meet stakeholders' expectations.
   f. **Resource** processes identify, obtain, and manage what is needed for successful completion.
   g. **Communications** processes should result in timely and appropriate use (planning and collection to monitoring and disposition) of relevant information.
   h. **Risk** management processes range from planning and identifying to response and monitoring.
   i. **Procurement** processes relate to products, services, or results to be obtained other than from the project team.
   j. **Stakeholder** processes (1) identify individuals and entities that could affect or be affected and (2) analyze their expectations and effects on the project. The purpose is to determine the means of engaging stakeholders in decisions and execution of the work.
10. The **project management process groups** are sets of processes used to achieve objectives. They are distinct from (a) applications (e.g., IT or accounting) or (b) the nature of the industry (e.g., banking, manufacturing, or social media).
    a. The following are the five process groups and examples of processes:
       1) **Initiating** processes define a new project or phase by securing authorization to begin. Stakeholder expectations should be consistent with the project's objectives and scope. The initial scope and financial investment are defined, and stakeholders who will influence outcomes are identified.
          a) A project **charter** is developed to authorize the use of resources for project activities.
          b) **Stakeholders** are identified, and their interests, influence, and involvement are documented (e.g., in a stakeholder register).
       2) **Planning** processes define the project scope, objectives, and actions to achieve those objectives. Also, the project management plan and project documents are developed. As more information is obtained, planning and initiating processes may need to be repeated to revise the project management plan. This iterative approach is known as **progressive elaboration** and includes 24 processes as follows:
          a) Developing the **project management plan** defines and consolidates its components to specify the basis and methods of work.
          b) **Planning scope** management is documenting a plan for the definition, validation, and control of the project and its scope.
          c) **Collecting requirements** documents and manages stakeholder needs and requirements to achieve objectives as a basis for defining scope.
          d) **Defining scope** describes the project in detail, including acceptance criteria.

e) **Creating a work breakdown structure (WBS)** reduces the deliverables and work to manageable parts by developing a framework for what is to be done.
f) **Planning schedule management** guides how the schedule will be managed, executed, and controlled.
g) **Definition of activities** identifies the actions needed to generate deliverables as a basis for controlling work.
h) **Sequencing of activities** identifies relationships and permits work to be performed in a logical, efficient order.
i) **Estimating activity durations** projects the work times required given specified resources.
j) **Developing a schedule** given activity sequences, durations, etc., establishes dates for completing activities.
k) **Planning cost management** determines methods for estimating and controlling costs.
l) **Estimating costs** results in a projection of the financial resources necessary to complete the work.
m) **Determining the budget** combines the costs of activities or work packages to create a baseline for comparison with actual results.
n) **Planning quality management**
   i) Identifies requirements or standards,
   ii) Documents methods of compliance, and
   iii) Directs the management of quality.
o) **Planning resource management** addresses how physical and team resources are to be estimated, obtained, and used to determine the required management effort.
p) **Estimating activity resources** determines the kinds, amounts, and nature of materials, equipment, and supplies required to complete the work.
q) **Planning communication management** involves determining an approach given available assets and the information needs of the project, stakeholders, and groups.
r) **Planning risk management** determines the necessary activities commensurate with the project's risks and importance to stakeholders.
s) **Identifying risks**
   i) Describes the aspects of individual and overall project risks and
   ii) Collects information for effective responses.
t) **Qualitative risk analysis** establishes risk priorities based on probabilities and potential effects.
u) **Quantitative risk analysis** mathematically aggregates the effects of uncertainties on project objectives as a basis for
   i) Estimating total risk exposure and
   ii) Responding to risks.
v) **Planning risk responses** identifies approaches, strategies, relevant actions, necessary resources, and amendments to the project management plan and project documents to cope with overall risks and individual risks.
w) **Planning procurement management** applies to decisions about what, how, when, and from whom (internal or external to the project) to obtain goods and services.
x) **Planning stakeholder engagement** results in an executable plan for interacting with various parties based on their effects on the project, expectations, etc.

3) **Executing** processes complete planned work in accordance with project requirements. They coordinate resources, integrate and perform activities, and manage stakeholder engagement. Thus, they consume much of the project's budget, resources, and time. They also may result in approved **change requests** that amend the plan, documents, and baselines.

   a) **Directing and managing project work** includes performing planned work and making approved changes.
   b) **Managing project knowledge** involves reaching objectives and improving the entity's learning by using current, and generating new, knowledge.
   c) **Managing quality** determines the quality activities to be performed to attain quality objectives and eliminate bad quality.
   d) **Acquiring resources** (employees, equipment, etc.) entails their selection and allocation to activities.
   e) **Developing the team** involves raising levels of competence and employees' interaction and bettering their environment. The objectives include lower turnover and higher motivation.
   f) **Managing the team** requires evaluating performance, giving feedback, managing conflict, and settling disputes.
   g) **Managing communications** should provide efficient and effective information flow (collection to disposition) to and from the team and stakeholders.
   h) **Implementing risk responses** is the execution of planned actions to address specific risks and overall exposure and to optimize project outcomes.
   i) **Conducting procurements** is the process of choosing qualified sellers and entering into binding contracts.
   j) **Managing stakeholder engagement** entails communication to obtain support through meeting expectations, resolving problems, and promoting involvement.

4) **Monitoring and controlling** processes track, review, and regulate progress and performance. They also (a) determine whether **changes** are needed in the **project management plan** and (b) initiate those changes. Monitoring collects data, generates performance measures, and reports the resulting information. Controlling analyzes the variances when performance differs from expectations. It also evaluates trends and options for improvement and recommends needed corrections.

   a) **Monitoring and controlling project work** is ongoing. It results in communicating the project's current state to stakeholders. This understanding facilitates recognition of corrective steps and anticipation of the future status of the project based on forecasts.

   b) **Integrated change** control processes review, approve, and manage changes (e.g., in deliverables, process assets, documents, and the plan). They also communicate the decisions. The benefit is documentation of integrated changes after consideration of project risk.

   c) **Validating scope** is formal acceptance of each deliverable.

   d) **Controlling scope** monitors project status and product scope and manages changes in the scope baseline.

   e) **Controlling the schedule** monitors status to update the schedule and manage changes in its baseline.

   f) **Controlling costs** involves reviewing the project's status, updating costs, and managing change in the cost baseline.

   g) **Controlling quality** records results of quality activities to evaluate performance and determine that outputs (deliverables and work) are appropriate for acceptance by stakeholders.

   h) **Controlling resources** verifies that physical resources are available when and where needed (and released if not needed) in accordance with the plan. It also compares planned and actual usage and takes corrective action.

   i) **Monitoring communications** ensures information flow to meet project and stakeholder needs.

   j) **Monitoring risks** addresses (1) implementation of risk responses, (2) tracking of risks, (3) analysis of newly identified risks, and (4) assessment of risk process effectiveness.

   k) **Controlling procurement** (1) manages relationships with sellers, (2) monitors performance, (3) makes needed changes, and (4) closes contracts.

   l) **Monitoring stakeholder engagement** applies to relationships and tailoring (modifying) engagement strategies and plans as necessary.

5) **Closing** processes formally terminate a project, phase, or contract. Thus, processes should be completed within every process group to close the project, etc.

   a) Closing a **project or phase** ends all activities. Information is archived, work is completed, and resources are released.

b. Specific processes in the groups may be repeated (and may interact) prior to closing depending on the requirements of a project. Most processes may be classified as follows:

1) Some processes occur once or at a defined time. An example is closing a project.
2) Some processes, e.g., obtaining resources, are repeated as required.
3) Some processes, e.g., monitoring and controlling, are continuous until the end of the project.

c. Ordinarily, outputs of processes (e.g., the project management plan and project documents resulting from the planning processes, such as a risk register of outputs of risk management processes) are inputs to other processes (e.g., executing processes).

11. Projects are influenced by certain internal and external factors.

a. **Organizational process assets (OPAs)** are specific (internal) to an entity. They are its plans, processes, policies, procedures, and knowledge bases that affect project management.

1) Examples are change controls, financial controls, work instructions, and knowledge repositories (such as historical information and lessons learned repositories).

b. **Enterprise environmental factors (EEFs)** are external to the project but influence, limit, or direct the project. They may be internal or external to the entity.

1) An example category of **internal** EEFs may consist of the entity's culture, structure, and governance (e.g., mission, cultural norms, hierarchy, ethics, and leadership style).
2) An example category of **external** EEFs may consist of financial factors (e.g., exchange and interest rates, inflation, tariffs, and location).

12. Management of a specific, unique project requires tailoring project artifacts.
    a. **Artifacts** in the project management context are processes, inputs, outputs, OPAs, EEFs, etc. **Tailoring** is selection of the artifacts relevant to the unique project.
    b. The **project management plan** is the most commonly used artifact.
        1) Its many possible components include the following:
            a) A description of the project's life cycle
            b) Baselines (e.g., scope, schedule, performance measurement, and cost)
                i) A **baseline** is an approved work product changeable only by formal procedures. It is a basis for comparison with an actual result.
            c) Subsidiary management plans
                i) A subsidiary plan relates to a particular element of the project or to 1 of the 10 project management knowledge areas described on page 122.
        2) Tailoring the project management plan involves determining the components required for a specific project.
            a) The plan is an input, and **updates** of the plan are outputs of many processes described in the ANSI standard.
                i) However, the input and output examples in the standard are **not** required. Moreover, other inputs and updates may be appropriate in the circumstances.
    c. **Project documents** are artifacts **not** included in the plan but that may be used to manage the project.
        1) The choice of such documents is a function of the requirements of the project and the project manager's judgment.
            a) Updated project documents are outputs of processes.
            b) Examples of project documents are those that may relate to scope, requirements, resources, activities, costs, milestones (significant points or events), communications, scheduling, quality, risks, and lessons learned.
    d. The source of a **business document** is external to the project. But it may be an input to the project.
        1) Examples include the business case and benefits management plan.

STOP & REVIEW

You have completed the outline for this subunit.
Study multiple-choice questions 1 through 7 beginning on page 140.

4.2 PROJECT MANAGEMENT -- TECHNIQUES

1. Project management is the process of managing the tradeoff between the two major inputs (time and cost) and the major output (quality). The project management triangle graphically depicts this relationship.

Project Management Triangle

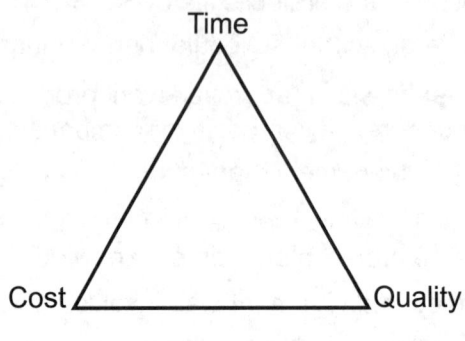

Figure 4-1

   a. The implication is that a high-quality deliverable can be achieved only by devoting a large number of employee hours to a project or by spending a lot of money.

EXAMPLE 4-1	Project Management -- Tradeoffs

In the days before widespread computer use, old-fashioned job-order print shops used to display signs saying, "You Want It Fast -- Cheap -- Correct. Pick Two."

Designers of submarines often speak of their classic tradeoff of depth, speed, and stealth. A vessel with sufficient shielding to be silent and to survive at great depths is too heavy to go very fast.

   b. Project management software is available and is used by most firms today.
   c. Common techniques for project management include Gantt charts, PERT, and CPM. They are suitable for any project having a target completion date and single start.
   d. Project management includes managing teams assigned to special projects.
      1) A dummy activity allows concurrent activities on a PERT/CPM network to end on separate nodes.
      2) The latest finish is the latest that an activity can finish without causing delay in the completion of the project.
      3) Optimistic time is the time for completing a project if all goes well.

2. **Gantt Charts**
   a. Gantt charts are simple to construct and use. To develop a Gantt chart,
      1) Divide the project into logical subprojects called activities or tasks,
      2) Estimate the start and completion times for each activity, and
      3) Prepare a bar chart showing each activity as a horizontal bar along a time scale.

b. Below is an example of a Gantt chart:

Gantt Chart

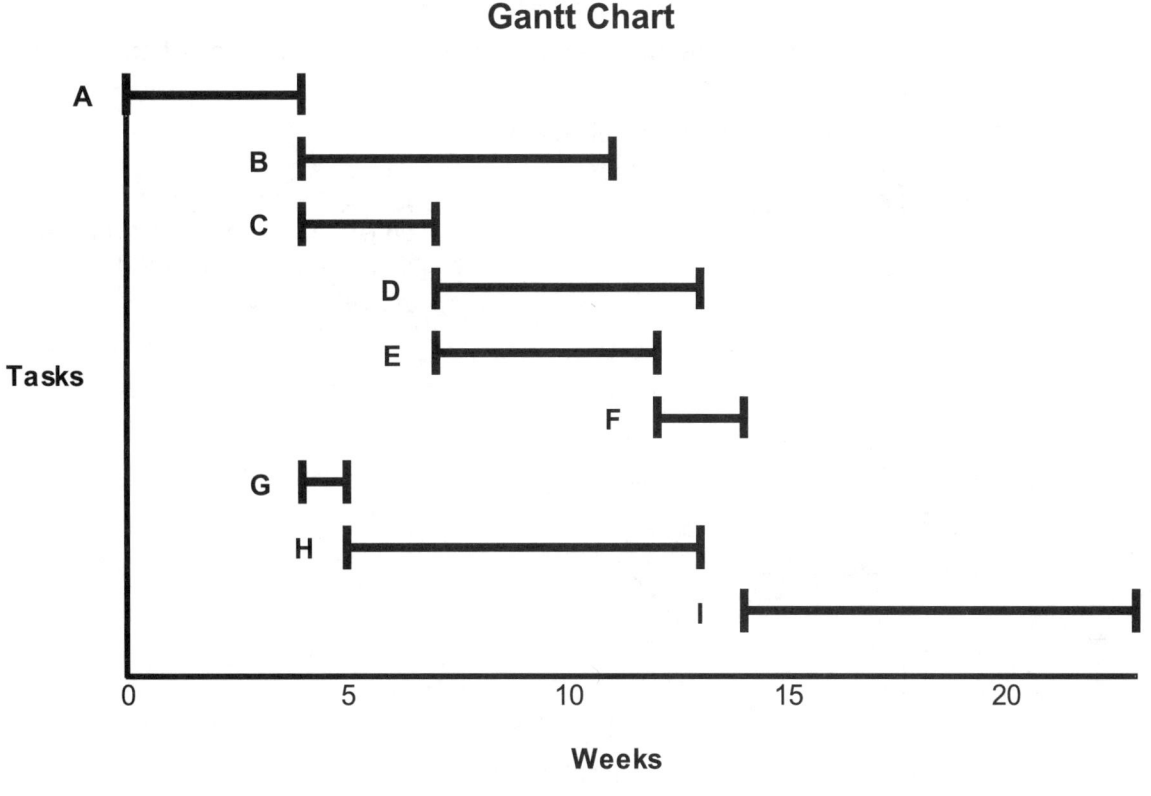

Figure 4-2

c. Gantt charts show the projected start and finish times for each task as well as for the project as a whole.

1) They also show, in a limited way, the interdependencies among tasks, i.e., which tasks can be performed simultaneously and which must be completed before other tasks can begin.

2) In Figure 4-2 above, tasks B, C, and G can begin as soon as task A is complete, but task I cannot begin until all others are complete.

d. The major advantage of the Gantt chart is its simplicity—it requires no special tools or mathematics. It forces the planner to think ahead and define logical activities.

e. The major disadvantage of the Gantt chart is that it is unsuitable for a very large-scale project. The interdependencies among tasks become unmanageable.

3. **Program Evaluation and Review Technique (PERT)**

a. PERT was developed to control large-scale, complex projects.

1) PERT diagrams are free-form networks showing each activity as a line between events.

a) A sequence of lines shows interrelationships among activities.

2) PERT diagrams are more complex than Gantt charts, but they have the advantages of incorporating probabilistic time estimates and identifying the critical path.

b. A PERT network consists of two components:

1) Events are moments in time representing the start or finish of an activity.

   a) They consume no resources and are depicted on a network diagram with circles (called nodes).

2) Activities are tasks to be accomplished.

   a) They consume resources (including time) and have a duration over time. They are depicted as lines connecting nodes.

PERT Network

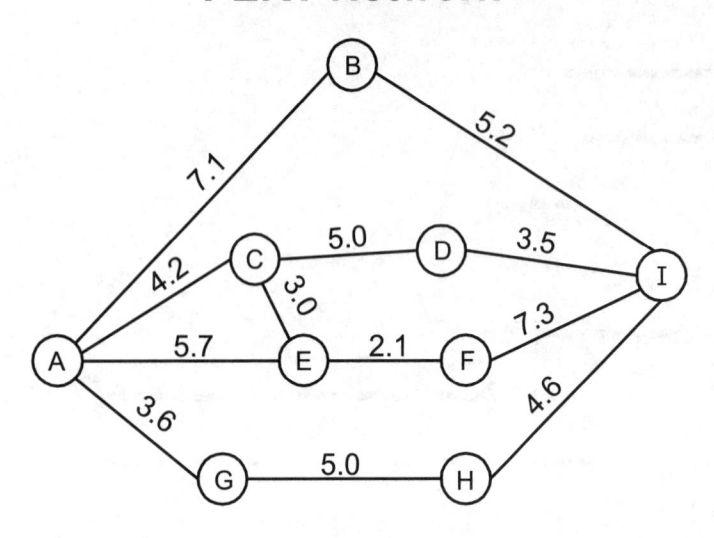

Figure 4-3

3) The network depicted above has five paths. To calculate their durations, the project manager makes a forward pass through the network.

Path	Time (days)	
A-B-I	7.1 + 5.2	= 12.3
A-C-D-I	4.2 + 5.0 + 3.5	= 12.7
A-C-E-F-I	4.2 + 3.0 + 2.1 + 7.3	= 16.6
A-E-F-I	5.7 + 2.1 + 7.3	= 15.1
A-G-H-I	3.6 + 5.0 + 4.6	= 13.2

c. Some processes contain activities that are performed simultaneously because they have the same start node and end node.

1) Concurrent activities cannot be depicted graphically on a PERT network. Every path between nodes must be unique. Thus, two paths cannot both be designated B-I in Figure 4-3 above.

4. **Calculating the Length of the Critical Paths**

   a. The critical path is the **longest** path in time through the network. It is critical because, if any activity on the critical path takes longer than expected, the entire project will be delayed.

   1) Every network has at least one critical path. In Figure 4-3 above, path A-C-E-F-I is the critical path because it has the longest time (16.6 days).

   2) The critical path is the **shortest** amount of time in which a project can be completed if all paths are begun simultaneously.

   b. Any activity that does not lie on the critical path has **slack time**, i.e., unused resources that can be diverted to the critical path.

5. **Expected Duration**

    a. A major advantage of PERT is that activity times can be expressed probabilistically.

        1) Three estimates are made: optimistic, most likely, and pessimistic. The usual weighting of the three estimates is 1:4:1. (The most likely time for the duration of a task is the one indicated on the PERT diagram.)

        2) In Figure 4-3 on the previous page, the most likely duration of task B-I is 5.2 days. The organization estimates the optimistic time at 5.0 and the pessimistic time at 5.8. The expected duration of task B-I is calculated as follows:

	Estimates		Weights		
Optimistic	5.0	×	1	=	5.0
Most likely	5.2	×	4	=	20.8
Pessimistic	5.8	×	1	=	5.8
Totals			6		31.6

Expected duration: 31.6 ÷ 6 = 5.27 days

6. **Critical Path Method (CPM)**

    a. CPM was developed independently of PERT and is widely used in the construction industry. Like PERT, CPM is a network technique, but it has two distinct differences:

        1) PERT uses probabilistic time estimates, but CPM is a deterministic method.

        2) PERT considers only the time required to complete a project. CPM incorporates cost amounts.

    b. Two estimates are made for each time and cost combination: a normal estimate and a crash estimate. A crash estimate consists of the time and cost required to complete an activity if all available resources are applied to it.

        1) Crashing a project applies all available resources to activities on the critical path (crashing a noncritical-path activity is not cost-effective).

EXAMPLE 4-2   CPM

Figure 4-3 on the previous page can be converted to a CPM network with the addition of the following time and cost data for the critical path:

Critical Path Activity	Normal Time & Cost		Crash Time & Cost	
A-C	4.2	US $20,000	4.0	US $35,000
C-E	3.0	10,000	2.0	20,000
E-F	2.1	18,000	2.0	21,000
F-I	7.3	60,000	6.5	90,000

These amounts can be used to determine the costs and gains of crashing a given activity:

Critical Path Activity	Crash Cost Minus Normal Cost		Incremental Cost of Crashing	Normal Time Minus Crash Time		Time Gained
A-C	US $35,000 − US $20,000	=	US $15,000	4.2 − 4.0	=	0.2
C-E	20,000 − 10,000	=	10,000	3.0 − 2.0	=	1.0
E-F	21,000 − 18,000	=	3,000	2.1 − 2.0	=	0.1
F-I	90,000 − 60,000	=	30,000	7.3 − 6.5	=	0.8

2) The most cost-effective activity to crash is determined with the following formula:

$$\text{Time-cost tradeoff} = \frac{\text{Crash cost} - \text{Normal cost}}{\text{Normal time} - \text{Crash time}}$$

> **EXAMPLE 4-3   Time-Cost Tradeoff -- Crashing**
>
> Using the data from Example 4-2, the ratio of crash cost to time gained reveals the best activity for crashing:
>
> | Critical Path Activity | Incremental Cost of Crashing | | Time Gained | | Cost per Day to Crash |
> |---|---|---|---|---|---|
> | A-C | US $15,000 | ÷ | 0.2 | = | US $75,000 |
> | C-E | 10,000 | ÷ | 1.0 | = | 10,000 |
> | E-F | 3,000 | ÷ | 0.1 | = | 30,000 |
> | F-I | 30,000 | ÷ | 0.8 | = | 37,500 |
>
> The most cost-effective activity to crash is C-E. Assuming this activity will be crashed, the network is recalculated to determine whether a new critical path will result. If so, the time-cost tradeoff of the activities on the new critical path are calculated and the process is repeated.

7. **Network Models**

   a. Network models are used to solve managerial problems pertaining to project scheduling, information systems design, and transportation systems design.

      1) Networks consisting of nodes and arcs may be created to represent in graphic form problems related to transportation, assignment, and transshipment.

   b. A shortest-route algorithm minimizes total travel time from one site to each of the other sites in a transportation system.

   c. The maximal flow algorithm maximizes throughput in networks with distinct entry (source node) and exit (sink node) points.

      1) Examples of applications are highway transportation systems and oil pipelines. Flows are limited by capacities.

   d. The minimal spanning tree algorithm identifies the set of connecting branches having the shortest combined length.

      1) A spanning tree is a group of branches (arcs) that connects each node in the network to every other node.

      2) An example problem is the determination of the shortest telecommunications linkage among users at remote sites and a central computer.

STOP & REVIEW

You have completed the outline for this subunit.
Study multiple-choice questions 8 through 11 beginning on page 143.

4.3 CHANGE MANAGEMENT

1. **Overview**
    a. Change management is important to all organizations. An appropriate balance between change and stability is necessary for an organization to thrive.
        1) Organizational change is conducted through change agents, who may include managers, employees, and consultants hired for the purpose.

2. **Types of Change**
    a. **Cultural change** is a change in attitudes and mindset, for example, when a total quality management approach is adopted.
    b. A **product change** is a change in a product's physical attributes and usefulness to customers.
    c. A **structural change** is a change in an organization's systems or structures.

3. **Resistance**
    a. Organizational and procedural changes often are resisted by the individuals and groups affected. This response may be caused by simple surprise, inertia, or fear of failure. But it also may arise from the following:
        1) Misunderstandings or lack of needed skills
        2) Lack of trust of, or conflicts with, management
        3) Emotional reactions when change is forced
        4) Bad timing
        5) Insensitivity to employees' needs
        6) Perceived threats to employees' status or job security
        7) Dissolution of tightly knit work groups
        8) Interference with achievement of other objectives
    b. Methods of coping with employee resistance include the following:
        1) Prevention through education and communication
        2) Participation in designing and implementing a change
        3) Facilitation and support through training and counseling
        4) Negotiation by providing a benefit in exchange for cooperation
        5) Manipulation of information or events
        6) Co-optation through allowing some participation but without meaningful input
        7) Coercion

4. **Organizational Development (OD)**

    a. OD provides a framework for managing change using the findings of the behavioral sciences.

    1) True OD has three distinctive characteristics:

        a) The change must be planned and deliberate.
        b) The change must actually improve the organization. Changes forced by regulatory requirements or changes that merely attempt to follow management trends and fads are not included.
        c) The change must be implemented using the findings of the behavioral sciences, such as organizational behavior and group psychology.

    2) The following are the objectives of OD:

        a) Deepen the sense of organizational purpose and align individuals with it
        b) Promote interpersonal trust, communication, cooperation, and support
        c) Encourage a problem-solving approach
        d) Develop a satisfying work experience
        e) Supplement formal authority with authority based on expertise
        f) Increase personal responsibility
        g) Encourage willingness to change

> **STOP & REVIEW**
> You have completed the outline for this subunit.
> Study multiple-choice questions 12 through 14 beginning on page 144.

4.4 CONTRACTS

1. **Contract Law**

    a. No part of commercial law is more important than contract law. Billions of contract-based agreements to transfer property and services are negotiated daily by individuals, businesses, and governments.

    b. Promise keeping is essential for planning in a modern complex society. Without a legal system committed to enforcement of private contracts, everyday transactions in a free-enterprise economy would be impossible.

    1) Contract law allows parties to enter into private agreements with assurance that they are enforceable against a party that fails to perform.

    c. A contract is a promise or an agreement that the law recognizes as establishing a duty of performance. It is enforceable by applying a remedy for its breach.

    d. The following are the **elements** of a contract:

    1) Mutual assent (offer and acceptance)
    2) Consideration (a bargain for exchange)
    3) Capacity of the parties
    4) Legality of the agreement

2. **Agreement**

    a. The most basic element of a contract is a voluntary agreement by the contracting parties. Agreement requires the **mutual assent** of the parties reached through an offer by the offeror and acceptance by the offeree.

    b. An **offer** is a statement or other communication that, if not terminated, gives upon the offeree the power of acceptance. An offer need not be in any particular form to be valid. It must

    1) Be communicated to an **offeree**,
    2) Manifest an objective intent to enter into a contract, and
    3) Be sufficiently definite and certain.

    c. **Communication** of an offer may be done in various ways and may occur over time. But at some moment in the formation of a contract, each party expresses an **intent** to enter into a legally binding and enforceable agreement.

    1) Whether an offer has been made is determined by an objective standard that uses the following test: Would a reasonable person assume that (s)he has been given the power of acceptance, i.e., that an offer has been made?

        a) An offer must be made with serious intent, not in anger, great excitement, or jest.

    2) The language of an offer differs from that merely soliciting or inviting offers. Communications between parties may simply be preliminary negotiations about a possible contract. A party may start negotiations by suggesting the general nature of a possible contract.

    d. An offer also must be **definite and certain**. If an offer is indefinite or vague or lacking an essential provision, no agreement results from an attempt to accept it. A court cannot determine the responsibilities of the parties.

    1) However, minor details may be left for future determination if they do not make an agreement too vague to be an offer.

    e. An offer does not remain effective forever. The offer terminates under any of the following circumstances:

    1) Revocation by the offeror
    2) Rejection or counteroffer by the offeree
    3) Death or incompetency of either the offeror or offeree
    4) Destruction of the specific subject matter to which the offer relates
    5) Subsequent illegality of the offer
    6) End of a specified or reasonable time

    f. **Acceptance** of an offer is essential to the formation of a contract. An agreement consists of an offer and an acceptance.

    1) To be effective, an acceptance must relate to the terms of the offer. The acceptance must be positive, unequivocal, and unconditional. It may not change, subtract from, add to, or qualify in any way the terms of the offer.

3. **Consideration**

    a. Consideration is given to make a promise enforceable. It is the primary basis for the enforcement of agreements in contract law. If a promise is not supported by consideration, it is usually not enforceable.

    b. One requirement of consideration is **mutuality of obligation**. Both parties must give consideration. Consequently, something of legal value must be given in a bargained-for exchange when the parties intend an exchange.

    c. The second required element of consideration is legal sufficiency (something of legal value). Consideration is legally sufficient to make a promise enforceable if the promisor receives a **legal benefit** or the promisee incurs a **legal detriment**.

    1) To incur a legal detriment, the promisee must do (or promise to do) something that (s)he is not legally obligated to do. A legal detriment also consists of not doing (or promising not to do) something (s)he is legally entitled to do.

        a) A cause-and-effect relationship must exist between the promise made by one party and the detriment incurred by the other.

4. **Capacity**

    a. Parties to a contract must have legal capacity. Capacity is the mental ability to make a rational decision. It includes the ability to perceive and appreciate all relevant facts.

    1) Three classes of parties are legally limited in their capacity to contract: (a) minors (also known as infants), (b) mentally incompetent persons, and (c) intoxicated parties.

        a) For public policy reasons, parties in these three groups are protected from the enforcement of most contracts against them.

5. **Legality**

    a. Legality is an essential requirement for an agreement to be valid and enforceable.

    1) An agreement is illegal and unenforceable if formation or performance of the agreement

        a) Violates a criminal law,
        b) Is a civil wrong upon which a suit may be filed, or
        c) Is determined by a court to be contrary to public policy.

    b. An agreement that is contrary to **public policy** has a negative effect on society that outweighs the interests of the parties. This principle reflects a balancing by the courts of freedom of contract and the public interest. Examples of agreements that may violate public policy are

    1) Agreements to unduly restrain competition;
    2) Clauses that excuse one of the parties from any liability;
    3) Contracts calling for immoral or illegal acts; and
    4) Agreements found to be unfair, oppressive, or unconscionable.

6. **Written Contracts**

    a. An oral contract is as enforceable as a written contract. But the **statute of frauds** may require that some contracts be in writing to be enforceable. For example, the following are required to be in writing to be enforceable:

        1) Contracts for the sale of an interest in land
        2) Contracts that by their terms cannot possibly be performed within 1 year (e.g., some employment contracts)
        3) Contracts to answer for the debt or duty of another (e.g., a guarantee or a suretyship)
        4) Contracts for the sale of goods for US $500 or more

7. **Cost Contracts**

    a. A **firm-fixed-price** contract provides for a price that cannot be changed, even if costs increase unexpectedly. A firm-fixed-price contract should be used when there is

        1) Adequate price competition,
        2) Reasonable price comparisons,
        3) Reasonable estimates of costs, and
        4) Performance uncertainties can be identified.

    b. A **cost-plus-fixed fee** contract is a cost-reimbursement contract that provides for a fixed fee in addition to incurred costs. A cost-plus-fixed fee contract should be used when a firm-fixed-price contract is unsuitable, such as when costs cannot be reasonably estimated because of performance uncertainties.

    c. A **cost-plus-award-fee** contract is a cost-reimbursement contract that provides for an award amount in addition to incurred costs. The award amount is based on a judgmental evaluation of performance. A cost-plus-award-fee contract should be used when

        1) It is impractical to set predetermined incentive targets,
        2) The performing party will be motivated toward exceptional performance, and
        3) The expected benefits will exceed the costs required to monitor and evaluate performance.

    d. A **time-and-materials** contract provides for acquiring supplies or services based on (1) direct labor hours at a specified rate and (2) actual cost for materials. A time-and-materials contract should be used only when it is not possible to accurately estimate the extent or duration of work or to reasonably estimate costs.

You have completed the outline for this subunit.
Study multiple-choice questions 15 through 18 beginning on page 145.

STOP & REVIEW

4.5 CLASSIFICATION OF CONTRACTS

1. **Express and Implied Contracts**
    a. The terms of an **express contract** are stated, either in writing or orally.
    b. The terms of an **implied contract** are wholly or partially inferred from conduct and circumstances but not from written or spoken words.
        1) A contract is **implied in fact** when the facts indicate a contract was formed.

> **EXAMPLE 4-4   Implied Contract**
>
> Kelly makes an appointment with a hairdresser. Kelly keeps the appointment and permits the hairdresser to cut her hair. Kelly has promised through her actions to pay for the haircut. A court infers from Kelly's conduct that an implied contract was formed and a duty to pay was understood and agreed to.

        2) A contract **implied in law** (the equitable remedy of restitution or quasi-contract) is not a true contract. It prevents unjust enrichment of one party when the facts do not indicate that both parties had contractual intent.

2. **Unilateral and Bilateral Contracts**
    a. In a **unilateral contract**, only one party makes a promise. The other party is an actor, not a promisor. If (s)he performs a defined action (an acceptance), the promisor is obligated to keep the promise.

> **EXAMPLE 4-5   Unilateral Contract**
>
> Amy tells Bill, "I'll pay you US $10 to polish my car." This offer is for a unilateral contract. Amy (the promisor) expects Bill (the actor) to accept by the act of polishing her car, not by making a return promise.

    b. In a **bilateral contract**, both parties make promises.

> **EXAMPLE 4-6   Bilateral Contract**
>
> Amanda tells Bob that she will provide him lodging in September if he agrees to pay her US $200. This is an offer for a bilateral contract. If Bob accepts and promises to pay the US $200, a bilateral contract is formed.

3. **Executory and Executed Contracts**
    a. An **executory contract** is a contract that is not yet fully performed. If any duty remains to be performed under the contract, the contract is considered executory.

> **EXAMPLE 4-7   Executory Contract**
>
> Al says to Brian, "I'll pay you US $10,000,000 to play football for me next season." Brian agrees, creating an executory bilateral contract. It is executory because neither party has yet performed.
>
> If Al pays Brian the US $10,000,000 and Brian refuses to play, the contract is partially executed.

    b. An **executed contract** has been fully performed by all parties.

> **EXAMPLE 4-8   Executed Contract**
>
> If Brian plays football for Al the entire season and Al pays Brian US $10,000,000, the contract is fully executed.

4. **Other Classifications**

   a. A **valid** contract has all the elements of a contract, and the law provides a remedy if breached. A valid contract is legally binding on both parties.

   b. An **unenforceable** contract is a valid contract because it has all the elements of a contract. But the law will not enforce the contract because it does not comply with another legal requirement.

EXAMPLE 4-9	Unenforceable Contract

   Jane enters into an oral contract to sell land to Emily. To be enforceable, a contract for the sale of land must be in writing. The real estate contract is not enforceable because it was not written.

   c. A party may choose to either enforce or nullify a **voidable** contract.

EXAMPLE 4-10	Voidable Contract

   Adam was induced to enter into a contract by Ben's intentional deception (i.e., fraud). Adam can choose either to enforce the contract or void the contract because it was fraudulently induced. Adam also can collect damages against Ben for any loss sustained due to fraud.

   d. A **void** contract is not binding and is considered **void ab initio**, which means it was void since its inception. A void contract cannot be ratified and enforced.

EXAMPLE 4-11	Void Contract

   A contract requiring the commission of a crime is void. It is not recognizable as a contract, and the law provides no remedy to enforce it.

STOP & REVIEW

You have completed the outline for this subunit.
Study multiple-choice questions 19 and 20 on page 147.

QUESTIONS

4.1 Project Management -- Concepts

1. A project is an undertaking with a specific beginning and end, but it may have a long duration. A project

A. May be part of a phase consisting of related projects.
B. May contain multiple programs and related activities.
C. Should be documented in a business case.
D. Has deliverables that include a benefits management plan.

Answer (C) is correct.
REQUIRED: The true statement about a project.
DISCUSSION: A project should realize an opportunity consistent with an entity's strategic goals. A business case therefore is prepared prior to the project to document its objectives, investments, and success criteria.
Answer (A) is incorrect. The project life cycle is the set of phases of a project. For example, a project might have such phases as feasibility study, design, prototyping, and testing. A phase is a set of related activities that end with completion of a deliverable(s). **Answer (B) is incorrect.** A project may be part of a program, that is, a set of related projects and program activities managed together to obtain the benefits of synergy. **Answer (D) is incorrect.** A benefits management plan is prepared prior to the project. It states how and when benefits will be delivered and the measurement methods. This plan is a business document external to the project, not a project document.

2. Stakeholders of a project most likely include

A. External stakeholders, such as team members.
B. Only those who provide resources and support.
C. Parties as diverse as full sponsors and survey participants.
D. Such internal individuals and entities as suppliers and shareholders.

Answer (C) is correct.
REQUIRED: The most likely stakeholders.
DISCUSSION: Stakeholders are individuals, groups, and organizations that are affected by or affect the project. Stakeholders may be individuals or entities in a spectrum from survey participants to full sponsors providing financial and political support. Project success depends on engaging stakeholders and effectively managing their expectations.
Answer (A) is incorrect. External stakeholders are suppliers, customers, end users, shareholders, and regulators. Team members are considered internal stakeholders. **Answer (B) is incorrect.** Stakeholders may be individuals or entities in a spectrum from survey participants to full sponsors providing financial and political support. **Answer (D) is incorrect.** Examples of external stakeholders are suppliers, customers, end users, shareholders, and regulators.

3. A project charter is most likely developed in which project management process group?

A. Initiating.
B. Planning.
C. Definition of activities.
D. Defining scope.

Answer (A) is correct.
REQUIRED: The process group in which a project charter is most likely developed.
DISCUSSION: Initiating processes define a new project or phase by securing authorization to begin. Stakeholder expectations should be consistent with the project's objectives and scope. The initial scope and financial investment are defined, and stakeholders who will influence outcomes are identified. For example, a project charter is developed to authorize the use of resources for project activities.
Answer (B) is incorrect. Planning processes define the project scope, objectives, and actions to achieve those objectives. Also, the project management plan and project documents are developed. But developing a charter is an initiating process. **Answer (C) is incorrect.** Definition of activities is a planning process, not a project management process group. Definition of activities identifies the actions needed to generate deliverables as a basis for controlling work. **Answer (D) is incorrect.** Defining scope is a planning process, not a project management process group. Defining scope describes the project in detail, including acceptance criteria.

4. Which of the following is a project management process group?

A. Applying applications.
B. Executing.
C. Estimating costs.
D. Identifying stakeholders.

Answer (B) is correct.
REQUIRED: The project management process group.
DISCUSSION: Executing is a project management process group. Executing processes complete planned work in accordance with project requirements. They coordinate resources, integrate and perform activities, and manage stakeholder engagement. Thus, they consume much of the project's budget, resources, and time. They also may result in approved change requests that amend the plan, documents, and baselines.
Answer (A) is incorrect. The project management process groups are sets of processes used to achieve objectives. They are distinct from (1) applications (e.g., IT or accounting) or (2) the nature of the industry (e.g., banking, manufacturing, or social media). **Answer (C) is incorrect.** Estimating costs is a planning process, not a project management process group. **Answer (D) is incorrect.** Identifying stakeholders is an initiating process, not a project management process group.

5. Which of the following is a project management knowledge area?

A. Monitoring and controlling processes.
B. Organizational process assets.
C. Project documents.
D. Integration processes.

Answer (D) is correct.
REQUIRED: The project management knowledge area.
DISCUSSION: Project management knowledge areas are sets of processes required for most projects most of the time. For example, integration processes define, combine, and coordinate the processes and activities within the project management process groups.
Answer (A) is incorrect. Monitoring and controlling processes is a project management process group.
Answer (B) is incorrect. Organizational process assets (OPAs) are specific (internal) to an entity. They are its plans, processes, policies, procedures, and knowledge bases that affect project management. They are project artifacts. **Answer (C) is incorrect.** Project documents are artifacts not included in the project management plan but that may be used to manage the project.

6. The project management plan

A. Is tailored to the specific project.
B. Includes project documents.
C. Includes business documents internal to the project.
D. Is an output of the project.

Answer (A) is correct.
REQUIRED: The true statement about the project management plan.
DISCUSSION: Artifacts in the project management context are processes, inputs, outputs, organizational process assets, enterprise environmental factors, etc. Tailoring is selection of the artifacts relevant to the unique project. The project management plan is the most commonly used artifact. Tailoring the project management plan involves determining the components required for a specific project. The plan is an input, and updates of the plan are outputs of many processes described in the ANSI standard.
Answer (B) is incorrect. Project documents are artifacts not included in the project management plan but that may be used to manage the project. **Answer (C) is incorrect.** The source of a business document is external to the project. But it may be an input to the project. Examples include the business case and benefits management plan. **Answer (D) is incorrect.** The project management plan is an input to the project.

7. The project life cycle is the set of phases of a project. During the life cycle,

A. Costs of changes decrease as the project nears completion.
B. Stakeholders' ability to influence results without affecting schedules materially is lowest at the start.
C. Risk increases as deliverables are accepted.
D. The project may be terminated or changed at the control point.

Answer (D) is correct.
REQUIRED: The true statement about the project life cycle.
DISCUSSION: At the control point (also called a phase gate, phase review, or control gate), the project's charter (formal authorization by the initiator or sponsor) and business documents (e.g., business case and benefits management plan prepared before project initiation) are reviewed to compare performance with the project management plan. The result is the project's change, cancellation, or continuation.
Answer (A) is incorrect. Risk declines as decisions are made and deliverables are accepted. But costs of changes in the project significantly increase. **Answer (B) is incorrect.** Risk and stakeholders' ability to influence the final result without a material effect on cost and scheduling are highest at the start. **Answer (C) is incorrect.** Risk decreases as decisions are made and deliverables are accepted.

4.2 Project Management -- Techniques

8. A Gantt chart

A. Shows the critical path for a project.
B. Is used for determining an optimal product mix.
C. Shows only the activities along the critical path of a network.
D. Does not necessarily show the critical path through a network.

Answer (D) is correct.
REQUIRED: The true statement about a Gantt chart.
DISCUSSION: The major advantage of a Gantt chart is its simplicity: It requires no special tools or mathematics. However, it depicts only the interrelationships between tasks in a limited way. Thus, trying to identify a project's critical path from a Gantt chart may not be feasible.
Answer (A) is incorrect. The critical path is not shown on a Gantt chart. **Answer (B) is incorrect.** Linear programming is used to determine an optimal product mix. **Answer (C) is incorrect.** A Gantt chart shows all activities, not just those along the critical path.

9. When making a cost-time tradeoff in CPM analysis, the first activity that should be crashed is the activity

A. With the largest amount of slack.
B. With the lowest unit crash cost.
C. On the critical path with the maximum possible time reduction.
D. On the critical path with the lowest unit crash cost.

Answer (D) is correct.
REQUIRED: The first activity that should be crashed when making a cost-time tradeoff.
DISCUSSION: When making a cost-time tradeoff, the first activity to be crashed (have its completion time accelerated) is one on the critical path. To select an activity on another path would not reduce the total time of completion. The initial activity chosen should be the one with the completion time that can be accelerated at the lowest possible cost per unit of time saved.
Answer (A) is incorrect. Eliminating an activity with slack will not reduce the total time of the project. **Answer (B) is incorrect.** The activity with the lowest unit crash cost may not be on the critical path. **Answer (C) is incorrect.** The time reduction should be related to its cost. The maximum time reduction may not be cost effective.

10. In a critical path analysis, if slack time in an activity exists, the activity

A. Is not essential to the overall project.
B. Is a backup activity to replace a main activity should it fail.
C. Could be delayed without delaying the overall project.
D. Involves essentially no time to complete.

Answer (C) is correct.
REQUIRED: The implication of the existence of slack time.
DISCUSSION: Slack is the free time associated with activities not on the critical path. Slack represents unused resources that can be diverted to the critical path.
Answer (A) is incorrect. An activity with slack may nevertheless be essential to the overall project. **Answer (B) is incorrect.** An activity with slack time is not a backup activity. **Answer (D) is incorrect.** Time is involved in a slack activity.

11. A shortest-route algorithm is used in network models to

A. Identify bottlenecks in a network and identify the longest path.
B. Minimize total travel time from one site to each of the other sites in a transportation system.
C. Maximize throughput in networks with distinct entry (source node) and exit (sink node) points.
D. Identify the set of connecting branches having the shortest combined length.

Answer (B) is correct.
REQUIRED: The purpose of a shortest-route algorithm used in network models.
DISCUSSION: Network models are used to solve managerial problems pertaining to project scheduling, information systems design, and transportation systems design. Networks consisting of nodes and arcs may be created to represent in graphic form problems related to transportation, assignment, and transshipment. The shortest-route, minimal spanning tree, and maximal flow problems are other applications of network models. A shortest-route algorithm minimizes total travel time from one site to each of the other sites in a transportation system.
Answer (A) is incorrect. The critical path method (CPM) is intended to identify bottlenecks in a network and identify the longest path. Answer (C) is incorrect. The maximal flow algorithm maximizes throughput in networks with distinct entry (source node) and exit (sink node) points. Examples of applications are highway transportation systems and oil pipelines. Flows are limited by capacities of the arcs (e.g., highways or pipes). Answer (D) is incorrect. The minimal spanning tree algorithm identifies the set of connecting branches having the shortest combined length. A spanning tree is a group of branches (arcs) that connects each node in the network to every other node. An example problem is the determination of the shortest telecommunications linkage among users at remote sites and a central computer.

4.3 Change Management

12. An organization's management perceives the need to make significant changes. Which of the following factors is management **least** likely to be able to change?

A. The organization's members.
B. The organization's structure.
C. The organization's environment.
D. The organization's technology.

Answer (C) is correct.
REQUIRED: The factor management is least likely to be able to change.
DISCUSSION: The environment of an organization consists of external forces outside its direct control that may affect its performance. These forces include competitors, suppliers, customers, regulators, climate, culture, politics, technological change, and many other factors. The organization's members are a factor that managers are clearly able to change.

13. Co-optation is a

A. Method of coping with employee resistance.
B. Cause of resistance to change.
C. Model for categorizing organizational changes.
D. Way of allowing meaningful input by resistant employees.

Answer (A) is correct.
REQUIRED: The definition of co-optation.
DISCUSSION: Methods of coping with employee resistance include co-optation through allowing some participation but without meaningful input.
Answer (B) is incorrect. Co-optation is a method of coping with employee resistance. Answer (C) is incorrect. Co-optation is a method of coping with employee resistance. Answer (D) is incorrect. Co-optation is a way of allowing some participation but without meaningful input.

14. Organizational change must be considered in the light of potential employee resistance. Resistance

A. May occur even though employees will benefit from the change.
B. Will be greatest when informal groups are weakest.
C. Will be insignificant if no economic loss by employees is expected.
D. Is centered mostly on perceived threats to psychological needs.

Answer (A) is correct.
REQUIRED: The true statement about resistance to organizational change.
DISCUSSION: Resistance to change may be caused by fear of the personal adjustments that may be required. Employees may have a genuine concern about the usefulness of the change, perceive a lack of concern for workers' feelings, fear the outcome, worry about downgrading of job status, and resent deviations from past procedures for implementing change (especially if new procedures are less participative than the old). Social adjustments also may be required that violate the behavioral norms of informal groups or disrupt the social status quo within groups. Economic adjustments may involve potential economic loss or insecurity based on perceived threats to jobs. In general, any perceived deterioration in the work situation that is seen as a threat to economic, social, and/or psychological needs will produce resistance. The various adjustments required are most likely to be resisted when imposed unilaterally by higher authority. However, employees who share in finding solutions to the problems requiring change are less likely to resist because they will have some responsibility for the change.
Answer (B) is incorrect. Strong informal groups are likely to offer more resistance. **Answer (C) is incorrect.** Resistance arises from threats to a complex pattern of economic, social, and psychological needs. **Answer (D) is incorrect.** Resistance arises from threats to a complex pattern of economic, social, and psychological needs.

4.4 Contracts

15. Carol dictated an offer she intended to make to Deanna. Irvin, her secretary, drafted an email based on Carol's dictation. During lunch and before the offer had been sent, Irvin saw Deanna and told her about it. Deanna promptly sent an acceptance to Carol. What was the effect of this attempted acceptance?

A. No contract was formed because the offer was not communicated to the offeree.
B. No contract was formed because the offer was not communicated to the offeree by the means chosen by the offeror.
C. A contract was formed because Irvin was Carol's agent.
D. A contract was formed because Carol intended to make an offer and Deanna learned of the offer in time to make a valid acceptance.

Answer (B) is correct.
REQUIRED: The effect of communication of an offer by a means not intended by the offeror.
DISCUSSION: An offer is not effective until it is communicated to the offeree. The communication, however, must be by a means chosen by the offeror. Carol evidently intended to communicate the offer by email. When the offeree learned of the offer in an unauthorized manner, she could only make an offer, not a valid acceptance.
Answer (A) is incorrect. The offer was actually communicated but not as intended by the offeror. **Answer (C) is incorrect.** The facts do not indicate that Irvin was an agent for purposes of communicating offers. **Answer (D) is incorrect.** The offer must be communicated as intended by the offeror.

16. Gudrun owned a 2,000-acre country estate. She signed a written agreement with Johann, selling the house on the property and "a sufficient amount of land surrounding the house to create a park." The price was stated to be US $200,000. When Gudrun refused to honor the agreement, Johann sued. Who will prevail and why?

A. Gudrun will win because the agreement is not reasonably definite.
B. Johann will win because the quantity of land is implied.
C. Johann will win because the parties intended to make a contract.
D. Gudrun will win because no financing term was included in the agreement.

Answer (A) is correct.
REQUIRED: The result when a contract for the sale of land does not state the quantity.
DISCUSSION: For an agreement between the parties to be enforceable, it must be reasonably definite and certain (not ambiguous). A court must be able to determine with reasonable accuracy what the parties agreed upon. In this case, the writing is not reasonably clear as to what amount of land Gudrun agreed to sell.
Answer (B) is incorrect. Some objective basis must exist for measuring the implied term. The court has no means of determining how much land is needed for a park. Answer (C) is incorrect. A court must be able to determine with reasonable accuracy what the parties agreed upon. Answer (D) is incorrect. The quantity term is more significant than the financing term. The price is given and payment in cash (or its equivalent) is implied.

17. Egan, a minor, purchased Baker's used computer for Egan's personal use. Egan paid US $200 down on delivery and was to pay US $200 thirty days later. Twenty days later, the computer was damaged seriously as a result of Egan's negligence. Five days after the damage occurred and 1 day after Egan reached the age of majority, Egan attempted to disaffirm the contract with Baker. Egan will

A. Be able to disaffirm even though Egan was not a minor at the time of disaffirmance.
B. Be able to disaffirm only if Egan does so in writing.
C. Not be able to disaffirm because Egan had failed to pay the balance of the purchase price.
D. Not be able to disaffirm because the computer was damaged as a result of Egan's negligence.

Answer (A) is correct.
REQUIRED: The true statement about disaffirming a contract made by a minor.
DISCUSSION: Most contracts entered into by a minor may be disaffirmed if (s)he acts during minority or a short time thereafter. Tender of goods is usually required. However, a minor may disaffirm even though (s)he cannot return the property or can return it only in damaged condition.
Answer (B) is incorrect. A writing was not required to disaffirm the voidable contract. Note that a minor's power to disaffirm is not dependent on the UCC. Answer (C) is incorrect. Payment of the balance would be performance, which is not a condition of disaffirming. Answer (D) is incorrect. Egan may still disaffirm the contract but may be liable for negligence in tort.

18. In determining whether the consideration requirement to form a contract has been satisfied, the consideration exchanged by the parties to the contract must be

A. Of approximately equal value.
B. Legally sufficient.
C. Exchanged simultaneously by the parties.
D. Fair and reasonable under the circumstances.

Answer (B) is correct.
REQUIRED: The nature of the consideration required to support an enforceable contract.
DISCUSSION: Consideration must be legally sufficient and intended as a bargained-for exchange. A promisee has provided legally sufficient consideration if (s)he incurs a legal detriment or if the promisor receives a legal benefit.
Answer (A) is incorrect. Legally sufficient consideration exchanged may be disparate in value. Answer (C) is incorrect. As long as a genuine bargained-for exchange is intended, the consideration need not be simultaneously exchanged. Answer (D) is incorrect. The amount of consideration is set in the market, not the courts. But extreme disparity of value may evidence fraud, unconscionability, a gift, etc.

4.5 Classification of Contracts

19. When a client accepts the services of an accountant without an agreement concerning payment, the result is

A. An implied-in-fact contract.
B. An implied-in-law contract.
C. An express contract.
D. No contract.

Answer (A) is correct.
REQUIRED: The type of contract formed when a client accepts an accountant's services.
DISCUSSION: Enforceable contracts may be formed without an express agreement of terms if the facts of the situation indicate (imply) an objective intent of both parties to contract. Objective intent means the apparent intent of an ordinary, reasonable person and not the actual (subjective) intent. When a client accepts the services of an accountant, an agreement to pay for them is implied. Because the facts indicate a contract was formed, it is an implied-in-fact contract.
Answer (B) is incorrect. The equitable remedy of restitution or quasi-contract (contract implied in law) prevents unjust enrichment of one party when the facts do not indicate both parties intended to form a contract. **Answer (C) is incorrect.** An express contract is one in which the terms (such as payment) are specifically agreed upon. **Answer (D) is incorrect.** A contract implied in fact was formed.

20. Which of the following represents the basic distinction between a bilateral contract and a unilateral contract?

A. Specific performance is available if the contract is unilateral but not if it is bilateral.
B. Only one promise is involved if the contract is unilateral, but two are involved if it is bilateral.
C. The statute of frauds applies to a bilateral contract but not to a unilateral contract.
D. Rights under a bilateral contract are assignable, whereas rights under a unilateral contract are not assignable.

Answer (B) is correct.
REQUIRED: The basic distinction between a unilateral and a bilateral contract.
DISCUSSION: In a bilateral contract, the promise of one party to perform is consideration for the promise of the other. In a unilateral contract, one party makes a promise in exchange for the other party's act, instead of in exchange for a promise from the other party (as in a bilateral contract). Thus, a unilateral contract involves only one promise, but a bilateral contract involves two promises.
Answer (A) is incorrect. The availability of specific performance is not affected by the distinction between unilateral and bilateral contracts. They may apply to either a unilateral or bilateral contract. **Answer (C) is incorrect.** The applicability of the statute of frauds is not affected by the distinction between unilateral and bilateral contracts. They may apply to either a unilateral or bilateral contract. **Answer (D) is incorrect.** The assignability of rights is not affected by the distinction between unilateral and bilateral contracts. They may apply to either a unilateral or bilateral contract.

Access the **Gleim CIA Premium Review System** featuring our SmartAdapt technology from your Gleim Personal Classroom to continue your studies. You will experience a personalized study environment with exam-emulating multiple-choice questions.

STUDY UNIT FIVE
WORKSTATIONS, DATABASES, AND APPLICATIONS

(24 pages of outline)

5.1	Workstations and Databases	149
5.2	Application Development and Maintenance	163

This study unit is the first of four covering **Domain III: Information Technology** from The IIA's CIA Exam Syllabus. This domain makes up 20% of Part 3 of the CIA exam and is tested at the **basic** cognitive level. Refer to the complete syllabus located in Appendix A to view the relevant sections covered in Study Unit 5.

5.1 WORKSTATIONS AND DATABASES

1. **Workstations**

    a. A workstation is any combination of input, output, and computing hardware that can be used for work. It may take the form of a personal computer (PC) or a powerful microcomputer, which is used for scientific or engineering work.

    1) Workstations belong to the hardware component of the IT system infrastructure. Thus, they may be included in the audit of hardware controls.

        a) Auditors can evaluate hardware controls in different ways. Examples include

            i) Interviewing users,
            ii) Comparing actual downtime with normal expectations, and
            iii) Reviewing failure logs.

2. **Binary Storage**

    a. Digital computers store all information in binary format, that is, as a pattern of ones and zeros. This makes arithmetic operations and true/false decisions on the lowest level extremely straightforward.

    b. A **bit** is either 0 or 1 (off or on) in binary code. Bits can be strung together to form a binary (i.e., base 2) number.

EXAMPLE 5-1	Bit
	0

c. A **byte** is a group of bits, most commonly eight. A byte can be used to signify a character (a number, letter of the alphabet, or symbol, such as a question mark or asterisk).

EXAMPLE 5-2	8-Bit Byte Representing the Capital Letter P
	01010000

1) Quantities of bytes are measured with the following units:

$$1,024\ (2^{10})\ \text{bytes} = \textbf{1 kilobyte} = 1\ \text{KB}$$
$$1,048,576\ (2^{20})\ \text{bytes} = \textbf{1 megabyte} = 1\ \text{MB}$$
$$1,073,741,824\ (2^{30})\ \text{bytes} = \textbf{1 gigabyte} = 1\ \text{GB}$$
$$1,099,511,627,776\ (2^{40})\ \text{bytes} = \textbf{1 terabyte} = 1\ \text{TB}$$

Author's Note: Please do not memorize these numbers. The intent is to demonstrate the difference in size for each unit to help you better grasp these terms.

d. A **field**, also called a data item, is a group of bytes. The field contains a unit of data about some entity, e.g., a composer's name.

EXAMPLE 5-3	Field
	Paul Hindemith

e. A **record** is a group of fields. All the fields contain information pertaining to an entity, e.g., a specific performance of an orchestral work.

EXAMPLE 5-4	Record
Paul Hindemith	Violin Concerto	Chicago Symphony	Claudio Abbado	Josef Suk

1) Some field or combination of fields on each record is designated as the **key**. The criterion for a key is that it contains enough information to uniquely identify each record; i.e., there can be no two records with the same key.

   a) The designation of a key allows records to be sorted and managed with much greater efficiency. If all the records are sorted in the order of the key, searching for a particular one becomes much easier.

   b) In Example 5-4, the key is the combination of the first two fields.

      i) The first field alone is not enough because there could be several works by each composer. The second field alone is likewise not enough since there could be many pieces with the same title.

      ii) The combination of the composer's name and title uniquely identify each piece of music.

f. A **file** is a group of records. All the records in the file contain the same pieces of information about different occurrences, e.g., performances of several orchestral works.

EXAMPLE 5-5 File

Paul Hindemith	Violin Concerto	Chicago Symphony	Claudio Abbado	Josef Suk
Gustav Mahler	Das Lied von der Erde	New York Philharmonic	Leonard Bernstein	Dietrich Fischer-Dieskau
Bela Bartok	Piano Concerto No. 2	Chicago Symphony	Sir Georg Solti	Etsko Tazaki
Arnold Schoenberg	Gurrelieder	Boston Symphony	Seiji Ozawa	James McCracken
Leos Janacek	Sinfonietta	Los Angeles Philharmonic	Simon Rattle	None
Dmitri Shostakovich	Symphony No. 6	San Francisco Symphony	Kazuhiro Koizumi	None
Carl Orff	Carmina Burana	Berlin Radio Symphony	Eugen Jochum	Gundula Janowitz

3. **Electronic Data Interchange (EDI)**

    a. EDI is the communication of electronic documents directly from a computer in one organization to a computer in another organization. Examples are ordering goods from a supplier and a transfer of funds. EDI was the first step in the evolution of e-business.

    1) EDI was developed to enhance JIT (just-in-time) inventory management.

    b. Advantages of EDI include (1) reduction of clerical errors, (2) higher speed of transactions, and (3) elimination of repetitive clerical tasks. EDI also eliminates document preparation, processing, and mailing costs.

    c. A disadvantage of EDI is that it cannot handle a large volume of custom orders. The lack of standardization imposes unacceptable cost.

    d. An extension of EDI is computer-stored records, a less expensive medium than traditional physical file storage.

4. **Electronic Funds Transfer (EFT)**

    a. EFT is a service provided by financial institutions worldwide that is based on electronic data interchange (EDI) technology.

    1) EFT transaction costs are lower than for manual systems because documents and human intervention are eliminated from the transaction process. Moreover, transfer customarily requires less than a day.

    2) Common consumer applications of EFT are

        a) The direct deposit of payroll checks in employees' accounts and

        b) The automatic withdrawal of payments for cable and telephone bills, mortgages, etc.

    b. The most important application of EFT is check collection. To reduce the enormous volume of paper, the check-collection process has been computerized.

    1) The result is reduction of the significance of paper checks. EFT allows payments and deposits without manual transfer of negotiable instruments. Thus, wholesale EFTs among financial institutions and businesses (commercial transfers) are measured in trillions of U.S. dollars.

5. Governance, Risk, and Compliance (GRC) Systems

a. **Data governance** encompasses information systems (IS) and information technology (IT). IS and IT are vital to ensure the successful implementation of an organization's strategy. IT strategy should be driven by the business needs and not by the functions of available technology when formulating a plan to achieve goals.

1) An IT strategic plan should be aligned with organizational goals and integrated with the overall business strategy.

2) Individual departments may function well in terms of their own goals but still not serve the goals of the organization.

3) IS infrastructure purchases need to be implemented in accordance with the IT strategic plan to ensure business needs are met.

4) Business owners, employees, customers, and financers such as banks have a vested interest in the strategy.

5) The IIA Global Technology Audit Guide (GTAG) on information technology controls discusses IT roles in the organization. Key people are involved in determining and supporting an entity's overall vision and strategy. Examples include but are not limited to the following:

   a) **Board of directors.** All major corporate decisions (including establishment of IT governance and strategy) are made or approved by the board. The board has an oversight role.

   b) **Management.** The corporation's officers (i.e., executive management) are responsible for carrying out the entity's day-to-day operations, such as implementing effective security governance.

      i) Officers include the chief executive officer (CEO), chief information officer (CIO), and chief information security officer (CISO).

   c) **Internal auditors.** Internal auditors' IT roles include performing IT risk assessments, advising on internal control issues, and performing IT audits of enterprise-level, general, and applications controls.

b. Organizations generally develop strategies at three different levels.

1) **Corporate-level strategy** is concerned with market definition (i.e., business and markets to focus resources).

2) **Business-level strategy** applies to organizations that have independent business units that each develop their own strategy.

3) **Functional-level strategy** concentrates on a specific functional area of the organization such as treasury, information systems, human resources, and operations.

c. Strategic drivers are the critical elements that help determine the success or failure of an organization's strategy. IS has become a strategic driver in most, if not all, organizations.
   1) New technologies create opportunities for improvement and competitive advantage.
   2) **Customer relationship management (CRM)** is a term that refers to practices, strategies, and technologies that companies use to manage and analyze customer interactions and data throughout the customer lifecycle. CRM
      a) Has a goal of improving business relationships with customers, assisting in customer retention, and driving sales growth.
      b) Is designed to compile information on customers across different channels or points of contact between the customer and the company.
      c) Should manage customer relationships on a long-term basis to add value.
d. A well-functioning governance program generally concentrates on the following:
   1) **Strategic alignment** between the organization's goals and IT's strategy for meeting those goals.
   2) **Risk management** involves identifying the controls in place to monitor, analyze, and address risks.
   3) **Value delivery** is assessed by the organization to determine the benefits provided by and the worth of IT (i.e., return on investment, productivity, and implementation results).
   4) **Performance measurement** involves analysis of whether IT has accomplished set goals and comparison to industry standards. The IIA has categorized the key components of successful IT governance as follows:
      a) IT processes that are used to provide services to all areas within the organization
      b) Organizational structure (i.e., roles and relationships) that communicates the carrying out of IT services within the organization
      c) Mechanisms or courses of action that coordinate, evaluate, and measure IT performance
   5) **Resource management** involves ensuring that infrastructure is meeting short-term expectations and identifying IT enhancements and advancements that are necessary to meet long-term expectations.
e. GRC software enables organizations to manage the governance program strategy.
   1) GRC systems assist management with monitoring, evaluating, and enforcing policies, standards, and procedures established to ensure compliance.
   2) Characteristics associated with successful GRC systems implementation include but are not limited to
      a) Compliance with laws and regulations
      b) Increased efficiency and effectiveness of business operations while reducing costs
      c) Risk management, control monitoring, and an information sharing focus
      d) Identification of the roles of management and who owns each risk, controls risk content, and approves those risks
      e) Cascade of information throughout the organization improving various functions

6. **Data, Databases, and Database Management System (DBMS)**
    a. A **database** is an organized collection of data in a computer system.
    b. Data in the database are integrated to eliminate redundancy of data items. A single integrated system allows for improved data accessibility.
        1) When systems within the organization are not integrated, they not only may contain different data but also may define and update data in inconsistent ways. Thus, determining the location of data and ensuring their consistency are more difficult.
    c. A DBMS is an integrated set of computer programs that (1) create the database, (2) maintain the elements, (3) safeguard the data from loss or destruction, and (4) make the data available to applications programs and inquiries.
        1) The DBMS allows programmers and designers to work independently of the technical structure of the database.
            a) Before the development of DBMSs, designing and coding programs that used databases was extremely time-consuming (and therefore expensive) because programmers had to know the exact contents and characteristics of the data in every database.
            b) DBMSs provide a common language for referring to databases, easing the design and coding of application programs.
            c) A DBMS includes security features. Thus, a specified user's access may be limited to certain data fields or logical views depending on the individual's assigned duties.
            d) DB2 (IBM), Oracle (Oracle Corp.), SQL Server (Microsoft), and Access (Microsoft) are examples of DBMSs.
    d. The term "database" often includes the DBMS.

EXAMPLE 5-6	Data Redundancy

The various files related to human resources in the conventional record systems of most organizations include payroll, work history, and permanent personnel data.

An employee's name must appear in each of these files when they are stored and processed separately. The result is redundancy. When data are combined in a database, each data item is usually stored only once.

e. The data are stored physically on direct-access storage devices (e.g., magnetic disks, cloud). They are also stored for efficient access.

1) The most frequently accessed items are placed in the physical locations permitting the fastest access.
2) When these items were stored in separate files under older file-oriented systems, the physical locations were usually similar to the logical structure of the data. Items that logically belonged together were stored in physical proximity to one another.
3) A logical data model is a user view. It is the way a user describes the data and defines their interrelationships based on the user's needs, without regard to how the data are physically stored.
4) A fundamental characteristic of databases is that applications are independent of the database structure; when writing programs or designing applications to use the database, only the name of the desired item is necessary.
5) A data item is identified using the data manipulation language, after which the DBMS locates and retrieves the desired item(s).
   a) The data manipulation language is used to add, delete, retrieve, or modify data or relationships.
6) The physical structure of the database can be completely altered without having to change any of the programs using the data items. Thus, different users may define different views of the data (subschemas).
   a) A **database view** is a virtual database table that allows the user to query data. The view can be read-only or updatable.
      i) Insert, update, and delete commands can be executed on updatable views.
7) Databases and the associated DBMS permit efficient storage and retrieval of data for formal system applications.
   a) They also permit increased ad hoc accessing of data (e.g., to answer inquiries for data not contained in formal system outputs) as well as updating of files by transaction processing.
   b) These increased capabilities, however, result in increased cost because they require
      i) The use of sophisticated hardware (direct-access devices)
      ii) Sophisticated software (the DBMS)
      iii) Highly trained technical personnel (database administrator, staff)
      iv) Increased security controls

7. **Two Early Database Structures**

    a. Storing all related data on one storage device creates security problems.

        1) Should hardware or software malfunctions occur, or unauthorized access be achieved, the results could be disastrous.

        2) Greater emphasis on security is required to provide backup and restrict access to the database.

            a) For example, the system may employ **dual logging**, that is, use of two transaction logs written simultaneously on separate storage media.

            b) It may also use a snapshot technique to capture data values before and after transaction processing.

            c) The files that store these values can be used to reconstruct the database in the event of data loss or corruption.

    b. To understand the vast improvement in performance brought about by database technology, it is helpful to review the development of file structures.

        1) The early mainframe computers used flat files, meaning that all the records and all the data elements within each record followed one behind the other. Much of the early mainframe storage was on magnetic tape, which naturally stored data in this fashion.

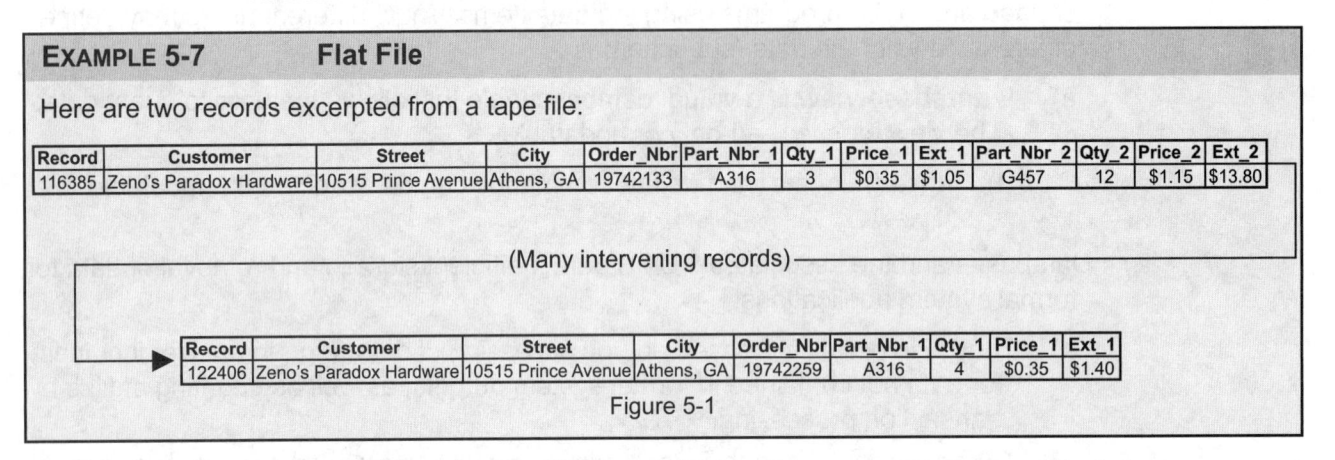

EXAMPLE 5-7	Flat File

Here are two records excerpted from a tape file:

Record	Customer	Street	City	Order_Nbr	Part_Nbr_1	Qty_1	Price_1	Ext_1	Part_Nbr_2	Qty_2	Price_2	Ext_2
116385	Zeno's Paradox Hardware	10515 Prince Avenue	Athens, GA	19742133	A316	3	$0.35	$1.05	G457	12	$1.15	$13.80

———————————— (Many intervening records) ————————————

Record	Customer	Street	City	Order_Nbr	Part_Nbr_1	Qty_1	Price_1	Ext_1
122406	Zeno's Paradox Hardware	10515 Prince Avenue	Athens, GA	19742259	A316	4	$0.35	$1.40

Figure 5-1

        2) Two inefficiencies are apparent at once in this method of accessing data:

            a) The customer's address has to be stored with every order the customer places, taking up much unnecessary storage.

            b) All intervening records must be read and skipped over in order to find both records pertaining to this customer.

c. Database technology overcame these two difficulties. The main ways to organize a database include tree or hierarchical, network, relational, and non-relational databases.

1) A tree or **hierarchical structure** arranges data in a one-to-many relationship in which each record has one antecedent but may have an unlimited number of subsequent records.

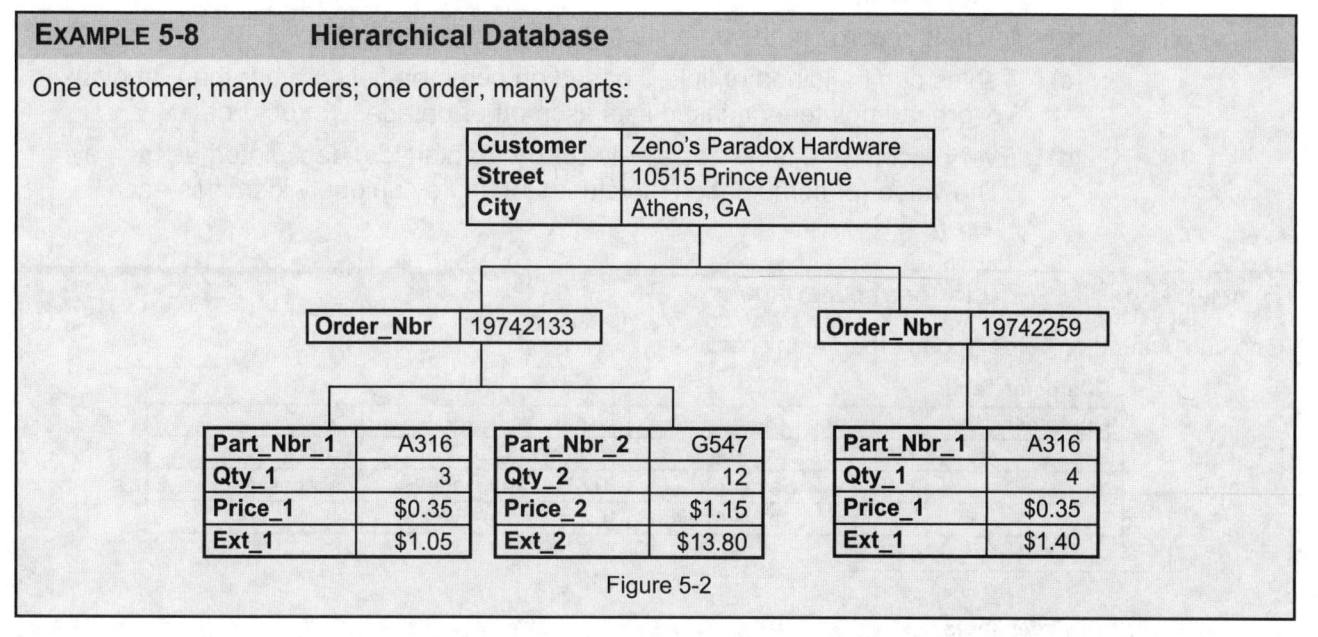

EXAMPLE 5-8   Hierarchical Database

One customer, many orders; one order, many parts:

Customer	Zeno's Paradox Hardware
Street	10515 Prince Avenue
City	Athens, GA

Order_Nbr	19742133

Order_Nbr	19742259

Part_Nbr_1	A316
Qty_1	3
Price_1	$0.35
Ext_1	$1.05

Part_Nbr_2	G547
Qty_2	12
Price_2	$1.15
Ext_2	$13.80

Part_Nbr_1	A316
Qty_1	4
Price_1	$0.35
Ext_1	$1.40

Figure 5-2

---

a) Because the records are not stored one after the other, a tree database structure stores a pointer with each record. The pointer is the storage address of the next record.

b) The tree structure cuts down on data redundancy but retains the necessity of searching every record to fulfill a query.

i) Thus, like the flat file, adding new records is awkward and ad hoc queries are inefficient.

2) The **network structure** connects every record in the database with every other record.

a) This was an attempt to make queries more efficient. However, the huge number of cross-references inherent in this structure makes maintenance far too complex.

8. **Relational Database Structure**
    a. A relational structure organizes data in a conceptual arrangement.
        1) An individual data item is called a field or column (e.g., name, date, amount).
            a) Related fields are brought together in a record or row (e.g., for a single sales transaction).
            b) Multiple records make up a file or table (e.g., sales).
            c) Tables can be joined or linked based on common fields rather than on high-overhead pointers or linked lists as in other database structures.
            d) Every record in a table has a field (or group of fields) designated as the key. The value (or combination of values) in the key uniquely identifies each record.

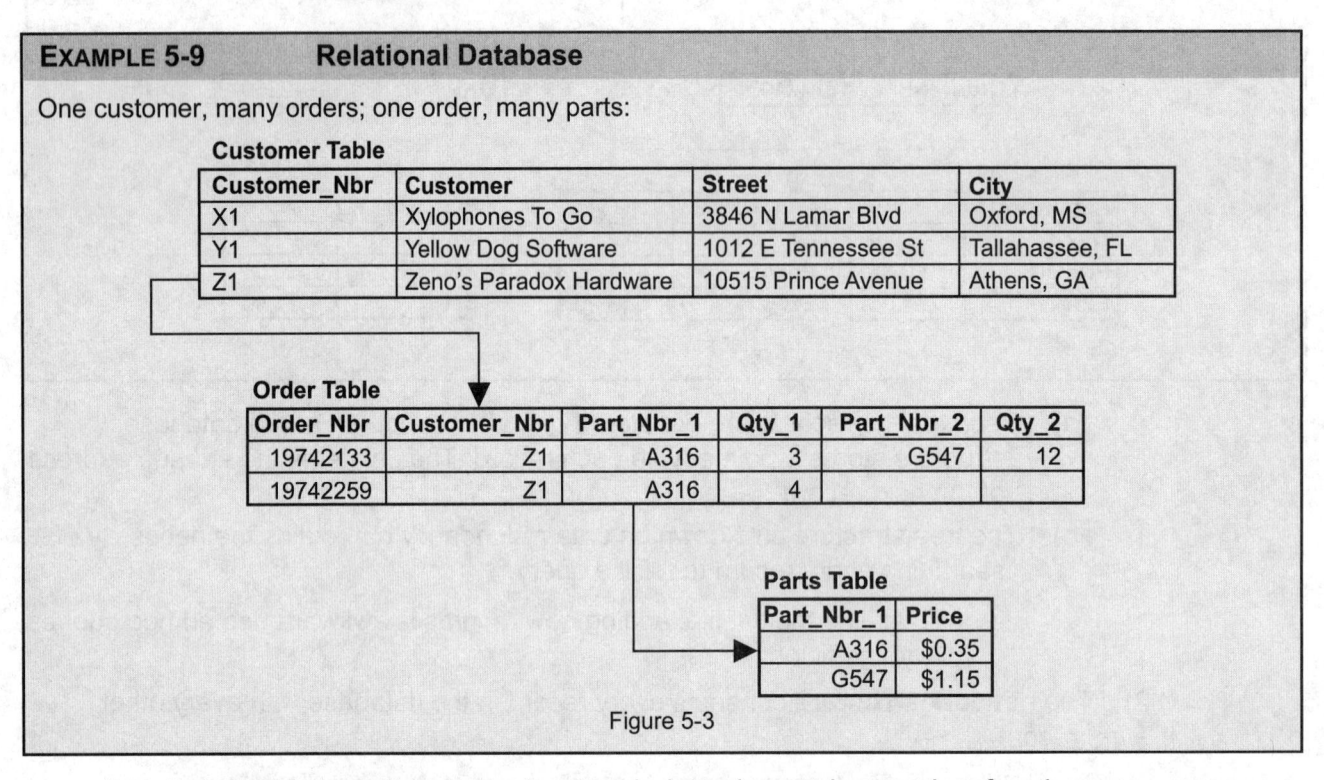

EXAMPLE 5-9   Relational Database

One customer, many orders; one order, many parts:

Customer Table

Customer_Nbr	Customer	Street	City
X1	Xylophones To Go	3846 N Lamar Blvd	Oxford, MS
Y1	Yellow Dog Software	1012 E Tennessee St	Tallahassee, FL
Z1	Zeno's Paradox Hardware	10515 Prince Avenue	Athens, GA

Order Table

Order_Nbr	Customer_Nbr	Part_Nbr_1	Qty_1	Part_Nbr_2	Qty_2
19742133	Z1	A316	3	G547	12
19742259	Z1	A316	4		

Parts Table

Part_Nbr_1	Price
A316	$0.35
G547	$1.15

Figure 5-3

---

   b. Note that in a relational structure, each data element is stored as few times as necessary. This is accomplished through the process of normalization. Normalization prevents inconsistent deletion, insertion, and updating of data items.
        1) The relational structure requires careful planning, but it is easy to maintain and processes queries efficiently.
   c. The three basic operations in the relational model are selecting, joining, and projecting.
        1) Selecting creates a subset of records that meet certain criteria.
        2) Joining is the combining of relational tables based on a common field or combination of fields.
        3) Projecting results in the requested subset of columns from the table. This operation creates a new table containing only the required information.

d. Two features that make the relational data structure stand out are cardinality and referential integrity.

   1) **Cardinality** refers to how close a given data element is to being unique.

      a) A data element that can only exist once in a given table has high cardinality. In Figure 5-3 on the previous page, Customer_Nbr has high cardinality in the Customer Table.

      b) A data element that is not unique in a given table but that has a restricted range of possible values is said to have normal cardinality. Order_Nbr in the Order Table is an example.

      c) A data element that has a very small range of values is said to have low cardinality. A field that can contain only male/female or true/false is an example.

   2) **Referential integrity** means that for a record to be entered in a given table, there must already be a record in some other table(s).

      a) For example, the Order Table in Figure 5-3 on the previous page cannot contain a record where the part number is not already present in the Parts Table.

e. The tremendous advantage of a relational data structure is that searching for records is greatly facilitated.

   1) For example, a user can specify a customer and see all the parts that customer has ordered, or the user can specify a part and see all the customers who have ordered it. Such queries were extremely resource-intensive, if not impossible, under older data structures.

f. A distributed database is stored in two or more physical sites using either replication or partitioning.

   1) The replication or snapshot technique makes duplicates to be stored at multiple locations.

      a) Changes are periodically copied and sent to each location. If a database is small, storing multiple copies may be cheaper than retrieving records from a central site.

   2) Fragmentation or partitioning stores specific records where they are most needed.

      a) For example, a financial institution may store a particular customer's data at the branch where (s)he usually transacts his or her business. If the customer executes a transaction at another branch, the pertinent data are retrieved via communication lines.

      b) One variation is the central index. A query to this index obtains the location in a remote database where the complete record is to be found.

      c) Still another variation is the ask-the-network distributed database. In this system, no central index exists. Instead, the remote databases are polled to locate the desired record.

3) Updating data in a distributed system may require special protocols.

    a) Thus, a two-phase commit disk-writing protocol is used. If data are to be updated in two places, databases in both locations are cleared for updating before either one performs (commits) the update.

    b) In the first phase, both locations agree to the update. In the second phase, both perform the update.

4) A deadly embrace (deadlock) occurs when each of two transactions has a lock on a single data resource.

    a) When deadly embraces occur, the database management system (DBMS) must have an algorithm for undoing the effects of one of the transactions and releasing the data resources it controls so that the other transaction can run to completion. Then, the other transaction is restarted and permitted to run to completion.

    b) If deadly embraces are not resolved, response time worsens or the system eventually fails.

9. **Non-Relational Databases**

   a. Non-relational databases provide a mechanism for storage and retrieval of data other than the tabular relations used in relational databases.

    1) The data structures used by NoSQL databases do not require joining tables, which allow operations to run faster.

    2) They capture all kinds of data (e.g., structured, semi-structured, and unstructured data), which allows for a flexible database that can easily and quickly accommodate any new type of data and is not disrupted by content structure changes.

    3) They provide better "horizontal" scaling to clusters of machines, which solves the problem when the number of concurrent users skyrockets for applications that are accessible via the Web and mobile devices.

    4) Impedance mismatch between the object-oriented approach to write applications and the schema-based tables and rows of relational databases is eliminated. For instance, storing all information on one document, in contrast to joining multiple tables together, results in less code to write, debug, and maintain.

10. **Additional Terminology**

    a. The **database administrator (DBA)** is the individual who has overall responsibility for developing and maintaining the database and for establishing controls to protect its integrity.

    1) Thus, only the DBA should be able to update data dictionaries. In small systems, the DBA may perform some functions of a DBMS. In larger applications, the DBA uses a DBMS as a primary tool.

    2) The responsibility for creating, maintaining, securing, restricting access to, and redefining and restructuring the database belongs to the database administrator.

    3) The **data control language** specifies the privileges and security rules governing database users.

    4) The **data manipulation language** is used to retrieve, store, modify, delete, insert, and update data in databases.

    5) The **data definition language** is used to create and modify the structure of database objects in databases.

    b. The **data dictionary** is a file that describes both the physical and logical characteristics of every data element in a database.

    1) The data dictionary includes, for example, the name of the data element (e.g., employee name, part number), the amount of disk space required to store the data element (in bytes), and what kind of data is allowed in the data element (e.g., alphabetic, numeric).

    2) Thus, the data dictionary contains the size, format, usage, meaning, and ownership of every data element. This greatly simplifies the programming process.

    c. Data from a relational database can be displayed in graphs and reports, changed, and otherwise controlled using a program called **Query Management Facility (QMF)**.

    d. The **schema** is a description of the overall logical structure of the database using data-definition language, which is the connection between the logical and physical structures of the database.

    1) A subschema describes a particular user's (application's) view of a part of the database using data definition language.

    e. The **database mapping facility** is software that is used to evaluate and document the structure of the database.

    f. **Data command interpreter languages** are symbolic character strings used to control the current state of DBMS operations.

    g. An **object-oriented database** is a response to the need to store not only numbers and characters but also graphics and multimedia applications.

    1) Translating these data into tables and rows is difficult. However, in an object-oriented database, they can be stored, along with the procedures acting on them, within an object.

h. In a **hypermedia database**, blocks of data are organized into nodes that are linked in a pattern determined by the user so that an information search need not be restricted to the predefined organizational scheme. A node may contain text, graphics, audio, video, or programs.

1) Hybrid systems containing object-oriented and relational database capabilities have also been developed.

i. Advanced database systems provide for **online analytical processing (OLAP)**, also called multidimensional data analysis, which is the ability to analyze large amounts of data from numerous perspectives.

1) OLAP is an integral part of the data warehouse concept.
2) Using OLAP, users can compare data in many dimensions, such as sales by product, sales by geography, and sales by salesperson.
3) The following technologies are replacing OLAP:

   a) **In-memory analytics** is an approach that queries data when it resides in a computer's random access memory (RAM), as opposed to querying data that is stored on physical disks. This results in shortened query response times and allows business intelligence and analytic applications to support faster business decisions.

   b) **Search engine technology** stores data at a document/transaction level, and data is not pre-aggregated like it would be when contained in an OLAP or in-memory technology application. Users are able to have full access to their raw data and create the aggregations themselves.

j. A **data warehouse** contains not only current operating data but also historical information from throughout the organization. Thus, data from all operational systems are integrated, consolidated, and standardized in an organization-wide database into which data are copied periodically. These data are maintained on one platform and can be read but not changed.

1) **Data cleansing** cleans up data in a database that is incorrect, incomplete, or duplicated before loading it into the database. It improves the quality of data. The need for data cleansing increases when multiple data sources are integrated.
2) Data mining is facilitated by a data warehouse. **Data mining** is the process of analyzing data from different perspectives and summarizing it into useful information. Data mining software ordinarily is used.

   a) For example, data mining software can help to find abnormal patterns and unforeseen correlations among the data.
   b) Internal auditors can use data mining techniques to detect fraud.

3) A **data mart** is a subset of a data warehouse.

STOP & REVIEW

You have completed the outline for this subunit.
Study multiple-choice questions 1 through 12 beginning on page 173.

5.2 APPLICATION DEVELOPMENT AND MAINTENANCE

1. **Organizational Needs Assessment**

    a. The organizational needs assessment is a detailed process of study and evaluation of how information systems can be deployed to help the organization meet its goals. The steps in the assessment are as follows:

    1) Determine whether current systems support organizational goals
    2) Determine needs unmet by current systems
    3) Determine capacity of current systems to accommodate projected growth
    4) Propose path for information systems deployment to achieve organizational goals within budgetary constraints

2. **Business Process Design**

    a. A business process is a flow of actions performed on goods and/or information to accomplish a discrete objective.

    1) Examples include hiring a new employee, recruiting a new customer, and filling a customer order.

    b. Some business processes are contained entirely within a single functional area; e.g., hiring a new employee is performed by the human resources function.

    1) Other processes cross functional boundaries. Filling a customer order requires the participation of the sales department, the warehouse, and accounts receivable.

    c. In the early days of automated system deployment, hardware and software were very expensive. Systems tended to be designed to serve a single process or even a single functional area. Tremendous gains in processing power and storage capacity have made integrated systems, i.e., those that combine multiple processes, the norm.

    1) The most advanced of these are enterprise resource planning (ERP) systems.

    d. The automation of a process, or the acquisition of an integrated system, presents the organization with an opportunity for business process reengineering.

    1) **Business process reengineering** involves a complete rethinking of how business functions are performed to provide value to customers, that is, radical innovation instead of mere improvement and a disregard for current jobs, hierarchies, and reporting relationships.

3. **Participants in Business Process Design**

    a. The everyday functioning of a business process affects multiple stakeholder groups.

        1) Input from each group should be considered in the design of the process. However, some stakeholders will be more active participants.

    b. End-users are generally the drivers of a new or redesigned process.

        1) For example, the customers of a multi-division business may have open accounts with several of the divisions. Whenever a customer calls, the customer relations department would like the most up-to-date customer balance information for all divisions to be accessible at once.

        2) Although the motivation for the new process begins with the customer service department, personnel in various divisions as well as the central IT function will be affected.

    c. Because IT pervades every aspect of operations in a modern organization, the **IT steering committee** must study each request for a new process and either approve or deny it.

        1) Typical members of the steering committee include the chief information officer and the head of systems development from the IT function. Executive management from each division is also represented.

        2) The committee members have an understanding of the interactions of the organization's current systems and how they will affect and be affected by new or redesigned business processes.

    d. Once a new process or system has been approved, a project team is assembled, consisting of representatives of the end-users who requested it and the IT personnel who will design and build the software components that will support it.

    e. Upper management supports process design by making sufficient resources available to ensure successful implementation of the new process.

    f. If the new process or system crosses organizational boundaries, as is the case with electronic data interchange (EDI) systems, external parties, such as representatives of the vendor or customer businesses, are participants.

4. **Build or Buy**

    a. When an organization acquires a new system by purchasing from an outside vendor, contract management personnel oversee the process. The future end-users of the system as well as IT personnel are also involved, drawing up specifications and requirements.

        1) However, when a new system is to be created in-house, planning and managing the development process is one of the IT function's most important tasks.

        2) The needs of the end-users must be balanced with budget and time constraints; the decision to use existing hardware vs. the purchase of new platforms must be weighed.

    b. Extensive time and resources are devoted to the creation of a new application, and generally, the more important the business function being automated, the more complex the application is. Thus, having a well-governed methodology for overseeing the development process is vital and could lead to the development of a killer application.

        1) A **killer application** is one that is so useful that it may justify widespread adoption of a new technology.

c. Both the end-users who specified the new system's functionality and IT management who are overseeing the development process must approve progress toward the completion of the system at the end of each of the stages described below and on the following pages. This requirement for ongoing review and approval of the project is a type of implementation control.

5. **Systems Development Life Cycle (SDLC)**

    a. The SDLC approach is the traditional methodology applied to the development of large, highly structured application systems. A major advantage of the life-cycle approach is enhanced management and control of the development process. SDLC consists of the following five steps:

    1) **Systems strategy** requires understanding the organization's needs.
    2) **Project initiation** is the process by which systems proposals are assessed.
    3) **In-house development** is generally chosen for unique information needs.
    4) **Commercial packages** are generally chosen for common needs rather than developing a new system from scratch.
    5) **Maintenance and support** involves ensuring the system accommodates changing user needs.

6. The **phases and component steps of the traditional SDLC** can be described as follows:

    a. **Initiation, Feasibility, and Planning**

    1) The SDLC begins with recognizing there is a need for a new system, gaining an understanding of the situation to determine whether it is feasible to create a solution, and formulating a plan.

    b. **Requirements Analysis and Definition**

    1) A formal proposal for a new system is submitted to the IT steering committee, describing the need for the application and the business function(s) that it will affect.
    2) Feasibility studies are conducted to determine
        a) What technology the new system will require
        b) What economic resources must be committed to the new system
        c) How the new system will affect current operations
    3) The steering committee gives its go-ahead for the project.

    c. **System Design**

    1) Logical design consists of mapping the flow and storage of the data elements that will be used by the new system and the new program modules that will constitute the new system.
        a) Data flow diagrams and structured flowcharts are commonly used in this step.
        b) Some data elements may already be stored in existing databases. Good logical design ensures that they are not duplicated.
    2) Physical design involves planning the specific interactions of the new program code and data elements with the hardware platform (existing or planned for purchase) on which the new system will operate.
        a) Systems analysts are heavily involved in these two steps.

d. **Build and Development**

   1) The actual program code and database structures that will be used in the new system are written.
   2) Hardware is acquired and physical infrastructure is assembled.

e. **Testing and Quality Control**

   1) Debugging (the process of testing and resolving problems) is performed during system development with the intent of identifying errors or other defects. The job of testing is an iterative process because when one error is corrected, it can illuminate other errors or even create new ones. Testing determines whether the system

      a) Meets the requirements that guided its design and development
      b) Responds correctly to all kinds of inputs
      c) Performs its functions within an acceptable time
      d) Achieves the general result its stakeholders desire

   2) Although the number of possible tests to apply is almost limitless, developers cannot test everything. All testing uses strategy to select tests that are feasible for the available time and resources.

      a) Combinatorial test design identifies the minimum number of tests needed to get the coverage developers want.

   3) The following are various methods available to test systems:

      a) **Static testing** examines the program's code and its associated documentation through reviews, walkthroughs, or inspections but does not require the program to be executed.
      b) **Dynamic testing** involves executing programmed code with a given set of test cases.
      c) **White-box testing** tests internal structures or workings of a program, as opposed to the functionality exposed to the end-user.
      d) **Black-box testing** treats the software as a "black box," examining functionality without any knowledge of the source code.
      e) **Gray-box testing** involves having knowledge of internal data structures and algorithms for purposes of designing tests, while executing those tests at the user, or black-box, level.

   4) There are four levels of tests:

      a) **Unit testing** refers to tests that verify (1) the functionality of a specific section of code and (2) the handling of data passed between various units or subsystems components.
      b) **Integration testing** is any type of software testing that seeks to verify the interfaces between components against a software design. Integration testing works to expose defects in the interfaces and interaction between integrated components (modules).
      c) **System testing**, or end-to-end testing, tests a completely integrated system to verify that the system meets its requirements.
      d) **Acceptance testing** is conducted to determine whether the systems meets the organization's needs and is ready for release.

f. **Acceptance, Installation, and Implementation**
    1) User acceptance testing is the final step before placing the system in live operation.
        a) IT must demonstrate to the users that submitted the original request that the system performs the desired functionality.
        b) Once the users are satisfied with the new system, they acknowledge formal acceptance and implementation begins.
    2) Four strategies for converting to the new system can be used.
        a) With **parallel** operation, the old and new systems both are run at full capacity for a given period.
            i) This strategy is the safest. The old system is still producing output because the new system may have major problems. But it is also the most expensive and time-consuming.
        b) With **direct changeover** (direct cutover) conversion, the old system is shut down and the new one takes over processing at once.
            i) This is the least expensive and time-consuming strategy, but it is also the riskiest because the new system cannot be reverted to the original.
        c) Under **pilot** conversion, one branch, department, or division at a time is fully converted to the new system.
            i) Experience gained from each installation is used to benefit the next one. One disadvantage of this strategy is the extension of the conversion time.
        d) In some cases, **phased** conversion is possible. Under this strategy, one function of the new system at a time is placed in operation.
            i) For instance, if the new system is an integrated accounting application, accounts receivable could be installed, then accounts payable, cash management, materials handling, etc.
            ii) The advantage of this strategy is allowing the users to learn one part of the system at a time.
    3) Training and documentation are critical.
        a) The users must feel comfortable with the new system and have plenty of guidance available, either hard copy or online.
        b) Documentation consists of more than just operations manuals for the users. Layouts of the program code and database structures must also be available for the programmers who must modify and maintain the system.

g. **Operations and Maintenance**
    1) After a system becomes operational, the system should be monitored to ensure ongoing performance and continuous improvement.
    2) Systems follow-up or post-audit evaluation is a subsequent review of the efficiency and effectiveness of the system after it has operated for a substantial time (e.g., 1 year).

7. **Change Management**
    a. Failing to effectively manage changes in the IT environment can negatively affect system and service availability and the achievement of organizational objectives.
        1) A key characteristic of organizations with high-performing IT environments is effective change management.
    b. **Change management** is the processes executed within an organization's IT environment designed to manage the changes to **production systems** (e.g., enhancements, updates, incremental fixes, and patches). Furthermore, such changes should result in minimal impact on, and risk to, production systems.
    c. IT **components** subject to change management include
        1) Hardware (e.g., mainframes, servers, and workstations)
        2) Software (e.g., operating systems and applications)
        3) Information, data, and data structures (e.g., files and databases)
        4) Security controls (e.g., antivirus software and firewalls)
        5) Processes, policies, and procedures
        6) Roles and responsibilities (e.g., over authorization, authority to act, and access controls)
    d. Change management generally involves supervising IT functions such as
        1) Creation, modification, and/or implementation of infrastructure (e.g., equipment, software, networks, etc.)
        2) Programming enhancements
        3) System fixes and/or updates
        4) Data transfigurations
    e. Change management's primary IT objective is to ensure that change requests are processed on time, accurately, and competently.

8. **Effective Change Management**
    a. To be effective, change management **must** provide the organization's management with knowledge of the following:
        1) What is being changed, the reason(s) for the change, and when the change will occur
        2) How efficiently and effectively changes are implemented
        3) Problems caused by the changes and their severity
        4) Cost of the changes
        5) Benefits of the changes
    b. Ultimately, effective change management depends on implementing **effective controls**, including adequate management supervision, over the change management process.

SU 5: Workstations, Databases, and Applications

9. **Change Management Process**

    a. The primary **goal** of the change management process is to sustain and improve the organization's operations.

    b. To this effect, changes must be managed in a **repeatable, defined, and predictable** manner. Accordingly, the change management process typically includes the following steps:

    1) **Identify** the need for the change.
    2) **Prepare** for the change.

        a) Document and write step-by-step procedures on the

            i) Details of the change,
            ii) Test plan, and
            iii) Rollback plan (i.e., the plan implemented in the event of change failure).

        b) Submit the change procedures in the form of a change request.

    3) **Justify and obtain approval.** Review and assess the cost, benefits, and risks (including regulatory impact) of the change request.
    4) **Authorize.** Authorize, reject, or request more information about the change request, and prioritize change requests.
    5) **Schedule, coordinate, and implement.** Schedule and assign a change implementer and change tester, test the change in a preproduction environment, communicate the change to affected stakeholders, obtain final approval, and implement the requested change.
    6) **Verify and review.** Report lessons learned based on assessing whether

        a) The change was successful,
        b) The change process was followed,
        c) Variances existed between the planned and implemented change, and
        d) Compliance requirements (e.g., internal control, operations, and regulatory) were maintained.

    7) **Back out.** Back out the change if unsuccessful.
    8) **Close.** Close the change request and communicate with the affected stakeholders.
    9) **Publish.** Produce and release the change schedule.
    10) **Change processes.** Make improvements to the change management process.

    c. An organization can immediately improve its change management processes by implementing the following steps:

    1) Create a **tone at the top** for a culture of change management across the entire organization.
    2) Consistently **monitor** the number of unplanned outages because they are indicative of unauthorized change and ineffective change control.
    3) Define and enforce change **freeze and maintenance** windows to decrease the number of risky changes and unplanned outages.
    4) Use a **change success rate** as a change management performance indicator.
    5) Use **unplanned work** as a key indicator of the effectiveness of change management processes and controls.

10. **Risks and Controls**

    a. The **risks** resulting from ineffective change management include lost market opportunities, unsatisfactory product or service quality, and increased potential for fraud. The top **risk indicators** of ineffective change management are

    1) Unauthorized changes,
    2) Unplanned outages,
    3) Low change success rate,
    4) High number of emergency changes, and
    5) Delayed project implementation.

    b. Effective change management requires preventive, detective, and corrective controls to manage the risks associated with changes to production systems.

    1) **Preventive** controls include **segregation of duties** (e.g., the separation of preparer, tester, implementer, and approver roles), change authorization, and limiting persons who may update access to production data and production programs.

        a) **Users** (i.e., end users) should have the ability to update access for production data but not production programs.
        b) **Programmers** should not have the ability to update access for production data or production programs.

    2) **Detective** controls include monitoring, reconciling actual changes to approved changes, and assurance services performed by internal or external auditors.

    3) **Corrective** controls include post-implementation reviews.

11. **Role of Internal Auditors**

    a. Internal auditors assist in change management by

    1) Understanding the organization's IT objectives,
    2) Assisting in identifying risks to IT objectives,
    3) Assessing whether such risks are aligned with the organization's risk appetite and tolerances,
    4) Assisting in deciding the appropriate risk management response (e.g., avoid, accept, reduce, or share),
    5) Understanding the controls used to manage risks and carry out risk responses, and
    6) Promoting a culture of effective change management.

    b. Internal audit engagements associated with systems and application development include but are not limited to

    1) An access control review that evaluates whether controls are effective at preventing and detecting unauthorized access
    2) An application control review that evaluates whether application controls effectively manage related risks
    3) A source code review that evaluates whether the program's source code is effectively managed and controlled
    4) A system design review that evaluates whether the system to be developed meets business requirements
    5) A post-implementation review that evaluates whether the system or application meets expectations

12. Rapid Application Development

a. **Prototyping** is an alternative approach to application development. Prototyping involves creating a working model of the system requested, demonstrating it for the user, obtaining feedback, and making changes to the underlying code.

   1) This process repeats through several iterations until the user is satisfied with the system's functionality.
   2) Formerly, this approach was derided as being wasteful of resources and tending to produce unstable systems, but with vastly increased processing power and high-productivity development tools, prototyping can, in some cases, be an efficient means of systems development.

b. **Computer-aided software engineering (CASE)** applies the computer to software design and development.

   1) It provides the capacity to
      a) Maintain on the computer all of the system documentation, e.g., data flow diagrams, data dictionaries, and pseudocode (structured English);
      b) Develop executable input and output screens; and
      c) Generate program code in at least skeletal form.
   2) Thus, CASE facilitates the creation, organization, and maintenance of documentation and permits some automation of the coding process.

13. End-User vs. Centralized Computing

a. End-user computing (EUC) involves user-created or user-acquired systems that are maintained and operated outside of traditional information systems controls.

   1) Certain environmental control risks are more likely in EUC. They include copyright violations that occur when unauthorized copies of software are made or when software is installed on multiple computers.
   2) Unauthorized access to application programs and related data is another concern. EUC lacks physical access controls, application-level controls, and other controls found in mainframe or networked environments.
   3) Moreover, EUC may not have adequate backup, recovery, and contingency planning. The result may be an inability to recreate the system or its data.

b. Program development, documentation, and maintenance also may lack the centralized control found in larger systems.

   1) The risk of allowing end-users to develop their own applications is decentralization of control. These applications may not be reviewed by independent outside systems analysts and are not created using a formal development methodology. They also may not be subject to appropriate standards, controls, and quality assurance procedures.
      a) End-user applications may not receive the independent testing associated with traditional development.
      b) End-user applications may not be adequately documented to facilitate review.
      c) Segregation of duties is inadequate if the same person performs programmer and operator functions.
      d) End-user applications generally do not follow a structured and controlled application development and change management life cycle.
      e) Review and analysis of user needs may be insufficient when user and analyst functions are no longer separate.

SU 5: Workstations, Databases, and Applications

2) When end-users create their own applications and files, private information systems in which data are largely uncontrolled may proliferate. Systems may contain the same information, but EUC applications may update and define the data in different ways. Thus, determining the location of data and ensuring data consistency become more difficult.

3) The auditor should determine that EUC applications contain controls that allow users to rely on the information produced. Identification of applications is more difficult than in a traditional centralized computing environment because few people know about and use them. There are three steps that the auditor should take:

　　a) The first step is to discover their existence and their intended functions. One approach is to take an organization-wide inventory of major EUC applications. An alternative is for the auditors and the primary user (a function or department) to review major EUC applications.

　　b) The second step is risk assessment. EUC applications that represent high-risk exposures are chosen for audit, for example, because they support critical decisions or are used to control cash or physical assets.

　　c) The third step is to review the controls included in the applications chosen in the risk assessment.

c. In a personal computer setting, the user is often the programmer and operator. Thus, the protections provided by segregation of duties are eliminated.

d. The audit trail is diminished because of the lack of history files, incomplete printed output, etc.

e. In general, available security features for stand-alone machines are limited compared with those in a network.

f. Responsibility for the control of EUC exists at the organizational, departmental, and individual user levels. The end-user is directly responsible for security of equipment. Acquisition of hardware and software, taking equipment inventories, and strategic planning of EUC are organizational- and departmental-level responsibilities.

STOP & REVIEW

You have completed the outline for this subunit.
Study multiple-choice questions 13 through 20 beginning on page 177.

QUESTIONS

5.1 Workstations and Databases

1. Of the following, the greatest advantage of a database (server) architecture is

- A. Data redundancy can be reduced.
- B. Conversion to a database system is inexpensive and can be accomplished quickly.
- C. Multiple occurrences of data items are useful for consistency checking.
- D. Backup and recovery procedures are minimized.

Answer (A) is correct.
REQUIRED: The greatest advantage of a database architecture.
DISCUSSION: In a database system, storage structures are created that render the applications programs independent of the physical or logical arrangement of the data. Because separate files for different applications programs are unnecessary, data redundancy can be substantially reduced.
Answer (B) is incorrect. Conversion to a database is often costly and time consuming. **Answer (C) is incorrect.** A traditional flat-file system, not a database, has multiple occurrences of data items. **Answer (D) is incorrect.** Given the absence of data redundancy and the quick propagation of data errors throughout applications, backup and recovery procedures are just as critical in a database as in a flat-file system.

2. A file-oriented approach to data storage requires a primary record key for each file. Which of the following is a primary record key?

- A. The vendor number in an accounts payable master file.
- B. The vendor number in a closed purchase order transaction file.
- C. The vendor number in an open purchase order master file.
- D. All of the answers are correct.

Answer (A) is correct.
REQUIRED: The item(s) used as a primary record key.
DISCUSSION: The primary record key uniquely identifies each record in a file. Because there is only one record for each vendor in an accounts payable master file, the vendor number would be the appropriate key.
Answer (B) is incorrect. Purchase order files can have multiple purchase orders made out to the same vendor. The primary key in purchase order files would be the purchase order number because it is the only unique identifier for the record. **Answer (C) is incorrect.** Purchase order files can have multiple purchase orders made out to the same vendor. The primary key in purchase order files would be the purchase order number because it is the only unique identifier for the record. **Answer (D) is incorrect.** Not all of the answer choices are correct.

3. In an inventory system on a database management system (DBMS), one stored record contains part number, part name, part color, and part weight. These individual items are called

- A. Fields.
- B. Stored files.
- C. Bytes.
- D. Occurrences.

Answer (A) is correct.
REQUIRED: The term for the data elements in a record.
DISCUSSION: A record is a collection of related data items (fields). A field (data item) is a group of characters representing one unit of information.
Answer (B) is incorrect. A file is a group or set of related records ordered to facilitate processing. **Answer (C) is incorrect.** A byte is a group of bits (binary digits). It represents one character. **Answer (D) is incorrect.** Occurrences is not a meaningful term in this context.

4. In a database system, locking of data helps preserve data integrity by permitting transactions to have control of all the data needed to complete the transactions. However, implementing a locking procedure could lead to

A. Inconsistent processing.
B. Rollback failures.
C. Unrecoverable transactions.
D. Deadly embraces (retrieval contention).

Answer (D) is correct.
REQUIRED: The potential problem of a locking procedure.
DISCUSSION: In a distributed processing system, the data and resources a transaction may update or use should be held in their current status until the transaction is complete. A deadly embrace occurs when two transactions need the same resource at the same time.
Answer (A) is incorrect. Inconsistent processing occurs when a transaction has different effects depending on when it is processed. Data locking ensures consistent processing. **Answer (B) is incorrect.** Rollback failure is the inability of the software to undo the effects of a transaction that could not be run to completion. A rollback failure is not caused by data locking. However, data locking may lead to situations in which rollback is required. **Answer (C) is incorrect.** Unrecoverable transactions are not a typical symptom of locking procedures.

5. Which of the following should **not** be the responsibility of a database administrator?

A. Design the content and organization of the database.
B. Develop applications to access the database.
C. Protect the database and its software.
D. Monitor and improve the efficiency of the database.

Answer (B) is correct.
REQUIRED: The item not the responsibility of a database administrator.
DISCUSSION: The database administrator (DBA) is the person who has overall responsibility for developing and maintaining the database. One primary responsibility is designing the content of the database. Another responsibility of the DBA is to protect and control the database. A third responsibility is to monitor and improve the efficiency of the database. The responsibility of developing applications to access the database belongs to systems analysts and programmers.
Answer (A) is incorrect. Designing the content and organization of the database is a responsibility of the database administrator. **Answer (C) is incorrect.** Protecting the database and its software is a responsibility of the database administrator. **Answer (D) is incorrect.** Monitoring and improving the efficiency of the database is a responsibility of the database administrator.

6. Which of the following outcomes is a likely benefit of information technology used for internal control?

A. Processing of unusual or nonrecurring transactions.
B. Enhanced timeliness of information.
C. Potential loss of data.
D. Recording of unauthorized transactions.

Answer (B) is correct.
REQUIRED: The benefit from using information technology.
DISCUSSION: The use of information technology typically increases the timeliness of information. Transactions are often recorded in real time, and information is available almost instantaneously.
Answer (A) is incorrect. Technology is most useful to process numerous, routine transactions. **Answer (C) is incorrect.** Technology allows the capture of many attributes of transactions and typically increases the availability of information. **Answer (D) is incorrect.** The possibility of recording unauthorized transactions would not be considered a benefit of technology.

7. Which of the following is a primary function of a database management system (DBMS)?

A. Report customization.
B. Capability to create and modify the database.
C. Financial transactions input.
D. Database access authorizations.

Answer (B) is correct.
REQUIRED: The primary function of a database management system.
DISCUSSION: A database management system (DBMS) is an integrated set of software tools superimposed on the data files that helps maintain the integrity of the underlying database. It allows programmers and designers to work independently of the physical and logical structure of the database. With a DBMS, the physical structure of the database can be completely altered without having to change any of the programs using the data items.
Answer (A) is incorrect. Although report customization may be an aspect of a DBMS, it is not the primary function. **Answer (C) is incorrect.** Financial transactions input would be accomplished through the transaction processing system. **Answer (D) is incorrect.** The database administrator, not the database management system, is responsible for providing database access authorizations.

8. Information technology (IT) strategy is determined by

A. Business needs.
B. Individual department needs.
C. The technology available.
D. Competitors' strategies.

Answer (A) is correct.
REQUIRED: The item that determines information technology strategy formulation.
DISCUSSION: Information systems (IS) and IT are vital to the successful implementation of an organization's strategy. IT strategy should be driven by the business needs and not by the functions of available technology when formulating a plan to achieve goals.
Answer (B) is incorrect. Individual departments may function well in terms of their own goals but still not serve the goals of the organization. **Answer (C) is incorrect.** Technology is vital to the successful implementation of an organization's strategy. IS infrastructure purchases need to be implemented in accordance with the IT strategic plan to ensure business needs are met. **Answer (D) is incorrect.** Although being familiar with the strategies of competitors is useful, strategy should be driven by the business's needs. Competitors' strengths and weaknesses may differ from those of the business.

9. Which of the following statements is **not** indicative of governance, risk, and compliance (GRC) systems?

A. GRC systems are associated with monitoring controls.
B. Federal and local government rules are considered when implementing GRC systems.
C. GRC systems are not tasked with identifying the source of risks.
D. GRC systems enable organizations to manage the governance program strategy.

Answer (C) is correct.
REQUIRED: The functionality of governance, risk, and compliance (GRC) systems.
DISCUSSION: GRC systems assist management with monitoring, evaluating, and enforcing policies, standards, and procedures established to ensure compliance. GRC systems assist with the identification of the roles of management and who owns each risk, controls risk content, and approves those risks.
Answer (A) is incorrect. Risk management, control monitoring, and information sharing are some of the characteristics associated with GRC systems. **Answer (B) is incorrect.** Compliance with laws and regulations is a characteristic of successful GRC systems. **Answer (D) is incorrect.** GRC systems enable organizations to manage the governance program strategy.

10. Which of the following is (are) a type(s) of business strategy(ies)?

A. Corporate-level strategy.
B. Business-level strategy.
C. Functional-level strategy.
D. All are types of strategies.

Answer (D) is correct.
REQUIRED: The item(s) that is (are) a type of business strategy.
DISCUSSION: Organizations generally develop strategies at three different levels. Corporate-level strategy is concerned with market definition (i.e., business and markets to focus resources). Business-level strategy applies to organizations that have independent business units that each develop their own strategy. Functional-level strategy concentrates on a specific functional area of the organization such as treasury, information systems, human resources, and operations.
Answer (A) is incorrect. Corporate-level strategy is concerned with market definition (i.e., business and markets to focus resources). **Answer (B) is incorrect.** Business-level strategy applies to organizations that have independent business units that each develop their own strategy. **Answer (C) is incorrect.** Functional-level strategy concentrates on a specific functional area of the organization such a treasury, information systems, human resources, and operations.

11. Which of the following is (are) true about strategic drivers that help determine the outcome of an organization's strategy?

1. New technologies create opportunities for improvement and competitive advantage.
2. Customer relationship management (CRM) is a term that refers to practices, strategies, and technologies that companies use to manage and analyze customer interactions and data throughout the customer lifecycle.
3. Information systems (IS) has become a strategic driver in most, if not all, organizations.

A. 1 only.
B. 2 only.
C. 3 only.
D. 1, 2, and 3.

Answer (D) is correct.
REQUIRED: The true statement(s) about strategic drivers that help determine the outcome of an organization's strategy.
DISCUSSION: Strategic drivers are the critical elements that help determine the success or failure of an organization's strategy. New technologies create opportunities for improvement and competitive advantage. Customer relationship management (CRM) is a term that refers to practices, strategies, and technologies that companies use to manage and analyze customer interactions and data throughout the customer lifecycle. IS has become a strategic driver in most, if not all, organizations.

12. Governance, risk, and compliance (GRC) systems are representative of all of the following statements **except**

A. GRC systems enable organizations to implement governance programs.
B. GRC systems concentrate on an individual function within an organization.
C. GRC systems assist with compliance with government requirements.
D. GRC systems have the potential of identifying and lowering costs.

Answer (B) is correct.
REQUIRED: The characteristics associated with governance, risk, and compliance (GRC) systems.
DISCUSSION: A characteristic of successful GRC systems is that information cascades throughout the organization, improving various functions. Thus, GRC systems concentrate on multiple functions within an organization.
Answer (A) is incorrect. GRC systems enable organizations to manage the governance program strategy. GRC systems assist management with monitoring, evaluating, and enforcing policies, standards, and procedures established to ensure compliance. **Answer (C) is incorrect.** A characteristic of successful GRC systems is compliance with laws and regulations. **Answer (D) is incorrect.** A characteristic of successful GRC systems is increasing the efficiency and effectiveness of business operations while reducing costs.

5.2 Application Development and Maintenance

13. An insurance firm that follows the systems development life cycle concept for all major information system projects is preparing to start a feasibility study for a proposed underwriting system. Some of the primary factors the feasibility study should include are

A. Possible vendors for the system and their reputation for quality.
B. Exposure to computer viruses and other intrusions.
C. Methods of implementation, such as parallel or cutover.
D. Technology and related costs.

Answer (D) is correct.
REQUIRED: The primary factors the feasibility study should include.
DISCUSSION: The feasibility study should consider the activity to be automated, the needs of the user, the type of equipment required, the cost, and the potential benefit to the specific area and the company in general. Thus, technical feasibility and cost are determined during this stage.
Answer (A) is incorrect. Possible vendors for the system and their reputation for quality would be determined after the feasibility study. **Answer (B) is incorrect.** Exposure to computer viruses and other intrusions is part of the information requirements phase. **Answer (C) is incorrect.** Methods of implementation, such as parallel or cutover, would be determined during the implementation and operations stage.

14. Responsibility for the control of end-user computing (EUC) exists at the organizational, departmental, and individual user level. Which of the following should be a direct responsibility of the individual users?

A. Acquisition of hardware and software.
B. Taking equipment inventories.
C. Strategic planning of end-user computing.
D. Physical security of equipment.

Answer (D) is correct.
REQUIRED: The direct responsibility of an individual user.
DISCUSSION: EUC involves user-created or user-acquired systems that are maintained and operated outside of traditional information systems controls. In this environment, an individual user is ordinarily responsible for the physical security of the equipment (s)he uses.
Answer (A) is incorrect. The acquisition of hardware and software is an organizational- and departmental-level responsibility. **Answer (B) is incorrect.** Taking equipment inventories is an organizational-level responsibility. **Answer (C) is incorrect.** Strategic planning is an organizational- and departmental-level responsibility.

15. Which of the following risks is more likely to be encountered in an end-user computing (EUC) environment as compared with a centralized environment?

A. Inability to afford adequate uninterruptible power supply systems.
B. User input screens without a graphical user interface (GUI).
C. Applications that are difficult to integrate with other information systems.
D. Lack of adequate utility programs.

Answer (C) is correct.
REQUIRED: The risk more likely to be encountered in an EUC environment.
DISCUSSION: The risks arising from allowing end users to develop their own applications are the risks associated with decentralization of control. These applications may lack appropriate standards, controls, and quality assurance procedures.
Answer (A) is incorrect. Inability to afford adequate uninterruptible power supply systems is a risk in all computing environments. **Answer (B) is incorrect.** Almost all EUC environments have some form of GUI. **Answer (D) is incorrect.** Lack of adequate utility programs is a risk in all computing environments.

16. The process of learning how the current system functions, determining the needs of users, and developing the logical requirements of a proposed system is referred to as

A. Systems maintenance.
B. Systems analysis.
C. Systems feasibility study.
D. Systems design.

Answer (B) is correct.
REQUIRED: The item that refers to learning how a system functions, determining the needs of users, and developing the logical requirements of a proposed system.
DISCUSSION: A systems analysis requires a survey of the existing system, the organization itself, and the organization's environment to determine (among other things) whether a new system is needed. The survey results determine not only what, where, how, and by whom activities are performed but also why, how well, and whether they should be done at all. Ascertaining the problems and informational needs of decision makers is the next step. The systems analyst must consider the entity's key success variables (factors that determine its success or failure), the decisions currently being made and those that should be made, the factors important in decision making (timing, relation to other decisions, etc.), the information needed for decisions, and how well the current system makes those decisions. Finally, the systems analysis should establish the requirements of a system that will meet user needs.
Answer (A) is incorrect. Maintenance is the final stage of the life cycle in that it continues throughout the life of the system; maintenance includes the redesign of the system and programs to meet new needs or to correct design flaws. **Answer (C) is incorrect.** The systems feasibility study does not involve the process of learning how the current system works. **Answer (D) is incorrect.** Systems design is the process of developing a system to meet specified requirements.

17. The process of monitoring, evaluating, and modifying a system as needed is referred to as

A. Systems analysis.
B. Systems feasibility study.
C. Systems maintenance.
D. Systems implementation.

Answer (C) is correct.
REQUIRED: The term for the process of monitoring, evaluating, and modifying a system.
DISCUSSION: Systems maintenance must be undertaken by systems analysts and applications programmers continuously throughout the life of a system. Maintenance is the redesign of the system and programs to meet new needs or to correct design flaws. Ideally, these changes should be made as part of a regular program of preventive maintenance.
Answer (A) is incorrect. Systems analysis is the process of determining user problems and needs, surveying the organization's present system, and analyzing the facts. **Answer (B) is incorrect.** A feasibility study determines whether a proposed system is technically, operationally, and economically feasible. **Answer (D) is incorrect.** Systems implementation involves training and educating system users, testing, conversion, and follow-up.

18. A benefit of using computer-aided software engineering (CASE) technology is that it can ensure that

A. No obsolete data fields occur in files.
B. Users become committed to new systems.
C. All programs are optimized for efficiency.
D. Data integrity rules are applied consistently.

Answer (D) is correct.
REQUIRED: The benefit of CASE.
DISCUSSION: CASE is an automated technology (at least in part) for developing and maintaining software and managing projects. A benefit of using CASE technology is that it can ensure that data integrity rules, including those for validation and access, are applied consistently across all files.
Answer (A) is incorrect. Obsolete data fields must be recognized by developers or users. Once recognized, obsolete data fields can be treated consistently in CASE procedures. **Answer (B) is incorrect.** Using CASE will not ensure user commitment to new systems if they are poorly designed or otherwise do not meet users' needs. **Answer (C) is incorrect.** Although it has the potential to accelerate system development, CASE cannot ensure that all programs are optimized for efficiency. In fact, some CASE-developed modules may need to be optimized by hand to achieve acceptable performance.

19. Change control typically includes procedures for separate libraries for production programs and for test versions of programs. The reason for this practice is to

A. Promote efficiency of system development.
B. Segregate incompatible duties.
C. Facilitate user input on proposed changes.
D. Permit unrestricted access to programs.

Answer (B) is correct.
REQUIRED: The reason for having separate libraries for production programs and for test versions of programs.
DISCUSSION: Separating production and test versions of programs ensures operators use the programs to fulfill their everyday responsibilities and do not have access to change programs. The effect is to segregate the incompatible functions of operators and programmers.
Answer (A) is incorrect. Production and test programs can be separated only if a specific procedure exists for placing programs in production libraries. Thus, maintaining the separation requires its own procedure, which may decrease development efficiency. **Answer (C) is incorrect.** Separating production and test versions of programs is independent of facilitating user input on proposed changes. **Answer (D) is incorrect.** Separating production and test versions of programs restricts access to programs.

20. A company often revises its production processes. The changes may entail revisions to processing programs. Ensuring that changes have a minimal impact on processing and result in minimal risk to the system is a function of

A. Security administration.
B. Change control.
C. Problem tracking.
D. Problem-escalation procedures.

Answer (B) is correct.
REQUIRED: The approach to ensure changes have a minimal impact on processing.
DISCUSSION: Change control is the process of authorizing, developing, testing, and installing coded changes so as to minimize the impact on processing and the risk to the system.
Answer (A) is incorrect. Security administration is concerned with access to data. **Answer (C) is incorrect.** Problem tracking is concerned with collecting data to be analyzed for corrective action. **Answer (D) is incorrect.** Problem escalation-procedures are a means of categorizing problems so that the least-skilled person can address them.

Access the **Gleim CIA Premium Review System** featuring our SmartAdapt technology from your Gleim Personal Classroom to continue your studies. You will experience a personalized study environment with exam-emulating multiple-choice questions.

STUDY UNIT SIX
IT INFRASTRUCTURE

(19 pages of outline)

6.1	Functional Areas of IT Operations	182
6.2	Web Infrastructure	184
6.3	IT System Communications and Software Licensing	188
6.4	Systems that Support Routine Processes	197

This study unit is the second of four covering **Domain III: Information Technology** from The IIA's CIA Exam Syllabus. This domain makes up 20% of Part 3 of the CIA exam and is tested at the **basic** cognitive level. Refer to the complete syllabus located in Appendix A to view the relevant sections covered in Study Unit 6.

6.1 FUNCTIONAL AREAS OF IT OPERATIONS

> **SUCCESS TIP**
>
> In the early days of computing, maintaining a rigid segregation of duties was a simple matter because the roles surrounding a mainframe computer were so specialized. As IT became more and more decentralized over the years, clear lines that once separated jobs such as systems analyst and programmer blurred and then disappeared. Candidates for the CIA exam must be aware of the evolving roles of IT personnel.

1. **Segregation of Duties**
   a. Organizational controls concern the proper segregation of duties and responsibilities within the information systems department.
   b. Controls should ensure the efficiency and effectiveness of IT operations. They include proper segregation of the duties within the IT environment. Thus, the responsibilities of systems analysts, programmers, operators, file librarians, the control group, and others should be assigned to different individuals, and proper supervision should be provided.
   c. Segregation of duties is vital because a traditional segregation of responsibilities for authorization, recording, and access to assets may not be feasible in an IT environment.
      1) For example, a computer may print checks, record disbursements, and generate information for reconciling the account balance, which are activities customarily segregated in a manual system.
         a) If the same person provides the input and receives the output for this process, a significant control weakness exists. Accordingly, certain tasks should not be combined.
         b) Thus, compensating controls may be necessary, such as library controls, computer logs, effective supervision, and rotation of personnel. Segregating test programs makes concealment of unauthorized changes in production programs more difficult.

2. **Responsibilities of IT Personnel**
   a. **Systems analysts** are specifically qualified to analyze and design computer information systems. They survey the existing system, analyze the organization's information requirements, and design new systems to meet those needs. The design specifications guide the preparation of specific programs by computer programmers.
      1) Because systems analysts may be able to modify programs, controls, and data files, systems analysts should not have access to data center operations, production programs, or data files.
   b. The **database administrator (DBA)** is the individual who has overall responsibility for developing and maintaining the database and for establishing controls to protect its integrity.
   c. **Programmers** design, write, test, and document the specific programs according to specifications developed by the systems analysts.
      1) Programmers may be able to modify programs, data files, and controls. Thus, they should have no access to the data center operations, production programs, or data files.
   d. The **webmaster** is responsible for the content of the organization's website. (S)he works closely with programmers and network technicians to ensure that the appropriate content is displayed and that the site is reliably available to users.

e. **Operators** are responsible for the day-to-day functioning of the data center, whether the organization runs a mainframe, servers, or anything else.

   1) Operators load data, mount storage devices, and operate the equipment. Operators should not be assigned programming duties or responsibility for systems design. Accordingly, they also should have no opportunity to make changes in programs and systems as they operate the equipment.

      a) Ideally, computer operators should not have programming knowledge or access to documentation not strictly necessary for their work.

f. **Help desks** are usually a responsibility of computer operations because of the operational nature of their functions. Help desk personnel log reported problems, resolve minor problems, and forward more difficult problems to the appropriate information systems resources, such as a technical support unit or vendor assistance.

g. **Information security officers** are typically in charge of developing information security policies, commenting on security controls in new applications, and monitoring and investigating unsuccessful login attempts.

h. **Network technicians** maintain the bridges, hubs, routers, switches, cabling, and other devices that interconnect the organization's computers. They are also responsible for maintaining the organization's connection to other networks, such as the Internet.

i. **End users** must be able to change production data but not programs.

j. The **network administrator** manages data and network communication which includes, but is not limited to, managing local area networks (LANs), metropolitan area networks (MANs), wide area networks (WANs), Internet systems or other forms of data, and network communication.

   1) Network administrator responsibilities include installing network systems (e.g., switched networks, routed networks, and wireless networks), maintaining and upgrading network systems, and resolving network problems.

k. The **system administrator** is in charge of all the parts that make a computer function, such as hardware and software, data backup and recovery, and maintenance of the computer system.

   1) System administrator responsibilities overlap with network administrator responsibilities at times.

   2) System administrator responsibilities include installing and testing computer equipment network systems, resolving help desk requests, designing and upgrading systems and processes, and monitoring the system daily for potential problems.

You have completed the outline for this subunit.
Study multiple-choice questions 1 through 5 beginning on page 200.

STOP & REVIEW

6.2 WEB INFRASTRUCTURE

1. **Overview**
   a. The **Internet** is a network of networks all over the world. The Internet is descended from the original ARPANet, a product of the Defense Department's Advanced Research Projects Agency (ARPA), introduced in 1969.
      1) The idea was to have a network that could not be brought down during an enemy attack by bombing a single central location. ARPANet connected computers at universities, corporations, and government.
         a) In view of the growing success of the Internet, ARPANet was retired in 1990.
      2) A **network** is a collection of hardware devices that are interconnected so they can communicate among themselves. This allows different hardware to share software and communicate data.
         a) The Internet is an example of a network, but many offices have intranets through which office computers can communicate with other office computers.
   b. The Internet facilitates inexpensive communication and information transfer among computers, with gateways allowing mainframe computers to interface with personal computers.
      1) Very high-speed Internet backbones carry signals around the world and meet at network access points.
      2) Computer programs such as web-crawlers (spiders or bots) access and read information on websites.
   c. Most Internet users obtain connections through **Internet service providers (ISPs)** that in turn connect either directly to a backbone or to a larger ISP with a connection to a backbone.
      1) The topology of the backbone and its interconnections may once have resembled a spine with ribs connected along its length but is now almost certainly more like a fishing net wrapped around the world with many circular paths.
   d. The three main parts of the Internet are the servers that hold information, the clients that view the information, and the Transmission Control Protocol/Internet Protocol (TCP/IP) suite of protocols that connect the two.
   e. A **gateway** makes connections between dissimilar networks possible by translating between two or more different protocol families.
   f. A **bridge** joins two similar networks so that they look like one network.

2. **Mainframe Communication**
   a. Large mainframe computers dominated the electronic data processing field in its first decades. Mainframes were arranged so that all processing and data storage were done in a single, centralized location.
   b. Communication with the mainframe was accomplished with the use of dumb terminals, simple keyboard-and-monitor combinations with no processing power (i.e., no CPU) of their own.

3. **Increasing Decentralization**

    a. Improvements in technology have led to the increasing decentralization of information processing.

    1) The mainframe-style computer was the only arrangement available in the early days of data processing. International Business Machines (IBM) dominated the marketplace.

    2) Mainframes are still in use at large institutions, such as governments, banks, insurance companies, and universities. However, remote connections to them are usually through personal computers rather than through dumb terminals. This is known as terminal emulation.

    3) As minicomputers evolved, the concept of distributed processing arose.

        a) **Distributed processing** involves the decentralization of processing tasks and data storage and assigning these functions to multiple computers, often in separate locations.

        b) This allowed for a drastic reduction in the amount of communications traffic because data needed locally could reside locally.

    b. During the 1980s, personal computers and the knowledge needed to build information systems became widespread.

    1) In the early part of this period, the primary means of moving data from one computer to another was through the laborious process of copying the data to a diskette and physically carrying it to the destination computer.

    2) It was clear that a reliable way of wiring office computers together would lead to tremendous gains in productivity.

4. **Servers**

    a. A server is generally a dedicated computer or device that manages specific resources.

    1) A file server is a computer in a network that operates as a librarian.

    2) A web server hosts a website.

    3) An enterprise server manages computer programs that collectively serve the needs of an organization.

    b. One of the risks associated with having data centrally located is that data files may be subject to change by unauthorized users without proper documentation or any indication of who made the changes.

5. **Languages and Protocols**
    a. The Internet was initially restricted to email and text-only documents.
        1) In the 1980s, English computer scientist Tim Berners-Lee conceived the idea of allowing users to click on a word or phrase (a hyperlink) on their screens and having another document automatically be displayed.
        2) Berners-Lee created a simple coding mechanism called **Hypertext Markup Language (HTML)** to perform this function. He also created a set of rules called **Hypertext Transfer Protocol (HTTP)** to allow hyperlinking across the Internet rather than on just a single computer. He then created a piece of software, called a **browser**, that allowed users to read HTML from any brand of computer. The result was the **World Wide Web** (often simply called the Web).
        3) As the use of HTML and its successor languages spread, it became possible to display rich graphics and stream audio and video in addition to displaying text.
    b. **Extensible Markup Language (XML)** was developed by an international consortium and released in 1998 as an open standard usable with many programs and platforms.
        1) XML is a variation of HTML, which uses fixed codes (tags) to describe how web pages and other hypermedia documents should be presented.
        2) XML codes all information in such a way that a user can determine not only how it should be presented but also what it is; i.e., all computerized data may be tagged with identifiers.
        3) Unlike HTML, XML uses codes that are extensible, not fixed. Thus, if an industry can agree on a set of codes, software for that industry can be written that incorporates those codes.
        4) For example, XML allows the user to label the Uniform Product Code (UPC), price, color, size, etc., of goods so that other systems will know exactly what the tag references mean. In contrast, HTML tags would only describe how items are placed on a page and provide links to other pages and objects.
    c. **Extensible Business Reporting Language (XBRL)** for financial statements is the specification developed by an AICPA-led consortium for commercial and industrial entities that report in accordance with U.S. GAAP.
        1) XBRL is a variation of XML that decreases the costs of generating financial reports, reformulating information for different uses, and sharing business information using electronic media.
6. **Uses**
    a. With the explosive growth of the World Wide Web in the 1990s, new distribution channels opened up for businesses. Consumers could browse a vendor's catalog using the rich graphics of the Web, initiate an order, and remit payment, all from the comfort of their homes.
        1) An organization's presence on the Web is constituted in its website. The website consists of a home page, which is the first screen encountered by users, and subsidiary web pages (screens constructed using HTML or a similar language).

2) Every resource on the Web has a unique address, made up of alphanumeric characters, periods, and forward slashes, called a **uniform resource locator (URL)**. A URL is recognizable by any web-enabled device. An example is https://www.gleim.com. However, just because the address is recognizable does not mean it is accessible to every user; security is a major feature of any organization's website.

   a) **Domain names** are used in URLs to identify specific web pages.

      i) A domain name contains a descriptive suffix, e.g., .gov for governmental agencies, .com for commercial businesses, and .edu for educational institutions.

3) **Cookies** are small text files created by a website as a means of recognizing users and tracking their preferences and activity on the website.

b. An **intranet** permits sharing of information throughout an organization by applying Internet connectivity standards and web software (e.g., browsers) to the organization's internal network.

   1) An intranet addresses the connectivity problems of an organization with many types of computers. It is ordinarily restricted to those within the organization and to outsiders after appropriate identification.

   2) An **extranet** consists of the linked intranets of two or more organizations, for example, of a supplier and its customers. It typically uses the public Internet as its transmission medium but requires a password for access.

c. **Cloud computing** ("the cloud") provides on-demand access to resources that are on the Internet and may be shared by others.

   1) Advantages of using cloud computing include fast access to software, a reduced need for investment in IT infrastructure, and the ability to use "pay as you go" services.

   2) IT security in the cloud is potentially more difficult due to the convenience and ease of access to sensitive data provided by cloud computing services.

   3) There are three primary cloud services:

      a) **Infrastructure-as-a-Service (IaaS)**
      b) **Platform-as-a-Service (PaaS)**
      c) **Software-as-a-Service (SaaS)**

   4) Cloud computing also has benefited from the rise of smartphones and tablets.

      a) Because these devices have limited memory, personal data (e.g., pictures, contacts, etc.) may be stored on the cloud (to be retrieved later) so that memory can be available for application software.

You have completed the outline for this subunit.
Study multiple-choice questions 6 through 9 beginning on page 202.

STOP & REVIEW

6.3 IT SYSTEM COMMUNICATIONS AND SOFTWARE LICENSING

1. **Systems Software**

    a. Systems software performs the fundamental tasks needed to manage computer resources. The most basic piece of systems software is the operating system.

    b. An **operating system** is a combination of programs that coordinates the actions of a computer, including its peripheral devices and memory.

    1) z/OS is the most recent operating system for the IBM mainframe.
    2) Server operating systems include Unix, Linux, Microsoft Windows Server, and Apple MacOS X Server. Inherent networking capabilities are an important part of server operating systems.
    3) Microsoft Windows, Apple MacOS, and Linux are operating systems for desktop computers.

    c. **Controls** over operating systems are essential because they may affect the entire database.

    1) Those controls include

        a) Segregation of duties

            i) System programmers should not be allowed to perform applications programming.

        b) Testing before use
        c) Making back-out plans and implementing changes in off-hours
        d) Keeping detailed logs of all changes

    2) Other controls include error notification for failed hardware and detection of abnormalities.

    d. Internal auditors should review the controls over operating systems. They should monitor change procedures and determine whether

    1) System programmers have sufficient training.
    2) The operating system is up to date.
    3) An error tracking system exists.

    e. A computer program is a set of instructions that directs a computer to perform certain tasks and produce certain results.

f. **Utility programs** are sometimes called privileged software.
   1) Utilities perform basic data maintenance tasks, such as
      a) Sorting, e.g., arranging all the records in a file by invoice number;
      b) Merging, i.e., combining the data from two files into one; and
      c) Copying and deleting entire files.
   2) Utilities are extremely powerful.
      a) For instance, a utility program could be used to read a file that contains all user access codes for the network. A control feature to negate this vulnerability is to encrypt passwords before storing them in the file.
      b) In any case, the use of utility programs should be restricted to appropriate personnel, and each occurrence should be logged.
g. A **graphical user interface (GUI)** is a link to a system that allows users to use icons, buttons, windows, and menus rather than command words to initiate processing.
   1) GUIs simplify the process of moving data from one application to another (e.g., copying a chart from a spreadsheet and pasting the chart into a word processing document).

2. **Network Equipment**
   a. Networks consist of
      1) The hardware devices being connected and
      2) The medium through which the connection is made.
   b. **Client devices.** Devices of all sizes and functions (mainframes, laptop computers, personal digital assistants, MP3 players, printers, scanners, cash registers, ATMs, etc.) can be connected to networks.
      1) Connecting a device to a network requires a network interface card (NIC). The NIC allows the device to speak that particular network's "language," that is, its protocol.
      2) A development in the late 1990s called the thin client explicitly mimics the old mainframe-and-terminal model.
         a) A typical thin client consists merely of a monitor, a keyboard, and a small amount of embedded memory. The key is that it has no local hard drive.
         b) Essentially all processing and data storage is done on the servers. Just enough of an application is downloaded to the client to run it.
         c) An advantage of this architecture is the large amount of IT staff time and effort saved that formerly went to configuring and troubleshooting desktop machines. A disadvantage is that there must be 100% server availability for any work to be done by users.
         d) The thin client architecture has not been widely used because the cost of hard drives has continued to steadily decrease, defying predictions.

3. **Data and Network Communication**

   a. A **protocol** is a set of standards for message transmission among the devices on the network.

   b. A **network** consists of multiple connected computers at multiple locations. Computers that are electronically linked permit an organization to assemble and share transaction and other information among different physical locations.

   c. A **local area network (LAN)** connects devices within a single office or home or among buildings in an office park. The LAN is owned entirely by a single organization.

      1) The LAN is the network familiar to office workers all over the world. In its simplest form, it can consist of a few desktop computers and a printer.

      2) A **peer-to-peer network** operates without a mainframe or file server, but does processing within a series of personal computers.

         a) Very small networks with few devices can be connected using a peer-to-peer arrangement, where every device is directly connected to every other.

         b) Peer-to-peer networks become increasingly difficult to administer with each added device.

      3) The most cost-effective and easy-to-administer arrangement for LANs uses the client-server model.

         a) **Client-server networks** differ from peer-to-peer networks in that the devices play more specialized roles. Client processes (initiated by the individual user) request services from server processes (maintained centrally).

         b) In a client-server arrangement, **servers** are centrally located and devoted to the functions that are needed by all network users.

            i) Examples include mail servers (to handle electronic mail), application servers (to run application programs), file servers (to store databases and make user inquiries more efficient), Internet servers (to manage access to the Internet), and web servers (to host websites).

            ii) Whether a device is classified as a server is not determined by its hardware configuration but rather by the function it performs. A simple desktop computer can be a server.

         c) Technically, a **client** is any object that uses the resources of another object. Thus, a client can be either a device or a software program.

            i) In common usage, however, "client" refers to a device that requests services from a server. This understanding of the term encompasses anything from a powerful graphics workstation to a smartphone.

            ii) A client device normally displays the user interface and enables data entry, queries, and the receipt of reports. Moreover, many applications, e.g., word processing and spreadsheet software, run on the client computer.

SU 6: IT Infrastructure

- d) The key to the client-server model is that it runs processes on the platform most appropriate to that process while attempting to minimize traffic over the network.
    - i) This model is commonly referred to as the three-tiered architecture of **client**, **application**, and **database**.
    - ii) Because of the specialized roles, client-server systems often contain equipment from multiple vendors.
- e) Security for client-server systems may be more difficult than in a highly centralized system because of the numerous access points.

d. A **metropolitan area network (MAN)** connects devices across an urban area, for example, two or more office parks.
   1) This concept had limited success as a wire-based network, but it may be more widely used as a microwave network.

e. A **wide area network (WAN)** consists of a group of LANs operating over widely separated locations. A WAN can be either publicly or privately owned.
   1) WANs come in many configurations. The simplest consists of one desktop computer using a slow dialup line to connect to an Internet service provider.
   2) Publicly owned WANs, such as the public telephone system and the Internet, are available to any user with a compatible device. The assets of these networks are paid for by means other than individually imposed user fees.
      a) **Public-switched networks** use public telephone lines to carry data. This arrangement is economical, but the quality of data transmission cannot be guaranteed, and security is questionable.
   3) Privately owned WANs are profit-making enterprises. They offer fast, secure data communication services to organizations that do not wish to make their own large investments in the necessary infrastructure.
      a) **Value-added networks (VANs)** are private networks that provide their customers with reliable, high-speed, secure transmission of data.
         i) To compete with the Internet, these third-party networks add value by providing their customers with (a) error detection and correction services, (b) electronic mailbox facilities for EDI purposes, (c) EDI translation, and (d) security for email and data transmissions.
      b) **Virtual private networks (VPNs)** are a relatively inexpensive way to solve the problem of the high cost of leased lines.
         i) A company connects each office or LAN to a local Internet service provider and routes data through the shared, low-cost public Internet.
         ii) The success of VPNs depends on the development of secure encryption products that protect data while in transit.
      c) A **private branch exchange (PBX)** is a specialized computer used for both voice and data traffic.
         i) A PBX can switch digital data among computers and office equipment, e.g., printers, copiers, and fax machines. A PBX uses telephone lines, so its data transmission capacity is limited.

f. A **distributed network** connects multiple computers for communication and data transmission and enables each connected computer to process its own data.

4. **Classifying Networks by Protocol**

    a. As previously stated, a protocol is a set of standards for message transmission among the devices on the network.

    b. LAN Protocols

    1) **Ethernet** has been the most successful protocol for LAN transmission. The Ethernet design breaks up the flow of data between devices into discrete groups of data bits called "frames."

        a) Ethernet is described as following the "polite conversation" method of communicating.

            i) Each device "listens" to the network to determine whether another conversation is taking place, that is, whether the network is busy moving another device's message.

            ii) When the network is determined to be free of traffic, the device sends its message.

    c. Switched Networks

    1) As described on page 190, in a LAN, all the devices and all the transmission media belong to one organization.

        a) This single ownership of infrastructure assets plus the ability to unify all communication on a single protocol make for great efficiency and security.

    2) When communication must cross organizational boundaries or travel beyond a limited geographical range, this single ownership principle no longer applies. A WAN is the applicable model.

        a) A WAN, with its hundreds of users and much greater distances, could never function using the collision-detection-and-retransmission method of Ethernet. To overcome this, the technique called switching is used.

    3) Switching takes two basic forms:

        a) In circuit switching, a single physical pathway is established in the public telephone system, and that pathway is reserved for the full and exclusive use of the two parties for the duration of their communication.

            i) An example is an ordinary landline telephone call or a dial-up connection from a modem. This is obviously a slow and insecure alternative for data transmission.

        b) In packet switching, the data bits making up a message are broken into "packets" of predefined length. Each packet has a header containing the electronic address of the device for which the message is intended.

    4) **Switches** are the networking devices that read the address on each packet and send it along the appropriate path to its destination.

        a) A convenient analogy is a group of 18-wheelers loaded with new machinery destined for a remote plant site. The trucks leave the machinery vendor's factory headed to the destination.

            i) As each truck arrives at a traffic light, it stops while vehicles going in other directions pass through the intersection.

            ii) As the trucks arrive at the plant site, they are unloaded and the machinery is installed.

5) By allowing message flow from many different organizations to pass through common points, switches spread the cost of the WAN infrastructure.

   a) Frame relay and ATM (asynchronous transfer mode) are examples of fast packet switched network protocols.

d. Routed Networks

   1) Routers have more intelligence than hubs, bridges, or switches.

      a) Routers have tables stored in memory that tell them the most efficient path along which each packet should be sent.

      b) An analogy is the trucks leave the machinery vendor's factory with the same destination.

         i) As the trucks stop at each intersection, traffic cops redirect them down different routes depending on traffic conditions.

         ii) As the trucks arrive in unknown sequence at the plant site, they are held until the machinery can be unloaded in the correct order.

   2) Routing is what makes the Internet possible.

      a) **Transmission Control Protocol/Internet Protocol (TCP/IP)** is the suite of routing protocols that makes it possible to interconnect thousands of devices from dozens of manufacturers all over the world through the Internet.

      b) The use of Internet Protocol addresses **(IP addresses)** is the heart of Internet routing. It allows any device anywhere in the world to be recognized on the Internet through the use of a standard-format IP address.

         i) The most well-known version of IP address is the Internet Protocol version 4 (IPv4) address, also known as dotted-decimal addressing. Each of the four decimal-separated elements of the IPv4 address is a numeral ranging from 0 to 255, e.g., 128.67.11.25.

         ii) Due to the depletion of available IPv4 addresses, a new version of IP address, Internet Protocol version 6 (IPv6), was developed and has been slowly deployed. Each of the 8 colon-separated elements of the IPv6 address is a hexadecimal number ranging from 0000 to ffff, e.g., 5937:bc04:751c:2fc1:e628:fca8:7fe6:e79d.

      c) **Dynamic host configuration protocol (DHCP)** allows tremendous flexibility on the Internet by enabling the constant reuse of IP addresses.

         i) Routers generally have their IP addresses hardcoded when they are first installed. However, the individual client devices on most organizational networks are assigned an IP address by DHCP from a pool of available addresses every time they boot up.

e. Wireless Networks

1) The Wi-Fi family of protocols supports client devices within a radius of about 300 feet around a wireless router. This usable area is called a hot spot.

   a) Wi-Fi avoids the collisions inherent in Ethernet by constantly searching for the best frequency within its assigned range to use.

   b) Security was a problem in early incarnations of Wi-Fi. Later versions alleviated some of these concerns with encryption.

2) The Bluetooth standard operates within a much smaller radius of about 30 feet.

   a) This distance permits the creation of what has come to be called the personal area network (PAN), which is a network of devices for a single user.

   b) Bluetooth is considerably slower than Wi-Fi.

3) The WiMax standard uses microwaves to turn an entire city into a hot spot, reviving the old MAN model. The radius is about 10 miles, and it is generally faster than traditional Wi-Fi.

4) Radio-frequency identification (RFID) technology involves the use of a combined microchip with antenna to store data about a product, pet, vehicle, etc. Common applications include

   a) Inventory tracking
   b) Lost pet identification
   c) Tollbooth collection

5. **Network Topology**

   a. Network topologies are either physical or logical. Physical topology is the set of physical connection points between devices on a LAN or similar network. Logical topology describes the path data travel through the network.

   b. The following are the basic topology arrangements:

   1) A **bus** network has a main line, and each node is connected to the line. It is the simplest and most common method of networking computers.

      a) If a bus network is interrupted (e.g., Ethernet cable becomes unplugged or one device malfunctions), the access points on one side of the network cannot access the computers and other devices on the other side of the network.

   2) A **ring** network is arranged in a circle, so two paths for data are available. Thus, if an interruption occurs at one point, the data can travel in the opposite direction and still be received.

   3) In a **star** network, cable segments from each computer are connected to centralized components. If one computer becomes unplugged, the remaining computers are still connected to the network.

   4) In a **mesh** network, each computer is connected to every other computer by separate cabling. This configuration provides redundant paths throughout the network. If one cable fails, another will take over the traffic.

SU 6: IT Infrastructure

6. **Voice Communications**

   a. Voice communication channels differ from the data channels connecting the CPU and peripheral equipment. They are the communications media for transmitting voice signals and are classified according to their capacity.

      1) An example of a voiceband channel is a telephone line.
      2) Internet telephony, known as **voice-over IP (VoIP)**, is any transmission of two-way voice communication that uses the Internet for all or part of its path. This can be performed with

         a) Traditional telephone devices;
         b) Desktop computers equipped with a sound card, microphone, and speakers; or
         c) Terminals dedicated to this function.

   b. Voice recognition input devices are still another alternative to keyboard input. These systems compare the speaker's voice patterns with prerecorded patterns. Advanced systems now have large vocabularies and shorter training periods. They allow for dictation and are not limited to simple commands.

   c. A voice output device converts digital data into speech using prerecorded sounds.

   d. A cell phone uses radio waves to transmit voice and data through antennas in a succession of cells or defined geographic areas.

   e. Personal communications service(s) (PCS) is a cellular technology based on lower-power, higher-frequency radio waves. The cells (i.e., the geographic areas of signal coverage) must be smaller and more numerous, but the phones should be smaller and less expensive and be able to operate where other such devices cannot.

   f. Voicemail converts spoken messages from analog to digital form, transmits them over a network, and stores them on a disk. Messages are then converted back to analog form when the recipient listens to them. Afterward, they may be saved, forwarded, or deleted.

   g. Conducting an electronic meeting among several parties at remote sites is teleconferencing. It can be accomplished by telephone or electronic mail group communication software.

      1) Videoconferencing permits the conferees to see each other on video screens.
      2) These practices have grown in recent years as companies have attempted to cut their travel costs.

7. **Rights Pertaining to Software**
   a. Software is copyrightable, but a substantial amount is in the public domain. Networks of computer users may share such software.
      1) **Shareware** is software made available for a fee (usually with an initial free trial period) by the owners to users through a distributor (or websites or electronic bulletin board services).
   b. Software piracy is a problem for vendors. Any duplication of the software beyond what is allowed in the software license agreement is illegal.
      1) The best way to detect an illegal copy of application software is to compare the serial number on the screen with the vendor's serial number.
      2) Use of unlicensed software increases the risk of introducing computer viruses into the organization. Such software is less likely to have been carefully tested.
      3) To avoid legal liability, controls also should be implemented to prevent use of unlicensed software that is not in the public domain.
         a) A **software licensing agreement** permits a user to employ either a specified or an unlimited number of copies of a software product at given locations, at particular machines, or throughout the organization. The agreement may restrict reproduction or resale, and it may provide subsequent customer support and product improvements.
      4) Software piracy can expose an organization's personnel to both civil and criminal penalties. The Business Software Alliance (BSA) is a worldwide trade group that coordinates software vendors' efforts to prosecute the illegal duplication of software.
   c. Diskless workstations increase security by preventing the copying of software to a flash drive from a workstation. This control not only protects the company's interests in its data and proprietary programs but also guards against theft of licensed third-party software.
   d. To shorten the installation time for revised software in a network, an organization may implement electronic software distribution (ESD), which is the computer-to-computer installation of software on workstations.
      1) Instead of weeks, software distribution can be accomplished in hours or days and can be controlled centrally.
      2) Another advantage of ESD is that it permits the tracking of PC program licenses.

STOP & REVIEW

You have completed the outline for this subunit.
Study multiple-choice questions 10 through 15 beginning on page 203.

6.4 SYSTEMS THAT SUPPORT ROUTINE PROCESSES

> **BACKGROUND 6-1   Information Resources Management**
>
> The tremendous variety of forms that information systems can take and the diverse needs of users have led to the concept of information resources management (IRM), which takes a global view of the information holdings and needs of an organization. This view is promoted by the Information Resources Management Association of Hershey, PA (www.irma-international.org).

1. **Management Information System (MIS)**

    a. A MIS typically receives input from a transaction processing system, aggregates it, then reports it in a format useful to middle management in running the business. For this reason, MISs are often classified by function or activity, such as the following:

        1) Accounting: general ledger, accounts receivable, accounts payable, payroll processing, fixed asset management, and tax accounting. Other aspects of accounting information systems are described in item 2. below.

        2) Finance: capital budgeting, operational budgeting, and cash management

        3) Manufacturing: production planning, cost control, and quality control

        4) Logistics: inventory management and transportation planning

        5) Marketing: sales analysis and forecasting

        6) Human resources: projecting payroll, projecting benefits obligations, employment-level planning, and employee evaluation tracking

    b. These single-function systems, often called stovepipe systems because of their limited focus, are gradually being replaced by integrated systems that link multiple business activities across the enterprise.

        1) The most comprehensive integrated system is termed an enterprise resource planning (ERP) system (discussed in item 3. beginning on the next page).

2. **Accounting Information System (AIS)**

    a. An AIS is a subsystem of a MIS that processes routine, highly structured financial and transactional data relevant to managerial as well as financial accounting. An AIS is concerned with

        1) Transactions with external parties (e.g., customers, suppliers, governments, owners, and creditors) reflected in financial statements prepared in conformity with GAAP and

        2) The internal activities recorded in the cost accounting system and the preparation of related reports and analyses (e.g., production reports, pro forma financial statements, budgets, and cost-volume-profit analyses).

3. **Enterprise Resource Planning (ERP)**

   > **BACKGROUND 6-2   ERP**
   >
   > Because ERP software is costly and complex, it is usually installed only by the largest enterprises, although mid-size organizations are increasingly likely to buy ERP software. Major ERP packages include SAP ERP Central Component from SAP SE and Oracle e-Business Suite, PeopleSoft, and JD Edwards EnterpriseOne, all from Oracle Corp.

   a. ERP is intended to integrate enterprise-wide information systems by creating one database linked to all of an organization's applications.

      1) ERP subsumes traditional MISs.
      2) The illustration below contrasts the less integrated MIS with the more integrated ERP system.

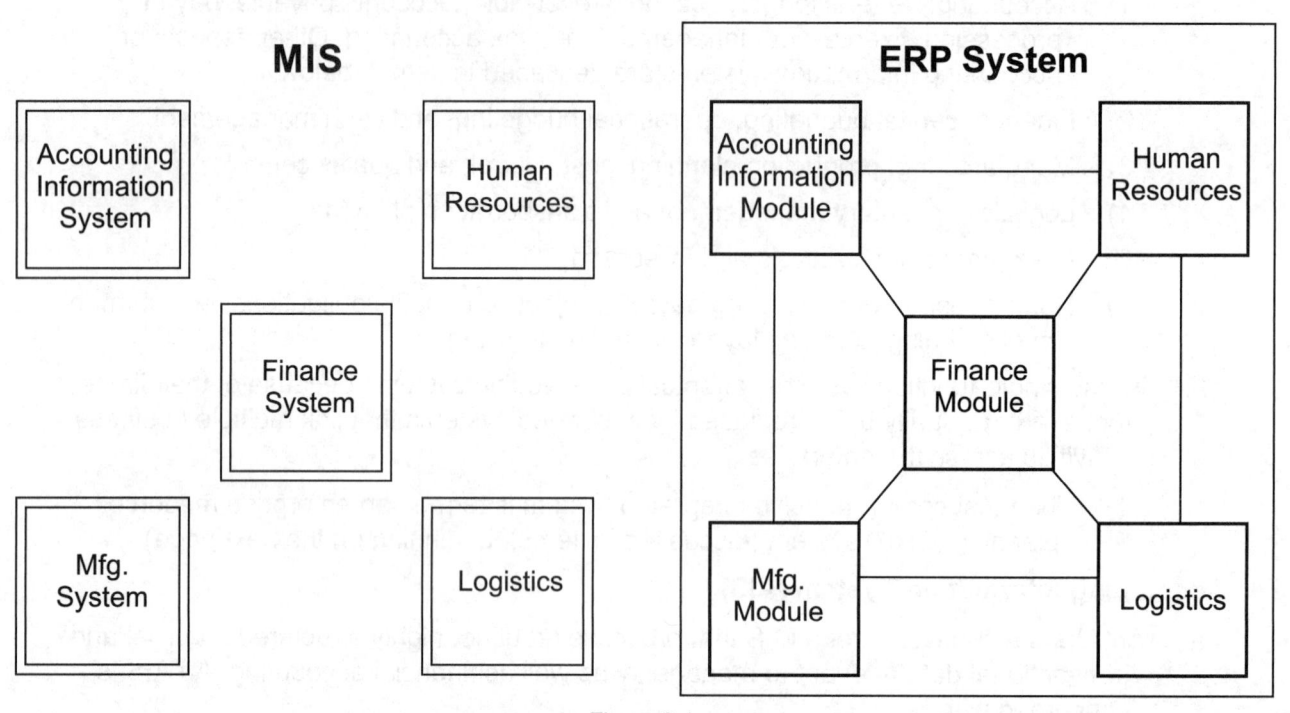

Figure 6-1

- b. In the traditional ERP system, subsystems share data and coordinate their activities. Thus, if sales receives an order, it can quickly verify that inventory is sufficient to notify shipping to process the order.
    1) Otherwise, production is notified to manufacture more of the product, with a consequent automatic adjustment of output schedules.
    2) If materials are inadequate for this purpose, the system will issue a purchase order.
    3) If more labor is needed, human resources will be instructed to reassign or hire employees.
    4) The foregoing business processes (and others) should interact seamlessly in an ERP system.
- c. The subsystems in a traditional ERP system are internal to the organization. Hence, they are often called **back-office functions**. The information produced is principally (but not exclusively) intended for **internal** use by the organization's managers.
- d. The current generation of ERP software has added **front-office functions**. These connect the organization with customers, suppliers, owners, creditors, and strategic allies (e.g., the members of a trading community or other business association).
    1) Moreover, the current generation of ERP software also provides the capability for smooth (and instant) interaction with the business processes of **external** parties.
    2) A newer ERP system's integration with the firm's back-office functions enables supply-chain management (SCM), customer relationship management (CRM), and partner relationship management (PRM).
- e. The disadvantages of ERP are its extent and complexity, which make implementation difficult and costly.
- f. Companies with legacy ERP systems are moving to cloud-based ERP systems. Advantages include
    1) Flexibility and agility of the cloud ERP's centralized data storage
    2) Sharing of data-processing tasks
    3) Internet-based access to services and resources

STOP & REVIEW

You have completed the outline for this subunit.
Study multiple-choice questions 16 through 22 beginning on page 206.

QUESTIONS

6.1 Functional Areas of IT Operations

1. For control purposes, which of the following should be organizationally segregated from the computer operations function?

A. Data conversion.
B. Surveillance of screen display messages.
C. Systems development.
D. Minor maintenance according to a schedule.

Answer (C) is correct.
REQUIRED: The activity that should be segregated from computer operations.
DISCUSSION: Systems development is performed by systems analysts and application programmers.
Answer (A) is incorrect. Data conversion may be assigned to computer operations. **Answer (B) is incorrect.** Surveillance of screen display messages may be assigned to computer operations. **Answer (D) is incorrect.** Minor maintenance according to a schedule may be assigned to computer operations.

2. An organization's computer help-desk function is usually a responsibility of the

A. Applications development unit.
B. Systems programming unit.
C. Computer operations unit.
D. User departments.

Answer (C) is correct.
REQUIRED: The entity in charge of a computer help desk.
DISCUSSION: Help desks are usually a responsibility of computer operations because of the operational nature of their functions. A help desk logs reported problems, resolves minor problems, and forwards more difficult problems to the appropriate information systems resources, such as a technical support unit or vendor assistance.
Answer (A) is incorrect. Applications development is responsible for developing systems, not providing help to end users. **Answer (B) is incorrect.** The responsibility of systems programming is to implement and maintain system-level software, such as operating systems, access control software, and database systems software. **Answer (D) is incorrect.** User departments usually lack the expertise to solve computer problems.

3. In a large organization, the biggest risk in not having an adequately staffed information center help desk is

A. Increased difficulty in performing application audits.
B. Inadequate documentation for application systems.
C. Increased likelihood of use of unauthorized program code.
D. Persistent errors in user interaction with systems.

Answer (D) is correct.
REQUIRED: The risk in not having an adequately staffed information center help desk.
DISCUSSION: The biggest risk in not having an adequately staffed help desk is that users will unknowingly persist in making errors in their interaction with the information systems.
Answer (A) is incorrect. Application audits should be about the same difficulty with or without an adequately staffed help desk. **Answer (B) is incorrect.** Preparation of documentation is a development function, not a help desk function. **Answer (C) is incorrect.** The likelihood of use of unauthorized program code is a function of change control, not of a help desk.

4. The practice of maintaining a test program library separate from the production program library is an example of

A. An organizational control.
B. Physical security.
C. An input control.
D. A concurrency control.

Answer (A) is correct.
REQUIRED: The type of control represented by separating the test and production program libraries.
DISCUSSION: This separation is an organizational control. Organizational controls concern the proper segregation of duties and responsibilities within the information systems department. Although proper segregation is desirable, functions that would be considered incompatible if performed by a single individual in a manual activity are often performed through the use of an information systems program or series of programs. Thus, compensating controls may be necessary, such as library controls, effective supervision, and rotation of personnel. Segregating test programs makes concealment of unauthorized changes in production programs more difficult.
Answer (B) is incorrect. Physical security (e.g., climate control and restrictions on physical access) is another aspect of organizational control. **Answer (C) is incorrect.** Input controls validate the completeness, accuracy, and appropriateness of input. **Answer (D) is incorrect.** Concurrency controls manage situations in which two or more programs attempt to use a file or database at the same time.

5. Which of the following terms best describes the type of control practice evidenced by a segregation of duties between computer programmers and computer operators?

A. Systems development control.
B. Hardware control.
C. Applications control.
D. Organizational control.

Answer (D) is correct.
REQUIRED: The type of control practice evidenced by a segregation of duties between computer programmers and computer operators.
DISCUSSION: Organizational control concerns the proper segregation of duties and responsibilities within the information systems function. For example, programmers should not have access to the equipment, and operators should not have programming ability. Although proper segregation is desirable, functions that would be considered incompatible if performed by a single individual in a manual activity are often performed through the use of an information systems program or series of programs. Therefore, compensating controls may be necessary, such as library controls and effective supervision.
Answer (A) is incorrect. Systems development controls concern systems analysis, design, and implementation. **Answer (B) is incorrect.** Hardware controls are incorporated into the equipment. **Answer (C) is incorrect.** Applications controls pertain to specific programs. They include input, processing, and output controls.

6.2 Web Infrastructure

6. Which of the following is true concerning HTML?

- A. The acronym stands for HyperText Material Listing.
- B. The language is among the most difficult to learn.
- C. The language is independent of hardware and software.
- D. HTML is the only language that can be used for Internet documents.

Answer (C) is correct.
REQUIRED: The true statement concerning HTML.
DISCUSSION: HTML is the most popular language for authoring web pages. It is hardware and software independent, which means that it can be read by several different applications and on many different kinds of computer operating systems. HTML uses tags to mark information for proper display on web pages.
Answer (A) is incorrect. HTML is the acronym for Hypertext Markup Language. **Answer (B) is incorrect.** The language is relatively easy to learn. Almost anyone can learn and use HTML, not just computer programmers. **Answer (D) is incorrect.** A number of other languages can be used for Internet transmissions, including Java and XML.

7. Using standard procedures developed by information center personnel, staff members download specific subsets of financial and operating data as they need it. The staff members analyze the data on their own personal computers and share results with each other. Over time, the staff members learn to modify the standard procedures to get subsets of financial and operating data that were not accessible through the original procedures. The greatest risk associated with this situation is that

- A. The data obtained might be incomplete or lack currency.
- B. The data definition might become outdated.
- C. The server data might be corrupted by staff members' updates.
- D. Repeated downloading might fill up storage space on staff members' personal computers.

Answer (A) is correct.
REQUIRED: The risk associated with downloading additional subsets of financial data.
DISCUSSION: Staff members may not be aware of how often they need to download data to keep it current, or whether their queries, especially the ones they modified, obtain all the necessary information. Users may employ faulty parameters or logic. Poorly planned queries may also use computing resources inefficiently.
Answer (B) is incorrect. Downloading data does not affect the data definitions. **Answer (C) is incorrect.** Staff members are downloading, not uploading, so the staff members are unlikely to corrupt server data. **Answer (D) is incorrect.** The downloading procedures could replace previously downloaded files on the staff members' personal computers.

8. The Internet consists of a series of networks that include

- A. Gateways to allow personal computers to connect to mainframe computers.
- B. Bridges to direct messages through the optimum data path.
- C. Repeaters to physically connect separate local area networks (LANs).
- D. Routers to strengthen data signals between distant computers.

Answer (A) is correct.
REQUIRED: The composition of the Internet.
DISCUSSION: The Internet facilitates information transfer among computers. Gateways are hardware or software products that allow translation between two different protocol families. For example, a gateway can be used to exchange messages between different email systems.
Answer (B) is incorrect. Routers are used to determine the best path for data. **Answer (C) is incorrect.** Bridges connect LANs. **Answer (D) is incorrect.** Repeaters strengthen signals.

SU 6: IT Infrastructure

9. In general, mainframe or server production programs and data are adequately protected against unauthorized access. Certain utility software may, however, have privileged access to software and data. To compensate for the risk of unauthorized use of privileged software, IT management can

A. Prevent privileged software from being installed on the mainframe.
B. Restrict privileged access to test versions of applications.
C. Limit the use of privileged software.
D. Keep sensitive programs and data on an isolated machine.

Answer (C) is correct.
REQUIRED: The best alternative information systems management can take to minimize unauthorized use of privileged software.
DISCUSSION: Since certain utility software may have privileged access to software and data stored on the mainframe or server, management must control the use of this utility software. Management should limit the use of this software to only those individuals with appropriate authority.
Answer (A) is incorrect. Privileged software may be needed to modify programs and data. **Answer (B) is incorrect.** Privileged access may be necessary to modify the final versions of applications. **Answer (D) is incorrect.** Authorized users must access sensitive programs and data through their workstations that are connected to the mainframe or server.

6.3 IT System Communications and Software Licensing

10. A local area network (LAN) is best described as a(n)

A. Computer system that connects computers of all sizes, workstations, terminals, and other devices within a limited proximity.
B. System to allow computer users to meet and share ideas and information.
C. Electronic library containing millions of items of data that can be reviewed, retrieved, and analyzed.
D. Method to offer specialized software, hardware, and data-handling techniques that improve effectiveness and reduce costs.

Answer (A) is correct.
REQUIRED: The best description of a LAN.
DISCUSSION: A LAN is a local distributed computer system, often housed within a single building. Computers, communication devices, and other equipment are linked by cable. Special software facilitates efficient data communication among the hardware devices.
Answer (B) is incorrect. A LAN is more than a system to allow computer users to share information. In addition, it is an interconnection of a computer system. **Answer (C) is incorrect.** A LAN is not a library. **Answer (D) is incorrect.** A LAN does not require specialized hardware.

11. Which of the following represents the greatest exposure to the integrity of electronic funds transfer data transmitted from a remote terminal?

A. Poor physical access controls over the data center.
B. Network viruses.
C. Poor system documentation.
D. Leased telephone circuits.

Answer (D) is correct.
REQUIRED: The greatest exposure to the integrity of EFT data transmitted from a remote terminal.
DISCUSSION: Leased telephone circuits represent a direct exposure to the risk of breached data integrity. They use public lines that can be easily identified and tapped.
Answer (A) is incorrect. Poor physical access controls represent a secondary exposure for compromise of remote data communications lines. **Answer (B) is incorrect.** Network viruses represent a secondary exposure for compromise of remote data communications lines. **Answer (C) is incorrect.** Poor system documentation represent a secondary exposure for compromise of remote data communications lines.

12. A type of network that is used to support interconnections within a building is known as a

A. Local area network.
B. Wide area network.
C. Metropolitan area network.
D. Value-added network.

Answer (A) is correct.
REQUIRED: The type of network that is used to support interconnections within a building.
DISCUSSION: A communication network consists of one or more computers and their peripheral equipment linked together. Local area networks (LANs) link together hardware and other equipment within a limited area such as a building so that users can share data and hardware devices.
Answer (B) is incorrect. Wide area networks consist of a conglomerate of LANs over widely separated locations. **Answer (C) is incorrect.** A metropolitan area network connects devices across an urban area. **Answer (D) is incorrect.** A value-added network is a type of privately owned WAN.

13. Which of the following would be the most appropriate starting point for a compliance evaluation of software licensing requirements for an organization with more than 15,000 computer workstations?

A. Determine if software installation is controlled centrally or distributed throughout the organization.
B. Determine what software packages have been installed on the organization's computers and the number of each package installed.
C. Determine how many copies of each software package have been purchased by the organization.
D. Determine what mechanisms have been installed for monitoring software usage.

Answer (A) is correct.
REQUIRED: The most appropriate starting point for a compliance evaluation of software licensing requirements in a large entity.
DISCUSSION: The logical starting point is to determine the point(s) of control. Evidence of license compliance can then be assessed. For example, to shorten the installation time for revised software in a network, an organization may implement electronic software distribution (ESD), which is the computer-to-computer installation of software on workstations. Instead of weeks, software distribution can be accomplished in hours or days and can be controlled centrally. Another advantage of ESD is that it permits tracking or metering of PC program licenses.
Answer (B) is incorrect. Before taking this step, an auditor should first determine whether installation is controlled centrally. This determination affects how the auditor will gather information about the installed software. **Answer (C) is incorrect.** This procedure helps an auditor determine whether software was legitimately purchased. However, a better starting point is determining where the software is installed. **Answer (D) is incorrect.** Monitoring usage is not as important as determining installation procedures when evaluating licensing compliance.

14. When two devices in a data communications system are communicating, there must be agreement as to how both data and control information are to be packaged and interpreted. Which of the following terms is commonly used to describe this type of agreement?

A. Asynchronous communication.
B. Synchronous communication.
C. Communication channel.
D. Communication protocol.

Answer (D) is correct.
REQUIRED: The agreement as to how both data and control information are to be packaged and interpreted.
DISCUSSION: A protocol is a set of formal rules or conventions governing communication between a sending and a receiving device. It prescribes the manner by which data are transmitted between these communications devices. In essence, a protocol is the envelope within which each message is transmitted throughout a data communications network.
Answer (A) is incorrect. Asynchronous communication is a mode of transmission. Communication is in disjointed segments, typically character by character, preceded by a start code and ended by a stop code. **Answer (B) is incorrect.** Synchronous communication is a mode of transmission in which a continuous stream of blocks of characters result in faster communications. **Answer (C) is incorrect.** A communication channel is a transmission link between devices in a network. The term is also used for a small processor that controls input-output devices.

15. Auditors often make use of computer programs that perform routine processing functions, such as sorting and merging. These programs are made available by computer companies and others and are specifically referred to as

A. Compiler programs.
B. Supervisory programs.
C. Utility programs.
D. User programs.

Answer (C) is correct.
REQUIRED: The term for programs used to perform routine functions.
DISCUSSION: Utility programs are provided by manufacturers of equipment to perform routine processing tasks required by both clients and auditors, such as extracting data, sorting, merging, and copying. Utility programs are pretested, are independent of the client's own programming efforts, and furnish useful information without the trouble of writing special programs for the engagement.
Answer (A) is incorrect. Compiler programs convert source programs written in a higher-level language into computer-readable object programs, i.e., into machine language. **Answer (B) is incorrect.** Supervisory programs, also termed operating systems, are master programs responsible for controlling operations within a computer system. **Answer (D) is incorrect.** User programs are those prepared for a particular application.

6.4 Systems that Support Routine Processes

16. An accounting information system (AIS) must include certain source documents in order to control purchasing and accounts payable. For a manufacturing organization, the best set of documents should include

A. Purchase requisitions, purchase orders, inventory reports of goods needed, and vendor invoices.

B. Purchase orders, receiving reports, and inventory reports of goods needed.

C. Purchase orders, receiving reports, and vendor invoices.

D. Purchase requisitions, purchase orders, receiving reports, and vendor invoices.

Answer (D) is correct.
REQUIRED: The best set of documents to be included in an AIS to control purchasing and accounts payable.
DISCUSSION: An AIS is a subsystem of a management information system that processes financial and transactional data relevant to managerial and financial accounting. The AIS supports operations by collecting and sorting data about an organization's transactions. An AIS is concerned not only with external parties but also with the internal activities needed for management decision making at all levels. An AIS is best suited to solve problems when reporting requirements are well defined. A manufacturer has well-defined reporting needs for routine information about purchasing and payables. Purchase requisitions document user department needs, and purchase orders provide evidence that purchase transactions were appropriately authorized. A formal receiving procedure segregates the purchasing and receiving functions and establishes the quantity, quality, and timeliness of goods received. Vendor invoices establish the liability for payment and should be compared with the foregoing documents.
Answer (A) is incorrect. Receiving reports should be included. **Answer (B) is incorrect.** Requisitions and vendor invoices should be included. **Answer (C) is incorrect.** Purchase requisitions should be included.

17. Which one of the following statements about an accounting information system (AIS) is **false**?

A. AIS supports day-to-day operations by collecting and sorting data about an organization's transactions.

B. The information produced by AIS is made available to all levels of management for use in planning and controlling an organization's activities.

C. AIS is best suited to solve problems where there is great uncertainty and ill-defined reporting requirements.

D. AIS is often referred to as a transaction processing system.

Answer (C) is correct.
REQUIRED: The false statement about an accounting information system (AIS).
DISCUSSION: An AIS is a subsystem of a management information system that processes financial and transactional data relevant to managerial and financial accounting. The AIS supports operations by collecting and sorting data about an organization's transactions. An AIS is concerned not only with external parties but also with the internal activities needed for management decision making at all levels. An AIS is best suited to solve problems when reporting requirements are well defined. A decision support system is a better choice for problems in which decision making is less structured.

18. The current generation of ERP software (ERP II) has added such front-office functions as

A. Inventory control.
B. Human resources.
C. Purchasing.
D. Customer service.

Answer (D) is correct.
REQUIRED: The front-office function addressed by ERP II.
DISCUSSION: The current generation of ERP software (ERP II) has added front-office functions. Customer relationship management applications in ERP II extend to customer service, finance-related matters, sales, and database creation and maintenance. Integrated data are helpful in better understanding customer needs, such as product preference or location of retail outlets. Thus, the organization may be able to optimize its sales forecasts, product line, and inventory levels.

19. A principal advantage of an ERP system is

A. Program-data dependence.
B. Data redundancy.
C. Separate data updating for different functions.
D. Centralization of data.

Answer (D) is correct.
REQUIRED: The principal advantage of an ERP system.
DISCUSSION: ERP integrates enterprise-wide information systems by creating one database linked to all of an organization's applications, resulting in the centralization of data.
Answer (A) is incorrect. An ERP system uses a central database and a database management system. A fundamental characteristic of a database is that applications are independent of the physical structure of the database. Writing programs or designing applications to use the database requires only the names of desired data items, not their locations. **Answer (B) is incorrect.** An ERP system eliminates data redundancy. **Answer (C) is incorrect.** An ERP system is characterized by one-time data updating for all organizational functions.

20. An enterprise resource planning (ERP) system has which of the following advantages over multiple independent functional systems?

A. Modifications can be made to each module without affecting other modules.
B. Increased responsiveness and flexibility while aiding in the decision-making process.
C. Increased amount of data redundancy since more than one module contains the same information.
D. Reduction in costs for implementation and training.

Answer (B) is correct.
REQUIRED: The advantage of an ERP system over multiple independent functioning systems.
DISCUSSION: ERP is the latest phase in the development of computerized systems for managing organizational resources. ERP is intended to integrate enterprise-wide information systems by creating one database linked to all of an organization's applications. The current generation of ERP software connects the organization with customers, suppliers, owners, creditors, and strategic allies. This increased integration allows for quicker response time and more flexibility.
Answer (A) is incorrect. In an ERP system, enterprise-wide information is integrated by creating one database linked to all of an organization's applications. Because of the integration, a change to one module will likely affect another. **Answer (C) is incorrect.** ERP is intended to integrate enterprise-wide information systems by creating one database linked to all of an organization's applications. This reduces data redundancy. **Answer (D) is incorrect.** The disadvantages of ERP are its extent and complexity, which make implementation difficult and costly.

21. In a traditional ERP system, the receipt of a customer order may result in

1. Customer tracking of the order's progress
2. Automatic issue of a purchase order
3. Hiring or reassigning of employees
4. Automatic adjustment of output schedules

A. 2, 3, and 4 only.
B. 1 and 3 only.
C. 3 and 4 only.
D. 1, 2, 3, and 4.

Answer (A) is correct.
REQUIRED: The possible effects of receipt of a customer order by a traditional ERP system.
DISCUSSION: The traditional ERP system is one in which subsystems share data and coordinate their activities. Thus, if marketing receives an order it can quickly verify that inventory is sufficient to notify shipping to process the order. Otherwise, production is notified to manufacture more of the product with a consequent automatic adjustment of output schedules. If materials are inadequate for this purpose the system will issue a purchase order. If more labor is needed human resources will be instructed to reassign or hire employees. However, the subsystems in a traditional ERP system are internal to the organization. Hence, they are often called back-office functions. The information produced is principally (but not exclusively) intended for internal use by the organization's managers.
The current generation of ERP software (ERP II) has added front-office functions. Consequently, ERP II, but not traditional ERP, is capable of customer tracking of the order's progress.
Answer (B) is incorrect. ERP II, but not traditional ERP, is capable of customer tracking of the order's progress. Additionally, traditional ERP can automatically issue a purchase order and adjust output schedules.
Answer (C) is incorrect. ERP II, but not traditional ERP, is capable of customer tracking of the order's progress. Additionally, if more labor is needed human resources will be instructed to reassign or hire employees. **Answer (D) is incorrect.** ERP II, but not traditional ERP, is capable of customer tracking of the order's progress.

22. An enterprise resource planning (ERP) system is designed to

A. Allow nonexperts to make decisions about a particular problem.
B. Help with the decision-making process.
C. Integrate data from all aspects of an organization's activities.
D. Present executives with the information needed to make strategic plans.

Answer (C) is correct.
REQUIRED: The primary function of an ERP system.
DISCUSSION: An ERP system is intended to integrate enterprise-wide information systems by creating one database linked to all of an organization's applications.
Answer (A) is incorrect. Problems should be solved by those individuals who are knowledgeable about the issue. **Answer (B) is incorrect.** An ERP system can help with the decision-making process. However, that is not what it is designed to do. **Answer (D) is incorrect.** An ERP system is more useful for day-to-day operations, not strategic management.

Access the **Gleim CIA Premium Review System** featuring our SmartAdapt technology from your Gleim Personal Classroom to continue your studies. You will experience a personalized study environment with exam-emulating multiple-choice questions.

STUDY UNIT SEVEN
IT FRAMEWORK AND DATA ANALYTICS

(27 pages of outline)

7.1	*IT Control Frameworks and International Organization for Standardization (ISO) Framework*	209
7.2	*Aspects of Automated Information Processing*	223
7.3	*IT Controls*	225
7.4	*Data Analytics*	230

This study unit is the third of four covering **Domain III: Information Technology** from The IIA's CIA Exam Syllabus. This domain makes up 20% of Part 3 of the CIA exam and is tested at the **basic** cognitive level. This study unit also covers Data Analytics, the final topic area of **Domain I: Business Acumen** from The IIA's CIA Exam Syllabus. This domain makes up 35% of Part 3 of the CIA exam, and this topic area of the domain is tested at the **basic** cognitive level. Refer to the complete syllabus located in Appendix A to view the relevant sections covered in Study Unit 7.

7.1 IT CONTROL FRAMEWORKS AND INTERNATIONAL ORGANIZATION FOR STANDARDIZATION (ISO) FRAMEWORK

SUCCESS TIP

The increasing integration of controls over automated systems with the organization's overall system of internal control is most clearly displayed in the eSAC and COBIT frameworks. These documents discuss at some length the role played by automated systems in pursuing the organization's mission, safeguarding assets, etc.

Candidates for the CIA exam must be aware not just of detailed controls, such as field checks, but also of the role that control over IT plays in the organization's strategy implementation.

1. **Control Framework**

    a. A control framework is a model for establishing a system of internal control.

    1) The framework does not prescribe the actual controls themselves, but it does influence management to focus on risk areas and design controls accordingly.

    2) Often, a control framework describes "families" of controls, that is, conceptual groupings of controls that attempt to address a particular type of risk exposure.

    3) **ITIL**, a product of AXELOS, assists organizations by focusing on allocating IT efforts to the needs of the business and supporting core processes.

2. **COSO**

   a. Probably the most well-known control framework in the U.S. is *Internal Control – Integrated Framework*, published in 1992 by the Committee of Sponsoring Organizations of the Treadway Commission (COSO). The framework is commonly referred to as "the COSO Framework."

      1) The importance and durability of the COSO Framework was reinforced when the U.S. Securities and Exchange Commission acknowledged it as an appropriate model for designing internal controls under the requirements of the Sarbanes-Oxley Act of 2002.

   b. The COSO Framework defines internal control as

      A process, effected by an organization's board of directors, management, and other personnel, designed to provide reasonable assurance regarding the achievement of objectives in the following categories:

      - *Effectiveness and efficiency of operations*
      - *Reliability of financial reporting*
      - *Compliance with applicable laws and regulations*

   c. COSO further describes five components of an internal control system:

      1) Control environment
      2) Risk assessment
      3) Control activities
      4) Information and communication
      5) Monitoring activities

3. **eSAC**

   a. *Electronic Systems Assurance and Control (eSAC)* is a publication of The IIA. The purpose of eSAC is to provide an internal control framework for e-business. In the eSAC model, the organization's internal processes accept inputs and produce outputs.

      1) Inputs: Mission, values, strategies, and objectives
      2) Outputs: Results, reputation, and learning

   b. The eSAC model's broad control objectives are influenced by those in the COSO Framework:

      1) Operating effectiveness and efficiency
      2) Reporting of financial and other management information
      3) Compliance with laws and regulations
      4) Safeguarding of assets

   c. eSAC's IT business assurance objectives fall into five categories:

      1) **Availability.** The organization must assure that information, processes, and services are available at all times.

      2) **Capability.** The organization must assure reliable and timely completion of transactions.

      3) **Functionality.** The organization must assure that systems are designed to user specifications to fulfill business requirements.

      4) **Protectability.** The organization must assure that a combination of physical and logical controls prevents unauthorized access to, or use of, system data.

      5) **Accountability.** The organization must assure that transaction processing is accurate, complete, and non-refutable.

SU 7: IT Framework and Data Analytics 211

4. **COBIT 4.1**

    a. Specifically for IT controls, the best-known framework is *Control Objectives for Information and Related Technology (COBIT)*. Version 4.1 of this framework was published in 2007 by the IT Governance Institute.

        1) ISACA released COBIT 5 in April 2012 (described in item 5. beginning on the next page). COBIT 5 consolidates the principles of COBIT 4.1.

    b. Automated information systems have been woven into every function of the modern organization, making IT governance an integral part of overall organizational governance. The COBIT model for IT governance contains five focus areas:

        1) Strategic alignment
        2) Value delivery
        3) Resource management
        4) Risk management
        5) Performance measurement

    c. The COBIT framework embodies four characteristics:

        1) Business-focused
        2) Process-oriented
        3) Controls-based
        4) Measurement-driven

    d. Each characteristic contains multiple components.

        1) Business-focused.

            a) This characteristic lists seven distinct but overlapping information criteria: effectiveness, efficiency, confidentiality, integrity, availability, compliance, and reliability.

            b) Business goals must feed IT goals, which in turn allow the organization to design the appropriate enterprise architecture for IT.

            c) IT resources include applications, information, infrastructure, and people.

        2) Process-oriented. This part of the model contains four domains:

            a) Plan and organize
            b) Acquire and implement
            c) Deliver and support
            d) Monitor and evaluate

        3) Controls-based. "An IT control objective is a statement of the desired result or purpose to be achieved by implementing control procedures in a particular IT activity." COBIT describes controls in three areas:

            a) Process controls. "Operational management uses processes to organize and manage ongoing IT activities."

            b) Business controls. These affect IT at three levels: the executive management level, the business process level, and the IT support level.

            c) IT general controls and application controls. This distinction for IT controls is of very long standing.

                i) "General controls are those controls embedded in IT processes and services. . . . Controls embedded in business process applications are commonly referred to as application controls."

4) Measurement-driven.
    a) The centerpiece of the COBIT framework in this area is the **maturity model**.
        i) The maturity model focuses on three dimensions of maturity: capability, coverage, and control.
        ii) "The organization must rate how well managed its IT processes are. The suggested scale employs the rankings of non-existent, initial, repeatable, defined, managed, and optimized."
        iii) Its benefits include the following:
            - It helps professionals explain where IT process management shortcomings exist.
            - It is used for comprehensive assessment, gap analyses, and improvement planning.
    b) Performance measurement. Goals and metrics are defined in COBIT at three levels:
        i) *IT goals and metrics that define what the business expects from IT*
        ii) *Process goals and metrics that define what the IT processes must deliver to support IT's objectives*
        iii) *Process performance metrics*

5. **COBIT 5 -- A Framework for IT Governance and Management**
    a. As was previously mentioned, COBIT is the best-known control and governance framework that addresses information technology.
        1) In its original version, COBIT was focused on controls for specific IT processes.
        2) Over the years, information technology has gradually pervaded every facet of the organization's operations. IT can no longer be viewed as a function distinct from other aspects of the organization.
            a) The evolution of COBIT has reflected this change in the nature of IT within the organization.
        3) Control frameworks are intended for use by anyone in the organization who has control responsibilities, not just auditors or senior management.
    b. **Information Criteria**
        1) **Effectiveness** deals with information's relevance to the business process and receipt in a timely, correct, consistent, and usable manner.
        2) **Efficiency** concerns the provision of information through the optimal (most productive and economical) use of resources.
        3) **Confidentiality** concerns the protection of sensitive information from unauthorized disclosure.
        4) **Integrity** relates to the accuracy and completeness of information as well as to its validity in accordance with business values and expectations.
        5) **Availability** relates to information being available when required by the business process now and in the future. It also concerns the safeguarding of necessary resources and associated capabilities.

6) **Compliance** deals with complying with the laws, regulations, and contractual arrangements to which the business process is subject, i.e., externally imposed business criteria as well as internal policies.

7) **Reliability** relates to the provision of appropriate information for management to operate the entity and exercise its fiduciary and governance responsibilities.

c. **IT Governance Focus Areas**

1) **Strategic alignment** focuses on ensuring the linkage of business and IT plans; defining, maintaining, and validating the IT value proposition; and aligning IT operations with enterprise operations.

2) **Value delivery** is about executing the value proposition throughout the delivery cycle, ensuring that IT delivers the promised benefits against the strategy, concentrating on optimizing costs, and proving the intrinsic value of IT.

3) **Resource management** is about the optimal investment in, and the proper management of, critical IT resources.

4) **IT risk** is the business risk associated with the use, ownership, operation, involvement, influence, and adaption of IT within an enterprise or organization.

5) **Risk management** involves risk awareness by senior corporate officers, understanding of compliance requirements, transparency about the significant risks to the enterprise, and embedding of risk management responsibilities into the organization.

6) **Performance measurement** tracks and monitors strategy implementation, project completion, resource usage, process performance, and service delivery.

d. COBIT 5 divides governance and management objectives into five domains (key areas).

1) Governance

a) **Evaluate, Direct, and Monitor (EDM)**

i) Evaluate. Evaluate stakeholder needs, conditions, and options.
ii) Direct. Set direction through prioritization and decision making.
iii) Monitor. Monitor performance and compliance.

2) Management

a) **Align, Plan, and Organize (APO).** Plan how IT can be used to achieve the company's goals and objectives.

b) **Build, Acquire, and Implement (BAI).** Identify IT requirements, build or acquire the technology, and incorporate it into business processes.

c) **Deliver, Service, and Support (DSS).** Execute and support the application of the technology in business processes.

d) **Monitor, Evaluate, and Assess (MEA).** Monitor and evaluate whether the current IT system and internal control system meet the company's goals and objectives.

3) Processes under each of the domains above are also defined.

e. **Five Key Principles**
  1) **Principle 1: Meeting Stakeholder Needs**
     a) COBIT 5 asserts that value creation is the most basic stakeholder need. Thus, the creation of stakeholder value is the fundamental goal of any enterprise, commercial or not.
        i) Value creation in this model is achieved by balancing three components:
           - Realization of benefits
           - Optimization (not minimization) of risk
           - Optimal use of resources
     b) COBIT 5 also recognizes that stakeholder needs are not fixed. They evolve under the influence of both internal factors (e.g., changes in organizational culture) and external factors (e.g., disruptive technologies).
        i) These factors are collectively referred to as stakeholder drivers.
     c) In response to the identified stakeholder needs, enterprise goals are established.
        i) COBIT 5 supplies 17 generic enterprise goals that are tied directly to the balanced scorecard model.
        ii) Next, IT-related goals (referred to as alignment goals in COBIT 2019) are drawn up to address the enterprise goals.
        iii) Finally, enablers are identified that support pursuit of the IT-related goals. The categories of enablers are identified in Principle 4 on the next page.
        iv) COBIT 5 refers to the process described above as the goals cascade.
  2) **Principle 2: Covering the Enterprise End-to-End**
     a) COBIT 5 takes a comprehensive view of all of the enterprise's functions and processes. Information technology pervades them all; it cannot be viewed as a function distinct from other enterprise activities.
        i) Thus, IT governance must be integrated with enterprise governance.
     b) IT must be considered enterprise-wide and end-to-end, i.e., all functions and processes that govern and manage information "wherever that information may be processed."
  3) **Principle 3: Applying a Single, Integrated Framework**
     a) In acknowledgment of the availability of multiple IT-related standards and best practices, COBIT 5 provides an overall framework for enterprise IT within which other standards can be consistently applied.
     b) COBIT 5 was developed to be an overarching framework that does not address specific technical issues; i.e., its principles can be applied regardless of the particular hardware and software in use.

4) **Principle 4: Enabling a Holistic Approach**

   a) COBIT 5 describes seven categories of enablers that support comprehensive IT governance and management:

   i) **Principles, policies, and frameworks** to translate desired behavior into guidance.

   ii) **Processes** are sets of practices to achieve the objectives.

   iii) **Organizational structures** are decision-making entities.

   iv) **Culture, ethics, and behavior** of individuals and the enterprise.

   v) **Information** produced and used by the enterprise.

   vi) **Services, infrastructure, and applications** provide the enterprise with IT processing and services.

   vii) **People, skills, and competencies** are required for operations, error detections, and corrections.

   b) The last three of these enablers are also classified as resources, the use of which must be optimized.

   c) Enablers are interconnected because they

   i) Need the input of other enablers to be fully effective and
   ii) Deliver output for the benefit of other enablers.

5) **Principle 5: Separating Governance from Management**

   a) The complexity of the modern enterprise requires governance and management to be treated as distinct activities.

   i) In general, governance is the setting of overall objectives and monitoring progress toward those objectives. COBIT 5 associates governance with the board of directors.

   - Within any governance process, three practices must be addressed: evaluate, direct, and monitor.

   ii) Management is the carrying out of activities in pursuit of enterprise goals. COBIT 5 associates these activities with executive management under the leadership of the CEO.

   - Within any management process, four responsibility areas must be addressed: plan, build, run, and monitor.

6. **COBIT 5 Conversion to COBIT 2019**
    a. COBIT 2019 expands on COBIT 5's key principles for a governance system applicable to IT governance to include six **governance system** principles and three **governance framework** principles. A governance system is the rules, practices, and processes that direct and regulate an entity. A governance framework is the structure upon which the governance system is built.
        1) The six principles for a **governance system** are summarized as follows:
            a) Provide **stakeholder value**. Achieving value requires a strategy and a governance system.
            b) **Holistic** approach. Create synergies among the components interconnected in the system.
                i) Governance system **components** were called "enablers" under COBIT 5. Components can be **generic** (components applied in principle to any circumstances) or **variant** (components designed for a given purpose or context in a focus area).
            c) **Dynamic** governance system. The governance system must be dynamic when dealing with a change in design factors (e.g., personnel, infrastructure, applications, etc.) and must be accompanied by consideration of its systemic effects.
            d) Governance **distinct** from management. Governance tasks should be differentiated from management tasks and not combined.
            e) Tailored to **enterprise needs**. The governance system must be designed to meet an organization's requirements.
                i) **Design factors** affect the blueprint of a governance system.
                ii) Design factors include, but are not limited to, threat landscape, technology adoption strategy, and enterprise strategy and goals.
            f) **End-to-end** enterprise coverage. The emphasis is not solely on the IT function but on all information, processes, and technology that contribute to organizational goal achievement.
        2) The following are three principles for a governance **framework**:
            a) It is **based on a conceptual model**. The governance framework achieves consistency and automation by identifying components and their relationships.
            b) It is **open and flexible**. The governance framework is flexible and permits inclusion of new content and issues without loss of consistency and integrity.
            c) It is **aligned with major standards**. The governance framework aligns with relevant regulations, standards, frameworks, and best practices (e.g., the latest IT standards and compliance regulations).
        3) The COBIT implementation approach comprises seven phases, and each phase is represented by a question.
            a) Program initiation: What are the drivers?
                i) This phase involves recognizing change drivers and establishing management's desire to change.

b) Problems and opportunities definition: Where are we now?

　　i) This phase involves assessing the current state or capability and forming an implementation team.

c) Road map definition: Where do we want to be?

　　i) This phase involves defining the target state and identifying the gap and potential solutions.

d) Program planning: What needs to be done?

　　i) This phase involves planning for the implementation to close the gap.

e) Plan execution: How do we get there?

　　i) This phase involves implementing the plan and establishing monitoring systems.

f) Benefits realization: Did we get there?

　　i) This phase involves monitoring progress and achievement.

g) Effectiveness review: How do we keep the momentum going?

　　i) This phase involves reviewing the overall program and reinforcing improvements.

4) Generally, these phases can be matched with the principles of the governance system. However, note that Principle 6 and Phase 7 are not matched.

Governance System Principle	Implementation Phases
1. Provide stakeholder value	1. What are the drivers?
2. Holistic approach 3. Dynamic governance system	2. Where are we now? 3. Where do we want to be? 4. What needs to be done?
4. Governance distinct from management	5. How do we get there?
5. Tailored to enterprise needs	6. Did we get there?
6. End-to-end enterprise coverage	
	7. How do we keep the momentum going?

b. COBIT 2019 includes 40 governance and management objectives organized into five domains, expanded from 37 processes organized into the same five domains under COBIT 5.

　1) Candidates need not memorize these objectives. They are included here because they represent one of the foundational shifts from COBIT 5 to COBIT 2019.

c. Performance management is a crucial element of a governance and management system. It directs all of the components at work towards accomplishing the goals of the organization by providing reliable and relevant outcomes.

　1) The **COBIT Performance Management (CPM)** model measures performance using capability and maturity levels.

　　a) **Capability levels.** The CPM measures performance by using the capability level to quantify how well a **process** is operating, ranging from 0 (no capability or not meeting the intent of any process practices) to 5 (well defined process or continuous improvement enabled).

b) **Maturity levels.** The CPM measures performance by using focus area maturity levels. The six maturity levels, presented in order of maturity, are listed below.

    0 – Incomplete
    1 – Initial
    2 – Managed
    3 – Defined
    4 – Quantitative
    5 – Optimizing

    i) A **focus area** is a governance issue, domain, or topic that is associated with a group of objectives and their components. COBIT 2019 added new focus areas, including cloud computing, cybersecurity, privacy, and small and medium enterprises.

BACKGROUND 7-1   COBIT Content

The COBIT 2019 product family currently includes the following documents:
1. COBIT 2019 Framework: Introduction and Methodology
2. COBIT 2019 Framework: Governance and Management Objectives
3. COBIT 2019 Design Guide: Designing an Information and Technology Governance Solution
4. COBIT 2019 Implementation Guide: Implementing and Optimizing an Information and Technology Governance Solution

These documents can be obtained from www.isaca.org/COBIT/Pages/COBIT-2019-Publications-Resources.aspx

---

7. **Global Technology Audit Guide (GTAG)**

    a. The IIA GTAG on information technology risk and controls recognizes three "families" of controls:

        1) General and application controls, described in Subunit 7.3

        2) Preventive, detective, and corrective controls

            a) Preventive controls "prevent errors, omissions, or security incidents from occurring."

EXAMPLE 7-1   Preventive Physical Controls

Examples of physical controls include
- Storing petty cash in a locked safe
- Segregation of duties

EXAMPLE 7-2   Preventive IT Controls

Examples of IT controls include
- Designing a database so that users cannot enter a letter in the field that stores a Social Security number
- Requiring the number of invoices in a batch to be entered before processing begins
- Establishing a formal security policy
- Using only clean and certified copies of software
- Not using shareware software
- Checking new software with antivirus software
- Restricting access
- Educating users
- Using edit (field) checks to prevent certain types of incorrect data from entering a system
- Preformatting a data entry screen so that certain fields must be filled before proceeding

b) Detective controls "detect errors or incidents that elude preventive controls."

   i) Detective controls alert the proper people after an unwanted event. They are effective when detection occurs before material harm occurs.

EXAMPLE 7-3   Detective Controls

Examples of detective controls include

- Automatic reporting to the accounts payable department of all rejected batches of invoices
- Using hash totals [defined in Subunit 7.3, item 8.d.3)] to detect data entry errors and/or test for completeness
- Installing burglar alarms
- Examining system logs of actions that require scrutiny, such as repeated failed login attempts and the use of powerful utility programs

---

c) Corrective controls "correct errors, omissions, or incidents once they have been detected."

EXAMPLE 7-4   Corrective Controls

Examples of corrective controls include

- Requiring that all cost variances over a certain amount are justified
- Correcting errors reported on error listings
- Isolating and removing viruses
- Restarting from system crashes

---

3) Governance, management, and technical controls

   a) "Governance controls . . . are linked with the concepts of corporate governance, which are driven both by organizational goals and strategies and by outside bodies such as regulators."

   b) Management controls "are deployed as a result of deliberate actions by management to recognize risks to the organization, its processes, and assets; and enact mechanisms and processes to mitigate and manage risks."

   c) Technical controls "are specific to the technologies in use within the organization's IT infrastructures."

b. The same GTAG also recommends that each organization use the applicable components of existing frameworks to categorize and assess IT controls and to provide and document its own framework for

   1) Compliance with applicable regulations and legislation,
   2) Consistency with the organization's objectives, and
   3) Reliable evidence (reasonable assurance) that activities comply with management's governance policies and are consistent with the organization's risk appetite.

8. **The International Organization for Standardization (ISO)**
    a. In 1987, the ISO introduced **ISO 9000**, a group of 11 voluntary standards and technical reports that provide guidance for establishing and maintaining a **quality management system (QMS)**.

    NOTE: ISO is not an acronym. It means equal, suggesting that entities certified under ISO 9000 have equal quality.

        1) The ISO's rules specify that its standards be revised every 5 years to reflect technical and market developments.
    b. The intent of the standards is to ensure the quality of the process, not the product. The marketplace determines whether a product is good or bad.
        1) For this reason, the ISO deems it unacceptable for phrases referring to ISO certification to appear on individual products or packaging.
    c. ISO 9001:2015 is a generic standard that states requirements for a QMS. It applies when an entity needs to demonstrate its ability to (1) sell a product that meets customer and regulatory requirements and (2) increase customer satisfaction through improving the QMS and ensuring conformity with requirements.
    d. ISO 9000:2015 expands on the concepts found in ISO 9001:2015 and makes them more accessible to all types of enterprises.

9. **Aspects of ISO Certification**
    a. Some entities are obtaining ISO certification because of concern that the European Union will require compliance with the standards in an attempt to restrict imports.
        1) The standards are not yet mandatory. However, they are required for certain regulated products (for which health and safety are concerns), such as medical devices, telecommunications equipment, and gas appliances.
        2) Some customers demand that suppliers register.
        3) ISO 9000 registration may be necessary to be competitive. It makes customers more comfortable with suppliers' products and services.
        4) Many entities implementing the standards make internal process and quality improvements as a result. ISO 9000 forces them to share information and understand who internal customers and users are.
    b. A registrar, or external auditor, must be selected. Registrars are usually specialists within certain Standard Industrial Classification (SIC) codes. Certification by a registrar avoids the need for each customer to audit a supplier.
        1) Following an onsite visit, the registrar, if convinced that a quality system conforms to the selected standard, issues a certificate describing the scope of the registration. Registration is usually granted for a 3-year period.
        2) All employees are subject to being audited. They must have the ability to explain what they do and to demonstrate that they do what they say.

10. **Basic Requirements of an ISO QMS**
    a. **Key Process Identification**
        1) Key processes affecting quality must be identified and included.
        2) A process management approach must be used. It manages the entity as a set of linked processes that are controlled for continuous improvement.

b. **General Requirements**

   1) The entity must have a quality policy and quality goals. It also must design a QMS to control process performance. Quality goals are measurable and specific.

   2) The QMS is documented in the

      a) Quality policy,
      b) Quality manual,
      c) Procedures,
      d) Work instructions, and
      e) Records.

   3) The entity also must demonstrate its ability to increase customer satisfaction through improving the QMS and ensuring conformity with requirements.

c. **Management Responsibility**

   1) Management (a) reviews the quality policy, (b) analyzes data about QMS performance, and (c) assesses opportunities for improvement and the need for change.

   2) Management ensures that systems exist to determine and satisfy customer requirements.

d. **Resource Management**

   1) The resources needed to improve the QMS and satisfy customer requirements must be provided.

e. **Product Realization**

   1) These processes result in products or services received by customers. They must be planned and controlled.

   2) Issues are (a) means of control, (b) objectives, (c) documentation and records needed, and (d) acceptance criteria.

f. **Measurement, Analysis, and Improvement**

   1) The entity must have processes for (a) inspection, (b) testing, (c) measurement, (d) analysis, and (e) improvement.

11. **Other Areas of Standardization**

    a. The ISO also has issued ISO 14000, a set of environmental standards. These standards are comparable in purpose to ISO 9000 but apply to environmental quality systems.

       1) Although they have not been as widely adopted as the ISO 9000 standards, they may become necessary for conducting international business. Some European countries already have environmental systems standards in place, and the relationship of these single-country standards with ISO 14000 is not clear. However, individual countries' standards are typically more strict.

    b. The scope of ISO 19011:2018 extends to (1) the principles of auditing, (2) managing audit programs, (3) conducting management system audits, and (4) the competence of individuals engaged in the audits.

       1) It applies to all entities that must (a) perform internal or external audits of management systems or (b) manage an audit program.

       2) ISO 19011 may apply to other types of audits if due consideration is given to identifying the specific competence required.

c. ISO 10012:2003 is a generic standard. It addresses the management of measurement processes and confirmation of measuring equipment used to support compliance with required measures.
　　1) It states quality management requirements of a **measurement management system (MMS)** that can be used as part of the overall management system.
　　2) It is not to be used as a requirement for demonstrating conformance with other standards. Interested parties may agree to use ISO 10012:2003 as an input for satisfying MMS requirements in certification activities.
　　　　a) Other standards apply to specific elements affecting measurement results, e.g., details of measurement methods, competence of personnel, or comparisons among laboratories.
d. ISO 14063:2006 states principles, policies, strategies, and activities for environmental communications, whether external or internal. It addresses the unique circumstances of environmental communications and applies to every entity regardless of whether it has an EMS.
e. ISO Guide 64:2008 applies to environmental questions in the setting of product standards. Its purpose is to help standard setters minimize negative environmental effects at each step in the product life cycle.
f. ISO 14050:2009 is a glossary of environmental management vocabulary.
g. Author's note: It is not necessary to commit the ISO numbers to memory. Simply having a general understanding of these concepts and their implications will be sufficient to help you pass the exam.
h. The ISO/IEC 27000 family of information security management systems (ISMS) standards (also referred to as ISO 27000 series) is published by ISO and the International Electrotechnical Commission (IEC).
　　1) ISO 27000 was created to provide globally recognized ISMS standards for organizations in all industries regardless of the size of the organization.
　　2) As advances in technology occur, new ISMS standards are developed in order to keep pace with security needs.
　　　　a) ISO 27000 contains overview and vocabulary.
　　　　b) ISO 27001 contains requirements.
　　　　c) All other ISO 27000 standards contain best-practice guidelines.

STOP & REVIEW

You have completed the outline for this subunit.
Study multiple-choice questions 1 through 5 beginning on page 236.

7.2 ASPECTS OF AUTOMATED INFORMATION PROCESSING

1. **Characteristics of Automated Processing**

    a. The use of computers in business information systems has fundamental effects on the nature of business transacted, the procedures followed, the risks incurred, and the methods of mitigating those risks.

    1) These effects flow from the characteristics that distinguish computer-based from manual processing.

    b. **Transaction Trails**

    1) A complete trail useful for audit and other purposes might exist for only a short time or only in computer-readable form.

    2) The nature of the trail is often dependent on the transaction processing mode, for example, whether transactions are batched prior to processing or whether they are processed immediately as they happen.

    c. **Uniform Processing of Transactions**

    1) Computer processing uniformly subjects similar transactions to the same processing instructions and thus virtually eliminates clerical error, but programming errors (or other similar systematic errors in either the hardware or software) will result in all similar transactions being processed incorrectly when they are processed under the same conditions.

    d. **Segregation of Functions**

    1) Many controls once performed by separate individuals may be concentrated in computer systems. Hence, an individual who has access to the computer may perform incompatible functions. As a result, other controls may be necessary to achieve the control objectives ordinarily accomplished by segregation of functions.

    e. **Potential for Errors and Fraud**

    1) The potential for individuals, including those performing control procedures, to gain unauthorized access to data, to alter data without visible evidence, or to gain access (direct or indirect) to assets may be greater in computer systems.

    2) Decreased human involvement in handling transactions can reduce the potential for observing errors and fraud.

    3) Errors or fraud in the design or changing of application programs can remain undetected for a long time.

    f. **Potential for Increased Management Supervision**

    1) Computer systems offer management many analytical tools for review and supervision of operations. These additional controls may enhance internal control.

        a) For example, traditional comparisons of actual and budgeted operating ratios and reconciliations of accounts are often available for review on a more timely basis. Furthermore, some programmed applications provide statistics regarding computer operations that may be used to monitor actual processing.

g. **Initiation or Subsequent Execution of Transactions by Computer**

1) Certain transactions may be automatically initiated or certain procedures required to execute a transaction may be automatically performed by a computer system. The authorization of these transactions or procedures may not be documented in the same way as those in a manual system, and management's authorization may be implicit in its acceptance of the design of the system.

h. **Dependence of Controls in Other Areas on Controls over Computer Processing**

1) Computer processing may produce reports and other output that are used in performing manual control procedures. The effectiveness of these controls can be dependent on the effectiveness of controls over the completeness and accuracy of computer processing. For example, the effectiveness of a manual review of a computer-produced exception listing is dependent on the controls over the production of the listing.

2. **Two Basic Processing Modes**

    a. **Batch Processing**

    1) In this mode, transactions are accumulated and submitted to the computer as a single batch. In the early days of computers, this was the only way a job could be processed.

    2) In batch processing, the user cannot influence the process once the job has begun (except to ask that it be aborted completely). (S)he must wait until the job is finished running to see if any transactions in the batch were rejected and failed to post.

    3) Despite huge advances in computer technology, this accumulation of transactions for processing on a delayed basis is still widely used. It is very efficient for such applications as payroll because large numbers of routine transactions must be processed on a regular schedule.

    4) **Memo posting** is used by banks for financial transactions when batch processing is used. It posts temporary credit or debit transactions to an account if the complete posting to update the balance will be done as part of the end-of-day batch processing. Information can be viewed immediately after updating.

        a) Memo posting is an intermediate step between batch processing and real-time processing.

    b. **Online, Real-Time Processing**

    1) In some systems, having the latest information available at all times is crucial to the proper functioning of the system. An airline reservation system is a common example.

    2) In an online, real-time system, the database is updated immediately upon entry of the transaction by the operator. Such systems are referred to as **online transaction processing (OLTP)** systems.

STOP & REVIEW

You have completed the outline for this subunit.
Study multiple-choice questions 6 through 10 beginning on page 238.

7.3 IT CONTROLS

1. **Classification of Controls**

    a. *Control Objectives for Information and Related Technology* (COBIT) has achieved widespread acceptance. It provides a model for the impact of an organization's internal controls on IT:

    *At the **executive management level**, business objectives are set, policies are established and decisions are made on how to deploy and manage the resources of the enterprise to execute the enterprise strategy.*

    *At the **business process level**, controls are applied to specific business activities. Most business processes are automated and integrated with IT application systems, resulting in many of the controls at this level being automated as well. These controls are known as application controls.*

    *To **support the business processes**, IT provides IT services, usually in a shared service to many business processes, as many of the development and operational IT processes are provided to the whole enterprise, and much of the IT infrastructure is provided as a common service (e.g., networks, databases, operating systems and storage). The controls applied to all IT service activities are known as IT general controls.*

    b. Internal control objectives remain essentially the same although technology, risks, and control methods change.

    1) Many control concepts (management's responsibility, the role of the control environment, reasonable assurance, monitoring, and cost-benefit analysis) are relevant regardless of IT changes.

    c. The organization must implement appropriate controls at each of the three levels described in the COBIT model.

    1) For example, at the executive level, an IT steering committee should be established, composed of senior managers from both the IT function and the end-user functions. The committee approves development projects, assigns resources, and reviews their progress.

    2) The steering committee also ensures that requests for new systems are aligned with the overall strategic plan of the organization.

    d. The interaction between general and application controls is crucial for an audit. According to COBIT,

    The reliable operation of these general controls is necessary for reliance to be placed on application controls.

    1) Because general controls affect the organization's entire processing environment, the auditor must become satisfied about their proper operation before relying on application controls.

    e. The following are the categories of **general controls**: systems development, change management, security, and computer operations.

    1) Effective IT general controls are measured by the number of

        a) Incidents that damage public reputation,
        b) Systems that do not meet security criteria, and
        c) Violations in segregation of duties.

f. The following are examples of types of **application controls**: completeness, accuracy, validity, authorization, error notification, and segregation of duties.

1) This classification reflects that a computer application is the automation of a business process and has the same control objectives.

a) For example, control objectives for an accounts receivable system should include

i) Customers' payments applied (credited to) the appropriate accounts
ii) Credit ratings timely updated
iii) Financial statements correctly stated

2. **General controls** are the umbrella under which the IT function operates.

a. They affect the organization's entire processing environment and commonly include controls over

1) Data center and network operations;
2) Systems software acquisition, change, and maintenance;
3) Access security; and
4) Application system acquisition, development, and maintenance.

3. IT Administration Controls over Operations

a. A modern organization should recognize information technology as a separate function with its own set of management and technical skills. An organization that allows every functional area to acquire and administer its own systems in isolation is not serious about proper control.

b. Treating IT as a separate functional area of the organization involves the designation of a chief information officer (CIO) or chief technology officer (CTO) and the establishment of an information systems steering committee to set a coherent direction for the organization's systems and prioritize information technology projects.

4. Change management controls permit management to supervise change requests such as the creation, modification, and/or implementation of IT infrastructure (e.g., equipment, software, networks, etc.) in a timely, accurate, and competent fashion while simultaneously using resources in an economical and feasible way.

a. Effectively implemented change management controls enhance an organization's operations by providing a recurring, measurable, and auditable process that captures all IT infrastructure changes.

1) Generally, effective change management is associated with less high-level systems management (i.e., administrators) and more productive and competent IT personnel.

5. **Segregation of duties** is vital because a separation of functions (authorization, recording, and access to assets) may not be feasible in an IT environment. For example, a computer may print checks, record disbursements, and generate information for reconciling the account balance.

a. These activities customarily are segregated in a manual system.
b. Segregation of duties within the IT function is discussed in Study Unit 6, Subunit 1.

6. Controls over software acquisition, change, and maintenance include

a. **Controls over systems software,** which ensure that operating systems, utilities, and database management systems are acquired and changed only under close supervision and that vendor updates are routinely installed.

b. **Controls over application software,** which ensure that programs used for transaction processing (e.g., payroll and accounts receivable) are cost-effective and stable.

7. **Hardware controls** are built into the equipment by the manufacturer. They ensure the proper internal handling of data as they are moved and stored.

    a. They include parity checks, echo checks, read-after-write checks, and any other procedure built into the equipment to ensure data integrity.

8. **Application Controls**

    a. According to GTAGs, application controls pertain to the scope of individual business processes or application systems. The objective of application controls is to ensure that

        1) Input data is accurate, complete, authorized, and correct.
        2) Data is processed as intended in an acceptable time period and processed only once.
        3) Data stored is accurate and complete.
        4) Outputs are accurate and complete.
        5) A record is maintained to track the process of data from input to storage and to the eventual output.
        6) Processing results are received by the intended user.

    b. When designing data input controls, primary consideration should be given to authorization, validation, and error notification.

    c. The most economical point for correcting input errors in an application is the time at which the data are entered into the system.

        1) For this reason, input controls are a primary focus of an internal auditor's assessment of application controls. Each of the two major types of processing modes has its own controls.

    d. **Batch Input Controls**

        1) **Financial totals** summarize monetary amounts in an information field in a group of records. The total produced by the system after the batch has been processed is compared to the total produced manually beforehand.
        2) **Record counts** track the number of records processed by the system for comparison to the number that the user expected to be processed.
        3) **Hash totals** are control totals without a defined meaning, such as the total of vendor numbers or invoice numbers, that are used to verify the completeness of the data.
        4) **Management release.** A batch is not released for processing until a manager reviews and approves it.

EXAMPLE 7-5   **Batch Input Controls -- Hash Totals**

A company has the following invoices in a batch:

Invoice Number	Product	Quantity	Unit Price
303	G7	100	US $15
305	A48	200	5
353	L30	125	10
359	Z26	150	20

The hash total is a control total without a defined meaning, such as the total of employee numbers or invoice totals, that is used to verify the completeness of data. Using invoice numbers, the hash total would be 1320.

e. **Online Input Controls**
1) **Preformatting** of data entry screens, i.e., to make them imitate the layout of a printed form, can aid the operator in keying to the correct fields.
2) The **dialogue** approach is a screen prompting method for data entry. It is most appropriate when information is received orally (e.g., by phone).
3) **Field (edit)/format checks** are tests of the characters in a field to verify that they are of an appropriate type for that field. For example, the system is programmed to reject alphabetic characters entered in the field for Social Security number.
4) **Validity checks** compare the data entered in a given field with a table of valid values for that field. For example, the vendor number on a request to cut a check must match the table of current vendors, and the invoice number must match the approved invoice table.
5) **Limit (reasonableness) and range checks** are based on known limits for given information. For example, hours worked per week must be between 0 and 100, with anything above that range requiring management authorization.
6) **Check digits** are an extra reference number that follows an identification code and bears a mathematical relationship to the other digits. This extra digit is input with the data. The identification code can be subjected to an algorithm and compared to the check digit.
7) **Sequence checks** are based on the logic that processing efficiency is greatly increased when files are sorted on some designated field, called the "key," before operations such as matching are performed. If the system discovers a record out of order, it may indicate that the files were not properly prepared for processing.
8) **Zero balance checks** will reject any transaction or batch thereof in which the sum of all debits and credits does not equal zero.
9) **Completeness checks** test whether all data items for a transaction have been entered by the person entering the data.
10) **Closed-loop verification** occurs when inputs by a user are transmitted to the computer, processed, and displayed back to the user for verification.
11) An **edit routine** is a program initiated prior to regular input to discover errors in data before entry.

f. **Processing controls** provide reasonable assurance that (1) all data submitted for processing are processed and (2) only approved data are processed. These controls are built into the application code by programmers during the systems development process.
1) Some processing controls repeat the steps performed by the **input controls**, such as limit checks and batch controls.
2) **Concurrency controls** manage situations where two or more users attempt to access or update a file or database simultaneously. These controls ensure the correct results are generated while getting those results as quickly as possible. An auditor is most concerned that concurrency controls are in place when evaluating database access controls with regard to end-user-developed applications.
3) **Validation.** Identifiers are matched against master files to determine existence. For example, any accounts payable transaction in which the vendor number does not match a number on the vendor master file is rejected.
4) **Completeness.** Any record with missing data is rejected.

5) **Arithmetic controls.** Cross-footing compares an amount with the sum of its components. Zero-balance checking adds the debits and credits in a transaction or batch to ensure that their sum is zero.

6) **Sequence check.** Computer effort is expended most efficiently when data are processed in a logical order, such as by customer number. This check ensures the batch is sorted in the proper order before processing begins.

7) **Run-to-run control totals.** The controls associated with a given batch are checked after each stage of processing to ensure all transactions have been processed.

8) **Key integrity.** A record's key is the group of values in designated fields that uniquely identify the record. No application process should be able to alter the data in these key fields.

g. **Output controls** provide assurance that the processing result (such as account listings or displays, reports, files, invoices, or disbursement checks) is accurate and that only authorized personnel receive the output.

1) These procedures are performed at the end of processing to ensure that all transactions the user expected to be processed were actually processed.

   a) **Transaction Logs**
      i) Every action performed in the application is logged along with the date, time, and ID in use when the action was taken.

   b) **Error Listings**
      i) All transactions rejected by the system are recorded and distributed to the appropriate user department for resolution.

   c) **Record Counts**
      i) The total number of records processed by the system is compared to the number the user expected to be processed.

   d) **Run-to-Run Control Totals**
      i) The new financial balance should be the sum of the old balance plus the activity that was just processed.

   e) Periodically reconciling output reports

   f) Maintaining formal procedures and documentation specifying authorized recipients of output

h. **Integrity controls** monitor data being processed and in storage to ensure it remains consistent and correct.

i. **Management trails** (or audit trails) are processing history controls that enable management to track transactions from their source to their output.

STOP & REVIEW

You have completed the outline for this subunit.
Study multiple-choice questions 11 through 16 beginning on page 240.

7.4 DATA ANALYTICS

1. The Institute of Internal Auditors defines data analytics (DA) as follows:

    The process whereby data is identified, consolidated and quality checked and put into a format where analysis can be done with the goal of identifying useful information that better supports corporate decision making.

2. Data analytics involves qualitative and quantitative methodologies and procedures to retrieve data out of data sources and then inspect the data (in accordance to predetermined requirements) based on data type to facilitate the decision-making process.

    a. A **data type** specifies the type of value and the applicable mathematical, relational and non-relational, or logical operation methodologies that can be applied without resulting in an error. Data types include, but are not limited to, the following:

    1) A **string** is used to classify text (e.g., MEEN85).
    2) **Float** is a number containing a decimal point (e.g., 10.98).
    3) An **integer** classifies whole numbers (e.g., 10).
    4) **Boolean** represents logical outcomes (e.g., Yes or No).
    5) An **array** is a collection of objects of the same data type.

    b. Data are processed with analytic and algorithmic tools to reveal meaningful information.

3. For-profit entities, not-for-profit entities, and government agencies (federal, state, and local) utilize DA to reach a conclusion based on evidence and reasoning to make well supported decisions and formulate strong business models.

    a. Organizations can also use business analytics to rule out proposed strategic plans and models which would not be beneficial or work for the organization.

4. Internal auditors utilize DA to evaluate operational, financial, and other data to identify any deviations from the norm (e.g., anomaly detection, potential risks) and opportunities for enhancement or advancement.

5. Data analytics contains five stages as follows:

    a. **Define questions**

    1) Identifying goals and objectives of what the organization is trying to achieve.

        a) Key performance indicators (KPI) must be identified to assist with measuring whether an organization is progressing towards its goals and objectives. Examples of KPIs include

            i) Current ratio
            ii) Net profit margin
            iii) Budget variance
            iv) Debt to equity ratio
            v) Payment error rate

        b) Clearly defined goals and objectives assist the IT team with selecting the most appropriate technology source to use for the analysis.

        c) Early adoption of goals and KPIs helps keep the analysis on course and avoid worthless analysis.

b. **Obtain relevant data** (commonly referred to as **information discovery**)
   1) Access to every piece of data available allows for
      a) Valuable analysis,
      b) More precise correlations,
      c) Construction of meaningful analysis models and forecasts, and
      d) Identification of actionable insights.

c. **Clean/normalize data**
   1) Cleaning data consists of, but is not limited to, flushing out useless information and identifying missing data.
   2) Data governance assists with ensuring data is accurate and usable.
   3) Normalizing data involves storing each data element as few times as necessary. It results in a reduction in data and strengthened data integrity for use of a specific purpose.
      a) **Integrity** is ensuring that data accurately reflect the business events underlying them and that any anomalies are rectified.

d. **Analyze data**
   1) As the data collected is analyzed, a determination can be made as to whether the data is the exact data needed. The determination includes, but is not limited to,
      a) Assessing whether additional data is needed,
      b) Collecting new and/or different data,
      c) Revising the original question, and
      d) Formulating additional questions.
   2) Data analytics methods in internal auditing include the following application types:
      a) **Descriptive analysis** is the most basic and most used method. It concentrates on reporting of actual results.
      b) **Diagnostic analysis** provides insight on the reason certain results occurred.
      c) **Predictive analysis** involves applying assumptions to data and predicting future results.
      d) **Prescriptive analysis** concentrates on what an organization needs to do in order for the predicted future results to actually occur.
      e) **Anomaly detection** is used to identify unusual patterns or deviations from the norm or expected results.
      f) **Network analysis** consists of analyzing network data and statistics to find patterns.
      g) **Text analysis** involves the utilization of text mining and natural language algorithms to find patterns in unstructured text.
   3) Internal audit personnel generally will select data to trace to supporting source documentation, such as invoices, contracts, and payments, and perform the following additional procedures:
      a) Review and confirm the details of the data selected.
      b) Analyze the findings and determine compliance or non-compliance with policy.
      c) Analyze the findings for accuracy.
      d) Identify internal controls requiring enhancement or, if no controls exist, assist with the creation of a control.

e. **Communicate results**

1) Prior to issuing the final communication, the internal auditor should discuss conclusions and recommendations with appropriate management at an exit meeting.

   a) The discussion provides management with an opportunity for clarification and an expression of views.

   b) The primary purpose of an exit meeting is to ensure the accuracy of the information used by the internal auditor.

2) Data visualization or graphic illustrations (e.g., charts, graphs, network analysis, etc.), written repetition (e.g., summaries), and itemized lists (bulleted or numbered) are good ways of emphasizing information.

   a) Using visual aids to support a discussion of major points results in the most retention of information.

3) Generally, language should be fact-based and neutral. But if the internal auditor's objective is to persuade an individual to accept recommendations, words with strong or emotional connotations should be used.

   a) Using too strong a word or a word inappropriate for the particular recipient may induce an unwanted response. Thus, high-connotation language should be chosen carefully to appeal to the specific recipient.

6. **Big data** is an evolving term that describes any voluminous amount of structured, semi-structured, or unstructured data that has the potential to be mined for information.

   a. **Structured data** refers to data with a high level of organization (e.g., data stored in a relational database).

   b. **Semi-structured data** does not conform with the formal structure of data models associated with relational databases or other forms of data tables; however, there exists some aspect of organization (e.g., HTML data).

   c. **Unstructured data** refers to information that is not organized in a pre-defined manner (e.g., text-heavy documents, audio files, videos, and images).

7. Big data includes information collected from social media, data from Internet-enabled devices, machine data, videos, and voice recordings.

   a. The information collected is converted from low-density data into high-density data (data that has value).

SU 7: IT Framework and Data Analytics

8. Big data is often characterized by the "4 Vs."

   a. **Volume**

      1) The term "volume" is used to describe the extreme amount of data captured over time.

         a) Depending on the amount of data required to be captured, the number of servers required could range from a single server to thousands.

      2) Real-time sensors used in the Internet of Things (IoT) have become one of the top sources of data.

         a) The Internet of Things is the network of interrelated computing devices embedded within physical devices, such as vehicles, home appliances, and other everyday objects.

            i) These physical devices are provided with real-time sensors and the ability to transfer data over a network without requiring human-to-human or human-to-computer interaction.

   b. **Variety**

      1) Data exist in a wide variety of file types.

         a) Structured data file types are generally maintained by Structured Query Language (SQL), which is used for managing relational databases and performing various operations on the data in them.

         b) Unstructured data file types (i.e., streaming data from sensors, text, audio, images, and videos) are maintained by non-relational databases (i.e., NoSQL).

   c. **Velocity**

      1) The term "velocity" refers to the speed at which big data must be analyzed.

         a) Analysts must have a detailed understanding of the available data and possess some sense of what answer(s) they are looking for.

         b) The computing power required to quickly process huge volumes and varieties of data can overwhelm a single server or multiple servers. Organizations must apply adequate computing power to big data tasks to achieve the desired velocity.

         c) Businesses are hesitant to invest in an extensive server and storage infrastructure that might only be used occasionally to complete big data tasks. As a result, cloud computing has emerged as a primary source for hosting big data projects.

   d. **Veracity**

      1) The term "veracity" refers to the trustworthiness of the data (inherent discrepancies in the data collected).

         a) Can the user rely on the fact the data is representative?

9. The "5th V"
    a. More and more businesses are using big data because of the **value** of the information resulting from the culmination of analyzing large information flows and identifying opportunities for improvement.
    b. Use of big data is only as valuable as the business outcomes it makes possible. It is how businesses make use of data that allows full recognition of its true value and potential to improve decision-making capabilities and enhance positive business outcomes.
        1) **Volume-based value.** The more data businesses have on customers, both recent and historical, the greater the insights. This leads to generating better decisions around acquiring, retaining, increasing, and managing those customer relationships.
        2) **Variety-based value.** In the digital era, the capability to acquire and analyze varied data is extremely valuable. This in turn provides deep insights into successfully developing and personalizing customer platforms for businesses to be more engaged and aware of customer needs and expectations.
        3) **Velocity-based value.** The faster businesses process data, the more time they will have to ask the right questions and seek answers. Rapid analysis capabilities provide businesses with the right data in time to achieve their customer relationship management goals.
        4) **Veracity-based value.** Once data is validated, the data transforms to "smart data." Collecting large amounts of statistics and numbers is of little value if they cannot be relied upon and used.
10. Big data uses inductive statistics and concepts from nonlinear system identification (i.e., output is not directly proportional to the input) to infer laws from large sets of data to reveal relationships and dependencies or to perform predictions of outcomes and behaviors.
    a. It can be used to analyze data to identify opportunities that include, but are not limited to, (1) cost reductions, (2) time reductions, (3) new product development and optimized offerings, and (4) new customers.
    b. Big data analytics tools complete missing pieces through **data fusion**, which is the process of integration of data and knowledge representing the same real-world object into a consistent, accurate, and useful representation.
11. Key Technologies
    a. **Data management.** Data need to be high quality and well-governed before they can be reliably analyzed. Thus, businesses need to
        1) Establish repeatable processes to build and maintain standards for data quality.
        2) Establish a master data management program.
    b. **Data mining** examines large amounts of data to discover patterns in the data.
        1) Data mining sifts through all the chaotic and repetitive noise in data, pinpoints what is relevant, uses that information to assess likely outcomes, and then accelerates the pace of making informed decisions.

c. **Hadoop** is an open source software framework that stores large amounts of data and runs applications on clusters of commodity hardware.

d. **In-memory analytics**

1) Analyzes data from system memory instead of secondary storage

2) Derives immediate results by removing data preparation and analytical processing delays

3) Enables iterative and interactive analytic scenarios more efficiently

e. **Predictive analytics** uses data, statistical algorithms, and machine-learning techniques to identify the likelihood of future outcomes based on historical data.

f. **Text mining**

1) Analyzes text data from the Web, comment fields, books, and other text-based sources through the use of machine learning or natural language processing technology

2) Identifies new topics and term relationships

12. A 2015 Data Analytics and Leadership Survey conducted by The Institute of Internal Auditors Research Foundation (IIARF) and Grant Thornton (GT) identified what internal audit professionals recognize as the benefits of DA. The results of the survey are as follows:

Audit process is streamlined	56%
Fieldwork time is reduced	50%
Fraudulent transactions are identified	45%
Audit scope is more consistent	40%
More audits are capable of being performed	28%

a. Additionally, the survey revealed the following with regard to the top uses of DA:

Analyzing trends	72%
Compliance monitoring	56%
Detecting fraud	54%
Evaluating business/operation performance	48%
Data visualization	40%
Predictive analytics	17%
Modeling	12%

STOP & REVIEW

You have completed the outline for this subunit.
Study multiple-choice questions 17 through 20 beginning on page 243.

QUESTIONS

7.1 IT Control Frameworks and International Organization for Standardization (ISO) Framework

1. Which of the following types of controls is **not** described in the IT Governance Institute's *Control Objectives for Information and Related Technology* (COBIT)?

    A. General controls.
    B. Exchange controls.
    C. Business controls.
    D. Process controls.

Answer (B) is correct.
REQUIRED: The type of control not described in COBIT.
DISCUSSION: COBIT describes controls in three areas: process controls, business controls, and IT general and application controls.

2. Control objectives regarding effectiveness and efficiency, reliability, and compliance are the basis of which control framework?

    A. ITGI.
    B. eSAC.
    C. COBIT.
    D. COSO.

Answer (D) is correct.
REQUIRED: The appropriate control framework.
DISCUSSION: Probably the most well-known control framework in the U.S. is *Internal Control – Integrated Framework*, published in 1992 by the Committee of Sponsoring Organizations of the Treadway Commission (COSO). The document is commonly referred to as "the COSO Framework." The COSO Framework defines internal control as

A process, effected by an organization's board of directors, management, and other personnel, designed to provide reasonable assurance regarding the achievement of objectives in the following categories:

- *Effectiveness and efficiency of operations*
- *Reliability of financial reporting*
- *Compliance with applicable laws and regulations*

Answer (A) is incorrect. IT Governance Institute (ITGI) is the organization that copyrighted COBIT (*Control Objectives for Information and Related Technology*), which is an IT control framework. **Answer (B) is incorrect.** The IIA's *Electronic Systems Assurance and Control*, eSAC, is not the source of these three control objectives. **Answer (C) is incorrect.** COBIT, the ITGI's *Control Objectives for Information and Related Technology*, is not the source of these three control objectives.

3. Why have many European Union countries **not** adopted ISO 14000 environmental standards?

A. Following ISO 14000 standards will not reduce monitoring and inspection by regulatory agencies.
B. Individual European Union countries' standards are typically more strict than ISO 14000 standards.
C. Regulators are permitted to use voluntary audits as a basis for punitive action.
D. ISO 14000 standards will not make it easier to do business across borders.

Answer (B) is correct.
REQUIRED: The reason many European Union countries have not adopted ISO 14000 standards.
DISCUSSION: Some European countries already have environmental systems in place, and individual countries' standards are typically more strict than the ISO 14000 standards. Furthermore, the relationship of these single-country standards with ISO 14000 is unclear.
Answer (A) is incorrect. Many believe following ISO 14000 standards will reduce monitoring or inspection by regulatory agencies. **Answer (C) is incorrect.** Many countries in the European Union have adopted measures similar to the ones in the US to prevent self-incrimination during voluntary ISO audits. **Answer (D) is incorrect.** ISO 14000 establishes internationally recognized standards that are intended to diminish trade barriers and make it easier to do business across borders.

4. According to eSAC, accountability is

A. Usually an issue with regard to trade secrets and other intellectual property.
B. The control attribute that identifies the source of a transaction.
C. The restriction of access to processing and storage devices.
D. Most often applicable to personal information about employees and customers.

Answer (B) is correct.
REQUIRED: The definition of accountability according to eSAC.
DISCUSSION: Accountability is the control attribute that identifies the source of a transaction. It specifies employees' roles, actions, and responsibilities. Thus, the person who caused a transaction is identifiable. Fundamental concepts of accountability are data ownership, identification, and authentication.
Answer (A) is incorrect. Confidentiality is usually an issue with regard to trade secrets and other intellectual property. **Answer (C) is incorrect.** Physical security is the restriction of access to processing and storage devices. **Answer (D) is incorrect.** Privacy is the attribute most often applicable to personal information about employees and customers.

5. Which of the following statements is **not** true regarding ISO 9000 standards?

A. Compliance with the standards is voluntary.
B. The ISO 9000 standards are revised every 5 years to account for technical and market developments.
C. The objective of ISO 9000 standards is to ensure high quality products and services.
D. ISO 9000 is a set of standards for establishing and maintaining a quality system within an entity.

Answer (C) is correct.
REQUIRED: The false statement regarding ISO 9000 standards.
DISCUSSION: The objective of ISO 9000 standards is to ensure consistent quality of the process even if the product quality is poor. The market determines the quality of the product.
Answer (A) is incorrect. Compliance is voluntary, but many entities are adopting the standards for competitive reasons or because of concern that the standards will be required in foreign markets. **Answer (B) is incorrect.** The ISO rules specify that standards are periodically revised every 5 years to reflect technical and market developments. **Answer (D) is incorrect.** ISO 9000 standards provide guidance for establishing and maintaining a quality management system (QMS).

7.2 Aspects of Automated Information Processing

6. Which of the following statements accurately describes the impact that automation has on the controls normally present in a manual system?

A. Transaction trails are more extensive in a computer-based system than in a manual system because there is always a one-for-one correspondence between data entry and output.

B. Responsibility for custody of information assets is more concentrated in user departments in a computer-based system than it is in a manual system.

C. Controls must be more explicit in a computer-based system because many processing points that present opportunities for human judgment in a manual system are eliminated.

D. The quality of documentation becomes less critical in a computer-based system than it is in a manual system because data records are stored in machine-readable files.

Answer (C) is correct.
REQUIRED: The impact that automation has on the controls normally present in a manual system.
DISCUSSION: Using a computer does not change the basic concepts and objectives of control. However, the use of computers may modify the control techniques used. The processing of transactions may be combined with control activities previously performed separately, or control function may be combined within the information system activity.
Answer (A) is incorrect. The "paper trail" is less extensive in an automated system. Combining processing and controls within the system reduces documentary evidence. **Answer (B) is incorrect.** Information assets are more likely to be under the control of the information system function. **Answer (D) is incorrect.** Documentation is more important in an information system. This is because information is more likely to be stored in machine-readable form than in hard copy, requiring specialized knowledge for retrieval.

7. A small client recently put its cash disbursements system on a server. About which of the following internal control features would an auditor most likely be concerned?

A. Programming of the applications are in Visual Basic rather than Java.

B. The server is operated by employees who have cash custody responsibilities.

C. Only one employee has the password to gain access to the cash disbursement system.

D. There are restrictions on the amount of data that can be stored and on the length of time that data can be stored.

Answer (B) is correct.
REQUIRED: The control feature of most concern to an auditor.
DISCUSSION: Segregation of duties is a basic category of control activities. Functions are incompatible if a person is in a position both to perpetrate and conceal fraud or errors. Hence, the duties of authorizing transactions, recording transactions, and custody of assets should be assigned to different people. Those employees that operate the server may be able to override the controls to change records to conceal a theft of cash.
Answer (A) is incorrect. The choice of language would have little effect on internal control. **Answer (C) is incorrect.** The limitation on access would be considered a strength. **Answer (D) is incorrect.** Restrictions on the amount of data that can be stored and on the length of time that data can be stored do not constitute a control weakness.

SU 7: IT Framework and Data Analytics

8. Which of the following statements most likely represents a disadvantage for an entity that keeps data files on a server rather than on a manual system?

A. Attention is focused on the accuracy of the programming process rather than errors in individual transactions.
B. It is usually easier for unauthorized persons to access and alter the files.
C. Random error associated with processing similar transactions in different ways is usually greater.
D. It is usually more difficult to compare recorded accountability with the physical count of assets.

Answer (B) is correct.
REQUIRED: The disadvantage of server-based data files.
DISCUSSION: In a manual system, one individual is usually assigned responsibility for maintaining and safeguarding the records. However, in a server environment, the data files may be subject to change by others without documentation or an indication of who made the changes.
Answer (A) is incorrect. The focus on programming is an advantage of using a server. A software program allows transactions to be processed uniformly.
Answer (C) is incorrect. It describes a disadvantage of a manual system. **Answer (D) is incorrect.** The method of maintaining the files is independent of the ability to compare this information in the file with the physical count of assets.

9. A small company has changed from a system of recording time worked on clock cards to a computerized payroll system in which employees record time in and out with magnetic cards. The computer system automatically updates all payroll records. Because of this change,

A. A generalized computer audit program must be used.
B. Part of the audit trail is altered.
C. The potential for payroll-related fraud is diminished.
D. Transactions must be processed in batches.

Answer (B) is correct.
REQUIRED: The effect of computerization of a payroll system.
DISCUSSION: In a manual payroll system, a paper trail of documents is created to provide audit evidence that controls over each step in processing are in place and functioning. One element of a computer system that differentiates it from a manual system is that a transaction trail useful for auditing purposes might exist only for a brief time or only in computer-readable form.
Answer (A) is incorrect. Use of generalized audit software is only one of many ways of auditing a computer-based system. **Answer (C) is incorrect.** Conversion to a computer system may actually increase the chance of fraud by eliminating segregation of incompatible functions and other controls. **Answer (D) is incorrect.** Automatic updating indicates that processing is not in batch mode.

10. Batch processing

A. Is not used by most businesses because it reduces the audit trail.
B. Allows users to inquire about groups of information contained in the system.
C. Accumulates transaction records into groups for processing against the master file on a delayed basis.
D. Can only be performed on a centralized basis.

Answer (C) is correct.
REQUIRED: The true statement about batch processing.
DISCUSSION: Batch processing is the accumulation and grouping of transactions for processing on a delayed basis. The batch approach is suitable for applications that can be processed against the master file at intervals and involve large volumes of similar items, such as payroll, sales, inventory, and billing.
Answer (A) is incorrect. Batch processing provides as much of an audit trail as any computerized operation. **Answer (B) is incorrect.** Batch processing refers to the input of data, not inquiry. **Answer (D) is incorrect.** Batch processing can also be performed on a decentralized basis.

7.3 IT Controls

11. When assessing application controls, which one of the following input controls or edit checks is most likely to be used to detect a data input error in the customer account number field?

A. Limit check.
B. Validity check.
C. Control total.
D. Hash total.

Answer (B) is correct.
REQUIRED: The input control or edit check most likely to be used to detect a data input error in the customer account number field.
DISCUSSION: Validity checks are tests of identification numbers or transaction codes for validity by comparison with items already known to be correct or authorized. For example, Social Security numbers on payroll input records can be compared with Social Security numbers authorized by the personnel department.
Answer (A) is incorrect. Reasonableness, limit, and range checks are based upon known limits for given information. For example, the hours worked per week is not likely to be greater than 45. **Answer (C) is incorrect.** A record count is a control total of the number of records processed during the operation of a program. Financial totals summarize dollar amounts in an information field in a group of records. **Answer (D) is incorrect.** A hash total is the number obtained from totaling the same field value for each transaction in a batch. The total has no meaning or value other than as a comparison with another hash total.

12. If a control total were to be computed on each of the following data items, which would best be identified as a hash total for a payroll computer application?

A. Hours worked.
B. Total debits and total credits.
C. Net pay.
D. Department numbers.

Answer (D) is correct.
REQUIRED: The example of a hash total.
DISCUSSION: The three types of control totals are record counts, financial totals, and hash totals. Record counts establish the number of source documents and reconcile it to the number of output records. Financial totals compute dollar totals from source documents (e.g., the total dollar amount of invoices processed) and reconcile them with the output records. Hash totals add numbers on input documents that are not normally added (e.g., department numbers), resulting in a total that is "meaningless" for any purpose other than this control.
Answer (A) is incorrect. Hours worked is an example of a financial total. **Answer (B) is incorrect.** Total debits and total credits is a financial total. **Answer (C) is incorrect.** Net pay is a financial total.

13. A catalog company has been experiencing an increasing incidence of problems in which the wrong products have been shipped to the customer. Most of the customer orders come in over the telephone, and an operator enters the data into the order system immediately. Which of the following control procedures, if properly implemented, would address the problem?

1. Have the computer automatically assign a sequential order number to each customer order.
2. Implement a self-checking digit algorithm for each product number and request entries by product number.
3. Request entries by product number, have the computer program identify the product and price, and require the operator to orally verify the product description with the customer.

A. 2 only.
B. 1, 2, and 3.
C. 2 and 3 only.
D. 1 and 2 only.

Answer (C) is correct.
REQUIRED: The procedure(s) to prevent incorrect shipments.
DISCUSSION: A self-checking digit detects incorrect codes. The digit is generated by applying an algorithm to the code. During input, the digit is recomputed by applying the algorithm to the code actually entered. Oral verification also addresses the problem of incorrectly identifying the product number. Assigning a sequential number to the customer's order helps build an audit trail but does not address the product identification issue.
Answer (A) is incorrect. Oral verification also would address the problem. **Answer (B) is incorrect.** Assigning a sequential number to the customer's order helps build an audit trail but does not address the product identification issue. **Answer (D) is incorrect.** Assigning a sequential number to the customer's order helps build an audit trail but does not address the product identification issue.

14. The two broad groupings of information systems control activities are general controls and application controls. General controls include controls

A. Relating to the correction and resubmission of faulty data.
B. For developing, modifying, and maintaining computer programs.
C. Designed to ensure that only authorized users receive output from processing.
D. Designed to ensure that all data submitted for processing have been properly authorized.

Answer (B) is correct.
REQUIRED: The characteristics of general controls in relation to information systems control activities.
DISCUSSION: General controls are policies and procedures that relate to many information systems applications and support the effective functioning of application controls by helping to ensure the continued proper operation of information systems. General controls include controls over (1) data center and network operations; (2) systems software acquisition and maintenance; (3) access security; and (4) application systems acquisition, development, and maintenance.

15. An accounts payable program posted a payable to a vendor not included in the online vendor master file. A control that would prevent this error is a

A. Validity check.
B. Range check.
C. Reasonableness test.
D. Parity check.

Answer (A) is correct.
REQUIRED: The control that would prevent the posting of a payable to a vendor not included in the online vendor master file.
DISCUSSION: Validity checks are tests of identification numbers or transaction codes for validity by comparison with items already known to be correct or authorized. For example, Social Security numbers on payroll input records can be compared with Social Security numbers authorized by the personnel department.
Answer (B) is incorrect. A range check is based on known limits for given information. **Answer (C) is incorrect.** A reasonableness test is based on known limits for given information. **Answer (D) is incorrect.** A parity check adds the bits in a character or message and checks the sum to determine if it is odd or even, depending on whether the computer has odd or even parity.

16. The purpose of check digit verification of an account number on an update transaction is to

A. Verify that the account number corresponds to an existing account in the master file.
B. Detect a transposition of an account number entered into the system.
C. Ensure that supporting documentation exists for the update transaction.
D. Require the account number to have the correct logical relationship with other fields.

Answer (B) is correct.
REQUIRED: The purpose of check digit verification of an account number on an update transaction.
DISCUSSION: A major control used to guard against errors made in transcribing or keying data is a check digit. A check digit is a detective control designed to establish the validity and appropriateness of numerical data elements, such as account numbers. The check digit within the code is a mathematical function of the other digits. Recalculation of the digit tests the accuracy of the other characters in the code. Check digit verification prevents single-digit errors from leading to erroneous updates.
Answer (A) is incorrect. Verifying that the account number corresponds to an existing account in the master file is a master file reference check. **Answer (C) is incorrect.** Ensuring that supporting documentation exists for update transactions is a document reconciliation control. **Answer (D) is incorrect.** Requiring a field to have the correct logical relationship with other fields is a dependency check.

7.4 Data Analytics

17. All of the following are correct statements regarding big data **except**

A. Big data is an evolving term that describes any voluminous amount of structured, semi-structured, and unstructured data that has the potential to be mined for information.

B. Big data includes information collected from social media, data from Internet-enabled devices, machine data, video, and voice recordings. The information collected is converted from high-density data into low-density data.

C. Big data is often characterized by the "4 Vs" – volume, variety, velocity, and veracity.

D. Big data processes data with analytic and algorithmic tools to reveal meaningful information.

Answer (B) is correct.
  REQUIRED: Knowledge of the general concepts of big data.
  DISCUSSION: Big data includes information collected from social media, data from Internet-enabled devices, machine data, video, and voice recordings. The information collected is converted from low-density data into high-density data. Thus, the statement regarding big data is not correct.

18. Which of the following best describes unstructured data?

A. Data with a high level of organization.

B. Data systematically stored with markers to enforce hierarchies of records and fields within the data.

C. Information that is not organized in a pre-defined manner (e.g., text-heavy facts, dates, numbers, and images).

D. Conforms with the organization of data models associated with relational databases.

Answer (C) is correct.
  REQUIRED: Knowledge of the general concepts of big data.
  DISCUSSION: Unstructured data refers to information that is not organized in a pre-defined manner (e.g., text-heavy facts, dates, numbers, and images).
  Answer (A) is incorrect. Structured data refers to data with a high level of organization. **Answer (B) is incorrect.** Semi-structured data does not conform with the formal structure of data models associated with relational databases or other forms of data tables; however, markers exist to enforce hierarchies of records and fields within the data. **Answer (D) is incorrect.** Structured data conforms with the organization of data models associated with relational databases.

19. Which of the following is a correct statement regarding Hadoop?

A. It is open source software framework that stores large amounts of data and runs applications on clusters of commodity hardware.
B. It analyzes data from system memory instead of hard drives.
C. It is a technology that uses data, statistical algorithms, and machine-learning techniques to identify the likelihood of future outcomes based on historical data.
D. It analyzes text data from the web, comment fields, books, and other text-based sources through the use of machine learning or natural language processing technology.

Answer (A) is correct.
REQUIRED: The correct statement regarding Hadoop.
DISCUSSION: Hadoop is an open source software framework that stores large amounts of data and runs applications on clusters of commodity hardware.
Answer (B) is incorrect. In-memory analytics analyzes data from system memory instead of hard drives. **Answer (C) is incorrect.** Predictive analytics is technology that uses data, statistical algorithms, and machine-learning techniques to identify the likelihood of future outcomes based on historical data. **Answer (D) is incorrect.** Text mining analyzes text data from the web, comment fields, books, and other text-based sources through the use of machine learning or natural language processing technology.

20. All of the following are correct statements regarding businesses deciding to utilize cloud computing for big data projects **except**

A. Businesses are hesitant to invest in an extensive server and storage infrastructure that might only be used occasionally to complete big data tasks.
B. Businesses only pay for the storage and computing time actually used.
C. A public cloud provider can store petabytes of data and scale up thousands of servers just long enough to accomplish the big data project.
D. Analysts are not required to have a detailed understanding of the available data and possess some sense of what answer(s) they're looking for.

Answer (D) is correct.
REQUIRED: Knowledge of the general concepts of big data.
DISCUSSION: Analysts are not required to have a detailed understanding of the available data and possess some sense of what answer(s) they're looking for is an incorrect statement. Analysts must have a detailed understanding of the available data and possess some sense of the answers they are looking for. The value of data is only as valuable as the business outcomes it makes possible. It is how businesses make use of data that allows full recognition of its true value and the potential to improve decision-making capabilities and measure them against the results of positive business outcomes.

Access the **Gleim CIA Premium Review System** featuring our SmartAdapt technology from your Gleim Personal Classroom to continue your studies. You will experience a personalized study environment with exam-emulating multiple-choice questions.

STUDY UNIT EIGHT
INFORMATION SECURITY AND DISASTER RECOVERY

(26 pages of outline)

8.1	Information Security and Cybersecurity Related Policies and Controls	246
8.2	Authentication, Authorization, and Encryption	252
8.3	Information Protection	254
8.4	Contingency Planning and Disaster Recovery	265

This study unit covers **Domain II: Information Security** and is the fourth of four covering **Domain III: Information Technology** from The IIA's CIA Exam Syllabus. These domains make up 25% and 20%, respectively, of Part 3 of the CIA exam and are tested at the **basic** cognitive level. Refer to the complete syllabus located in Appendix A to view the relevant sections covered in Study Unit 8.

8.1 INFORMATION SECURITY AND CYBERSECURITY RELATED POLICIES AND CONTROLS

1. Organizations need to be aware of the unique risks associated with a computer-based business information system.
   a. Safe computing can be achieved by using carefully crafted policies and procedures in conjunction with antivirus and access control software.
   b. The most comprehensive indicator of an information system's compliance with prescribed procedures is the control the system has over the data. This includes the capacity and complexity of the system as well as the accessibility of the data to the end-user.
2. Information security and cybersecurity are commonly viewed as synonymous terms; however, information security is more expansive than cybersecurity.
   a. Information security involves securing data in any form (e.g., locking paper documents in filing cabinets and file storage rooms and storing electronic data on IT equipment), whereas cybersecurity concentrates on protecting electronic data.
   b. Cybersecurity is information security applied to computer hardware, software, and networks.
      1) The Committee on National Security Systems (CNSS) defines information security as the protection of information and its critical elements, including the systems and hardware that use, store, and transmit the information.
   c. **Three Goals of Information Security**
      1) **Availability** is the ability of the intended and authorized users to access computer resources to meet organizational goals.
      2) **Confidentiality** is assurance of the secrecy of information that could adversely affect the organization if revealed to unauthorized persons.
      3) **Integrity** is ensuring that data accurately reflect the business events underlying them and preventing the unauthorized or accidental modification of programs or data.
3. Policies form the foundation of effective information security and cybersecurity measures.
   a. The successful planning, design, and implementation of security procedures are initiated by strong policies and management support.
   b. Policies govern how to resolve issues and the use of IT infrastructure to resolve issues.
      1) Effective policy must
         a) Comply with laws and regulations
         b) Be communicated and explained to applicable personnel
         c) Be accepted by applicable personnel
         d) Be enforced

4. Standards assist the implementation of policies by detailing what actions must occur to comply with policy. Standards are categorized as de facto and de jure.

    a. **De facto standards** are informal standards that have been widely adopted and accepted.

    b. **De jure standards** are formal standards that have been assessed, approved, and sanctioned.

5. Guidelines and procedures illustrate how to comply with policies by providing detailed instructions.

> **SUCCESS TIP**: Broadly conceived, "security" can extend to almost any aspect of automated systems. An internal auditor's awareness of information security should encompass three general types: logical, physical, and communication.

6. **Data Integrity**

    a. The difficulty of maintaining the integrity of the data is the most significant limitation of computer-based audit tools.

        1) Electronic evidence is difficult to authenticate and easy to fabricate.

        2) Internal auditors must be careful not to treat computer printouts as traditional paper evidence. The data security factors pertaining to electronic evidence must be considered.

        3) The degree of the auditor's reliance on electronic evidence depends on the effectiveness of the controls over the system from which such evidence is taken.

        4) When making recommendations regarding the costs and benefits of computer security, the auditor should focus on

            a) Potential loss if security is not implemented,

            b) The probability of the occurrences, and

            c) The cost and effectiveness of the implementation and operation of computer security.

        5) The most important control is to enact an organization-wide network security policy. This policy should promote at a minimum the objectives of availability, privacy, and integrity.

    b. Many controls once performed by separate individuals may be concentrated in computer systems. Hence, an individual who has access to the computer may perform incompatible functions. As a result, other control procedures may be necessary to achieve the control objectives ordinarily accomplished by segregation of functions.

        1) These controls can be classified as either physical controls or logical controls. Physical controls are further divided into two subcategories: physical access controls and environmental controls.

7. **Physical Security Controls**
   a. **Physical access controls** limit who can physically access systems.
      1) Keypad devices allow entry of a password or code to gain entry to a physical location or computer system.
      2) Card reader controls are based on reading information from a magnetic strip on a credit, debit, or other access card. Controls then can be applied to information about the cardholder contained on the magnetic strip.
      3) Biometric technologies are automated methods of establishing an individual's identity using physiological or behavioral traits. These characteristics include fingerprints, retina patterns, hand geometry, signature dynamics, speech, and keystroke dynamics.
   b. **Environmental controls** are also designed to protect the organization's physical information assets. The most important are
      1) Temperature and humidity control
      2) Gaseous fire-suppression system (not water)
      3) Data center not located on an outside wall
      4) Building housing data center not located in a flood plain

8. **Logical Controls**
   a. Logical security controls are needed because of the use of communications networks and connections to external systems. User identification and authentication, restriction of access, and the generation of audit trails are required in this environment. Thus, access controls have been developed to prevent improper use or manipulation of data files and programs. They ensure that only those persons with a bona fide purpose and authorization have access to computer systems.
      1) **Access control** software (a) protects files, programs, data dictionaries, processing, etc., from unauthorized access; (b) restricts use of certain devices (e.g., terminals); and (c) may provide an audit trail for both successful and unsuccessful access attempts. For example, a firewall separates internal from external networks.
      2) **Passwords and ID numbers.** The use of passwords and identification numbers is an effective control in an online system to prevent unauthorized access to computer files. Lists of authorized persons are maintained in the computer. The entry of passwords or ID numbers; a prearranged set of personal questions; and the use of badges, magnetic cards, or optically scanned cards may be combined to avoid unauthorized access.
         a) A security card may be used with a personal computer so that users must sign on with an ID and a password. The card controls the machine's operating system and records access data (date, time, duration, etc.).
         b) Proper user authentication by means of a password requires password-generating procedures to ensure that valid passwords are known only by the proper individuals. Thus, a password should not be displayed when entered at a keyboard.

- c) Password security also may be compromised in other ways. For example, log-on procedures may be cumbersome and tedious.
    - i) Thus, users often store log-on sequences on their personal computers and invoke them when they want to use mainframe facilities. A risk of this practice is that anyone with access to the personal computers could log on to the mainframe.
- d) To be more effective, passwords should consist of random letters, symbols, and numbers. They should not contain words or phrases.

3) **File attributes** can be assigned to control access to and the use of files. Examples are read/write, read only, archive, and hidden.

4) A **device authorization table** restricts file access to those physical devices that should logically need access. For example, because it is illogical for anyone to access the accounts receivable file from a manufacturing terminal, the device authorization table will deny access even when a valid password is used.
   - a) Such tests are often called compatibility tests because they ascertain whether a code number is compatible with the potential information usage.
     - i) Thus, a user may be authorized to enter only certain kinds of data, have access only to certain information, have access but not updating authority, or use the system only at certain times.
     - ii) The lists or tables of authorized users or devices are sometimes called access control matrices.

5) A **system access** log records all attempts to use the system. The date and time, codes used, mode of access, data involved, and operator interventions are recorded.

6) **Encryption** uses a fixed algorithm to manipulate plaintext.

7) **Controlled disposal** of documents is a method of enforcing access restrictions by destroying data when they are no longer in use. Thus, paper documents may be shredded and magnetic media may be erased.

8) **Automatic log-off** (disconnection) of inactive data terminals may prevent the viewing of sensitive data on an unattended data terminal.

9) **Security personnel.** An organization may need to hire security specialists. For example, developing an information security policy for the organization, commenting on security controls in new applications, and monitoring and investigating unsuccessful access attempts are appropriate duties of the information security officer.

9. **Internet Security**

   a. Connection to the Internet presents security issues.

      1) Thus, the organization-wide network security policy should at the very least include

         a) A user account management system
         b) Installation of an Internet firewall
         c) Methods such as encryption to ensure that only the intended user receives the information and that the information is complete and accurate

      2) User account management involves installing a system to ensure that

         a) New accounts are added correctly and assigned only to authorized users
         b) Old and unused accounts are removed promptly
         c) Passwords are changed periodically and employees are educated on how to choose a password that cannot be easily guessed (e.g., a password of at least six diverse characters that do not form a word)

      3) A **firewall** separates an internal network from an external network (e.g., the Internet) and prevents passage of specific types of traffic. It identifies names, Internet Protocol (IP) addresses, applications, etc., and compares them with programmed access rules.

         a) A firewall may have any of the following features:

            i) A **packet filtering system** examines each incoming network packet and drops (does not pass on) unauthorized packets.
            ii) A **proxy server** acts as an intermediary for requests between a client application and the real server.
            iii) An **application gateway** is an application-level proxy that limits traffic to specific applications and prevents malicious requests from being submitted to web applications.
            iv) A **circuit-level gateway** connects an internal device, e.g., a network printer, with an outside TCP/IP port. It can identify a valid TCP session.
            v) **Stateful inspection** stores information about the state of a transmission and uses it as background for evaluating messages from similar sources.

         b) Firewall systems ordinarily produce reports on organization-wide Internet use, unusual usage patterns, and system penetration attempts. These reports are very helpful to the internal auditor as a method of continuous monitoring, or logging, of the system.

            i) Firewalls do not provide adequate protection against computer viruses. Thus, an organization should include one or more antivirus measures in its network security policy.

      4) Data traveling across the network can be encoded so that it is indecipherable to anyone except the intended recipient.

5) Other Controls

   a) **Authentication** measures verify the identity of the user, thus ensuring that only the intended and authorized users gain access to the system.

      i) Most firewall systems provide authentication procedures.
      ii) Access controls are the most common authentication procedures.

   b) **Checksums** help ensure data integrity by checking whether the file has been changed.

      i) The system computes a value for a file and then checks whether this value equals the last known value for this file.
      ii) If the numbers are the same, the file has likely remained unchanged.

10. **Data Storage**

    a. Storing all related data on one storage device creates security problems.

       1) If hardware or software malfunctions occur or unauthorized access is achieved, the results could be disastrous.
       2) Greater emphasis on security is required to provide backup and restrict access to the database.

          a) For example, the system may employ dual logging, that is, use of two transaction logs written simultaneously on separate storage media.

             i) It may also use a snapshot technique to capture data values before and after transaction processing.
             ii) The files that store these values can be used to reconstruct the database in the event of data loss or corruption.

       3) The responsibility for creating, maintaining, securing, and restricting access to the database belongs to the database administrator (DBA).
       4) A database management system (DBMS) includes security features. Thus, a specified user's access may be limited to certain data fields or logical views depending on the individual's assigned duties.

    b. **Cloud computing** relieves organizations of the need to manage the storage of both applications and data because all of the software and data are stored on the Internet.

       1) Cloud computing is defined as a standardized IT capability (services, software, infrastructure) delivered via the Internet in a pay-per-use, self-service way.
       2) Advantages of cloud computing include lower infrastructure investments and maintenance costs, increased mobility, and lower personnel and utility costs.
       3) Disadvantages of cloud computing include less control than there would be over an internal IT department, more difficulty ensuring data security and privacy, and less compatibility with existing tools and software.

STOP & REVIEW

You have completed the outline for this subunit.
Study multiple-choice questions 1 through 7 beginning on page 271.

8.2 AUTHENTICATION, AUTHORIZATION, AND ENCRYPTION

1. **Application Authentication**

    a. Application authentication is a means of taking a user's identity from the operating system on which the user is working and passing it to an authentication server for verification. This can be designed into an application from its inception.

    b. **Two-level authentication** (also referred to as **two-factor authentication**) requires

    1) A username and password and
    2) Information known only to the user (e.g., information such as "make and model of the user's first car" or "favorite food") or something (s)he immediately has on hand (i.e., a physical hardware token).

    c. There are three classes of authentication information.

    1) Remembered information: name, birthdate, account number, password, PIN
    2) Possessed objects: badge, plastic card, key, finger ring
    3) Personal characteristics: fingerprint, voiceprint, hand size, signature, retinal pattern

2. **Encryption Overview**

    a. Encryption technology converts data into a code. A program codes data prior to transmission. Another program decodes it after transmission. Unauthorized users still may be able to access the data, but without the encryption key, they cannot decode the information.

    b. Encryption software uses a fixed algorithm (a step-by-step, usually mathematical, procedure) to manipulate plaintext (the understandable form of the encrypted text) and an encryption key to introduce variation.

    1) The information is sent in its manipulated form (cyphertext), and the receiver translates the information back into plaintext.
    2) Although data may be accessed by tapping into the transmission line, the encryption key is necessary to understand the data being sent.
    3) The machine instructions necessary to code and decode data can constitute a 20%-30% increase in system overhead.

    c. Encryption technology may be either hardware- or software-based. Two major types of encryption software exist: public-key and private-key.

3. **Public-Key (Asymmetric) Encryption**
   a. Public-key (asymmetric) encryption requires a pair of keys: one public and one private. These pairs of keys are issued by a trusted third party called a certificate authority (e.g., VeriSign, Thawte, GoDaddy).
      1) Every recipient's public key is available in the certificate authority's directory, but the associated private key is known only to the recipient.
      2) Any party who wishes to send a secure message encrypts it using the intended recipient's public key. The recipient then decrypts the message using the private key. The two keys are mathematically related so that a message encrypted with one key can be decrypted only with the other key.
   b. This arrangement is more secure than a single-key system, in which the parties must agree on and transmit a single key that could be intercepted.
      1) RSA, named for its developers (Rivest, Shamir, and Adelman), is the most commonly used public-key method.
   c. A **digital signature** is a means of authentication of an electronic document, for example, of the validity of a purchase order, acceptance of a contract, or financial information.
      1) The sender uses its private key to encode all or part of the message, and the recipient uses the sender's public key to decode it. Hence, if that key decodes the message, the sender must have written it.
      2) One variation is to send the message in both plaintext and cyphertext. If the decoded version matches the plaintext version, no alteration has occurred.
   d. A **digital certificate** is another means of authentication used in e-business. The certificate authority issues a coded electronic certificate that contains (1) the holder's name, (2) a copy of its public key, (3) a serial number, and (4) an expiration date. The certificate verifies the holder's identity.
      1) The recipient of a coded message sent by the holder uses the certificate authority's public key (available on the Internet) to decode the certificate included in the message. The recipient then determines that the certificate was issued by the certificate authority. Moreover, the recipient can use the sender's public key and identification data to send a coded response.
         a) Such methods may be used for transactions between sellers and buyers using credit cards.
      2) A certificate also may be used to provide assurance to customers that a website is genuine.
   e. The public key infrastructure permits secure monetary and information exchange over the Internet. Thus, it facilitates e-business.
      1) The two main cryptographic protocols for secure communications over the Internet are SSL (Secure Sockets Layer) and TLS (Transport Layer Security).
         a) When HTTP (Hypertext Transfer Protocol, a higher-level protocol that makes the graphics-intensive World Wide Web possible) is used in conjunction with SSL or TLS, it is called HTTPS (HTTP Secure).
         b) The URLs of secure web pages where shoppers enter their credit card numbers most often change from http:// to https://.
      2) Digital time stamping services verify the time (and possibly the place) of a transaction. For example, a document may be sent to a service, which applies its digital stamp and then forwards the document.

4. **Private-Key (Symmetric) Encryption**
   a. Private-key, or symmetric, encryption is less secure than the public-key method because it requires only a single (secret) key for each pair of parties that want to send each other coded messages.
      1) Data Encryption Standard (DES), a shared private-key method developed by the U.S. government, is the most prevalent secret-key method. It is based on numbers with 56 binary digits.
      2) The Advanced Encryption Standard (AES) is a cryptographic algorithm for use by U.S. government organizations to protect sensitive information.
         a) The National Institute of Standards and Technology started development of AES in 1997, when it announced the need for a successor algorithm for DES, which was becoming vulnerable to brute force attacks.

> You have completed the outline for this subunit.
> Study multiple-choice questions 8 through 10 beginning on page 273.

8.3 INFORMATION PROTECTION

1. **Business Objectives**
   a. According to the eSAC model (*Electronic Systems Assurance and Control*) published by The IIA, the following five categories are IT business assurance objectives:
      1) **Availability.** The organization must ensure that information, processes, and services are available at all times.
      2) **Capability.** The organization must ensure reliable and timely completion of transactions.
      3) **Functionality.** The organization must ensure that systems are designed to user specifications to fulfill business requirements.
      4) **Protectability.** The organization must ensure that a combination of physical and logical controls prevents unauthorized access to, or use of, system data.
      5) **Accountability.** The organization must ensure that transaction processing is accurate, complete, and non-refutable.
   b. One of the primary concerns of protectability relates to malicious software (malware). IT assets should have safeguards in place to prevent unauthorized access, use, or harm.
      1) Controls over access and change management processes should be in place to achieve the objective of protectability.
      2) Moreover, security awareness by all concerned should be heightened. Consequently, the business assurance objective of accountability is also pertinent. The roles, actions, and responsibilities for security should be defined.

2. **Malicious Software (Malware)**
    a. Malicious software may exploit a known hole or weakness in an application or operating system program to evade security measures.
        1) Such a vulnerability may have been caused by a programming error. It also may have been intentionally (but not maliciously) created to permit a programmer simple access (a back door) for correcting the code.
        2) Having bypassed security controls, the intruder can do immediate damage to the system or install malicious software. In some cases, malware infection may have few or no effects noticeable by users.
    b. A **Trojan horse** is an apparently innocent program (e.g., a spreadsheet) that includes a hidden function that may do damage when activated.
        1) For example, it may contain a virus, which is a program code that copies itself from file to file. The virus may destroy data or programs. Viruses commonly spread through email attachments and downloads.
        2) A Trojan horse may act as a back door to bypass normal authentication and provide unauthorized, remote access to data, computers, and networks.
    c. A **worm** copies itself not from file to file but from computer to computer, often very rapidly. Repeated replication overloads a system by depleting memory or overwhelming network traffic capacity.
    d. A **logic bomb** is much like a Trojan horse, except it activates only upon some occurrence, e.g., on a certain date such as Friday the 13th, April Fool's Day, etc.
    e. Malware may create a **denial of service** by overwhelming a system or website with more traffic than it can handle.
    f. **Ransomware** is a type of malware that threatens to publish the victim's data or prevents users from accessing their system or personal files and demands ransom payment in order to regain access.

3. **Controls against Malware**
    a. Controls to prevent or detect infection by malware are particularly significant for file servers in large networks. The following are broad control objectives:
        1) A policy should require use only of authorized software.
        2) A policy should require adherence to licensing agreements.
        3) A policy should create accountability for the persons authorized to maintain software.
        4) A policy should require safeguards when data or programs are obtained by means of external media.
        5) Antivirus software should continuously monitor the system for viruses (or worms) and eradicate them. It should also be immediately upgraded as soon as information about new threats becomes available.
        6) Software and data for critical systems should be regularly reviewed.
        7) Investigation of unauthorized files or amendments should be routine.
        8) Email attachments and downloads (and files on unauthorized media or from networks that are not secure) should be checked.
        9) Procedures should be established and responsibility assigned for coping with malware.
            a) Procedures should reflect an understanding that another organization that has transmitted malware-infected material may have done so unwittingly and may need assistance.
                i) If such events occur repeatedly, however, termination of agreements or contracts may be indicated.
            b) Procedures and policies should be documented, and employees must understand the reasons for them.
        10) Business continuity (recovery) plans should be drafted, e.g., data and software backup.
        11) Information about malware should be verified and appropriate alerts given.
        12) Responsible personnel should be aware of the possibility of hoaxes, which are false messages intending to create fear of a malware attack.
            a) For example, a spurious email message may be received instructing users to delete supposedly compromised files.
        13) Qualified personnel should be relied upon to distinguish hoaxes from malware.

b. The following are specific controls to prevent or detect infection by malware:
   1) All computer media (incoming or outgoing) may be scanned by sheep dip (dedicated) computers.
   2) Nonscreened media should not be allowed on the organization's computers.
   3) Scanning may be done of standalone computers or those on networks as another line of defense if media control fails.
   4) Software may reside in memory to scan for malware communicated through a network.
   5) Email gateways may have software to scan attachments.
   6) Network servers may have software to detect and erase or store malware.
   7) Scanning software on a standalone device should be upgraded when it is networked.
c. Use of external rather than internal expertise for coping with malware problems may be more costly and time consuming but less risky.
   1) External service providers should be subject to the terms of a contract, and access and other controls should be in place.
d. Off-site computers and media of employees should be subject to malware controls, such as screening.
e. Responses to threats via covert channels and Trojan horse programs include the following:
   1) Purchases should be of evaluated products from trusted suppliers.
   2) Purchases should be in source code so that they are verifiable. This code should be inspected and tested prior to use.
   3) Access to and changes in code should be restricted after it is put in use.
   4) The availability of security patches for bugs in programs should be monitored constantly, especially regarding such items as network operating systems, email servers, routers, and firewalls. Patches should be tested and installed promptly.
   5) Trusted employees should be assigned to key systems.
   6) Known Trojan horses can be detected by scanning.
   7) Reviewing data outflows, for example, through the firewall, may detect suspicious activity meriting investigation.
f. Hosts are the most common targets in a network because they furnish services to other requesting hosts.
   1) Protective measures include promptly installing the most recent patches, fixes, and updates.
      a) The effects of protective measures on other elements of the system should be considered.
      b) Updates should be tested before installation.

4. **Types of Attacks**
    a. **Password Attacks**
        1) A **brute-force attack** uses password-cracking software to try large numbers of letter and number combinations to access a network.
            i) A simple variation is the use of password-cracking software that tries all the words in a dictionary.
        2) Passwords (and user accounts) also may be discovered by Trojan horses, IP spoofing, and packet sniffers.
            a) Phishing (spoofing) is identity misrepresentation in cyberspace. **Phishing** is a method of electronically obtaining confidential information through deceit.
                i) The perpetrator sets up a website that appears to be legitimate but actually serves no purpose other than to obtain the victim's information.
                ii) Phishing scams are often initiated through email spoofing, in which the perpetrator sends out emails that appear to be from a real financial institution. When the victim clicks on the link to what (s)he thinks is the institution's website, the victim is unknowingly redirected to the perpetrator's website.
            b) **Sniffing** is the use of software to eavesdrop on information sent by a user to the host computer of a website.
        3) Once an attacker has access, (s)he may do anything the rightful user could have done.
            a) If that user has privileged access, the attacker may create a back door to facilitate future entry despite password and status changes.
            b) The attacker also may be able to leverage the initial access to obtain greater privileges than the rightful user.
        4) If a user has the same password for multiple hosts, cracking that password for one compromises all.
        5) Expressive methods of thwarting password attacks are one-time password and cryptographic authentication.
        6) Optimal passwords are randomly generated, eight-character or longer combinations of numbers, uppercase and lowercase letters, and special symbols.
            a) A disadvantage is that users often write down passwords that are hard to remember. However, software has been developed that encrypts passwords to be kept on a handheld computer. Thus, the user only needs to know one password.
    b. A **man-in-the-middle attack** takes advantage of networking, packet sniffing, and routing and transport protocols.
        1) These attacks may be used to
            a) Steal data
            b) Obtain access to the network during a rightful user's active session
            c) Analyze the traffic on the network to learn about its operations and users
            d) Insert new data or modify the data being transmitted
            e) Deny service
        2) Encryption is the effective response to man-in-the-middle attacks. The encrypted data will be useless to the attacker unless it can be decrypted.

c. A **denial-of-service (DoS)** attack is an attempt to overload a system (e.g., a network or web server) with false messages so that it cannot function (a system crash).

　1) A distributed DoS (DDoS) attack comes from multiple sources, for example, the machines of innocent parties infected by Trojan horses. When activated, these programs send messages to the target and leave the connection open.

　2) A DoS may establish as many network connections as possible to exclude other users, overloading primary memory, or corrupting file systems.

　3) Responses

　　a) Firewalls should not permit use of Internet relay chat channels or other TCP/IP ports unless for business purposes. Thus, the organization should determine what relay kits have been installed, e.g., by employees connected to virtual private networks via cable or DSL.

　　　i) These methods, intrusion detection systems, and penetration testing may prevent a system from being used to make a DoS attack.

　　b) The best protection by the target is the Internet service provider (ISP). The ISP can establish rate limits on transmissions to the target's website.

　　　i) Thus, only a defined amount of message packets with certain characteristics are allowed to reach the site.

d. **Software piracy** is a problem for vendors. Any duplication of software beyond what is allowed in the software license agreement is illegal.

　1) The best way to detect an illegal copy of application software is to compare the serial number on the screen with the vendor's serial number.

　2) Use of unlicensed software increases the risk of introducing computer viruses into the organization. Such software is less likely to have been carefully tested.

　3) To avoid legal liability, controls also should be implemented to prevent use of unlicensed software that is not in the public domain.

　　a) A software licensing agreement permits a user to employ either a specified or an unlimited number of copies of a software product at given locations, at particular machines, or throughout the organization. The agreement may restrict reproduction or resale, and it may provide subsequent customer support and product improvements.

　4) Software piracy can expose an organization's personnel to both civil and criminal penalties. The Business Software Alliance (BSA) is a worldwide trade group that coordinates software vendors' efforts to prosecute the illegal duplication of software.

e. **Computer tampering** is unauthorized access to programs, data, or computers that is used for fraudulent purposes or to damage another computer, data, or program.

f. **Hacking** refers to unauthorized intrusion into a computer or network for modification or alteration (i.e., tampering) of the computer software or hardware to accomplish a goal outside the creator's original objective.

5. **Countermeasures -- Intrusion Detection System (IDS)**
    a. If an organization's computer system has external connections, an IDS is needed to respond to security breaches.
        1) The IDS complements the computer system's firewalls. It responds to attacks on
            a) The network infrastructure (protected by the network IDS component)
                i) Routers
                ii) Switches
                iii) Bandwidth
            b) Servers (protected by the host IDS component)
                i) Operating systems
                ii) Applications
        2) An IDS responds to an attack by
            a) Taking action itself
            b) Alerting the management system
    b. A host IDS provides maximum protection only when the software is installed on each computer. It may operate in the following ways:
        1) The aggressive response is to monitor every call on the operating system and application as it occurs.
        2) A less effective method of preventing attacks is analysis of access log files.
        3) A host IDS may also identify questionable processes and verify the security of system files.
    c. A network IDS works by using sensors to examine packets traveling on the network. Each sensor monitors only the segment of the network to which it is attached. A packet is examined if it matches a signature.
        1) String signatures (certain strings of text) are potential signs of an attack.
        2) Port signatures alert the IDS that a point subject to frequent intrusion attempts may be under attack.
            a) A port in this sense (as opposed to the physical serial and parallel ports on a personal computer) is a logical connection to the system.
            b) A port number included in the message header stipulates how the message will be handled. Because many port numbers are widely known, an attacker may be able to send messages to determine whether ports are open and therefore vulnerable.
        3) A header signature is a suspicious combination in a packet header.
    d. The preferable IDS combines host IDS and network IDS components.
        1) A host IDS has greater potential for preventing a specific attack, but the network IDS provides a necessary overall perspective. Thus, a host IDS should be in place for each host, with a network IDS for the whole system.

e. Knowledge-based detection is based on information about the system's weaknesses and searches for intrusions that take advantage of them.

1) This type of IDS depends on frequent and costly updating of information about intrusion methods. It is also specialized with respect to those methods and operating system methods.

a) Problems are compounded when different versions of the operating system (or different operating systems) are in place.

f. Behavior-based detection presumes that an attack will cause an observable anomaly. Actual and normal system behavior (a model of expected operations) are compared. A discrepancy results in an alert.

1) This approach is more complete than the knowledge-based approach because every attack should be detected. However, the level of accuracy is lower. False alarms may be generated, so the model must be updated whenever operational changes are made.

2) The advantages of behavior-based detection are that

a) Knowledge of specific new intrusion techniques is not necessary.
b) It is less specific to particular operating systems.

g. Responses to detection of an intrusion normally include an automatic component. Continuous monitoring and response by individuals may not be feasible or sufficiently rapid.

1) An automatically acting IDS provides continuous security. It responds without the presence of humans. Responses may include

a) Disconnecting the entire network from outside access
b) Locking access to all or part of the system
c) Slowing the system's activity to reduce injury
d) Validating the external user
e) Sending console, email, pager, or phone messages to appropriate personnel

2) Alarmed systems resources are dummy files or accounts, for example, a default administrator account with a default password set. They are traps for an intruder.

a) Access to a dummy resource results in automatic action or notice to appropriate employees.
b) The advantage of this method is that it is uncomplicated and inexpensive.
c) The disadvantage is that authorized persons may inadvertently cause an alarm.

6. **Information Integrity and Reliability**

    a. Internal auditors often assess the organization's information integrity and reliability practices.

        1) Internal auditors determine whether senior management and the board have a clear understanding that information reliability and integrity is a management responsibility. This responsibility includes all critical information of the organization regardless of how the information is stored. Information reliability and integrity includes accuracy, completeness, and security.

        2) The chief audit executive (CAE) determines whether the internal audit activity possesses, or has access to, competent audit resources to evaluate information reliability and integrity and associated risk exposures. This includes both internal and external risk exposures, and exposures relating to the organization's relationships with outside entities.

        3) Internal auditors assess the effectiveness of preventive, detective, and mitigation measures against past attacks, as appropriate, and future attempts or incidents deemed likely to occur. Internal auditors determine whether the board has been appropriately informed of threats, incidents, vulnerabilities exploited, and corrective measures.

        4) Internal auditors periodically assess the organization's information reliability and integrity practices and recommend, as appropriate, enhancements to, or implementation of, new controls and safeguards. Such assessments can either be conducted as separate stand-alone engagements or integrated into other audits or engagements conducted as part of the internal audit plan.

7. **Privacy**

    a. Management is responsible for ensuring that an organization's privacy framework is in place. Internal auditors' primary role is to ensure that relevant privacy laws and other regulations are being properly communicated to the responsible parties.

        1) Risks associated with the privacy of information encompass personal privacy (physical and psychological); privacy of space (freedom from surveillance); privacy of communication (freedom from monitoring); and privacy of information (collection, use, and disclosure of personal information by others).

            a) Personal information is information associated with a specific individual.

        2) Effective control over the protection of personal information is an essential component of the governance, risk management, and control processes of an organization.

            a) The board is ultimately accountable for identifying the principal risks to the organization and implementing appropriate control processes to mitigate those risks. This includes establishing the necessary privacy framework for the organization and monitoring its implementation.

3) In conducting such an evaluation of the management of the organization's privacy framework, the internal auditor

   a) Considers the laws, regulations, and policies relating to privacy in the jurisdictions where the organization operates and where information travels and is stored;

   b) Liaisons with in-house legal counsel to determine the exact nature of laws, regulations, and other standards and practices applicable to the organization and the country/countries in which it operates;

   c) Liaisons with information technology specialists to determine that information security and data protection controls are in place and regularly reviewed and assessed for appropriateness; and

   d) Considers the level or maturity of the organization's privacy practices. Depending upon the level, the internal auditor may have differing roles.

4) Violations of privacy laws and regulations may result in fines, civil suits, and damage to the organization's reputation.

b. The European Union's (EU) General Data Protection Regulation (GDPR), enacted on May 25, 2018, stipulates that any organization with an Internet presence in the EU is required to comply with the following or be subject to fines of up to 4% based on an organization's worldwide sales or €20 million, whichever is greater:

1) Gaining approval of EU citizens before processing or moving personal data

2) Providing data breach notifications

3) For specific organizations, requiring the appointment of a data protection officer to oversee GDPR compliance

8. **Emerging Technology Practices and Their Effects on Security**

   a. Organizations (including internal auditors) must assess the effects on information security as technology is improved and replaced with more advanced technology such as the following:

   1) **Smart machines** are automation technology that enable processes or procedures to be performed without human assistance.

      a) Generally, smart machine technology characteristics include but are not limited to (1) learning and operating on their own, (2) adapting their behavior based on experience (learning), and (3) generating unanticipated results.

      b) Smart machines include (1) self-driving cars, (2) robots, and (3) self-service checkout counters at a supermarket.

   2) **Bring your own device (BYOD)** is the use by people associated with the organization (i.e., business owners, employees, customers, vendors, etc.) of their own computing devices (e.g., computers, tablets, and smartphones) to access the organization's computer applications to conduct business.

   3) The **Internet of things (IoT)** is the connection of devices other than typical items such as computers and smartphones to the Internet. Cars, medical monitors, residential and commercial alarms, and locator chips implanted in animals are examples of devices that can be connected via IoT.

b. Risks associated with the use of smart technology (including BYOD) accessing an organization's information systems include the following:
1) **Compliance** risks involve the users of the smart technology not complying with policies, procedures, and controls or failing to install updates that subject the organization to vulnerabilities and lead to system downtime.
2) **Privacy** risks range from protecting personal information accessed or stored on a smart device to concerns of the users that the organization is surveilling the user.
3) Security risks include physical security and data security.
   a) **Physical security** risks are associated with smart devices as a result of their portability. Information might become vulnerable to misuse in the event of theft or loss of the smart device or if the device is not cleaned of all data associated with the organization when the user leaves the organization.
   b) **Data security** risks involve unauthorized access to information through methods that include but are not limited to unsecure network connections, unauthorized applications, and bypassing security protocols of smart device operating systems [e.g., jailbreaking (Apple OS) or rooting (Android OS)].

c. Controls that generally lessen or eliminate the risks associated with the use of smart technology accessing an organization's information systems include the following:
1) **Authentication** restricts the use of the smart device to only authorized users.
2) **Remote wipe** is the process of deleting data and applications without physical access to the smart device.
3) **Encryption** of data in transit and stored on the smart device.
4) **Anti-malware software** guards against malicious software.
5) A **BYOD policy** that encompasses controls such as
   a) Approved devices
   b) Reporting lost or stolen devices
   c) Use of secured networks only
   d) Use of authorized applications only
   e) Not bypassing security protocols of smart device operating systems
   f) Backups and transfers among devices
   g) Replacing currently used devices with new devices

STOP & REVIEW

You have completed the outline for this subunit.
Study multiple-choice questions 11 through 16 beginning on page 274.

8.4 CONTINGENCY PLANNING AND DISASTER RECOVERY

1. **Overview**

    a. The information security goal of data availability is primarily the responsibility of the IT function.

    b. Contingency planning is the name commonly given to this activity.

    1) **Disaster recovery** is the process of resuming normal information processing operations after the occurrence of a major interruption.

    2) **Business continuity** is the continuation of business by other means during the period in which computer processing is unavailable or less than normal.

    c. Plans must be made for two major types of contingencies: those in which the data center is physically available and those in which it is not.

    1) Examples of the first type of contingency are (a) power failure, (b) random intrusions such as viruses, and (c) deliberate intrusions such as hacking incidents. The organization's physical facilities are sound, but immediate action is required to continue normal processing.

    2) The second type of contingency is much more serious. It is caused by disasters such as floods, fires, hurricanes, or earthquakes. An occurrence of this type requires an alternate processing facility.

2. **Backup and Rotation**

    a. Periodic backup and offsite rotation of computer files is the most basic part of any disaster recovery or business continuity plan. A database system requires a more elaborate backup procedure than other systems.

    1) An organization's data are more valuable than its hardware. Hardware can be replaced for a price, but each organization's data are unique and indispensable to operations. If they are destroyed, they cannot be replaced. For this reason, periodic backup and rotation are essential.

    b. A typical backup routine duplicates all data files and application programs once a month. Incremental changes are then backed up and taken to an offsite location once a week. (Application files and data must be backed up because both change.)

    1) In case of an interruption of normal processing, the organization's systems can be restored so that, at most, 7 days of business information is lost.

    2) Retaining each day's transaction files is good business practice because information processed since the last backup file can be restored.

    c. Checkpoint/restart information is not needed. The backups are created after all processing is finished for the day.

    d. The offsite location must be temperature- and humidity-controlled and guarded against physical intrusion. Just as important, it must be far enough away from the site of main operations not to be affected by the same natural disaster. Adequate backup is useless if the files are not accessible or have been destroyed.

3. **Risk Assessment Steps**

    a. Identify and prioritize the organization's critical applications.

    1) Not all of an organization's systems are equally important. The firm must decide which vital applications it simply cannot do business without and in what order they should be brought back into operation.

    b. Determine the minimum recovery time frames and minimum hardware requirements.

    1) How long will it take to reinstall each critical application, and what platform is required? If the interruption has been caused by an attack, such as a virus or hacker, how long will it take to isolate the problem and eliminate it from the system?

    c. Develop a recovery plan.

4. **Disaster Recovery Plan (DRP)**

    a. Disaster recovery is the process of regaining access to data (e.g., hardware, software, and records), communications, work areas, and other business processes.

    b. Thus, a DRP that is established and tested must be developed in connection with the business continuity plan. It should describe IT recovery strategies, including details about procedures, vendors, and systems.

    1) Detailed procedures must be updated when systems and businesses change. A plan could quickly become out of date as a result of changes in equipment, data, and software. The following are examples of items addressed by the DRP:

        a) Data center
        b) Applications and data needed
        c) Servers and other hardware
        d) Communications
        e) Network connections
        f) IT infrastructure (e.g., log-on services and software distribution)
        g) Remote access services
        h) Process control systems
        i) File rooms
        j) Document management systems

    c. The following are considerations for choosing DRP strategies:

    1) The DRP should be based on the business impact analysis (discussed in detail on page 269).
    2) The recovery abilities of critical service providers must be assessed.
    3) The recovery of IT components often must be combined to recover a system.
    4) Service providers (internal and external) must furnish recovery information, such as their

        a) Responsibilities,
        b) Limitations,
        c) Recovery activities,
        d) Recovery time and point objectives, and
        e) Costs.

    5) Strategies for components may be developed independently. The objective is the best, most cost-effective solution that (a) allows user access and (b) permits components to work together, regardless of where systems are recovered.
    6) Security and compliance standards must be considered.

5. **Contingencies with Data Center Available**

    a. The purchase of backup electrical generators protects against power failures. These can be programmed to begin running automatically as soon as a dip in electric current is detected. This practice is widespread in settings such as hospitals where 24-hour availability is crucial.

    b. Attacks such as viruses and denial-of-service require a completely different response. The system must be brought down gracefully to halt the spread of the infection. The IT staff must be well trained in the nature of the latest virus threats to know how to isolate the damage and bring the system back to full operation.

6. **Contingencies with Data Center Unavailable**

    a. The most extreme contingency is a disaster that makes the organization's main facility unusable. To prepare for these cases, organizations contract for alternate processing facilities.

    b. An **alternate processing facility** is a physical location maintained by an outside contractor for the purpose of providing processing facilities for customers in case of disaster.

    1) The recovery center, like the off-site storage location for backup files, must be far enough from the main facility that it is not affected by the same natural disaster. Usually, organizations contract for backup facilities in another city.

    2) When processing is no longer possible at the principal site, the backup files are retrieved from the secure storage location and taken to the recovery center.

    c. Recovery centers take three basic forms. Organizations determine which facility is best by calculating the trade-off between the cost of the contract and the cost of downtime.

    1) A **hot site** is a fully operational processing facility that is immediately available. The organization generally contracts with a service provider.

        a) For a fee, the service provider agrees to have a hardware platform and communications lines substantially identical to the organization's ready for use 24 hours a day, 365 days a year.

        b) This solution is the least risky and most expensive.

        c) Any contract for a hot site must include a provision for annual testing.

            i) The service provider agrees to a window of time in which the organization can declare a fake disaster, load its backup files onto the equipment at the hot site, and determine how long it takes to resume normal processing.

    2) A **cold site** is a shell facility with sufficient electrical power, environmental controls, and communications lines to permit the organization to install its own newly acquired equipment.

        a) On an ongoing basis, this solution is much less expensive.

        b) However, the time to procure replacement equipment can be weeks or months. Also, emergency procurement from equipment vendors can be very expensive.

    3) A **warm site** is a compromise between a cold and hot site, combining features of both.

        a) Resources are available at the site but may need to be configured to support the production system.

        b) Some data may need to be restored.

        c) Typical recovery time ranges from 2 days to 2 weeks.

7. **Fault Tolerance**

    a. A fault-tolerant computer has additional chips and disk storage as well as a backup power supply. This technology is used for mission-critical applications that cannot afford to suffer downtime. Accordingly, the user has the ability to continue processing at all sites except a nonfunctioning one.

        1) The technology that permits fault-tolerance is the redundant array of inexpensive (or independent) disks, or RAID. It is a group of multiple hard drives with special software that allows for data delivery along multiple paths. If one drive fails, the other disks can compensate for the loss.

    b. High-availability computing is used for less-critical applications because it provides for a short recovery time rather than the elimination of recovery time.

8. **Business Continuity Management (BCM) Overview**

    a. The objective of BCM is to restore critical processes and to minimize financial and other effects of a disaster or business disruption.

    b. BCM is the third component of an **emergency management program**. Its time frame is measured in hours and days if not weeks. The other components are

        1) **Emergency response**, the goal of which is lifesaving, safety, and initial efforts to limit the effects of a disaster to asset damage. Its time frame is measured in hours if not minutes.

        2) **Crisis management**, the focus of which is managing communications and senior management activities. Its time frame is measured in days if not hours.

9. **Elements of BCM**

    a. **Management Support**

        1) Management must assign adequate resources to preparing, maintaining, and practicing a business continuity plan.

    b. **Risk Assessment and Mitigation**

        1) The assessment identifies risks from such threats (disruptive events) as

            a) Natural disasters.
            b) IT events (e.g., cyberterrorism, viruses, and denial-of-service attack).
            c) Supplier failures.
            d) Industrial events (e.g., fires and toxic waste spills).
            e) Labor disruptions.
            f) Human failures (e.g., fraud, other criminal acts, and errors).

        2) BCM then assesses their probability and effects and develops mitigation strategies.

c. **Business Impact Analysis**

1) This analysis identifies critical business processes necessary to function in a disaster and determines how soon they should be recovered.

2) The organization (a) identifies critical processes, (b) defines the recovery time objective (RTO) and the recovery point objective (RPO) for processes and resources, and (c) identifies the other parties (e.g., vendors and other divisions of the organization) and physical resources (e.g., critical equipment and records) needed for recovery.

   a) A **recovery time objective** is the duration of time and service level within which a process must be restored. A **recovery point objective** is the amount of data the organization can afford to lose.

   b) The cost of a recovery solution ordinarily increases as either objective decreases.

d. **Business Recovery and Continuity Strategy**

1) A crucial element of business recovery is the existence of a comprehensive and current disaster recovery plan, which addresses the actual steps, people, and resources required to recover a critical business process. (Disaster recovery plans were discussed in greater detail earlier.)

2) The organization plans for

   a) Alternative staffing (e.g., staff remaining at the site, staff at another site, or staff of another organization),

   b) Alternative sourcing (e.g., use of nonstandard products and services, use of diverse suppliers, outsourcing to organizations that provide standard services, or reciprocal disaster recovery agreements with competitors),

      i) When reviewing **reciprocal disaster recovery agreements**, the primary concern is whether the hardware and software of the participating organizations are compatible.

   c) Alternative work spaces (e.g., another organization facility, remote access with proper security, or a commercial recovery site), and

   d) The return to normal operations (e.g., entry of manually processed data, resolution of regulatory and financial exceptions, return of borrowed equipment, and replenishment of products and supplies).

e. **Education, Awareness, and Maintenance**

1) Education and awareness (including training exercises) are vital to BCM and execution of the business continuity plan.

2) The BCM capabilities and documentation must be maintained to ensure that they remain effective and aligned with business priorities.

f. **Business Continuity**

1) According to The IIA, large-scale exercises (or testing) of the BCM programs and BC plans should be conducted at least annually.
2) The following are different types of exercises:
    a) A **desk check** is a review of the written plan to ensure accuracy of the documentation. It is the least invasive type of exercise or test.
    b) The **orientation** or plan walk-through method ensures that all team members understand their new roles and the basic plan content and format.
        i) This method allows the employees expected to implement the plan to walk through the document informally.
        ii) Normally, this type of low-intensity event **does not** constitute a test.
    c) A **tabletop exercise** simulates an emergency situation in an informal, stress-free environment. The purpose is to help team members understand the importance of their roles and responsibilities.
    d) **Communication testing** normally involves actual contact with business partners and employees. The objectives include
        i) Validating the contact information of key stakeholders,
        ii) Training participants in how to use mass notification and otherwise perform any roles they have in the response,
        iii) Properly configuring mass notification tools, and
        iv) Identifying communication gaps where timely communication could falter during a disaster.
    e) An **IT environment walk-through** involves conducting an announced or unannounced disaster simulation and executing documented system recovery procedures.
    f) **End-to-end testing** determines whether an application is performing as designed from start to finish. The test validates connectivity to the organization's production site.

You have completed the outline for this subunit.
Study multiple-choice questions 17 through 23 beginning on page 276.

STOP & REVIEW

QUESTIONS

8.1 Information Security and Cybersecurity Related Policies and Controls

1. An Internet firewall is designed to provide adequate protection against which of the following?

A. A computer virus.
B. Unauthenticated logins from outside users.
C. Insider leaking of confidential information.
D. A Trojan horse application.

Answer (B) is correct.
REQUIRED: The protection provided by an Internet firewall.
DISCUSSION: A firewall is a combination of hardware and software that separates two networks and prevents passage of specific types of network traffic while maintaining a connection between the networks. Generally, an Internet firewall is designed to protect a system from unauthenticated logins from outside users, although it may provide several other features as well.
Answer (A) is incorrect. A firewall cannot adequately protect a system against computer viruses.
Answer (C) is incorrect. Industrial spies need not leak information through the firewall. A telephone or flash drive are much more common means of sharing confidential information.
Answer (D) is incorrect. A firewall cannot adequately protect against a Trojan horse (a program, such as a game, that appears friendly but that actually contains applications destructive to the computer system) or any other program that can be executed in the system by an internal user.

2. Authentication is the process by which the

A. System verifies that the user is entitled to enter the transaction requested.
B. System verifies the identity of the user.
C. User identifies himself or herself to the system.
D. User indicates to the system that the transaction was processed correctly.

Answer (B) is correct.
REQUIRED: The definition of authentication.
DISCUSSION: Identification is the process of uniquely distinguishing one user from all others. Authentication is the process of determining that individuals are who they say they are. For example, a password may identify but not authenticate its user if it is known by more than one individual.
Answer (A) is incorrect. Authentication involves verifying the identity of the user. This process does not necessarily confirm the functions the user is authorized to perform.
Answer (C) is incorrect. User identification to the system does not imply that the system has verified the identity of the user.
Answer (D) is incorrect. This procedure is an application control for accuracy of the transaction.

3. Which of the following issues would be of most concern to an auditor relating to an organization's information security policy?

A. Auditor documentation.
B. System efficiency.
C. Data integrity.
D. Rejected and suspense item controls.

Answer (C) is correct.
REQUIRED: The item of most concern to the auditor relating to Internet security.
DISCUSSION: Controls are intended to ensure the integrity, confidentiality, and availability of information. An auditor relies on the integrity of the system's data and programs in making critical decisions throughout the audit process.
Answer (A) is incorrect. Auditor documentation is not as crucial as data integrity.
Answer (B) is incorrect. Efficiency does not affect the basis for critical auditor decisions using information provided by the system.
Answer (D) is incorrect. Rejected and suspense item controls represent a portion of the techniques used to ensure data integrity.

4. Passwords for personal computer software programs are designed to prevent

A. Inaccurate processing of data.
B. Unauthorized access to the computer.
C. Incomplete updating of data files.
D. Unauthorized use of the software.

Answer (D) is correct.
REQUIRED: The function of passwords.
DISCUSSION: The use of passwords is an effective control in an online system to prevent unauthorized access to computer files. Lists of authorized users are maintained in the computer. The entry of passwords or ID numbers; a prearranged set of personal questions; and use of badges, magnetic cards, or optically scanned cards may be combined to avoid unauthorized access.
Answer (A) is incorrect. Passwords concern authorization, not accuracy of data. **Answer (B) is incorrect.** Passwords do not prevent physical access to the computer. **Answer (C) is incorrect.** Passwords concern authorization, not completeness of data.

5. A client installed sophisticated controls using the biometric attributes of employees to authenticate user access to the computer system. This technology most likely replaced which of the following controls?

A. Use of security specialists.
B. Reasonableness tests.
C. Passwords.
D. Virus protection software.

Answer (C) is correct.
REQUIRED: The control most likely replaced by biometric technologies.
DISCUSSION: The use of passwords is an effective control in an online system to prevent unauthorized access to computer systems. However, biometric technologies are more sophisticated and difficult to compromise.
Answer (A) is incorrect. Biometric technologies do not eliminate the need for specialists who evaluate and monitor security needs. **Answer (B) is incorrect.** Reasonableness tests are related to input controls, not access controls. **Answer (D) is incorrect.** Virus protection software prevents damage to data in a system, not access to a system.

6. Which of the following statements is **incorrect** regarding information security and cybersecurity?

A. Cybersecurity is information security applied to computer hardware, software, and networks.
B. Standards associated with information security and cybersecurity include de facto and de jure types.
C. Availability of data is one of the objectives of information security and cybersecurity.
D. Information security and cybersecurity are commonly viewed as synonymous terms; however, cybersecurity is more expansive than information security.

Answer (D) is correct.
REQUIRED: The incorrect statement about information security and cybersecurity.
DISCUSSION: Information security and cybersecurity are commonly viewed as synonymous terms; however, information security is more expansive than cybersecurity. Information security involves securing data in any form (e.g., locking paper documents in filing cabinets and file storage rooms and storing electronic data on IT equipment), whereas cybersecurity concentrates on protecting electronic data.
Answer (A) is incorrect. Cybersecurity is information security applied to computer hardware, software, and networks. **Answer (B) is incorrect.** Standards assist the implementation of policies by detailing what actions must occur to comply with policy. Standards are categorized as de facto standards and de jure standards. **Answer (C) is incorrect.** The main objectives of information security and cybersecurity are safeguarding against unauthorized access to data (paper or electronic form) and maintaining the integrity and availability of the data.

7. The basis of effective information security and cybersecurity are

A. De facto standards.
B. Policies.
C. De jure standards.
D. Procedures.

Answer (B) is correct.
REQUIRED: The basis of effective information security and cybersecurity policies.
DISCUSSION: Policies form the foundation of effective information security and cybersecurity measures. The successful planning, design, and implementation of security procedures are initiated by strong policies and management support. Policies govern how to resolve issues and the use of IT infrastructure to resolve issues.
Answer (A) is incorrect. Standards assist the implementation of policies by detailing what actions must occur to comply with policy. Standards are categorized as de facto and de jure. De facto standards are informal standards that have been widely adopted and accepted.
Answer (C) is incorrect. De jure standards are formal standards that have been assessed, approved, and sanctioned. Standards assist the implementation of policies by detailing what actions must occur to comply with policy. Standards are categorized as de facto and de jure. **Answer (D) is incorrect.** Guidelines and procedures illustrate how to comply with policies by providing detailed instructions.

8.2 Authentication, Authorization, and Encryption

8. A client communicates sensitive data across the Internet. Which of the following controls would be most effective to prevent the use of the information if it were intercepted by an unauthorized party?

A. A firewall.
B. An access log.
C. Passwords.
D. Encryption.

Answer (D) is correct.
REQUIRED: The most effective control for preventing the use of intercepted information.
DISCUSSION: Encryption technology converts data into a code. Encoding data before transmission over communications lines makes it more difficult for someone with access to the transmission to understand or modify its contents.
Answer (A) is incorrect. A firewall tries to prevent access from specific types of traffic to an internal network. After someone has obtained information from the site, a firewall cannot prevent its use. **Answer (B) is incorrect.** An access log only records attempted usage of a system. **Answer (C) is incorrect.** Passwords prevent unauthorized users from accessing the system. If information has already been obtained, a password cannot prevent its use.

9. To ensure privacy in a public-key encryption system, knowledge of which of the following keys would be required to decode the received message?

1. Private
2. Public

A. 1.
B. 2.
C. Both 1 and 2.
D. Neither 1 nor 2.

Answer (A) is correct.
REQUIRED: The key(s) required to decode messages in a public-key system to ensure privacy.
DISCUSSION: In a public-key system, the public key is used to encrypt the message prior to transmission, and the private key is needed to decrypt (decode) the message.

10. The use of two-level authentication

A. Requires a username and password only.
B. Protects against a Trojan horse attack.
C. Requires information known only to the user.
D. Protects against a logic bomb.

Answer (C) is correct.
REQUIRED: The various forms of user authentication and authorization controls.
DISCUSSION: Two-level authentication (also referred to as two-factor authentication) requires (1) a username and password and (2) information known only to the user (e.g., information such as "make and model of the user's first car" or "favorite food") or something (s)he immediately has on hand (i.e., a physical hardware token).
Answer (A) is incorrect. Two-level authentication requires other information in addition to a username and password. **Answer (B) is incorrect.** A Trojan horse is an apparently innocent program (e.g., a spreadsheet) that includes a hidden function that may do damage when activated. For example, it may contain a virus, which is a program code that copies itself from file to file. The virus may destroy data or programs. Viruses commonly spread through email attachments and downloads. Anti-virus software is generally used to protect against Trojan horses. **Answer (D) is incorrect.** A logic bomb is much like a Trojan horse except it activates only upon some occurrence, e.g., on a certain date. Anti-virus software is generally used to protect against Trojan horses.

8.3 Information Protection

11. All of the following are correct statements regarding smart devices **except**

A. The portability of smart devices is a major factor when assessing physical security risks.
B. Smart machines are automation technology.
C. Remote wipe is the process of deleting data and applications without physical access to the smart device.
D. Although smart devices have the capability of adapting their behavior based on experience, smart devices are not able to learn and operate on their own.

Answer (D) is correct.
REQUIRED: The incorrect statement about emerging technology practices and their impact on security.
DISCUSSION: Generally, smart machine technology characteristics include but are not limited to (1) learning and operating on their own, (2) adapting their behavior based on experience (learning), and (3) generating unanticipated results.
Answer (A) is incorrect. Physical security risks are associated with smart devices as a result of their portability. Information might become vulnerable to misuse in the event of theft or loss of the smart device or if the device is not cleaned of all data associated with the organization when the user leaves the organization. **Answer (B) is incorrect.** Smart machines are automation technology that enable processes or procedures to be performed without human assistance. Generally, smart machine technology characteristics include but are not limited to (1) learning and operating on their own, (2) adapting their behavior based on experience (learning), and (3) generating unanticipated results. **Answer (C) is incorrect.** Controls that generally lessen or eliminate the risks associated with the use of smart technology accessing an organization's information systems include but are not limited to remote wipe, authentication, encryption, and anti-malware software.

12. Which of the following is an indication that a computer virus is present?

A. Frequent power surges that harm computer equipment.
B. Unexplainable losses of or changes to data.
C. Inadequate backup, recovery, and contingency plans.
D. Numerous copyright violations due to unauthorized use of purchased software.

Answer (B) is correct.
REQUIRED: The indicator of a computer virus.
DISCUSSION: The effects of computer viruses range from harmless messages to complete destruction of all data within the system. A symptom of a virus would be the unexplained loss of or change to data.
Answer (A) is incorrect. Power surges are caused by hardware or power supply problems. Answer (C) is incorrect. Inadequate backup, recovery, and contingency plans are operating policy weaknesses. Answer (D) is incorrect. Copyright violations represent policy or compliance problems.

13. Which of the following is a computer program that appears to be legitimate but performs some illicit activity when it is run?

A. Hoax virus.
B. Web crawler.
C. Trojan horse.
D. Killer application.

Answer (C) is correct.
REQUIRED: The apparently legitimate computer program that performs an illicit activity.
DISCUSSION: A Trojan horse is a computer program that appears friendly, for example, a game, but that actually contains an application destructive to the computer system.
Answer (A) is incorrect. A hoax virus is a false notice about the existence of a computer virus. It is usually disseminated through use of distribution lists and is sent by email or via an internal network. Answer (B) is incorrect. A web crawler (a spider or bot) is a computer program created to access and read information on websites. The results are included as entries in the index of a search engine. Answer (D) is incorrect. A killer application is one that is so useful that it may justify widespread adoption of a new technology.

14. The reliability and integrity of all critical information of an organization, regardless of the media in which the information is stored, is the responsibility of

A. Shareholders.
B. IT department.
C. Management.
D. All employees.

Answer (C) is correct.
REQUIRED: The responsibility for information reliability and integrity.
DISCUSSION: Internal auditors determine whether senior management and the board have a clear understanding that information reliability and integrity is a management responsibility. Information reliability and integrity includes accuracy, completeness, and security.
Answer (A) is incorrect. Management has a responsibility to shareholders and other stakeholders (customers, vendors, etc.) to ensure information is secure and reliable. Answer (B) is incorrect. The IT department is generally the functional department charged by management to monitor and ensure all information is controlled in accordance with company policies and rules. Answer (D) is incorrect. Management has a responsibility to employees to ensure employee information (employee Social Security numbers, direct deposit account information, etc.) is secure and accurate.

15. Select the cyberattack which is best associated with extorting an individual or an organization.

A. Ransomware.
B. Phishing.
C. Software piracy.
D. Hacking.

Answer (A) is correct.
REQUIRED: The various forms of cyberattacks.
DISCUSSION: Ransomware is a type of malware that threatens to publish the victim's data or prevents users from accessing their system or personal files and demands ransom payment in order to regain access.
Answer (B) is incorrect. Phishing is a method of electronically obtaining confidential information through deceit. The perpetrator sets up a website that appears to be legitimate but actually serves no purpose other than to obtain the victim's information. **Answer (C) is incorrect.** Software piracy is any duplication of software beyond what is allowed in the software license agreement. Software piracy is illegal, and use of unlicensed software increases the risk of introducing computer viruses into the organization. Such software is less likely to have been carefully tested. **Answer (D) is incorrect.** Hacking refers to unauthorized intrusion into a computer or network and modifying or altering (i.e., tampering) the computer software or hardware to accomplish a goal outside the creator's original objective.

16. The best preventive measure against a computer virus is to

A. Compare software in use with authorized versions of the software.
B. Execute virus exterminator programs periodically on the system.
C. Allow only authorized software from known sources to be used on the system.
D. Prepare and test a plan for recovering from the incidence of a virus.

Answer (C) is correct.
REQUIRED: The best preventive measure against a computer virus.
DISCUSSION: Preventive controls are designed to prevent errors before they occur. Detective and corrective controls attempt to identify and correct errors. Preventive controls are usually more cost beneficial than detective or corrective controls. Allowing only authorized software from known sources to be used on the system is a preventive measure. The authorized software from known sources is expected to be free of viruses.
Answer (A) is incorrect. Comparing software with authorized versions is a detective control used to determine whether only authorized versions of the software are being used on the system. **Answer (B) is incorrect.** Executing virus exterminator programs is a corrective control against a computer virus. **Answer (D) is incorrect.** Preparing and testing a plan for virus recovery is a corrective control against a computer virus.

8.4 Contingency Planning and Disaster Recovery

17. Business continuity management (BCM) provides for all of the following **except**?

A. Segregation of duties.
B. Alternative work spaces.
C. Business impact analysis.
D. Alternative sourcing.

Answer (A) is correct.
REQUIRED: The item not included in business continuity management.
DISCUSSION: As part of an entity's business recovery and continuity strategy, it plans for alternative staffing, sourcing, and work spaces as well as for the return to normal operations. Segregation of duties, however, is a category of controls.
Answer (B) is incorrect. BCM provides for alternative work spaces. **Answer (C) is incorrect.** BCM provides for business impact analysis. **Answer (D) is incorrect.** BCM provides for alternative sourcing.

18. Contingency plans for information systems should include appropriate backup agreements. Which of the following arrangements would be considered too vendor-dependent when vital operations require almost immediate availability of computer resources?

A. A "hot site" arrangement.
B. A "cold site" arrangement.
C. A "cold and hot site" combination arrangement.
D. Using excess capacity at another data center within the organization.

Answer (B) is correct.
REQUIRED: The contingency plan that is too vendor-dependent.
DISCUSSION: Organizations should maintain contingency plans for operations in the case of a disaster. These plans usually include off-site storage of important backup data and an arrangement for the continuation of operations at another location. A cold site has all needed assets in place except the needed computer equipment and is vendor-dependent for timely delivery of equipment.
Answer (A) is incorrect. A hot site has all needed assets in place and is not vendor-dependent. Answer (C) is incorrect. A cold and hot site combination allows the hot site to be used until the cold site is prepared and is thus not too vendor-dependent. Answer (D) is incorrect. Excess capacity would ensure that needed assets are available and would not be vendor-dependent.

19. In conducting an audit of an organization's disaster recovery capability, which of the following would an auditor consider to be the most serious weakness?

A. Tests use recovery scripts.
B. Hot-site contracts are 2 years old.
C. Backup media are stored on-site.
D. Only a few systems are tested annually.

Answer (C) is correct.
REQUIRED: The most serious weakness in an organization's disaster recovery capability.
DISCUSSION: A crucial element of business recovery is the existence of a comprehensive and current disaster recovery plan. A comprehensive plan provides for (1) emergency response procedures, (2) alternative communication systems and site facilities, (3) information systems backup, (4) disaster recovery, (5) business impact assessments and resumption plans, (6) procedures for restoring utility services, and (7) maintenance procedures for ensuring the readiness of the organization in the event of an emergency or disaster. Storing backup media on-site is a weakness in the plan. They should not be located where they can be affected by the same event that interrupted the system's activities.
Answer (A) is incorrect. Use of scripts is a common practice to sequence the activities required for resumption of business. Answer (B) is incorrect. Contracts for off-site facilities are not updated frequently. Answer (D) is incorrect. Generally, the limited test-time window will only permit testing a few systems.

20. A company updates its accounts receivable master file weekly and retains the master files and corresponding update transactions for the most recent 2-week period. The purpose of this practice is to

A. Verify run-to-run control totals for receivables.
B. Match internal labels to avoid writing on the wrong volume.
C. Permit reconstruction of the master file if needed.
D. Validate groups of update transactions for each version.

Answer (C) is correct.
REQUIRED: The purpose of periodic retention of master files and transaction data.
DISCUSSION: Periodic backup and retention of both master files and transaction files is an integral part of any business continuity plan. If the data center is unavailable, these can be used to restore the master file and resume processing.
Answer (A) is incorrect. Comparison of batch totals is a control over the completeness of processing, not a recovery procedure. Answer (B) is incorrect. Internal labels may avoid destruction of data but do not aid in recovery. Answer (D) is incorrect. Validation may avoid destruction of data but does not aid in recovery.

21. If a corporation's disaster recovery plan requires fast recovery with little or no downtime, which of the following backup sites should it choose?

A. Hot site.
B. Warm site.
C. Cold site.
D. Quick site.

Answer (A) is correct.
REQUIRED: The type of backup facility that has fast recovery and little or no downtime.
DISCUSSION: A company uses a hot site backup when fast recovery is critical. The hot site includes all software, hardware, and other equipment necessary for a company to carry out operations. Hot sites are expensive to maintain and may be shared with other organizations with similar needs.
Answer (B) is incorrect. A warm site provides an intermediate level of backup. Its use results in more downtime than a hot site. Answer (C) is incorrect. A cold site is a shell facility suitable for quick installation of computer equipment. Disaster recovery would take more time in a cold site than a hot site. Answer (D) is incorrect. There is no backup site called a quick site.

22. Which of the following series identifies recovery solutions and sites for which a recovery plan exists?

A. Red, yellow, green.
B. High, medium, low.
C. Fast, moderate, slow.
D. Hot, warm, cold.

Answer (D) is correct.
REQUIRED: The series used to identify recovery solutions and sites for which a recovery plan exists.
DISCUSSION: The following are recovery solutions and sites for which a recovery plan exists:
 Hot -- Resources are available at the site(s), and data are synchronized in real time to permit recovery immediately or within hours.
 Warm -- Resources are available at the site(s) but may need to be configured to support the production system. Some data may need to be restored. Typical recovery time is 2 days to 2 weeks.
 Cold -- Sites have been identified with space and base infrastructure. Resources are not available at the sites. Data will likely need to be restored. Typical recovery time is 2 weeks to a month.

23. Which component of an emergency management program of a business normally has the longest time frame?

A. Emergency response.
B. Crisis management.
C. Continuity management.
D. Communications management.

Answer (C) is correct.
REQUIRED: The component of an EMP with the longest time frame.
DISCUSSION: The objective of business continuity management is to restore critical processes and to minimize the financial effects of a disaster or business disruption. Its time frame is measured in hours and days if not weeks.
Answer (A) is incorrect. The time frame of emergency response is measured in hours if not minutes. Answer (B) is incorrect. The time frame of crisis management is typically measured in days if not hours. Answer (D) is incorrect. Communicating with stakeholders (including the public) about a crisis and the steps for restoring business processes is the focus of crisis management.

STUDY UNIT NINE

CONCEPTS AND UNDERLYING PRINCIPLES OF FINANCIAL ACCOUNTING

(41 pages of outline)

9.1	Concepts of Financial Accounting	280
9.2	Financial Statements	283
9.3	The Accrual Basis of Accounting	290
9.4	The Accounting Process	293
9.5	Cash, Accounts Receivable, and Inventory	296
9.6	Property, Plant, and Equipment and Intangible Assets	301
9.7	Accounts Payable, Accrued Expenses, and Deposits and Other Advances	305
9.8	The Time Value of Money	309
9.9	Bonds	311
9.10	Pensions	314
9.11	Leases and Contingencies	316

This study unit is the first of six covering **Domain IV: Financial Management** from The IIA's CIA Exam Syllabus. This domain makes up 20% of Part 3 of the CIA exam and is tested at the **basic** and **proficient** cognitive levels. Refer to the complete syllabus located in Appendix A to view the relevant sections covered in Study Unit 9.

SUCCESS TIP: The majority of financial management questions on the CIA exam test conceptual understanding, not the ability to perform calculations. However, many of our financial management questions require you to perform calculations. They are an effective means of reinforcing your conceptual understanding.

9.1 CONCEPTS OF FINANCIAL ACCOUNTING

1. **The Objective of General-Purpose Financial Reporting**

    a. The objective of general-purpose financial reporting is to report financial information that is **useful in making decisions** about **providing resources** to the reporting entity.

    b. The **primary users** of financial information are current or prospective investors and creditors who cannot obtain it directly.

    1) Their decisions depend on expected returns.
    2) Accordingly, users need information that helps them to assess the potential for future net cash inflows.

    c. The information reported relates to the entity's **economic resources and claims** to them (financial position) and to changes in them (financial performance).

    1) This information helps to evaluate liquidity, solvency, financing needs, and the probability of obtaining financing.

    d. Changes in economic resources and claims to them may result from (1) the entity's performance (e.g., the income statement) or (2) other events and transactions, such as issuing debt and equity (balance sheet). Information about financial performance is useful for

    1) Understanding the return on economic resources, its variability, and its components;
    2) Evaluating management; and
    3) Predicting future returns.

    e. Financial statement analysis is described in Study Unit 10, Subunits 6 through 10.

2. **Accounting Assumptions**

    a. Certain assumptions about the environment in which the reporting entity operates are used in the preparation of the financial statements.

    b. **Going-concern assumption.** It is assumed that the entity

    1) Will operate indefinitely and
    2) Will not be liquidated.

    c. **Economic-entity assumption.** The reporting entity is separately identified for the purpose of economic and financial accountability. The economic affairs of owners and managers are segregated from those of the reporting entity.

    1) The legal entity and the economic entity are not necessarily the same. For example, consolidated reporting is permitted, if not required, even though the parent and its subsidiaries are legally distinct entities.

    d. **Monetary-unit (unit-of-money) assumption.** Accounting records are stated in units of money. Changes in purchasing power are assumed not to be material.

    e. **Periodicity (time period) assumption.** Financial statements are prepared periodically throughout the life of an entity to ensure the timeliness of information.

    1) The periodicity assumption requires reporting estimates in the financial statements. It sacrifices some degree of faithful representation for increased relevance and timeliness.

SU 9: Concepts and Underlying Principles of Financial Accounting

3. **Qualitative Characteristics of Useful Financial Information**

    a. For financial information to be useful in decision making, it must have the following qualitative characteristics:

    1) **Relevance.** Relevant information is able to make a difference in user decisions. To do so, it must have predictive value, confirmatory value, or both.

        a) Something has predictive value if it can be used as an input in a predictive process.

        b) Something has confirmatory value with respect to prior evaluations if it provides feedback that confirms or changes (corrects) them.

        c) **Materiality.** Information is material if its omission or misstatement can influence user decisions.

    2) **Faithful representation.** Useful information faithfully represents the economic phenomena that it purports to represent.

        a) A representation is perfectly faithful if it is **complete** (containing what is needed for user understanding), **neutral** (unbiased in its selection and presentation), and **free from error** (but not necessarily perfectly accurate).

    3) **Comparability.** Information should be comparable with similar information for (a) other entities and (b) the same entity for another period or date. Comparability allows users to understand similarities and differences.

        a) Consistency is a means of achieving comparability. It is the use over time of the same principles for the same items.

    4) **Verifiability.** Information is verifiable (directly or indirectly) if knowledgeable and independent observers can agree (not necessarily unanimously) that it is faithfully represented.

    5) **Timeliness.** Information is timely when it is available in time to influence decisions.

    6) **Understandability.** Understandable information is clearly and concisely classified, characterized, and presented.

4. **Accounting Principles**

    a. The following four principles provide guidelines for recording financial information.

    1) **Historical cost principle.** Transactions are recorded initially at cost because that is the most objective determination of fair value.

    2) **Full-disclosure principle.** Financial statement users should be able to assume that financial information that could influence users' judgment is reported in the financial statements.

    3) **Revenue recognition principle.** Revenues and gains should be recognized **when (a) realized or realizable and (b) earned**.

        a) Revenues and gains are realized when goods or services have been exchanged for cash or claims to cash. Revenues and gains are realizable when goods or services have been exchanged for assets that are readily convertible into cash or claims to cash.

        b) Revenues are earned when the earning process has been substantially completed, and the entity is entitled to the resulting benefits or revenues.

        c) Thus, revenue on sales can be recognized in the statement of income even if the cash from sales is not received yet.

d) The core principle for recognition of revenue from contracts with customers is that an entity recognizes revenue for the transfer of promised goods or services to customers in an amount that reflects the consideration to which the entity expects to be entitled in the exchange.

i) This principle reflects the **contractual relationship** between the provider of goods or services and the recipient of such goods or services.

ii) The **five-step model** for recognizing revenue from contracts with customers is below.

Step 1:	Identify the contract(s) with a customer.
Step 2:	Identify the performance obligations in the contract.
Step 3:	Determine the transaction price.
Step 4:	Allocate the transaction price to the performance obligations in the contract.
Step 5:	Recognize revenue when (or as) a performance obligation is satisfied.

e) The **revenue cycle** starts with the sale of the good or service and ends with the receipt of payment for the sale.

4) **Matching principle.** Expenses should be recognized in the same period as directly related revenues. Matching is essentially the same as associating cause and effect. For example, this direct relationship exists when cost of goods sold is recognized in the same period as the revenue from the sale of the goods.

5. **Measurement Attributes**

   a. **Measurement** is the determination of the amounts at which the items are to be recognized in the financial statements.

   b. **Historical cost** is the acquisition price of an asset. It is ordinarily adjusted subsequently for amortization (which includes depreciation) or other allocations.

   c. **Current (replacement) cost** is the amount of cash that would have to be paid for a current acquisition of the same or an equivalent asset.

   d. **Net realizable value** is the cash or equivalent expected to be received for an asset in the due course of business, minus the costs of completion and sale.

   e. **Fair value** is the price that would be received to sell an asset or paid to transfer a liability in an orderly transaction between market participants at the measurement date.

   f. **Present value** incorporates the time value of money concept. Determination of the present value of an asset or liability requires discounting, at an appropriate interest rate, the related future cash flows expected to occur in the due course of business.

STOP & REVIEW

You have completed the outline for this subunit.
Study multiple-choice questions 1 and 2 on page 320.

9.2 FINANCIAL STATEMENTS

1. **A Full Set of Financial Statements**

    a. Financial statements are the primary means of communicating financial information to external parties. Additional information is provided by financial statement notes, supplementary information, and other disclosures. Information typically disclosed in notes is essential to understanding the financial statements.

    b. A full set of financial statements includes the following statements:

    1) Statement of financial position **(balance sheet)**
    2) Income statement
    3) Statement of comprehensive income
    4) Statement of changes in equity
    5) Statement of cash flows

    c. A full set of financial statements can be found in Appendix C.

2. **Statement of Financial Position**

    a. The statement of financial position reports the amounts in the accounting equation at a moment in time, such as at the end of the fiscal year. This equation reports resources (assets) on one side and claims to those resources (liabilities and equity) on the other side.

    ### The Accounting Equation

    Assets = Liabilities + Equity (net assets)

    1) **Assets** are resources controlled by the entity as a result of past events. They are probable future economic benefits. Examples are inventory; accounts receivable; investments; and property, plant, and equipment.

    2) **Liabilities** are present obligations of the entity arising from past events. Their settlement is expected to result in an outflow of economic benefits. Examples include loans, bonds issued by the entity, and accounts payable.

    3) **Equity** is the residual interest in the net assets of the entity. Examples include common stock, preferred stock, and retained earnings.

        a) Equity is affected not only by operations but also by transactions with owners, such as dividends and contributions.

b. Assets and liabilities are separated into **current** and **noncurrent** categories.

1) Current assets are generally expected to be realized in cash or sold or consumed in 1 year from the balance sheet date.
2) Current liabilities are generally expected to be settled or liquidated in 1 year from the balance sheet date.
3) Some variation of the following classifications is used by most entities:

Assets
Current assets:
  Cash
  Certain investments
  Accounts and notes receivable
  Inventories
  Prepaid expenses
Noncurrent assets:
  Certain investments and funds
  Property, plant, and equipment (PPE)
  Intangible assets
  Deferred tax assets
  Other noncurrent assets

Liabilities
Current liabilities:
  Accounts payable
  Current notes payable
  Current maturities of noncurrent liabilities
  Accrued expenses
Noncurrent liabilities:
  Noncurrent notes payable
  Bonds payable
  Employee-related obligations
  Deferred tax liabilities
  Other noncurrent liabilities

Equity
Investments by owners
Retained earnings (income reinvested)
Accumulated other comprehensive income
Noncontrolling interest in a consolidated entity

c. A comprehensive example of a statement of financial position is in Appendix C.
d. The following are the major limitations of the statement of financial position:

1) Many items, such as fixed assets, are measured at historical cost, which may not equal their fair value.
2) Preparation requires estimates and management judgment.
3) An entity's financial position is reported at a moment in time. Balances may vary significantly during the accounting period.

3. **Income Statement**

   a. The income statement reports the results of an entity's operations over a period of time, such as a year. Its elements are recorded in temporary accounts (e.g., income or loss) that are periodically closed to permanent accounts (e.g., retained earnings).

   ### The Income Equation

   Income (loss) = Revenues + Gains − Expenses − Losses

   1) **Revenues** are inflows or other enhancements of assets or settlements of liabilities (or both) from delivering or producing goods, providing services, or other activities that qualify as ongoing major or central operations.

   2) **Gains** are increases in equity (or net assets) other than from revenues or investments by owners.

   3) **Expenses** are outflows or other usage of assets or incurrences of liabilities (or both) from delivering or producing goods, providing services, or other activities that qualify as ongoing major or central operations.

   4) **Losses** are decreases in equity (or net assets) other than from expenses or distributions to owners.

EXAMPLE 9-1 **Income Statement Format**

Net sales	US $ 200,000
Cost of goods sold	(150,000)
Gross profit	US $ 50,000
Selling expenses	(6,000)
Administrative expenses	(5,000)
Income from operations	US $ 39,000
Other revenues and gains	3,500
Other expenses and losses	(2,500)
Income before taxes	US $ 40,000
Income taxes	(8,000)
Net income	US $ 32,000

A more detailed example format is in Appendix C.

---

   b. A **discontinued operation**, if one exists, is presented net of tax in a separate section of the income statement after income from continuing operations. It reports (1) income or loss from operations of the component that has been disposed of or is classified as held for sale and (2) gain or loss on the disposal of the component.

   c. The following are major limitations of the income statement:

   1) The financial statements report accrual-basis results for the period. An entity may recognize revenue and report net income before any cash was actually received.

      a) For example, the data from the income statement itself do not suffice for assessing liquidity. This statement must be analyzed with other statements, e.g., the balance sheet and the statement of cash flows.

   2) The income statement does not always show all items of income and expense. Some items are reported on a statement of other comprehensive income and are not included in the calculation of net income.

   3) The preparation of the income statement requires estimates and management judgment.

4. **Statement of Comprehensive Income**

    a. All nonowner changes in equity must be presented either in one continuous statement or in two separate but consecutive statements (an income statement and a statement of other comprehensive income).

    1) Comprehensive income for a period consists of (a) net income or loss (the bottom line of the income statement) and (b) **other comprehensive income (OCI)**.
    2) The following are examples of components of OCI:
        a) The effective portion of a gain or loss on a hedging instrument in a cash flow hedge
        b) A gain or loss on remeasurement of certain financial assets
        c) Translation gains and losses for financial statements of foreign operations
        d) Certain amounts associated with accounting for defined benefit postretirement plans

---

EXAMPLE 9-2   **Statement of Other Comprehensive Income Format**

Net income		US $ 32,000
OCI (net of tax):		
Loss on defined benefit postretirement plans	US $(2,000)	
Gains on foreign currency translation	4,500	
Gains on remeasuring certain financial assets	1,100	
Effective portion of losses on cash flow hedges	(800)	2,800
Total comprehensive income		US $ 34,800

---

5. **Statement of Changes in Equity**

    a. This statement reconciles the beginning balance for each component of equity to the ending balance.
    b. Each change is disclosed separately in the statement. The following are common changes in equity balances during the accounting period:
        1) Net income (loss) for the period increases (decreases) retained earnings.
        2) Distributions to owners (dividends paid) decreases retained earnings.
        3) An issue of common stock increases common stock. If the amount paid is above the par value of the stock, additional paid-in capital also increases.
        4) OCI increases accumulated OCI.
    c. The accounting for equity is described in Study Unit 10, Subunit 5.
    d. A comprehensive example of statement of changes in equity is in Appendix C.

6. **Statement of Cash Flows**

    a. The primary purpose of the statement of cash flows is to provide relevant information about the cash receipts and cash payments of an entity during the period. It reports the cash inflows and outflows from the operating, investing, and financing activities of the entity.

    b. The statement of cash flows explains the change in cash and cash equivalents during the period. It reconciles the beginning balance with the ending balance.

EXAMPLE 9-3   Statement of Cash Flows -- Summarized Format

The following is an example of the summarized format of the statement of cash flows (headings only). The amounts of cash and cash equivalents at the beginning and end of the year are taken from the balance sheet.

Entity A's Statement of Cash Flows for the Year Ended December 31, Year 1

Net cash provided by (used in) operating activities	US $XXX
Net cash provided by (used in) investing activities	XXX
Net cash provided by (used in) financing activities	XXX
Net increase (decrease) in cash and cash equivalents during the year	US $XXX
Cash and cash equivalents at beginning of year (January 1, Year 1)	XXX
Cash and cash equivalents at end of year (December 31, Year 1)	US $XXX

A more detailed example format is in Appendix C.

---

    c. **Operating activities** are all transactions and other events that are not financing or investing activities. Most cash flows from operating activities are from the principal revenue-producing activities of the entity. The following are the acceptable methods of presentation:

      1) The **direct method** presents major classes of gross operating cash receipts and payments and their sum (net cash flow from operating activities). Also, a reconciliation of net income to net operating cash flow must be disclosed separately.

2) The **indirect method** reconciles net income to cash flow from operating activities. The reconciliation must disclose major classes of operating items. Adjustments to net income must be made. Net income is reported on the accrual basis, not the cash basis, and certain financing and investing cash flows are reported in net income.

   a) The following must be **added to net income**:
      i) Increases in current operating liabilities (e.g., accounts payable and interest payable)
      ii) Decreases in current operating assets (e.g., inventory and receivables)
      iii) Noncash losses and expenses (e.g., depreciation expense)
      iv) Losses and expenses whose cash effects are related to investing or financing cash flows (e.g., a loss on disposal of equipment related to investing activities)

   b) The following must be **subtracted from net income**:
      i) Decreases in current operating liabilities (e.g., accounts payable and interest payable)
      ii) Increases in current operating assets (e.g., inventory and receivables)
      iii) Noncash revenues and gains
      iv) Revenues and gains whose cash effects are related to investing or financing cash flows (e.g., a gain on extinguishment of debt related to financing activities)

   NOTE: The net operating cash flow is the same under both methods.

d. Cash flows from **investing activities** represent the extent to which payments have been made for resources intended to generate future income and cash flows.

   1) The following are examples of **cash flows** from investing activities:
      a) Cash payments to acquire (cash receipts from sale of)
         i) Property, plant, and equipment
         ii) Intangible assets
         iii) Other long-lived assets
      b) Cash payments to acquire (cash receipts from sale and maturity of) equity and debt securities of other entities

e. Cash flows from **financing activities** generally involve the cash effects of transactions and other events that relate to the issuance, settlement, or reacquisition of the entity's debt and equity instruments.

   1) The following are examples of **cash inflows** from financing activities:
      a) Cash proceeds from issuing shares and other equity instruments (obtaining resources from owners)
      b) Cash proceeds from issuing loans, notes, bonds, and other short-term or long-term borrowings

   2) The following are examples of **cash outflows** from financing activities:
      a) Cash repayments of amounts borrowed
      b) Payments of cash dividends

7. **Notes to the Financial Statements**

    a. Notes

    1) Describe the basis of preparation and the significant policies applied,
    2) Make required disclosures not presented on the face of the statements, and
    3) Provide additional information needed for a fair presentation.

    b. The first note accompanying any set of complete financial statements generally describes significant accounting policies, such as the use of estimates and rules for revenue recognition.

    c. Note disclosures and schedules specifically related to the balance sheet include

    1) Investment securities;
    2) Maturity patterns of bond issues;
    3) Significant uncertainties, such as pending litigation; and
    4) Details of capital stock issues.

    d. Note disclosures and schedules specifically related to the income statement include

    1) Earnings per share,
    2) Depreciation schedules, and
    3) Components of income tax expense.

8. **Financial Statement Relationships**

    a. Financial statements complement each other. They describe different aspects of the same transactions, and more than one statement is necessary to provide information for a specific economic decision.

    b. The components of one statement relate to those of other statements. Among the relationships are the following:

    1) Net income or loss from the statement of income is reported and accumulated in the retained earnings account, a component of the equity section of the statement of financial position.
    2) The components of cash and equivalents from the statement of financial position are reconciled with the corresponding items in the statement of cash flows.
    3) Items of equity from the statement of financial position are reconciled with the beginning balances on the statement of changes in equity.
    4) Ending inventories are reported in current assets on the statement of financial position and are reflected in the calculation of cost of goods sold on the statement of income.
    5) Amortization and depreciation reported in the statement of income also are reflected in asset and liability balances in the statement of financial position.

    NOTE: Appendix C contains a complete set of financial statements. The complementary relationships among these statements are lettered.

STOP & REVIEW

You have completed the outline for this subunit.
Study multiple-choice questions 3 through 5 on page 321.

9.3 THE ACCRUAL BASIS OF ACCOUNTING

1. **Accrual Basis**

    a. Financial statements are prepared under the accrual basis of accounting. Accrual accounting records the financial effects of transactions and other events and circumstances when they occur rather than when their associated cash is paid or received.

       1) Revenues are recognized when they were earned even if the cash will be received in a future period.

       2) Expenses are recognized when they were incurred even if the cash will be paid in a future period.

       NOTE: Under the cash basis, revenues are recognized when cash is received, and expenses are recognized when cash is paid. The cash basis is not permitted under U.S. GAAP and IFRS.

2. **Accruals and Deferrals**

    a. **Accruals** anticipate future cash flows. They reflect the amounts of cash that must be paid or received at some later date for goods or services received or provided today.

       1) For example, an entity incurs an expense by having its carpets cleaned, with the price due within 10 days according to the invoice. The entity has incurred a liability (owes money) because it has already received the benefits of the service.

       2) The entity records an accrued expense to acknowledge that it must pay cash to compensate another party for a service already performed and recognizes an expense for the services that were already received.

          (Dr) Maintenance expense   US $800
             (Cr) Accounts payable   US $800

          a) No cash has passed from the entity to the cleaner, but both the income statement and the statement of financial position are affected. The debit to an expense reflects a current consumption of economic benefit, and the credit to accounts payable reflects the future cash outflow.

b. **Deferrals** result from past cash flows. They are amounts paid or received for goods or services to be received or provided at a later date.

   1) For example, a magazine publisher has received cash from subscribers entitling them to receive the next 12 issues. The publisher must deliver a product over the next year, but it has already received the benefits of the cash.

   2) The publisher must record a **contract liability**, also called **deferred revenue**, to acknowledge its obligation to other parties.

   (Dr) Cash   US $24,000
      (Cr) Contract liability (subscription income)   US $24,000

      a) Cash has passed from the customers to the publisher, and the publisher must now satisfy its performance obligation by providing a product. The debit to an asset reflects the cash inflow, and the credit to a liability reflects the outstanding obligation.

   3) Another common deferral is **prepaid expense**. It is a cash prepayment for goods or services to be received over a specified period. In this example, an entity paid at the beginning of the year for 3 years of insurance premiums in advance.

   (Dr) Prepaid insurance   US $120,000
      (Cr) Cash   US $120,000

      a) Cash has passed from the entity to the insurer, who must now provide a service. The debit to an asset reflects the future benefit expected, and the credit to cash reflects the immediate cash payment.

3. **Allocation**

   a. Allocation is the accrual-accounting process of distributing an amount according to a plan or formula. Assigning a total cost to the accounting periods expected to be benefited is a common allocation.

   1) In the prepaid insurance example in item 2.b.3) above, the entity received a third of the benefit during the first year after the prepayment. Thus, it allocates one-third of the prepayment to expense recognized in Year 1 (US $120,000 ÷ 3 = US $40,000).

   (Dr) Insurance expense   US $40,000
      (Cr) Prepaid insurance   US $40,000

   2) Depreciation of capital assets and amortization of intangible assets (other than goodwill) over their estimated useful lives also are time-based allocations.

4. Relationship between Cash Amounts and Accrual-Basis Amounts

a. Financial statement accrual-basis amounts can be calculated based on the relationship among receivables, payables, accruals, and deferrals.

b. The following calculations relate the amount of cash paid or received and the accrual-basis amount of revenue or expense recognized in the income statement.

Cash collected from customers	US $ XXX	Cash paid to suppliers	US $ XXX
Ending accounts receivable	XXX	Ending accounts payable	XXX
Beginning accounts receivable	(XXX)	Beginning accounts payable	(XXX)
Net sales (accrual basis)	US $ XXX	Purchases (accrual basis)	US $ XXX
Expenses paid during the period	US $ XXX	Cash received during the period	US $ XXX
Beginning prepaid expenses	XXX	Beginning deferred income	XXX
Ending prepaid expenses	(XXX)	Ending deferred income	(XXX)
Expenses recognized (accrual basis)	US $ XXX	Income recognized (accrual basis)	US $ XXX

EXAMPLE 9-4   Conversion of Cash Basis to Accrual Basis

On January 1 and December 31 of the current year, an entity had the following balances:

	January 1	December 31
Accounts receivable	US $15,000	US $25,000
Prepaid expenses	7,000	5,000

During the year, cash collections totaled US $40,000, and cash expenses paid totaled US $27,000.

The amount of sales revenue recognized for the year is US $50,000 ($40,000 + $25,000 – $15,000). The increase in receivables is an earned amount with no cash inflow. This increase should be added to the amount of cash collected to calculate the amount of accrual-basis revenues.

The amount of expenses recognized for the year is US $29,000 ($27,000 + $7,000 – $5,000). The decrease in prepaid expenses is an expense recognized with no cash outflow. This decrease should be added to the amount of cash expenses paid to calculate the amount of accrual-basis expenses.

NOTE: The easiest way to solve questions about converting cash-basis amounts to accrual-basis amounts and vice versa is by using the calculations described above.

STOP & REVIEW

You have completed the outline for this subunit.
Study multiple-choice questions 6 and 7 on page 322.

9.4 THE ACCOUNTING PROCESS

1. **The Accounting System**

    a. An accounting system consists of a set of **accounts**, recorded in a **journal** and posted to a **ledger**.

        1) The accounting system records the effects of the transactions and other events and circumstances that must be recognized by the entity.

        2) The accounting system classifies the items, summarizes their effects, and reports the results in the form of **financial statements**.

    b. The accounting system is based on the **debit-credit** and **double-entry** convention.

        1) In accordance with the convention, a debit is an increase (decrease) in a given account, and a credit is a decrease (increase) in the same account.

        2) For each account, the balance equals the sum of the amounts debited and credited.

        3) Moreover, the monetary amount of the total debits must equal the total credits.

2. **Permanent and Temporary Accounts**

    a. Assets, liabilities, and equity are recorded in **permanent (real) accounts**. Their balances at the end of one accounting period (the balance sheet date) are carried forward as the beginning balances of the next accounting period.

    b. Revenues, expenses, gains, losses, and dividends are recorded in **temporary (nominal) accounts** because they record the transactions, events, and other circumstances during a period of time. These accounts are closed (reduced to zero) at the end of each accounting period, and their balances are transferred to real accounts.

        1) For example, the total of nominal accounts for the period (the net income or loss and the dividends) is transferred to the retained earnings (real) account. The ending retained earnings account equals the beginning amount, plus net income for the period (or minus net loss), minus dividends.

    c. An entity's **chart of accounts** names the accounts used in that entity's accounting system.

    d. The following table summarizes the application of the debit-credit convention:

	Permanent (Real) Accounts			Temporary (Nominal) Accounts	
	Balance Sheet			Income Statement	
	Assets	Liabilities	Equity (Net Assets)	Revenues & Gains	Expenses & Losses
Increase	Debit	Credit	Credit	Credit	Debit
Decrease	Credit	Debit	Debit	Debit	Credit

294   SU 9: Concepts and Underlying Principles of Financial Accounting

3. **Journal Entries and the Accounting Cycle**

   a. **Journal entries** record the financial effects of transactions, events, and other circumstances in the accounting system.

      1) For every journal entry, the total debited must equal the total credited.
      2) Every journal entry therefore must affect at least two accounts, and the effects (debit and credit) must be posted to specific accounts.

   b. The **accounting cycle** is the series of steps taken to maintain financial records in accordance with the accrual basis. After identification and measurement of items to be recorded, the steps in the accounting cycle are as in the table below.

Step 1:	Journalize transactions
Step 2:	**Post** journal entries to the ledgers
Step 3:	Prepare an unadjusted trial balance
Step 4:	Record entries to **adjust** accrued and deferred accounts
Step 5:	Prepare an adjusted trial balance
Step 6:	Prepare financial statements
Step 7:	Record entries to **close** temporary (nominal) accounts
Step 8:	Prepare a post-closing trial balance (optional)
Step 9:	Record entries to **reverse** the accrual entries (optional)

      1) Journal entries are recorded in books of original entry (journals).
      2) Accounts' balances are maintained in the **general ledger**. Journal entries may be posted to the appropriate ledgers either immediately (in real-time automated systems) or overnight (in batch systems).
      3) The financial records must be closed at the end of each period before preparation of accrual-basis financial statements. The first three steps in the closing process are preparing an unadjusted trial balance.

         a) A **trial balance** is a report of the balances of every account in the general ledger, providing proof that total debits equal total credits.

      4) **Adjusting entries** are made as of the balance sheet date to record the effects on periodic revenue and expense of (a) deferrals (prepaid expenses and contract liabilities) and (b) accruals (revenues recognized but not yet realized in cash and expenses incurred but not yet paid in cash). Other adjustments also may be necessary, e.g., recognition of depreciation and amortization expense.

         a) The adjusting journal entry depends on how the transaction was recorded initially.

SU 9: Concepts and Underlying Principles of Financial Accounting

> **EXAMPLE 9-5   Adjusting Entries**
>
> In the prepaid insurance example on page 291, assume that the premium payment for 3 years of insurance was recognized as insurance expense at the beginning of the year:
>
> (Dr) Insurance expense   US $120,000
>   (Cr) Cash   US $120,000
>
> The insurance expense account and prepaid insurance account are reported in the unadjusted trial balance at US $120,000 and US $0, respectively. But only one-third of the amount paid is for current-year insurance. The accrual-basis balances are US $40,000 for insurance expense and US $80,000 for prepaid insurance. Thus, the year-end adjusting entry is to decrease insurance expense by US $80,000 (Cr) and recognize prepaid insurance of US $80,000 (Dr):
>
> (Dr) Prepaid insurance   US $80,000
>   (Cr) Insurance expense   US $80,000
>
> After the adjusting entry, the adjusted balance of insurance expense is US $40,000 ($120,000 – $80,000), and the adjusted balance of prepaid insurance is US $80,000.
>
> If the premium payment for 3 years of insurance was recognized as prepaid insurance at the beginning of the year, the following is the entry:
>
> (Dr) Prepaid insurance   US $120,000
>   (Cr) Cash   US $120,000
>
> The insurance expense account and prepaid insurance account are reported in the unadjusted trial balance at US $0 and US $120,000, respectively. The year-end adjusting entry therefore is to recognize insurance expense of US $40,000 (Dr) and decrease prepaid insurance by US $40,000 (Cr):
>
> (Dr) Insurance expense   US $40,000
>   (Cr) Prepaid insurance   US $40,000
>
> After the adjusting entry, the adjusted balance of insurance expense is US $40,000, and the adjusted balance of prepaid insurance is US $80,000 ($120,000 – $40,000).

5) An adjusted trial balance is prepared to prove that total debits in the general ledger still equal total credits after the posting of adjusting entries.

6) The adjusted trial balance is used to prepare financial statements.

7) The temporary (nominal) accounts must now be closed (reduced to zero). Closing entries transfer (close) temporary account balances to the **income summary account** (net income or loss for the period). The income summary account then is transferred to retained earnings.

8) A post-closing trial balance can be prepared to prove that total debits in the general ledger still equal total credits after closing the nominal accounts.

9) Reversing entries reverse the effects of adjusting entries to simplify the future bookkeeping process.

STOP & REVIEW

You have completed the outline for this subunit.
Study multiple-choice questions 8 and 9 beginning on page 322.

9.5 CASH, ACCOUNTS RECEIVABLE, AND INVENTORY

1. **Cash**

    a. All cash balances on hand and on deposit that are readily available for current operating purposes are reported as cash. Restricted cash is reported under a separate caption. Because cash is the most liquid asset, it is usually the first asset listed on the balance sheet.

2. **Bank Reconciliation**

    a. A bank reconciliation is a schedule comparing the cash balance per books with the balance per bank statement (usually received monthly). The common approach is to reconcile both the bank balance and the book balance to reach the true balance. The bank and book balances usually vary. Thus, the reconciliation permits the entity to determine whether the difference is attributable to normal conditions, errors, or fraud. It is also a basis for entries to adjust the books to reflect unrecorded items.

        1) **Items known to the entity but not to the bank** include

            a) Outstanding checks and other disbursements,
            b) Deposits in transit, and
            c) Errors made by the bank.

        2) **Items known to the bank but not to the entity** include amounts added (collections and interest) or subtracted (or not added) by the bank (insufficient funds checks and service charges).

Common Reconciliation Items

	To Book Balance	To Bank Balance
Additions	Interest earned Deposits collected Errors	Deposits in transit Errors
Subtractions	Service charges NSF checks Errors	Outstanding checks and other disbursements Errors

3. **Accounts Receivable**
   a. Accounts receivable, often called trade receivables, are the amounts owed to an entity by its customers.
   b. Because collection in full of all accounts receivable is often unlikely, they are reported at **net realizable value (NRV)**.
      1) The NRV of accounts receivable equals gross accounts receivable minus the allowance for credit losses.
      2) Thus, an allowance contra to accounts receivable is established. This method attempts to match credit loss expense with the related revenue.
         a) The **credit loss** expense recognized for the period increases the allowance for credit losses. The allowance is a contra account to accounts receivable. Thus, the recognition of credit loss expense decreases the balance of accounts receivable.
      3) The direct write-off method expenses bad debts when they are determined to be uncollectible.
         a) This method is **not acceptable under GAAP** because it does not match revenue and expense when the receivable and the write-off are recorded in different periods.
         b) However, this method is used for tax purposes.
   c. The two common methods of measuring credit loss expense and the allowance are the **percentage-of-sales** method (an income statement approach) and the **percentage-of-receivables** method (a balance sheet approach).
   d. The **allowance method** systematically records credit loss expense as a percentage of either sales or the balance of accounts receivable on an annual basis.
      1) Some customers are unwilling or unable to pay their debts. As specific accounts receivable are written off, they are charged to the allowance.

Allowance for credit losses	US $XXX	
Accounts receivable		US $XXX

      2) The write-off of a particular account has no effect on credit loss expense. Write-offs do not affect the carrying amount of net accounts receivable because the reductions of gross accounts receivable and the allowance are the same.

e. The **income statement approach** calculates credit loss expense as a percentage of credit sales reported on the income statement.

EXAMPLE 9-6   Income Statement Approach -- Credit Loss Expense

A company's year-end unadjusted trial balance reports the following amounts:

Gross accounts receivable	US $100,000 Dr
Allowance for credit losses (year-beginning balance)	1,000 Cr
Sales on credit	250,000 Cr

According to past experience, 1% of the company's credit sales have been uncollectible. The company uses the income statement approach to calculate credit loss expense.

The credit loss expense recognized for the year is US $2,500 ($250,000 × 1%). The company records the following adjusting journal entry:

Credit loss expense	US $2,500	
Allowance for credit losses		US $2,500

The total adjusted balances of the allowance for credit losses and credit loss expense are US $3,500 ($1,000 + $2,500) and US $2,500, respectively. The company reports net accounts receivable of US $96,500 ($100,000 – $3,500) in its balance sheet and credit loss expense of US $2,500 in its statement of income.

---

f. The **balance sheet approach** estimates the balance that should be recorded in the allowance based on the collectibility of ending gross accounts receivable. Credit loss expense is the amount necessary to adjust the allowance.

1) An entity rarely has a single rate of uncollectibility for all accounts. Accordingly, it generally prepares an **aging schedule** for accounts receivable.

EXAMPLE 9-7   Aging Schedule

	Balance		Percentage Historically Uncollectible		Balance Needed in Allowance
31 - 60 days old	US $440,000	×	2%	=	US $ 8,800
61 - 90 days old	120,000	×	8%	=	9,600
91 - 120 days old	75,000	×	11%	=	8,250
Over 120 days old	13,000	×	16%	=	2,080
Totals	US $648,000				US $28,730

---

2) If the beginning balance of the allowance was a credit of US $9,010, and the ending balance of the allowance needs to be US $28,730, the entry is as follows:

Credit loss expense (US $28,730 – $9,010)	US $19,720	
Allowance for credit losses		US $19,720

g. A customer might pay an amount previously written off.

1) The first entry is to **reestablish the account** for the sum the customer has agreed to pay (any remainder remains written off).

Accounts receivable	US $XXX	
Allowance for credit losses		US $XXX

2) The second entry records the receipt of cash.

Cash	US $XXX	
Accounts receivable		US $XXX

h. Credit loss expense is not affected when
   1) An account receivable is written off or
   2) An account previously written off becomes collectible.

> **SUCCESS TIP**
>
> The following equation illustrates the reconciliation of the beginning and ending balances of the allowance for credit losses:
>
> | | |
> |---|---|
> | Beginning allowance for credit losses | US $XXX |
> | Credit loss expense **recognized** for the period | XXX |
> | Accounts receivable written off | (XXX) |
> | Collection of accounts receivable previously written off | XXX |
> | Ending allowance for credit losses | US $XXX |
>
> Under the income statement approach, credit loss expense is a percentage of sales on credit, and the ending balance of the allowance is calculated using the equation above.
>
> Under the balance sheet approach, the ending balance of the allowance is a percentage of the ending balance of accounts receivable, and credit loss expense is calculated using the equation above.

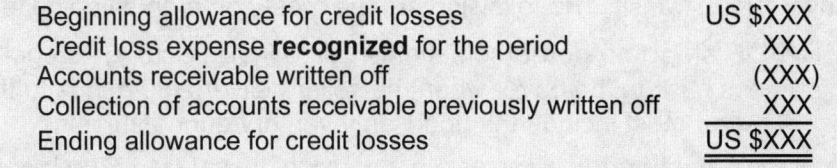

4. **Costs Included in Inventory**

   a. The **cost of inventory** includes all costs incurred in bringing the inventories to their existing location and ready-to-use condition.

   b. The **cost of purchased inventories** includes

   1) The price paid or consideration given to acquire the inventory (net of trade discounts, rebates, and other similar items);

   2) Import duties and other unrecoverable taxes; and

   3) Handling, insurance, freight-in, and other costs directly attributable to (a) acquiring finished goods and materials and (b) bringing them to their present location and condition (salable or usable condition).

   4) The following is the calculation of net purchases:

	Purchases
−	Returns and allowances
−	Purchase discounts
+	Transportation-in
=	Net purchases

   c. The **cost of manufactured inventories** (work-in-process and finished goods) includes the costs of direct materials used and conversion costs. Conversion costs consist of (1) direct labor costs and (2) manufacturing overhead costs.

d. For a physical count to be accurate, the entity must count all items considered to be inventory and eliminate all items that are not. Items to be counted as inventory include the following:

1) **Goods in transit** – Items in transit are inventories that on the physical count date (a) are not on the entity's premises and are on the way to the desired location and (b) whose legal title is held by the entity; i.e., the entity bears the risk of loss on inventory in transit. The following are the most common shipping terms:

   a) **FOB shipping point** (sometimes called FOB Factory) – Legal title and risk of loss pass to the buyer when the seller delivers the goods to the carrier. The **buyer** must include the goods in inventory during shipping.

   b) **FOB destination** – Legal title and risk of loss pass to the buyer when the seller delivers the goods to a specified destination. The **seller** must include the goods in inventory during shipping.

2) **Goods out on consignment** – A consignment sale is an arrangement between the owner of goods (consignor) and the sales agent (consignee). Consigned goods are not sold but rather transferred to an agent for possible sale. The consignor records sales only when the goods are sold to third parties by the consignee.

   a) Goods out on consignment are included in the **consignor's** inventory at cost. Costs of transporting the goods to the consignee are inventoriable costs, not selling expenses.

   b) The **consignee** never records the consigned goods as an asset.

EXAMPLE 9-8   Inventory Shipping Terms

Kew Co.'s accounts payable balance at December 31, Year 3, was US $2.2 million before considering the following:

- Goods shipped to Kew **FOB shipping point** on December 22, Year 3, were lost in transit. The invoice cost of US $40,000 was not recorded by Kew. On January 7, Year 4, Kew filed a US $40,000 claim against the common carrier.

- On December 27, Year 3, a vendor authorized Kew to return, for full credit, goods shipped and billed at US $70,000 on December 3, Year 3. The returned goods were shipped by Kew on December 28, Year 3. A US $70,000 credit memo was received and recorded by Kew on January 5, Year 4.

- Goods shipped to Kew **FOB destination** on December 20, Year 3, were received on January 6, Year 4. The invoice cost was US $50,000.

When goods are shipped FOB shipping point, inventory and a payable are recognized at the time of shipment. Thus, Kew should currently recognize a US $40,000 payable for the goods lost in transit. The US $70,000 purchase return should be recognized currently because the seller authorized the credit on December 27. However, the goods shipped FOB destination and not received until January should be excluded. Kew should not recognize inventory and a payable until the goods are tendered at the destination. Accordingly, the ending accounts payable balance is US $2,170,000 ($2,200,000 + $40,000 – $70,000).

---

e. The valuation of inventory is discussed in Study Unit 14.

You have completed the outline for this subunit.
Study multiple-choice question 10 on page 323.

9.6 PROPERTY, PLANT, AND EQUIPMENT AND INTANGIBLE ASSETS

1. **Overview**

   a. Property, plant, and equipment (PPE), also called fixed assets, consists of tangible property expected to benefit the entity for more than 1 year that is held for the production or supply of goods or services, rental to others, or administrative purposes.

2. **PPE -- Initial Measurement**

   a. The historical (initial) cost of PPE includes

      1) The net purchase price (minus trade discounts and rebates, plus purchase taxes and import duties) and

      2) The directly attributable costs of bringing the asset to the location and condition needed for its intended operation, such as architects' and engineers' fees, site preparation, delivery and handling, installation, assembly, and testing.

   b. Interest (borrowing costs) attributable to the acquisition, construction, or production of a PPE asset constructed for internal use is included in its initial cost.

3. **PPE -- Subsequent Expenditures**

   a. **Capital expenditures** provide additional benefits by improving the quality of services rendered by the asset, extending its useful life, or increasing its output. These expenditures are capitalized to the asset's cost.

   b. **Revenue expenditures** (expenses) maintain an asset's normal service capacity. These costs are recurring, are not expected to benefit future periods, and are expensed as incurred.

      1) Routine, minor expenditures made to maintain the operating efficiency of PPE ordinarily are expensed as incurred.

4. **PPE -- Measurement Subsequent to Initial Recognition**

   a. An item of PPE is reported in the financial statements at its carrying amount. This amount is equal to the historical cost minus accumulated depreciation and impairment losses.

Historical cost	US $ XXX
Accumulated depreciation	(XXX)
Impairment losses	(XXX)
Asset's carrying amount	US $ XXX

5. **PPE -- Depreciation**

    a. **Depreciation** is the process of systematically and rationally allocating the depreciable base of a tangible capital asset over its expected useful life. The periodic depreciation expense is recognized in the income statement. Accumulated depreciation is a contra-asset account.

        1) The debit is to depreciable expense, and the credit is to accumulated depreciation.

    b. The asset's **depreciable base** (i.e., the amount to be allocated) is calculated as follows:

    Depreciable base = Historical cost − Estimated salvage value (residual value)

    c. **Estimated useful life** is the period over which the entity expects to receive services/economic benefits from the asset.

    d. **Salvage value** is the amount that the entity expects to obtain from disposal of the asset at the end of the asset's useful life.

    e. Land has an indefinite useful life and therefore must not be depreciated. Thus, the depreciable base of property that consists of land and a building is the depreciable base of the building.

EXAMPLE 9-9   Depreciable Base Calculation

At the beginning of Year 1, a manufacturer paid US $270,000 for a new machine.

The entity estimates that, at the end of the machine's 5-year useful life, it will be able to sell the machine for US $20,000.

Depreciable base = US $270,000 − $20,000 = US $250,000

---

6. **Depreciation Methods**

    a. **Straight-line** (S-L) depreciation allocates the depreciable base evenly over the estimated useful life of the asset.

    $$\text{Periodic depreciation expense} = \frac{\text{Depreciable base}}{\text{Estimated useful life}}$$

EXAMPLE 9-10   Straight-Line Depreciation

A manufacturer applies straight-line depreciation:

Year	Depreciable Base	Estimated Useful Life	Depreciation Expense	Accumulated Depreciation	Carrying Amount at Year End
1	US $250,000	5	US $50,000	US $ 50,000	US $220,000
2	250,000	5	50,000	100,000	170,000
3	250,000	5	50,000	150,000	120,000
4	250,000	5	50,000	200,000	70,000
5	250,000	5	50,000	250,000	20,000

---

    b. The **units-of-production** method allocates a proportional amount of the asset's cost based on its output.

    $$\text{Periodic depreciation expense} = \text{Depreciable base} \times \frac{\text{Units produced during current period}}{\text{Estimated total lifetime units}}$$

    c. Accelerated depreciation methods, such as the declining balance and sum-of-the-years'-digits methods, result in decreasing depreciation charges over the life of the asset.

SU 9: Concepts and Underlying Principles of Financial Accounting

7. **PPE -- Disposal**

   a. When an item of PPE is sold, the gain or loss on disposal is the difference between the net proceeds and the carrying amount of the asset. Depreciation (if any) is recognized to the date of sale, the carrying amount is removed from the books, the proceeds are recorded, and any gain or loss is recognized.

      1) A gain is recognized if the proceeds exceed the carrying amount.
      2) A loss is recognized if the proceeds are less than the carrying amount.

8. **PPE -- Reconciliation Equation**

   a. The following calculation illustrates the changes in the carrying amount of the PPE account during the period:

Beginning PPE	US $ XXX
Purchases during the period	XXX
Depreciation expense	(XXX)
Disposals during the period	(XXX)
Ending PPE	US $ XXX

9. **Intangible Assets -- Definition**

   a. An intangible asset is an identifiable, nonmonetary asset that lacks physical substance.

      1) Examples of intangible assets include licenses, patents, copyrights, franchises, and trademarks.

   b. Internally generated goodwill must not be recognized as an asset, but goodwill acquired in a business combination is recognized as an intangible asset.

10. **Intangible Assets -- Amortization**
    a. An intangible asset is carried at cost minus any accumulated amortization and impairment losses.
    b. Amortization of an intangible asset with a **finite useful life** begins when it is available for use. Its amortizable amount is systematically allocated over its useful life (much like depreciation for PPE items).
    c. An intangible asset with an **indefinite useful life** is not amortized. Instead, it is tested for impairment at least annually.

11. **Internally Developed Intangible Assets**
    a. Under U.S. GAAP, **research and development** (R&D) costs must be **expensed as incurred** and are never capitalized. Thus, **internally developed** intangible assets are not recognized on the balance sheet. For example, R&D cost incurred in developing a patent must be expensed, and no intangible asset is recognized. However, an acquired patent must be recognized as an intangible asset at cost.
        1) **Research** is planned search or critical investigation aimed at discovery of new knowledge.
        2) **Development** is translation of research findings or other knowledge into a plan or design for a new or improved product or process.
    b. Under IFRS, research costs must be expensed as incurred. But development costs may result in recognition of intangible assets if certain criteria are met.

STOP & REVIEW

You have completed the outline for this subunit.
Study multiple-choice questions 11 through 13 beginning on page 324.

9.7 ACCOUNTS PAYABLE, ACCRUED EXPENSES, AND DEPOSITS AND OTHER ADVANCES

1. **Current Liabilities**

    a. A current liability is an obligation that will be either paid using current assets or replaced by another current liability. Thus, a liability is classified as current if it is expected to be paid within the entity's operating cycle or 1 year, whichever is longer.

    b. Current liabilities (accounts payable) should be recorded at **net settlement value**. Thus, they are measured at the undiscounted amounts of cash expected to be paid to liquidate an obligation.

    1) Obligations that are callable by the creditor **within 1 year** because of a violation of a debt agreement also are classified as current liabilities.

        a) An obligation callable at **any time** by the creditor is not a current liability.

        b) If the creditor waives or loses the right to demand repayment for more than 1 year (or the entity's operating cycle, if longer) from the balance sheet date, the obligation is noncurrent.

    c. **Checks** written before the end of the period but not mailed to creditors should not be accounted for as cash payments for the period. The amounts remain current liabilities until control of the checks has been surrendered.

2. **Accounts Payable**

    a. Accounts payable (trade payables) are **liabilities**. They are obligations to sellers incurred when an entity purchases inventory, supplies, or services on credit.

    b. Accounts payable are usually **noninterest-bearing** unless they are not settled when due or payable.

    1) They also are usually **not** secured by collateral.

    c. **Gross Method vs. Net Method**

    1) Cash discounts are offered to induce early payment. Purchases and related accounts payable may be recorded using the gross method or the net method.

    2) The **gross method** ignores cash discounts. It accounts for payables at their face amount.

        a) **Purchase discounts taken** are credited to a contra purchases account and closed to cost of goods sold.

    3) The **net method** records payables net of the cash (sales) discount for early payment.

        a) When the discount is taken (the payment is within the discount period), no additional adjustment is required.

        b) Purchase discounts lost is recognized (debited) when payment is not made within the discount period.

3. **Accrual Expenses**

   a. Ordinarily, accrued expenses meet **recognition criteria** in the current period but have **not been paid** as of year end. Thus, they do not affect cash flows and are accounted for using basic accrual entries.

   b. Accruals may be used to facilitate accounting for expenses incurred but not paid at the end of an accounting period. For example, the year-end **accrual entry** for wages payable is

Wages expense	US $XXX	
Wages payable		US $XXX

   c. The reversing entry at the beginning of the next period is

Wages payable	US $XXX	
Wages expense		US $XXX

   d. No allocation between the liability and wages expense is needed when wages are paid in the subsequent period. The full amount of expenses paid in the next period can be debited to expense. The entry is simply

Wages expense	US $XXX	
Cash		US $XXX

   e. At year end, the **liability** is adjusted to the balance owed at that date. For example, if the liability for accrued wages has decreased, the adjusting entry is

Wages payable	US $XXX	
Wages expense		US $XXX

EXAMPLE 9-11   Accrued Expenses

Mike Co.'s salaried employees are paid monthly. The payment is always on the fifth day of the next month. In Year 1, the total monthly salary was US $100,000. In Year 2, the employees received a 5% raise to US $105,000.

On December 31, Year 1, Mike must accrue a liability of US $100,000 for December salaries expense that will be paid on January 5, Year 2.

Salaries expense	US $100,000	
Salaries payable		US $100,000

In Year 2, the journal entries recorded by Mike depend on its bookkeeping approach to expense accrual.

1) Reversing Journal Entries

January 1, Year 2 – Reversal of December 31, Year 1, entry

Salaries payable	US $100,000	
Salaries expense		US $100,000

January 5, Year 2 – Payment of December Year 1 salaries

Salaries expense	US $100,000	
Cash		US $100,000

February 5, Year 2, through December 5, Year 2: Monthly entry

Salaries expense	US $105,000	
Cash		US $105,000

December 31, Year 2 – Accrual of a liability for December Year 2 salaries

Salaries expense	US $105,000	
Salaries payable		US $105,000

NOTE: The annual salaries expense for Year 2 is US $1,260,000 ($105,000 monthly salary × 12 months). The salaries payable balance on December 31, Year 2, is US $105,000.

-- Continued on next page --

SU 9: Concepts and Underlying Principles of Financial Accounting

> **EXAMPLE 9-11 -- Continued**
>
> **2) No Reversing Journal Entries**
>
> January 5, Year 2 – Payment of December Year 1 salaries
>
> | | | |
> |---|---|---|
> | Salaries expense | US $100,000 | |
> | Cash | | US $100,000 |
>
> February 5, Year 2, through December 5, Year 2: Monthly entry
>
> | | | |
> |---|---|---|
> | Salaries expense | US $105,000 | |
> | Cash | | US $105,000 |
>
> December 31, Year 2 – The liability is adjusted to the balance owed. The credit is US $5,000 ($105,000 amount owed for December Year 2 – $100,000 unadjusted balance).
>
> | | | |
> |---|---|---|
> | Salaries expense | US $5,000 | |
> | Salaries payable | | US $5,000 |
>
> NOTE: The annual salaries expense for Year 2 is US $1,260,000 [$100,000 on 1/5/Year 2 + ($105,000 × 11 months) + $5,000 on 12/31/Year 2]. The salaries payable balance on December 31, Year 2, is US $105,000 ($100,000 beginning balance + $5,000 adjustment on 12/31/Year 2).

f. **Effects of Nonaccrual**

   1) If an entity fails to accrue expenses at year end, **income** is overstated in that period and understated in the next period (when they are paid and presumably expensed).

      a) Moreover, expenses incurred but unpaid and not recorded result in understated **accrued liabilities** and possibly understated assets (e.g., if the amounts should be inventoried).

      b) In addition, working capital (Current assets – Current liabilities) will be overstated, but cash flows will not be affected.

> **EXAMPLE 9-12**   **Year-End Accruals**
>
> Windy Co. must determine the December 31, Year 2, year-end accruals for advertising and rent expenses. A US $500 advertising bill was received January 7, Year 3. It related to costs of US $375 for advertisements in December Year 2 and US $125 for advertisements in January Year 3. A lease, effective December 16, Year 1, calls for fixed rent of US $1,200 per month, payable beginning 1 month from the effective date. In addition, rent equal to 5% of net sales over US $300,000 per calendar year is payable on January 31 of the following year. Net sales for Year 2 were US $550,000.
>
> The US $375 of advertising expense should be accrued in Year 2 because this amount can be directly related to events in that period. The US $125 amount is related to events in Year 3 and should not be accrued in Year 2.
>
> The fixed rental is due at mid-month. Thus, the fixed rental for the last half month of Year 2 (US $1,200 ÷ 2 = $600) and the rental based on annual sales [(US $550,000 – $300,000) × 5% = $12,500] also should be accrued.
>
> In its December 31, Year 2, balance sheet, Windy should report accrued liabilities of US $13,475 ($375 + $600 + $12,500).

4. **Deposits and Other Advances**

   a. A deposit, advance sale, service contract, or other advance is a **contract liability**. It does not qualify for revenue recognition.

   b. A contract liability is an obligation to transfer goods or services to a customer for which the consideration already has been received from the customer.

   c. Alternative descriptions of a contract liability, such as **deferred revenue**, may be used in the statement of financial position.

   d. Cash advances (such as sales of gift cards) are recorded as follows:

Cash	US $XXX	
Contract liability (deferred revenue)		US $XXX

   e. The entity should derecognize the contract liability and recognize revenue when the promised goods or services are transferred to the customer or when items such as gift cards are redeemed or expire.

Contract liability	US $XXX	
Revenue		US $XXX

   f. Cash received from customers for **magazine subscriptions** creates a contract liability for deferred subscription revenue.

EXAMPLE 9-13   Revenue -- Nonrefundable Advances

Nepal Co. requires advance payments with special orders for machinery constructed to customer specifications. These advances are nonrefundable. Revenue is recognized when control of the machinery is transferred to the customer (e.g., when the order is shipped). Information for Year 2 is as follows:

Customer advances -- balance 12/31/Year 1	US $236,000
Advances received with orders in Year 2	368,000
Advances applied to orders shipped in Year 2	328,000
Advances applicable to orders canceled in Year 2	100,000

In Nepal's December 31, Year 2, balance sheet, the amount reported as a current liability is US $176,000 ($236,000 beginning balance + $368,000 advances received − $328,000 advances credited to revenue after shipment of orders − $100,000 for canceled orders) for customer advances. Deposits or other advance payments are contract liabilities because they were received before Nepal transferred machinery to customers. The nonrefundable advances applicable to canceled orders qualify for revenue recognition (debit the liability, credit revenue) because the entity's performance obligations have been satisfied.

STOP & REVIEW

You have completed the outline for this subunit.
Study multiple-choice question 14 on page 325.

9.8 THE TIME VALUE OF MONEY

1. **Time Value and Interest**

   a. A quantity of money to be received or paid in the future ordinarily is worth less than the same amount now. The difference is measured in terms of interest calculated using the appropriate discount rate.

      1) Interest is paid by a borrower or investee to a lender or investor for the use of money. It is a percentage of the amount (the principal) borrowed or invested.

   b. Time value of money concepts have many applications. For example, they affect the accounting for noncurrent receivables and payables (bonds and notes), leases, and certain employee benefits.

2. **The Present Value of an Amount**

   a. The present value (PV) of an amount is the value today of some future payment. It equals the future payment times the present value of 1 (a factor found in a standard table) for the given number of periods and interest rate.

EXAMPLE 9-14	Factors for PV of an Amount			
			Present Value	
	No. of Periods	6%	8%	10%
	1	0.943	0.926	0.909
	2	0.890	0.857	0.826
	3	0.840	**0.794**	0.751
	4	0.792	0.735	0.683
	5	0.747	0.681	0.621

The present value of US $1,000 to be received in 3 years and discounted at 8% is US $794 ($1,000 × 0.794).

3. **Present Value of Annuities**

    a. An annuity is a series of equal payments at equal intervals of time, e.g., US $1,000 at the end of every year for 10 years.

        1) An **ordinary annuity** (annuity in arrears) is a series of payments occurring at the end of each period.
        2) An **annuity due** (annuity in advance) is a series of payments occurring at the beginning of each period.

    b. The PV of an annuity is the value today of a series of future equal payments at equal intervals discounted at a given rate.

| EXAMPLE 9-15 | PV -- Ordinary Annuity vs. Annuity Due |

	Present Value		
No. of Periods	6%	8%	10%
1	0.943	0.926	0.909
2	1.833	1.783	1.736
3	2.673	2.577	2.487
4	3.465	3.312	3.170
5	4.212	3.993	3.791

To calculate the present value of an **ordinary annuity** of four payments of US $1,000 each discounted at 10%, multiply US $1,000 by the appropriate factor (US $1,000 × 3.170 = $3,170).

Using the same table, the present value of an **annuity due** of four payments of US $1,000 each also may be calculated. This value equals US $1,000 times the factor for one less period (4 − 1 = 3), increased by 1.0. Thus, the present value of the annuity due for four periods at 10% is US $3,487 [$1,000 × (2.487 + 1.0)].

The present value of the annuity due (US $3,487) is greater than the present value of the ordinary annuity (US $3,170) because the payments occur 1 year sooner.

4. **The Future Value (FV) of an Amount**

    a. The FV of an amount is the amount available at a specified time in the future based on a single investment (deposit) today.

    b. The interest factor for the FV of a present amount equals the reciprocal of the interest factor for the PV of a future amount, assuming the same interest rate and number of periods.

        1) For example, the factor for the FV of an amount is 1.191 for 3 periods at 6%. Thus, the factor for the PV of an amount for three periods at 6% is 0.840 (1 ÷ 1.191).

| EXAMPLE 9-16 | FV of an Amount |

	Future Value Factor of an Amount		
No. of Periods	6%	8%	10%
1	1.060	1.080	1.100
2	1.124	1.166	1.210
3	1.191	1.260	1.331
4	1.262	1.360	**1.464**
5	1.338	1.469	1.610

The future value of US $1,000 invested today for 4 years at 10% interest will be US $1,464 ($1,000 present value of an amount × 1.464 future value factor).

5. **The FV of Annuities**

    a. The FV of an annuity is the value that a series of equal payments will have at a certain moment in the future if interest is earned at a given rate.

| EXAMPLE 9-17 | FV -- Ordinary Annuity vs. Annuity Due |

	Future Value		
No. of Periods	6%	8%	10%
1	1.0000	1.0000	1.0000
2	2.0600	2.0800	2.1000
3	3.1836	3.2464	3.3100
4	4.3746	4.5061	4.6410
5	5.6371	5.8667	6.1051

To calculate the FV of a 3-year **ordinary annuity** with payments of US $1,000 each at 6% interest, multiply US $1,000 by the appropriate factor (US $1,000 × 3.184 = $3,184).

The FV of an **annuity due** also may be determined from the same table. Multiply the US $1,000 payment by the factor for one additional period (3 + 1 = 4) decreased by 1.0 (4.375 – 1.0 = 3.375) to arrive at a FV of US $3,375 ($1,000 × 3.375).

The future value of the annuity due (US $3,375) is greater than the future value of an ordinary annuity (US $3,184). The deposits are made earlier.

STOP & REVIEW

You have completed the outline for this subunit.
Study multiple-choice question 15 on page 325.

9.9 BONDS

1. **Nature of Bonds**

    a. A bond is a formal contract to pay an amount of money (face amount) at the maturity date plus interest at the stated rate at specific intervals.

| EXAMPLE 9-18 | Accounting for a Bond Issue |

At the beginning of the year, a company issues 200 8%, 5-year, US $5,000 bonds. Annual cash interest payments will be made at the end of each year. The total face amount of bonds issued is US $1,000,000 (200 bonds × $5,000 face amount), and the annual interest payment is US $80,000 ($1,000,000 face amount × 8% stated rate).

    b. The proceeds received on the day the bonds are sold equal the present value of the sum of the future cash flows expected to be received from the bonds. These proceeds equal

        1) The present value of the face amount plus
        2) The present value of the annuity of interest payments.

    c. The bonds are recognized in the financial statements at the amount of proceeds paid or received, i.e., the face amount plus any premium or minus any discount, as a(n)

        1) Debt in the issuer's financial statements
        2) Investment in the investors' financial statements

2. **Bond Issuance**
   a. The cash proceeds from the sale of bonds can be equal to, less than, or greater than the face amount of the bonds. The measurement depends on the relationship of the bonds' stated rate of interest to the market rate of interest on the date the bonds are sold.
      1) If the stated rate is equal to the market rate, the cash proceeds equal the face amount of the bonds.
      2) If the stated rate is greater than the current market rate, the cash proceeds are greater than the face amount, and the bonds are sold at **premium**.
      3) If the stated rate is lower than the current market rate, the cash proceeds are lower than the face amount, and the bonds are sold at **discount**.
   b. The current market rate of interest is used to discount the cash flows expected to be received by the investor (paid by the issuer) from the bonds.

EXAMPLE 9-19   Calculation of Premium or Discount

The following calculation uses the data from Example 9-18 and the following present value factors:

	At 6%	At 10%
Present value of 1 for 5 periods	0.747	0.621
Present value of ordinary annuity of 1 for 5 periods	4.212	3.791

(1) Assume that the market interest rate was 6% on the date the bonds were issued.

Present value of face amount (US $1,000,000 × 0.747)	US $ 747,000
Present value of cash interest (US $80,000 × 4.212)	336,960
Cash proceeds from bonds issue	US $1,083,960

The amount of premium is US $83,960 ($1,083,960 proceeds − $1,000,000 face amount).

(2) Assume that the market interest rate was 10% on the date the bonds were issued.

Present value of face amount (US $1,000,000 × 0.621)	US $621,000
Present value of cash interest (US $80,000 × 3.791)	303,280
Cash proceeds from bonds issue	US $924,280

The amount of discount is US $75,720 ($1,000,000 face amount − $924,280 proceeds).

---

3. **Amortization of Premium or Discount**
   a. Bond premium or discount must be amortized over the life of the bonds using the **effective-interest method** (the market interest rate on the date the bond was sold). Under this method, interest expense changes every period and equals the following:

   $$\text{Annual interest expense} = \text{Carrying amount of the bond at the beginning of the period} \times \text{Effective interest rate}$$

   b. The annual interest expense consists of the cash interest paid plus the effect of amortization of premium or discount.
      1) When the bond is issued at premium, annual interest expense equals cash interest paid minus the amount of premium amortized.
      2) When the bond is issued at discount, annual interest expense equals cash interest paid plus the amount of discount amortized.
      3) The carrying amount of bonds as they are presented in the financial statements equals the face amount plus the premium (or minus the discount).

EXAMPLE 9-20 — Amortization of a Premium and Discount

Using the data from Example 9-19, the following interest expense will be recognized by the company in the first 2 years of the bonds:

(1) When market interest rate was 6% and bonds were issued at premium:

	A				B		A − B
Year	Beginning Carrying Amount of Bonds	Market Interest Rate	Interest Expense	Cash Interest Paid	Premium Amortized	Remaining Premium	Ending Carrying Amount of Bonds
1	US $1,083,960	× 6%	= US $65,038	− US $80,000	= US $14,962	US $68,998	US $1,068,998
2	1,068,998	× 6%	= 64,140	− 80,000	= 15,860	53,138	1,053,138

(2) When market interest rate was 10% and bonds were issued at discount:

	A				B		A + B
Year	Beginning Carrying Amount of Bonds	Market Interest Rate	Interest Expense	Cash Interest Paid	Discount Amortized	Remaining Discount	Ending Carrying Amount of Bonds
1	US $924,280	× 10%	= US $92,428	− US $80,000	= US $12,428	US $63,292	US $936,708
2	936,708	× 10%	= 93,671	− 80,000	= 13,671	49,621	950,379

  4) At the maturity date, the discount or premium is fully amortized, and the carrying amount of the bonds equals the face amount.

4. **Investment in Debt Securities**

   a. A **debt security** represents a **creditor** relationship with the issuer.

   b. Debt securities are classified at acquisition into one of **three categories**. The classification is reassessed at each reporting date.

Category	Criteria
Held-to-maturity	Debt securities that the reporting entity has the positive intent and ability to hold to maturity
Trading	Debt securities intended to be sold in the near term
Available-for-sale	Debt securities not classified as held-to-maturity or trading

   c. Debt securities are measured and presented as follows:

      1) **Held-to-maturity** securities are reported at amortized cost and presented net of any unamortized premium or discount. Realized gains and losses and interest income (including amortization of premium or discount) are recognized in the income statement.

      2) **Trading** securities are measured at fair value. The changes in fair value (unrealized holding gains and losses) are recognized in the income statement.

      3) **Available-for-sale** securities are measured at fair value. The changes in fair value (unrealized holding gains and losses) are recognized in other comprehensive income.

STOP & REVIEW

You have completed the outline for this subunit.
Study multiple-choice question 16 on page 326.

9.10 PENSIONS

1. **Definition**

    a. A pension plan is a type of retirement plan to which an employer makes periodic contributions of assets to be set aside for employees' future benefit.

    b. The two main types of pension plans are the defined contribution plan and the defined benefit plan.

2. **Defined Contribution Plan**

    a. A defined contribution plan provides an individual account for each participating employee. Benefits that the employees will receive during retirement depend on

    1) The amount contributed to the plan by the employer and the employee and
    2) The returns earned on investments of those contributions.

    b. The employer's only obligation is to make periodic deposits of the amounts defined by the plan's formula in return for the services rendered by employees.

    1) Thus, the employer does not guarantee the amount of benefits that the employees will receive during retirement.
    2) The employees bear the investment risk (the benefit of gain or risk of loss from assets contributed to the plan).

    c. The employer's **annual pension expense** is the amount of the contribution required by the pension plan's formula.

    1) The employer reports an **asset** only if the contribution made is greater than the amount required by the pension plan's formula.
    2) The employer reports a **liability** only if the contribution made is less than the amount required by the pension plan's formula.

3. **Defined Benefit Plan**

    a. A defined benefit plan defines an amount of pension benefit to be provided to each employee. The employer is responsible for providing the agreed benefits and, therefore, bears actuarial risk and investment risk.

    b. The benefits that the employer is required to pay depend on future events, such as how long an employee lives, how many years of service the employee renders, and the employee's compensation before retirement.

    1) Many of these events cannot be controlled by the employer. Thus, the total benefit is not precisely determinable and can only be estimated by using actuarial assumptions.

c. The projected benefit obligation (PBO) is the actuarial present value of all benefits attributed by the pension benefit formula to employee service rendered prior to that date.

d. Plan assets are contributions to the pension plan made by the employer to at least partially cover the PBO.

1) These plan assets are usually stocks, bonds, and other investments. They are segregated and restricted, generally in a trust, to provide for pension benefits.

e. Statement of financial position (balance sheet). The employer recognizes a noncurrent liability or asset depending on whether the projected benefit obligation is underfunded or overfunded.

1) A pension liability is recognized in the employer's year-end balance sheet if the PBO exceeds the fair value of plan assets.

Pension liability = Underfunded PBO

2) A pension asset is recognized if the fair value of plan assets exceeds the PBO.

Pension asset = Overfunded PBO

f. Income statement. The employer recognizes periodic pension expense based on many factors. These include employee service performed in the current period, interest on the benefit obligation, the return on the investments of the pension fund, etc.

STOP & REVIEW

You have completed the outline for this subunit.
Study multiple-choice questions 17 and 18 beginning on page 326.

9.11 LEASES AND CONTINGENCIES

1. **Definition of a Lease**
   a. A **lease** is a contractual agreement in which the **lessor** (owner) conveys to the **lessee** the right to control the use of specific **property, plant, or equipment** for a stated period in exchange for a stated payment.
   b. The amount and timing of lease revenue recognized by the lessor and lease expenses recognized by the lessee depend on the initial classification of the lease.

2. **Lease Classification**
   a. A lease is classified as a **finance lease by the lessee** and as a **sales-type lease by the lessor** if, at lease commencement, **at least one** of the **five criteria** below is met:
      1) The lease **transfers ownership** of the leased asset to the lessee by the end of the lease term.
      2) The lease includes an **option to purchase** the leased asset that the lessee is reasonably certain to exercise.
      3) The lease term is for the major part of the remaining **economic life** of the leased asset.
         a) A lease term of **75%** or more of the remaining economic life of the leased asset generally is considered to be a major part of its remaining economic life.
         b) This criterion is inapplicable if the beginning of the lease term is at or near the end of the economic life of the leased asset. This period generally is considered to be the last 25% of the leased asset's total economic life.
      4) The present value of the sum of (a) the **lease payments** and (b) any **residual value guaranteed by the lessee** equals or exceeds substantially all of the **fair value** of the leased asset.
         a) A present value of **90%** or more of the fair value of the leased asset generally is considered to be substantially all of its fair value.
      5) The leased asset is so specialized that it is expected to have **no alternative use** to the lessor at the end of the lease term.
   b. When none of the five classification criteria described above are met, the lease is classified as
      1) An **operating lease** by the **lessee**.
      2) An **operating lease** or a **direct financing lease** by the **lessor**.
   c. The lessor classifies a lease as a **direct financing lease** only when
      1) The lease is not a sales-type lease,
      2) The present value of the sum of (a) the lease payments and (b) any residual value guaranteed by the lessee **or any other third party** equals or exceeds substantially all of the fair value of the leased asset, and
      3) It is probable that the lease payments and any residual value guarantee will be collected.

d. If the lease is **not** a direct financing lease, it is classified as an **operating lease** by the lessor.

1) Classification of a lease as a direct financing lease is rare. It happens only when the lease includes residual value guaranteed by a third party other than the lessee that results in meeting the "substantially all of the fair value" classification criterion (the 90% of the fair value of the leased asset criterion).

    a) Thus, a lessor classifies a lease without residual value guaranteed by a third party (not the lessee) as either

        i) A sales-type lease or
        ii) An operating lease.

    b) In most cases, when none of the five classification criteria are met (when the lease is not a sales-type lease), the **lessor classifies the lease as an operating lease**.

Decision Tree: Classification of the Lease by the Lessor

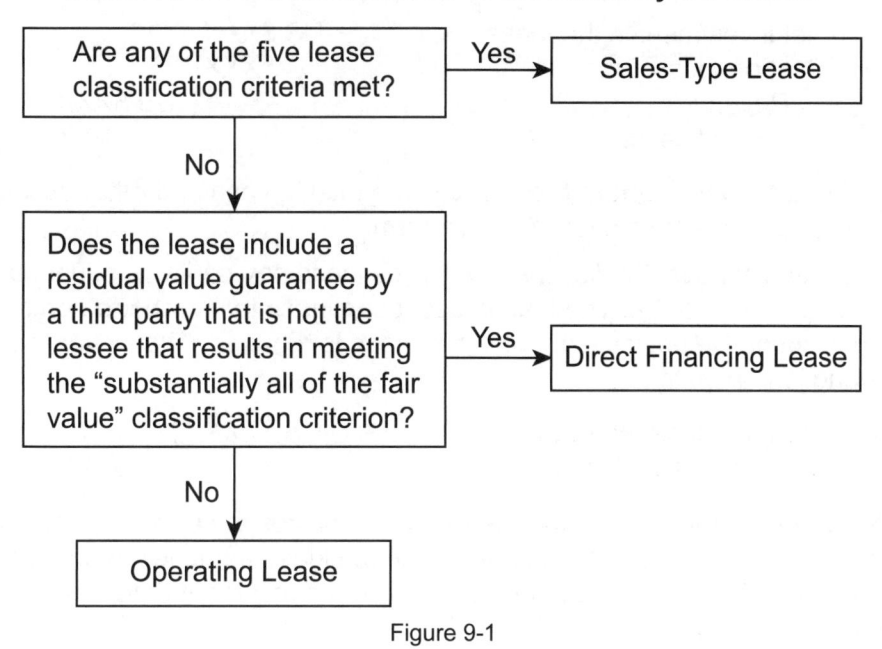

```
┌─────────────────────────┐  Yes  ┌──────────────────┐
│ Are any of the five     │──────▶│ Sales-Type Lease │
│ lease classification    │       └──────────────────┘
│ criteria met?           │
└─────────────────────────┘
            │ No
            ▼
┌─────────────────────────┐
│ Does the lease include a│
│ residual value guarantee│
│ by a third party that is│
│ not the lessee that     │  Yes  ┌────────────────────────┐
│ results in meeting the  │──────▶│ Direct Financing Lease │
│ "substantially all of   │       └────────────────────────┘
│ the fair value"         │
│ classification criterion│
└─────────────────────────┘
            │ No
            ▼
┌─────────────────┐
│ Operating Lease │
└─────────────────┘
```

Figure 9-1

3. **Accounting for Leases**
    a. For **finance** and **operating leases**, a **lessee** must recognize a lease liability and a right-of-use asset at the lease commencement date.
        1) A **right-of-use asset** is a lessee's right to use a leased asset for the lease term.
        2) At the lease commencement date, a **lease liability** is measured at the present value of the **lease payments** to be made by the lessee over the lease term.
        3) For finance leases, each periodic lease payment made by the lessee has two components: **interest expense** and the **reduction of the lease liability**. The right-of-use asset is amortized on a straight-line basis.
        4) For operating leases, each periodic lease payment made by the lessee is recognized as a single (equal) lease expense. It has two components: **interest expense** on the lease liability and **amortization of the right-of-use asset**.
    b. For **sales-type leases**, the **lessor** must derecognize the leased asset and record the following journal entry at the lease commencement date:

Net investment in the lease	US $XXX	
Cost of goods sold	XXX	
Revenue		US $XXX
Leased asset		XXX

      1) The **net investment in the lease** is the total of cash and other assets that the lessor expects to receive over the lease term.
    c. For **operating leases**, the **lessor** recognizes lease payments as equal periodic amounts of lease (rental) income. The leased asset continues to be reported on the lessor's balance sheet. No net investment in the lease is required. The lessor records the following journal entry:

Cash or lease receivable	US $XXX	
Rental (lease) income		US $XXX

    d. For **direct financing leases**, the **lessor** derecognizes the carrying amount of the leased asset and recognizes the net investment in the lease at the lease commencement date. No selling profit is recognized on the lease commencement date. The lessor records the following journal entry:

Net investment in the lease	US $XXX	
Leased asset		US $XXX

4. **Contingencies**
    a. A contingency is an existing condition, situation, or set of circumstances involving **uncertainty** as to (1) possible loss (a loss contingency) or (2) gain (a gain contingency). It ultimately will be resolved when one or more future events do or do not occur.
    b. A **contingent liability** or asset valuation allowance (credit) and a **loss contingency** (debit) are recognized prior to resolution. A contingent loss must be probable and capable of reasonable estimation. The following are examples of loss contingencies:
        1) Pending or threatened litigation
        2) **Warranties** and obligations for product defects
        3) Uncollectibility of receivables
        4) Guarantees, e.g., of the residual value of a leased asset or of the debt of another
            a) A liability is recognized for a guarantee even if the probability of loss is remote.
        5) Coupons (premiums) offered to customers
    c. A gain contingency is recognized in the financial statements only when it is **realized**.
    d. A **contingent asset** is a possible asset resulting from past events and the existence of which will be confirmed only by uncertain future events not wholly within the entity's control. An example is a potential recovery on a legal claim with an uncertain outcome.
        1) A contingent asset is not recognized but should be disclosed if an inflow of economic benefits is probable.
            a) Disclosures include a description of the contingent asset and an estimate of its financial effects.
        2) A contingent asset is not recognized because the income may not be realized. However, if realization is virtually certain, the asset is not contingent and may be recognized.

STOP & REVIEW

You have completed the outline for this subunit.
Study multiple-choice questions 19 and 20 on page 327.

QUESTIONS

9.1 Concepts of Financial Accounting

1. A newly acquired plant asset is to be depreciated over its useful life. The rationale for this process is the

A. Economic entity assumption.
B. Monetary unit assumption.
C. Materiality assumption.
D. Going concern assumption.

Answer (D) is correct.
REQUIRED: The rationale for depreciation.
DISCUSSION: A basic feature of financial accounting is that the entity is assumed to be a going concern in the absence of evidence to the contrary. The going concern concept is based on the empirical observation that many entities have an indefinite life. The reporting entity is assumed to have a life long enough to fulfill its objectives and commitments and therefore to depreciate wasting assets over their useful lives.
Answer (A) is incorrect. The economic entity assumption provides that economic activity can be identified with a particular unit of accountability.
Answer (B) is incorrect. The monetary unit assumption provides that all transactions and events can be measured in terms of a common denominator, for instance, the euro. **Answer (C) is incorrect.** Materiality is an entity-specific aspect of relevance, a fundamental qualitative characteristic. Information is material if it can influence a user's decision. Thus, in the case of plant assets, certain items may be expensed rather than capitalized and depreciated because they are not material. The difference in treatment is not large enough to influence users if the item is not material.

2. An objective of financial reporting is

A. Providing information useful to investors, creditors, donors, and other users for decision making.
B. Assessing the adequacy of internal control.
C. Evaluating management results compared with standards.
D. Providing information on compliance with established procedures.

Answer (A) is correct.
REQUIRED: The objective of financial reporting.
DISCUSSION: The objective is to report financial information that is useful in making decisions about providing resources to the reporting entity. Primary users of financial information are current or prospective investors and creditors who cannot obtain it directly. Their decisions depend on expected returns.
Answer (B) is incorrect. Assessing the adequacy of internal control is a function of internal auditing, not financial reporting. **Answer (C) is incorrect.** Evaluating management results compared with standards is a function of internal auditing, not financial reporting. **Answer (D) is incorrect.** Providing information on compliance with established procedures is a function of internal auditing, not financial reporting.

9.2 Financial Statements

3. The management of ABC Corporation is analyzing the financial statements of XYZ Corporation because ABC is strongly considering purchasing a block of XYZ ordinary shares that would give ABC significant influence over XYZ. Which financial statement should ABC primarily use to assess the amounts, timing, and certainty of future cash flows of XYZ Company?

A. Income statement.
B. Statement of changes in equity.
C. Statement of cash flows.
D. Statement of financial position.

Answer (C) is correct.
REQUIRED: The financial statement used to assess the amounts, timing, and uncertainty of future cash flows.
DISCUSSION: A statement of cash flows provides information about the cash receipts and cash payments of an entity during a period. This information helps investors, creditors, and other users to assess the entity's ability to generate cash and cash equivalents and the needs of the entity to use those cash flows. Historical cash flow data indicate the amount, timing, and certainty of future cash flows. It is also a means of verifying past cash flow assessments and of determining the relationship between profits and net cash flows and the effects of changing prices.
Answer (A) is incorrect. The statement of income is prepared on an accrual basis and is not meant to report cash flows. **Answer (B) is incorrect.** The statement of changes in equity is prepared on the accrual basis. **Answer (D) is incorrect.** The statement of financial position reports on financial position at a moment in time.

4. Suppose that an entity has paid one of its liabilities twice during the year, in error. The effects of this mistake would be

A. Assets, liabilities, and equity are understated.
B. Assets, net income, and equity are unaffected.
C. Assets and liabilities are understated.
D. Assets and net income and equity are understated, and liabilities are overstated.

Answer (C) is correct.
REQUIRED: The effects of paying a liability twice.
DISCUSSION: When a liability is paid, an entry debiting accounts payable and crediting cash is made. If an entity erroneously pays a liability twice, the accounts payable and cash accounts will be understated by the amount of the liability. Thus, assets and liabilities will be understated.
Answer (A) is incorrect. The double payment of a liability does not affect expenses of the period so it does not affect net income and equity. **Answer (B) is incorrect.** Assets will be reduced. **Answer (D) is incorrect.** Both assets and liabilities will be understated, and net income and equity will be unaffected.

5. In a statement of cash flows (indirect method), depreciation expense should be presented as

A. An inflow of cash.
B. An outflow of cash.
C. An addition to net income in converting net income or loss to net cash flows from operating activities.
D. A deduction from net income in converting net income or loss to net cash flows from operating activities.

Answer (C) is correct.
REQUIRED: The presentation of depreciation expense in a statement of cash flows (indirect method).
DISCUSSION: Under the indirect method, net income is reconciled to cash flow from operating activities. The net income for the period was calculated using the accrual method of accounting. Depreciation expense is a noncash expense included in net income. Thus, it must be added to net income to determine the net cash flow from operating activities.
Answer (A) is incorrect. Depreciation does not involve an inflow or outflow of cash. Depreciation is a noncash operating expense. **Answer (B) is incorrect.** Depreciation is a noncash operating expense. **Answer (D) is incorrect.** Depreciation expense should be added.

9.3 The Accrual Basis of Accounting

6. To calculate net sales, an increase in <List A> must be <List B> cash receipts from customers.

	List A	List B
A.	Accounts receivable	Added to
B.	Accounts receivable	Subtracted from
C.	Accounts payable	Added to
D.	Accounts payable	Subtracted from

Answer (A) is correct.
REQUIRED: The calculation of net sales.
DISCUSSION: To convert from the cash basis (cash receipts) to the accrual basis (net sales), the increase in net accounts receivable must be added to cash receipts from customers.

7. The publisher of a popular magazine offers a special discounted price for a 3-year subscription. At the end of the reporting period, the amount that has already been collected but for which a performance obligation has not been satisfied is best referred to as

A. Accrued subscriptions revenue (an asset account).
B. A contract liability.
C. Earned subscriptions revenue (a revenue account).
D. Precollected subscriptions receivable (a deferred asset account).

Answer (B) is correct.
REQUIRED: The best description of revenue that has already been collected but pertains to future periods.
DISCUSSION: Revenue is recognized when the performance obligation is satisfied. When it is received in advance, the amount applicable to future periods is a contract liability. But, the entity still must satisfy an obligation to perform in the future before it is entitled to the future economic benefits. The amount received in advance is a liability because it represents a present obligation resulting from a past event. Accordingly, a contract liability is an amount that has been received but that has not met the recognition criteria for revenue.
Answer (A) is incorrect. An accrued revenue is revenue that has met the recognition criteria but has not been received. **Answer (C) is incorrect.** The revenue will be recognized in future periods when a performance obligation has been satisfied by distributing issues of the magazine to the subscribers. **Answer (D) is incorrect.** "Precollected receivable" is not a standard accounting term.

9.4 The Accounting Process

8. The correct order of the following steps of the accounting cycle is

A. Posting, closing, adjusting, reversing.
B. Posting, adjusting, closing, reversing.
C. Posting, reversing, adjusting, closing.
D. Adjusting, posting, closing, reversing.

Answer (B) is correct.
REQUIRED: The proper sequence of steps in the accounting cycle.
DISCUSSION: After identification and measurement of items to be recorded, the steps in the accounting cycle are, in order, (1) journalizing transactions, (2) posting journal entries to the ledgers, (3) preparing an unadjusted trial balance, (4) recording adjusting entries, (5) preparing an adjusted trial balance, (6) preparing financial statements, (7) closing temporary (nominal) accounts, (8) preparing a post-closing trial balance (optional), and (9) reversing the accrual entries (optional).
Answer (A) is incorrect. Adjusting entries are made prior to closing. **Answer (C) is incorrect.** Reversing entries are made after adjustments and closing entries. **Answer (D) is incorrect.** Posting is done prior to adjusting.

9. In performing an audit, you encounter an adjusting journal entry recorded at year end that contains a debit to rental revenue and a credit to a contract liability. The purpose of this journal entry is to record an

A. Accrued revenue.
B. Unexpired cost.
C. Expired cost.
D. Adjustment.

Answer (D) is correct.
REQUIRED: The purpose of an adjusting entry debiting rental revenue and crediting a contract liability.
DISCUSSION: A contract liability is a revenue item that has been received but for which a performance obligation has not been satisfied. The journal entry described in the question is an adjusting entry to transfer an amount from the revenue account to a contract liability. The initial collection of cash in advance from the tenant was apparently recorded by a credit to revenue. An adjusting entry is therefore required at year end to transfer any remaining amount that does not qualify for revenue recognition.
Answer (A) is incorrect. An accrued revenue has met the recognition criteria but has not yet been received. The journal entry described indicates that collection has been made. **Answer (B) is incorrect.** The entry concerns a revenue rather than an expense transaction. **Answer (C) is incorrect.** The entry concerns a revenue rather than an expense transaction.

9.5 Cash, Accounts Receivable, and Inventory

10. On January 1, a new landscaping firm, Bandit27 Co., acquired a fleet of vehicles, all the necessary tools and equipment, and a parking and storage facility. It began operations immediately. It is now the end of the first year of operations, and the first set of year-end financial statements is being prepared.

During the first year of operations, the company experienced a 5% credit loss rate on sales. None of the credit losses are expected to be recovered, given that 5% is the industry average level of credit losses. Total credit sales for the year were US $400,000. The year-end balance of accounts receivable includes uncollected overdue accounts of US $100,000. Half of the uncollected overdue amounts are estimated to be uncollectible. If Bandit27 Co. uses the <List A> approach to estimate credit loss expense, the estimated credit loss expense will be <List B>.

	List A	List B
A.	Statement of financial position	US $20,000
B.	Statement of financial position	US $100,000
C.	Income statement	US $20,000
D.	Income statement	US $50,000

Answer (C) is correct.
REQUIRED: The estimated credit loss expense.
DISCUSSION: Using the income statement approach, the credit loss expense is determined using a percentage of total credit sales. Credit loss expense is therefore US $20,000 ($400,000 credit sales × 5% estimated credit loss rate).
Answer (A) is incorrect. The amount of US $20,000 is the credit loss expense calculated using the income statement approach. **Answer (B) is incorrect.** Under the statement of financial position approach, the amount estimated to be uncollectible is US $50,000 ($100,000 × 50%). **Answer (D) is incorrect.** The estimated credit loss expense using the statement of financial position approach is US $50,000.

9.6 Property, Plant, and Equipment and Intangible Assets

11. A theme park purchased a new, exciting ride and financed it through the manufacturer. The following facts pertain:

Purchase price	US $800,000
Delivery cost	50,000
Installation cost	70,000

The straight-line method is to be used. Compute the depreciation on the equipment for the first year assuming an estimated service life of 5 years.

A. US $160,000
B. US $174,000
C. US $184,000
D. US $170,000

Answer (C) is correct.
 REQUIRED: The depreciation expense.
 DISCUSSION: Under the straight-line method, the annual depreciation expense for an asset equals the asset's amount (Cost – Residual value) divided by the asset's estimated useful life. The cost of the asset includes its price and the directly attributable costs of bringing it to working condition for intended use. Thus, the depreciation expense is US $184,000 [($800,000 purchase price + $50,000 delivery cost + $70,000 installation cost) ÷ 5-year estimated service life].
 Answer (A) is incorrect. The amount of US $160,000 excludes the delivery and installation costs. **Answer (B) is incorrect.** The amount of US $174,000 excludes the delivery cost. **Answer (D) is incorrect.** The amount of US $170,000 excludes the installation cost.

12. An entity sells a piece of machinery, for cash, prior to the end of its estimated useful life. The sale price is less than the carrying amount of the asset on the date of sale. The entry that the entity uses to record the sale is

A. Cash
   Accumulated depreciation -- machinery
   Loss on disposal of machinery
      Machinery
B. Cash
   Accumulated depreciation -- machinery
      Gain on disposal of machinery
      Machinery
C. Cash
   Expense -- disposal of machinery
      Accumulated depreciation -- machinery
      Machinery
D. Cash
   Machinery
      Accumulated depreciation -- machinery
      Gain on disposal of machinery

Answer (A) is correct.
 REQUIRED: The entry to record sale of machinery at less than its carrying amount.
 DISCUSSION: Cash is debited for the amount of the sale proceeds. Machinery and the related accumulated depreciation are eliminated by a credit and a debit, respectively. Because the sale price was less than the carrying amount of the asset on the date of sale, a loss on disposal should be recognized in net income or loss.
 Answer (B) is incorrect. A loss on disposal should be recognized in net income. **Answer (C) is incorrect.** Accumulated depreciation should be debited. **Answer (D) is incorrect.** A loss and accumulated depreciation should be debited.

SU 9: Concepts and Underlying Principles of Financial Accounting

13. An entity purchases office equipment for US $525,000 on account. Select the appropriate journal entry to record this transaction.

A. Office expense US $525,000
    Accounts payable US $525,000

B. Office equipment US $525,000
    Accounts payable US $525,000

C. Accounts payable US $525,000
    Office expense US $525,000

D. Accounts payable US $525,000
    Office equipment US $525,000

Answer (B) is correct.
REQUIRED: The appropriate journal entry to record a purchase of equipment on account.
DISCUSSION: The purchase of office equipment represents the acquisition of an asset. An increase in an asset is recorded by a debit. The purchase on account increases liabilities. An increase in a liability is recorded by a credit.
Answer (A) is incorrect. The charge is to an expense account only if the amount were immaterial.
Answer (C) is incorrect. An increase in accounts payable is recorded by a credit. The purchase of equipment results in an asset that is recorded by a debit to an asset account. Also, the charge is to an expense account only if the amount were immaterial. **Answer (D) is incorrect.** An increase in a liability is recorded by a credit. An increase in an asset is recorded by a debit.

9.7 Accounts Payable, Accrued Expenses, and Deposits and Other Advances

14. Which of the following is usually associated with payables classified as accounts payable and expected to be settled?

	Periodic Payment of Interest	Secured by Collateral
A.	No	No
B.	No	Yes
C.	Yes	No
D.	Yes	Yes

Answer (A) is correct.
REQUIRED: The characteristic(s) usually associated with accounts payable.
DISCUSSION: Accounts payable, commonly termed trade accounts payable, are liabilities reflecting the obligations to sellers that are incurred when an entity purchases inventory, supplies, or services on credit. Accounts payable should be recorded at their settlement value. Short-term liabilities, such as accounts payable, do not usually provide for a periodic payment of interest unless the accounts are not settled when due or payable. They also are usually not secured by collateral.

9.8 The Time Value of Money

15. If the amount to be received in 4 years is US $137,350, and given the correct factor from the 10% time-value-of-money table below, what is the current investment?

Interest Factors for 10%

Periods	PV	PV of Ordinary Annuity
1	.9091	.9091
2	.8264	1.7355
3	.7513	2.4869
4	.6830	3.1699
5	.6029	3.7908

A. US $30,034.33

B. US $43,329.44

C. US $93,810.05

D. US $201,098.09

Answer (C) is correct.
REQUIRED: The current investment required to receive a future amount of money at a given interest rate.
DISCUSSION: The current investment is the present value of the given future amount. It equals the future amount multiplied by the factor for the present value of US $1 for four periods at 10%. Accordingly, the current investment is US $93,810.05 ($137,350 × .6830).
Answer (A) is incorrect. The amount of US $30,034.33 cannot be derived from any of the time value factors given. **Answer (B) is incorrect.** The amount of US $43,329.44 results from incorrectly dividing by the factor for the present value of an ordinary annuity for four periods. **Answer (D) is incorrect.** The amount of US $201,098.09 results from incorrectly dividing by the factor for the present value of US $1 for 4 periods.

9.9 Bonds

16. If bonds are initially sold at a discount and the effective-interest method of amortization is used, interest expense

A. In the earlier periods will be less than interest expense in the later periods.
B. In the earlier periods will be greater than interest expense in the later periods.
C. Will equal the cash interest payment each period.
D. Will be less than the cash interest payment each period.

Answer (A) is correct.
REQUIRED: The effect on interest expense if bonds are initially sold at a discount and the effective-interest method of amortization is used.
DISCUSSION: Interest expense equals the carrying amount of the liability at the beginning of the period times the effective interest rate. The carrying amount of the liability equals the face amount of the bond minus the discount. As the discount is amortized over the life of the bond, the carrying amount increases. Consequently, the interest expense increases over the term of the bond.
Answer (B) is incorrect. Interest expense will increase over the term of the bonds. **Answer (C) is incorrect.** Interest expense exceeds the cash interest payment when bonds are issued at a discount. The reason is that the effective rate is higher than the nominal rate. The excess of interest expense over the cash payment is the amount of discount amortized each period. **Answer (D) is incorrect.** Interest expense exceeds the cash interest payment when bonds are issued at a discount. The reason is that the effective rate is higher than the nominal rate. The excess of interest expense over the cash payment is the amount of discount amortized each period.

9.10 Pensions

17. On December 31, Year 1, Entity A determines the following information in relation to its defined benefit pension plan:

Fair value of plan assets US $210,000
Projected benefit obligation (PBO) US $260,000

In its Year 1 financial statements, Entity A reports a pension <List A> of <List B> for the <List C> PBO.

	List A	List B	List C
A.	Liability	US $50,000	Underfunded
B.	Asset	US $210,000	Overfunded
C.	Liability	US $260,000	Underfunded
D.	Liability	US $50,000	Overfunded

Answer (A) is correct.
REQUIRED: The proper reporting of the pension-related balance.
DISCUSSION: Entity A recognizes a pension liability to the extent its PBO is underfunded. This excess of the PBO over the fair value of the plan assets is US $50,000 ($260,000 – $210,000).
Answer (B) is incorrect. A pension asset is recognized if the fair value of plan assets is greater than the PBO. **Answer (C) is incorrect.** The amount of US $260,000 is the PBO, not the underfunded amount of the PBO. **Answer (D) is incorrect.** An overfunded PBO results in recognition of a pension asset.

18. Which of the following statements is true for a defined contribution pension plan?

A. The employer is required to contribute a certain amount each period based on the plan's formula.
B. The employer bears the risk of the plan's investment performance.
C. Retirement benefits received by employees are defined by the plan's formula.
D. The employer and employees are required to contribute equal amounts to the pension fund.

Answer (A) is correct.
REQUIRED: The true statement about a defined contribution plan.
DISCUSSION: Under a defined contribution plan, the employer's only obligation is to periodically deposit a certain amount in the pension fund.
Answer (B) is incorrect. The employees bear the risk of the plan's investment performance. Answer (C) is incorrect. The benefits received by employees are defined by the plan's formula under a defined benefit plan, not a defined contribution plan. Answer (D) is incorrect. Equal contributions are not required for a defined contribution plan.

9.11 Leases and Contingencies

19. Sales-type leases and operating leases differ in that the lessor

A. Obtains use of the asset only under a sales-type lease.
B. Must recognize a lease liability and a right-of-use asset for an operating lease.
C. Makes rent payments that are actually installment payments constituting a payment of both principal and interest only under an operating lease.
D. Must derecognize the leased asset under a sales-type lease.

Answer (D) is correct.
REQUIRED: The difference between sales-type and operating leases.
DISCUSSION: For sales-type leases, the lessor must derecognize the leased asset. For operating leases, the lessor recognizes lease payments as lease (rental) income. The leased asset continues to be reported on the lessor's balance sheet.
Answer (A) is incorrect. The lessor transfers use of the asset under both types of leases to the lessee. The lessor does not obtain use of the asset. Answer (B) is incorrect. For finance and operating leases, a lessee (not a lessor) must recognize a lease liability and a right-of-use asset at the lease commencement date. Answer (C) is incorrect. The lessee makes payments to the lessor under both types of leases. The lessor does not make payments.

20. Which of the following is an example of a contingent liability?

A. A retail store in a shopping mall pays the lessor a minimum monthly rent plus an agreed-upon percentage of sales.
B. An entity is refusing to pay the invoice for a completed annual audit because it seems higher than the amount agreed upon with the public accounting entity's partner.
C. An entity accrues income tax payable in its interim financial statements.
D. A lessee agrees to reimburse a lessor for a shortfall in the residual value of an asset under lease.

Answer (D) is correct.
REQUIRED: The example of a contingent liability.
DISCUSSION: The liability resulting from a guarantee is contingent on the lessor's not receiving the full residual value from a third party. A liability is recognized for a guarantee even if the probability of loss is remote.
Answer (A) is incorrect. The amount of rent is not uncertain. Rent expense can be accrued as sales occur. Answer (B) is incorrect. A service was received, and the entity owes an amount. The amount is not contingent on a future event. The entity can accrue the amount that it expected the invoice to show. Answer (C) is incorrect. As of the date of the interim financial statements, the income tax is payable because earnings have occurred. The amount or the timing of the payment as of the date of the statements is not uncertain.

328 Notes

STUDY UNIT TEN
ADVANCED FINANCIAL ACCOUNTING CONCEPTS AND ANALYSIS

(33 pages of outline)

10.1	Risk and Return	330
10.2	Derivatives	333
10.3	Foreign Currency Transactions	337
10.4	Business Combinations and Consolidated Financial Statements	340
10.5	Corporate Equity Accounts and Partnerships	344
10.6	Financial Statement Analysis -- Liquidity Ratios	346
10.7	Financial Statement Analysis -- Activity Ratios	349
10.8	Financial Statement Analysis -- Solvency Ratios and Leverage	354
10.9	Financial Statement Analysis -- ROI and Profitability	356
10.10	Financial Statement Analysis -- Corporate Valuation and Common-Size Financial Statements Ratios	359

This study unit is the second of six covering **Domain IV: Financial Management** from The IIA's CIA Exam Syllabus. This domain makes up 20% of Part 3 of the CIA exam and is tested at the **basic and proficient** cognitive levels. Refer to the complete syllabus located in Appendix A to view the relevant sections covered in Study Unit 10.

SUCCESS TIP: The majority of financial management questions on the CIA exam test conceptual understanding, not the ability to perform calculations. However, many of our financial management questions require you to perform calculations. They are an effective means of reinforcing your conceptual understanding.

10.1 RISK AND RETURN

1. **Rate of Return**

    a. A return is the amount received by an investor as compensation for taking on the risk of the investment.

    $$\text{Return} = \text{Amount received} - \text{Amount invested}$$

    > **EXAMPLE 10-1   Return on Investment**
    >
    > An investor paid US $100,000 for an investment that returned US $112,000. The investor's return is US $12,000 ($112,000 − $100,000).

    b. The rate of return is the return stated as a percentage of the amount invested.

    $$\text{Rate of return} = \frac{\text{Return}}{\text{Amount invested}}$$

    > **EXAMPLE 10-2   Rate of Return**
    >
    > The investor's rate of return is 12% (US $12,000 ÷ $100,000).

    SUCCESS TIP: Note that the return formula presented above differs from the return on investment (ROI) formula presented in Subunit 10.9. The return looks at a specific investment's profitability relative to the amount invested, whereas the ROI formula indicates how well a business is using its resources to generate operating income.

2. **Residual Income**

    a. Residual income is calculated as follows:

    $$\text{Residual income} = \text{Operating income} - \text{Target return on invested capital}$$

    1) The target return equals average invested capital times an imputed interest rate. This rate ordinarily is the weighted-average cost of capital (defined in Study Unit 12, Subunit 3), but it may be a hurdle rate reflecting the specific risks of a project.

    b. Projects with a positive residual income should be accepted, and projects with a negative residual income should be rejected.

    c. Residual income is often considered to be superior to ROI (discussed in Subunit 10.9). ROI is a percentage measure, and residual income is a monetary measure. Residual income therefore may be more consistent with maximizing profits.

3. **Investment Securities**

    a. Financial managers may select from many financial instruments for investments and capital acquisition.

b. The safety of an investment and its potential return are inversely related. To the right is a short list of widely available investment securities.

Instrument	Risk and Potential Return
Equity { Common stock Convertible preferred stock Preferred stock Debt { Income bonds Subordinated debentures Second mortgage bonds First mortgage bonds U.S. Treasury bonds	Highest Lowest

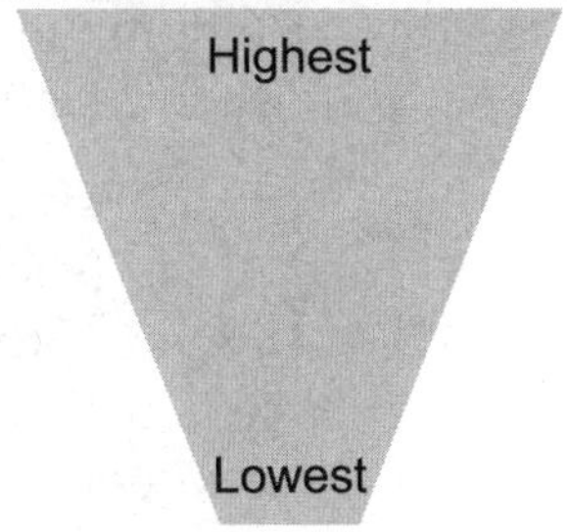

Figure 10-1

c. The reasons for the varying risk and potential return of these securities can be summarized as follows:

1) Equity securities are necessarily more risky than debt because an entity's owners are not contractually guaranteed a return.
2) Issuers of debt securities are contractually obligated to redeem them. Because these returns are guaranteed, they are lower than those for equity investments.

4. **Asset Valuation -- CAPM**

   a. The capital asset pricing model (CAPM) quantifies the expected return on an equity security by relating the security's risk to the average return available in the market.
   b. The investor must be compensated for the time value of money and risk.

   1) The time value component is the **risk-free rate (R_F)**. It is the return provided by the safest investments, e.g., U.S. Treasury securities.
   2) The risk component is determined by the following:

      a) The **market risk premium ($R_M - R_F$)** is the return provided by the market above the risk-free rate.
      b) The effect of an individual security on the volatility of a portfolio is measured by its sensitivity to movements by the overall market. This sensitivity is stated in terms of a stock's **beta coefficient (β)**.

         i) The beta of the market portfolio equals 1, and the beta of U.S. Treasury securities is 0.

      c) The **security risk premium** is the market risk premium weighted by beta.

CAPM Formula

$$\text{Required rate of return} = R_F + \beta(R_M - R_F)$$

If: R_F = Risk-free return
R_M = Market return
β = Measure of the systematic risk or volatility of the individual security in comparison with the market (diversified portfolio)

EXAMPLE 10-3   Required Rate of Return -- CAPM

An investor is considering the purchase of a stock with a beta of 1.2. Treasury bills currently return 8.6%, and the average return on the market is 10.1%. (U.S. Treasuries are as close to a risk-free investment as possible.) The return that the investor requires is calculated as follows:

$$\begin{aligned}\text{Required rate of return} &= R_F + \beta(R_M - R_F) \\ &= 8.6\% + 1.2(10.1\% - 8.6\%) \\ &= 8.6\% + 1.8\% \\ &= 10.4\%\end{aligned}$$

5. **Two Basic Types of Investment Risk**
   a. **Systematic risk**, or **market risk**, is unavoidable. Changes in the economy as a whole, such as inflation or the business cycle, affect all market participants.
      1) Systematic risk is sometimes called **undiversifiable risk**. All investments are affected, and this risk cannot be reduced by diversification.
   b. **Unsystematic risk**, or **firm-specific risk**, is the risk inherent in a specific investment. This type of risk is determined by the firm's industry, products, customer loyalty, degree of leverage, management competence, etc.
      1) Unsystematic risk is **diversifiable risk**. Because individual investments are affected by the strengths and weaknesses of the firm, this risk can be reduced by diversification.

6. **Types of Investment Risk**
   a. **Credit default risk** is the risk that the borrower will default and will not be able to repay principal or interest. This risk is estimated by credit-rating agencies.
   b. **Liquidity risk** is the risk that a security cannot be sold on short notice for its market value.
   c. **Maturity risk**, or **interest rate risk**, is the risk that an investment security will fluctuate in value between the time it was issued and its maturity date. The longer the time until maturity, the greater the maturity risk.
   d. **Inflation risk** is the risk that the purchasing power of the currency will decline.
   e. **Political risk** is the probability of loss from actions of governments, such as from changes in tax laws or environmental regulations or from expropriation of assets.
   f. **Exchange rate risk** is the risk of loss because of fluctuation in the relative value of foreign currency.
   g. **Business risk** (or **operations risk**) is the risk of fluctuations in earnings before interest and taxes or in operating income when the firm has no debt. It is the risk inherent in its operations that excludes **financial risk**, which is the risk to the shareholders from the use of financial leverage. Business risk depends on factors such as the variability of demand, sales prices, and input prices. It also is affected by operating leverage.

7. **Portfolio Management -- Diversification**
   a. The goal of portfolio management is to hold a group of securities that generates a return without the risks associated with one security. An investor wants to maximize return and minimize risk when choosing a portfolio of investments.
      1) Portfolio **return** is the weighted average of the returns on the individual securities.
      2) Portfolio **risk** is usually less than a simple average of the risks of the securities in the portfolio. One goal of diversification is to offset the unsystematic risk.
   b. The **coefficient of correlation** measures the degree to which the prices of two variables (e.g., two equity securities) are related. It has a range from 1.0 to –1.0.
      1) Perfect positive correlation (1.0) means that the prices of two securities always move together.
      2) Perfect negative correlation (–1.0) means that the prices of two securities always move in opposite directions.
      3) If a pair of securities has a coefficient of correlation of 1.0, the risk of the two together is the same as the risk of each security by itself. If a pair of securities has a coefficient of correlation of –1.0, all unsystematic (firm-specific) risk has been eliminated.
   c. The ideal portfolio consists of securities with a wide enough variety of coefficients of correlation so that only market risk remains.

SU 10: Advanced Financial Accounting Concepts and Analysis

8. **Efficient Markets Hypothesis**

   a. The efficient markets hypothesis states that current stock prices immediately and fully reflect all relevant information. Hence, the market is continuously adjusting to new information and acting to correct pricing errors. The efficient markets hypothesis has three forms.

Strong Form	All public and private information is instantaneously reflected in securities' prices.
Semistrong Form	All publicly available data are reflected in security prices, but private or insider data are not immediately reflected.
Weak Form	Current securities prices reflect all recent price movement data.

STOP & REVIEW

You have completed the outline for this subunit.
Study multiple-choice questions 1 and 2 on page 362.

10.2 DERIVATIVES

1. **Overview**

   a. A **derivative instrument** is an investment in which the parties' gain or loss is derived from some other economic event, for example, the price of a given stock, a foreign currency exchange rate, or the price of a certain commodity.

      1) One party enters into the transaction to speculate (incur risk), and the other enters into it to hedge (avoid risk).

   b. Derivatives are a type of financial instrument, along with cash, accounts receivable, notes receivable, bonds, preferred shares, etc.

2. **Options**

   a. A party who buys an option has bought the right to demand that the counterparty (the seller or "writer" of the option) buy or sell an underlying asset on or before a specified future date. The buyer holds all of the rights, and the seller has all of the obligations. The buyer pays a fee to determine whether the seller buys (sells) the underlying asset from (to) the buyer.

      1) A **call option** gives the buyer (holder) the right to purchase (i.e., the right to call for) the underlying asset (stock, currency, commodity, etc.) at a fixed price.

      2) A **put option** gives the buyer (holder) the right to sell (i.e., the right to put onto the market) the underlying asset (stock, currency, commodity, etc.) at a fixed price.

      3) The asset that is subject to being bought or sold under the terms of the option is the **underlying**.

      4) The party buying an option is the **holder**. The seller is the **writer**.

      5) The exercise of an option is always at the discretion of the option holder (the buyer) who has, in effect, bought the right to exercise the option or not.

         a) The seller of an option has no choice. (S)he must perform if the holder chooses to exercise.

      6) An option has an expiration date after which it can no longer be exercised.

3. **Components of the Option Price**

    a. The price of an option (the option premium) consists of two components: intrinsic value and the time premium, also called extrinsic value.

    Option premium = Intrinsic value + Time premium

    b. The **exercise price** (the strike price) is the price at which the holder can purchase (call option) or sell (put option) the underlying.

    c. The **intrinsic value** of an option is the value of the option today if it is exercised today. If intrinsic value is zero, market value would still be positive because of market volatility, interest rates, and the time value of money.

      1) The **intrinsic value of a call option** is the amount by which the exercise price is less than the current price of the underlying.

          a) If an option has a positive intrinsic value, it is in-the-money.

EXAMPLE 10-4   Intrinsic Value of a Call Option

An investor holds call options for 200 shares of Locksley Corporation with an exercise price of US $48 per share. Locksley stock is currently trading at US $50 per share. The investor's options have an intrinsic value of US $2 each ($50 − $48).

---

          b) If an option has an intrinsic value of US $0, it is out-of-the-money.

EXAMPLE 10-5   Out-of-the-Money Call Option

An investor holds call options for 200 shares of Locksley Corporation with an exercise price of US $48 per share. Locksley stock is currently trading at US $45 per share. The investor's options are out-of-the-money.

---

    d. The **intrinsic value of a put option** is the amount by which the exercise price is greater than the current price of the underlying.

      1) If an option has a positive intrinsic value, it is in-the-money.

EXAMPLE 10-6   Intrinsic Value of a Put Option

An investor holds put options for 200 shares of Locksley Corporation with an exercise price of US $48 per share. Locksley stock is currently trading at US $45 per share. The investor's options have an intrinsic value of US $3 each ($48 − $45).

---

      2) If an option has an intrinsic value of US $0, it is out-of-the-money.

EXAMPLE 10-7   Out-of-the-Money Put Option

An investor holds put options for 200 shares of Locksley Corporation with an exercise price of US $48 per share. Locksley stock is currently trading at US $50 per share. The investor's options are out-of-the-money.

---

    e. Time Premium

      1) The more time between the writing of an option and its expiration, the greater the probability that the price of the underlying will change and the option will be in-the-money. Because the buyer's loss on an option is limited to the option premium, an increase in the term of an option (call or put) increases the time premium.

4. **Forward Contracts**

    a. One method of mitigating risk is the simple forward contract. The two parties agree that, at a set future date, one will perform and the other will pay a specified amount for the performance.

        1) A common example is that of a retailer and a wholesaler who agree in September on the prices and quantities of merchandise that will be shipped to the retailer's stores in time for the winter holiday season. The retailer has locked in a price and a source of supply, and the wholesaler has locked in a price and a customer.

    b. In a forward contract, each party has an obligation, i.e., to deliver merchandise or to pay. Neither has the option of nonperformance.

        1) Forward contracts often are used in foreign currency exchange transactions.

5. **Futures Contracts**

    a. A futures contract is a commitment to buy or sell an asset at a fixed price during a specific future period. Unlike a forward contract, the counterparty is unknown.

    b. Futures contracts are standardized forward contracts with predetermined quantities and dates. They are essentially commodities that are actively traded on futures exchanges.

        1) A clearinghouse randomly matches sellers who will deliver during a given period with buyers who are seeking delivery during the same period.

    c. Because futures contracts are actively traded, the result is a **liquid market** that permits buyers and sellers to net their positions.

    d. Another aspect of futures contracts is that the market price is posted and netted to each person's account at the close of every business day. This practice is called **mark-to-market**.

        1) A mark-to-market provision minimizes a futures contract's chance of default. Profits and losses on the contracts must be received or paid each day through a clearinghouse that guarantees (underwrites) the transactions to eliminate the risk of nonperformance.

6. **Margin Requirements**

    a. A margin account is a brokerage account in which the investor borrows money (obtains credit) from a broker to purchase securities, such as derivatives. The broker charges interest on the credit provided.

    b. A **margin requirement** (set in the U.S. by the Federal Reserve Board's Regulation T) is the minimum down payment that the purchasers of securities must deposit in the margin account. When the balance is below the margin requirement, the broker notifies the investor to add funds to the account. This notice is a margin call.

7. **Hedging**
    a. Hedging is the process of using offsetting commitments to minimize or avoid the effects of adverse price movements. Hedging transactions often are used to protect positions in commodity buying, foreign currency, and future cash flows.
        1) The purchase or sale of a derivative or other instrument is a hedge if it is expected to minimize the risk of loss.
            a) In theory, the hedging instrument should be perfectly but negatively correlated with the hedged items.
        2) An example of the hedging approach is financing an asset with a financial instrument of the same approximate maturity as the life of the asset. The basic concept is that that entity has the entire life of the asset to recover the amount invested before having to pay the lender.
    b. **Long-position** hedges are futures contracts that are purchased to protect against price increases.
        1) For example, if a flour company buys and uses 1 million bushels of wheat each month, it may wish to guard against increases in wheat costs. If so, it will purchase futures contracts to buy 1 million bushels of wheat at the current price one month from today. This long position hedge will result in gains if the price of wheat increases (offsetting the actual increased costs).
    c. **Short-position** hedges are futures contracts that are sold to protect against price declines.

STOP & REVIEW

You have completed the outline for this subunit.
Study multiple-choice questions 3 and 4 on page 363.

10.3 FOREIGN CURRENCY TRANSACTIONS

1. **Definitions**

    a. The **functional currency** is the currency of the primary economic environment in which the entity operates. Normally, that environment is the one in which it primarily generates and expends cash.

    b. A **foreign currency** is any currency other than the entity's functional currency.

    c. The **reporting currency** is the currency in which an entity prepares its financial statements.

    d. **Foreign currency transactions** are fixed in a currency other than the functional currency. They result when an entity

    1) Buys or sells on credit;
    2) Borrows or lends;
    3) Is a party to a derivative instrument; or,
    4) For other reasons, acquires or disposes of assets, or incurs or settles liabilities, fixed in a foreign currency.

2. **Exchange Rate Exposure**

    a. When a U.S. firm purchases from, or sells to, an entity in a foreign country, the transaction is recorded in U.S. dollars (the firm's domestic currency).

    Foreign sale:
    Accounts receivable   US $100,000
        Sales   US $100,000

    Foreign purchase:
    Inventory   US $100,000
        Accounts payable   US $100,000

    1) The dollar, however, might not be the currency in which the transaction will have to be settled (typically 30 days later).
    2) If the exchange rate of the two currencies (i.e., the units of one currency required to purchase a single unit of the other) is fixed, the existence of a foreign-denominated receivable or payable raises no measurement issue.

EXAMPLE 10-8   Initial Recognition -- Foreign Currency Transaction

On November 15, Year 1, JRF Corporation, a U.S. entity, purchases and receives inventory from Paris Corporation, a French entity. The transaction is fixed in euros and calls for JRF to pay Paris €500,000 on January 15, Year 2. On November 15, Year 1, the euro-dollar exchange rate is US $1.2 to €1.

November 15, Year 1:
Inventory   US $600,000
    Accounts payable (€500,000 × 1.2 exchange rate)   US $600,000

3. **Accounting for Transaction Gains and Losses**
   a. A **transaction gain (loss)** results from a change in exchange rates between the functional currency and the currency in which the transaction is denominated. It is the change in functional currency cash flows
      1) Actually realized on settlement and
      2) Expected on unsettled transactions.
   b. Transactions are recorded at the spot rate in effect at the transaction date.
   c. Transaction gains and losses are recorded at each balance sheet date and at the date the receivable or payable is settled. The gains or losses ordinarily are **included in earnings**.
   d. When the amount of the functional currency exchangeable for a unit of the currency in which the transaction is fixed increases, a transaction gain or loss is recognized on a receivable or payable, respectively. The opposite occurs when the exchange rate (functional currency to foreign currency) decreases.

EXAMPLE 10-9   Gain or Loss -- Foreign Currency Transaction

In continuation of Example 10-8, the euro-dollar exchange rate was US $1.4 to €1 on December 31, Year 1, and US $1.55 to €1 on January 15, Year 2.

December 31, Year 1 (financial statements day):

Loss on foreign currency transactions	US $100,000	
Accounts payable [US $600,000 − (€500,000 × 1.4 year-end exchange rate)]		US $100,000

For the period between the initial recognition of the transaction (November 15, Year 1) and the financial statements date (December 31, Year 1), the dollar has depreciated against the euro. Now the €500,000 cost US $700,000 (500,000 × 1.4). On December 31, Year 1, accounts payable are reported at US $700,000, and loss on foreign currency transaction is reported at US $100,000.

January 15, Year 2 (transaction settlement day):

Accounts payable	US $700,000	
Loss on foreign currency transactions [500,000 × (1.55 − 1.4)]	75,000	
Cash (€500,000 × 1.55 settlement date exchange rate)		US $775,000

The loss of US $75,000 on foreign currency transactions is included in the Year 2 income statement.

NOTE: The total loss recognized on the exchange rate difference is US $175,000 [500,000 × (1.2 − 1.55)].

> **EXAMPLE 10-10**   **Transaction Gains and Losses**
>
> On December 15, Year 1, Boise Co. purchased electronic components from Kinugasa Corporation. Boise must pay Kinugasa ¥15,000,000 on January 15, Year 2. The exchange rate in effect on December 15, Year 1, was US $.01015 per yen, giving the transaction a value on Boise's books of US $152,250 (¥15,000,000 × $.01015).
>
>   Transaction Date:
>   Inventory   US $152,250
>   Accounts payable   US $152,250
>
> The exchange rate on December 31, Year 1, Boise's reporting date, has fallen to US $.01010 per yen. The balance of the payable must be adjusted in the amount of US $750 [(¥15,000,000 × ($.01015 − $.01010)].
>
>   Reporting Date:
>   Accounts payable   US $750
>   Transaction gain   US $750
>
> The exchange rate on January 15, Year 2, has risen to US $.01020 per yen. To settle the payable, the balance must be adjusted in the amount of US $1,500 [¥15,000,000 × ($.01010 − $.01020)].
>
>   Settlement Date:
>   Accounts payable (US $152,250 − $750)   US $151,500
>   Transaction loss   1,500
>   Cash   US $153,000

     e.   The occurrence of transaction gains and losses can be summarized as follows:

Effects of Exchange Rate Fluctuations

Transaction That Will Be Settled in a Foreign Currency	Results in a Foreign-Denominated	Foreign Currency Appreciates	Foreign Currency Depreciates
Sale	Receivable	Transaction gain	Transaction loss
Purchase	Payable	Transaction loss	Transaction gain

STOP & REVIEW

You have completed the outline for this subunit.
Study multiple-choice question 5 on page 364.

10.4 BUSINESS COMBINATIONS AND CONSOLIDATED FINANCIAL STATEMENTS

1. **Investment in Equity Securities**

    a. The accounting for an investment in common stock of an investee depends on the influence that the investor has over the investee.

Voting Interest	Presumed Influence	Accounting Method
100% – 50%	Control	Consolidation
50% – 20%	Significant	Equity Method or Fair Value Option (FVO)
20% – 0%	Little or None	Fair Value Measurement

    b. The fair value option (FVO) may be elected when the investor does not have control over the investee.

    c. When the investor has **little or no influence** over the investee (holds less than 20% of the voting interests), the investment is measured at fair value.

       1) The changes in its fair value (unrealized holding gains and losses) are recognized in the income statement.

    d. When the investor has **significant influence** over the investee (holds between 20% and 50% of the voting interests), the investment in equity securities is accounted for using the **equity method** if the investor has not elected the FVO.

       1) The investment is initially recognized at cost.
       2) The investor recognizes in income its share of the investee's net income or loss for the period.
       3) Dividends from the investee are treated as a return of an investment and decrease the investment balance.

2. **Business Combination**

    a. A business combination is a transaction or event in which an acquirer obtains control of one or more businesses.

       1) **Control** (controlling financial interest) is the direct or indirect ability to determine the direction of management and policies of the investee.

          a) An entity is presumed to have control when it acquires **more than 50%** of the voting interests (e.g., shares of common stock) of a second entity.
          b) However, a controlling financial interest is not deemed to exist when control does not rest with the majority owner, such as when the entity is in bankruptcy, in legal reorganization, or under severe governmentally imposed uncertainties.

       2) A **parent** is an entity that controls one or more subsidiaries.
       3) A **subsidiary** is an entity in which another entity, known as its parent, holds a controlling financial interest.

3. **Acquisition Method**

   a. A business combination must be accounted for using the acquisition method. This method involves

      1) Identifying the acquirer and
      2) Identifying the acquisition date, i.e., the date on which the acquirer obtains control of the acquiree.

   b. At the acquisition date, the acquirer (parent) must recognize and measure

      1) Identifiable assets acquired,
      2) Liabilities assumed,
      3) Any noncontrolling interest, and
      4) Goodwill or a gain from bargain purchase.

   c. **Measurement principle.** The identifiable assets acquired, liabilities assumed, and any noncontrolling interest in the subsidiary are recognized separately from goodwill and must be measured at **acquisition-date fair value**.

   d. The **noncontrolling interest** (NCI) is the portion of equity (net assets) in a subsidiary not attributable, directly or indirectly, to the parent.

      1) At the acquisition date, any NCI is measured at fair value.
      2) Any NCI is reported in the equity section of the consolidated balance sheet separately from the parent's shareholders' equity.
      3) If the parent holds all the subsidiary's outstanding common stock, no NCI is recognized.

   e. Goodwill recognized in a business combination is an intangible asset reflecting the future economic benefits resulting from those assets acquired in the combination that are not individually identified and separately recognized.

      1) Goodwill equals the excess of (a) the sum of the acquisition-date fair values of (1) the consideration transferred, (2) any noncontrolling interest in the acquiree, and (3) any prior interest held by the acquirer over (b) the acquisition-date fair value of the net identifiable assets acquired.
      2) Goodwill has an indefinite useful life. Thus, it must not be amortized subsequent to its initial recognition and is instead periodically tested for impairment.
      3) The parent presents any goodwill recognized in its consolidated balance sheet as one amount under noncurrent assets.
      4) Goodwill can be recognized only in a business combination. Internally generated goodwill must not be recognized in the financial statements.

5) Goodwill recognized equals the excess of a) over b) below:

 a) The sum of the acquisition-date **fair value** of the consideration transferred, any NCI recognized, and any previously held equity interest in the acquiree

 b) The acquisition-date fair value of identifiable assets acquired and liabilities assumed (fair value of net assets acquired)

EXAMPLE 10-11   Noncontrolling Interest

Entity C acquired 80% of the outstanding common stock of Entity D for US $192,000. Entity D's acquisition-date fair values of identifiable assets and liabilities were US $350,000 and US $140,000, respectively. The acquisition-date fair value of NCI was US $48,000. The goodwill is calculated as follows:

Consideration transferred		US $192,000
Noncontrolling interest		48,000
Acquisition-date fair value of identifiable net assets (Assets – Liabilities) acquired:		
Assets	US $350,000	
Liabilities	(140,000)	(210,000)
Goodwill		US $ 30,000

---

6) If b) exceeds a) above, an ordinary **gain from a bargain purchase** must be recognized in the parent's consolidated statement of income.

4. **Consolidated Financial Statements**

 a. When one entity (parent) controls another (subsidiary), consolidated financial statements must be issued by the parent regardless of the percentages of ownership.

 1) Consolidated reporting is required even when majority ownership is indirect, i.e., when a subsidiary holds a majority interest in another subsidiary.

 b. **Consolidated financial statements** are the general-purpose financial statements of a parent with one or more subsidiaries. They present amounts for the parent and all its subsidiaries as if they were a **single economic entity**.

 c. Required consolidated reporting is an example of substance over form. Even if the two entities remain legally separate, the financial statements are more meaningful to users if they see the effects of control by one over the other.

 d. **Consolidated procedures.** The starting point of the consolidation process is the parent-only and subsidiary-only adjusted trial balances (parent's and subsidiary's separate financial statements). The following steps must be performed when preparing consolidated financial statements:

 1) All line items of assets, liabilities, revenues, expenses, gains, losses, and OCI items of a subsidiary are added item by item to those of the parent. These items are reported at the consolidated amounts.

 2) The periodic net income or loss of a consolidated subsidiary attributable to NCI is presented separately from the periodic net income or loss attributable to the shareholders of the parent.

 3) All the equity amounts of the subsidiary are eliminated (not presented in the consolidated financial statements).

 4) The carrying amount of the parent's investment in the subsidiary as it is presented in the parent-only financial statements is eliminated (not presented in the consolidated financial statements).

5) Goodwill recognized at the acquisition date is presented separately as an intangible asset.
6) Any NCI is reported separately in one line item in the equity section. It must be adjusted for its proportionate share of (a) the subsidiary's net income (increase) or net loss (decrease) for the period, (b) dividends declared by the subsidiary (decrease), and (c) items of OCI recognized by the subsidiary.
7) Intraentity balances, transactions, income, and expenses must be eliminated in full.
   a) Reciprocal balances, such as (1) receivables and payables and (2) interest income and interest expense, between a parent and a subsidiary are eliminated in their entirety, regardless of the portion of the subsidiary's stock held by the parent.

EXAMPLE 10-12   Intraentity Eliminations -- Reciprocal Balances

Platonic's separate balance sheet reports a US $12,600 receivable from and a US $8,500 payable to Socratic. Socratic's separate balance sheet reports a US $8,500 receivable from and a US $12,600 payable to Platonic. These balances are not reported on the consolidated balance sheet.

---

   b) Consolidating entities routinely conduct business with each other. The effect of these intraentity transactions must be eliminated in full during the preparation of the consolidated financial statements.
   c) Consolidated financial statements report the financial position, results of operations, and cash flows as if the consolidated entities were a single economic entity. Thus, all line items in the consolidated financial statements must be presented at the amounts that would have been reported if the intraentity transactions had never occurred.
   d) After adding together all the assets, liabilities, and income statement items of a parent and a subsidiary, eliminating journal entries for intraentity transactions must be recorded for proper presentation of the consolidated financial statements.

e. An example of a full set of consolidated financial statements can be found in Appendix C.

STOP & REVIEW

You have completed the outline for this subunit.
Study multiple-choice questions 6 and 7 on page 364.

10.5 CORPORATE EQUITY ACCOUNTS AND PARTNERSHIPS

1. **Corporate Equity**

    a. The equity accounts of a corporation include contributed capital, treasury stock, retained earnings, and items included in accumulated other comprehensive income.

2. **Corporate Equity -- Contributed Capital**

    a. Contributed capital represents amounts invested by owners in exchange for stock (common or preferred).

        1) **Common stock.** The common shareholders are the owners of the entity. They have voting rights and may receive dividends at the discretion of the board of directors.

        2) **Preferred stock.** Preferred shareholders have the right to receive (a) dividends at a specified rate (before common shareholders may receive any) and (b) distributions before common shareholders (but after creditors) upon liquidation. Preferred stock can be cumulative, callable, or redeemable.

            a) The dividends on preferred stock equal the par value of the stock times its stated rate.

    b. **Issuance of shares.** Cash received is debited, the appropriate class of capital stock is recognized (credited) for the total **par value**, and **additional paid-in capital** is recognized (credited) for the difference.

> **EXAMPLE 10-13   Common Stock Issuance**
>
> A company issued 50,000 shares of its US $1 par value common stock. The market price was US $17 per share on the day of issue.
>
> | | | |
> |---|---|---|
> | Cash (50,000 shares × US $17 market price) | US $850,000 | |
> | Common stock (50,000 shares × US $1 par value per share) | | US $ 50,000 |
> | Additional paid-in capital (difference) | | 800,000 |
>
> A company also issued 10,000 shares of US $50 par value, 6% preferred stock. The market price was US $62 per share on the day of issue.
>
> | | | |
> |---|---|---|
> | Cash (10,000 shares × US $62 market price) | US $620,000 | |
> | 6% preferred stock (10,000 shares × US $50 par value per share) | | US $500,000 |
> | Additional paid-in capital (difference) | | 120,000 |

    c. When an entity reacquires its previously issued and outstanding shares, these shares are held as **treasury stock**. The acquisition of treasury shares results in a direct decrease in equity. This acquisition reduces the shares outstanding but not the shares authorized.

        1) Treasury shares are not assets, and dividends are not paid on them.

        2) The most common method for recording shares held as treasury stock is the cost method. Under this method, reacquired shares are recorded at their acquisition cost (debit treasury stock, credit cash).

3. **Corporate Equity -- Retained Earnings and Dividends**

   a. Retained earnings is accumulated net income or loss. It is increased by net income and decreased by net loss and dividends.

   b. The following entries are recorded when the dividend is declared and paid:

Declaration		Payment	
Retained earnings US $XXX		Dividends payable US $XXX	
Dividends payable	US $XXX	Cash	US $XXX

   c. The amount of retained earnings (ending balance) as it is reported in the balance sheet can be calculated as follows:

Beginning retained earnings	US $XXX
Plus: Net income for the period (or minus net loss)	XXX
Minus: Dividends declared this period	(XXX)
Ending retained earnings	US $XXX

   d. The beginning balance of retained earnings is adjusted for the cumulative effect on the income statement of (1) changes in accounting principle and (2) corrections of errors in prior-period financial statements. Accordingly, these items must not be included in the calculation of current-period net income.

4. **Corporate Equity -- Stock Dividends and Splits**

   a. A **stock dividend** involves no distribution of cash or other property. Stock dividends are accounted for as a reclassification of equity (transfer from retained earnings to common stock), not as liabilities.

      1) The recipient does not recognize income. It has the same proportionate interest in the entity and the same total carrying amount as before the stock dividend.

   b. **Stock splits** are issuance of shares that do not affect the total par or stated value of shares issued and outstanding or total equity.

      1) No entry is made, and no transfer from retained earnings occurs.

5. **Partnership Formation**

   a. A partnership is an association of two or more persons to carry on, as co-owners, a business for profit.

   b. Partners **contribute cash and other property** as the basis of their equity in a partnership. Cash is recorded at its nominal amount and property at its **fair value**.

   c. Partnership equity includes only the partners' capital accounts.

6. **Partnership Income or Loss**

   a. Profit and loss are distributed equally among partners unless the partnership agreement provides otherwise.

      1) If the partnership agreement specifies how profits, but not losses, are to be shared, losses are shared in the same manner as profits.

7. **Liquidation of a Partnership -- Process**
   a. When the partners dissolve their partnership, the process of liquidating noncash assets and settling liabilities begins. The liquidation process has four steps:
      1) Any gain or loss realized from the actual sale of assets is allocated to the partners' capital accounts in accordance with the profit-and-loss ratio.
      2) Remaining noncash assets are assumed to have a fair value of zero, resulting in an assumed loss equal to their carrying amounts. This amount is allocated to the partners' accounts in accordance with the profit-and-loss ratio.
      3) If at least one of the partners' capital accounts has a deficit balance, the deficit is allocated to the remaining partners' accounts.
      4) The final balances in the partnership accounts equal the amounts of cash, if any, that may be distributed to the partners.
   b. If a partner account has a debit balance after the fourth step, (s)he is liable for that balance.

> **STOP & REVIEW**
> You have completed the outline for this subunit.
> Study multiple-choice questions 8 and 9 on page 365.

10.6 FINANCIAL STATEMENT ANALYSIS -- LIQUIDITY RATIOS

1. **Liquidity**
   a. Liquidity is an entity's ability to pay its current obligations as they come due and remain in business in the short run.
   b. Liquidity depends on the ease with which current assets can be converted to cash. Liquidity ratios measure this ability by relating an entity's liquid assets to its current liabilities at a moment in time.

RESOURCES	CAPITAL STRUCTURE
	Debt / **Equity**
Current Assets	**Current Liabilities**
Noncurrent Assets	Noncurrent Liabilities / Stockholders' Equity

Figure 10-2

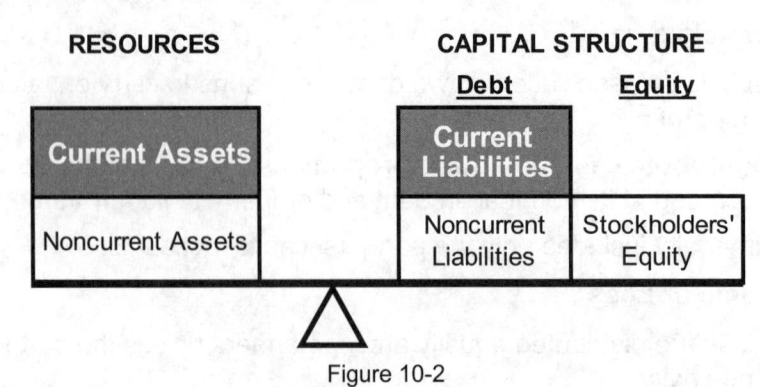

   c. Current assets are the most liquid. They are expected to be converted to cash, sold, or consumed within 1 year or the operating cycle, whichever is longer. Ratios involving current assets thus measure a firm's ability to continue operating in the short run.
      1) Current assets include, in descending order of liquidity, cash and equivalents; marketable securities; receivables (net of allowance for credit losses); inventories; and prepaid items.

d. Current liabilities, by the same token, are ones that must be settled the soonest. Specifically, they are expected to be settled or converted to other liabilities within 1 year or the operating cycle, whichever is longer.

1) Current liabilities include accounts payable, notes payable, current maturities of long-term debt, unearned revenues, taxes payable, wages payable, and other accruals.

EXAMPLE 10-14   Statement of Financial Position

RESOURCES	Current Year End	Prior Year End		FINANCING	Current Year End	Prior Year End
CURRENT ASSETS:			**CURRENT LIABILITIES:**			
Cash and equivalents	US $ 325,000	US $ 275,000	Accounts payable		US $ 150,000	US $ 75,000
Available-for-sale securities	165,000	145,000	Notes payable		50,000	50,000
Accounts receivable (net)	120,000	115,000	Accrued interest on note		5,000	5,000
Notes receivable	55,000	40,000	Current maturities of L.T. debt		100,000	100,000
Inventories	85,000	55,000	Accrued salaries and wages		15,000	10,000
Prepaid expenses	10,000	5,000	Income taxes payable		70,000	35,000
Total current assets	US $ 760,000	US $ 635,000	Total current liabilities		US $ 390,000	US $ 275,000
NONCURRENT ASSETS:			**NONCURRENT LIABILITIES:**			
Equity-method investments	US $ 120,000	US $ 115,000	Bonds payable		US $ 500,000	US $ 600,000
Property, plant, and equip.	1,000,000	900,000	Long-term notes payable		90,000	60,000
Less: Accum. depreciation	(85,000)	(55,000)	Employee-related obligations		15,000	10,000
Goodwill	5,000	5,000	Deferred income taxes		5,000	5,000
Total noncurrent assets	US $1,040,000	US $ 965,000	Total noncurrent liabilities		US $ 610,000	US $ 675,000
			Total liabilities		US $1,000,000	US $ 950,000
			STOCKHOLDERS' EQUITY:			
			Preferred stock, US $50 par		US $ 120,000	US $ 0
			Common stock, US $1 par		500,000	500,000
			Additional paid-in capital		110,000	100,000
			Retained earnings		70,000	50,000
			Total stockholders' equity		US $ 800,000	US $ 650,000
Total assets	US $1,800,000	US $1,600,000	Total liabilities and stockholders' equity		US $1,800,000	US $1,600,000

2. **Working Capital**

   a. Net working capital consists of the resources the company would have to continue operating in the short run if it had to settle all of its current liabilities at once.

   Working Capital = Current assets − Current liabilities

EXAMPLE 10-15   Change in Working Capital

Current year: US $760,000 − $390,000 = US $370,000
Prior year: US $635,000 − $275,000 = US $360,000

Although the company's current liabilities increased, its current assets increased by US $10,000 more. The company has more working capital. If current liabilities had increased by the same amount as current assets, the working capital balance would not have changed.

3. **Current Ratio**

   a. The current ratio, also called the working capital ratio, is the most common measure of liquidity.

   $$\text{Current ratio} = \frac{\text{Current assets}}{\text{Current liabilities}}$$

EXAMPLE 10-16	Current Ratio

   Current year: US $760,000 ÷ $390,000 = 1.95
   Prior year: US $635,000 ÷ $275,000 = 2.31

   Although working capital increased in absolute terms (US $10,000), current assets now provide less proportional coverage of current liabilities than in the prior year.

   1) A low ratio indicates a possible solvency problem.

      a) A firm with a low current ratio may become insolvent. Therefore, care should be taken when determining whether to extend credit to a firm with a low ratio.

   2) An overly high ratio indicates that management may not be investing idle assets productively.

   3) The quality of accounts receivable and merchandise inventory should be considered before evaluating the current ratio.

      a) Obsolete or overvalued inventory or receivables can artificially inflate the current ratio.

   4) The general principle is that the current ratio should be proportional to the operating cycle. Thus, a shorter cycle may justify a lower ratio.

      a) For example, a grocery store has a short operating cycle and can survive with a lower current ratio than could a gold mining company, which has a much longer operating cycle.

4. **Quick (Acid-Test) Ratio**

   a. The quick (acid-test) ratio excludes inventories and prepaid expenses from the numerator because they are difficult to liquidate at their stated amounts. The quick ratio is therefore a more conservative measure than the basic current ratio.

   $$\text{Quick (acid-test) ratio} = \frac{\text{Cash and equivalents + Marketable securities + Net receivables}}{\text{Current liabilities}}$$

EXAMPLE 10-17	Quick (Acid-Test) Ratio

   Current year: (US $325,000 + $165,000 + $120,000 + $55,000) ÷ $390,000 = 1.71
   Prior year: (US $275,000 + $145,000 + $115,000 + $40,000) ÷ $275,000 = 2.09

   Despite its increase in total working capital, the company's position in its most liquid assets declined.

   1) This ratio measures the firm's ability to easily pay its short-term debts while avoiding the problem of inventory valuation.

You have completed the outline for this subunit.
Study multiple-choice questions 10 through 12 beginning on page 366.

STOP & REVIEW

10.7 FINANCIAL STATEMENT ANALYSIS -- ACTIVITY RATIOS

1. **Income Statement to Balance Sheet**
   a. Activity ratios measure how quickly the two major noncash assets are converted to cash.
      1) Activity ratios measure results over a period of time and thus draw information from the firm's income statement as well as from the balance sheet.

EXAMPLE 10-18   **Balance Sheet**

RESOURCES

CURRENT ASSETS:	Current Year End	Prior Year End
Cash and equivalents	US $ 325,000	US $ 275,000
Available-for-sale securities	165,000	145,000
Accounts receivable (net)	120,000	115,000
Notes receivable	55,000	40,000
Inventories	85,000	55,000
Prepaid expenses	10,000	5,000
Total current assets	**US $ 760,000**	**US $ 635,000**
NONCURRENT ASSETS:		
Equity-method investments	US $ 120,000	US $ 115,000
Property, plant, and equip.	1,000,000	900,000
Less: Accum. depreciation	(85,000)	(55,000)
Goodwill	5,000	5,000
Total noncurrent assets	**US $1,040,000**	**US $ 965,000**
Total assets	**US $1,800,000**	**US $1,600,000**

FINANCING

CURRENT LIABILITIES:	Current Year End	Prior Year End
Accounts payable	US $ 150,000	US $ 75,000
Notes payable	50,000	50,000
Accrued interest on note	5,000	5,000
Current maturities of L.T. debt	100,000	100,000
Accrued salaries and wages	15,000	10,000
Income taxes payable	70,000	35,000
Total current liabilities	**US $ 390,000**	**US $ 275,000**
NONCURRENT LIABILITIES:		
Bonds payable	US $ 500,000	US $ 600,000
Long-term notes payable	90,000	60,000
Employee-related obligations	15,000	10,000
Deferred income taxes	5,000	5,000
Total noncurrent liabilities	**US $ 610,000**	**US $ 675,000**
Total liabilities	**US $1,000,000**	**US $ 950,000**
STOCKHOLDERS' EQUITY:		
Preferred stock, US $50 par	US $ 120,000	US $ 0
Common stock, US $1 par	500,000	500,000
Additional paid-in capital	110,000	100,000
Retained earnings	70,000	50,000
Total stockholders' equity	**US $ 800,000**	**US $ 650,000**
Total liabilities and stockholders' equity	**US $1,800,000**	**US $1,600,000**

EXAMPLE 10-19   **Income Statement**

	Current Year	Prior Year
Net sales	US $ 1,800,000	US $ 1,400,000
Cost of goods sold	(1,450,000)	(1,170,000)
Gross profit	US $ 350,000	US $ 230,000
SG&A expenses	(200,000)	(160,000)
Operating income	**US $ 150,000**	**US $ 70,000**
Other income and expenses	(65,000)	(25,000)
Income before interest and taxes	US $ 85,000	US $ 45,000
Interest expense	(15,000)	(10,000)
Income before taxes	US $ 70,000	US $ 35,000
Income taxes (40%)	(28,000)	(14,000)
Net income	**US $ 42,000**	**US $ 21,000**

2. **Receivables Activity Formulas**
   a. The **accounts receivable turnover ratio** is the number of times in a year the total balance of receivables is converted to cash.

   $$\text{Accounts receivable turnover} = \frac{\text{Net credit sales}}{\text{Average accounts receivable}}$$

   1) Average accounts receivable equals beginning accounts receivable plus ending accounts receivable, divided by two.
      a) If a business is highly seasonal, a simple average of beginning and ending balances is inadequate. The monthly balances should be averaged instead.

   EXAMPLE 10-20   Accounts Receivable Turnover

   All of the company's sales are on credit. Net trade receivables at the reporting date of the second prior year were US $105,000.

   Current year: US $1,800,000 ÷ [($120,000 + $115,000) ÷ 2] = 15.3 times
   Prior year: US $1,400,000 ÷ [($115,000 + $105,000) ÷ 2] = 12.7 times

   The company turned over its trade receivables balance 2.6 more times during the current year, even as receivables were growing in absolute terms. Thus, the company's effectiveness at collecting accounts receivable has improved.

   ---

   2) A higher turnover implies that customers may be paying their accounts promptly.
      a) Because sales are the numerator, higher sales without an increase in receivables will result in a higher turnover. Because receivables are the denominator, encouraging customers to pay quickly (thereby lowering the balance in receivables) also results in a higher turnover ratio.
   3) A lower turnover implies that customers are taking longer to pay.
      a) If the discount period is extended, customers will be able to wait longer to pay while still getting the discount.

   b. The **average collection period**, also called the **days' sales in receivables** or **days' sales outstanding**, measures the average number of days between the time of sale and receipt of the invoice amount.

   $$\text{Days' sales in receivables} = \frac{\text{Days in year}}{\text{Accounts receivable turnover ratio}}$$

   EXAMPLE 10-21   Days' Sales in Receivables

   Current year: 365 days ÷ 15.3 times = 23.9 days
   Prior year: 365 days ÷ 12.7 times = 28.7 days

   The denominator (calculated in Example 10-20) increased, and the numerator is a constant. Accordingly, days' sales in receivables must decrease. In addition to improving its collection practices, the company also may have become better at assessing the creditworthiness of its customers.

3. Inventory Activity Ratios

a. Two ratios measure the efficiency of inventory management.

b. **Inventory turnover** measures the number of times in a year the total balance of inventory is converted to cash or receivables.

$$\text{Inventory turnover} = \frac{\text{Cost of goods sold}}{\text{Average inventory}}$$

1) Average inventory equals beginning inventory plus ending inventory, divided by two.

    a) If a business is highly seasonal, a simple average of beginning and ending balances is inadequate. The monthly balances should be averaged instead.

EXAMPLE 10-22	Inventory Turnover

The balance in inventories at the balance sheet date of the second prior year was US $45,000.

Current year: US $1,450,000 ÷ [($85,000 + $55,000) ÷ 2] = 20.7 times
Prior year: US $1,170,000 ÷ [($55,000 + $45,000) ÷ 2] = 23.4 times

The company did not turn over its inventory as often during the current year as in the prior year. A lower turnover is expected during a period of growing sales (and increasing inventory). It is not necessarily a sign of poor inventory management.

2) A higher turnover implies strong sales or that the firm may be carrying low levels of inventory.

3) A lower turnover implies that the firm may be carrying excess levels of inventory or inventory that is obsolete.

    a) Because cost of goods sold is the numerator, higher sales without an increase in inventory balances result in a higher turnover.

    b) Because inventory is the denominator, reducing inventory levels also results in a higher turnover ratio.

4) The ideal level for inventory turnover is industry specific, with the nature of the inventory items impacting the ideal ratio. For example, spoilable items such as meat and dairy products will mandate a higher turnover ratio than would natural resources such as gold, silver, and coal. Thus, a grocery store should have a much higher inventory turnover ratio than a uranium mine or a jewelry store.

c. **Days' sales in inventory**, also called the **inventory conversion period**, measures the average number of days that pass between the acquisition of inventory and its sale.

$$\text{Days' sales in inventory} = \frac{\text{Days in year}}{\text{Inventory turnover ratio}}$$

EXAMPLE 10-23	Days' Sales in Inventory

Current year: 365 days ÷ 20.7 times = 17.6 days
Prior year: 365 days ÷ 23.4 times = 15.6 days

Because the numerator is a constant, the decreased turnover means that days' sales in inventory increased. This is a common phenomenon during a period of increasing sales.

4. **Operating Cycle**

    a. A firm's **operating cycle** is the amount of time that passes between the acquisition of inventory and the collection of cash on the sale of that inventory.

    Operating cycle = Days' sales in inventory + Days' sales in receivables

EXAMPLE 10-24	Operating Cycle
Current year: 17.6 days + 23.9 days = 41.5 days
Prior year: 15.6 days + 28.7 days = 44.3 days
The entity has slightly reduced its operating cycle while increasing sales and inventory.

5. **Cash Conversion Cycle**

    a. A firm's cash conversion cycle is the amount of time that passes between the actual outlay of cash for inventory purchases and the collection of cash from the sale of that inventory.

    Cash conversion cycle = Average collection period + Days' sales in inventory − Average payables period

    1) The accounts payable turnover ratio is the number of times during a period that the firm pays its accounts payable.

    $$\text{Accounts payable turnover} = \frac{\text{Total purchases}}{\text{Average accounts payable}}$$

    a) Average accounts payable equals beginning accounts payable plus ending accounts payable, divided by two.

    i) If a business is highly seasonal, a simple average of beginning and ending balances is inadequate. The monthly balances should be averaged instead.

EXAMPLE 10-25	Accounts Payable Turnover
The company had current- and prior-year purchases of US $1,480,000 and US $1,180,000, respectively. Net accounts payable at the beginning of the prior year was US $65,000.
Current Year: US $1,480,000 ÷ [($150,000 + $75,000) ÷ 2] = 13.2 times
Prior Year: US $1,180,000 ÷ [($75,000 + $65,000) ÷ 2] = 16.9 times
The company is now carrying a much higher balance in payables, so it is not surprising that the balance is turning over less often. It also may be the case that the company was paying invoices too soon in the prior year.

    b) A higher turnover implies that the firm is taking less time to pay off suppliers and may indicate that the firm is taking advantage of discounts.

    c) A lower turnover implies that the firm is taking more time to pay off suppliers and forgoing discounts.

2) The average payables period (also called payables turnover in days, or payables deferral period) is the average time between the purchase of inventories and the payment of cash.

$$\text{Average payables period} = \frac{\text{Days in year}}{\text{Accounts payable turnover}}$$

b. The difference between the operating cycle and the cash conversion cycle is attributable to credit purchases of inventory. The cash conversion cycle therefore is equal to the operating cycle minus the average payables period.

6. **Other Turnover Ratios**

   a. The total assets turnover and fixed assets turnover are broader-based ratios that measure the efficiency with which assets are used to generate revenue.

   1) Both cash and credit sales are included in the numerator.

   $$\text{Total assets turnover} = \frac{\text{Net total sales}}{\text{Average total assets}}$$

   $$\text{Fixed assets turnover} = \frac{\text{Net total sales}}{\text{Average net fixed assets}}$$

   a) Average total net fixed assets equal beginning total net fixed assets plus ending total net fixed assets, divided by two.

EXAMPLE 10-26   Turnover Ratios for Total Assets and Fixed Assets

Current-year total assets turnover: US $1,800,000 ÷ [($1,800,000 + $1,600,000) ÷ 2] = 1.06 times
Current-year fixed assets turnover: US $1,800,000 ÷ [($915,000 + $845,000) ÷ 2]   = 2.04 times

NOTE: The current- and prior-year net carrying amounts of fixed assets are US $915,000 ($1,000,000 – $85,000) and US $845,000 ($900,000 – $55,000), respectively.

STOP & REVIEW

You have completed the outline for this subunit.
Study multiple-choice questions 13 and 14 beginning on page 367.

10.8 FINANCIAL STATEMENT ANALYSIS -- SOLVENCY RATIOS AND LEVERAGE

1. **Solvency**

    a. Solvency is an entity's ability to pay its noncurrent obligations as they come due and remain in business in the long run. The key ingredients of solvency are the entity's capital structure and degree of leverage.

        1) By contrast, liquidity relates to the ability to remain in business for the short run.

    b. A firm's capital structure includes its sources of financing, both long- and short-term. These sources can be in the form of debt (external sources) or equity (internal sources).

        1) Capital structure decisions affect the **risk profile** of a firm. For example, a company with a higher percent of debt capital will be riskier than a firm with a high percentage of equity capital. Thus, when there is a lot of debt, equity investors will demand a higher rate of return on their investments to compensate for the risk brought about by the high use of financial leverage.

        2) Alternatively, a company with a high level of equity capital will be able to borrow at lower rates because debt holders will accept lower interest in exchange for the lower risk indicated by the equity cushion.

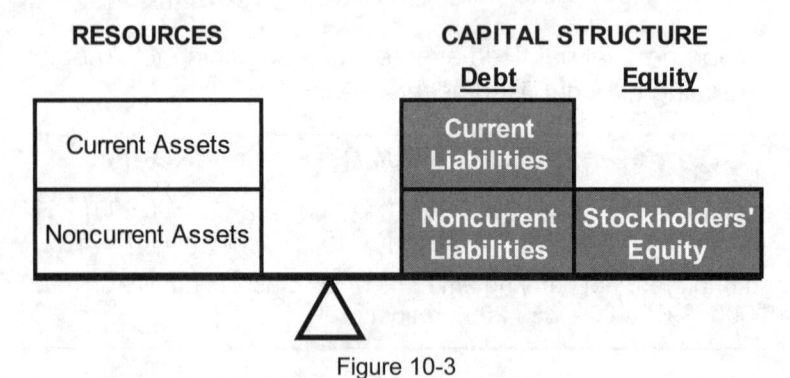

RESOURCES	**CAPITAL STRUCTURE**
Current Assets	Current Liabilities (Debt)
Noncurrent Assets	Noncurrent Liabilities (Debt) / Stockholders' Equity

    Figure 10-3

2. **Debt to Total Assets and Debt to Total Equity**

    a. The **debt to total assets ratio** (also called the debt ratio) reports the entity's debt per monetary unit of assets.

    $$\text{Debt ratio} = \frac{\text{Total liabilities}}{\text{Total assets}}$$

EXAMPLE 10-27	Debt Ratio
Current year:	US $1,000,000 ÷ $1,800,000 = 0.556
Prior year:	US $ 950,000 ÷ $1,600,000 = 0.594
The company became slightly less reliant on debt in its capital structure during the current year. The company is thus less leveraged than before.	

b. The **debt-to-equity ratio** is a direct comparison of the firm's debt and equity.

$$\text{Debt-to-equity ratio} = \frac{\text{Total debt}}{\text{Shareholders' equity}}$$

EXAMPLE 10-28	Debt-to-Equity Ratio

Current year: US $1,000,000 ÷ $800,000 = 1.25
Prior year: US $ 950,000 ÷ $650,000 = 1.46

The amount by which the company's debts exceed its equity stake declined in the current year.

1) Like the previous ratio, the debt-to-equity ratio reflects long-term debt-payment ability. A low ratio means lower relative debt and better debt repayment ability.

3. **Earnings Coverage**

   a. Earnings coverage is a creditor's best measure of an entity's ongoing ability to generate the earnings that will allow it to satisfy its debts and remain solvent.

   b. The **times-interest-earned ratio** is an income statement approach to evaluating the ongoing ability to meet interest payments on debt obligations.

$$\text{Times-interest-earned ratio} = \frac{\text{Earnings before interest and taxes (EBIT)}}{\text{Interest expense}}$$

   1) An increased times-interest-earned ratio signifies that more profit is available to pay interest on debt and solvency has improved.

EXAMPLE 10-29	Times-Interest-Earned Ratio

Current year: US $85,000 ÷ $15,000 = 5.67
Prior year: US $45,000 ÷ $10,000 = 4.50

The entity has improved its ability to pay interest expense. In the prior year, EBIT was only four-and-a-half times interest expense, but in the current year, it is more than five-and-a-half times.

4. **Leverage**

   a. Leverage is the relative amount of fixed cost in a firm's overall cost structure. Leverage creates solvency risk because fixed costs must be covered regardless of the level of sales.

   1) Total costs (TC) equals fixed costs (FC) plus variable costs (VC).
   2) A firm's total leverage consists of an operating leverage component and a financial leverage component.

   b. **Operating leverage** is the extent to which a firm's costs of operating are fixed as opposed to variable. The following ratio is one of the ways to measure operating leverage.

   Operating leverage = Fixed costs (FC) ÷ Total costs (FC + VC)

   1) High operating leverage means that a high percentage of a firm's total costs is fixed.
   2) A firm with a high percentage of fixed costs is more risky than a firm in the same industry that relies more on variable costs, but by the same token, it will generate more earnings by increasing sales.

c. **Financial leverage** is the degree of debt (fixed financial costs) in the firm's financial structure. The following ratio is one of the ways to measure financial leverage.

$$\text{Financial leverage} = \text{Total assets} \div \text{Total equity}$$

EXAMPLE 10-30 — Financial Leverage

Current-year financial leverage ratio: US $1,800,000 ÷ $800,000 = 2.25

---

1) High financial leverage means that a high percentage of a firm's total assets is financed by debt.
2) When a firm has a high percentage of fixed financial costs, the firm takes more risk to increase its earnings per share. (Earnings per share is explained in item 6. on page 358.)

STOP & REVIEW

You have completed the outline for this subunit.
Study multiple-choice questions 15 and 16 on page 368.

10.9 FINANCIAL STATEMENT ANALYSIS -- ROI AND PROFITABILITY

1. **Return on Invested Capital**

    a. Return on investment, or ROI (also called return on invested capital), is a broad concept for measures that reflect how efficiently an entity is using the resources contributed by its shareholders to generate a profit.

$$\text{Return on investment (ROI)} = \frac{\text{Measure of profit}}{\text{Measure of capital}} = \frac{\text{Operating income}}{\text{Average invested capital}}$$

    NOTE: The examples in this subunit use the statement of financial position on page 347 and the income statement on page 349.

2. **Return on Assets**

    a. Return on assets, or ROA (also called return on total assets, or ROTA), is the most basic form of the ROI ratio.

$$\text{Return on assets (ROA)} = \frac{\text{Net income}}{\text{Average total assets}}$$

EXAMPLE 10-31 — Return on Assets

Current year: US $42,000 ÷ [($1,800,000 + $1,600,000) ÷ 2] = 0.025

During the current year, the company generated US $0.025 in net income for each US $1 invested in the company's assets.

---

3. **DuPont Model**

   a. The original DuPont model treats ROA as the product of a two-component ratio.

   $$\underset{\text{ROA}}{\frac{\text{Net income}}{\text{Average total assets}}} = \underset{\text{Profit Margin}}{\frac{\text{Net income}}{\text{Net sales}}} \times \underset{\text{Total Assets Turnover}}{\frac{\text{Net sales}}{\text{Average total assets}}}$$

   1) The advantage of this analysis is that it examines both the results of operations and the efficiency of asset usage in generating sales.

   EXAMPLE 10-32   DuPont Model -- ROA

   Current-year profit margin: US $42,000 net income ÷ $1,800,000 total sales = 0.0233

   1. Profit margin of 0.0233 means that the company generates US $0.0233 of net income from each US $1 of sales.
   2. The total assets turnover is 1.06 (as calculated on page 353).
   3. The ROA is 0.025 (0.0233 × 1.06).
   ---

4. **Return on Equity**

   a. Return on equity (ROE) is the second version of the ROI ratio.

   $$\text{Return on equity (ROE)} = \frac{\text{Net income}}{\text{Average total equity}}$$

   1) Average total equity equals beginning total equity plus ending total equity, divided by two.
   2) This ratio measures the return available to all shareholders.

   EXAMPLE 10-33   Return on Equity

   Current-year ROE: US $42,000 net income ÷ [($800,000 + $650,000) ÷ 2] = 0.058
   ---

   b. The DuPont model has been adapted and expanded. One widely used variation treats ROE as the product of three components.

   $$\text{ROE} = \text{Profitability} \times \text{Turnover} \times \text{Equity multiplier}$$

   $$\text{ROE} = \frac{\text{Net income}}{\text{Net sales}} \times \frac{\text{Net sales}}{\text{Average total assets}} \times \frac{\text{Average total assets}}{\text{Average total equity}}$$

5. **Other Profitability Ratios**

    a. Three common percentages measure profitability directly from the income statement:

    $$\text{Gross profit margin} = \frac{\text{Gross profit}}{\text{Net sales}}$$

    $$\text{Operating income margin} = \frac{\text{Operating income}}{\text{Net sales}}$$

    $$\text{Net income margin} = \frac{\text{Net income}}{\text{Net sales}}$$

EXAMPLE 10-34	Other Profitability Ratios
Current-year gross profit margin:	US $350,000 ÷ $1,800,000 = 19.4%
Current-year operating income margin:	US $150,000 ÷ $1,800,000 = 8.3%
Current-year net income margin:	US $ 42,000 ÷ $1,800,000 = 2.3%

    b. A vertical common-size analysis (discussed in Subunit 10.10) can be useful in measurement of these ratios.

6. **Earnings per Share**

    a. **Basic** earnings per share (EPS) is a ratio of particular interest to the corporation's common shareholders. It is a profitability ratio that measures the amount of current-period earnings that can be associated with a single share of a corporation's common stock.

    $$\text{EPS} = \frac{\text{Net income} - \text{Preferred dividends}}{\text{Weighted-average number of common shares outstanding}}$$

    1) The numerator often is called income available to common shareholders.

    2) EPS is calculated only for common stock because common shareholders are the residual owners of a corporation.

    3) The weighted-average number of common shares outstanding is determined by relating the portion of the period that the shares were outstanding to the total time in the period.

    b. An entity that has **potential common shares** (e.g., convertible bonds, convertible preferred stock, and share options) must report **diluted** EPS in addition to basic EPS. The calculation includes the effects of dilutive potential common shares. Dilution is a reduction in basic EPS resulting from the assumption that potential common shares were converted to common stock.

STOP & REVIEW

You have completed the outline for this subunit.
Study multiple-choice questions 17 and 18 on page 369.

10.10 FINANCIAL STATEMENT ANALYSIS -- CORPORATE VALUATION AND COMMON-SIZE FINANCIAL STATEMENTS RATIOS

1. **Book Value per Common Share**

    a. Book value per common share equals the amount of net assets available to shareholders divided by the number of shares outstanding.

    $$\text{Book value per common share} = \frac{\text{Total equity} - \text{Liquidation value of preferred stock}}{\text{Common stock outstanding}}$$

    1) Book value per common share is the amount per share of the company's net assets at their book value (carrying amounts) that will be received by the common shareholders upon the liquidation of the company.

    2) The limitation of book value per share is that it is a valuation based solely on the amounts recorded in the books.

        a) Unlike market value, book value does not consider future earnings potential in determining a company's valuation.

        b) The recorded values of assets on the books are subject to accounting estimates (e.g., choice of depreciation method) that may vary across companies within the same industry. Consequently, net assets may be overstated if estimates are inaccurate.

        c) Additionally, those same assets may be pledged as collateral on a loan. However, a pledge of collateral is not recorded as a liability on the books. Thus, book value will not account for this potential liability.

        d) A well-managed firm's stock should sell at high multiples of its book value.

2. **Price-Earnings (P/E) Ratio**

    a. The price-earnings ratio measures the amount that investors are willing to pay for US $1 of the company's earnings.

    $$\text{Price-earnings ratio} = \frac{\text{Market price of share}}{\text{Earnings per share (EPS)}}$$

    1) Growth companies are likely to have high P/E ratios. A high P/E ratio reflects the stock market's positive assessment of the firm's earnings quality and prospects.

    2) Because of the widespread use of the P/E ratio and other measures, the relationship between accounting data and stock prices is crucial. Thus, managers have an incentive to "manage earnings," sometimes by fraudulent means.

        a) A decrease in investors' required rate of return will cause share prices to go up, which will result in a higher P/E ratio.

        b) A decline in the rate of dividend growth will cause the share price to decline, which will result in a lower P/E ratio.

        c) An increasing dividend yield indicates that share price is declining, which will result in a lower P/E ratio.

3. **Dividend Payout Ratio**

   a. Increasing shareholder wealth is the fundamental goal of any business. The dividend payout ratio measures the portion of available earnings the entity actually distributed to shareholders.

   $$\text{Dividend payout ratio} = \frac{\text{Dividend paid per share}}{\text{Earnings per share}} = \frac{\text{Total dividends}}{\text{Net income}}$$

   1) Growing entities tend to have a low payout. They prefer to use earnings for expansion.

4. **Dividend Yield Ratio**

   a. The dividend yield measures the percentage of a share's market price that was returned as dividends. This ratio can be applied to both common and preferred stock.

   $$\text{Dividend yield ratio} = \frac{\text{Dividends per share}}{\text{Market price per share}}$$

5. **Effect of Price Inflation on Financial Ratio Analysis**

   a. Inflation is the decrease over time of the purchasing power of money. Because statement of financial position amounts are expressed in terms of money, historical cost amounts for different periods are measured in units representing different levels of purchasing power.

   b. Net income or loss is also distorted because of inflation's effect on depreciation expense and inventory costs.

   1) Inflation therefore impairs the comparability of financial statement items, whether for the same entity over time or for entities of differing ages.

6. **Common-Size Financial Statements and Multiple Ratios**

   a. **Common-size financial statements** are expressed in percentages.

   1) **Horizontal common-size analysis** focuses on changes in operating results and financial position during two or more accounting periods. The changes are expressed in terms of percentages of corresponding amounts in a base period.

   2) **Vertical common-size analysis** relates to the relationships among financial statement items of a single accounting period expressed in terms of a percentage relationship to a base item (the base is 100%).

      a) For example, income statement items may be expressed as percentages of sales, and balance sheet items may be expressed as a percentage of total assets.

EXAMPLE 10-35   **Vertical Analysis -- Income Statement**

	Current Year	Prior Year
Net sales	100.0%	100.0%
Cost of goods sold	(80.6%)	(83.6%)
Gross profit	**19.4%**	**16.4%**
SG&A expenses	(11.1%)	(11.4%)
Operating income	**8.3%**	**5.0%**
Other income and expenses	(3.6%)	(1.8%)
Income before interest and taxes	4.7%	3.2%
Interest expense	(0.8%)	(0.7%)
Income before taxes	3.9%	2.5%
Income taxes (40%)	(1.6%)	(1.0%)
Net income	**2.3%**	**1.5%**

    b.   The income statement above is presented in the **common-size** format. Line items on common-size statements are expressed as percentages of net sales (on the income statement) or total assets (on the statement of financial position).

        1)   On a common-size income statement, net sales is 100%, and all other amounts are a percentage of net sales. On the statement of financial position, total assets and the total of liabilities and equity are each 100%.

        2)   Each line item can be interpreted in terms of its proportion of the baseline amount. This process is **vertical analysis**.

    c.   Preparing common-size statements makes it easier to analyze differences among companies of various sizes or comparisons between a similar company and an industry average.

        1)   For example, comparing the efficiency of a company with US $1,800,000 of revenues to a company with US $44 billion in revenues is difficult unless the numbers are reduced to a common denominator.

STOP & REVIEW

You have completed the outline for this subunit.
Study multiple-choice questions 19 and 20 on page 370.

QUESTIONS

10.1 Risk and Return

1. The risk that securities cannot be sold at a reasonable price on short notice is called

A. Default risk.
B. Interest-rate risk.
C. Purchasing-power risk.
D. Liquidity risk.

Answer (D) is correct.
REQUIRED: The term for the risk that securities cannot be sold at a reasonable price on short notice.
DISCUSSION: An asset is liquid if it can be converted to cash on short notice. Liquidity (marketability) risk is the risk that assets cannot be sold at a reasonable price on short notice. If an asset is not liquid, investors will require a higher return than for a liquid asset. The difference is the liquidity premium.
Answer (A) is incorrect. Default risk is the risk that a borrower will not pay the interest or principal on a loan. **Answer (B) is incorrect.** Interest-rate risk is the risk to which investors are exposed because of changing interest rates. **Answer (C) is incorrect.** Purchasing-power risk is the risk that inflation will reduce the purchasing power of a given sum of money.

2. Systematic risk explains why

A. Stock values tend to move in the same direction.
B. Diversification reduces overall risk.
C. Stock values move in different directions.
D. Diversification increases overall risk.

Answer (A) is correct.
REQUIRED: The effect of systematic risk on stock values and overall risk.
DISCUSSION: Systematic risk, also called market risk, is the risk faced by all firms. Changes in the economy as a whole, such as the business cycle, affect all players in the market. Since all firms are affected by systematic risk, all of their stock values move somewhat in the same direction.
Answer (B) is incorrect. Systematic risk is also known as undiversifiable risk. Therefore, diversification has no effect on systematic risk. **Answer (C) is incorrect.** Systematic risk affects all firms equally. Therefore, it causes the stock values to move in the same general direction. **Answer (D) is incorrect.** Systematic risk is also known as undiversifiable risk. Therefore, diversification has no effect on systematic risk.

10.2 Derivatives

3. A call option on an ordinary share is more valuable when there is a lower

A. Market value of the underlying share.
B. Exercise price on the option.
C. Time to maturity on the option.
D. Variability of market price on the underlying share.

Answer (B) is correct.
REQUIRED: The circumstance under which a call option is more valuable.
DISCUSSION: The lower the exercise price, the more valuable the call option. The exercise price is the price at which the call holder has the right to purchase the underlying share.
Answer (A) is incorrect. A call option is the right to purchase an ordinary share at a set price for a set time period. If the underlying share has a lower market value, the call option is less, not more, valuable. **Answer (C) is incorrect.** A call option is less, not more, valuable given less time to maturity. When the option has less time to maturity, the chance that the share price will rise is smaller. **Answer (D) is incorrect.** A call option is less, not more, valuable if the price of the underlying share is less variable. Less variability means a lower probability of a price increase.

4. An entity has recently purchased some shares of a competitor as part of a long-term plan to acquire the competitor. However, it is somewhat concerned that the market price of these shares could decrease over the short run. The entity could hedge against the possible decline in the shares' market price by

A. Purchasing a call option on those shares.
B. Purchasing a put option on those shares.
C. Selling a put option on those shares.
D. Obtaining a warrant option on those shares.

Answer (B) is correct.
REQUIRED: The means of hedging against the possible decline in the shares' market price.
DISCUSSION: A put option is the right to sell shares at a given price within a certain period. If the market price falls, the put option may allow the sale of shares at a price above market, and the profit of the option holder will be the difference between the price stated in the put option and the market price, minus the cost of the option, commissions, and taxes. The entity that issues the shares has nothing to do with put (and call) options.
Answer (A) is incorrect. A call option is the right to purchase shares at a given price within a specified period. **Answer (C) is incorrect.** Selling a put option could force the entity to purchase additional shares if the option is exercised. **Answer (D) is incorrect.** A warrant gives the holder a right to purchase shares from the issuer at a given price (it is usually distributed along with debt).

10.3 Foreign Currency Transactions

5. When the U.S. dollar is expected to rise in value against foreign currencies, a U.S. company with foreign currency denominated receivables and payables should

A. Slow down collections and speed up payments.
B. Slow down collections and slow down payments.
C. Speed up collections and speed up payments.
D. Speed up collections and slow down payments.

Answer (D) is correct.
REQUIRED: The action a U.S. company with foreign currency denominated receivables should take if the dollar is expected to rise.
DISCUSSION: The U.S. firm should increase collections and decrease payments. Collections should be made quickly and converted into dollars to sustain the increase in their value as the dollar appreciates. Decreasing payments is profitable because, as the company exchanges dollars for foreign currency at a later date, it will receive more of the foreign currency, thus lowering its real cost.
Answer (A) is incorrect. Slowing collections and expediting payments increases the company's real cost. **Answer (B) is incorrect.** Slowing collections does not maximize the amount of U.S. dollars received. **Answer (C) is incorrect.** Expediting payments does not maximize the amount of U.S. dollars received.

10.4 Business Combinations and Consolidated Financial Statements

6. Entity X owns 90% of Entity Y. Early in the year, X lent Y US $1,000,000. No payments have been made on the debt by year end. Proper accounting at year-end in the consolidated financial statements would

A. Eliminate 100% of the receivable, the payable, and the related interest.
B. Eliminate 100% of the receivable and the payable but not any related interest.
C. Eliminate 90% of the receivable, the payable, and the related interest.
D. Eliminate 90% of the receivable and the payable but not any related interest.

Answer (A) is correct.
REQUIRED: The accounting treatment of a loan made by a parent to a subsidiary.
DISCUSSION: In a consolidated statement of financial position, reciprocal balances, such as receivables and payables, between a parent and a consolidated subsidiary should be eliminated in their entirety regardless of the portion of the subsidiary's shares held by the parent. Thus, all effects of the US $1,000,000 loan should be eliminated in the preparation of the year-end consolidated statement of financial position.

7. Entity A acquires all of the voting shares of Entity B for US $1,000,000. At the time of the acquisition, the net fair value of the identifiable assets acquired and liabilities assumed had a carrying amount of US $900,000 and a fair value of US $800,000. The amount of goodwill Entity A will record on the acquisition date is

A. US $0
B. US $100,000
C. US $200,000
D. US $300,000

Answer (C) is correct.
REQUIRED: The goodwill recorded.
DISCUSSION: Given no prior equity interest or noncontrolling interest, goodwill equals the excess of the acquisition-date fair value of the consideration transferred over the acquisition-date fair value of the net of the identifiable assets acquired and liabilities assumed. Consequently, goodwill is US $200,000 ($1,000,000 – $800,000).
Answer (A) is incorrect. Goodwill must be recorded. **Answer (B) is incorrect.** The amount of US $100,000 is the excess of the acquisition cost over the carrying amount. **Answer (D) is incorrect.** The amount of US $300,000 equals goodwill plus the excess of the carrying amount over fair value.

10.5 Corporate Equity Accounts and Partnerships

8. During the year, an entity's retained earnings increased by US $25,000. Profit for the year was US $42,000. The only other change in retained earnings was for the declaration of cash dividends. The amount of dividends declared was

A. US $25,000
B. US $17,000
C. US $42,000
D. US $67,000

Answer (B) is correct.
REQUIRED: The amount of dividends declared.
DISCUSSION: Retained earnings is accumulated net income or loss. It is increased by net income and decreased by net loss and dividends. Ending retained earnings equals beginning retained earnings plus net income, minus dividends declared in the period. Given the increase of retained earnings of US $25,000 and profits of US $42,000, dividends declared must have been US $17,000 ($42,000 – $25,000).
Answer (A) is incorrect. The amount of US $25,000 is the increase in retained earnings. **Answer (C) is incorrect.** The amount of US $42,000 is the profit for the year. **Answer (D) is incorrect.** The amount of US $67,000 equals profit plus the increase in retained earnings.

9. When property other than cash is invested in a partnership, at what amount should the noncash property be credited to the contributing partner's capital account?

A. Fair value at the date of contribution.
B. Contributing partner's original cost.
C. Assessed valuation for property tax purposes.
D. Contributing partner's tax basis.

Answer (A) is correct.
REQUIRED: The credit to the contributing partner's capital account when noncash assets are invested.
DISCUSSION: The capital account should be credited for the current fair value of the assets at the date of the contribution.
Answer (B) is incorrect. Cost does not reflect depreciation or appreciation of the property. **Answer (C) is incorrect.** Fair value best reflects the economic substance of the transaction. **Answer (D) is incorrect.** Tax basis is determined differently than the true economic value of the property.

10.6 Financial Statement Analysis -- Liquidity Ratios

Questions 10 through 12 are based on the following information.

RST Corporation's Statements of Financial Position End of Year 5 and Year 6

Assets	Year 6	Year 5
Current assets:		
Cash	US $ 5,000	US $ 4,000
Marketable securities	3,000	2,000
Accounts receivable (net)	16,000	14,000
Inventory	30,000	20,000
Total current assets	US $ 54,000	US $ 40,000
Noncurrent assets:		
Long-term investments	11,000	11,000
PP&E	80,000	70,000
Intangibles	3,000	4,000
Total assets	US $148,000	US $125,000
Liabilities and Equity		
Current liabilities:		
Accounts payable	US $ 11,000	US $ 7,000
Accrued payables	1,000	1,000
Total current liabilities	US $ 12,000	US $ 8,000
Bonds payable, 10%, due Year 12	30,000	30,000
Total liabilities	US $ 42,000	US $ 38,000
Equity:		
Common stock, 2,400 shares, US $10 par	US $ 24,000	US $ 24,000
Retained earnings	82,000	63,000
Total equity	US $106,000	US $ 87,000
Total liabilities and equity	US $148,000	US $125,000

The market value of RST's ordinary shares at the end of Year 6 was US $100 per share.

10. What is RST's current ratio at the end of Year 6?

A. 4.5 to 1.
B. 2.4 to 1.
C. 2.0 to 1.
D. 1.5 to 1.

Answer (A) is correct.
REQUIRED: The current ratio at the end of Year 6.
DISCUSSION: The current ratio equals current assets divided by current liabilities. At the end of Year 6, it was 4.5 to 1 (US $54,000 ÷ $12,000).
Answer (B) is incorrect. A ratio of 2.4 to 1 results from dividing current liabilities by the amount of cash, which is not a meaningful ratio. **Answer (C) is incorrect.** A ratio of 2.0 to 1 is the quick (acid-test) ratio (cash, marketable securities, and net receivables divided by total current liabilities). **Answer (D) is incorrect.** A ratio of 1.5 to 1 results from dividing total current liabilities by the sum of cash and marketable securities, which is not a meaningful ratio.

11. What is RST's acid-test (or quick) ratio at the end of Year 6?

A. 2.40 to 1.
B. 2.18 to 1.
C. 2.00 to 1.
D. 1.50 to 1.

Answer (C) is correct.
REQUIRED: The acid-test ratio at the end of Year 6.
DISCUSSION: The acid-test or quick ratio equals the sum of the quick assets (net accounts receivable, marketable securities, and cash) divided by current liabilities. This ratio at the end of Year 6 is 2.00 to 1 [(US $5,000 + $3,000 + $16,000) ÷ $12,000].
Answer (A) is incorrect. A ratio of 2.40 to 1 results from dividing total current liabilities (US $12,000) by the amount of cash (US $5,000), which is not a meaningful ratio. **Answer (B) is incorrect.** A ratio of 2.18 to 1 results from dividing quick assets (US $5,000 + $3,000 + $16,000) by accounts payable (US $11,000) results in 2.18. The denominator should include all current liabilities other than accounts payable. **Answer (D) is incorrect.** A ratio of 1.50 to 1 results from dividing total current liabilities (US $12,000) by the sum of cash (US $5,000) and marketable securities (US $3,000), which is not a meaningful ratio.

12. Based on a comparison of RST's quick ratios in Year 5 and Year 6, what is a likely conclusion?

A. RST has improved its management of long-term investments in Year 6.
B. RST has written off obsolete inventory in Year 6.
C. RST's ability to meet short-term financing needs has declined since Year 5.
D. RST's ability to meet short-term financing needs has improved since Year 5.

Answer (C) is correct.
REQUIRED: The likely conclusion based on a comparison of consecutive-year quick ratios.
DISCUSSION: RST's quick ratio decreased from 2.5 in Year 5 [(US $4,000 cash + $2,000 marketable securities + $14,000 net A/R) ÷ $8,000] to 2.0 in Year 6 [(US $5,000 + $3,000 + $16,000) ÷ $12,000]. RST has fewer assets that are easily convertible to cash available to meet current liabilities. Thus, its ability to meet short-term financing needs (i.e., liquidity) has declined.
Answer (A) is incorrect. The quick ratio compares the quick assets (current assets minus inventory) with current liabilities; it does not provide a basis for conclusions about long-term investments. **Answer (B) is incorrect.** The quick ratio does not consider inventory. **Answer (D) is incorrect.** RST is less liquid in Year 6.

10.7 Financial Statement Analysis -- Activity Ratios

13. An analysis of inventory turnover in a store's clothing department indicated extremely low turnover. Which of the following would most likely increase the turnover rate?

A. Increase inventories.
B. Increase sales incentives.
C. Increase selling prices.
D. Decrease the frequency of purchases but maintain the same level of inventory.

Answer (B) is correct.
REQUIRED: The action that would most likely increase the turnover rate.
DISCUSSION: Inventory turnover equals cost of sales divided by average inventory. Reducing inventory therefore increases turnover. Sales incentives to improve sales should lower inventory levels.
Answer (A) is incorrect. Increasing the denominator of the ratio would only further decrease turnover. **Answer (C) is incorrect.** Increasing price would probably decrease sales, thereby further decreasing turnover. **Answer (D) is incorrect.** A constant inventory level would not affect the turnover rate.

14. An entity has a high fixed assets turnover ratio. What conclusion can a financial analyst draw from this?

A. The entity may be overcapitalized.
B. The entity may have a problem with employees converting inventory to personal use.
C. The entity may be undercapitalized.
D. The entity has favorable profitability.

Answer (C) is correct.
REQUIRED: The implication of a high fixed-assets turnover ratio.
DISCUSSION: The fixed assets turnover ratio equals net sales divided by net fixed assets. A high ratio indicates either that the entity is undercapitalized, that is, it cannot afford to buy enough fixed assets, or that it uses fixed assets efficiently.
Answer (A) is incorrect. The ratio may indicate undercapitalization. **Answer (B) is incorrect.** Fluctuations in inventory do not affect fixed-assets turnover. **Answer (D) is incorrect.** The fixed assets turnover ratio is not a profitability indicator. It measures the efficiency of asset management.

10.8 Financial Statement Analysis -- Solvency Ratios and Leverage

15. An entity purchased a new machine for US $500,000 by borrowing the required funds from a bank for 180 days. What will be the direct impact of this transaction?

A. Decrease the current ratio and increase the debt ratio.
B. Increase the current ratio and decrease the debt ratio.
C. Increase the current ratio and increase the debt ratio.
D. Decrease the current ratio and decrease the debt ratio.

Answer (A) is correct.
REQUIRED: The direct effect of purchasing a new machine on the current and the debt ratios.
DISCUSSION: The borrowing of funds for 180 days constitutes short-term borrowing. The new machine is a fixed asset. Current liabilities have increased, and current assets have remained constant. Consequently, the current ratio (Current assets ÷ Current liabilities) has decreased. Total debt and total assets increased by the same absolute amount, and the debt ratio (Total debt ÷ Total assets) should have increased, assuming total debt is less than total assets.

16. The times-interest-earned ratio is primarily an indication of

A. Solvency.
B. Liquidity.
C. Asset management.
D. Profitability.

Answer (A) is correct.
REQUIRED: The purpose of the times-interest-earned ratio.
DISCUSSION: The times-interest-earned ratio equals profit or loss before taxes and interest divided by interest. It measures the extent to which operating profit can decline before the entity is unable to meet its annual interest cost. Thus, it is a measure of debt-paying capacity (solvency).
Answer (B) is incorrect. Liquidity ratios, e.g., the current ratio, indicate the relationship of current assets to current liabilities. **Answer (C) is incorrect.** Asset management ratios indicate how effectively the entity is using its assets. **Answer (D) is incorrect.** Profitability ratios measure operating results.

10.9 Financial Statement Analysis -- ROI and Profitability

17. Return on investment (ROI) is a very popular measure employed to evaluate the performance of corporate segments because it incorporates all of the major ingredients of profitability (revenue, cost, investment) into a single measure. Under which one of the following combination of actions regarding a segment's revenues, costs, and investment would a segment's ROI always increase?

	Revenues	Costs	Investment
A.	Increase	Decrease	Increase
B.	Decrease	Decrease	Decrease
C.	Increase	Increase	Increase
D.	Increase	Decrease	Decrease

Answer (D) is correct.
REQUIRED: The circumstances in which ROI always increases.
DISCUSSION: An increase in revenue and a decrease in costs will increase the ROI numerator. A decrease in investment will decrease the denominator. The ROI must increase in this situation.

18. The following ratios relate to an entity's financial situation compared with that of its industry:

	The Entity	Industry Average
Return on assets (ROA)	7.9%	9.2%
Return on equity (ROE)	15.2%	12.9%

What conclusion could a financial analyst validly draw from these ratios?

A. The entity's product has a high market share, leading to higher profitability.

B. The entity uses more debt than does the average entity in the industry.

C. The entity's profits are increasing over time.

D. The entity's shares have a higher market value to carrying amount than does the rest of the industry.

Answer (B) is correct.
REQUIRED: The conclusion from comparing ROA and ROE with industry averages.
DISCUSSION: The use of financial leverage has a multiplier effect on the return on assets. The extended DuPont formula illustrates this point by showing that the return on equity equals the return on assets times the equity multiplier (Total assets ÷ Ordinary equity). Thus, greater use of debt increases the equity multiplier and the return on equity. In this example, the equity multiplier is 1.92 (15.2% ROE ÷ 7.9% ROA), and the industry average is 1.40 (12.9% ROE ÷ 9.2% ROA). The higher equity multiplier indicates that the entity uses more debt than the industry average.
Answer (A) is incorrect. The question gave no information about market share. **Answer (C) is incorrect.** This comparison is with an industry average, not over time. **Answer (D) is incorrect.** Share valuation is a response to many factors. The higher-than-average return on equity does not mean that the entity has a more favorable market-to-carrying-amount ratio.

10.10 Financial Statement Analysis -- Corporate Valuation and Common-Size Financial Statements Ratios

19. An entity has 100,000 outstanding common shares with a market value of US $20 per share. Dividends of US $2 per share were paid in the current year, and the entity has a dividend-payout ratio of 40%. The price-to-earnings (P/E) ratio of the entity is

A. 2.5
B. 4
C. 10
D. 50

Answer (B) is correct.
REQUIRED: The P/E ratio.
DISCUSSION: The P/E ratio equals the share price divided by EPS. If the dividends per share equaled US $2 and the dividend-payout ratio was 40%, EPS must have been US $5 ($2 ÷ .4). Accordingly, the P/E ratio is 4 (US $20 share price ÷ $5 EPS).
Answer (A) is incorrect. EPS divided by dividends per share equals 2.5. **Answer (C) is incorrect.** Share price divided by dividends per share equals 10. **Answer (D) is incorrect.** Price per share divided by the dividend-payout percentage equals 50.

20. Which of the following financial statement analyses is most useful in determining whether the various expenses of a given entity are higher or lower than industry averages?

A. Horizontal.
B. Vertical.
C. Activity ratio.
D. Defensive-interval ratio.

Answer (B) is correct.
REQUIRED: The analysis most useful in determining whether various expenses of an entity are higher or lower than industry averages.
DISCUSSION: Vertical analysis is the expression of each item on a financial statement in a given period in relation to a base amount. On the income statement, each item is stated as a percentage of sales. Thus, the percentages for the entity in question can be compared with industry norms.
Answer (A) is incorrect. A horizontal analysis indicates the proportionate change over a period of time and is useful in trend analysis of an individual entity.
Answer (C) is incorrect. Activity ratio analysis includes the preparation of turnover ratios such as those for receivables, inventory, and total assets. **Answer (D) is incorrect.** The defensive-interval ratio is part of a liquidity analysis.

GLEIM
GO TO ONLINE COURSE

Access the **Gleim CIA Premium Review System** featuring our SmartAdapt technology from your Gleim Personal Classroom to continue your studies. You will experience a personalized study environment with exam-emulating multiple-choice questions.

STUDY UNIT ELEVEN
CURRENT ASSETS MANAGEMENT

(19 pages of outline)

11.1	Working Capital and Cash Management	371
11.2	Receivables Management	375
11.3	Managing Inventory Costs and Quantities	378
11.4	Inventory Management Methods	380
11.5	Inventory Systems	384

This study unit is the third of six covering **Domain IV: Financial Management** from The IIA's CIA Exam Syllabus. This domain makes up 20% of Part 3 of the CIA exam and is tested at the **basic and proficient** cognitive levels. Refer to the complete syllabus located in Appendix A to view the relevant sections covered in Study Unit 11.

NOTE: The revenue cycle is described in Study Unit 9, Subunit 1. The supply chain is described in Study Unit 3, Subunit 4. Accounts payable is described in Study Unit 9, Subunit 7.

11.1 WORKING CAPITAL AND CASH MANAGEMENT

1. **Working Capital**

    a. Working capital finance concerns the optimal level, mix, and use of **current assets** and the means used to acquire them, notably **current liabilities**.

       1) The objective is to minimize the cost of maintaining liquidity (quick convertibility to cash to pay current obligations) while guarding against the risk of insolvency (inability to pay obligations as they come due).

       2) Working capital policy applies to short-term decisions, and capital structure finance applies to long-term decisions.

       3) Net working capital equals current assets minus current liabilities.

       Net working capital = Current assets − Current liabilities

    b. Permanent working capital is the minimum level of current assets maintained by a firm.

       1) Permanent working capital should increase as the firm grows.

       2) Permanent working capital generally is financed with long-term debt. Financing with short-term debt is risky because assets may not be liquidated in time to pay off the debt at maturity, interest rates may rise, and loans may not be renewed.

    c. Temporary working capital fluctuates seasonally.

       1) As the firm's needs for current assets change on a seasonal basis, temporary working capital is increased and decreased.

2. **Working Capital Policy**
   a. A firm that adopts a **conservative** working capital policy seeks to minimize liquidity risk by increasing working capital.
      1) The firm seeks to ensure that adequate cash, inventory, and supplies are available and payables are minimized.
      2) The firm forgoes the potentially higher returns from investing in long-term assets and instead keeps that additional working capital available.
      3) This policy is reflected in a higher current ratio (Current assets ÷ Current liabilities) and acid-test ratio (Quick assets ÷ Current liabilities). Liquidity ratios are presented in Study Unit 10, Subunit 6.
   b. A firm that adopts an **aggressive** working capital policy seeks to increase profitability while accepting reduced liquidity and a higher risk of short-term cash flow problems.
      1) This policy is reflected in a lower current ratio and acid-test ratio.
3. **Spontaneous Financing of Working Capital**
   a. Spontaneous financing is the amount of current liabilities, such as trade payables and accruals, that occurs naturally in the ordinary course of business.
   b. Trade credit is an offer of credit terms by suppliers.

EXAMPLE 11-1   Trade Credit

A vendor has delivered goods and invoiced the company for US $160,000 on terms of net 30. The company has effectively received a 30-day interest-free US $160,000 loan.

---

   c. Accrued expenses, such as salaries, wages, interest, dividends, and taxes payable, are another source of (interest-free) spontaneous financing.
4. **Other Financing of Working Capital**
   a. The firm's temporary working capital usually cannot be financed only by spontaneous financing. The firm must decide whether to use short-term or long-term financing.
      1) The interest rate on long-term debt is higher than on the short-term. Thus, long-term financing is more expensive than short-term.
      2) But the shorter the maturity schedule of a firm's debt, the greater the risk that the firm will be unable to meet principal and interest payments.
   b. In general, short-term financing is more risky and less expensive than long-term financing.
5. **Maturity Matching of Temporary Working Capital**
   a. A firm ideally should be able to offset each element of its temporary working capital with a short-term liability of similar maturity. For example, a short-term loan could be obtained before the winter season and repaid with the collections from holiday sales.
6. **Managing the Level of Cash**
   a. The following are three motives for holding cash:
      1) The transactional motive, i.e., to use as a medium of exchange
      2) The precautionary motive, i.e., to provide for unexpected contingencies
      3) The speculative motive, i.e., to take advantage of unexpected opportunities
   b. The goal of cash management is to determine and maintain the firm's optimal cash balance.
      1) The optimal balance is rarely the largest. Because cash does not earn a return, only the amount needed to satisfy current obligations as they come due should be kept.

SU 11: Current Assets Management

c. The firm's optimal level of cash should be determined by a cost-benefit analysis.

1) The three motives must be balanced against the opportunity cost of missed investments in marketable securities or purchasing inventory when prices are low.

d. A **compensating balance** is a minimum amount that a bank requires the firm to keep in its demand (checking) account.

1) Compensating balances are noninterest-bearing and are meant to compensate the bank for various services rendered, such as unlimited check writing.
2) These funds are unavailable for short-term investment and incur an opportunity cost.

7. **Forecasting Future Cash Flows**

a. Managing cash flows begins with the cash budget. It states projected receipts and payments for the purpose of matching inflows and outflows.

1) The budget is for a specific period, but cash budgeting is an ongoing, cumulative activity. It is re-evaluated constantly to ensure all objectives are met.

b. Cash receipts are based on projected sales, credit terms, and estimated collection rates.

EXAMPLE 11-2   Projected Cash Collections

A firm forecasts the following cash collections for the next 4 months:

	Cash Sales	Credit Sales
July	US $40,000	US $160,000
August	60,000	220,000
September	80,000	340,000
October	70,000	300,000

On average, 50% of credit sales are paid for in the month of sale, 30% in the month after sale, and 15% in the second month after sale (5% are expected to be uncollectible). The firm's projected cash collections for October can be calculated as follows:

October cash sales		US $ 70,000
October credit sales:	US $300,000 × 50% =	150,000
September credit sales:	US $340,000 × 30% =	102,000
August credit sales:	US $220,000 × 15% =	33,000
Total October collections		US $355,000

---

c. Cash payments are based on budgeted purchases and total sales.

EXAMPLE 11-3   Projected Cash Payments

The firm forecasts the following cash payments for the next 4 months:

	Purchases	Total Sales
July	US $200,000	US $200,000
August	250,000	280,000
September	300,000	420,000
October	350,000	370,000

On average, the firm pays for 50% of purchases in the month of purchase and 25% in each of the 2 following months. Payroll is projected as 10% of that month's sales and operating expenses are 20% of the following month's sales (November's sales are projected to be US $280,000). Interest of US $5,000 is paid every month. The firm's projected cash payments for October can be calculated as follows:

October purchases:	US $350,000 × 50% =	US $175,000
September purchases:	US $300,000 × 25% =	75,000
August purchases:	US $250,000 × 25% =	62,500
October payroll:	US $370,000 × 10% =	37,000
October op. expenses:	US $280,000 × 20% =	56,000
Interest		5,000
Total October disbursements		US $410,500

8. **Speeding Cash Collections**

    a. The period of time from when a payor puts a check in the mail until the funds are available in the payee's bank is called float. Companies use various strategies to reduce the float time on receipts and to increase the float time on payments.

    b. A **lockbox** system expedites the receipt of funds.

        1) Customers submit their payments to a post office box. Bank personnel remove the envelopes from the mailbox and deposit the checks in the company's account immediately. The remittance advices are then transmitted to the company for entry into the accounts receivable system. The bank generally charges a flat monthly fee for this service.

        2) For firms doing business nationwide, a lockbox network is appropriate. The country is divided into regions according to customer population patterns. A lockbox arrangement then is established with a bank in each region.

    c. A firm using a lockbox network also engages in concentration banking. The regional banks that provide lockbox services automatically transfer their daily collections to the firm's principal bank, where they can be used for payments and short-term investment.

9. **Slowing Cash Payments**

    a. A **draft** is a three-party instrument in which one person (the drawer) orders a second person (the drawee) to pay money to a third person (the payee).

        1) A check is the most common form of draft. A check is an instrument payable on demand in which the drawee is a bank. Consequently, a draft can be used to delay the outflow of cash.

        2) A draft can be dated on the due date of an invoice and will not be processed by the drawee until that date, thereby eliminating the necessity of writing a check earlier than the due date or using an electronic funds transfer (EFT). Thus, the outflow is delayed until the check clears the drawee bank.

    b. A **payable through draft** (PTD) differs from a check. (1) It is not payable on demand and (2) the drawee is the payor, not a bank. After the payee presents the PTD to a bank, the bank in turn presents it to the issuer. The issuer then must deposit sufficient funds to cover the PTD. Use of PTDs therefore allows a firm to maintain lower cash balances.

        1) Drawbacks are that vendors prefer to receive an instrument that will be paid on demand, and banks generally impose higher processing charges for PTDs.

    c. A **zero-balance account** (ZBA) has a balance of US $0. At the end of each processing day, the bank transfers just enough from the firm's master account to cover all checks presented against the ZBA that day.

        1) This practice allows the firm to maintain higher balances in the master account from which short-term investments can be made. The bank generally charges a fee for this service.

    d. **Payment float** is the period of time from when the payor puts a check in the mail to withdrawal from the payor's account. To increase payment float, a firm may mail checks to vendors despite uncertainty about whether funds suffice to pay them all.

        1) For these situations, some banks offer overdraft protection, in which the bank guarantees (for a fee) to cover any shortage with a transfer from the firm's master account.

SU 11: Current Assets Management

10. **Idle Cash and Its Uses**

    a. Idle cash incurs an opportunity cost. To offset this cost, firms invest their idle cash balances in marketable securities.

    b. Beyond earning a modest return, the most important aspects of marketable securities management are liquidity and safety. Thus, marketable securities management applies to low-yield, low-risk instruments that are traded on highly active markets, commonly referred to as money market instruments.

    c. The money market is the market for short-term investments where companies invest their temporary surpluses of cash. The money market is not formally organized but consists of many financial institutions, companies, and government agencies offering many instruments of various risk levels and short- to medium-range maturities.

> **STOP & REVIEW**
> You have completed the outline for this subunit.
> Study multiple-choice questions 1 through 3 beginning on page 390.

11.2 RECEIVABLES MANAGEMENT

1. **Overview**

    a. Accounts receivable are carried for competitive and investment purposes.

        1) A firm almost always must offer credit if its competitors do.
        2) Customers who choose to pay beyond the stated time limit can be charged financing fees (interest income to the firm).
        3) Due to the interaction of these two factors, managing accounts receivable must involve the sales, finance, and accounting functions.

    b. Factors influencing the level of receivables include the soundness of the

        1) Procedures for evaluating customer creditworthiness,
        2) Formula for establishing standard credit terms,
        3) System for tracking accounts receivable and billing customers, and
        4) Procedures for following up on overdue accounts.

    c. The optimal credit policy does not seek merely to maximize sales.

        1) This result could be accomplished by increasing discounts, offering longer payment periods, or accepting riskier customers.

            a) But the firm cannot ignore the increase in credit losses and its negative effect on cash inflows.
            b) Thus, the firm must balance default risk (credit loss experience) and sales maximization.

d. **Default risk** is the probability that a particular customer will be unwilling or unable to pay a debt.

   1) To manage (not necessarily minimize) default risk, firms often require written agreements to be signed by the customer, outlining the terms of credit and the consequences for nonpayment.
   2) Firms often use credit scoring to determine whether to extend credit to a specific customer. Credit scoring assigns numerical values to the elements of credit worthiness.

2. **Aging Accounts Receivable**

   a. A common analytical tool is an aging schedule of accounts receivable. It stratifies the accounts depending on time outstanding.
   b. Since accounts that have been outstanding longest are also the least likely to be collected, an aging of accounts receivable provides useful information on collectability.

EXAMPLE 11-4   Aging Schedule for Accounts Receivable

A firm prepares the following aging schedule of its accounts receivable:

Balance Range	Less than 30 Days	31-60 Days	61-90 Days	Over 90 Days	Total Balances
US $0 - $100	US $ 5,000	US $ 200	US $ 100	US $ 100	US $ 5,400
US $100 - $1,000	8,000	3,800			11,800
US $1,000 - $5,000	20,000	2,000	1,900		23,900
US $5,000 - $10,000	38,000		8,000	900	46,900
Over US $10,000		12,000			12,000
Totals	US $71,000	US $18,000	US $10,000	US $1,000	US $100,000

The firm then applies an appropriate percentage to each stratum based on experience.

Aging Intervals	Balance	Estimated Uncollectible	Ending Allowance
Less than 30 days	US $ 71,000	2%	US $1,420
30-60 days	18,000	12%	2,160
61-90 days	10,000	15%	1,500
Over 90 days	1,000	20%	200
Total	US $100,000		US $5,280

3. **Basic Credit Terms**

   a. The most common credit terms offered are 2/10, net 30. This convention means that the customer may either deduct 2% of the invoice amount if the invoice is paid within 10 days or must pay the entire balance by the 30th day.

      1) Credit terms do not include quantity discounts, which affect the prices of purchases, not financing.

   b. The **average collection period** (also called the days sales outstanding in receivables) is the average number of days that pass between the time of a sale and payment of the invoice.

4. **Change in Credit Terms**

   a. Amounts of receivables are an opportunity cost, i.e., the return that could be earned if those amounts were invested elsewhere. A key aspect of any change in credit terms is balancing the competitive need to offer credit with the opportunity cost incurred.

   b. Factors considered in changing credit terms include the cost of borrowing and opportunity for repeat sales.

5. **Factoring**

   a. Factoring is a transfer of receivables to a third party (a factor) who assumes the responsibility of collection.

   b. A factor usually receives a high financing fee plus a fee for collection. Furthermore, the factor often operates more efficiently than its clients because of the specialized nature of its services.

   c. **Credit card sales** are a common form of factoring. The retailer benefits by prompt receipt of cash and avoidance of credit losses and other costs. In return, the credit card company charges a fee.

6. **Pledging**

   a. A pledge (a general assignment) is the use of receivables as collateral (security) for a loan. The borrower agrees to use collections of receivables to repay the loan.

      1) Upon default, the lender can sell the receivables to recover the loan proceeds.

      2) Because a pledge is a relatively informal arrangement, it is not reflected in the accounts.

STOP & REVIEW

You have completed the outline for this subunit.
Study multiple-choice questions 4 through 6 on page 391.

11.3 MANAGING INVENTORY COSTS AND QUANTITIES

1. **Costs of Inventory**

    a. An entity carries inventories because of the difficulty in predicting the amount, timing, and location of supply and demand.

        1) Thus, one purpose of inventory control is to determine the optimal level of inventory necessary to minimize costs.

    b. The **carrying costs** (also called **holding costs**) of inventory include warehousing insurance, cost of capital invested in inventories, inventory taxes, security costs, depreciation, and opportunity cost (i.e., the pretax return forgone by investing capital in inventory rather than the best alternative). Carrying costs may also include a charge for shrinkage, e.g., from spoilage of perishable items, obsolescence, theft, or waste.

        1) Shipping costs and the initial cost of the inventory are purchase costs.

        2) The annual opportunity cost of carrying inventory equals the average inventory level, times the per-unit purchase price, times the cost of capital.

EXAMPLE 11-5   Carrying Inventory -- Opportunity Cost

ABC Co. does not have beginning inventory and orders 1,000 units at a price of US $10 per unit, resulting in an average inventory of 500 units. If the entity has a cost of capital of 8%, its annual opportunity cost of carrying inventory is calculated as follows:

$$[(1,000 \text{ units} \div 2) \times \text{US \$10} \times .08] = \text{US \$400}$$

---

    3) Carrying costs are reduced by minimizing the amount of inventory. This practice risks stockouts, resulting in lost contribution margin on sales and customer ill will.

    4) Safety stock is the extra inventory kept to guard against stockouts.

    c. **Ordering costs** are the fixed costs of placing an order with a vendor and receiving the goods, independent of the number of units ordered.

        1) Frequent ordering of small quantities thus may not be cost-beneficial compared with the relevant carrying costs.

            a) If smaller orders are placed more frequently, fewer items are carried, reducing the effect of increased carrying costs. But ordering costs increase.

            b) Decreasing total orders increases inventory and carrying costs.

    d. Inventory management minimizes the total costs of inventory, i.e., the sum of carrying costs and ordering costs, as illustrated by the graph below:

Inventory Management

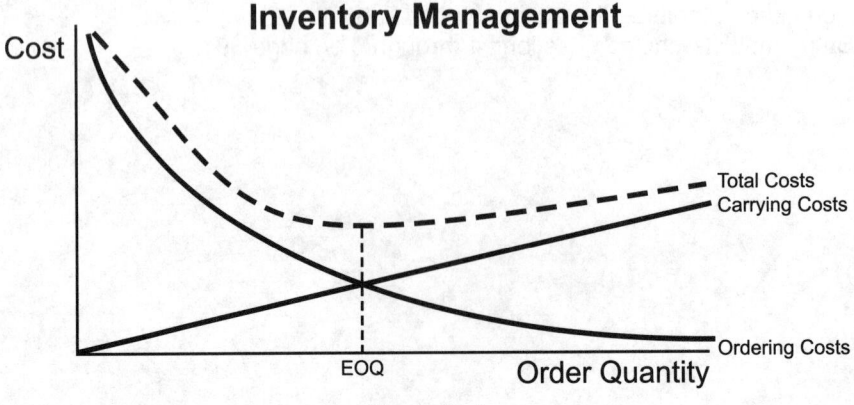

Figure 11-1

SU 11: Current Assets Management

2. **Economic Order Quantity (EOQ) Model**

   > **SUCCESS TIP**: EOQ is a frequently tested inventory management topic. Mastery of the EOQ model will increase your success on the exam.

   a. The objective of the EOQ model is to find an optimal order quantity that balances carrying and ordering costs.
   b. The EOQ results from using **differential calculus** to determine the minimum point on the total cost curve. It corresponds to the intersection of the carrying cost and ordering cost curves in Figure 11-1 on the previous page.

      1) The basic formula is

      $$EOQ = \sqrt{\frac{2aD}{k}}$$

      If: a = variable cost per order (or production setup)
      D = periodic demand in units
      k = unit periodic carrying cost

EXAMPLE 11-6   EOQ

If periodic demand is uniform at 1,000 units, the cost to place an order is US $4, and the cost to carry one unit in inventory for a period is US $2, the EOQ is calculated as follows:

$$EOQ = \sqrt{\frac{2(US\ \$4)(1{,}000)}{US\ \$2}} = 63.25 \text{ units per order}$$

---

      2) The formula shows that the EOQ

         a) Increases when demand or order costs increase
         b) Decreases when demand or order costs decrease
         c) Decreases when carrying costs increase
         d) Increases when carrying costs decrease

      3) The average level of inventory under this model is the safety stock plus one-half of the EOQ.
      4) The EOQ is a periodic model. The number of orders (production runs) per period is given by the periodic demand divided by the EOQ.
      5) The safety stock level is only indirectly related to the reorder point. It is the factor the internal auditor is least likely to consider when reviewing reorder point levels.
      6) The **optimal level of inventory** is affected by the factors in the EOQ model and delivery or production lead times.

         a) These factors are (1) the annual demand for inventory; (2) the carrying cost, which includes the interest on funds invested in inventory; (3) the usage rate; and (4) the cost of placing an order or making a production run.

EXAMPLE 11-7   EOQ -- Safety Stock

Using the data from Example 11-6, the company has determined it also desires a safety stock of 15 units. Given that demand is constant and the EOQ is 63.25 units, the average inventory level without regard to safety stock is 31.625 (63.25 ÷ 2). Adding safety stock results in an average level of 46.625 (31.625 + 15). Given that carrying costs are US $2 per unit, the annual inventory holding costs are calculated as follows:

46.625 × US $2 = US $93.25 annual inventory holding costs

c. The limitations of the EOQ model are its restrictive assumptions.

 1) The three variables in the formula (order placement or production setup cost, unit demand, per-unit carrying cost) are constant throughout the period.

 2) Full replenishment occurs instantly when the last item is used, stockout costs are zero, and no safety stock is held.

> **STOP & REVIEW**
> You have completed the outline for this subunit.
> Study multiple-choice questions 7 through 9 on page 392.

11.4 INVENTORY MANAGEMENT METHODS

1. **ABC Inventory Management**

 a. The ABC system is a simple inventory management method. It controls inventories by dividing items into three groups:

 1) Group A consists of high-monetary-value items, which account for a small portion (perhaps 10%) of the total inventory usage.

 2) Group B consists of medium-monetary-value items, which may account for perhaps 20% of the total inventory items.

 3) Group C consists of low-monetary-value items, which account for the remaining 70% of sales or usage.

 b. The ABC system permits managerial control over inventory to be exercised in the most cost-effective manner.

 1) The stocking levels and activity of group A items are reviewed on a regular basis.

 2) Group B items may not need review as often as group A items, but they may need review more often than group C items.

 3) For group C, extensive use of models and records is not cost effective. They are reviewed even less frequently.

2. **Just-in-Time (JIT)**

 a. Modern inventory control favors the just-in-time model. Companies have traditionally built parts and components for subsequent operations on a preset schedule.

 1) Such a schedule provides a cushion of inventory so that the next operation will always have parts to work with -- a just-in-case method.

 b. In contrast, JIT limits output to the amount required (the demand) by the next operation in the production process. Reductions in inventory result in fewer resources invested in idle assets; reduction of storage space requirements; and lower inventory taxes, pilferage, and obsolescence risks.

 1) High inventory often conceals production problems because defective parts can be overlooked when plenty of good parts are available. If only enough parts are made for the subsequent operation, however, any defects immediately stop production.

2) The focus of quality control under JIT changes from the discovery of defective parts to the prevention of quality problems. Zero machine breakdowns (achieved through preventive maintenance) and zero defects are ultimate goals, and higher quality and lower inventory can be achieved.

c. The ultimate objectives of JIT methods are increased competitiveness and higher profits through

1) Greater productivity
2) Reduced order costs and carrying costs
3) Faster and cheaper setups
4) Shorter manufacturing cycle times
5) Better due date performance
6) Improved quality
7) More flexible processes

d. JIT systems are based on a manufacturing philosophy that combines purchasing, production, and inventory control. It also treats many inventory-related activities as nonvalue-added. Carrying inventory is regarded as indicating problems, such as poor quality, long cycle times, and lack of coordination with suppliers.

1) A JIT system **reduces carrying costs** by eliminating inventories and increasing supplier deliveries that ideally should be received just in time to be used in manufacturing.

a) This system **increases the risk of stockout costs** because inventory is reduced or eliminated.

e. However, JIT also reorganizes the production process to eliminate waste of resources. JIT is a **pull system**. Items are pulled through production by current demand, not pushed through by anticipated demand. Thus, one operation produces only what is needed by the next operation, and components and materials arrive just in time to be used.

1) In a pull system, workers often may be idle if they are not multi-skilled.

a) Thus, (1) central support departments are reduced or eliminated, (2) space is saved, (3) fewer and smaller factories may be required, and (4) materials and tools are brought close to the point of use.

b) Manufacturing cycle time and setup time also are reduced.

c) As a result, on-time delivery performance and response to changes in markets are enhanced, and production of customized goods in small lots becomes feasible.

f. The lower inventory in a JIT system eliminates the need for some internal controls.

1) Frequent receipt of deliveries from suppliers often means less need for (a) a sophisticated inventory control system and (b) control personnel.

2) JIT also may eliminate central receiving areas, hard copy receiving reports, and storage areas. A central warehouse is not needed because deliveries are made by suppliers directly to the area of production.

3) The quality of parts provided by suppliers is verified by use of statistical controls, not inspection of incoming goods. Storage, counting, and inspecting are eliminated because they are not value-adding work.

382   SU 11: Current Assets Management

      g.   In a JIT system, the dependability of suppliers is crucial.

           1)   Organizations that adopt JIT systems therefore have strategic teaming agreements with a few carefully chosen suppliers who are extensively involved in the buyer's processes.

           2)   Long-term contracts are negotiated to reduce order costs.

           3)   Buyer-supplier relationships are facilitated by electronic data interchange (EDI), a technology that allows the supplier access to the buyer's online inventory management system.

               a)   Electronic messages replace paper documents (purchase orders and sales invoices), and the production schedules and deliveries of the parties can be more readily coordinated.

3.   **Materials Requirements Planning (MRP)**

      a.   MRP is an integrated computer-based system designed to plan and control materials used in production.

           1)   MRP is a push system. The demand for materials is pushed by the forecasted demand for the final product.

      b.   The MRP system consults the **bill of materials (BOM)**, a record of which (and how many) subassemblies are needed for the finished product. The system then generates a complete list of every part and component needed.

EXAMPLE 11-8   MRP

A manufacturer has the following bill of materials for a car:

Subunit	Quantity
Engine	1
Suspension	4

The bill of materials for the component subunits is as follows:

Subunit	Contains	Quantity
Engine	Cylinder Head	2
	Pistons	6
Suspension	Shock Absorber	4

Current inventory quantities are as follows:

Subunit	On Hand
Engine	25
Suspension	35
Shock Absorber	50
Cylinder Head	30
Pistons	40

The company has 20 units of the finished product in inventory and wishes to maintain this level throughout the year. Production of 40 units is scheduled for the upcoming month. The quantities of the principal subunits that must be produced are calculated below:

Subunit	Quantity per Finished Product		Production Run		Quantity Needed		Quantity on Hand		To Be Built
Engine	1	×	40	=	40	−	25	=	15
Suspension	4	×	40	=	160	−	35	=	125

The parts that must be ordered from vendors can thus be calculated as follows:

Subunit	Components	Component Quantity		Subunits to Be Built		Quantity Needed		Quantity on Hand		To Be Purchased
Engine	Cylinder Head	2	×	15	=	30	−	30	=	0
	Pistons	6	×	15	=	90	−	40	=	50
Suspension	Shock Absorber	4	×	125	=	500	−	50	=	450

SU 11: Current Assets Management

    c. MRP schedules when items of inventory are needed in the production departments.

        1) If parts are not in stock, the system automatically generates a purchase order on the proper date (considering lead times) so that deliveries will arrive on time. The timing of deliveries is vital to avoid both production delays and excessive inventory of materials.

4. **Manufacturing Resource Planning**

    a. Manufacturing resource planning (MRP-II) extends the scope of MRP to integrate all facets of a manufacturing business, including production, sales, inventories, schedules, and cash flows.

        1) The same system is used for financial reporting and management of operations (both use the same transactions and numbers).

        2) MRP-II uses a master production schedule (MPS), a statement of the anticipated manufacturing schedule for selected items and periods.

        3) A further refinement is the inclusion of a feedback loop that allows the continuous revision of a production plan.

5. **Computer-Integrated Manufacturing (CIM)**

    a. Computer technology has advanced beyond planning and controlling resource use to the automation of actual production processes.

    b. A CIM system (1) designs products using computer-aided design (CAD), (2) tests the design using computer-aided engineering (CAE), (3) manufactures products using computer-aided manufacturing (CAM), and (4) integrates all components with a computerized information system.

        1) CIM is a comprehensive approach to manufacturing in which design is translated into product by centralized processing and robotics. The concept also includes materials handling.

        2) The advantages of CIM include increased flexibility, productivity, integration, synergism, and cost minimization. Waste, scrap, rework, and spoilage are reduced.

    c. Flexibility is a key advantage. A traditional manufacturing system may be disrupted by an emergency change. But CIM can reschedule everything when a priority requirement is inserted into the system. The areas of flexibility include the following:

        1) Varying production volumes during a period
        2) Handling new parts added to a product
        3) Changing the proportion of parts being produced
        4) Adjusting to engineering changes of a product
        5) Adapting the sequence in which parts come to the machinery
        6) Adapting to changes in materials

STOP & REVIEW

You have completed the outline for this subunit.
Study multiple-choice questions 10 through 15 beginning on page 393.

11.5 INVENTORY SYSTEMS

1. **Inventory systems** track the flow of goods from vendors to an organization's inventory storage or retail facilities, then to the organization's customers. Inventory shrinkage must be considered when valuing inventory.

    a. A **perpetual inventory** system tracks every item purchased and sold. This system is generally more suitable for entities that sell relatively expensive and heterogeneous items and require continuous monitoring of inventory and cost of goods sold accounts. Automobile dealers are an example. Under this system,

       1) Purchases and other items related to inventory costing are charged directly to inventory.
       2) Inventory and cost of goods sold are adjusted as sales occur. The amount of inventory on hand and the cost of goods sold can be determined at any time.
       3) A disadvantage is that bookkeeping is more complex and expensive.

    b. In the **periodic inventory** system, inventory and cost of goods sold are updated at specific intervals, such as quarterly or annually, based on the results of a physical count. Bookkeeping is simpler. Entities with relatively inexpensive and homogeneous items, such as grain wholesalers, that have no need to monitor inventory and cost of goods sold generally use this method. Under the periodic system,

       1) Goods bought from suppliers and other items related to inventory costing usually are tracked during the period in a separate temporary account (purchases).
       2) The beginning inventory balance remains unchanged until the end of the period when the purchases account is closed.
       3) Changes in inventory and cost of goods sold are recorded only at the end of the period, based on the physical count.

2. **Ending Inventory and Cost of Goods Sold**

    a. Ending inventory affects both the statement of financial position (balance sheet) and the income statement.

       1) For a retailer, cost of goods sold is calculated based on changes in inventory:

Retailer	
Beginning inventory	US $ XXX
Plus: Net purchases	XXX
Plus: Freight-in	XXX
Goods available for sale	US $ XXX
Minus: Ending inventory	(XXX)
Cost of goods sold	US $ XXX

2) For a manufacturer, cost of goods sold is calculated as follows:

Manufacturer

Beginning materials inventory	US $ XXX	
Purchases during the period	XXX	
Ending materials inventory	(XXX)	
Direct materials used in production		US $XXX
Direct labor costs		XXX
Manufacturing overhead costs (fixed + variable)		XXX
Total manufacturing costs		US $ XXX
Beginning work-in-process inventory		XXX
Ending work-in-process inventory		(XXX)
Cost of goods manufactured		US $ XXX
Beginning finished goods inventory		XXX
Ending finished goods inventory		(XXX)
Cost of goods sold		US $ XXX

3. **Inventory Costing**

   a. **Specific Identification Method**

      1) The specific identification method requires determining which specific items are sold and thus reflects the actual physical flow of goods. Specific costs are attributed to identified items of inventory.

      2) This system is appropriate for items that are not ordinarily interchangeable and for items that are segregated for a specific project.

      3) Specific identification is the most accurate method. It identifies each item of inventory separately. But, it is also the most expensive because it requires detailed records.

   b. When the inventory items purchased or produced are identical and ordinarily interchangeable, the use of specific identification is inappropriate. In this case, an inventory cost flow assumption (e.g., average, FIFO, or LIFO) is made. The assumption used should be the one that, in the circumstances, most clearly reflects periodic income.

c. **Average Method**
1) The average method assumes that goods are indistinguishable and are therefore measured at an average of the costs incurred. The average may be calculated on the periodic basis or as each additional purchase occurs.
2) The **moving-average method** is used under the **perpetual** inventory accounting system. It requires determination of a new weighted-average inventory cost after each purchase. This cost is used for every sale until the next purchase.

EXAMPLE 11-9   **Moving-Average Method**

The following data relate to a company's Year 1 activities:

Date	Transaction	Number of units	Purchase price per unit (US $)	Sale price per unit (US $)
January 1	Beginning balance	100	20	
March 1	Purchase	20	32	
April 1	Sale	70		40
June 1	Purchase	30	14	
October 1	Sale	40		24

Under the moving-average method, the year-end inventory and Year 1 cost of goods sold are calculated as follows:

Date	Activity	Units	Price (US $)	Cost of inventory purchased (sold)	Inventory total balance	On-hand units	Cost per unit
January 1	Beg. bal.	100	20		US $2,000 (100 × $20)	100	**US $20**
March 1	Purchase	20	32	US $640 = 20 × US $32	US $2,640 ($2,000 + $640)	120	US $22 ($2,640 ÷ 120)
April 1	Sale	70	22	US $(1,540) = 70 × US $22	US $1,100 ($2,640 – $1,540)	50	US $22 ($1,100 ÷ 50)
June 1	Purchase	30	14	US $420 = 30 × US $14	US $1,520 ($1,100 + $420)	80	US $19 ($1,520 ÷ 80)
October 1	Sale	40	19	US $(760) = 40 × US $19	**US $760 ($1,520 – $760)**	40	**US $19 ($760 ÷ 40)**

The cost of **inventory** on December 31, Year 1, is **US $760**. The Year 1 **cost of goods sold** is **US $2,300**.

Beginning inventory	US $2,000
Purchases (US $640 + $420)	1,060
Ending inventory	(760)
Cost of goods sold (US $1,540 + $760)	**US $2,300**

---

3) The **weighted-average method** is used under the **periodic** inventory accounting system. The average cost is determined only once, at the end of the period. The weighted-average cost per unit is used to calculate the amounts of period-end inventory and the cost of goods sold for the period.

a) The weighted-average cost per unit is calculated as follows:

$$\frac{\text{Cost of period-beginning inventory} + \text{Cost of purchases during the period}}{\text{Number of period-beginning inventory} + \text{Number of units purchased during the period}}$$

EXAMPLE 11-10   **Weighted-Average Method**

Under the weighted-average method, the year-end inventory and Year 1 cost of goods sold are calculated as follows:

First, the weighted-average cost per unit should be calculated.

$$\frac{\text{Cost of year-beginning inventory} + \text{Cost of purchases during the period}}{\text{Number of year-beginning inventory} + \text{Number of units purchased}} = \frac{\text{US \$2,000} + \$1,060}{100 + 20 + 30} = \text{US \$20.4}$$

Then, by using the weighted-average cost per unit (WACPU), the year-end inventory and Year 1 cost of goods sold can be calculated:

Beginning inventory	US $2,000	
Purchases	1,060	
Ending inventory	(816)	(40 × US $20.4) = (WACPU × Year end, number of inventory units)
Cost of goods sold	**US $2,244**	(110 × US $20.4) = (WACPU × Number of units sold during the period)

d. **FIFO (First-In, First-Out) Method**
   1) The FIFO method assumes that the first items of inventory purchased or produced are the first sold.
      a) In an inflationary environment, ending inventory is highest under FIFO because less expensive items are assumed to be sold first.
   2) Ending inventory consists of the latest purchases or production output.
   3) Under the FIFO method, year-end inventory and cost of goods sold for the period will be the same regardless of whether the perpetual or the periodic inventory accounting system is used.

EXAMPLE 11-11   FIFO Method

Using the data from Example 11-9 on the previous page, the year-end cost of inventory is calculated as follows:

Under the FIFO method, the cost of these 40 units consists of the **latest purchases** and is equal to **US $740**.

Date of purchase	Units	Price per unit	Total cost
June 1, Year 1	30	US $14	US $420
March 1, Year 1	10	32	320
Year-end inventory	**40**		**US $740**

The Year 1 cost of goods sold is equal to **US $2,320**.

Beginning inventory	US $2,000
Purchases (US $640 + $420)	1,060
Ending inventory	(740)
Cost of goods sold	**US $2,320**

---

e. **LIFO (Last-In, First-Out) Method**
   1) The LIFO method assumes the newest items of inventory are sold first. Thus, the items remaining in inventory are recognized as if they were the oldest.
   2) Under the LIFO method, the perpetual and the periodic inventory accounting systems may result in different amounts for the cost of year-end inventory and cost of goods sold.
   3) LIFO is permissible under U.S. GAAP (U.S. generally accepted accounting principles) but not under IFRS (international financial reporting standards).
   4) Under the **periodic** inventory accounting system, the calculation of inventory and cost of goods sold is made at the end of the period.

EXAMPLE 11-12   LIFO Method

In Example 11-11, the number of units at year end was determined to be 40. The year-end cost of inventory is therefore calculated as follows:

Under the LIFO method, the cost of these 40 units consists of the **earliest purchases** (beginning inventory) equal to **US $800** ($20 × 40).

The Year 1 cost of goods sold is equal to **US $2,260**.

Beginning inventory	US $2,000
Purchases (US $640 + $420)	1,060
Year-end inventory	(800)
Cost of goods sold (US $1,540 + $760)	**US $2,260**

---

   5) Under the **perpetual** inventory accounting system, the cost of goods sold is calculated every time the sale occurs and consists of the most recent (latest) purchases.

4. **Inventory Estimation**

   a. An estimate of inventory may be needed when an exact count is not feasible, e.g., for interim reporting purposes or when inventory records have been destroyed. The gross profit method may be used for inventory estimation.

      1) Gross profit margin (gross profit percentage) equals gross profit divided by sales.
      2) The following calculation is used to estimate the ending inventory and cost of goods sold:

   Gross Profit Method

Beginning inventory		US $ XXX
Purchases		XXX
Goods available for sale		US $ XXX
Sales	US $ XXX	
Gross profit (Sales × Gross profit margin)	(XXX)	
Costs of goods sold [Sales × (1 – Gross profit margin)]		(XXX)
Ending inventory		US $ XXX

   EXAMPLE 11-13   Gross Profit Method

   A retailer needs to estimate ending inventory for quarterly reporting purposes. The firm's best estimate of the gross percentage is its historical rate of 25%. The following additional information is available:

Net sales	US $1,000,000
Purchases	300,000
Beginning inventory	800,000

   Estimated cost of goods sold for the quarter is US $750,000 [$1,000,000 × (1 – 25%)]. Estimated ending inventory is therefore US $350,000 ($800,000 + $300,000 – $750,000).

   ---

5. **Inventory Errors**

   a. These errors may have a material effect on current assets, working capital (current assets minus current liabilities), cost of goods sold, net income, and equity. A common error is inappropriate timing of the recognition of transactions.

      1) If a purchase on account is not recorded and the goods are not included in ending inventory, cost of goods sold (BI plus purchases minus EI) and net income are unaffected. But current assets and current liabilities are understated.
      2) If purchases and beginning inventory are properly recorded but items are excluded from ending inventory, cost of goods sold is overstated. Net income, inventory, retained earnings, working capital, and the current ratio are understated.

   b. Errors arising from recording transactions in the wrong period may reverse in the subsequent period.

      1) If ending inventory is overstated, the overstatement of net income will be offset by the understatement in the following year that results from the overstatement of beginning inventory.

c. An **overstatement error in year-end inventory** of the current year affects the financial statements of 2 different years.

1) The **first year's** effects may be depicted as follows:

Balance Sheet Effects		Income Statement Effects	
		Net sales revenue	US $XXX,XXX
		Beginning inventory	US $XXX,XXX
		Plus: Cost of goods acquired/produced	XXX,XXX
Current assets:		Goods available for sale	XXX,XXX
Ending inventory	Overstated ↑ → Minus: Ending inventory →	Overstated ↑	
		Cost of goods sold	Understated ↓
Stockholders' equity:		Gross profit	Overstated ↑
Retained earnings, 12/31/Yr 0	US $XXX,XXX	Expenses	(XX,XXX)
Plus: Net income	Overstated ↑ ← Net income ←		Overstated ↑
Retained earnings, 12/31/Yr 1	Overstated ↑		

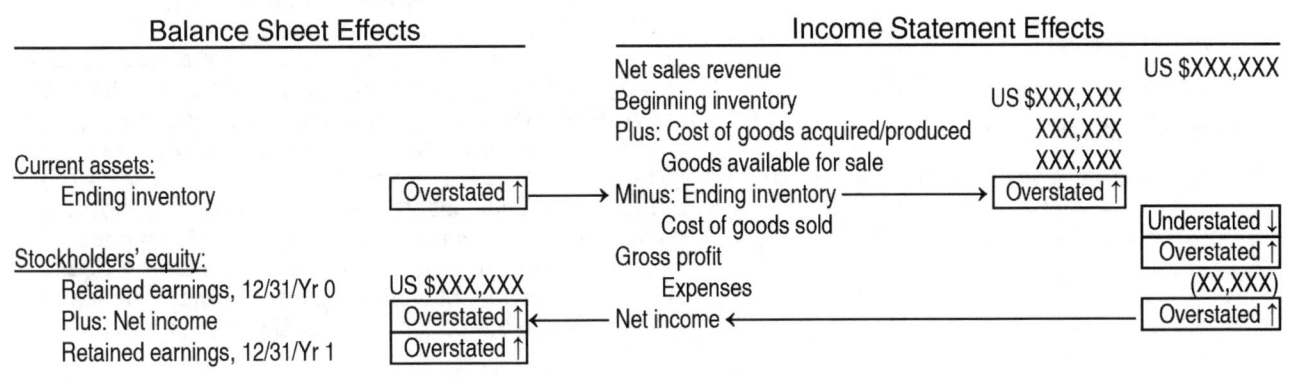

Figure 11-2

2) At the end of the **second year**, retained earnings is correctly stated as follows:

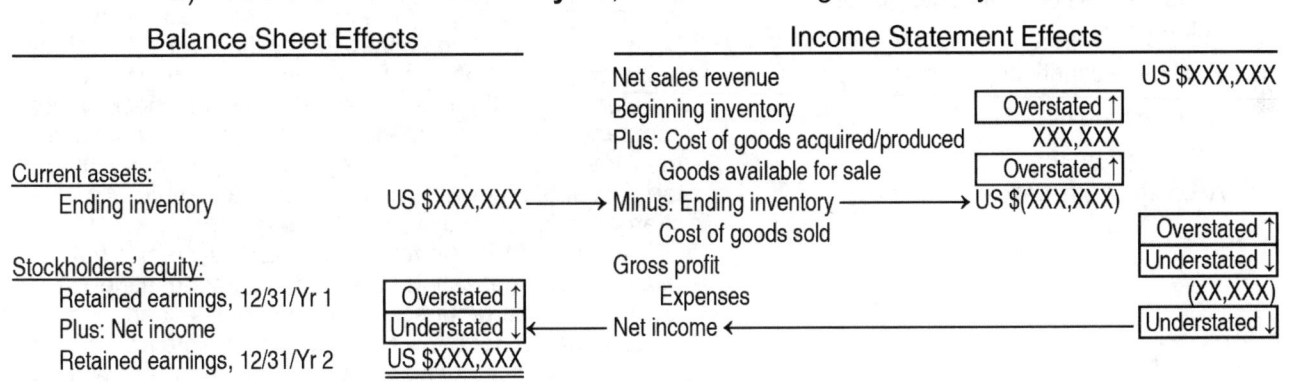

Balance Sheet Effects		Income Statement Effects	
		Net sales revenue	US $XXX,XXX
		Beginning inventory	Overstated ↑
		Plus: Cost of goods acquired/produced	XXX,XXX
Current assets:		Goods available for sale	Overstated ↑
Ending inventory	US $XXX,XXX → Minus: Ending inventory →	US $(XXX,XXX)	
		Cost of goods sold	Overstated ↑
Stockholders' equity:		Gross profit	Understated ↓
Retained earnings, 12/31/Yr 1	Overstated ↑	Expenses	(XX,XXX)
Plus: Net income	Understated ↓ ← Net income ←		Understated ↓
Retained earnings, 12/31/Yr 2	US $XXX,XXX		

Figure 11-3

STOP & REVIEW

You have completed the outline for this subunit.
Study multiple-choice questions 16 through 20 beginning on page 395.

QUESTIONS

11.1 Working Capital and Cash Management

1. Net working capital is the difference between

A. Current assets and current liabilities.
B. Fixed assets and fixed liabilities.
C. Total assets and total liabilities.
D. Shareholders' investment and cash.

Answer (A) is correct.
REQUIRED: The definition of net working capital.
DISCUSSION: Net working capital is defined by accountants as the difference between current assets and current liabilities. Working capital is a measure of liquidity.
Answer (B) is incorrect. Working capital refers to the difference between current assets and current liabilities; fixed assets are not a component. **Answer (C) is incorrect.** Total assets and total liabilities are not components of working capital; only current items are included. **Answer (D) is incorrect.** Shareholders' equity is not a component of working capital; only current items are included in the concept of working capital.

2. A lockbox system

A. Reduces the need for compensating balances.
B. Provides security for late night deposits.
C. Reduces the risk of having checks lost in the mail.
D. Accelerates the inflow of funds.

Answer (D) is correct.
REQUIRED: The true statement.
DISCUSSION: A lockbox system is one strategy for expediting the receipt of funds. Customers submit their payments to a mailbox controlled by the bank rather than to the company's offices. Bank personnel remove the envelopes from the mailbox and deposit the checks to the company's account immediately. The remittance advices must then be transported to the company for entry into the accounts receivable system. The bank generally charges a flat monthly fee for this service.
Answer (A) is incorrect. A lockbox system is not related to compensating balances; a compensating balance may be required by a covenant in a loan agreement that requires a company to maintain a specified balance during the term of the loan. **Answer (B) is incorrect.** A lockbox system is a process by which payments are sent to a bank's mailbox, which is checked during normal post office hours. **Answer (C) is incorrect.** The use of a lockbox system entails sending checks through the mail to a post office box. Thus, it does not reduce the risk of losing checks in the mail.

3. As a company becomes more conservative in its working capital policy, it tends to have a(n)

A. Decrease in its acid-test ratio.
B. Increase in the ratio of current liabilities to noncurrent liabilities.
C. Increase in the ratio of current assets to current liabilities.
D. Increase in funds invested in common stock and a decrease in funds invested in marketable securities.

Answer (C) is correct.
REQUIRED: The effect of a more conservative working capital policy.
DISCUSSION: A conservative working capital policy minimizes liquidity risk by increasing net working capital (Current assets – Current liabilities). The result is loss of the potentially higher returns available from using the additional working capital to acquire long-term assets. A conservative policy has a higher current ratio (Current assets ÷ Current liabilities) and acid-test ratio (Quick assets ÷ Current liabilities). Thus, the company increases current assets or decreases current liabilities. A conservative policy finances assets using long-term or permanent funds rather than short-term sources.
Answer (A) is incorrect. An acid-test ratio decrease suggests an aggressive policy. A conservative company wants a higher acid-test ratio, i.e., more liquid assets relative to liabilities. **Answer (B) is incorrect.** A conservative company wants working capital to be financed from long-term sources. **Answer (D) is incorrect.** A conservative company seeks more liquid (marketable) investments.

11.2 Receivables Management

4. The average collection period for a firm measures the number of days

- A. After a typical credit sale is made until the firm receives the payment.
- B. For a typical check to "clear" through the banking system.
- C. Beyond the end of the credit period before a typical customer payment is received.
- D. Before a typical account becomes delinquent.

Answer (A) is correct.
REQUIRED: The meaning of a firm's average collection period.
DISCUSSION: The average collection period measures the number of days between the date of sale and the date of collection. It should be related to a firm's credit terms. For example, a firm that allows terms of 2/15, net 30, should have an average collection period of somewhere between 15 and 30 days.
Answer (B) is incorrect. It describes the concept of float. **Answer (C) is incorrect.** The average collection period includes the total time before a payment is received, including the periods both before and after the end of the normal credit period. **Answer (D) is incorrect.** It describes the normal credit period.

5. An aging of accounts receivable measures the

- A. Ability of the firm to meet short-term obligations.
- B. Average length of time that receivables have been outstanding.
- C. Percentage of sales that have been collected after a given time period.
- D. Amount of receivables that have been outstanding for given lengths of time.

Answer (D) is correct.
REQUIRED: The item measured by an aging of accounts receivable.
DISCUSSION: The purpose of an aging of receivables is to classify receivables by due date. Those that are current (not past due) are listed in one column, those less than 30 days past due in another column, etc. The amount in each category can then be multiplied by an estimated credit loss percentage that is based on a company's credit experience and other factors. The theory is that the oldest receivables are the least likely to be collectible. Aging the receivables and estimating the uncollectible amounts is one method of arriving at the appropriate balance sheet valuation of the accounts receivable account.
Answer (A) is incorrect. An aging schedule is used for receivables, not liabilities. **Answer (B) is incorrect.** An aging schedule is based on specific accounts, not averages. **Answer (C) is incorrect.** An aging schedule focuses on uncollected receivables.

6. Consider the following factors affecting a company as it is reviewing its trade credit policy.

1. Operating at full capacity
2. Low cost of borrowing
3. Opportunity for repeat sales
4. Low gross margin per unit

Which of the above factors would indicate that the company should liberalize its credit policy?

- A. 1 and 2 only.
- B. 1, 2, and 3 only.
- C. 2 and 3 only.
- D. 3 and 4 only.

Answer (C) is correct.
REQUIRED: The factor indicating liberalization of credit policy.
DISCUSSION: If the cost of borrowing is low, the firm can satisfy its working capital needs otherwise than by encouraging early payment from customers. Also, loosening credit policies tends to increase repeat sales.
Answer (A) is incorrect. If the firm is operating at full capacity, it is selling all it can produce and has no need to loosen its credit policies. **Answer (B) is incorrect.** If the firm is operating at full capacity, it is selling all it can produce and has no need to loosen its credit policies. **Answer (D) is incorrect.** If the gross margin per unit is low, greater sales will not significantly improve the firm's profits.

11.3 Managing Inventory Costs and Quantities

7. With regard to inventory management, an increase in the frequency of ordering will normally

A. Reduce the total ordering costs.
B. Have no impact on total ordering costs.
C. Reduce total carrying costs.
D. Have no impact on total carrying costs.

Answer (C) is correct.
REQUIRED: The effect of an increase in the frequency of ordering.
DISCUSSION: If orders are placed more frequently, fewer items are carried and carrying costs fall.
Answer (A) is incorrect. Ordering costs are the fixed costs of placing an order with a vendor and receiving the goods. Consequently, an increase in the frequency of ordering will normally increase total ordering costs. **Answer (B) is incorrect.** Total ordering costs will increase. **Answer (D) is incorrect.** Total carrying costs are reduced.

8. Assuming other factors are constant, which action is the most appropriate when carrying costs of inventory are increasing significantly?

A. Increase total orders.
B. Decrease total orders.
C. Decrease the use of inventory in the production process.
D. Hire additional line managers.

Answer (A) is correct.
REQUIRED: The most appropriate action when carrying costs of inventory are increasing significantly.
DISCUSSION: If smaller orders are placed more frequently, fewer items are carried, reducing the effect of increased carrying costs. But ordering costs increase.
Answer (B) is incorrect. Decreasing total orders increases inventory and carrying costs. **Answer (C) is incorrect.** Decreased use of inventory is not feasible if other factors (e.g., inputs) are assumed to be constant. **Answer (D) is incorrect.** Hiring additional line managers has no effect on inventory management.

9. An increase in inventory carrying costs

A. Decreases the economic order quantity (EOQ).
B. Increases the reorder point.
C. Increases the economic order quantity (EOQ).
D. Does not change the economic order quantity (EOQ).

Answer (A) is correct.
REQUIRED: The effect of an increase in inventory carrying costs.
DISCUSSION: An increase in inventory carrying costs decreases the EOQ because, in the EOQ model, carrying cost is a denominator variable.
Answer (B) is incorrect. The reorder point is based on lead time, not the EOQ model. **Answer (C) is incorrect.** The EOQ increases when inventory carrying costs decrease. **Answer (D) is incorrect.** Carrying cost is a variable in the EOQ formula. Therefore, a change in carrying cost will result in a change in the EOQ.

11.4 Inventory Management Methods

10. Which of these inventory management techniques is the simplest?

A. Just-in-time.
B. Manufacturing resource planning.
C. ABC inventory management.
D. Materials requirements planning.

Answer (C) is correct.
REQUIRED: The simplest inventory management method.
DISCUSSION: The ABC system is a simple inventory management technique. It controls inventories by dividing items into three groups based on monetary value.
Answer (A) is incorrect. Just-in-time inventory management requires firm commitments from suppliers and very reliable delivery networks. **Answer (B) is incorrect.** Manufacturing resource planning is extremely complex. It integrates all facets of a manufacturing business, including production, sales, inventories, schedules, and cash flows. **Answer (D) is incorrect.** Materials requirements planning is an integrated computer-based system designed to plan and control materials used in production. It is a complex system.

11. A manufacturing firm has experienced a surge in demand for its products. The need to store steadily increasing supplies of raw materials has led the firm to rent warehouse space at an exorbitant cost. The most cost-effective inventory management technique for the company to improve its practices is most likely

A. Economic order quantity.
B. Electronic data interchange.
C. ISO 9000.
D. Just-in-time.

Answer (D) is correct.
REQUIRED: The best inventory management method.
DISCUSSION: Just-in-time inventory management views storing and handling inventory as nonvalue-added activities. The goal of just-in-time is to reduce the need for materials storage space by timing deliveries to arrive just as the materials are needed in production.
Answer (A) is incorrect. Instituting an economic order quantity system would not alleviate the increasing costs of storing raw materials. **Answer (B) is incorrect.** Electronic data interchange may reduce the amount of paper exchanged by trading parties, but it would not help reduce the firm's rising storage costs. **Answer (C) is incorrect.** The ISO 9000 set of standards addresses process quality, not inventory management.

12. An organization sells a product for which demand is certain and carrying costs are high. Management wants to minimize inventory costs. The organization should

A. Keep a large safety stock.
B. Use a just-in-time (JIT) inventory system.
C. Use a materials requirements planning (MRP) system.
D. Maintain a master production schedule.

Answer (B) is correct.
REQUIRED: The action management should take to minimize inventory costs.
DISCUSSION: A JIT system reduces inventory on hand. Decreased inventory reduces the effect of increased carrying costs. Also, constant demand encourages small, equal shipments of inventory that occur when needed.
Answer (A) is incorrect. Safety stock is inventory maintained to reduce the number of stockouts resulting from higher-than-expected demand during lead time. Maintaining a large safety stock during periods of stable demand results in unnecessary carrying costs. Stockouts are less likely. **Answer (C) is incorrect.** An MRP system schedules production and controls the level of inventory for components with dependent demand. **Answer (D) is incorrect.** A master production schedule states the timing and amounts of production.

13. Just-in-time (JIT) inventory systems have been adopted by large manufacturers to minimize the carrying costs of inventories. A weakness of JIT systems is

A. Increased production time.
B. Increased carrying costs.
C. Increased stockout costs.
D. Increased purchase costs.

Answer (C) is correct.
REQUIRED: The weakness of a JIT inventory system.
DISCUSSION: JIT minimizes inventory by relying on coordination with suppliers to provide deliveries when they are needed for production. Consequently, inventory shortages are more likely. Thus, stockouts increase because the inventory buffer is reduced or eliminated.
Answer (A) is incorrect. JIT systems allow continuous production when inventory is delivered as needed; bottlenecks should not arise even if inventory is eliminated. **Answer (B) is incorrect.** JIT systems significantly reduce and sometimes eliminate carrying costs. **Answer (D) is incorrect.** Assuming demand and purchase price are constant, purchase costs often remain the same in a JIT systems.

14. Which of the following is **not** a characteristic of a just-in-time (JIT) inventory management system?

A. JIT relies on good quality materials.
B. JIT reorganizes the production process to eliminate waste of resources.
C. The lower inventory in a JIT system eliminates the need for some internal controls.
D. The number of suppliers is relatively large in a JIT system.

Answer (D) is correct.
REQUIRED: The characteristic of a JIT inventory management system.
DISCUSSION: In a JIT system, the dependability of suppliers is crucial. Organizations that adopt JIT systems therefore have strategic teaming agreements with a few, not many, carefully chosen suppliers who are extensively involved in the buyer's processes.
Answer (A) is incorrect. The focus of quality control under JIT changes from the discovery of defective parts to the prevention of quality problems. Zero machine breakdowns (achieved through preventive maintenance) and zero defects are ultimate goals. Because lower quality materials are more likely to be defective, JIT relies on good quality materials. **Answer (B) is incorrect.** JIT reorganizes the production process to eliminate waste of resources. JIT is a pull system. Items are pulled through production by current demand, not pushed through by anticipated demand. Thus, one operation produces only what is needed by the next operation, and components and materials arrive just in time to be used. **Answer (C) is incorrect.** The lower inventory in a JIT system eliminates the need for some internal controls. Frequent receipt of deliveries from suppliers often means less need for a sophisticated inventory control system and for control personnel.

15. A major benefit of computer-integrated manufacturing (CIM) is

A. Increased amount of scrap available for resale.
B. Increased working capital.
C. Delivery of customized products with long lead times.
D. Increased flexibility.

Answer (D) is correct.
REQUIRED: The benefit of CIM.
DISCUSSION: CIM is a comprehensive approach to manufacturing in which design is translated into product by centralized processing and robotics. CIM can help an organization reduce costs of spoilage, increase flexibility, and increase productivity. Flexibility is the key benefit. A traditional manufacturing system might become disrupted from an emergency change. But CIM reschedules everything in the plant when a priority requirement is inserted into the system.
Answer (A) is incorrect. CIM decreases the amount of scrap available for resale. **Answer (B) is incorrect.** CIM does not change working capital. **Answer (C) is incorrect.** CIM allows production of customized high quality products with short lead times.

11.5 Inventory Systems

16. The cost of materials has risen steadily over the year. Which of the following methods of estimating the ending balance of the materials inventory account will result in the highest profit, assuming all other variables remain constant?

A. Last-in, first-out (LIFO).
B. First-in, first-out (FIFO).
C. Weighted average.
D. Specific identification.

Answer (B) is correct.
REQUIRED: The inventory flow assumption yielding the highest profit given rising prices.
DISCUSSION: Profit is higher when cost of goods sold is lower, other factors held constant. Cost of goods sold equals beginning inventory, plus purchases, minus ending inventory. Accordingly, cost of goods sold will be lowest when the ending inventory is highest. In an inflationary environment, ending inventory is highest under FIFO. The older, less expensive items are deemed to have been sold, leaving the more expensive items in the ending inventory.
Answer (A) is incorrect. LIFO yields the lowest profit. **Answer (C) is incorrect.** In an inflationary environment, weighted average results in a lower profit than FIFO. **Answer (D) is incorrect.** Under specific identification, the newest (most expensive) items are not necessarily in the ending inventory. The result is a higher cost of goods sold and lower profit than under FIFO.

17. Which of the following changes in accounting policies resulting from a significant change in the expected pattern of economic benefit will increase profit?

A. A change from FIFO to LIFO inventory valuation when costs are rising.
B. A change from FIFO to weighted-average inventory valuation when costs are falling.
C. A change from accelerated to straight-line depreciation in the later years of the depreciable lives of the assets.
D. A change from straight-line to accelerated depreciation in the early years of the depreciable lives of the assets.

Answer (B) is correct.
REQUIRED: The change in principle that increases retained earnings.
DISCUSSION: In a period of falling costs, FIFO results in higher cost of goods sold than the weighted-average method. FIFO includes the higher, earlier costs in cost of goods sold, and the weighted-average method averages the later, lower costs with the higher, earlier costs. Thus, a change from FIFO to weighted-average costing reduces cost of goods sold and increases reported profit.
Answer (A) is incorrect. If costs are rising, applying LIFO (last in, first out) expenses the more recently acquired and more costly inventory items. Its effect is to reduce profit compared with FIFO, which expenses the earlier acquired and less costly items (a change to LIFO is allowed under U.S. GAAP but not IFRS). **Answer (C) is incorrect.** In the later years of the depreciable life of an asset, accelerated depreciation results in lower depreciation expense than does the straight-line method. A change to straight line increases depreciation expense and reduces reported profit. **Answer (D) is incorrect.** In the early years of the depreciable life of an asset, straight-line depreciation results in lower depreciation expense than accelerated depreciation. A change to accelerated depreciation increases depreciation expense and reduces reported profit.

18. Which inventory pricing method generally approximates current cost for each of the following?

	Ending Inventory	Cost of Goods Sold
A.	FIFO	FIFO
B.	LIFO	FIFO
C.	FIFO	LIFO
D.	LIFO	LIFO

Answer (C) is correct.
REQUIRED: The inventory pricing method.
DISCUSSION: FIFO assigns the most recent acquisition costs to ending inventory and the earliest acquisition costs to cost of goods sold. LIFO assigns the earliest acquisition costs to ending inventory (it is permitted by U.S. GAAP but not by IFRS). Thus, FIFO approximates current cost for ending inventory, and LIFO approximates current cost of goods sold.
Answer (A) is incorrect. LIFO approximates current cost of goods sold. Answer (B) is incorrect. FIFO approximates current cost for ending inventory, and LIFO approximates current cost of goods sold. Answer (D) is incorrect. FIFO approximates current cost for ending inventory.

19. If ending inventory is underestimated due to an error in the physical count of items on hand, the cost of goods sold for the period will be <List A> and net earnings will be <List B>.

	List A	List B
A.	Underestimated	Underestimated
B.	Underestimated	Overestimated
C.	Overestimated	Underestimated
D.	Overestimated	Overestimated

Answer (C) is correct.
REQUIRED: The effect of underestimating ending inventory.
DISCUSSION: Cost of goods sold equals beginning inventory, plus purchases, minus ending inventory. If ending inventory is underestimated, cost of goods sold will be overestimated for the period. If cost of goods sold is overestimated, net earnings for the period will be underestimated.
Answer (A) is incorrect. Cost of goods sold will be overestimated. Answer (B) is incorrect. Cost of goods sold will be overestimated and profit will be underestimated. Answer (D) is incorrect. Net earnings will be underestimated.

20. If certain goods owned by an entity were **not** recorded as a purchase and were **not** counted in ending inventory, in error, then

A. Cost of goods sold for the period will be understated.
B. Cost of goods sold for the period will be overstated.
C. Net income for the period will be understated.
D. There will be no effect on cost of goods sold or profit for the period.

Answer (D) is correct.
REQUIRED: The effect of failing to record a purchase or to count the goods in inventory.
DISCUSSION: The effects of the errors on cost of goods sold are offsetting. Purchases, which increase cost of goods sold, and ending inventory, which decreases cost of goods sold, are understated by the same amount. Neither cost of goods sold nor net income is affected.
Answer (A) is incorrect. Cost of goods is not understated because the errors offset each other. Answer (B) is incorrect. Cost of goods is not overstated because the errors offset each other. Answer (C) is incorrect. Cost of goods sold is unaffected by the error, so net income is also unaffected.

STUDY UNIT TWELVE
CAPITAL STRUCTURE AND BUDGET, BASIC TAXATION, AND TRANSFER PRICING

(30 pages of outline)

12.1	Corporate Capital Structure -- Debt Financing	397
12.2	Corporate Capital Structure -- Equity Financing	400
12.3	Corporate Capital Structure -- Cost of Capital	404
12.4	Capital Budgeting	408
12.5	Short-Term Financing	414
12.6	Methods of Taxation	418
12.7	Transfer Pricing	422

This study unit is the fourth of six covering **Domain IV: Financial Management** from The IIA's CIA Exam Syllabus. This domain makes up 20% of Part 3 of the CIA exam and is tested at the **basic** and **proficient** cognitive levels. Refer to the complete syllabus located in Appendix A to view the relevant sections covered in Study Unit 12.

SUCCESS TIP: The majority of financial management questions on the CIA exam test conceptual understanding, not the ability to perform calculations. However, many of our financial management questions require you to perform calculations. They are an effective means of reinforcing your conceptual knowledge.

12.1 CORPORATE CAPITAL STRUCTURE -- DEBT FINANCING

1. **Debt vs. Equity**

   a. The balance sheet reports the firm's resources and its capital structure. Resources consist of the assets the firm used to earn a return. The capital structure consists of the amounts contributed by creditors (debt) and owners (equity).

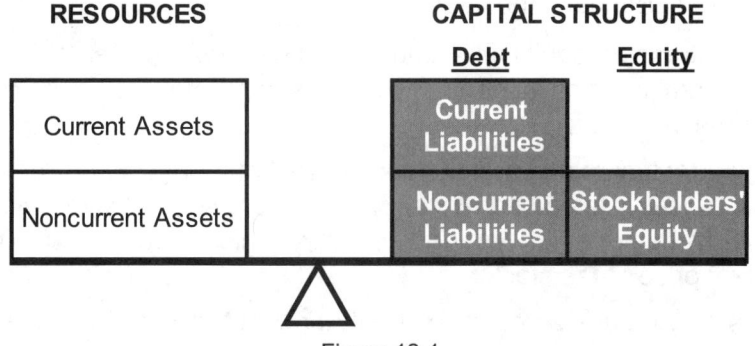

   Figure 12-1

   1) Each firm must determine the appropriate mix of debt and equity in the capital structure. Each component has a cost that changes as economic conditions change and as more or less of that component is used.

2. **Aspects of Bonds**

    a. Bonds are the principal form of long-term debt financing for corporations and governmental entities.

        1) A bond is a formal contractual obligation to pay an amount of money (par value, maturity amount, or face amount) to the holder at a certain date. Also, most bonds provide for a series of cash interest payments based on a specified percentage (stated rate or coupon rate) of the face amount at specified intervals.

        2) The agreement is stated in a legal document called an **indenture**.

    b. In general, the longer the term of a bond, the higher the return (yield) demanded by investors to compensate for increased risk. This relationship is the **term structure of interest rates**. It is depicted graphically by the yield curve.

    Positive (Normal) Yield Curve

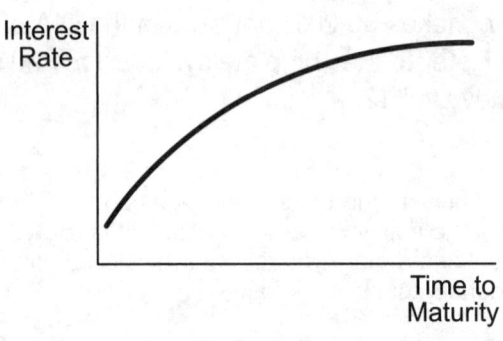

    Figure 12-2

    c. An indenture may require the issuer to maintain a **bond sinking fund**. The objective of the fund is to accumulate sufficient assets, including earnings of the fund, to pay the bond principal at maturity.

    d. Advantages of Bonds to the Issuer

        1) Interest paid on debt is tax deductible (the tax shield).
        2) Basic control of the firm is not shared with debtholders.

    e. Disadvantages of Bonds to the Issuer

        1) Unlike returns on equity investments, the payment of interest and principal on debt is a contractual obligation. If cash flow is insufficient to service debt, the firm could become insolvent.

        2) The contractual requirement to pay interest and principal increases a firm's risk and reduces retained earnings. Shareholders consequently will demand higher capitalization rates on retained earnings, which may result in a decline in the market price of the stock.

        3) Bonds may require some collateral that restricts the entity's assets.

        4) The amount of debt financing available to the individual firm is limited. Generally accepted standards of the investment community usually dictate a certain debt-equity ratio for an individual firm. Beyond this limit, the cost of debt may rise rapidly, or debt may not be available.

3. **Types of Bonds**
    a. Maturity Pattern
        1) A **term bond** has a single maturity date at the end of its term.
        2) A **serial bond** matures in stated amounts at regular intervals.
    b. Valuation
        1) **Variable (or floating) rate bonds** pay interest that is dependent on market conditions.
        2) **Zero-coupon or deep-discount bonds** bear no stated rate of interest and involve no periodic cash payments. The interest component consists entirely of the bond's discount.
        3) **Commodity-backed bonds** are payable at prices related to a commodity such as gold.
    c. Redemption Provisions
        1) **Callable bonds** may be repurchased by the issuer at a specified price before maturity. During a period of falling interest rates, the issuer can replace old high-interest debt with new low-interest debt. Callable bonds typically have higher interest rates than comparable noncallable bonds.
        2) **Convertible bonds** may be converted into equity securities of the issuer at the option of the holder under certain conditions. The ability to become equity holders is an inducement to potential investors, allowing the issuer to offer a lower coupon rate.
    d. Securitization
        1) **Mortgage bonds** are backed by specific assets, usually real estate.
        2) **Debentures** are backed by the borrower's general credit but not by specific collateral.
    e. Ownership
        1) **Registered bonds** are issued in the name of the holder. Only the registered holder may receive interest and principal payments.
        2) **Bearer bonds** are not individually registered. Interest and principal are paid to whoever presents the bond.
    f. Priority
        1) **Subordinated debentures** and second mortgage bonds are junior securities with claims inferior to those of senior bonds.
    g. Repayment Provisions
        1) **Income bonds** pay interest contingent on the issuer's profitability.
        2) **Revenue bonds** are issued by governmental units and are payable from specific revenue sources.

400   SU 12: Capital Structure and Budget, Basic Taxation, and Transfer Pricing

4. **Bond Ratings**

   a. Investors can judge the creditworthiness of a bond issue by consulting the rating assigned by a credit-rating agency. The higher the rating, the more likely the firm will pay the interest and principal.

   b. The three largest firms are Moody's, Standard & Poor's, and Fitch.

      1) **Investment-grade bonds** are safe investments and have the lowest yields. The highest rating assigned is AAA. Some fiduciary organizations (such as banks and insurance companies) are allowed to invest only in investment-grade bonds.

      2) **Noninvestment grade bonds**, also called speculative-grade bonds, high-yield bonds, or junk bonds, have high risk. Ratings range from BB+ to DDD.

STOP & REVIEW

You have completed the outline for this subunit.
Study multiple-choice questions 1 through 3 on page 427.

12.2 CORPORATE CAPITAL STRUCTURE -- EQUITY FINANCING

1. **Relevant Terminology**

   a. The most widely used classes of stock are common and preferred. The following basic terminology is related to stock.

      1) Stock **authorized** is the maximum amount of stock that a corporation is legally allowed to issue.

      2) Stock **issued** is the amount of stock authorized that has actually been issued by the corporation.

      3) Stock **outstanding** is the amount of stock issued that has been purchased and is held by shareholders. It excludes treasury stock.

2. **Common Stock**

   a. The **common shareholders** are the owners of the firm. They have voting rights, and they select the firm's board of directors and vote on resolutions. Common shareholders are not entitled to dividends unless so declared by the board of directors. A firm may choose not to declare any.

      1) Common shareholders are entitled to receive **liquidating distributions** only after all other claims have been satisfied, including those of preferred shareholders.

      2) Common shareholders ordinarily have **preemptive rights**.

         a) Preemptive rights give current common shareholders the right to purchase any additional stock issuances in proportion to their ownership percentages. This way the preemptive rights safeguard a common shareholder's proportionate interest in the firm.

      3) Equity ownership involves risk because shareholders are not guaranteed a return.

b. **Advantages to the Issuer**
   1) Dividends are not fixed. They are paid from profits when available.
   2) They have no fixed maturity date for repayment of the capital.
   3) The sale of common shares increases the creditworthiness of the entity by providing more equity.

c. **Disadvantages to the Issuer**
   1) New common shares dilute earnings per share available to existing shareholders because of the greater number of shares outstanding.
   2) Underwriting costs (costs of issuing common shares) are typically higher for shares than other forms of financing.
   3) Too much equity may raise the average cost of capital of the entity above its optimal level.
   4) Cash dividends on common shares are not tax-deductible. They must be paid out of after-tax profits.

d. **Common Stock Valuation** Based on Dividend Yield Models
   1) When the dividend per share of common stock is constant and expected to be paid continuously, the price per share is calculated as follows:

   $$P_0 = D \div r$$

   P_0 = Current price per share
   D = Dividend per share (constant)
   r = Required rate of return (cost of common stock)

   2) The **constant growth model** (dividend discount model) assumes that the dividend per share and price per share grow at the same constant rate. The price per share can be calculated as follows:

   $$P_0 = \frac{D_0(1+g)}{r-g} = \frac{D_1}{r-g}$$

   P_0 = Current price per share
   D_0 = Current dividend per share
   D_1 = Dividend per share expected next year
   r = Required rate of return (cost of common stock)
   g = Growth rate (constant)

   a) According to this model, the market value of an entity's outstanding stock is higher if investors have a lower required return on equity.

EXAMPLE 12-1 Constant Growth Model

A company pays dividends of US $10 per share. The dividends are expected to grow at a constant rate of 5% per year. If the investors' required rate of return is 8%, the current market value of the company's shares will be US $350.

$$P_0 = \frac{D_0(1+g)}{r-g} = \frac{US\ \$10(1+5\%)}{8\% - 5\%} = US\ \$350$$

---

   3) The required rate of return (the cost of common stock) can be derived from the dividend growth model.

   $$r = \frac{D_1}{P_0} + g$$

   4) The price per share (P_0) upon issuance equals the net proceeds from the issuance (Gross proceeds – Flotation costs). Flotation costs also are called issuance costs.

3. **Preferred Stock**

    a. Preferred stock has features of debt and equity. It has a fixed charge, but payment of dividends is not an obligation.

        1) Debt holders have priority over preferred shareholders in liquidation.

    b. Advantages to the Issuer

        1) Preferred stock is a form of equity and therefore increases the creditworthiness of the entity.

        2) Control is still held by common shareholders. Preferred shareholders generally do not have voting rights.

        3) Preferred stock does not require periodic payments, and failure to pay dividends will not lead to bankruptcy.

    c. Disadvantages to the Issuer

        1) Cash dividends paid are not deductible as a tax expense. They must be paid out of after-tax profits.

        2) In periods of economic difficulty, cumulative (past) dividends may create major managerial and financial problems for the firm.

    d. Typical Provisions of Preferred Stock Issues

        1) Par value. Par value is the liquidation value, and a percentage of par equals the preferred dividend.

        2) Priority in assets and earnings. If the entity goes bankrupt, the preferred shareholders have priority over common shareholders.

        3) Accumulation of dividends. If preferred dividends are cumulative, dividends in arrears must be paid before any common dividends can be paid.

        4) Convertibility. Preferred share issues may be convertible into common shares at the option of the shareholder.

        5) Participation. Preferred shares may receive the entity's earnings beyond the stated dividend level. For example, 8% participating preferred shares might pay a dividend each year greater than 8% when the entity is extremely profitable. But nonparticipating preferred shares will receive no more than is stated on the face of the share.

e. **Preferred Stock Valuation**

1) The future cash flows from the preferred stock are assumed to consist only of the estimated future annual dividends (D_p).

$$D_p = \text{Par value of preferred stock} \times \text{Preferred dividend rate}$$

2) The discount rate used is the investor's required rate of return (r).
3) Unlike a bond, which has a specific maturity date, preferred stock is assumed to be outstanding in perpetuity.

$$\text{Preferred stock price } (P_p) = \frac{D_p}{r}$$

EXAMPLE 12-2   Preferred Stock Valuation

The value of a share of preferred stock with a par value of US $100 and a dividend rate of 5% to an investor with a required rate of return of 10% is US $50 [($100 × 5%) ÷ 10%].

---

4. **Debt vs. Equity Financing**

   a. The main differences between debt financing (involving the payment of interest) and equity financing (involving the payment of dividends) can be summarized as follows:

	Equity Financing	Debt Financing
Effect on company's control	Yes	No
Cost of issuance	Higher	Lower
Effect on net income	No	Yes
Dilution of EPS	Yes	No
Effect on solvency risk	No	Yes
Tax deductibility of payments	No	Yes

5. **Cost of New Equity Financing**

   a. The cost of new equity is calculated by adding the expected dividend yield, based on the net proceeds of the new issue, to the expected dividend growth rate.

   1) The expected dividend at the end of the period equals the dividend at time zero times one plus the expected dividend growth rate.
   2) Net proceeds received by the entity when issuing one common share equals the market price of a share times one minus the flotation cost percentage.

      a) Flotation costs include items such as underwriting fees, printing, and advertising.
      b) The calculation of the cost of new equity is as follows:

      $$\frac{\text{Expected dividend at end of period}}{\text{Net proceeds of issuing one share}} + \text{Dividend growth rate}$$

STOP & REVIEW

You have completed the outline for this subunit.
Study multiple-choice questions 4 through 6 beginning on page 428.

12.3 CORPORATE CAPITAL STRUCTURE -- COST OF CAPITAL

1. **Overview**
    a. Investors provide funds to corporations with the understanding that management will use the funds to provide a return to investors.
        1) If management does not provide the investors' required rate of return, the investors will sell their stock on the secondary market, causing the value of the stock to drop. Creditors then demand higher rates on the firm's debt.
        2) For this reason, the investors' required rate of return (also called their opportunity cost of capital) becomes the firm's cost of capital.
    b. A firm's cost of capital is used to discount the future cash flows of long-term projects. Investments with a rate of return higher than the cost of capital increase the value of the firm and shareholders' wealth. (The cost of capital is not used in working capital finance because short-term needs are met with short-term funds.)
        1) Providers of equity capital are exposed to more risk than lenders because
            a) The firm is not required to pay them a return and
            b) Creditors have priority in case of liquidation.
        2) To compensate for this higher risk, equity investors demand a higher return, making equity financing more expensive than debt.

2. **Component Costs of Capital**
    a. A firm's financing structure consists of three components: long-term debt, preferred equity, and common equity (including retained earnings).
        1) The rate of return demanded by holders of each is the component cost for that form of capital.
    b. The component cost of **long-term debt** is the after-tax interest rate on the debt (interest payments are tax-deductible by the firm).

    $$\text{Effective rate} \times (1.0 - \text{Marginal tax rate})$$

    c. The component cost of **preferred stock** is calculated using the dividend yield ratio.

    $$\text{Cash dividend on preferred stock} \div \text{Market price of preferred stock}$$

    1) The market price of preferred stock upon issuance equals the net proceeds from the issuance (Gross proceeds – Flotation costs). Flotation costs, also called issuance costs, reduce the net proceeds received, thereby raising the cost of capital.

d. Generally, the component cost of **retained earnings** is considered to be the same as that for common stock (if the firm cannot find a profitable use for retained earnings, it should be distributed to the common shareholders in the from of dividends so that they can find their own alternative investments).

   1) While internally generated capital provides a supply of needed capital, a firm cannot rely solely on retained earnings to fund new projects. The cost of **external** common stock (also known as the cost of new common stock) anticipates that common shareholders will demand steadily increasing dividends over time. The firm also incurs issuance costs when raising new, outside funds. Therefore, the cost of retained earnings will be lower than the cost of external common stock.

EXAMPLE 12-3   Component Costs of Capital

A company has outstanding bonds with a coupon rate of 7% and an effective rate of 5%. The company's 9%, US $60 par-value preferred stock is currently trading at US $67.50 per share, while its US $1 par-value common stock trades at US $1.40 per share and pays a 14% dividend. The applicable tax rate is 35%.

The company's component costs of capital are calculated as follows:

Long-Term Debt	Preferred Equity	Common Equity
Cost = Effective rate × (1.0 − Tax rate)	Cost = Cash dividend ÷ Market price	Cost = Cash dividend ÷ Market price
= 5% × (1.0 − .35)	= (US $60 × 9%) ÷ $67.50	= (US $1 × 14%) ÷ $1.40
= 5% × .65	= US $5.40 ÷ $67.50	= US $.14 ÷ $1.40
= 3.25%	= 8%	= 10%

---

3. **Weighted-Average Cost of Capital (WACC)**

   a. Corporate management usually designates a target capital structure for the firm, i.e., the proportion of each component of capital.

   b. A firm's WACC is one composite rate of return on its combined components of capital. The weights are based on the firm's target capital structure.

EXAMPLE 12-4   Weighted-Average Cost of Capital (WACC)

Using the data from Example 12-3, the company has set a target capital structure of 20% long-term debt, 30% preferred equity, and 50% common equity. The weighted-average cost of capital can thus be calculated as follows:

	Target Weight		Cost of Capital		Weighted Cost
Long-term debt	20%	×	3.25%	=	0.65%
Preferred equity	30%	×	8%	=	2.40%
Common equity	50%	×	10%	=	5.00%
					8.05%

4. **Impact of Income Taxes on Capital Structure and Capital Decisions**
    a. Taxes are an important consideration because they can be anywhere from 25% to 50% of all costs.
    b. Corporate capital gains are taxed at a regular rate, and the capital gains of individuals are currently 16% or less.
    c. A dividends-received deduction renders free from taxation anywhere from 70% to 100% of dividends received by one company from investments in the stock of another company. This deduction prevents or reduces double taxation. It also encourages one company to invest in the stock of another company. However, a conflict may arise between the desires of corporate owners and individual owners in that individuals may sometimes prefer capital gains, while corporate owners would prefer dividends.
    d. Interest is a tax-deductible expense of the debtor company, but dividends are not deductible. Thus, a company needing capital would prefer to issue bonds rather than stock because the interest would be deductible. As a result, the issuer would prefer to issue debt because the interest is deductible, but the investor would prefer stock because interest on debt is fully taxable while the return on stock is only partially taxable or taxable at special low rates. Similarly, a corporation may be reluctant to issue common stock because it does not want to share control of the company, but the investor may prefer stock because of the favorable tax treatment.
    e. Multinational corporations frequently derive income from several countries. The government of each country in which a corporation does business may enact statutes imposing one or more types of tax on the corporation, so any capital decision affecting multiple countries must consider the tax provisions of each nation.

5. **Optimal Capital Structure**
    a. Standard financial theory provides a model for the optimal capital structure of every firm. This model holds that shareholder wealth-maximization results from **minimizing the weighted-average cost of capital**. Thus, management should not focus only on maximizing earnings per share. (EPS can be increased by assuming more debt, but debt increases risk.)
        1) The relevant relationships are depicted below:

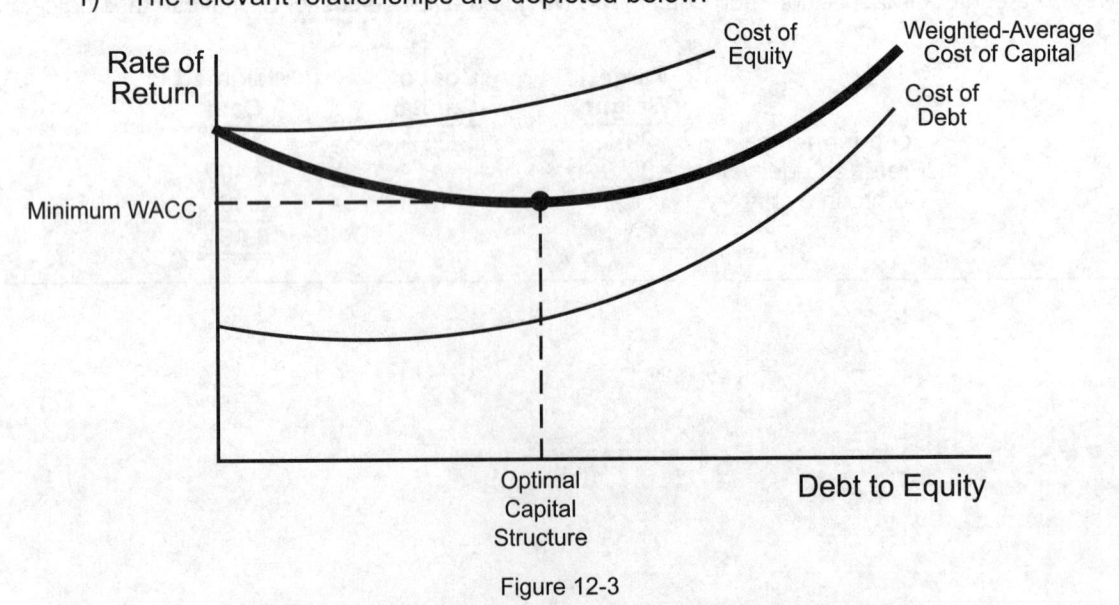

Figure 12-3

        a) Ordinarily, firms cannot identify this optimal point precisely. They should attempt to find an optimal range for the capital structure.

6. Marginal Cost of Capital

a. The marginal cost of capital (MCC) is the cost to the entity of the next monetary unit of new capital raised after existing internal sources are exhausted. Each additional monetary unit raised becomes increasingly expensive as investors demand higher returns to compensate for increased risk.

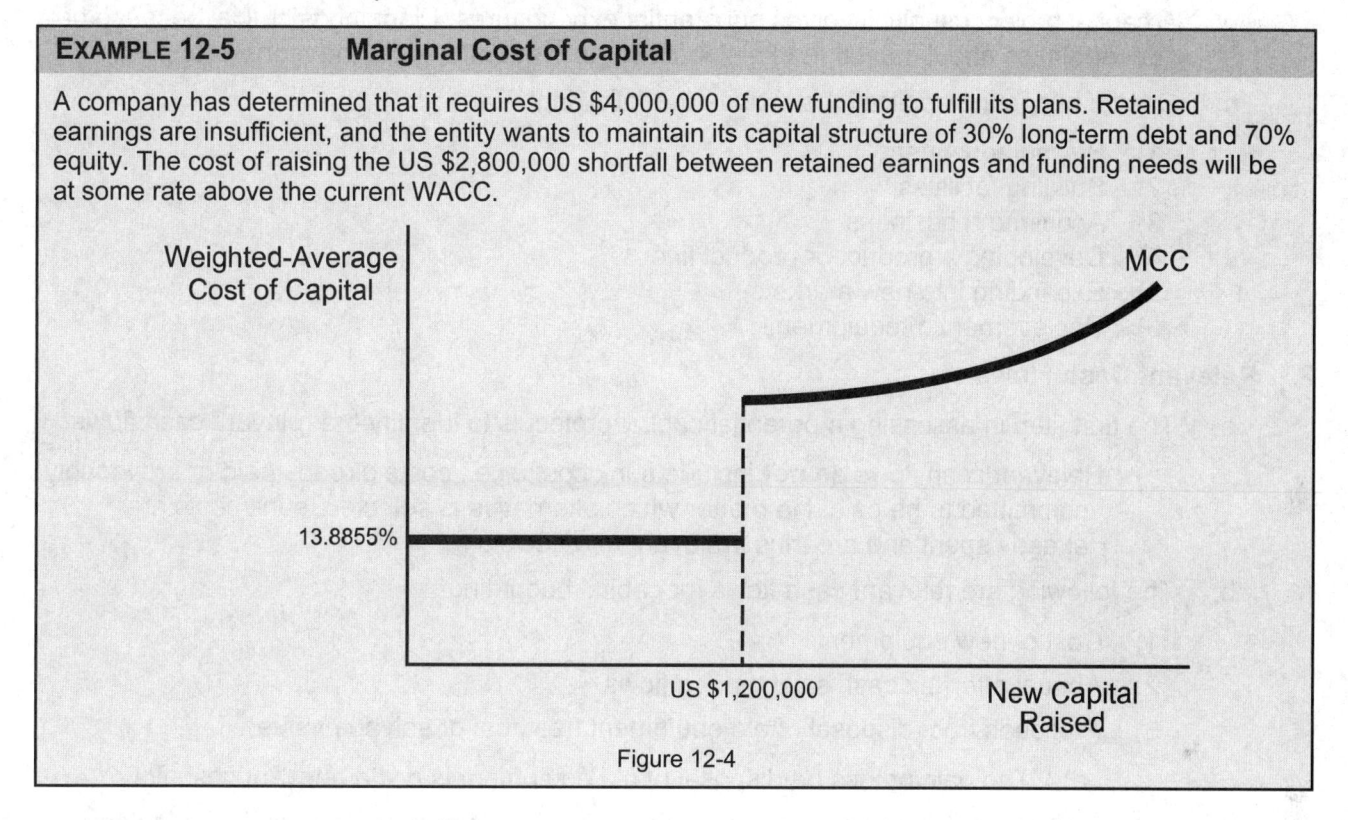

EXAMPLE 12-5 — Marginal Cost of Capital

A company has determined that it requires US $4,000,000 of new funding to fulfill its plans. Retained earnings are insufficient, and the entity wants to maintain its capital structure of 30% long-term debt and 70% equity. The cost of raising the US $2,800,000 shortfall between retained earnings and funding needs will be at some rate above the current WACC.

Figure 12-4

You have completed the outline for this subunit.
Study multiple-choice questions 7 through 9 beginning on page 429.

STOP & REVIEW

12.4 CAPITAL BUDGETING

1. **Capital Budgeting Basics**

   a. Capital budgeting is the process of planning and controlling investments for long-term projects.

   b. A capital project usually involves substantial expenditures. Planning is crucial because of uncertainties about capital markets, inflation, interest rates, and the money supply.

   c. Capital budgeting applications include the following:

      1) Buying equipment
      2) Building facilities
      3) Acquiring a business
      4) Developing a product or product line
      5) Expanding into new markets
      6) Replacement of equipment

2. **Relevant Cash Flows**

   a. The first step in assessing a potential capital project is to identify the relevant cash flows.

      1) Relevant cash flows do **not** include sunk costs, i.e., costs already paid or irrevocably committed to be paid. No matter which alternative is selected, sunk costs are already spent and are thus irrelevant to a decision.

   b. The following are relevant cash flows for capital budgeting:

      1) Cost of new equipment
      2) Annual after-tax cash savings or inflows
      3) Proceeds from disposal of old equipment (residual or salvage value)

         a) The gain or loss on disposal of old equipment is **not** a relevant cash flow.

      4) Adjustment for depreciation expense on new equipment (the depreciation tax shield that reduces taxable income and cash outflows for tax expense)

   c. As Example 12-6 on the following page indicates, tax considerations are essential when considering capital projects.

EXAMPLE 12-6   Projected Relevant Cash Flows

A company is determining the relevant cash flows for a potential capital project. The company has a 40% tax rate.

Net initial investment:

1) The project will require an initial outlay of US $500,000 for new equipment.
2) The company expects to commit US $12,000 of working capital for the duration of the project in the form of increased accounts receivable and inventories.
3) Calculating the after-tax proceeds from disposal of the existing equipment is a two-step process.

   a) First, the tax gain or loss is determined.

Disposal value	US $ 5,000
Less: Tax basis	(20,000)
Tax-basis loss on disposal	**US $(15,000)**

   b) The after-tax effect on cash can then be calculated.

Disposal value	US $ 5,000
Add: Tax savings on loss (US $15,000 × .40)	6,000
After-tax cash inflow from disposal	**US $11,000**

4) The cash outflow required for this project's net initial investment is therefore US $(501,000) [$(500,000) + $(12,000) + $11,000].

Annual net cash flows:

1) The project is expected to generate US $100,000 annually from ongoing operations.

   a) However, 40% of this will have to be paid out in the form of income taxes.

Annual cash collections	US $100,000
Less: Income tax expense (US $100,000 × .40)	(40,000)
After-tax cash inflow from operations	**US $ 60,000**

2) The project is slated to last 8 years.

   a) The new equipment is projected to have a salvage value of US $50,000 and will generate US $62,500 ($500,000 ÷ 8) per year in depreciation charges. The annual savings is US $25,000 [($62,500 – $0) × .40].
   b) Unlike the income from operations, the depreciation charges will generate a tax savings. This is referred to as the **depreciation tax shield**.

3) The annual net cash inflow from the project is thus US $85,000 ($60,000 + $25,000) for the last 8 years.

Project termination cash flows:

1) Proceeds of US $50,000 are expected from disposal of the new equipment at the end of the project.

   a) First, the tax gain or loss is determined.

Disposal value	US $50,000
Less: Tax basis	0
Tax-basis gain on disposal	**US $50,000**

   b) The after-tax effect on cash can then be calculated.

Tax basis gain on disposal	US $50,000
Less: Tax liability on gain (US $50,000 × .40)	(20,000)
After-tax cash inflow from disposal	**US $30,000**

2) Once the project is over, the company will recover the US $12,000 of working capital committed to it.
3) The net cash inflow upon project termination is therefore US $42,000 ($30,000 + $12,000).

3. **Net Present Value (NPV)**

   a. The net present value (NPV) method discounts the relevant cash flows using the required rate of return. This rate also is called the hurdle rate or opportunity cost of capital.

   b. A capital project's NPV is the difference between the present value of the net cash savings or inflows expected over the life of the project and the required monetary investment.

      1) If the difference is positive, the project should be undertaken. If the difference is negative, it should be rejected.

EXAMPLE 12-7   NPV

The Juan Fangio Co. is considering the purchase of a machine for US $250,000 that will have a useful life of 10 years with no residual (salvage) value. The machine is expected to generate an annual operating cash savings of US $60,000 over its useful life and would be depreciated on the straight-line basis, resulting in annual depreciation expense of US $25,000 ($250,000 ÷ 10 years). Fangio's internal rate of return is 12%, and its effective tax rate is 40%.

The present value of US $1 for 10 periods at 12% is 0.322, and the present value of an ordinary annuity of US $1 for 10 periods at 12% is 5.650. Fangio calculates the net present value of this potential investment as follows:

Present value of cash savings		
Annual operating cash savings/inflows		US $ 60,000
Annual tax expense:		
Tax expense on annual cash savings (60,000 × 40%)	US $(24,000)	
Depreciation tax shield (25,000 × 40%)	10,000	(14,000)
After-tax net annual cash savings		US $ 46,000
Times: PV factor for an ordinary annuity		× 5.650
Present value of net cash savings		US $259,900
Required investment		
Cost of new equipment		US $250,000
Net present value of investment		
Present value of net cash savings		US $259,900
Less: Required investment		(250,000)
Net present value of investment		US $ 9,900

The positive net present value indicates that the project should be undertaken.

---

   c. Use of the NPV method implicitly assumes that cash flows are reinvested at the entity's minimum required rate of return.

4. Internal Rate of Return (IRR)

a. The IRR of a project is the discount rate at which the investment's NPV equals zero. The IRR equates the present value of the expected cash inflows with the present value of the expected cash outflows.

   1) If the IRR is higher than the hurdle rate, the investment is desirable. If it is lower, the project should be rejected.

   IRR > Hurdle rate: Accept project

   IRR < Hurdle rate: Reject project

EXAMPLE 12-8   IRR

John Lauda, Inc., has a hurdle rate of 12% for all capital projects. The firm is considering a project that calls for a cash outlay of US $200,000 that will create savings in after-tax cash costs of US $52,000 for each of the next 5 years. The applicable present value factor is 3.846 (US $200,000 ÷ $52,000). Consulting a table of present value factors for an ordinary annuity for 5 periods places this factor between 9% and 10%. Lauda's hurdle rate is 12%, so the project should be rejected.

---

5. NPV vs. IRR

a. The reinvestment rate is important when choosing between the NPV and IRR methods.

   1) NPV assumes the cash flows from the investment can be reinvested at the project's discount rate, that is, the desired rate of return.

   2) The IRR method assumes that cash flows will be reinvested at the IRR.

      a) If the project's funds are not reinvested at the IRR, the ranking calculations obtained may be in error.

      b) The NPV method is preferable in many decision situations because the reinvestment is assumed to be at the desired rate of return.

b. The NPV and IRR methods give the same accept or reject decision if projects are independent. Independent projects have unrelated cash flows. Thus, all acceptable independent projects can be undertaken.

   1) However, if projects are **mutually exclusive**, only one project can be accepted. The others must be rejected.

   2) The NPV and IRR methods may rank projects differently if

      a) The cost of one project is greater than the cost of another.
      b) The timing, amounts, and directions of cash flows differ among projects.
      c) The projects have different useful lives.
      d) The cost of capital or desired rate of return varies over the life of a project. The NPV can easily be determined using different desired rates of return for different periods. The IRR determines one rate for the project.
      e) Multiple investments are involved in a project. NPV amounts are cumulative, but IRR rates are not. The IRR for the whole is not the sum of the IRRs for the parts.

6. **Payback Period**

   a. The payback period is the number of years required for the net cash savings or inflows to equal the original investment, i.e., the time necessary for an investment to pay for itself.

      1) Companies using the payback method set a maximum length of time within which projects must pay for themselves to be considered acceptable.

   b. If the cash flows are constant, the formula is

   $$\text{Payback period} = \frac{\text{Initial investment}}{\text{Annual after-tax cash savings or inflows}}$$

      1) This method ignores the time value of money.

   EXAMPLE 12-9   Payback Period -- Constant Cash Flows

   Using the data from Example 12-8, John Lauda also applies a 4-year payback period test on all capital projects.

   Payback period = US $200,000 ÷ $52,000 = 3.846 years

   Judged by this criterion, the project is acceptable because its payback period is less than the company's maximum.

   ---

   c. If the cash flows are not constant, the calculation must be in cumulative form.

   EXAMPLE 12-10   Payback Period -- Variable Cash Flows

   Assume that John Lauda's initial investment is US $160,000 and that, instead of the smooth inflows predicted in Example 12-8, the project's cash stream is expected to vary. The payback period is calculated as follows:

End of Year	Cash Savings	Remaining Initial Investment
Initial investment	US $ --	US $160,000
Year 1	48,000	112,000
Year 2	54,000	58,000
Year 3	54,000	4,000
Year 4	60,000	--

   The project is acceptable because its payback period is over 3 years and under 4 years and is less than the company's maximum.

   ---

   d. The advantage of the payback method is its simplicity.

      1) To some extent, the payback period measures risk. The longer the period, the more risky the investment.

   e. The payback method has the following two significant disadvantages:

      1) It does not recognize the time value of money. Weighting all cash inflows equally ignores the benefits of early receipts and delayed payments.

      2) It neglects total project profitability by disregarding all cash inflows after the payback cutoff date. Applying a single cutoff date to every project results in accepting many marginal projects and rejecting good ones.

7. **Accounting Rate of Return**

   a. The accounting rate of return is a measure used to assess potential capital projects that ignores the time value of money.

   $$\text{Accounting rate of return} = \frac{\text{Annual GAAP net income}}{\text{Required investment}} = \frac{\text{Annual cash inflow} - \text{Depreciation}}{\text{Initial investment}}$$

> **EXAMPLE 12-11   Accounting Rate of Return**
>
> A manufacturer is considering the purchase of a new piece of machinery that would cost US $250,000 and would decrease annual after-tax cash costs by US $40,000. The machine is expected to have a 10-year useful life, no salvage value, and would be depreciated on the straight-line basis. The firm calculates the accounting rate of return on this machine as follows:
>
> | | |
> |---|---:|
> | Annual cash savings | US $ 40,000 |
> | Minus: Annual depreciation expense (US $250,000 ÷ 10 years) | (25,000) |
> | Annual accounting net income | US $ 15,000 |
> | Divided by: Purchase price of new equipment | ÷ 250,000 |
> | Accounting rate of return | 6% |

1) The advantage of this method is that the financial statements are readily available.
2) The disadvantages of this method are that financial statements (a) are affected by the company's choices of accounting methods and (b) do not represent cash flows.

8. **Economic Value Added**

    a. Economic value added (EVA) is the formula for residual income adjusted for the opportunity cost of capital.

    b. The basic formula can be stated as follows:

After-tax operating income	US $XXX,XXX
Investment (capital used) × Cost of capital (WACC)	(XX,XXX)
Economic value added	US $ XX,XXX

> **EXAMPLE 12-12   Economic Value Added**
>
> A company invested US $200,000 in a new operating segment. The current-year net income of the segment was US $21,000. The company's cost of capital is 9%.
>
> | | |
> |---|---:|
> | Net income | US $21,000 |
> | Investment × Cost of capital (US $200,000 × 9%) | (18,000) |
> | Economic value added | US $ 3,000 |
>
> The economic value is positive. Thus, the investment in a new operating segment increased shareholder value.

   c. EVA is a business unit's true economic profit primarily because a charge for the cost of equity capital is implicit in the cost of capital.

      1) The cost of equity is an opportunity cost, that is, the return that could have been obtained on the best alternative investment of similar risk.
      2) EVA measures the marginal benefit obtained by using resources in a given way. It is useful for determining whether a segment of a business is increasing shareholder value.

STOP & REVIEW
You have completed the outline for this subunit.
Study multiple-choice questions 10 and 11 on page 430.

12.5 SHORT-TERM FINANCING

1. **Spontaneous Financing -- Trade Credit**

   a. All entities require financing from outside sources to carry on day-to-day operations. These usually are spontaneous financing in the form of trade credit offered by vendors or bank loans.

   b. If a supplier offers an early payment discount (e.g., terms of 2/10, n/30, meaning a 2% discount is given if the invoice is paid within 10 days or the entire balance is due in 30 days), the entity ordinarily should take the discount. The annualized cost of not taking a discount can be calculated with the following formula:

   Cost of Not Taking a Discount

   $$\frac{\text{Discount \%}}{100\% - \text{Discount \%}} \times \frac{\text{Days in year}}{\text{Total payment period} - \text{Discount period}}$$

   > **EXAMPLE 12-13   Cost of Not Taking a Discount**
   >
   > A vendor has delivered goods and invoiced the company on terms of 2/10, net 30. The company has chosen to pay on day 30. The effective annual rate the company paid by forgoing the discount is calculated as follows (using a 360-day year):
   >
   > Cost of not taking discount = [2% ÷ (100% − 2%)] × [360 days ÷ (30 days − 10 days)]
   > = (2% ÷ 98%) × (360 days ÷ 20 days)
   > = 2.0408% × 18
   > = 36.73%
   >
   > Only entities in dire cash flow situations would incur a 36.73% cost of funds.

2. **Formal Financing Arrangements**

   a. Commercial banks offer short-term financing in the form of term loans and lines of credit.

      1) A **term loan**, such as a note, must be repaid by a definite time.

      2) A **line of credit** allows the company to reborrow amounts continuously up to a certain ceiling if certain minimum payments are made each month.

         a) A line of credit may have a definite term, or it may be revolving; that is, the borrower can continuously pay off and reborrow from it. This arrangement is similar to a consumer's credit card.

         b) A line of credit is often an unsecured loan that is **self-liquidating**; that is, the assets acquired (e.g., inventory) provide the cash to pay the loan.

3. **Simple Interest Short-Term Loans**

   a. Interest on a simple interest loan is paid at the end of the loan term. The amount of interest to be paid is based on the nominal (stated) rate and the principal of the loan (amount needed).

   Interest expense = Principal of loan × Stated rate

   > **EXAMPLE 12-14   Simple Interest Short-Term Loans**
   >
   > A company obtained a short-term bank loan of US $15,000 at an annual interest rate of 8%. The interest expense on the loan is US $1,200 ($15,000 × 8%).
   >
   > The stated rate of 8% is also the effective rate.

b. The **effective rate** on any financing arrangement is the ratio of the amount paid to the amount usable.

$$\text{Effective interest rate} = \frac{\text{Interest expense (interest to be paid)}}{\text{Usable funds (net proceeds)}}$$

EXAMPLE 12-15   Effective Interest Rate -- Origination Fee

A company obtained a short-term bank loan of US $15,000 at an annual interest rate of 8%. The bank charges a loan origination fee of US $500.

$$\begin{aligned}\text{Effective rate} &= \text{Interest paid} \div \text{Net proceeds} \\ &= (\text{US } \$15{,}000 \times 8\%) \div (\$15{,}000 - \$500) \\ &= \text{US } \$1{,}200 \div \$14{,}500 \\ &= 8.27\%\end{aligned}$$

The effective interest rate (8.27%) is higher than the stated interest rate (8%) because the net proceeds are lower than the principal.

---

4. **Discounted Loans**

    a. The interest and finance charges on a discounted loan are paid at the beginning of the loan term.

    $$\text{Total borrowings} = \frac{\text{Amount needed}}{(1.0 - \text{Stated rate})}$$

EXAMPLE 12-16   Discounted Loans -- Total Borrowings

A company needs to pay a US $90,000 invoice. Its bank has offered to extend this amount at an 8% nominal rate on a discounted basis.

$$\begin{aligned}\text{Total borrowings} &= \text{Amount needed} \div (1.0 - \text{Stated rate}) \\ &= \text{US } \$90{,}000 \div (100\% - 8\%) \\ &= \text{US } \$90{,}000 \div 92\% \\ &= \text{US } \$97{,}826\end{aligned}$$

---

    b. Because the borrower receives a smaller amount, the effective rate on a discounted loan is higher than its nominal rate.

EXAMPLE 12-17   Discounted Loans -- Effective Rate

$$\begin{aligned}\text{Effective rate} &= \text{Net interest expense (annualized)} \div \text{Usable funds} \\ &= (\text{US } \$97{,}826 \times 8\%) \div \$90{,}000 \\ &= \text{US } \$7{,}826 \div \$90{,}000 \\ &= 8.696\%\end{aligned}$$

---

    c. In all financing arrangements, the effective rate can be calculated without reference to monetary amounts.

    $$\text{Effective rate on discounted loan} = \frac{\text{Stated rate}}{(1.0 - \text{Stated rate})}$$

EXAMPLE 12-18   Effective Rate Calculation -- No Monetary Amounts

The entity calculates the effective rate on this loan without using monetary amounts.

$$\begin{aligned}\text{Effective rate} &= \text{Stated rate} \div (1.0 - \text{Stated rate}) \\ &= 8\% \div (100\% - 8\%) \\ &= 8\% \div 92\% \\ &= 8.696\%\end{aligned}$$

5. Loans with Compensating Balances

a. To reduce risk, banks sometimes require borrowers to maintain a compensating balance during the term of a financing arrangement.

$$\text{Total borrowings} = \frac{\text{Amount needed}}{(1.0 - \text{Compensating balance \%})}$$

EXAMPLE 12-19   Compensating Balance Loan -- Total Borrowings

A company has received an invoice for US $120,000 with terms of 2/10, net 30. The entity's bank will lend it the necessary amount for 20 days so the discount can be taken on the 10th day at a nominal annual rate of 6% with a compensating balance of 10%.

Total borrowings = Amount needed ÷ (1.0 − Compensated balance %)
= (US $120,000 × 98%) ÷ (100% − 10%)
= US $117,600 ÷ 90%
= US $130,667

---

b. The borrower can use a smaller amount than the face amount of the loan, so the effective rate is higher than the nominal rate.

EXAMPLE 12-20   Compensating Balance Loan -- Effective Rate

Effective rate = Net interest expense (annualized) ÷ Usable funds
= (US $130,667 × 6%) ÷ $117,600
= US $7,840 ÷ $117,600
= 6.667%

---

c. Again, the monetary amounts are not needed to determine the effective rate.

$$\text{Effective rate with comp. balance} = \frac{\text{Stated rate}}{(1.0 - \text{Compensating balance \%})}$$

EXAMPLE 12-21   Compensating Balance -- Effective Rate with No Monetary Amounts

Effective rate = Stated rate ÷ (1.0 − Compensating balance %)
= 6% ÷ (100% − 10%)
= 6% ÷ 90%
= 6.667%

---

6. Money Market Instruments

a. Bankers' acceptances are drafts drawn by a nonfinancial entity on deposits at a bank.

1) The acceptance by the bank is a guarantee of payment at maturity. The payee can rely on the creditworthiness of the bank rather than on that of the (presumably riskier) drawer.
2) Because they are backed by the prestige of a large bank, these instruments are marketable after acceptance.

b. Commercial paper consists of short-term, unsecured notes payable issued in large denominations (US $100,000 or more) by large corporations with high credit ratings to other corporations and institutional investors, such as pension funds, banks, and insurance companies.

1) Maturities of commercial paper are at most 270 days. No general secondary market exists for commercial paper. Commercial paper is a lower-cost source of funds than bank loans. It is usually issued at below the prime rate.

7. **Treasury Securities**

    a. U.S. Treasury securities are considered to be the safest investment because they are backed by the U.S. government.

        1) **Treasury bills** (T-bills) have maturities of 1 year or less. They do not pay interest but are sold on a discount basis.

            a) They can be traded in international money markets.

        2) **Treasury notes** (T-notes) and **treasury bonds** (T-bonds) have maturities of 1 to 10 years and 10 years or longer, respectively. They provide the lender with a coupon (interest) payment every 6 months.

8. **Secured Financing**

    a. Loans can be secured by pledging receivables, i.e., committing the proceeds of the receivables to paying the loan. A bank often lends up to 80% of outstanding receivables, depending upon the average age of the accounts and the assessed likelihood of their collectibility.

    b. A **warehouse receipt** is secured short-term financing using inventory as security for the loan.

        1) A third party, such as a public warehouse, holds the collateral and serves as the creditor's agent. The creditor receives the terminal warehouse receipts as evidence of its rights in the collateral.

        2) A field warehouse is established when the warehouser takes possession of the inventory on the debtor's property. The inventory is released (often from a fenced-in area) as needed for sale. Warehouse receipts may be negotiable or nonnegotiable.

9. **Factoring Receivables and Securitization**

    a. When an entity pledges receivables, it retains ownership of the accounts and commits to sending the proceeds to a creditor. In a **factoring arrangement**, the entity sells the accounts receivable outright. The financing cost is usually high.

        1) However, an entity that uses a factor can eliminate its credit department and accounts receivable staff. Also, credit losses are eliminated from the statement of financial position.

        2) These reductions in costs do more than offset the fee charged by the factor. The factor often operates more efficiently than its clients because of the specialized nature of its service.

    b. **Securitization** is the transfer of a portfolio of financial assets to a trust, mutual fund, or other entity and the sale of beneficial interests in that entity to investors.

STOP & REVIEW

You have completed the outline for this subunit.
Study multiple-choice questions 12 through 14 beginning on page 431.

12.6 METHODS OF TAXATION

1. **Tax Uses**

    a. Government, at all levels, finances its expenditures by taxation. Thus, taxes generate government revenues. National governments also use taxation as a means of implementing fiscal policy regarding inflation, full employment, economic growth, etc.

    b. One view of taxation is that individuals should pay tax based on the benefits received from the services (e.g., paying for the use of a public park or swimming pool). Another view is that consumers should pay taxes based on their ability to pay (e.g., taxes on income and wealth).

2. **Tax Rate Structures**

    a. **Progressive.** Higher income persons pay a higher percentage of their income in taxes.

       1) Indexing is a means of avoiding the unfairness that results when inflation increases nominal but not real taxable income, subjecting it to higher tax rates. Adjusting tax bracket, deduction, and exemption amounts by reference to some index of inflation avoids this problem.

    b. **Proportional.** At all levels of income, the percentage paid in taxes is constant.

    c. **Regressive.** As income increases, the percentage paid in taxes decreases (e.g., sales, payroll, property, or excise taxes). For example, an excise tax is regressive because its burden falls disproportionately on lower-income persons. As personal income increases, the percentage of income paid declines because an excise tax is a flat amount per quantity of the good or service purchased.

       1) An **excise tax** increases the selling price of the product. This price increase will have a less negative effect on sales volume for products with less elastic demand. Examples of products with low elasticity of demand include gasoline, tobacco, and alcohol. The tax revenue generated by an increase in excise taxes is therefore higher if the tax is levied on products with less elastic demand.

          a) Demand is price elastic if a given percentage change in price results in a greater percentage change in revenues in the opposite direction.

3. **Tax Rates**
    a. The marginal tax rate is the rate applied to the last unit of taxable income.
        1) The **average tax rate** is the total tax liability divided by the amount of taxable income.
        2) The **effective tax rate** is the total tax liability divided by total economic income (includes amounts that do not have tax consequences).

4. **Direct vs. Indirect**
    a. Direct taxes are imposed upon the taxpayer and paid directly to the government, e.g., the personal income tax.
        1) Indirect taxes are levied against others and therefore only indirectly on the individual taxpayer, e.g., corporate income taxes.

5. **Tax Credits**
    a. Tax credits, e.g., the Investment Tax Credit, are deductions on the income tax return that lower investment cost and increase a project's net present value.

6. **Incidence of Taxation**
    a. Who actually bears a particular tax is not always obvious. Accordingly, the person who actually bears an indirect tax may not be the one who pays the tax to the government.
    b. The incidence of taxation is important when a government wants to change the tax structure. Because taxation is a form of fiscal policy, the government needs to know who will actually bear the burden of a tax, not only who will statutorily pay it.
    c. Taxes such as the corporate income tax and corporate property and excise taxes are often shifted to customers in the form of higher prices.
        1) However, sellers ordinarily must bear part of the burden. Passing on the entire tax might reduce unit sales unacceptably by raising the price too high. Thus, the effect of the tax is to reduce supply (because suppliers' costs increase) and quantity demanded by buyers (because the price increases).
        2) The combined loss of sellers and buyers is called the deadweight loss or excess burden of taxation.
    d. Taxes such as windfall profits taxes are not shifted to customers via higher prices. This type of one-time-only tax levied on part of the output produced does not increase the equilibrium price of the taxed good.

e. Supply-side economists use the Laffer Curve to attempt to explain how people react to varying rates of income taxation. For example, if the income tax rate is 0%, zero revenue will be raised by government. Similarly, if the tax rate is 100%, income tax revenue will probably be zero because an earner who faces a tax rate of 100% will not work.

  1) The optimal income tax rate will bring in the most revenue possible. A rate that is either too high or too low will generate less than optimal tax revenues.

  2) Supply-side economists do not state that lowering income tax rates will produce more revenue. Instead, they claim that, if the rates are too high, lowering rates will produce more revenue because output and national income will increase. This result, in theory, should follow because of increased incentives to work, invest, and save.

  3) However, economic policy should not be confused with political considerations. Obvious political reasons exist for having higher or lower tax rates on certain income levels. Thus, the theory underlying the Laffer Curve does not address questions of redistributionist politics.

  4) A criticism of the Laffer Curve is that it does not prescribe the optimal tax rate. The only way to know whether the current tax rates are too high or too low is to change them and see whether revenues increase.

     a) Critics also have observed that the incentives provided by tax cuts may have relatively small supply-side effects and that those effects may be felt only in the very long run.

     b) Another potential problem is that cutting taxes in an expanding economy may overstimulate demand, thereby increasing inflation.

7. **International Tax Considerations**

  a. Multinational corporations frequently derive income from several countries. The government of each country in which a corporation does business may enact statutes imposing one or more types of tax on the corporation.

  b. Treaties. To avoid double taxation, two or more countries may adopt treaties to coordinate or synchronize the effects of their taxing statutes.

  1) Treaties also are used to integrate other governmental goals, e.g., providing incentives for desired investment.

  2) A treaty might modify the rules in a country's statutes that designate the source country of income or the domicile of an entity.

c. Multinational Corporations

1) Most countries tax only the income sourced to that country.
2) But some countries tax worldwide income (from whatever source derived) of a domestic corporation. Double taxation is avoided by allowing a credit for income tax paid to foreign countries or by treaty provisions.
3) In the case of foreign corporations, a country may tax only income sourced to it. Ordinarily, such income is effectively connected with engaging in a trade or business of the country. Certain source income, e.g., gain on the sale of most shares, may not be taxed.

8. **Value-Added Tax (VAT)**

   a. Many major industrial nations have adopted a value-added tax (VAT).

   1) The tax is levied on the value added to goods by each business unit in the production and distribution chain. The amount of value added is the difference between sales and purchases.

      a) Each entity in the chain collects the tax on its sales, takes a credit for taxes paid on purchases, and remits the difference to the government.

   2) The consumer ultimately bears the tax through higher prices.
   3) A VAT encourages consumer savings because taxes are paid only on consumption, not on savings. Because the VAT is based on consumption, people in the lower income groups spend a greater proportion of their income on this type of tax. Thus, the VAT is regressive.
   4) Only those businesses that make a profit have to pay income taxes. The VAT, however, requires all businesses to pay taxes, regardless of income.
   5) The VAT tax is not a useful tool for fiscal policy purposes.

You have completed the outline for this subunit.
Study multiple-choice questions 15 through 17 beginning on page 432.

STOP & REVIEW

12.7 TRANSFER PRICING

1. **Overview**

    a. Transfer prices are charged by one segment of an organization for goods and services it provides to another segment of the same organization.

    1) Transfer pricing is used by profit and investment centers (a cost center's costs are allocated to producing departments).

    b. Upper management's challenge is to set transfer-pricing policy such that segment managers achieve overall entity goals by pursuing their segment goals.

    c. Thus, transfer pricing should motivate managers by encouraging goal congruence and managerial effort.

    1) **Goal congruence** is alignment of a manager's individual goals with those of the organization.

    2) **Managerial effort** is the extent to which a manager attempts to accomplish a goal.

2. **Three Basic Methods for Determining Transfer Prices**

    a. **Cost plus** pricing sets price at the selling segment's full cost of production plus a reasonable markup.

    b. **Market** pricing uses the price the selling segment could obtain on the open market.

    c. **Negotiated** pricing gives the segments the freedom to bargain among themselves to agree on a price.

EXAMPLE 12-22   Transfer Price Calculation

A conglomerate refines nitrogen and manufactures fertilizer. Upper management is considering the factors involved in setting transfer-pricing policy. External markets exist for both products. The Fertilizer Division would like to pay only the Nitrogen Division's cost plus 10%. The Nitrogen Division wants to sell at the market price. When forced to compromise, management of the two divisions settled on an average of the two prices. The Nitrogen Division's results under the three alternatives are calculated as follows:

Nitrogen Division	Full Cost Plus 10%	Market Price	Negotiated Price
Revenues:			
Revenue per cubic-foot	US $ 3.30	US $ 4.00	US $ 3.65
Times: Cubic feet	× 10,000	× 10,000	× 10,000
Total division revenue	**US $ 33,000**	**US $ 40,000**	**US $ 36,500**
Costs (for all three prices):			
Purchase cost per cubic foot	US $ 2.00		
Division variable costs	0.25		
Division fixed costs	0.75		
Per-cubic-foot division costs	US $ 3.00		
Times: Cubic feet	× 10,000		
Total division costs	**US $ 30,000**		
Operating income:			
Total division revenue	US $ 33,000	US $ 40,000	US $ 36,500
Total division costs	(30,000)	(30,000)	(30,000)
Division operating income	**US $ 3,000**	**US $ 10,000**	**US $ 6,500**

-- Continued on next page --

EXAMPLE 12-22 -- Continued

The Fertilizer Division's results under the three alternatives are calculated as follows:

Fertilizer Division

Revenues:
Revenue per pound	US $ 14.00
Times: Pounds	× 5,000
Total division revenue	**US $ 70,000**

Costs:
Division variable costs	US $ 4.00
Division fixed costs	0.50
Per-pound division costs	US $ 4.50
Times: Pounds	× 5,000
Total division costs	**US $ 22,500**

Operating income:	Full Cost Plus 10%	Market Price	Negotiated Price
Total division revenue	US $ 70,000	US $ 70,000	US $ 70,000
Transferred-in costs	(33,000)	(40,000)	(36,500)
Total division costs	(22,500)	(22,500)	(22,500)
Division operating income	**US $ 14,500**	**US $ 7,500**	**US $ 11,000**

The motive of each manager to set a different price is clear. However, the following calculation shows that the choice among the three methods is irrelevant to the organization as a whole. Motivating management is the main concern of transfer pricing.

	Full Cost Plus 10%	Market Price	Negotiated Price
Nitrogen Division operating income	US $ 3,000	US $10,000	US $ 6,500
Fertilizer Division operating income	14,500	7,500	11,000
Combined operating incomes	**US $17,500**	**US $17,500**	**US $17,500**

3. **Minimum Transfer Price**

    a. The minimum price that a seller is willing to accept is calculated as follows:

    $$\text{Minimum transfer price} = \text{Incremental cost to date} + \text{Opportunity cost of selling internally}$$

    1) The opportunity cost of selling internally varies depending on two factors: the existence of an external market for the product and whether the seller has excess capacity.

4. **Choice of Transfer Price**

    a. Scenario 1 -- External market exists and seller has no excess capacity

    1) The opportunity cost to sell internally is the contribution margin the seller would have received selling on the external market.
    2) The seller can sell everything it produces on the open market, so this margin must be included in the transfer price to make selling internally worthwhile.

    b. Scenario 2 -- External market exists and seller has excess capacity

    1) Both segments benefit from any price between the floor of the incremental cost to date and a ceiling of the market price.
    2) The seller cannot demand the full contribution margin because the open market may not purchase its full output.

    c. Scenario 3 -- No external market exists

    1) The seller cannot demand anything above its incremental cost to date.

Transfer Price Decision Tree

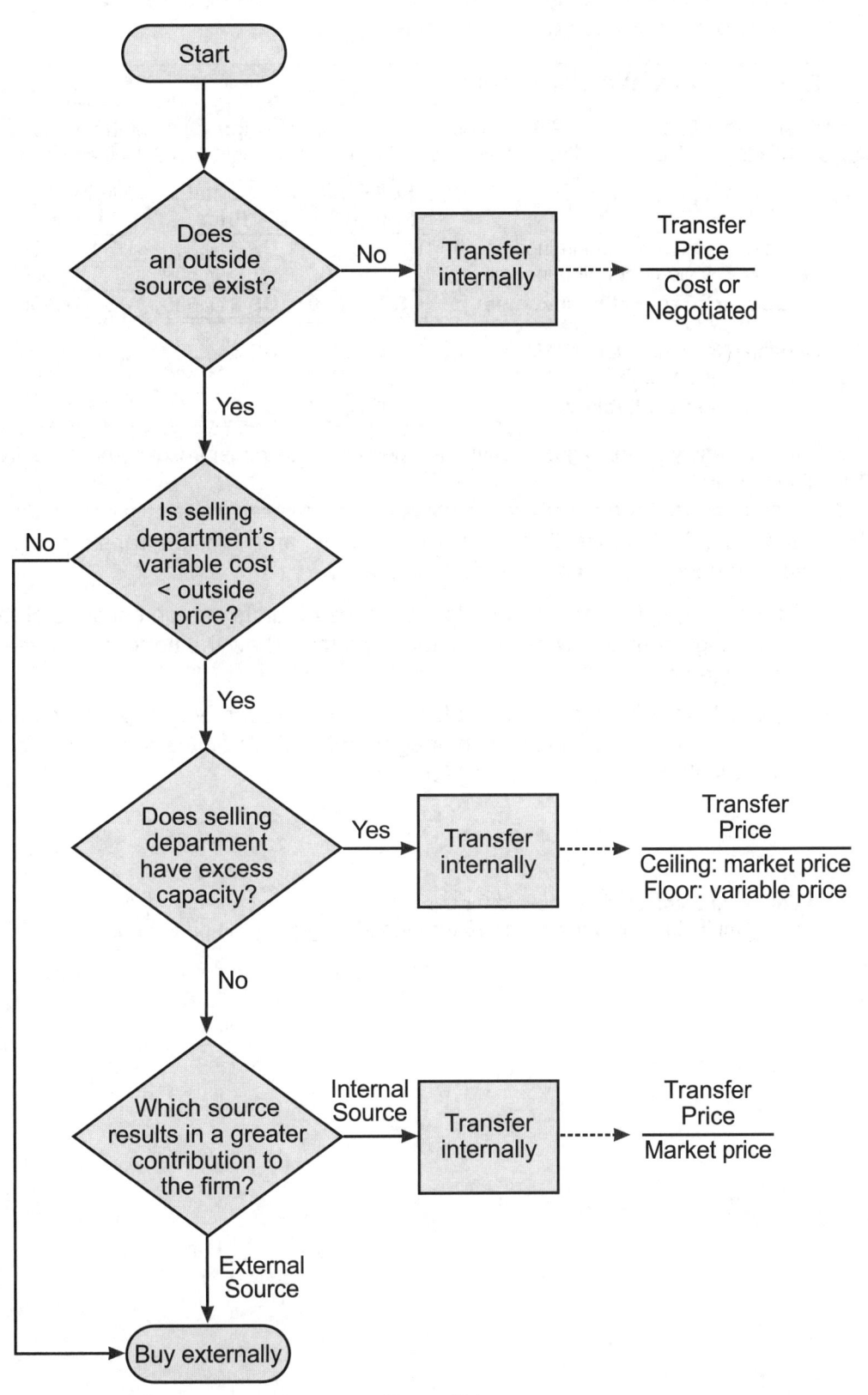

```
Start
  │
  ▼
Does an outside source exist? ──No──▶ Transfer internally ┈┈▶ Transfer Price / Cost or Negotiated
  │
  Yes
  ▼
Is selling department's variable cost < outside price? ──No──▶ Buy externally
  │
  Yes
  ▼
Does selling department have excess capacity? ──Yes──▶ Transfer internally ┈┈▶ Transfer Price / Ceiling: market price, Floor: variable price
  │
  No
  ▼
Which source results in a greater contribution to the firm? ──Internal Source──▶ Transfer internally ┈┈▶ Transfer Price / Market price
  │
  External Source
  ▼
Buy externally
```

Figure 12-5

5. **Multinational Considerations**

    a. When segments are located in different countries, taxes and tariffs may override any other considerations when setting transfer prices.

    > **EXAMPLE 12-23   Multinational Pricing**
    >
    > The Nitrogen Division from Example 12-22 is located in Canada, which imposes a combined tax and tariff burden of 45%, while the Fertilizer Division located in the U.S. is subject only to a 20% income tax.
    >
    > | | Full Cost Plus 10% | Market Price | Negotiated Price |
    > | --- | --- | --- | --- |
    > | Nitrogen Division operating income | US $ 3,000 | US $10,000 | US $ 6,500 |
    > | Fertilizer Division operating income | 14,500 | 7,500 | 11,000 |
    > | **Combined operating incomes** | **US $17,500** | **US $17,500** | **US $17,500** |
    > | Canadian taxes and tariffs (45%) | US $ 1,350 | US $ 4,500 | US $ 2,925 |
    > | U.S. income tax (20%) | 2,900 | 1,500 | 2,200 |
    > | **Combined tax liability** | **US $ 4,250** | **US $ 6,000** | **US $ 5,125** |
    >
    > If tax minimization is the entity's overall goal, upper management is no longer unconcerned about which transfer-pricing policy to select.

    b. Exchange rate fluctuations, threats of expropriation, and limits on transfers of profits outside the host country are additional concerns.

        1) The best transfer price may be low because of tariffs or high because of foreign exchange controls. These considerations may skew the performance statistics of management.

        2) The high transfer price may result in foreign management's reports of lower returns on investment than domestic management. But the difference may be explained by use of different transfer-pricing formulas.

STOP & REVIEW

You have completed the outline for this subunit.
Study multiple-choice questions 18 through 20 beginning on page 433.

SU 12: Capital Structure and Budget, Basic Taxation, and Transfer Pricing

QUESTIONS

12.1 Corporate Capital Structure -- Debt Financing

1. Capital structure decisions involve determining the proportions of financing from

A. Short-term or long-term debt.
B. Debt or equity.
C. Short-term or long-term assets.
D. Retained earnings or common equity.

Answer (B) is correct.
REQUIRED: Capital structure decisions.
DISCUSSION: Debt and equity are the two elements of an entity's capital structure.
Answer (A) is incorrect. The capital structure also includes equity. **Answer (C) is incorrect.** Assets are not part of the capital structure. **Answer (D) is incorrect.** The capital structure also includes debt and preferred equity.

2. Which of the following scenarios would encourage a company to use short-term loans to retire its 10-year bonds that have 5 years until maturity?

A. The company expects interest rates to increase over the next 5 years.
B. Interest rates have increased over the last 5 years.
C. Interest rates have declined over the last 5 years.
D. The company is experiencing cash flow problems.

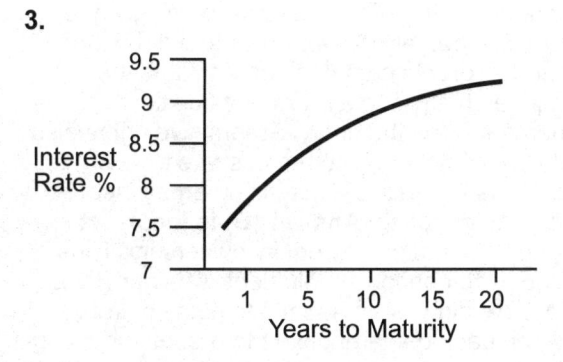

Answer (C) is correct.
REQUIRED: The scenario that encourages a company to use short-term debt to retire long-term debt.
DISCUSSION: If interest rates have declined, refunding with short-term debt may be appropriate. The bonds pay a higher interest rate than the new short-term debt. Assuming that rates continue to fall, the short-term debt can itself be refunded with debt having a still lower interest charge. The obvious risk is that interest rates may rise, thereby compelling the company to choose between paying off the debt or refunding it at higher rates.
Answer (A) is incorrect. The company will not benefit from short-term loans if interest rates rise. **Answer (B) is incorrect.** The company should maintain the existing debt if prevailing interest rates are higher. **Answer (D) is incorrect.** The company increases the cash flow problem by shifting to short-term loans.

3.

The yield curve shown implies that the

A. Credit risk premium of corporate bonds has increased.
B. Credit risk premium of municipal bonds has increased.
C. Long-term interest rates have a higher annualized yield than short-term rates.
D. Short-term interest rates have a higher annualized yield than long-term rates.

Answer (C) is correct.
REQUIRED: The implication of the yield curve.
DISCUSSION: The term structure of interest rates is the relationship between yield to maturity and time to maturity. This relationship is depicted by a yield curve. Assuming the long-term interest rate is an average of expected future short-term rates, the curve will be upward sloping when future short-term interest rates are expected to rise. Furthermore, the normal expectation is for long-term investments to pay higher rates because of their higher risk. Thus, long-term interest rates have a higher annualized yield than short-term rates.
Answer (A) is incorrect. The yield curve does not reflect the credit risk premium of bonds. **Answer (B) is incorrect.** The yield curve does not reflect the credit risk premium of bonds. **Answer (D) is incorrect.** Long-term interest rates should be higher than short-term rates.

12.2 Corporate Capital Structure -- Equity Financing

4. An entity must select from among several methods of financing arrangements when meeting its capital requirements. To acquire additional growth capital while attempting to maximize earnings per share, an entity should normally

A. Attempt to increase both debt and equity in equal proportions, which preserves a stable capital structure and maintains investor confidence.
B. Select debt over equity initially, even though increased debt is accompanied by interest costs and a degree of risk.
C. Select equity over debt initially, which minimizes risk and avoids interest costs.
D. Discontinue dividends and use current cash flow, which avoids the cost and risk of increased debt and the dilution of EPS through increased equity.

Answer (B) is correct.
REQUIRED: The financing arrangement that acquires additional growth capital while maximizing EPS.
DISCUSSION: Earnings per share ordinarily are higher if debt is used to raise capital instead of equity, provided that the entity is not over-leveraged. The reason is that the cost of debt is lower than the cost of equity because interest is tax deductible. However, the prospect of higher EPS is accompanied by greater risk to the entity resulting from required interest costs, creditors' liens on the entity's assets, and the possibility of a proportionately lower EPS if sales volume fails to meet projections.
Answer (A) is incorrect. EPS is not a function of investor confidence and is not maximized by concurrent proportional increases in both debt and equity. EPS are usually higher if debt is used instead of equity to raise capital, at least initially. **Answer (C) is incorrect.** Equity capital is initially more costly than debt. **Answer (D) is incorrect.** Using only current cash flow to raise capital is usually too conservative an approach for a growth-oriented entity. Management is expected to be willing to take acceptable risks to be competitive and attain an acceptable rate of growth.

5. Common shareholders with preemptive rights are entitled to

A. Vote first at annual meetings.
B. Purchase any additional bonds sold by the entity.
C. Purchase any additional shares sold by the entity.
D. Gain control of the entity in a proxy fight.

Answer (C) is correct.
REQUIRED: The privilege enjoyed by common shareholders with preemptive rights.
DISCUSSION: Preemptive rights protect common shareholders' proportional ownership interests from dilution in value. A secondary purpose is to maintain the shareholders' control of the entity. Accordingly, the preemptive right, whether granted by statute or by the corporate charter, grants common shareholders the power to acquire on a pro rata basis any additional common shares sold by the entity. Preemptive rights also apply to debt convertible into common shares.
Answer (A) is incorrect. There is no prescribed order of shareholder voting. **Answer (B) is incorrect.** Preemptive rights concern only equity ownership. Thus, they do not apply to nonconvertible debt. **Answer (D) is incorrect.** A proxy fight is an attempt to gain control of an entity by persuading shareholders to grant their voting rights to others.

6. Participating preferred shareholders are entitled to

A. Monitor any sinking funds for the purchase and retirement of debt.
B. Vote at all annual meetings.
C. Convert their shares into common shares.
D. Share in the entity's earnings beyond the stated dividend level.

Answer (D) is correct.
REQUIRED: The right of participating preferred shareholders.
DISCUSSION: Participating preferred shareholders are entitled to share in the earnings of the entity. They participate in earnings distributions under set terms and conditions. Thus, after the stated preferred dividend is paid, and common shareholders receive an equal dividend, any remaining dividends are allocated to all shareholders in proportion to the par values of their shares.
Answer (A) is incorrect. The participation privilege is unrelated to monitoring privileges. **Answer (B) is incorrect.** Preferred shareholders do not have voting rights except in circumstances in which the entity has not paid the preferred share dividends for a specified period. **Answer (C) is incorrect.** A conversion feature, not a participation feature, allows conversion to common shares.

12.3 Corporate Capital Structure -- Cost of Capital

7. An entity has made the decision to finance next year's capital projects through debt rather than additional equity. The benchmark cost of capital for these projects should be the

A. Before-tax cost of new-debt financing.
B. After-tax cost of new-debt financing.
C. Cost of equity financing.
D. Weighted-average cost of capital.

Answer (D) is correct.
REQUIRED: The benchmark cost of capital.
DISCUSSION: A weighted average of the costs of all financing sources should be used, with the weights determined by the usual financing proportions. The terms of any financing raised at the time of initiating a particular project do not represent the cost of capital for the entity. When an entity achieves its optimal capital structure, the weighted-average cost of capital is minimized. The cost of capital is a composite, or weighted average, of all financing sources in their usual proportions. The cost of capital should also be calculated on an after-tax basis.
Answer (A) is incorrect. The weighted-average cost of capital is calculated on an after-tax basis. **Answer (B) is incorrect.** The weighted-average cost of capital consists of both debt and equity components calculated on an after-tax basis. **Answer (C) is incorrect.** The cost of capital is an after-tax composite, or weighted average, of all financing sources in their usual proportions.

8. The marginal cost of capital (MCC) curve for an entity rises twice, first when the entity has raised US $75 million and again when US $175 million of new funds has been raised. These increases in the MCC are caused by

A. Increases in the returns on the additional investments undertaken.
B. Decreases in the returns on the additional investments undertaken.
C. Decreases in the cost of at least one of the financing sources.
D. Increases in the cost of at least one of the financing sources.

Answer (D) is correct.
REQUIRED: The reason for the increases in the MCC.
DISCUSSION: The MCC is a weighted average of the costs of various new financing sources. If the cost of any source of new financing increases, the MCC curve will rise. The curve shifts upward with each incremental increase in financing cost because the lowest-cost sources are assumed to be used first.
Answer (A) is incorrect. Financing costs do not directly depend on rates of return on investment. **Answer (B) is incorrect.** Financing costs do not directly depend on rates of return on investment. **Answer (C) is incorrect.** As additional funds are raised, an increase in the cost of a source of financing, not a decrease, will result in an increase in the MCC.

9. A firm seeking to optimize its capital budget has calculated its marginal cost of capital and projected rates of return on several potential projects. The optimal capital budget is determined by

A. Calculating the point at which marginal cost of capital meets the projected rate of return, assuming that the most profitable projects are accepted first.

B. Calculating the point at which average marginal cost meets average projected rate of return, assuming the largest projects are accepted first.

C. Accepting all potential projects with projected rates of return exceeding the lowest marginal cost of capital.

D. Accepting all potential projects with projected rates of return lower than the highest marginal cost of capital.

Answer (A) is correct.
REQUIRED: The determinant of the optimal capital budget.
DISCUSSION: In economics, a basic principle is that a firm should increase output until marginal cost equals marginal revenue. Similarly, the optimal capital budget is determined by calculating the point at which marginal cost of capital (which increases as capital requirements increase) and marginal efficiency of investment (which decreases if the most profitable projects are accepted first) intersect.
Answer (B) is incorrect. The intersection of average marginal cost with average projected rates of return when the largest (not most profitable) projects are accepted first offers no meaningful capital budgeting conclusion.
Answer (C) is incorrect. The optimal capital budget may exclude profitable projects as lower-cost capital goes first to projects with higher rates of return. **Answer (D) is incorrect.** Accepting projects with rates of return lower than the cost of capital is not rational.

12.4 Capital Budgeting

10. A project has an initial outlay of US $1,000. The projected cash inflows are

Year 1	US $200
Year 2	200
Year 3	400
Year 4	400

What is the investment's payback period?

A. 4.0 years.

B. 3.5 years.

C. 3.4 years.

D. 3.0 years.

Answer (B) is correct.
REQUIRED: The payback period.
DISCUSSION: Cash inflows are assumed to occur equally throughout the Years 1 through 4. At the end of Year 3, US $800 ($200 + $200 + $400) will have been received. The remaining US $200 will be received in one half of Year 4 (US $200 ÷ $400).
Answer (A) is incorrect. The total cash inflow over 4.0 years is US $1,200 ($200 + $200 + $400 + $400).
Answer (C) is incorrect. Cash inflows over 3.4 years will total US $960 [($200 + $200 + $400) + ($400 × 0.4)].
Answer (D) is incorrect. The 3-year total is US $800 ($200 + $200 + $400).

11. Which of the following phrases defines the internal rate of return on a project?

A. The number of years it takes to recover the investment.

B. The discount rate at which the net present value of the project equals zero.

C. The discount rate at which the net present value of the project equals one.

D. The weighted-average cost of capital used to finance the project.

Answer (B) is correct.
REQUIRED: The definition of the IRR.
DISCUSSION: The IRR is the discount rate at which the investment's NPV equals zero. Accordingly, it is the rate that equates the present value of the expected cash inflows with the present value of the expected cash outflows.
Answer (A) is incorrect. The payback period is the number of years it takes to recover the investment.
Answer (C) is incorrect. The IRR is the discount rate at which the NPV is zero. **Answer (D) is incorrect.** The weighted-average cost of capital is the single, composite rate of return on the components of capital used to finance the project.

12.5 Short-Term Financing

12. The correct equation for calculating the approximate percentage cost, on an annual basis, of not taking trade discounts is

A. $\dfrac{\text{Discount \%}}{100 - \text{Discount \%}} \times \dfrac{360}{[\text{Days credit is outstanding} - \text{Discount period}]}$

B. $\dfrac{\text{Discount \%}}{100} \times \dfrac{360}{[\text{Days credit is outstanding} - \text{Discount period}]}$

C. $\dfrac{100 - \text{Discount \%}}{\text{Discount \%}} \times \dfrac{360}{[\text{Days credit is outstanding} - \text{Discount period}]}$

D. $\dfrac{\text{Discount \%}}{100 - \text{Discount \%}} \times \dfrac{[\text{Days credit is outstanding} - \text{Discount period}]}{360}$

Answer (A) is correct.
REQUIRED: The equation for calculating the percentage cost of not taking trade discounts.
DISCUSSION: The first term of the formula is the periodic cost of the trade discount, calculated as the cost per unit of trade credit (discount %) divided by the funds made available by not taking the discount (100% − discount %). The second term represents the number of times per year this cost is incurred. The product of these terms is the approximate annual percentage cost of not taking the trade discount. A precise formula would incorporate the effects of compounding when calculating the annual cost.
Answer (B) is incorrect. The denominator of the first term should represent the funds made available by not taking the discount (100% − discount %). **Answer (C) is incorrect.** The first term is the reciprocal of the correct term. **Answer (D) is incorrect.** The second term is the reciprocal of the correct term.

13. An entity has accounts payable of US $5 million with terms of 2% discount within 15 days net, 30 days (2/15, net 30). It can borrow funds from a bank at an annual rate of 12%, or it can wait until the 30th day when it will receive revenues to cover the payment. Which of the following would be the most appropriate way to calculate the more cost-effective strategy?

A. Calculate the amount saved under the 2% discount and compare to the face value of the payable.

B. Calculate the amount saved under the 2% discount and compare to the amount that would be paid if the payable were satisfied at 30 days.

C. Calculate the amount saved under the 2% discount, compute the amount of interest due to the bank when returning the borrowed funds, and determine the difference.

D. Calculate the amount of interest due to the bank when returning the borrowed funds and compare that amount to the face value of the payable.

Answer (C) is correct.
REQUIRED: The proper calculation to determine the most cost-effective payment strategy.
DISCUSSION: In order to determine the optimal payment strategy, the entity should compare the amount saved with the discount to the amount of interest due when borrowed funds would be returned at 30 days. As the discount savings is higher than the interest due after 15 days, the most cost-effective strategy is to borrow funds in time to pay the payable within the discount period and pay back the borrowed funds on the 30th day when revenues are available.
Answer (A) is incorrect. This calculation does not take into account the cost of borrowed funds. **Answer (B) is incorrect.** This calculation does not take into account the cost of borrowed funds. **Answer (D) is incorrect.** This calculation does not take into account the savings resulting from paying the payable within the discount period.

14. Factoring is the

A. Selling of accounts receivable by one entity to another.
B. Selling of inventory by one entity to another.
C. Conversion of accounts receivable to credit losses on financial statements for accounts that are long overdue.
D. Adjustment of inventories on financial statements for supplies that have become obsolete.

Answer (A) is correct.
REQUIRED: The definition of factoring.
DISCUSSION: A factor purchases an entity's accounts receivable and assumes the risk of collection. The seller receives money immediately to reinvest in new inventories. The financing cost is usually high: about 2 points or more above prime, plus a fee for collection. Factoring has been traditional in the textile industry for years, and companies in many industries have recently found it an efficient means of operation. An entity that uses a factor can eliminate its credit department, accounts receivable staff, and credit losses. These reductions in costs can more than offset the fee charged by the factor, which can often operate more efficiently than its clients because of the specialized nature of its service.

12.6 Methods of Taxation

15. A taxpayer who earns US $50,000 during the year and pays a 15% tax rate on the first US $30,000 of income and a 30% tax rate on all earnings over US $30,000 has a(n)

A. Marginal tax rate of 15%.
B. Marginal tax rate of 21%.
C. Average tax rate of 21%.
D. Average tax rate of 22.5%.

Answer (C) is correct.
REQUIRED: The nature and amount of the tax rate.
DISCUSSION: The average tax rate is calculated using the weighted-average method. The weight assigned to each rate is determined by the proportion of taxable income subject to it. The average tax rate is 21% [(US $30,000 ÷ $50,000) × .15 + ($20,000 ÷ $50,000) × .30].
Answer (A) is incorrect. The marginal tax rate is 30%. The marginal tax rate equals the highest rate paid. Answer (B) is incorrect. The marginal tax rate is 30%. The marginal tax rate equals the highest rate paid. Answer (D) is incorrect. A rate of 22.5% is a simple numerical average.

16. General sales taxes tend to be regressive with respect to income because

A. A larger portion of a lower income person's income is subject to the tax.
B. A smaller portion of a lower income person's income is subject to the tax.
C. The tax rate is higher for person with lower income.
D. The tax claims an increasing amount of income as income rises.

Answer (A) is correct.
REQUIRED: The reason general sales taxes tend to be regressive with respect to income.
DISCUSSION: A sales tax is regressive with respect to income even though the rate is the same regardless of the buyer's income. The reason is that a greater percentage of a low-income individual's income is exposed to the tax. A higher-income individual should be able to save more and therefore shield a greater percentage of his or her income from the tax.
Answer (B) is incorrect. A larger portion of a lower-income person's income is subject to the tax. Answer (C) is incorrect. The general sales tax rate is uniform for all taxpayers. Answer (D) is incorrect. If the tax claims an increasing amount of income as income rises, it is progressive, not regressive.

17. On what basis is value-added tax collected?

A. The difference between the value of an entity's sales and the value of its purchases from other domestic entities.
B. The difference between the selling price of a real estate property and the amount the entity originally paid for the property.
C. The value of an entity's sales to related companies.
D. The profit earned on an entity's sales.

Answer (A) is correct.
REQUIRED: The basis for collecting a value-added tax.
DISCUSSION: A value-added tax (VAT) is collected on the basis of the value created by the entity. This tax is measured by the difference between the value of the entity's sales and the value of its purchases. A VAT is, in effect, a retail sales tax. Because a consumer can avoid the tax by not purchasing, a VAT encourages saving and discourages consumption.
Answer (B) is incorrect. The difference between the selling price of a real estate property and the amount the entity originally paid for the property is a capital gain. **Answer (C) is incorrect.** The value of an entity's sales to related companies is the internal transfer price. **Answer (D) is incorrect.** The profit earned on an entity's sales is subject to the income tax.

12.7 Transfer Pricing

18. The price that one division of a company charges another division for goods or services provided is called the

A. Market price.
B. Transfer price.
C. Outlay price.
D. Distress price.

Answer (B) is correct.
REQUIRED: The price that one division of a company charges another for goods or services provided.
DISCUSSION: A transfer price is charged by one segment of an organization for a product or service supplied to another segment of the same organization.
Answer (A) is incorrect. Market price is an approach to determine a transfer price. **Answer (C) is incorrect.** Outlay price is an approach to determine a transfer price. **Answer (D) is incorrect.** Distress price is an approach to determine a transfer price.

19. A carpet manufacturer maintains a retail division consisting of stores stocking its brand and other brands, and a manufacturing division that makes carpets and pads. An outside market exists for carpet padding material in which all padding produced can be sold. The proper transfer price for padding transferred from the manufacturing division to the retail division is

A. Variable manufacturing division production cost.
B. Variable manufacturing division production cost plus allocated fixed factory overhead.
C. Variable manufacturing division production cost plus variable selling and administrative cost.
D. The market price at which the retail division could purchase padding.

Answer (D) is correct.
REQUIRED: The proper transfer price for padding transferred from the manufacturing division to the retail division.
DISCUSSION: The three basic criteria that the transfer pricing system in a decentralized company should satisfy are to (1) provide information allowing central management to evaluate divisions with respect to total company profit and each division's contribution to profit, (2) stimulate each manager's efficiency without losing each division's autonomy, and (3) motivate each divisional manager to achieve his or her own profit goal in a manner contributing to the company's success. The market price should be used as the transfer price to avoid waste and maximize efficiency in a competitive economy (an outside market in which all padding produced can be sold). This price also measures the product's profitability and the division managers' performance in a competitive environment.

20. An entity produces a good in country A and sells some of its output in country B. Selling prices are identical in the two countries. The corporate tax rates are 40% in country A and 20% in country B. Assuming that the entity does not increase or decrease production, it should <List A> sales in country B and set as <List B> a transfer price as possible, in order to minimize global taxes.

	List A	List B
A.	Maximize	High
B.	Maximize	Low
C.	Minimize	High
D.	Minimize	Low

Answer (B) is correct.
REQUIRED: The strategy for minimizing global taxes.
DISCUSSION: The tax-minimizing strategy is to minimize taxable income where tax rates are high and to maximize taxable income where tax rates are low. Consequently, the entity should sell more in country B but set a low transfer price. This dual strategy minimizes sales and profits in country A, minimizes cost of sales in country B, and maximizes sales and profits in country B.
Answer (A) is incorrect. If selling prices are identical, the tax-minimizing strategy involves maximizing sales in country B. However, to report the highest possible profits in the lower tax country, input costs must be minimized. The transfer price paid to the production facility in country A must therefore be set as low as possible. **Answer (C) is incorrect.** A strategy of minimizing sales in country B and maximizing reported cost of goods sold in country B would result in the lowest reported profit in the lower tax country, thereby maximizing taxes paid. **Answer (D) is incorrect.** The tax-minimizing strategy involves maximizing sales revenue in the lower tax country, not minimizing it.

Access the **Gleim CIA Premium Review System** featuring our SmartAdapt technology from your Gleim Personal Classroom to continue your studies. You will experience a personalized study environment with exam-emulating multiple-choice questions.

STUDY UNIT THIRTEEN
MANAGERIAL ACCOUNTING: GENERAL CONCEPTS

(23 pages of outline)

13.1	Cost Management Terminology	435
13.2	Budget Systems	437
13.3	Budget Methods	446
13.4	Cost-Volume-Profit (CVP) Analysis and Cost-Benefit Analysis	449
13.5	Responsibility Accounting	456

This study unit is the fifth of six covering **Domain IV: Financial Management** from The IIA's CIA Exam Syllabus. This domain makes up 20% of Part 3 of the CIA exam and is tested at the **basic** and **proficient** cognitive levels. Refer to the complete syllabus located in Appendix A to view the relevant sections covered in Study Unit 13.

SUCCESS TIP: The majority of financial management questions on the CIA exam test conceptual understanding, not the ability to perform calculations. However, many of our financial management questions require you to perform calculations. They are an effective means of reinforcing your conceptual understanding.

13.1 COST MANAGEMENT TERMINOLOGY

1. **Basic Definitions**

    a. A **cost** is the measure of a resource used up for some purpose.

    1) For financial reporting, a cost can be either capitalized as an asset or expensed.

    b. A **cost object** is any entity to which costs can be attached.

    1) Examples are products, processes, employees, departments, and facilities.

    c. A **cost driver** is the basis used to assign costs to a cost object.

    1) A cost driver is an activity measure, such as direct labor hours or machine hours, that is a factor in causing the incurrence of cost.

2. **Manufacturing vs. Nonmanufacturing**
   a. The costs of manufacturing a product can be classified as follows:
      1) **Direct materials** are tangible inputs to the manufacturing process that feasibly can be traced to the product, e.g., sheet metal welded together for a piece of heavy equipment.
         a) All costs of bringing materials to the production line, e.g., transportation-in, are included in the cost of direct materials.
      2) **Direct labor** is the cost of human labor that feasibly can be traced to the product, e.g., the wages of the welder.
      3) **Manufacturing overhead** consists of all costs of manufacturing that are not direct materials or direct labor.
         a) Indirect materials are tangible inputs to the manufacturing process that feasibly cannot be traced to the product, e.g., the welding compound used to put together a piece of heavy equipment.
         b) Indirect labor is the cost of human labor connected with the manufacturing process that feasibly cannot be traced to the product, e.g., the wages of assembly line supervisors and janitorial staff.
         c) Other manufacturing costs include utilities, real estate taxes, insurance, and depreciation on factory equipment.
   b. Manufacturing costs also may be classified as follows:
      1) **Prime cost** equals **direct materials plus direct labor**, the costs directly attributable to a product.
      2) **Conversion cost** equals **direct labor plus manufacturing overhead**, the costs of converting materials into the finished product.
   c. The following are nonmanufacturing (operating) costs:
      1) Selling (marketing) costs are incurred in getting the product to the consumer, e.g., sales personnel salaries and product transportation.
      2) Administrative expenses are not directly related to producing or marketing the product, e.g., executive salaries and depreciation on the headquarters building.

3. **Product vs. Period**
   a. An important issue in managerial accounting is whether to capitalize a cost as part of finished goods inventory or to expense it as incurred.
      1) **Product costs** (inventoriable costs) are capitalized as part of finished goods inventory. They eventually become a component of cost of goods sold.
      2) **Period costs** are expensed as incurred. They are not capitalized in finished goods inventory and are excluded from cost of goods sold.
   b. This distinction is crucial because of the required treatment of manufacturing costs for external financial reporting purposes.

4. **Direct vs. Indirect**
   a. **Direct costs** can be traced to a cost object in an economically feasible way.
      1) Examples are direct materials and direct labor inputs.
   b. **Indirect costs** cannot be traced to a cost object in an economically feasible way. They must be allocated to that object.
      1) Examples are indirect materials and indirect labor inputs.
      2) To simplify allocation, indirect costs often are collected in cost pools.
         a) A cost pool is an account in which similar cost elements with a common cause (cost driver) are accumulated.
         b) Manufacturing overhead is a commonly used cost pool in which various indirect costs of manufacturing are accumulated.
   c. **Common costs** are indirect costs shared by two or more users.
      1) Because common costs cannot be directly traced to the users that generate the costs, they must be allocated on a systematic and rational basis.
      2) An example is depreciation on a headquarters building. It is a direct cost when accounting for the building as a whole. However, it is a common cost of the departments located in the building and must be allocated to them.

STOP & REVIEW

You have completed the outline for this subunit.
Study multiple-choice questions 1 through 4 beginning on page 458.

13.2 BUDGET SYSTEMS

1. **Purposes of a Budget**
   a. The budget is a plan.
      1) A budget forces management to evaluate the assumptions used and the objectives identified in the budgetary process.
   b. The budget is a control.
      1) A budget helps control costs by setting guidelines and provides a framework for manager performance evaluations.
   c. The budget is a motivator.
      1) A budget helps to motivate employees. Employees are especially motivated if they help prepare the budget.
   d. The budget is a means of communication and coordination.
      1) A budget states the entity's objectives in numerical terms. It therefore requires segments of the entity to communicate and cooperate.
   e. A principal advantage of budgeting is that it forces management to plan.
      1) Managers in a formal budget setting are compelled to examine the future and be prepared to respond to future conditions. Without budgets, many operations would fail because of inadequate planning.
      2) Additional advantages of budgeting include motivating employees, evaluating performance, and communicating the plan.

2. **Participation in the Budget Process**
    a. Participation in the budget preparation process is at all organizational levels.
        1) The budget process begins with the mission statement formulated by the **board of directors**.
        2) **Senior management** translates the mission statement into a strategic plan with measurable, realizable goals.
        3) A **budget committee** composed of top management is formed to draft the budget calendar and budget manual. The budget committee also reviews and approves the departmental budgets submitted by operating managers.
            a) A budget director's primary responsibility is to compile the budget and manage the budget process.
        4) **Middle and lower management** receive their budget instructions, draft their departmental budgets in conformity with the guidelines, and submit them to the budget committee.
    b. **Top-down (authoritative) budgeting** is imposed by upper management and therefore has less chance of acceptance by those on whom the budget is imposed.
        1) This approach has the advantage of ensuring consistency across functions. It is also far less complex and time-consuming than coordinating input from middle and lower levels.
    c. **Bottom-up (participative) budgeting** is based on general guidance from the highest levels of management, followed by extensive input from middle and lower management. Because of this degree of participation, the chance of acceptance is greater.
        1) Disadvantages of participative standards setting include its time and financial costs. Also, the quality of participation is affected by the goals, values, beliefs, and expectations of those involved.

	Advantages	Disadvantages
Top-Down Budgeting	• Ensures consistency across all functions • Is far less complex and time-consuming than coordinating input from the middle and lower levels	• An imposed budget is much less likely to promote a sense of commitment
Bottom-Up Budgeting	• Encourages employees to have a sense of ownership of the output of the process, resulting in acceptance of, and commitment to, objectives expressed in the budget • Enables employees to relate performance to rewards or penalties • Provides a broader information base (middle- and lower-level managers often are far better informed about operational realities than senior managers)	• Higher costs in time and money • Quality of participation is affected by the objectives, values, beliefs, and expectations of those involved • Creation of budgetary slack

d. Participation in developing a budget may result in a **padding** of the budget, also known as budgetary slack.

1) **Budgetary slack** is the excess of resources budgeted over the resources necessary to achieve organizational goals. Slack must be avoided if a budget is to have its desired effects.

   a) The tendency of a manager is to negotiate for a less stringent measure of performance so as to avoid unfavorable variances from expectations.

2) Management may create slack by overestimating costs and underestimating revenues.

   a) A firm may decrease slack by (1) emphasizing the consideration of all variables, (2) holding in-depth reviews during budget development, and (3) allowing for flexibility in making budget changes.

   b) A manager who expects his or her request to be reduced may inflate the amount.

   c) If a budget is to be used as a performance evaluator, a manager asked for an estimate may provide one that is easily attained.

3) Slack can have positive and negative effects on the budget. It reduces the planning benefits of a budget because of the lack of accuracy.

   a) For example, a cash budget might show that US $500,000 needs to be borrowed this month. But that amount may be overstated because of managerial caution.

   b) However, absence of slack may discourage managers from implementing new programs or performing routine maintenance when the budget is tighter.

3. **Cost Standards**

   a. Standard costs are **predetermined expectations** about how much a unit of input, a unit of output, or a given activity should cost.

   1) The standard-cost system alerts management when the actual costs of production differ significantly from the standards.

   b. A standard cost is not an average of past costs but an objectively determined estimate of what a cost should be. Standards may be based on accounting, engineering, or statistical quality control studies.

   1) Because of the importance of fixed costs in most businesses, a standard costing system is usually not effective unless the organization also adopts flexible budgeting.

4. **Developing Standards**

    a. **Activity analysis** identifies, describes, and evaluates the activities and resources needed for an output.

        1) Each operation requires a unique set of inputs and procedures. Activity analysis describes the inputs and who performs the procedures.

            a) Inputs include the amounts and kinds of equipment, facilities, materials, and labor. Engineering analysis, cost accounting, time-and-motion study, and other approaches may be useful.

        2) **Historical data** may be used to set standards by firms that lack the resources to perform the complex task of activity analysis.

    b. **Direct materials.** A direct relationship often exists between unit price and quality. To set cost standards, a manufacturer must decide whether to use an input that is

        1) Cheaper per unit but results in using a larger quantity because of low quality or

        2) More expensive per unit but results in using a smaller quantity because of lower waste and spoilage.

    c. **Direct labor.** The complexity of the production process and the restrictions on cost imposed by union agreements affect cost standards. The human resource function also must be consulted to project the costs of benefits.

    d. Standards can be based on a top-down (authoritative) approach or the bottom-up (participative) approach.

        1) Team development is a form of the bottom-up approach that involves line managers and their supervisors, accountants, engineers, and other interested employees. It is implemented before standards are accepted by top management.

5. **Theoretical vs. Practical Standards**

    a. **Ideal (theoretical) standards** are standard costs assuming optimal conditions. They also are called perfection or maximum efficiency standards.

        1) They are based on the work of the most skilled workers with no allowance for waste, spoilage, machine breakdowns, or other downtime.

        2) These tight standards may have positive behavioral effects if workers are motivated to strive for excellence. But they are not widely used because of the negative effects if they are perceived to be impossible to attain.

        3) Ideal standards have been adopted by some organizations that apply continuous improvement and other total quality management principles.

        4) Ideal standards ordinarily are replaced by currently attainable standards for cash budgeting, product costing, and budgeting departmental performance. Accurate financial planning otherwise is not feasible.

    b. **Currently attainable (practical) standards** define the performance expected of reasonably well-trained workers with an allowance for normal spoilage, waste, and downtime.

        1) An alternative definition is that practical standards are possible but difficult-to-attain results.

6. **The Master Budget**

    a. The master budget, also called the comprehensive budget or the annual profit plan, consists of the organization's operating and financial plans for a specified period (ordinarily a year or single operating cycle).

        1) Carefully drafting the **budget calendar** is important. Lower-level budgets are inputs to higher-level budgets.
        2) The master budget consists of the operating budget and the financial budget. Both have interrelated sub-budgets.

    b. The emphasis of the **operating budget** is (1) on obtaining and using current resources for short-term planning and (2) as a control method for evaluating management performance. The following are its components:

        1) Sales budget
        2) Production budget
        3) Direct materials budget
        4) Direct labor budget
        5) Manufacturing overhead budget
        6) Cost of goods sold budget
        7) Nonmanufacturing budget

            a) R&D budget
            b) Selling and administrative budget

                i) Design budget
                ii) Marketing budget
                iii) Distribution budget
                iv) Customer service budget
                v) Administrative budget

        8) Pro forma income statement

    c. The emphasis of the **financial budget** is on obtaining the funds needed to purchase operating assets. The following are its components:

        1) Capital budget (completed before the operating budget and cash budget are begun)
        2) Cash budget (completed before pro forma financial statements are begun)

            a) Projected cash payment schedule
            b) Projected cash collection schedule

        3) Pro forma statement of financial position (balance sheet)
        4) Pro forma statement of cash flows

7. **Sales Budget**

    a. The sales budget is the first budget prepared because sales volume affects production and purchasing levels, operating expenses, and cash flows.

        1) The budget process is based on expectations about sales.

    b. The next step is to decide how much a manufacturer produces or a retailer purchases.

        1) Sales usually are budgeted by product or department. The sales budget also establishes targets for sales personnel.
        2) Sales credit policies affect the sales budget.

EXAMPLE 13-1	Sales Budget		
		April	Ref.
Projected sales in units		1,000	SB1
Selling price		× US $ 400	
Projected total sales		US $400,000	SB2

8. **Production Budgets**

    a. Production budgets for manufacturers are based on sales in units (not dollars) plus or minus the planned inventory change.

        1) They are prepared for each department and each item.

    b. When the production budget has been completed, it is used to prepare three additional budgets:

        1) Materials purchases, similar to the purchases budget of a retailer
        2) Direct labor budget, including hours, wage rates, and total dollars
        3) Manufacturing overhead budget, similar to a departmental expenses budget

EXAMPLE 13-2	Production Budget		

Finished goods beginning inventory is 100 units at US $125 cost per unit, a total of US $12,500. The planned finished goods ending inventory is 120 units. The organization has no work-in-process.

	Source	April	Ref.
Projected sales in units	SB1	1,000	
Plus: Planned ending inventory		120	
Minus: Beginning inventory		(100)	
Units to be produced		1,020	PB

   c. The **purchases budget** of a retailer also is based on projected unit sales.

        1) It is prepared on a monthly or even a weekly basis.
        2) Purchases should be planned so that stockouts are avoided.
        3) Inventory should suffice to avoid unnecessary carrying costs.
        4) It is similar to the production budget above. But the units are purchased rather than produced.

   d. Comparing actual production with management forecasts detects whether finished goods inventory is excessive, and comparing actual costs with budgeted costs detects unfavorable cost variances.

9. Direct Materials Budget

a. The direct materials budget is stated in units and input prices.

1) Two dollar amounts are included: the cost of materials to be used in production and the total cost of materials to be purchased.

EXAMPLE 13-3   Direct Materials Budget

Materials beginning inventory is 1,000 units at US $18 cost per unit, and the planned direct materials ending inventory is 980 units. The current materials cost per unit is US $20. Also, 4 units of materials are required per finished product.

Materials Usage (Quantity)	Source	April	Ref.
Finished products to be produced	PB	1,020	
Times: Materials units per finished product		× 4	
Total units planned for production		4,080	DMB1

Materials Purchases	Source	April	Ref.
Units planned for production	DMB1	4,080	
Plus: Planned units in ending inventory		980	
Minus: Beginning inventory		(1,000)	
Direct materials purchases		4,060	
Times: Materials cost per unit		× US $ 20	
Cost of materials purchases		US $81,200	DMB2

Materials Usage	Source	April	Ref.
Beginning inventory (1,000 × US $18)		US $18,000	
Plus: Materials purchases	DMB2	81,200	
Minus: Planned ending inventory (980 × US $20)		(19,600)	
Cost of materials usage		US $79,600	DMB3

---

10. Direct Labor Budget

a. The direct labor budget depends on, for example, wage rates, amounts and types of production, and the numbers and skill levels of employees to be hired.

b. The total direct labor cost per hour may include the regular wage rate, employer FICA taxes, health insurance, life insurance, and pension contributions.

EXAMPLE 13-4   Direct Labor Budget

A unit of the finished product requires 2 direct labor hours. According to the human resources department, the total cost per direct labor hour is US $18.

	Source	April	Ref.
Units to be produced	PB	1,020	
Times: Direct labor hours per unit		× 2	
Projected total direct labor hours		2,040	DLB1
Times: Direct labor cost per hour		× US $ 18	
Total projected direct labor cost		US $36,720	DLB2

11. **Manufacturing Overhead Budget**
    a. Manufacturing overhead is a mixed cost with variable and fixed components. (Mixed costs are defined in Study Unit 14.)
    b. The elements of **variable overhead** vary with the level of production, such as the following:
        1) **Indirect** materials
        2) Some indirect labor
        3) Variable plant operating costs (e.g., electricity)

EXAMPLE 13-5   Variable Overhead Budget

Variable overhead is applied to production based on a rate of US $3 per direct labor hour.

	Source	April	Ref.
Projected total direct labor hours	DLB1	2,040	
Variable OH rate per direct labor hour		× US $ 3	
Projected variable overhead		US $6,120	MOB1

---

   c. The elements of **fixed overhead** are constant regardless of the level of production, such as the following:
        1) Real estate taxes
        2) Insurance
        3) Depreciation

EXAMPLE 13-6   Fixed Overhead Budget

Fixed overhead is applied to production based on a rate of US $4 per direct labor hour.

	April	Ref.
Projected fixed overhead	US $8,160	MOB2

---

12. **Cost of Goods Sold Budget**
    a. The cost of goods sold budget combines the projections for the three major inputs (materials, labor, and overhead). The result directly affects the pro forma income statement. Cost of goods sold is the largest cost for a manufacturer.

EXAMPLE 13-7   Cost of Goods Sold Budget

Ending finished goods inventory has a budgeted unit cost of US $130:

$$
\begin{aligned}
\text{DM: 4 units} \times \text{US \$20} &= \text{US \$ 80} \\
\text{DL: 12 DLH} \times 18 &= 36 \\
\text{VoH: 2 DLH} \times 3 &= 6 \\
\text{FoH: 2 DLH} \times (\text{US \$8,160} \div 2,040 \text{ DLH}) &= 8 \\
&\ \underline{\text{US \$130}}
\end{aligned}
$$

	Source	April	Ref.
Beginning finished goods inventory		US $ 12,500	
Manufacturing costs:			
Direct materials	DMB3	US $79,600	
Direct labor	DLB2	36,720	
Variable overhead	MOB1	6,120	
Fixed overhead	MOB2	8,160	
Cost of goods manufactured		130,600	
Cost of goods available for sale		US $143,100	
Ending finished goods inventory			
(120 units × US $130)		(15,600)	
Cost of goods sold		US $127,500	CGSB

13. Nonmanufacturing Budget

a. The nonmanufacturing budget consists of the individual budgets for R&D, design, marketing, distribution, customer service, and administrative costs. The development of separate budgets for these functions reflects a **value-chain** approach.

   1) An alternative is to prepare a single budget for selling and administrative (S&A) costs of nonproduction functions.

b. The variable and fixed portions of selling and administrative costs must be treated separately.

   1) Some S&A costs vary directly and proportionately with the level of sales. As more product is sold, sales representatives must travel more miles and serve more customers.

   2) Other S&A expenses, such as sales support staff, are fixed. They must be paid at any level of sales.

14. Pro Forma Income Statement

a. The pro forma income statement is the end of the operating budget process.

   1) Pro forma statements report projected results.

b. The pro forma income statement is used to decide whether the budgeted activities will result in an acceptable level of income. If the initial projection is a loss or an unacceptable level of income, adjustments can be made to the components of the master budget.

EXAMPLE 13-8   **Pro Forma Income Statement**

Manufacturing Company
Pro Forma Statement of Income
Month of April

Sales		US $400,000
Beginning finished goods inventory	US $ 12,500	
Plus: Cost of goods manufactured	130,600	
Goods available for sale	US $143,100	
Minus: Ending finished goods inventory	(15,600)	
Cost of goods sold		(127,500)
Gross margin		US $272,500
Minus: Selling and administrative expenses		(82,840)
Operating income		US $189,660
Minus: Other items		(15,000)
Earnings before interest and taxes		US $174,660
Minus: Interest expense		(45,000)
Earnings before income taxes		US $129,660
Minus: Income taxes (40%)		(49,200)
Net income		US $ 80,460

STOP & REVIEW

You have completed the outline for this subunit.
Study multiple-choice questions 5 through 10 beginning on page 459.

13.3 BUDGET METHODS

1. **Project Budgets**

    a. A project budget consists of all the costs expected to attach to a particular project, such as the design of a new airliner or the building of a single ship.

        1) The costs and profits associated with it are significant enough to be tracked separately.

    b. A project typically uses resources from many parts of the organization, e.g., design, engineering, production, marketing, accounting, and human resources.

        1) All of these aspects of the project budget must align with those of the entity's master budget.

EXAMPLE 13-9   Project Budget

Function	1st Quarter	2nd Quarter	3rd Quarter	4th Quarter	Totals
Design	US $ 800,000	US $ 200,000	US $ --	US $ --	US $1,000,000
Engineering	500,000	1,200,000	400,000	--	2,100,000
Production	--	2,100,000	1,500,000	1,500,000	5,100,000
Marketing	--	100,000	200,000	200,000	500,000
Accounting	100,000	100,000	100,000	100,000	400,000
Human Resources	20,000	20,000	20,000	20,000	80,000
Totals	**US $1,420,000**	**US $3,720,000**	**US $2,220,000**	**US $1,820,000**	**US $9,180,000**

---

2. **Activity-Based Budgeting (ABB)**

    a. ABB applies activity-based costing (ABC) principles to budgeting. (An outline of ABC is in Study Unit 14.) It focuses on the numerous activities necessary to produce and market goods and services and requires analysis of cost drivers.

        1) Budget line items are related to activities performed.

        2) This approach contrasts with the traditional emphasis on functions or spending categories. The costs of non-value-added activities are quantified.

    b. Activity-based budgeting provides greater detail than traditional budgeting, especially regarding indirect costs. It permits the isolation of numerous activities and the drivers of costs.

        1) A cost pool is established for each activity, and a cost driver is identified for each pool.

        2) The budgeted cost for each pool is determined by multiplying the demand for the activity by the estimated cost of a unit of the activity.

3. **Zero-Based Budgeting (ZBB)**

    a. ZBB is a budget and planning process in which each manager must justify his or her department's entire budget every budget cycle.

        1) ZBB differs from the traditional concept of incremental budgeting, in which the current year's budget is simply adjusted to allow for changes planned for the coming year.

        2) The managerial advantage of incremental budgeting is that the manager has to make less effort to justify changes in the budget.

    b. Under ZBB, a manager must begin the budget process every year from a base of zero. All expenditures must be justified regardless of variance from previous years.

        1) The objective is to encourage periodic reexamination of all costs in the hope that some can be reduced or eliminated.

    c. The major limitation of ZBB is that it requires more time and effort to prepare than a traditional budget.

4. **Continuous (Rolling) Budgeting**

    a. A continuous (rolling) budget is revised on a regular (continuous) basis. Typically, such a budget is continuously extended for an additional month or quarter in accordance with new data as the current month or quarter ends.

        1) For example, if the budget cycle is 1 year, a budget for the next 12 months will be available continuously as each month ends.

    b. The principal advantage of a rolling budget is that it requires managers to always be thinking ahead.

        1) The disadvantage is the amount of time managers must constantly spend on budget preparation.

5. **Kaizen Budgeting**

    a. The Japanese term "kaizen" means continuous improvement, and kaizen budgeting assumes the continuous improvement of products and processes. It requires estimates of the effects of improvements and the costs of their implementation.

        1) Accordingly, kaizen budgeting is based not on the existing system but on changes yet to be made.

        2) Budget targets, for example, target costs, cannot be reached unless those improvements occur.

6. **Static and Flexible Budgeting**

   a. The static (master) budget is **prepared before the period begins and is left unchanged**. The static budget is based on only one level of expected activity (output planned at the beginning of the period).

      1) **Standard costs** are predetermined expectations about how much a unit of input, a unit of output, or a given activity should cost.

         a) The use of standard costs in budgeting allows the standard-cost system to alert management when the actual costs of production differ significantly from the standard.

      Standard cost of input = Units of input per single unit of output × Price per unit of input

      2) A standard cost is not just an average of past costs but an objectively determined estimate of what a cost should be. Standards may be based on accounting, engineering, or statistical quality control studies.

EXAMPLE 13-10   Static Budget

A company has the following static budget for the upcoming month based on production and sales of 1,000 units:

Sales revenue (US $400 per unit)	US $400,000
Minus: Variable costs (US $160 per unit)	(160,000)
Contribution margin	US $240,000
Minus: Fixed costs	(200,000)
Operating income	US $ 40,000

---

   b. A flexible budget based on standard costs is prepared for the actual level of output achieved for the period.

EXAMPLE 13-11   Flexible Budget

A company has the following flexible budget for the upcoming month based on production and sales of 800 units, 1,000 units, and 1,200 units.

	Flexible Budget Based on 800 Units	Static Budget Based on 1,000 Units	Flexible Budget Based on 1,200 Units
Sales revenue (US $400 per unit)	US $320,000	US $400,000	US $480,000
Minus: Variable costs (US $160 per unit)	(128,000)	(160,000)	(192,000)
Contribution margin	US $192,000	US $240,000	US $288,000
Minus: Fixed costs	(200,000)	(200,000)	(200,000)
Operating income	US $ (8,000)	US $ 40,000	US $ 88,000

Operating income is highly sensitive to the activity level.

STOP & REVIEW

You have completed the outline for this subunit.
Study multiple-choice questions 11 through 13 beginning on page 462.

13.4 COST-VOLUME-PROFIT (CVP) ANALYSIS AND COST-BENEFIT ANALYSIS

1. **Purpose**
   a. Also called **breakeven analysis**, CVP analysis is a means of understanding the interaction of revenues with fixed and variable costs.
      1) It explains how changes in assumptions about cost behavior and the relevant ranges in which those assumptions are valid may affect the relationships among revenues, variable costs, and fixed costs at various production levels.
      2) Thus, CVP analysis allows management to determine the probable effects of changes in sales volume, sales price, product mix, etc.
   b. The **breakeven point** is the output at which total revenues equal total expenses.
      1) All fixed costs have been recovered and operating income is zero.

2. **Assumptions of CVP**
   a. Cost and revenue relationships are predictable and linear. These relationships are true over the relevant range of activity and specified time span.
   b. Unit selling prices do not change.
   c. Inventory levels do not change, i.e., production equals sales.
   d. Total variable costs change proportionally with volume, but unit variable costs do not change.
   e. Fixed costs are constant over the relevant range of volume, but unit fixed costs vary indirectly with volume.
   f. The relevant range of volume may vary based on the time frame (e.g., operating period) considered. Therefore, the classification of fixed and variable costs may vary each time frame.
   g. The revenue (sales) mix does not change.
   h. The time value of money is ignored.

3. **Contribution Margin (CM)**
   a. The contribution margin formatted income statement is utilized in accounting as it facilitates making decisions, such as those found in CVP analysis.
   b. Variable and fixed cost behaviors are highlighted in the preparation of the contribution margin formatted income statement.
   c. Contribution margin, in total and per unit, is key to calculating various items in CVP analysis.

   $$\text{UCM} = \text{Unit sales price} - \text{Unit variable cost}$$

   1) Contribution margin per unit can also be referred to as unit contribution margin (UCM).

   d. Contribution margin ratio (CMR) is the contribution margin as a percentage of sales. This ratio can be calculated using totals or per-unit data and is also key to calculating various items in CVP analysis.

   $$\text{CMR} = \frac{\text{UCM}}{\text{Unit selling price}}$$

EXAMPLE 13-12   Contribution Margin Income Statement

Company X sells 10,000 units at a sales price of US $40 per unit. Variable expenses are US $12 per unit and fixed costs total US $200,000.

Sales (10,000 × US US $40)	US $400,000
Less: Variable expenses (10,000 × US $12)	(120,000)
Contribution margin	US $280,000
Less: Fixed expenses	(200,000)
Operating income	US $ 80,000

EXAMPLE 13-13   UCM

Using Example 13-12, UCM can be calculated by preparing the contribution margin income statement. Total contribution margin divided by the number of units equals UCM.

US $280,000 total contribution margin ÷ 10,000 units = US $28 UCM

Alternatively, use the per-unit data to find the contribution margin per unit as follows:

US $40 sales − $12 variable expenses = US $28 UCM

EXAMPLE 13-14   Total Contribution Margin

As illustrated in Example 13-12, the total contribution margin can be found by preparing the contribution margin income statement.

Alternatively, use the per-unit data to find the total contribution margin as follows:

US $40 sales − $12 variable expenses = US $28 UCM

US $28 UCM × 10,000 units = US $280,000

SU 13: Managerial Accounting: General Concepts   451

EXAMPLE 13-15   **CMR**

Using data from Example 13-12, CMR can be found using either total or per-unit data.

Alternative 1: Use totals

$$\text{Total CM} \div \text{Total sales} = \text{US } \$280,000 \div \$400,000 = 70\%$$

Alternative 2: Use per-unit data

$$\text{UCM} \div \text{Sales price per unit} = \text{US } \$28 \div \$40 = 70\%$$

EXAMPLE 13-16   **Summary**

The information from Examples 13-12 through 13-15 can be summarized as follows:

	Total	Per Unit	Percentage
Sales	US $400,000	US $40	100%
Less: Variable expenses	(120,000)	12	30%
Contribution margin	**US $280,000**	**US $28 UCM**	**70% CMR**
Less: Fixed expenses	(200,000)		
Operating income	US $ 80,000		

---

4. **Breakeven Point for a Single Product**

   a. The breakeven point can be calculated in units and in sales dollars.

      1) The breakeven point in units equals fixed costs divided by the unit contribution margin.

         $$\text{Breakeven point in units} = \frac{\text{Fixed costs}}{\text{UCM}}$$

      2) The breakeven point in sales dollars equals fixed costs divided by the contribution margin ratio.

         $$\text{Breakeven point in dollars} = \frac{\text{Fixed costs}}{\text{CMR}}$$

EXAMPLE 13-17   **Breakeven Point**

A manufacturer's product has a unit sales price of US $0.60 and a unit variable cost of US $0.20. Fixed costs are US $10,000.

Unit selling price	US $0.60
Minus: Unit variable costs	(0.20)
Unit contribution margin (UCM)	US $0.40

Breakeven point in units = Fixed costs ÷ UCM
= US $10,000 ÷ $0.40
= 25,000 units

The manufacturer's contribution margin ratio is 66.667% (US $0.40 ÷ $0.60).

Breakeven point in dollars = Fixed costs ÷ CMR
= US $10,000 ÷ .66667
= US $15,000

5. **Margin of Safety**

   a. The margin of safety is the excess of budgeted sales over breakeven sales.

      1) It is the amount by which sales can decline before losses occur.

      $$\text{Margin of safety} = \text{Planned sales} - \text{Breakeven sales}$$

      2) The margin of safety ratio is the percentage by which sales exceed the breakeven point.

      $$\text{Margin of safety ratio} = \frac{\text{Margin of safety}}{\text{Planned sales}}$$

EXAMPLE 13-18   Margin of Safety Ratio

<u>In units:</u>
Margin of safety = Planned sales − Breakeven sales
= 35,000 − 25,000
= 10,000 units

$$\text{Margin of safety ratio} = \frac{\text{Margin of safety}}{\text{Planned sales}}$$
$$= \frac{\text{US \$10,000}}{\text{US \$35,000}}$$
$$= 28.6\%$$

<u>In dollars:</u>
Margin of safety = Planned sales − Breakeven sales
= (35,000 units × US $0.60) − $15,000
= US $21,000 − $15,000
= US $6,000

$$\text{Margin of safety ratio} = \frac{\text{Margin of safety}}{\text{Planned sales}}$$
$$= \frac{\text{US \$ 6,000}}{\text{US \$21,000}}$$
$$= 28.6\%$$

---

6. **Target Operating Income**

   a. An amount of operating income, either in dollars or as a percentage of sales, is frequently required.

      1) By treating target income as an additional fixed cost, CVP analysis can be applied.

      $$\text{Target income in units} = \frac{\text{Fixed costs} + \text{Target operating income}}{\text{UCM}}$$

EXAMPLE 13-19   Units Sold for Target Operating Income

The manufacturer from Example 13-17 with the US $0.40 contribution margin per unit wants to determine how many units must be sold to generate US $25,000 of operating income.

Target unit volume = (Fixed costs + Target operating income) ÷ UCM
= (US $10,000 + $25,000) ÷ $0.40
= US $35,000 ÷ $0.40
= 87,500 units

7. Target Net Income

a. A variation of this problem asks for net income (an after-tax amount) instead of operating income (a pretax amount).

$$\text{Target income in units} = \frac{\text{Fixed costs} + [\text{Target net income} \div (1.0 - \text{Tax rate})]}{\text{UCM}}$$

EXAMPLE 13-20   Units Sold for Target Net Income

The manufacturer wants to generate US $30,000 of net income. The effective tax rate is 40%.

Target income in units = {Fixed costs + [Target net income ÷ (1.0 − .40)]} ÷ UCM
= [US $10,000 + ($30,000 ÷ .60)] ÷ $0.40
= 150,000 units

---

8. Other Target Income Applications

a. Analyses of other target income applications use the standard formula for operating income.

$$\text{Operating income} = \text{Sales} - \text{Variable costs} - \text{Fixed costs}$$

EXAMPLE 13-21   Units Sold for Target Income %

If units are sold at US $6.00 and variable costs are US $2.00, how many units must be sold to realize operating income of 15% (US $6.00 × .15 = $0.90 per unit) before taxes, given fixed costs of US $37,500?

Operating income = Sales − Variable costs − Fixed costs
US $0.90 × Q = ($6.00 × Q) − ($2.00 × Q) − $37,500
US $3.10 × Q = $37,500
Q = 12,097 units

Selling 12,097 units results in US $72,582 of revenues. Variable costs are US $24,194, and operating income is US $10,888 ($72,582 × 15%). The proof is that variable costs of US $24,194, plus fixed costs of US $37,500, plus operating income of US $10,888, equals US $72,582 of sales.

---

b. The operating income formula can also be used in this situation.

EXAMPLE 13-22   Pro Forma Target Net Income Statement

If variable costs are US $1.20, fixed costs are US $10,000, selling price is US $2, and the target is a US $5,000 after-tax profit when the tax rate is 30%, the calculation is as follows:

US $ 2Q = [$5,000 ÷ (1.0 − 0.3)] + $1.20Q + $10,000
US $.8Q = $7,142.86 + $10,000
US $.8Q = $17,142.86
Q = US $17,142.86 ÷ $.8
Q = 21,428.575 units

If planned sales are 21,429 units at US $2 each, revenue is US $42,858. The following is the pro forma income statement for the target net income:

Sales (21,429 × US $2)	US $ 42,858
Minus: Variable costs (21,429 × US $1.20)	(25,715)
Contribution margin	US $ 17,143
Minus: Fixed costs	(10,000)
Operating income	US $ 7,143
Income taxes (30%)	(2,143)
Net income	US $ 5,000

9. **Cost-Benefit Analysis**
   a. In deciding among risk responses, management must consider the costs and benefits of each risk response. A risk response should be ignored if its costs exceed its benefits.
   b. The costs associated with a risk response include both direct and indirect costs. Such costs include the costs incurred to design, implement, and maintain the risk response. Management should also consider the opportunity costs associated with each risk response.
   c. The costs and related benefits of each risk response can be measured quantitatively or qualitatively.
   d. The Application Techniques portion of the COSO Framework provides the following guidance on preparing a cost-benefit analysis:

   Virtually every risk response will incur some direct or indirect cost that is weighed against the benefits it creates. The initial cost to design and implement a response (processes, people, and technology) is considered, as is the cost to maintain the response on an ongoing basis. The costs, and associated benefits, can be measured quantitatively or qualitatively, with the unit of measure typically consistent with that used in establishing the related objective and risk tolerance. A cost–benefit analysis is illustrated [below and on the following page].

   [EXAMPLE] Evaluating the Costs and Benefits of Alternative Risk Responses

   A supplier to the automotive industry manufactures aluminum suspension modules. The supplier is in a "tandem" relationship with an original equipment manufacturer (OEM), where the vast majority of revenue is generated with the OEM. This OEM traditionally revises its forecasted demand by an average of 20%, always late in the cycle, creating a high degree of uncertainty for the supplier's production and scheduling activities. If the OEM were not to significantly revise demand late in the cycle, the supplier would be able to increase plant utilization by increasing its manufacturing of products for other customers, thereby increasing profitability. The supplier seeks to optimize scheduling and capacity planning for plant utilization to achieve 95% average monthly utilization. Management assessed the most significant risk to this objective – that is, the high level of uncertainty regarding actual demand from the OEM – and assessed costs and benefits of the following risk responses:

   Accept – Absorb the cost of having to respond to late changes in OEM demand, and consider the extent to which it can produce and sell product to other customers within the constraints of the OEM relationship

   Avoid – Exit the relationship with the OEM, and establish relationships with new customers offering more stable demand

   Share – Negotiate a revision to the current contract, stipulating a "take or pay" clause to ensure a certain rate of return

   Reduce – Install a more sophisticated forecasting system, which analyzes external factors (e.g., public information on consumer budgets, OEM and dealership inventories) and internal factors (historical orders from various sources) to better project actual demand from all customers

The following table compares the costs and benefits of these responses. Costs relate predominantly to supply chain management, marketing, information technology, and legal functions. Benefits are expressed using the unit of measure for the objective – plant utilization – and the resulting effect on targeted earnings before interest and taxes (EBIT).

Response	Cost	Description	Benefits
Accept	US $750,000	Marketing/sales efforts required to generate additional customers, and additional transportation costs, US $750,000	Management predicts it can sell an additional 2% to other customers, bringing utilization up to 82% Effect on EBIT: increase of US $1,250,000
Avoid	US $1,500,000	Unit price drops 2% due to smaller customers paying less than premium price	Marketing efforts allow utilization of 97%
		US $750,000 in increased salary costs for personnel required to identify, win, and sustain new customers	Effect on EBIT: increase of US $1,560,000
		US $250,000 in increased outbound logistics costs due to larger number of suppliers	
		US $500,000 in legal fees to negotiate and finalize new agreements	
Share	US $350,000	Unit price drops 5% due to increased pressure from OEM in response to "take or pay" nature of relationship	New contract allows utilization of 99%
		US $250,000 in legal fees to negotiate and revise contract agreement	Effect on EBIT: increase of US $100,000
		US $100,000 to improve data sharing, forecasting, and planning	
Reduce	US $1,050,000	Average unit price drops 1% due to smaller customers not paying premium price	Improved forecasting provides sufficient time to win alternative customers for a utilization of 98%
		US $500,000 for purchasing new software	Effect on EBIT: increase of US $3,170,000
		US $50,000 for new software training	
		US $500,000 for increased forecasting and analysis	

With this analysis, and considering the likelihood of each alternative and sustainability of results, management decided on [the risk reduction response].

STOP & REVIEW

You have completed the outline for this subunit.
Study multiple-choice questions 14 through 16 beginning on page 463.

13.5 RESPONSIBILITY ACCOUNTING

1. **Overview**

    a. The primary distinction between centralized and decentralized organizations is the degree of freedom of decision making by managers at many levels. **Centralization** assumes decision making must be consolidated so that activities throughout the organization may be more effectively coordinated.

    1) In **decentralization**, decision making occurs at as low a level as possible. The premise is that a local manager can make better decisions than a centralized manager.
    2) Decentralization typically reflects larger companies that are divided into multiple segments.
    3) In most organizations, a mixture of these approaches is used.

2. **Types of Responsibility Centers**

    a. A well-designed responsibility accounting system establishes responsibility centers (also called strategic business units). Their purposes are to

    1) Encourage managerial effort to attain organizational objectives,
    2) Motivate managers to make decisions consistent with those objectives, and
    3) Provide a basis for managerial compensation.

    b. A **cost center**, e.g., a maintenance department, is responsible for costs only.

    1) Cost drivers are the relevant performance measures.
    2) A disadvantage of a cost center is the potential for cost shifting. For example, variable costs for which a manager is responsible might be replaced with fixed costs for which (s)he is not.
        a) Another disadvantage is that long-term issues may be disregarded when the emphasis is on, for example, annual cost amounts.
        b) Another issue is allocation of service department costs to cost centers.
    3) Service centers exist primarily (and sometimes solely) to provide specialized support to other organizational subunits. They are usually operated as cost centers.

    c. A **revenue center**, e.g., a sales department, is responsible for revenues only.

    1) Revenue drivers are the relevant performance measures. They are factors that influence unit sales, such as changes in prices and products, customer service, marketing efforts, and delivery terms.

    d. A **profit center**, e.g., an appliance department in a retail store, is responsible for revenues and expenses.

    e. An **investment center**, e.g., a branch office, is responsible for revenues, expenses, and invested capital.

    1) The performance of investment centers can be evaluated on a return on investment basis, i.e., on the effectiveness of asset use.

3. **Performance Measures and Manager Motivation**

    a. Each responsibility center is structured such that a logical group of operations is under the direction of a single manager.

    1) Measures are designed for every responsibility center to monitor performance.

- b. **Controllability.** The performance measures on which the manager's incentive package are based must be, as far as practicable, under the manager's direct influence.
    1) Controllable factors can be thought of as those factors that a manager can influence in a given time period.
        a) Inevitably, some costs (especially common costs, such as the costs of central administrative functions) cannot be traced to particular activities or responsibility centers.
    2) Controllable cost is not synonymous with variable cost. Often, this classification is particular to the level of the organization.
        a) For instance, the fixed cost of depreciation may not be a controllable cost of the manager of a revenue center but may be controllable by the division vice president to which that manager reports.
- c. **Goal congruence.** The performance measures must be designed such that the manager's pursuit of them ties directly to accomplishment of the organization's overall goals.
    1) Suboptimization results when segments of the organization pursue goals that are in that segment's own best interests rather than those of the organization as a whole.
- d. Along with the responsibility, a manager must be granted sufficient authority to control those factors on which his or her incentive package is based.

4. **Common Costs**
    a. Common costs are the costs of products, activities, facilities, services, or operations shared by two or more cost objects. The term "joint costs" is frequently used to describe the common costs of a single process that yields two or more joint products.
        1) The costs of service centers and headquarters are common examples.
    b. Because common costs are indirect costs, identification of a direct cause-and-effect relationship between a common cost and the actions of the cost object to which it is allocated can be difficult.
        1) Such a relationship promotes acceptance of common-cost allocation by managers who perceive the fairness of the procedure.

5. **Financial vs. Nonfinancial Measures**
    a. The following are appropriate financial performance measures for responsibility centers:
        1) Cost centers -- Variable costs and total costs
        2) Revenue centers -- Gross sales and net sales
        3) Profit centers -- Sales, gross margin, and operating income
        4) Investment centers
            a) Return on assets, return on equity, return on investment, and residual income are covered in Study Unit 10.
            b) Economic value added is covered in Study Unit 12.
    b. Nonfinancial performance measures are not standardized and thus can take any form appropriate to the SBU under review.

STOP & REVIEW

You have completed the outline for this subunit.
Study multiple-choice questions 17 through 20 beginning on page 464.

QUESTIONS

13.1 Cost Management Terminology

1. An example of a direct labor cost is wages paid to a

	Factory Machine Operator	Supervisor in a Factory
A.	No	No
B.	No	Yes
C.	Yes	Yes
D.	Yes	No

Answer (D) is correct.
REQUIRED: The direct labor cost(s).
DISCUSSION: Direct labor costs are wages paid to labor that can be specifically identified with the production of finished goods. Because the wages of a factory machine operator are identifiable with a finished product, those wages are considered a direct labor cost. Because the supervisor's salary is not identifiable with the production of finished goods, it is a part of manufacturing overhead and thus not a direct labor cost.
Answer (A) is incorrect. The machine operator's wages are directly identifiable with the production of finished goods. **Answer (B) is incorrect.** The machine operator's wages are directly identifiable with the production of finished goods, while the salary of a factory supervisor is not. **Answer (C) is incorrect.** The salary of a factory supervisor is not directly identifiable with the production of finished goods.

2. In cost terminology, conversion costs consist of

A. Direct and indirect labor.
B. Direct labor and direct materials.
C. Direct labor and manufacturing overhead.
D. Indirect labor and variable manufacturing overhead.

Answer (C) is correct.
REQUIRED: The components of conversion costs.
DISCUSSION: Conversion costs consist of direct labor and manufacturing overhead. These are the costs of converting direct materials into a finished product.
Answer (A) is incorrect. All manufacturing overhead is included in conversion costs, not just indirect labor. **Answer (B) is incorrect.** Direct materials are not an element of conversion costs; they are a prime cost. **Answer (D) is incorrect.** Direct labor is also an element of conversion costs.

3. Direct materials cost is a

	Conversion Cost	Prime Cost
A.	No	No
B.	No	Yes
C.	Yes	Yes
D.	Yes	No

Answer (B) is correct.
REQUIRED: The classification of direct materials cost.
DISCUSSION: Direct materials and direct labor are a manufacturer's prime costs. Conversion cost consists of direct labor and manufacturing overhead.
Answer (A) is incorrect. Direct materials cost is a prime cost. **Answer (C) is incorrect.** Direct materials cost is not a conversion cost. **Answer (D) is incorrect.** Direct materials cost is a prime cost but not a conversion cost.

4. A company experienced a machinery breakdown on one of its production lines. As a consequence of the breakdown, manufacturing fell behind schedule, and a decision was made to schedule overtime to return manufacturing to schedule. Which one of the following methods is the proper way to account for the overtime paid to the direct laborers?

A. The overtime hours times the sum of the straight-time wages and overtime premium would be charged entirely to manufacturing overhead.

B. The overtime hours times the sum of the straight-time wages and overtime premium would be treated as direct labor.

C. The overtime hours times the overtime premium would be charged to repair and maintenance expense, and the overtime hours times the straight-time wages would be treated as direct labor.

D. The overtime hours times the overtime premium would be charged to manufacturing overhead, and the overtime hours times the straight-time wages would be treated as direct labor.

Answer (D) is correct.
REQUIRED: The proper way to account for the overtime paid to the direct laborers.
DISCUSSION: Direct labor costs are wages paid to labor that can feasibly be specifically identified with the production of finished goods. Manufacturing overhead consists of all costs, other than direct materials and direct labor, that are associated with the manufacturing process. Thus, straight-time wages are treated as direct labor. However, because the overtime premium cost is a cost that should be borne by all production, the overtime hours times the overtime premium should be charged to manufacturing overhead.
Answer (A) is incorrect. The straight-time wages times the overtime hours should still be treated as direct labor. **Answer (B) is incorrect.** Only the straight-time wages times the overtime hours is charged to direct labor. **Answer (C) is incorrect.** Labor costs are not related to repairs and maintenance expense.

13.2 Budget Systems

5. A company has budgeted sales of 24,000 finished units for the forthcoming 6-month period. It takes 4 pounds of direct materials to make one finished unit. Given the following:

	Finished units	Direct materials (pounds)
Beginning inventory	14,000	44,000
Target ending inventory	12,000	48,000

How many pounds of direct materials should be budgeted for purchase during the 6-month period?

A. 48,000
B. 88,000
C. 92,000
D. 96,000

Answer (C) is correct.
REQUIRED: The pounds of direct materials budgeted for purchase during the period.
DISCUSSION: Required production of finished units is 22,000 units (12,000 target ending inventory + 24,000 sales – 14,000 beginning inventory). Thus, 88,000 pounds of direct materials (22,000 × 4 pounds per unit) must be available. Required purchases of direct materials equal 92,000 pounds (48,000 target ending inventory + 88,000 usage – 44,000 beginning inventory).
Answer (A) is incorrect. The target ending inventory is 48,000. **Answer (B) is incorrect.** The amount that must be available for production is 88,000 pounds of direct material. The desired 4,000-pound increase in direct materials inventory must also be added. **Answer (D) is incorrect.** The changes in finished goods and direct materials inventories were not considered.

6. The major objectives of any budget system are to

A. Define responsibility centers, provide a framework for performance evaluation, and promote communication and coordination among organization segments.
B. Define responsibility centers, facilitate the fixing of blame for missed budget predictions, and ensure goal congruence between superiors and subordinates.
C. Foster the planning of operations, provide a framework for performance evaluation, and promote communication and coordination among organization segments.
D. Foster the planning of operations, facilitate the fixing of blame for missed budget predictions, and ensure goal congruence between superiors and subordinates.

Answer (C) is correct.
REQUIRED: The major objectives of any budget system.
DISCUSSION: A budget is a realistic plan for the future expressed in quantitative terms. The process of budgeting forces a company to establish goals, determine the resources necessary to achieve those goals, and anticipate future difficulties in their achievement. A budget also is a control tool because it establishes standards and facilitates comparison of actual and budgeted performance. Because a budget establishes standards and accountability, it motivates good performance by highlighting the work of effective managers. Moreover, the nature of the budgeting process fosters communication of goals to company subunits and coordination of their efforts. Budgeting activities by entities within the company must be coordinated because they are interdependent. Thus, the sales budget is a necessary input to the formulation of the production budget. In turn, production requirements must be known before purchases and expense budgets can be developed, and all other budgets must be completed before preparation of the cash budget.
Answer (A) is incorrect. Responsibility centers are determined prior to budgeting. **Answer (B) is incorrect.** Responsibility centers are determined prior to budgeting, budgets do not fix blame but rather measure performance, and goal congruence is promoted but not ensured by budgets. **Answer (D) is incorrect.** Budgets do not fix blame but rather measure performance, and goal congruence is promoted but not ensured by budgets.

7. One of the primary advantages of budgeting is that it

A. Does not take the place of management and administration.
B. Bases the profit plan on estimates.
C. Is continually adapted to fit changing circumstances.
D. Requires departmental managers to make plans in conjunction with the plans of other interdependent departments.

Answer (D) is correct.
REQUIRED: The primary advantage of budgeting.
DISCUSSION: A budget is a quantitative model of a plan of action developed by management. A budget functions as an aid to planning, coordination, and control. Thus, a budget helps management to allocate resources efficiently and to ensure that subunit goals are congruent with those of other subunits and of the organization.
Answer (A) is incorrect. Budgeting, far from taking the place of management and administration, makes them even more important. **Answer (B) is incorrect.** Basing the profit plan on estimates is a necessity, not an advantage. **Answer (C) is incorrect.** Adaption to changing circumstances is a commitment that upper management must make; it is not inherent in a budget.

8. Budgets are a necessary component of financial decision making because they help provide a(n)

A. Efficient allocation of resources.
B. Means to use all the firm's resources.
C. Automatic corrective mechanism for errors.
D. Means to check managerial discretion.

Answer (A) is correct.
REQUIRED: The major benefit of budgets.
DISCUSSION: A budget is a quantitative model of a plan of action developed by management. A budget functions as an aid to planning, coordination, and control. Thus, a budget helps management to allocate resources efficiently.
Answer (B) is incorrect. Budgets are designed to use resources efficiently, not just use them. **Answer (C) is incorrect.** Budgets per se provide for no automatic corrections. **Answer (D) is incorrect.** Budgets are a management tool and are not designed to thwart managerial discretion.

9. The master budget

A. Shows forecasted and actual results.
B. Reflects controllable costs only.
C. Can be used to determine manufacturing cost variances.
D. Contains the operating budget.

Answer (D) is correct.
REQUIRED: The purpose of the master budget.
DISCUSSION: The operating and financial budgets are subsets of the master budget. Thus, quantified estimates by management from all functional areas are contained in the master budget. These results then are combined in a formal quantitative model recognizing the organization's objectives, inputs, and outputs.
Answer (A) is incorrect. The master budget does not contain actual results. **Answer (B) is incorrect.** The master budget reflects all applicable expected costs, whether or not controllable by individual managers. **Answer (C) is incorrect.** The master budget is not structured to allow determination of manufacturing cost variances, which requires using the flexible budget and actual results.

10. Individual budget schedules are prepared to develop an annual comprehensive or master budget. The budget schedule that provides the necessary input data for the direct labor budget is the

A. Sales forecast.
B. Materials purchases budget.
C. Schedule of cash receipts and disbursements.
D. Production budget.

Answer (D) is correct.
REQUIRED: The budget schedule that provides the input data for the direct labor budget.
DISCUSSION: A master budget typically begins with the preparation of a sales budget. The next step is to prepare a production budget. After the production budget has been completed, the next step is to prepare the direct labor, materials, and overhead budgets. Thus, the production budget provides the input necessary for the completion of the direct labor budget.
Answer (A) is incorrect. The sales forecast is insufficient for completion of the direct labor budget. **Answer (B) is incorrect.** The materials purchases budget is not needed to prepare a direct labor budget. **Answer (C) is incorrect.** The schedule of cash receipts and disbursements cannot be prepared until after the direct labor budget has been completed.

13.3 Budget Methods

11. The major feature of zero-based budgeting (ZBB) is that it

A. Takes the previous year's budgets and adjusts them for inflation.

B. Questions each activity and determines whether it should be maintained as it is, reduced, or eliminated.

C. Assumes all activities are legitimate and worthy of receiving budget increases to cover any increased costs.

D. Focuses on planned capital outlays for property, plant, and equipment.

Answer (B) is correct.
REQUIRED: The major feature of ZBB.
DISCUSSION: ZBB is a planning process in which each manager must justify his or her department's full budget for each period. The purpose is to encourage periodic reexamination of all costs in the hope that some can be reduced or eliminated.
Answer (A) is incorrect. Traditional or incremental budgeting adjusts the previous year's budgets for inflation. **Answer (C) is incorrect.** ZBB is a planning process in which each manager must justify his or her department's full budget for each period. The purpose is to encourage periodic reexamination of all costs in the hope that some can be reduced or eliminated. **Answer (D) is incorrect.** It is a definition of a capital budget.

12. Butteco has the following cost components for 100,000 units of product for the year just ended:

Raw materials	US $200,000
Direct labor	100,000
Manufacturing overhead	200,000
Selling/administrative expense	150,000

All costs are variable except for US $100,000 of manufacturing overhead and US $100,000 of selling and administrative expenses. The total costs to produce and sell 110,000 units during the year are

A. US $650,000
B. US $715,000
C. US $695,000
D. US $540,000

Answer (C) is correct.
REQUIRED: The flexible budget costs for producing and selling a given quantity.
DISCUSSION: Direct (raw) materials unit costs are variable at US $2 ($200,000 ÷ 100,000 units). Similarly, direct labor has a variable unit cost of US $1 ($100,000 ÷ 100,000 units). The US $200,000 of manufacturing overhead for 100,000 units is 50%. The variable unit cost is US $1. Selling costs are US $100,000 fixed and US $50,000 variable for production of 100,000 units, and the variable unit selling expense is US $0.50 ($50,000 ÷ 100,000 units). The total unit variable cost is therefore US $4.50 ($2 + $1 + $1 + $0.50). Fixed costs are US $200,000. At a production level of 110,000 units, variable costs are US $495,000 (110,000 units × $4.50). Thus, total costs are US $695,000 ($495,000 + $200,000).
Answer (A) is incorrect. The cost at a production level of 100,000 units is US $650,000. **Answer (B) is incorrect.** The amount of US $715,000 assumes a variable unit cost of US $6.50 with no fixed costs. **Answer (D) is incorrect.** Total costs are US $695,000 based on a unit variable cost of US $4.50 each.

13. Comparing actual results with a budget based on achieved volume is possible with the use of a

A. Monthly budget.
B. Master budget.
C. Rolling budget.
D. Flexible budget.

Answer (D) is correct.
REQUIRED: The budget that permits easy comparison of actual results with a budget based on achieved volume.
DISCUSSION: A flexible budget is essentially a series of several budgets prepared for many levels of sales or production. At the end of the period, management can compare actual costs or performance with the appropriate budgeted level in the flexible budget. New columns can quickly be made by interpolation or extrapolation, if necessary. A flexible budget is designed to allow adjustment of the budget to the actual level of activity before comparing the budgeted activity with actual results.
Answer (A) is incorrect. Comparing results using a monthly budget is no easier than using a budget of any other duration. Answer (B) is incorrect. A master budget is the overall budget. It will not facilitate comparisons unless it is also a flexible budget. Answer (C) is incorrect. A rolling (or continuous) budget is revised on a regular (continuous) basis. It will not facilitate comparisons unless it is also a flexible budget.

13.4 Cost-Volume-Profit (CVP) Analysis and Cost-Benefit Analysis

14. A company manufactures a single product. Estimated cost data regarding this product and other information for the product and the company are as follows:

Sales price per unit	US $40
Total variable production cost per unit	US $24
Fixed costs and expenses:	
Manufacturing overhead	US $5,598,720
General and administrative	US $3,732,480

The number of units the company must sell in the coming year in order to reach its breakeven point is

A. 233,280 units.
B. 349,920 units.
C. 583,200 units.
D. 145,800 units.

Answer (C) is correct.
REQUIRED: The number of units to reach the breakeven point.
DISCUSSION: The breakeven point is determined by dividing total fixed costs by the unit contribution margin (UCM). The total fixed costs are US $9,331,200 ($5,598,720 manufacturing overhead + $3,732,480 general and administrative). The UCM is US $16 ($40 sales price − $24 variable production cost). Thus, the breakeven point is 583,200 units (US $9,331,200 fixed costs ÷ $16 UCM).
Answer (A) is incorrect. Failing to subtract the variable costs per unit from the sales price results in 233,280 units. Answer (B) is incorrect. Failing to include general and administrative expenses in total fixed costs results in 349,920 units. Answer (D) is incorrect. Improperly adding variable cost per unit to sales price per unit results in 145,800 units.

15. The most likely strategy to reduce the breakeven point would be to

A. Increase both the fixed costs and the contribution margin.
B. Decrease both the fixed costs and the contribution margin.
C. Decrease the fixed costs and increase the contribution margin.
D. Increase the fixed costs and decrease the contribution margin.

Answer (C) is correct.
REQUIRED: The strategy to reduce the breakeven point.
DISCUSSION: A ratio can be reduced either by decreasing the numerator or increasing the denominator. The breakeven point in units equals fixed costs divided by the unit contribution margin. The breakeven point in sales dollars is the fixed costs divided by the contribution margin ratio. Because fixed costs are in the numerator and the contribution margin is in the denominator, decreasing the fixed costs and increasing the contribution margin reduces the breakeven point.
Answer (A) is incorrect. Increasing the fixed costs increases the breakeven point. **Answer (B) is incorrect.** Decreasing the contribution margin increases the breakeven point. **Answer (D) is incorrect.** Increasing fixed costs and decreasing the contribution margin increases the breakeven point.

16. A retail company determines its selling price by marking up variable costs 60%. In addition, the company uses frequent selling price markdowns to stimulate sales. If the markdowns average 10%, what is the company's contribution margin ratio?

A. 27.5%
B. 30.6%
C. 37.5%
D. 41.7%

Answer (B) is correct.
REQUIRED: The contribution margin ratio.
DISCUSSION: The selling price can be stated in terms of the unit variable cost (UVC):

Selling price = UVC × 1.6 markup × .90 markdown
= UVC × 1.44

Substitution in the formula for contribution margin ratio (CMR) results in the following:

CMR = UCM ÷ Selling price
= (Selling price − UVC) ÷ Selling price
= [(UVC × 1.44) − UVC] ÷ (UVC × 1.44)
= (UVC × .44) ÷ (UVC × 1.44)
= 30.56%

Answer (A) is incorrect. Improperly omitting markdowns from the denominator results in 27.5%. **Answer (C) is incorrect.** Improperly omitting markdowns results in 37.5%. **Answer (D) is incorrect.** Improperly omitting markdowns from the numerator results in 41.7%.

13.5 Responsibility Accounting

17. In a responsibility accounting system, managers are accountable for

A. Variable costs but not for fixed costs.
B. Product costs but not for period costs.
C. Incremental costs.
D. Costs over which they have significant influence.

Answer (D) is correct.
REQUIRED: The accountability of managers in a responsibility accounting system.
DISCUSSION: The most desirable measure for evaluating a departmental manager is one that holds the manager responsible for the revenues and expenses (s)he can control. Controllability is the basic concept of responsibility accounting.
Answer (A) is incorrect. All variable costs may not be controllable, but some, if not all, fixed costs might be controllable. **Answer (B) is incorrect.** Not all budgeted costs are controllable by managers. **Answer (C) is incorrect.** All product costs may not be controllable, but some, if not all, period costs might be controllable.

18. A company plans to implement a bonus plan based on segment performance. In addition, the company plans to convert to a responsibility accounting system for segment reporting. The following costs, which have been included in the segment performance reports that have been prepared under the current system, are being reviewed to determine if they should be included in the responsibility accounting segment reports:

1. Corporate administrative costs allocated on the basis of net segment sales.
2. Personnel costs assigned on the basis of the number of employees in each segment.
3. Fixed computer facility costs divided equally among each segment.
4. Variable computer operational costs charged to each segment based on actual hours used times a predetermined standard rate; any variable cost efficiency or inefficiency remains in the computer department.

Of these four cost items, the only item that could logically be included in the segment performance reports prepared on a responsibility accounting basis would be the

A. Corporate administrative costs.
B. Personnel costs.
C. Fixed computer facility costs.
D. Variable computer operational costs.

Answer (D) is correct.
REQUIRED: The item included in the segment performance reports prepared on a responsibility accounting basis.
DISCUSSION: The variable computer cost can be included. The segments are charged for actual usage, which is under each segment's control. The predetermined standard rate is set at the beginning of the year and is known by the segment managers. Moreover, the efficiencies and inefficiencies of the computer department are not passed on to the segments. Both procedures promote a degree of control by the segments.
Answer (A) is incorrect. Corporate administrative costs should be excluded from the performance report. The segments have no control over their incurrence or the allocation basis. The allocation depends upon the segment sales (controllable) as well as the sales of other segments (uncontrollable). **Answer (B) is incorrect.** The segments have no control over the incurrence of personnel costs or the method of assignment, which depends upon the number of employees in the segment (controllable) in proportion to the total number of employees in all segments (not controllable). **Answer (C) is incorrect.** The segments have no control over fixed computer facility costs, and the equal assignment is arbitrary and bears no relation to usage.

19. Which of the following is **not** true of responsibility accounting?

A. Managers should only be held accountable for factors over which they have significant influence.
B. The focus of cost center managers will normally be more narrow than that of profit center managers.
C. Every factor that affects a firm's financial performance ultimately is controllable by someone, even if that someone is the person at the top of the firm.
D. When a responsibility account system exists, operations of the business are organized into separate areas controlled by individual managers.

Answer (C) is correct.
REQUIRED: The false statement about responsibility accounting.
DISCUSSION: Responsibility accounting stresses that managers are responsible only for factors under their control. For this purpose, the operations of the business are organized into responsibility centers. Costs are classified as controllable and uncontrollable, implying that some revenues and costs can be changed through effective management. Management may then focus on deviations for either reinforcement or correction. Thus, the statement that every factor is ultimately controllable by someone is not a premise of responsibility accounting.
Answer (A) is incorrect. Responsibility accounting holds managers responsible only for what they can control. **Answer (B) is incorrect.** A cost center manager is concerned with costs only, whereas a profit center manager is concerned with costs and revenues. **Answer (D) is incorrect.** This is the essence of responsibility accounting. Each manager is held accountable for factors under their control.

20. The receipt of raw materials used in the manufacture of products and the shipping of finished goods to customers is under the control of the warehouse supervisor. The warehouse supervisor's time is spent approximately 60% on receiving activities and 40% on shipping activities. Separate staffs for the receiving and shipping operations are employed. The labor-related costs for the warehousing function are as follows:

Warehouse supervisor's salary	US $ 40,000
Receiving clerks' wages	75,000
Shipping clerks' wages	55,000
Employee benefit costs (30% of wage and salary costs)	51,000
	US $221,000

The company employs a responsibility accounting system for performance reporting purposes. The costs are classified on the report as period or product costs. The total labor-related costs that would be listed on the responsibility accounting performance report as product costs under the control of the warehouse supervisor for the warehousing function would be

A. US $97,500
B. US $128,700
C. US $130,000
D. US $221,000

Answer (A) is correct.
REQUIRED: The total labor-related costs listed as product costs under the control of the warehouse supervisor.
DISCUSSION: The responsibility accounting report should list only the costs over which the warehousing supervisor exercises control. The supervisor's salary should therefore be excluded because it is controlled by the warehouse supervisor's superior. Moreover, only the product costs are to be considered. These exclude the shipping clerks' wages and fringe benefits because they are period costs (shipping is a selling expense). Thus, the only product cost under the control of the warehouse supervisor is the receiving clerks' wages (US $75,000) and the related fringe benefits (US $75,000 × 0.3 = $22,500), or a total of US $97,500.

STUDY UNIT FOURTEEN

MANAGERIAL ACCOUNTING: COSTING SYSTEMS AND DECISION MAKING

(28 pages of outline)

14.1	Cost Behavior and Relevant Range	468
14.2	Activity-Based Costing	471
14.3	Process Costing	477
14.4	Absorption (Full) vs. Variable (Direct) Costing	483
14.5	Relevant Costs and Decision Making	487

This study unit is the sixth of six covering **Domain IV: Financial Management** from The IIA's CIA Exam Syllabus. This domain makes up 20% of Part 3 of the CIA exam and is tested at the **basic** and **proficient** cognitive levels. Refer to the complete syllabus located in Appendix A to view the relevant sections covered in Study Unit 14.

14.1 COST BEHAVIOR AND RELEVANT RANGE

1. **Variable Costs**

    a. Examples are direct materials, direct labor, and manufacturing supplies.

    b. Variable cost **per unit** is constant in the short run regardless of the level of production.

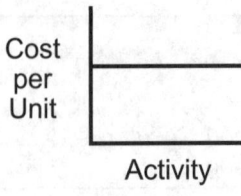

    Figure 14-1

    c. However, variable costs **in total** vary directly and proportionally with changes in volume.

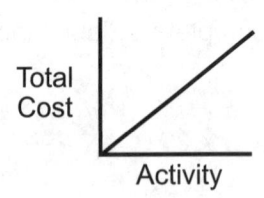

    Figure 14-2

    EXAMPLE 14-1   **Variable Cost**

    An entity requires one unit of direct material to be used in each finished good it produces.

Number of Outputs Produced	Input Cost per Unit	Total Cost of Inputs
0	US $10	US $ 0
100	10	1,000
1,000	10	10,000
5,000	10	50,000
10,000	10	100,000

    ---

2. **Fixed Costs**

    a. Examples are depreciation, rent, and insurance.

    b. Fixed costs in **total** are unchanged in the short run regardless of production level. For example, the amount paid for an assembly line is the same even if it is not used.

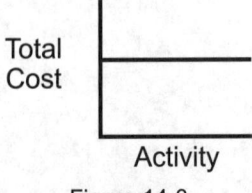

    Figure 14-3

c. However, fixed cost **per unit** varies indirectly with the activity level.

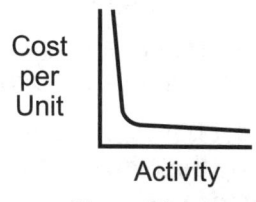

Figure 14-4

EXAMPLE 14-2   **Fixed Cost**

The historical cost of the assembly line is fixed, but its cost per unit decreases as production increases.

Number of Outputs Produced	Cost of Assembly Line	Per-Unit Cost of Assembly Line
100	US $1,000,000	US $10,000
1,000	1,000,000	1,000
5,000	1,000,000	200
10,000	1,000,000	100

---

3. **Other Cost Behaviors**

   a. Mixed (semivariable) costs combine fixed and variable elements, e.g., rental of a car for a flat fee per month plus an additional fee for each mile driven.

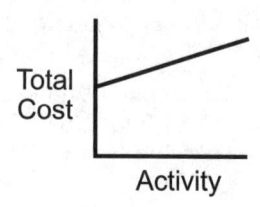

Figure 14-5

EXAMPLE 14-3   **Mixed Cost**

The entity rents a piece of machinery to make its production line more efficient. The rental is US $150,000 per year plus US $1 for every unit produced.

Number of Outputs Produced	Fixed Cost of Extra Machine	Variable Cost of Extra Machine	Total Cost of Extra Machine
0	US $150,000	US $ 0	US $150,000
100	150,000	100	150,100
1,000	150,000	1,000	151,000
5,000	150,000	5,000	155,000
10,000	150,000	10,000	160,000

b. The fixed and variable portions of a mixed cost may be estimated. Two methods of estimating mixed costs are in general use:

1) The high-low method generates a regression line by basing the equation on only the highest and lowest values in the series of observations.

    a) The difference in cost between the highest and lowest levels of activity (not output) is divided by the difference in the activity level to determine the variable portion of the cost.

EXAMPLE 14-4   High-Low Method

An entity has the following cost data:

Month	Machine Hours	Maintenance Costs
April	1,000	US $2,275
May	1,600	3,400
June	1,200	2,650
July	800	1,900
August	1,200	2,650
September	1,000	2,275

The numerator can be derived by subtracting the cost at the lowest level, July, from the cost at the highest level, May (US $3,400 − $1,900 = US $1,500).

The denominator equals the highest level of activity, May, minus the lowest level, July (1,600 − 800 = 800).

The variable portion of the cost is therefore US $1.875 per machine hour (US $1,500 ÷ 800).

The fixed portion can be calculated by inserting the appropriate values for either the high or low month in the range:

Fixed portion = Total cost − Variable portion
             = US $1,900 − ($1.875 × 800 hours)
             = US $1,900 − $1,500
             = US $400

The regression equation is y = US $400 + $1.875x

If: y = Total cost
    x = Machine hours

---

    b) The disadvantage of the high-low method is that the high and low points may not be representative of normal activity.

2) The regression (scattergraph) method is more complex. It determines the average rate of variability of a mixed cost rather than the variability between the high and low points in the range.

4. **Relevant Range**

    a. The **relevant range** defines the normal limits within which per-unit variable costs are constant and fixed costs do not change.

       1) The relevant range is established by such factors as the efficiency of an entity's current manufacturing plant and its agreements with labor unions and suppliers.

       2) The relevant range exists only for a specified time span. Thus, all costs are variable in the long run.

       3) Investment in new, more productive equipment results in higher total fixed costs and lower total and per-unit variable costs.

You have completed the outline for this subunit.
Study multiple-choice question 1 on page 495.

STOP & REVIEW

14.2 ACTIVITY-BASED COSTING

1. **Disadvantages of Volume-Based Systems**

    a. **Activity-based costing (ABC)** is a response to the increase in indirect costs resulting from changes in technology. ABC refines an existing costing system (job-order or process).

       1) Under a **traditional (volume-based)** system, overhead is accumulated in **one cost pool** and allocated to all end products using one allocation base, such as direct labor hours or direct machine hours used.

       2) Under **ABC**, indirect costs are assigned to **activities** and then rationally allocated to end products.

          a) ABC may be used by manufacturing, service, or retailing firms.
          b) ABC may be used in a job-order system or a process cost system.

    b. The inaccurate averaging or spreading of indirect costs over products or service units that use different amounts of resources is **peanut-butter costing**. Peanut-butter costing results in product-cost cross-subsidization. It miscosts one product and, as a result, miscosts other products.

c. The peanut-butter effect can be summarized as follows:

1) Direct labor and direct materials are traced to products or service units.
2) One pool of indirect costs (overhead) is accumulated for a given organizational unit.
3) Indirect costs from the pool are assigned using an allocative (rather than a tracing) procedure, such as a single overhead rate for an entire department, e.g., US $3 of overhead for every direct labor hour.

   a) The effect is an averaging of costs that may result in significant inaccuracy when products or service units do not use similar amounts of resources (cost shifting).

EXAMPLE 14-5   ABC vs. Volume-Based

The effect of product-cost cross-subsidization can be illustrated as follows:

- Two products are produced. Both require 1 unit of direct materials and 1 hour of direct labor. Materials costs are US $14 per unit, and direct labor is US $70 per hour. Also, the manufacturer has no beginning or ending inventories.
- During the month just ended, production equaled 1,000 units of Product A and 100 units of Product B. Manufacturing overhead for the month was US $20,000.

Volume-Based

Using direct labor hours as the overhead allocation base, per-unit costs and profits are calculated as follows:

	Product A	Product B	Total
Direct materials	US $ 14,000	US $ 1,400	
Direct labor	70,000	7,000	
Overhead {US $20,000 × [1,000 ÷ (1,000 + 100)]}	18,182		
Overhead {US $20,000 × [100 ÷ (1,000 + 100)]}		1,818	
Total costs	US $102,182	US $ 10,218	US $112,400
Selling price	US $ 119.99	US $ 139.99	
Cost per unit (US $102,182 ÷ 1,000)	(102.18)		
Cost per unit (US $10,218 ÷ 100)		(102.18)	
Profit per unit	US $ 17.81	US $ 37.81	

ABC

Overhead consists almost entirely of production line setup costs, and the two products require equal setup times. Allocating overhead on this basis has different results.

	Product A	Product B	Total
Direct materials	US $14,000	US $ 1,400	
Direct labor	70,000	7,000	
Overhead (US $20,000 × 50%)	10,000		
Overhead (US $20,000 × 50%)		10,000	
Total costs	US $94,000	US $ 18,400	US $112,400
Selling price	US $119.99	US $ 139.99	
Cost per unit (US $94,000 ÷ 1,000)	(94.00)		
Cost per unit (US $18,400 ÷ 100)		(184.00)	
Profit (loss) per unit	US $ 25.99	US $ (44.01)	

Under volume-based costing, Product B appeared to be profitable. But ABC revealed that high-volume Product A has been subsidizing the setup costs for the low-volume Product B.

d. Example 14-5 on the previous page assumes a single component of overhead for clarity. In reality, overhead consists of many components. The peanut-butter effect of volume-based overhead allocation is illustrated in the diagram below:

Overhead Allocation in Volume-Based Costing

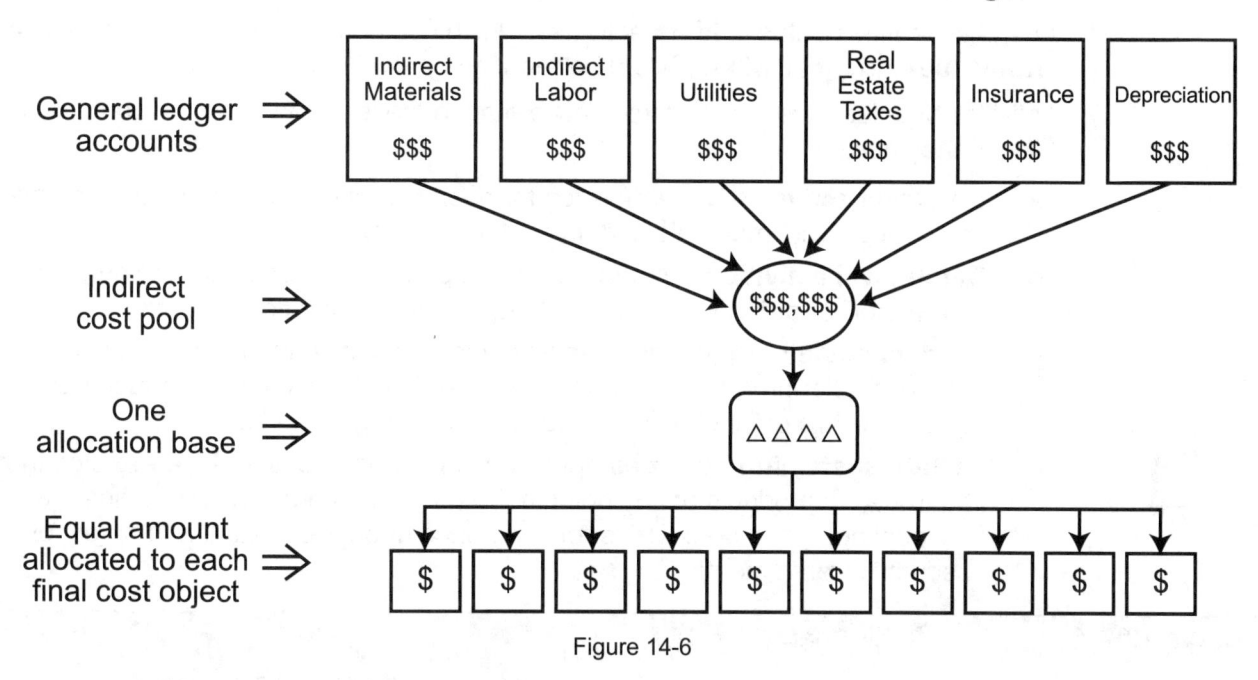

General ledger accounts ⇒ | Indirect Materials $$$ | Indirect Labor $$$ | Utilities $$$ | Real Estate Taxes $$$ | Insurance $$$ | Depreciation $$$ |

Indirect cost pool ⇒ $$$,$$$

One allocation base ⇒ △△△△

Equal amount allocated to each final cost object ⇒ $ $ $ $ $ $ $ $ $

Figure 14-6

2. **Volume-Based vs. Activity-Based**

    a. Volume-based systems are appropriate when most manufacturing costs are homogeneously consumed. In these cases, one volume-based cost driver can be used to allocate the overhead costs. However, overhead costs do not always fluctuate with volume. ABC addresses the increasing complexity and variety of overhead costs.

    b. Activity-based systems involve

    1) Identifying organizational activities that result in overhead.

    2) Assigning to activity cost pools the costs of resources consumed by the activities.

        a) A driver causes a change in cost. A **resource cost driver** is used as a cost assignment base to allocate overhead to activity cost pools.

    3) Assigning the costs accumulated in activity cost pools to final (or next) cost objects based on an activity cost driver.

        a) An **activity cost driver** is used as a cost assignment base to allocate overhead to final (or next) cost objects.

3. **Steps in Activity-Based Costing**

   a. **Step 1 – Activity Analysis**

      1) An activity is a set of work actions undertaken, and a cost pool is established for each activity.

      2) Analysis identifies **value-adding** activities, which contribute to customer satisfaction. **Nonvalue-adding** activities should be reduced or eliminated.

      3) Activities are classified in a hierarchy according to the level of the production process where they occur.

         a) **Unit-level activities** are performed for each unit of output produced. Examples are using direct materials and using direct labor.

         b) **Batch-level activities** occur for each group of outputs produced. Examples are materials ordering, materials handling, and production line setup.

         c) **Product-sustaining** (or service-sustaining) **activities** support the production of a particular product (or service), irrespective of the level of production. Examples are product design, engineering changes, and testing.

         d) **Facility-sustaining activities** apply to overall operations and therefore cannot be traced to products at any point in the production process. Examples are accounting, human resources, maintenance of physical plant, and safety or security arrangements.

EXAMPLE 14-6   Activity Analysis

Foundry, Inc., uses a job-order system to accumulate costs for its custom pipe fittings. The entity accumulates overhead costs in six general ledger accounts (indirect materials, indirect labor, utilities, real estate taxes, insurance, and depreciation). It combines them in one indirect cost pool and allocates the total to products based on machine hours.

- When this system was established, overhead was a relatively small percentage of total manufacturing costs.
- With increasing reliance on robots in the production process and computers for monitoring and control, overhead is now a greater percentage of the total. Direct labor costs have decreased.

To obtain better data about product costs, the entity refined its job-order costing system by switching to activity-based costing for the allocation of overhead.

- Management accountants interviewed production and sales personnel to determine how the incurrence of indirect costs can be viewed as activities that consume resources.
- The accountants identified five activities and created a cost pool for each:

Activity	Hierarchy
Product design	Product-sustaining
Production setup	Batch-level
Machining	Unit-level
Inspection & testing	Unit-level
Customer maintenance	Facility-sustaining

SU 14: Managerial Accounting: Costing Systems and Decision Making

b. **Step 2 – Assign Resource Cost Drivers to Resource Costs**

   1) Identifying resource costs is not as simple as in volume-based overhead allocation.

      a) A separate accounting system may be necessary to track resource costs separately from the general ledger.

   2) After resource costs have been identified, resource cost drivers are designated to allocate resource costs to the **activity cost pools**.

      a) **Resource cost drivers** (causes) are measures of the resources consumed by an activity.

EXAMPLE 14-7	Assignment of Resource Cost Drivers to Resource Costs

Foundry identified the following resources used by its indirect cost processes:

Resource	Resource Cost Driver
Computer processing	CPU cycles
Production line	Machine hours
Materials management	Hours worked
Accounting	Hours worked
Sales and marketing	Number of orders

c. **Step 3 – Allocate Resource Costs to Activity Cost Pools**

   1) This step is **first-stage allocation**.

   2) After resource cost drivers are assigned, the dollar amount of resources per resource cost driver is determined.

      a) One method is to divide the total resource cost by the total amount of the resource cost driver used by the entity.

   3) Costs of resources then are allocated to activity cost pools based on the amount of resource cost drivers used for each activity cost pool.

EXAMPLE 14-8	Allocation of Resource Costs to Activities

US $1,000,000 of materials management costs were incurred over a total of 100,000 hours worked. US $10 ($1,000,000 ÷ 100,000 hours) therefore is allocated to each activity pool for each hour of materials management worked for each cost pool.

Activity	Amount Allocated
Product design	US $250,000 for 25,000 hours
Production setup	US $270,000 for 27,000 hours
Machining	US $450,000 for 45,000 hours
Inspection and testing	US $30,000 for 3,000 hours
Customer maintenance	US $0 for 0 hours

   4) This allocation is done for each resource.

      a) A cost activity is not allocated resources if it did not use those resources.

d. **Step 4 – Assign Activity Cost Drivers to Activity Costs**
   1) After resource costs have been allocated to activity cost pools, activity cost drivers are designated to allocate these costs to final stage (or, if intermediate cost objects are used, next stage) cost objects on the basis of activity cost drivers.
      a) **Activity cost drivers** are measures of the demands on an activity by next-stage cost objects (e.g., the number of parts in a product used to measure an assembly activity).

EXAMPLE 14-9   **Assignment of Activity Cost Drivers to Activities**

The following activity cost drivers are assigned to corresponding activities:

Activity	Activity Cost Driver
Product design	Number of products
Production setup	Number of setups
Machining	Number of units produced
Inspection and testing	Number of units produced
Customer maintenance	Number of orders

---

e. **Step 5 – Allocate Amounts in Activity Cost Pools to Final Cost Objects**
   1) This final step is **second-stage allocation**.
   2) After activity cost drivers are assigned, the dollar amount of the costs in a pool per activity cost driver can be determined.
      a) One method is to divide the total cost assigned to an activity cost pool by the total amount of the activity cost driver used by the entire entity.

EXAMPLE 14-10   **Final Allocation of Activity Costs**

Knight Company is a manufacturer of pants and coats. The following information pertains to Knight's current-month activities:

Manufacturing overhead costs		Cost driver
Plant utilities and real estate taxes	US $150,000	Square footage
Materials handling	40,000	Pounds of direct material used
Inspection and testing	10,000	Number of units produced
	US $200,000	

Current-month activity level

	Pants	Coats	Total
Direct labor hours	20,000	5,000	25,000
Plant square footage	400	600	1,000
Pounds of direct material used	10,000	6,000	16,000
Number of units produced	15,000	3,000	18,000

-- Continued on next page --

> **EXAMPLE 14-10 -- Continued**
>
> Using direct labor hours as the overhead allocation base (traditional volume-based system), the manufacturing overhead costs are allocated as follows:
>
> Pants: US $200,000 × (20,000 ÷ 25,000) = US $160,000
> Coats: US $200,000 × (5,000 ÷ 25,000) = US $40,000
>
> Manufacturing overhead costs per pants: US $160,000 ÷ 15,000 = US $10.67
> Manufacturing overhead costs per coat: US $40,000 ÷ 3,000 = US $13.33
>
> Under an activity-based costing system, the manufacturing overhead costs are allocated as follows:
>
> | | Pants | | Coats | |
> |---|---|---|---|---|
> | Plant utilities and real estate taxes | US $150,000 × (400 ÷ 1,000) = | US $60,000 | US $150,000 × (600 ÷ 1,000) = | US $ 90,000 |
> | Materials handling | US $40,000 × (10,000 ÷ 16,000) = | 25,000 | US $40,000 × (6,000 ÷ 16,000) = | 15,000 |
> | Inspection and testing | US $10,000 × (15,000 ÷ 18,000) = | 8,333 | US $10,000 × (3,000 ÷ 18,000) = | 1,667 |
> | | | US $93,333 | | US $106,667 |
>
> Manufacturing overhead costs per pants: US $93,333 ÷ 15,000 = US $6.22
> Manufacturing overhead costs per coat: US $106,667 ÷ 3,000 = US $35.56

STOP & REVIEW

You have completed the outline for this subunit.
Study multiple-choice questions 2 through 5 beginning on page 495.

14.3 PROCESS COSTING

1. **Uses of Process Costing**

   a. Process cost accounting assigns costs to inventoriable goods or services. It applies to relatively homogeneous products that are mass produced on a continuous basis (e.g., petroleum products, thread, and computer monitors).

   b. Instead of using subsidiary ledgers to track specific jobs, process costing typically uses a **work-in-process** account for each department through which the production of output passes.

   c. Process costing calculates the average cost of all units as follows:

      1) Costs are accumulated for a **cost object** that consists of a large number of similar units of goods or services,

      2) Work-in-process is stated in terms of **equivalent units produced (EUP)**, and

      3) Cost per EUP is established.

2. Accumulation of Costs

a. The accumulation of costs under a process costing system is by department to reflect the continuous, homogeneous nature of the process.

b. The physical inputs required for production are obtained from suppliers.

Materials	US $XXX	
Accounts payable		US $XXX

c. Direct materials are added by the first department in the process.

Work-in-process -- Department A	US $XXX	
Materials		US $XXX

d. **Conversion costs** are the sum of direct labor and manufacturing overhead. The nature of process costing makes this accounting treatment more efficient. (Item 4., beginning on page 480, contains an outline of equivalent units.)

Work-in-process -- Department A	US $XXX	
Wages payable (direct labor)		US $XXX
Manufacturing overhead		XXX

e. Products move from one department to the next.

Work-in-process -- Department B	US $XXX	
Work-in-process -- Department A		US $XXX

f. The second department adds more direct materials and more conversion costs.

Work-in-process -- Department B	US $XXX	
Materials		US $XXX
Work-in-process -- Department B	US $XXX	
Wages payable (direct labor)		US $XXX
Manufacturing overhead		XXX

g. When processing is finished in the last department, all costs are transferred to finished goods.

Finished goods	US $XXX	
Work-in-process -- Department B		US $XXX

h. As products are sold, sales are recorded and the costs are transferred to cost of goods sold.

Accounts receivable	US $XXX	
Sales		US $XXX
Cost of goods sold	US $XXX	
Finished goods		US $XXX

i. The changes in these accounts during the period can be summarized as follows:

Direct Materials Inventory (DM)	Work-in-Progress Inventory (WIP)	Finished Goods Inventory (FG)
Beginning DM Purchases of DM (Ending DM)	Beginning WIP Conversion Costs Direct Material used (Ending WIP)	Beginning FG Cost of Goods Manufactured (Ending FG)
Direct Materials Used	Cost of Goods Manufactured	Cost of Goods Sold

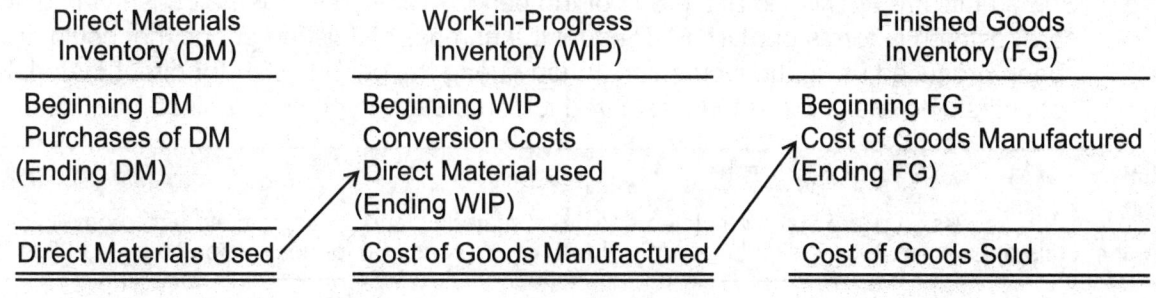

Figure 14-7

3. **Process Cost Flows**

Direct Materials
Beginning DM	Usage of direct materials
Purchase of materials	
Ending DM	

Wages Payable
| | Usage of direct and indirect labor |

Manufacturing Overhead
| Incurrence of manufacturing overhead | |

Work-in-Process Department A
Beginning WIP	Transferred out
Usage of direct materials	
Incurrence of conversion costs	
Ending WIP	

Work-in-Process Department B
Beginning WIP	Costs of goods manufactured
Transferred in	
Addition of direct materials	
Addition of conversion costs	
Ending WIP	

Finished Goods
Beginning FG	
Cost of goods manufactured	
Goods available for sale	To cost of goods sold
Ending FG	

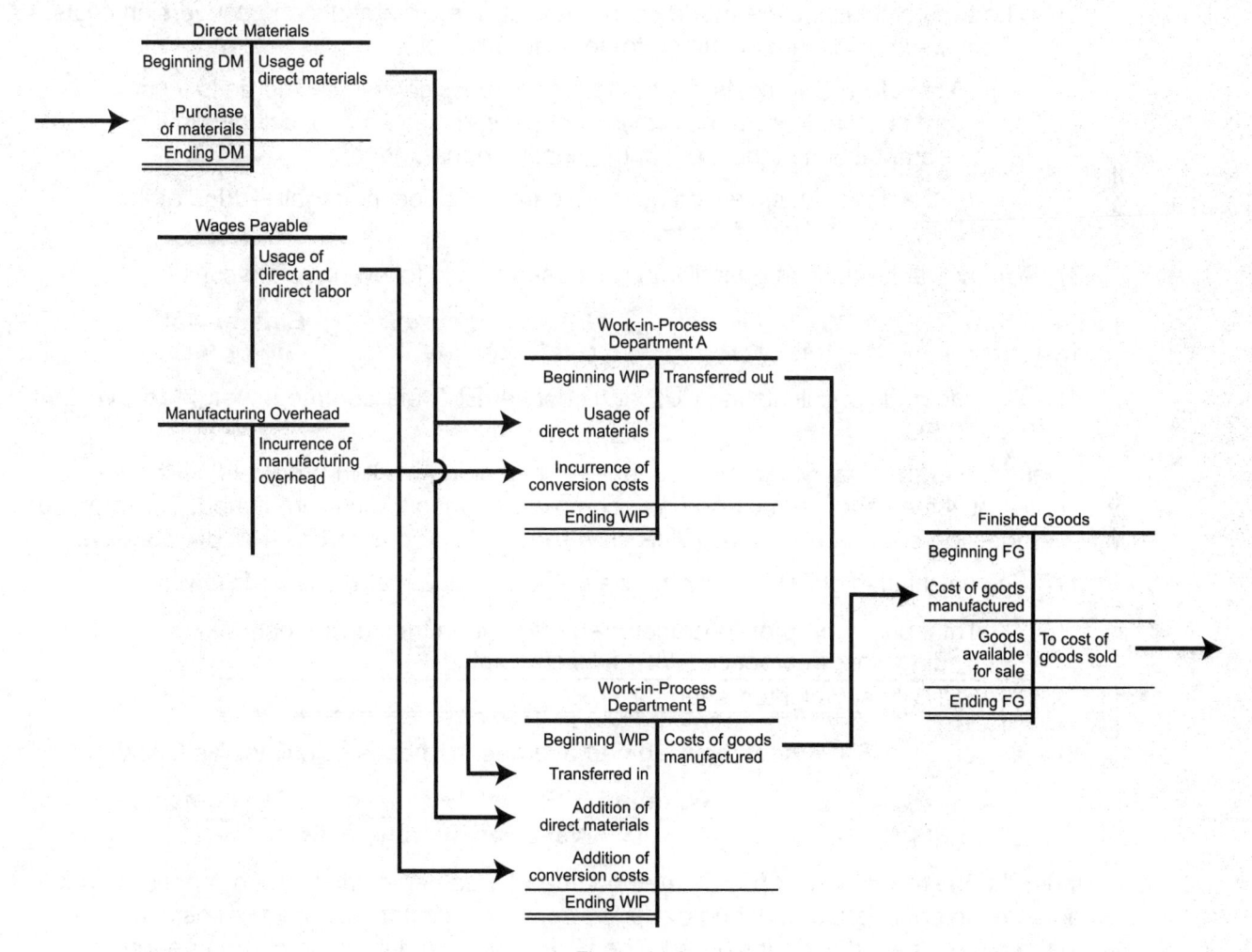

Figure 14-8

4. **Equivalent Units of Production (EUP)**

   a. Some units are unfinished at the end of the period. To account for their costs, the units are restated in terms of EUP. EUP equal the number of finished goods that could have been produced using the inputs consumed during the period. EUP for direct materials or conversion costs is the amount required to complete one physical unit of production.

   > **EXAMPLE 14-11   Calculation of EUP**
   >
   > If 1,000 work-in-process units are 80% complete as to direct materials and 60% complete as to conversion costs, the totals of EUP are 800 for direct materials (1,000 × 80%) and 600 for conversion costs (1,000 × 60%).

   1) Determining the costs of unfinished units requires two calculations: (a) calculating the EUP and (b) calculating the cost per EUP.
   2) The two calculations are made separately for direct materials and conversion costs. Conversion costs are assumed to be uniformly incurred.

      a) **Transferred-in** costs are by definition 100% complete. The units (costs) transferred in from the previous department should be included in the computation of the EUP of the second department.

         i) These costs are treated the same as direct materials added at the beginning of the period.

   3) The actual production quantity flow is based on the following relationship:

   Beginning work-in-process + Units started this period = Units transferred out (completed) + Ending work-in-process

   4) Two methods of calculating EUP and cost per EUP are common: **weighted-average** and **FIFO**.

   b. Under the **weighted-average** method, units in beginning work-in-process (WIP) are treated as if they had been started and completed during the current period. This method averages the costs of **beginning WIP with the costs of current-period production**.

   1) The calculation of EUP under the weighted-average method is as follows:

   Total units **completed** (transferred out) during the current period
   + Ending work-in-process (WIP) × % completed
   ───
   EUP under weighted-average

   2) The cost per EUP under the weighted-average method is calculated as follows:

   $$\text{Weighted-average cost per EUP} = \frac{\text{Beginning WIP costs + Current-period costs}}{\text{Weighted-average EUP}}$$

   c. Under the **first-in, first-out (FIFO)** method, the EUP in beginning work-in-process (work done in the prior period) must be excluded from the calculation. Only the costs incurred in the current period are considered. The EUP produced during the current period are based only on the work done during the current period.

   1) The calculation of EUP under the FIFO method is as follows:

   Beginning work-in-process (WIP) × % left to complete
   + Units **started and completed** during the current period
   + Ending work-in-process (WIP) × % completed
   ───
   EUP under FIFO

   NOTE: Units **started and completed** during the current period are equal to units started minus ending WIP (or equal to units completed minus beginning WIP).

2) Another equation for the calculation of EUP under the FIFO method is below:

Total units completed (transferred out) this period
+ Ending work-in-process (WIP) × % completed
− Beginning work-in-process (WIP) × % completed in the prior period
EUP under FIFO

3) The cost per EUP under FIFO is calculated as follows:

$$\text{FIFO cost per EUP} = \frac{\text{Current-period costs}}{\text{FIFO EUP}}$$

EXAMPLE 14-12 Weighted-Average vs. FIFO

	Units	Completed for Direct Materials (DM)	Completed for Conversion Costs (CC)
Beginning work-in-process (BWIP)	100	30%	40%
Units started during period	3,000		
Units completed (transferred out)	2,600		
Ending work-in-process (EWIP)	500	15%	20%

	DM	CC
Costs to account for:		
BWIP costs	US $ 1,200	US $ 2,200
Costs incurred during the period	30,000	33,000
	US $31,200	US $35,200

Step 1: Determine the equivalent units produced (EUP)

	Weighted-Average		FIFO	
	DM	CC	DM	CC
BWIP				
100 units × (1 − 30%)			70	
100 units × (1 − 40%)				60
Units completed	2,600	2,600		
Units started and completed				
2,600 units completed − 100 units BWIP			2,500	2,500
EWIP				
500 units × 15%	75		75	
500 units × 20%		100		100
EUP	**2,675**	**2,700**	**2,645**	**2,660**

Step 2: Determine the cost per EUP

	Weighted-Average		FIFO	
	DM	CC	DM	CC
(BWIP costs + Current-period costs) ÷ EUP				
(US $1,200 + $30,000) ÷ 2,675 units	US $11.66			
(US $2,200 + $33,000) ÷ 2,700 units		US $13.04		
Current-period costs ÷ EUP				
US $30,000 ÷ 2,645 units			US $11.34	
US $33,000 ÷ 2,660 units				US $12.41

d. After the EUP have been calculated, the cost per EUP under each method can be determined.

1) Under the **weighted-average method**, all direct materials and conversion costs incurred in the current period and in beginning work-in-process are averaged.

2) Under the **FIFO method**, only the costs incurred in the current period are included in the calculation.

e. When beginning work-in-process is zero, the two methods have the same results.

> **SUCCESS TIP**
>
> Beginning inventory is subtracted in the EUP calculation only when applying FIFO. The weighted-average method treats units in beginning inventory as if they had been started and completed during the current period.

5. **Other Cost Accumulation Systems**

    a. **Job-order** costing is appropriate when producing products with individual characteristics or when identifiable groupings are possible.

    1) Costs are attached to specific jobs. Each job results in a single, identifiable end product.

    2) Examples are any industries that generate custom-built products, such as shipbuilding.

    b. **Backflush** costing delays the assignment of costs until the goods are finished.

    1) After production is finished for the period, standard costs are flushed backward through the system to assign costs to products.

        a) The result is that detailed tracking of costs is eliminated.

    2) Backflush costing is best suited to companies that maintain low inventories because costs can flow directly to cost of goods sold.

        a) Backflush costing is often used with just-in-time (JIT) inventory, one of the goals of which is the maintenance of low inventory levels.

            i) It complements JIT because it simplifies costing.

6. **Spoilage and Scrap**

    a. **Normal spoilage** occurs under normal operating conditions. It is essentially uncontrollable in the short run.

    1) Because it is expected under efficient operations, it is treated as a product (inventoriable) cost, that is, absorbed into the cost of the good output.

    b. **Abnormal spoilage** is not expected to occur under normal, efficient operating conditions. It is typically treated as a period cost (a loss).

    1) Recognizing the loss resulting from abnormal spoilage under process costing is a multi-step process.

2) The manufacturer establishes inspection points, that is, the places in the production process where goods not meeting specifications are pulled from the process.

   a) The typical arrangement is to inspect units as they are being transferred from one department to the next.

   b) Each department has its own amount of spoilage, calculated using its own equivalent-unit costs.

3) The loss is equal to the number of units of abnormal spoilage multiplied by the department's equivalent-unit costs, whether weighted-average or FIFO.

   Loss on abnormal spoilage   US $XXX
         Work-in-process -- Department A   US $XXX

c. Waste has no monetary value but disposal may incur a cost.

d. Scrap consists of materials left over from the production process. If scrap is sold, it reduces manufacturing overhead. If it is discarded, it is absorbed into the cost of the good output.

STOP & REVIEW

You have completed the outline for this subunit.
Study multiple-choice questions 6 through 10 beginning on page 497.

14.4 ABSORPTION (FULL) VS. VARIABLE (DIRECT) COSTING

1. **Absorption Costing**

   a. Absorption (full) costing includes the fixed portion of manufacturing overhead in product cost.

      1) Product cost includes **all manufacturing costs** (fixed and variable).

      2) Sales minus absorption-basis cost of goods sold equals **gross profit** (gross margin).

      3) **Operating income** equals gross profit minus total selling and administrative (S&A) expenses (fixed and variable).

      4) This method is required under GAAP for external reporting purposes.

         a) The justification is that, for external reporting, product cost should include all costs to bring the product to the point of sale.

2. **Variable Costing**

   a. Variable costing includes only variable manufacturing costs in product cost.

      1) Variable costing is preferable for internal reporting.

         a) It better satisfies management's needs for operational planning and control information because it excludes arbitrary allocations of fixed costs.

         b) Furthermore, variable-costing net income varies directly with sales and is not affected by changes in inventory levels.

b. The **contribution margin** equals sales minus variable cost of goods sold and the variable portion of selling and administrative expenses.

   1) The contribution margin is an important element of the variable costing income statement.

      a) It is the amount available for covering fixed costs (fixed manufacturing, fixed selling and administrative, etc.).

EXAMPLE 14-13 **Contribution Margin Income Statement**

Company X sells 20,000 units in the current year at a sales price of US $60 per unit. X has the following costs:

Variable costs per unit		Total fixed costs	
Direct materials	US $8	Overhead	US $200,000
Direct labor	5	Selling and administrative	150,000
Overhead	2		
Selling	1		

Company X's contribution margin formatted income statement is prepared as follows:

Sales (US $60 × 20,000)		US $1,200,000
Less: Variable costs		
Direct materials (US $8 × 20,000)	US $160,000	
Direct labor (US $5 × 20,000)	100,000	
Overhead (US $2 × 20,000)	40,000	
Selling (US $1 × 20,000)	20,000	(320,000)
Contribution margin		US $ 880,000
Less: Fixed costs		
Overhead	US $200,000	
Selling and administrative	150,000	(350,000)
Operating income		US $ 530,000

---

3. **Variable vs. Absorption Costing**

   a. The accounting for variable production costs and fixed S&A expenses is identical under the two methods.
   b. The difference lies in the varying treatment of fixed production costs and presentation of variable S&A expenses.
   c. Absorption and variable costing income statements can be illustrated as follows:

Absorption Costing	**Variable Costing**
Sales	Sales
− Cost of goods sold:	− Variable expenses:
Direct materials	Direct materials
Direct labor	Direct labor
Variable overhead	Variable overhead
Fixed overhead	Variable S&A expenses
= Gross margin	= Contribution margin
− Total S&A expenses	− Fixed expenses:
= Operating income	Fixed overhead
	Fixed S&A expenses
	= Operating income

d. Note that ending finished goods inventory will differ between the two methods due to the different treatment of fixed production costs.

1) This leads to a difference in cost of goods sold and operating income.

EXAMPLE 14-14   Absorption Costing vs. Variable Costing

Beginning inventory is 0, 100 units are produced, and 80 units are sold. The following costs were incurred:

Direct materials	US $1,000
Direct labor	2,000
Variable overhead	1,500
Manufacturing costs for variable costing	US $4,500 (a)
Fixed overhead	3,000 (b)
Manufacturing costs for absorption costing	US $7,500

The following are the effects on the financial statements of using absorption or variable costing:

	Manufacturing costs	Divided by: Units produced	Equals: Per-unit cost	Times: Units in ending inventory	Equals: Cost of ending inventory
Absorption costing	US $7,500	100	US $75	20	US $1,500 (e)
Variable costing	4,500	100	45	20	900 (f)

The per-unit selling price of the finished goods was US $100, and US $200 (c) of variable selling and administrative expenses and US $600 (d) of fixed selling and administrative expenses were incurred.

The following are partial income statements prepared using the two methods:

		Absorption Costing (Required under GAAP)	Variable Costing (Internal reporting only)
	Sales	US $ 8,000	US $ 8,000
	Beginning inventory	US $ 0	US $ 0
Product Costs	Plus: Variable manufacturing costs	4,500 (a)	4,500 (a)
	Plus: Fixed manufacturing costs	3,000 (b)	
	Goods available for sale	US $7,500	US $4,500
	Minus: Ending inventory	(1,500) (e)	(900) (f)
	Cost of goods sold	US $(6,000)	US $(3,600)
	Minus: Variable S&A expenses		(200) (c)
	Gross profit (abs.) or contribution margin (var.)	US $ 2,000	US $ 4,200
Period Costs	Minus: Fixed manufacturing costs		(3,000) (b)
	Minus: Variable S&A expenses	(200) (c)	
	Minus: Fixed S&A expenses	(600) (d)	(600) (d)
	Operating income	US $ 1,200	US $ 600

Given no beginning inventory, the difference in operating income (US $1,200 – $600 = US $600) is the difference between the ending inventory amounts (US $1,500 – $900 = US $600).

Under the absorption method, 20% of the fixed overhead costs (US $3,000 × 20% = US $600) is recorded as an asset because 20% of the month's production (100 units available – 80 units sold = 20 units) is still in inventory.

e. The following table summarizes product and period costs under both methods:

	Absorption Costing (Required under GAAP)	Variable Costing (For Internal Reporting Only)
Product Costs (Included in Cost of Goods Sold)	Variable production costs	Variable production costs
	Fixed production costs	
Period Costs (Excluded from Cost of Goods Sold)		Fixed production costs
	Variable S&A expenses	Variable S&A expenses
	Fixed S&A expenses	Fixed S&A expenses

4. **Effects on Operating Income**

   a. As production and sales change, the two methods have varying effects on operating income.

   b. When production and sales are equal for a period, the two methods report the same operating income.

      1) Total fixed costs for the period are expensed during the period under both methods.

   c. When production and sales are not equal for a period, the two methods report different operating incomes as illustrated below.

When production △△△△△△△ exceeds sales, △△△ ending inventory increases. ↑↑↑↑↑↑↑↑↑↑↑↑↑↑	When production △△△ is less than sales, △△△△△△△ ending inventory decreases. ↓↓↓↓↓↓
Under absorption costing, some fixed manufacturing costs are included in ending inventory, reducing COGS.	**Under absorption costing,** fixed manufacturing costs included in beginning inventory are expensed, increasing COGS.
Under variable costing, all fixed costs of the current period are expensed. No fixed costs are included in ending inventory.	**Under variable costing,** all fixed costs of the current period are expensed. No fixed costs are included in ending inventory.
Operating income is higher under <u>absorption</u> costing.	**Operating income is higher under <u>variable</u> costing.**

Figure 14-9

You have completed the outline for this subunit.
Study multiple-choice questions 11 through 15 beginning on page 499.

STOP & REVIEW

14.5 RELEVANT COSTS AND DECISION MAKING

1. **Relevant vs. Irrelevant Factors**

    a. In decision making, an organization must focus only on relevant revenues and costs. To be relevant, the revenues and costs must

    1) Be received or incurred in the future.

        a) Costs that have already been incurred or to which the organization is committed, called sunk costs, have no bearing on any future decisions.

        b) EXAMPLE: A manufacturer is considering upgrading its production equipment owing to the obsolescence of its current machinery. The amounts paid for the existing equipment are sunk costs. They make no difference in the decision to modernize.

    2) Differ among the possible courses of action.

        a) EXAMPLE: A union contract may require 6 months of wage continuance in case of a plant shutdown. Thus, 6 months of wages must be disbursed regardless of whether the plant remains open.

    b. Only avoidable costs are relevant.

    1) An avoidable cost may be saved by not adopting a particular option. Avoidable costs might include variable materials costs, direct labor costs, and opportunity costs (e.g., idle space or unused workplace capacity).

    2) An unavoidable cost cannot be avoided if a particular action is taken.

        a) For example, if a company has a long-term lease on a building, closing the business in that building will not eliminate the need to pay rent. Thus, the rent is an unavoidable cost.

c. Incremental (marginal or differential) costs are inherent in the concept of relevance.

1) Throughout the relevant range, the incremental cost of an additional unit of output is the same. Once a certain level of output is reached, however, the current production capacity is insufficient, and another increment of fixed costs must be incurred.

2) In the short run, management decisions are based on incremental costs without regard to overhead costs that are fixed in the short run (fixed overhead). Thus, the emphasis in the short run should be on controllable costs.

a) For example, service department costs allocated as a part of overhead may not be controllable in the short run.

EXAMPLE 14-15 — **Special Order and Relevant Costs**

A firm produces a product for which it incurs the following unit costs:

Direct materials	US $2.00
Direct labor	3.00
Variable overhead	.50
Fixed overhead	.50
Total cost	US $6.00

The product normally sells for US $10 per unit. An application of marginal analysis is necessary if a foreign buyer, who has never before been a customer, offers to pay US $5.60 per unit for a special order of the firm's product. The immediate reaction might be to refuse the offer because the selling price is less than the average cost of production.

However, marginal analysis results in a different decision. Assuming that the firm has idle capacity, only the additional costs should be considered. In this example, the only marginal costs are for direct materials, direct labor, and variable overhead. No additional fixed overhead costs would be incurred. Because marginal revenue (the US $5.60 selling price) exceeds marginal costs (US $2 materials + $3 labor + $.50 variable OH = US $5.50 per unit), accepting the special order will be profitable.

If a competitor bids US $5.80 per unit, the firm can still profitably accept the special order while underbidding the competitor by setting a price below US $5.80 per unit but above US $5.50 per unit.

---

2. **Submitting Bids for the Lowest Selling Price**

a. Bids should be made at prices that meet or exceed incremental cost depending on how competitive the bid needs to be.

1) A bid lower than incremental cost can result in lower profit for the company.

a) However, lower bids are more competitive and are therefore closer to incremental cost.

2) The company must weigh quantitative and qualitative factors when deciding on a final bid.

a) Whether available capacity exists affects whether fixed costs will be included in the lowest possible bid price.

3. **Special Orders When Available Capacity Exists**

a. When a manufacturer has available production capacity, accepting a special order has no opportunity cost. Assuming the capacity needed for the special order is not greater than the idle capacity, no current production is displaced.

1) When capacity is available, fixed costs are **irrelevant**.

2) The order should be accepted if the minimum price for the product is equal to the variable costs.

EXAMPLE 14-16	Special Order -- Available Capacity

Normal unit pricing for a manufacturer's product is as follows:

Direct materials and labor	US $15.00
Variable overhead	3.00
Fixed overhead	5.00
Variable selling	1.50
Fixed selling and administrative	12.00
Total cost	US $36.50

If the manufacturer receives a special order for which capacity exists, the lowest bid the company could offer is US $19.50 ($15.00 + $3.00 + $1.50).

4. **Special Orders in the Absence of Available Capacity**

   a. When a manufacturer lacks available production capacity, the differential (marginal or incremental) costs of accepting the order must be considered.

      1) Although fixed costs are committed, the manufacturer must reduce current production to fill the special order. The firm must consider the opportunity cost of redirecting productive capacity away from (possibly more profitable) products.

      2) The revenue, variable costs, and fixed costs of the reduced production are **relevant**.

EXAMPLE 14-17	Special Order -- No Available Capacity

Using the information from Example 14-16, if the manufacturer receives a special order for which capacity does not exist, the lowest bid that can be offered is US $36.50.

In addition to fixed costs, any revenue lost from reducing or stopping production of other products is relevant when determining the lowest acceptable bid price.

5. **Make-or-Buy Decisions (Insourcing vs. Outsourcing)**

   a. The firm should use available resources as efficiently as possible before outsourcing.

      1) If the total relevant costs of production are **less** than the cost to buy the item, it should be made in-house.

      2) If the total relevant costs of production are **more** than the costs to buy the item, it should be bought (outsourced).

   b. As with a special order, the manager considers only the costs relevant to the investment decision. The key variable is total relevant costs, not all total costs.

      1) **Sunk** costs are irrelevant.

      2) Costs that do not differ between two alternatives should be ignored because they are not relevant to the decision being made.

      3) As described above, opportunity costs must be considered when idle capacity is not available.

   c. The firm also should consider the qualitative aspects of the decision.

      1) Will the product quality be as high if a component is outsourced rather than produced internally?

      2) How reliable are the suppliers?

6. **Make-or-Buy Decisions When Available Capacity Exists**

    a. When capacity is available, fixed costs are **irrelevant** in deciding whether to make or buy the product.

EXAMPLE 14-18	Make-or-Buy Decision -- Available Capacity

    Lawton must determine whether to make or buy an order of 1,000 frames. Lawton can purchase the frames for US $13 or choose to make them in-house. Lawton currently has adequate available capacity. Cost information for the frames is as follows:

Total variable costs	US $10
Allocable fixed costs	5
Total unit costs	US $15

    Because capacity is available, the allocable fixed costs are not relevant. The total relevant costs of US $10 are less than the US $13 cost to purchase. Lawton should make the frames.

7. **Make-or-Buy Decisions in the Absence of Available Capacity**

    a. When capacity is not available, the differential (marginal or incremental) costs of accepting the order must be considered.

    1) The revenue, variable costs, and fixed costs related to reduced production of existing product lines are **relevant** in deciding whether to make or buy the product.

EXAMPLE 14-19	Make-or-Buy Decision -- No Available Capacity

    Continuing from Example 14-18, Lawton has received another special order for 1,000 frames, but no capacity is available this month.

    Thus, allocable fixed costs are relevant. The total relevant costs of US $15 are more than the US $13 cost to purchase; therefore, Lawton should purchase the frames.

8. **Sell-or-Process-Further Decisions**

    a. In determining whether to sell a product at the split-off point or process the item further at additional cost, the joint cost of the product is irrelevant because it is a sunk cost.

    1) **Joint (common) costs** are incurred up to the point at which the products become separately identifiable (the split-off point).

        a) Joint costs include direct materials, direct labor, and manufacturing overhead. Because they are not separately identifiable, they must be allocated to the individual joint products.

    b. At the split-off point, the joint products become separate and costs incurred after the split-off point are separable costs.

    1) Separable costs can be identified with a particular joint product and are allocated to a specific unit of output.

    2) Separable costs are relevant when determining whether to sell or process further.

c. Because joint costs cannot be traced to individual products, they must be allocated. The methods available for this allocation include the following:

1) The physical-measure-based approach employs a physical measure, such as volume, weight, or a linear measure.
2) Market-based approaches assign a proportionate amount of the total cost to each product on a monetary basis.
   a) Sales-value at split-off method
   b) Estimated net realizable value (NRV) method
   c) Constant-gross-margin percentage NRV method

d. The **physical-unit method** allocates joint production costs to each product based on their relative proportions of the measure selected.

EXAMPLE 14-20   Physical-Unit Method

A refinery processes 1,000 barrels of crude oil and incurs US $100,000 of processing costs. The process results in the following outputs. Under the physical unit method, the joint costs up to split-off are allocated as follows:

Asphalt	US $100,000 × (300 barrels ÷ 1,000 barrels) =	US $ 30,000
Fuel oil	US $100,000 × (300 barrels ÷ 1,000 barrels) =	30,000
Diesel fuel	US $100,000 × (200 barrels ÷ 1,000 barrels) =	20,000
Kerosene	US $100,000 × (100 barrels ÷ 1,000 barrels) =	10,000
Gasoline	US $100,000 × (100 barrels ÷ 1,000 barrels) =	10,000
Joint costs allocated		US $100,000

---

1) The physical-unit method's simplicity makes it appealing, but it does not match costs with the individual products' revenue-generating potential.

e. The **sales-value at split-off method** is based on the relative sales values of the separate products at split-off.

EXAMPLE 14-21   Sales-Value at Split-Off Method

The refinery from Example 14-20 estimates that the five outputs can sell for the following prices at split-off:

Asphalt	300 barrels @ US $ 60/barrel =	US $ 18,000
Fuel oil	300 barrels @ US $180/barrel =	54,000
Diesel fuel	200 barrels @ US $160/barrel =	32,000
Kerosene	100 barrels @ US $ 80/barrel =	8,000
Gasoline	100 barrels @ US $180/barrel =	18,000
Total sales value at split-off		US $130,000

The total expected sales value for the entire production run at split-off is US $130,000. The total joint costs to be allocated are multiplied by the proportion of the total expected sales of each product:

Asphalt	US $100,000 × ($18,000 ÷ $130,000) =	US $ 13,846
Fuel oil	US $100,000 × ($54,000 ÷ $130,000) =	41,539
Diesel fuel	US $100,000 × ($32,000 ÷ $130,000) =	24,615
Kerosene	US $100,000 × ($ 8,000 ÷ $130,000) =	6,154
Gasoline	US $100,000 × ($18,000 ÷ $130,000) =	13,846
Joint costs allocated		US $100,000

f. The **estimated net realizable value (NRV)** method also allocates joint costs based on the relative market values of the products.

    1) The significant difference is that, under the estimated NRV method, all separable costs necessary to make the product salable are subtracted before the allocation is made.

EXAMPLE 14-22   **Estimated NRV Method**

The refinery from Example 14-20 estimates final sales prices as follows:

Asphalt	300 barrels @ US $ 70/barrel	=	US $ 21,000
Fuel oil	300 barrels @ US $200/barrel	=	60,000
Diesel fuel	200 barrels @ US $180/barrel	=	36,000
Kerosene	100 barrels @ US $ 90/barrel	=	9,000
Gasoline	100 barrels @ US $190/barrel	=	19,000

From these amounts, separable costs are subtracted (these costs are given):

Asphalt	US $21,000 − $1,000	=	US $ 20,000
Fuel oil	US $60,000 − $1,000	=	59,000
Diesel fuel	US $36,000 − $1,000	=	35,000
Kerosene	US $ 9,000 − $2,000	=	7,000
Gasoline	US $19,000 − $2,000	=	17,000
	Total net realizable value		US $138,000

The total joint costs to be allocated are multiplied by the proportion of the final expected sales of each product:

Asphalt	US $100,000 × ($20,000 ÷ $138,000)	=	US $ 14,493
Fuel oil	US $100,000 × ($59,000 ÷ $138,000)	=	42,754
Diesel fuel	US $100,000 × ($35,000 ÷ $138,000)	=	25,362
Kerosene	US $100,000 × ($ 7,000 ÷ $138,000)	=	5,072
Gasoline	US $100,000 × ($17,000 ÷ $138,000)	=	12,319
	Joint costs allocated		US $100,000

---

g. The **constant-gross-margin percentage NRV** method is based on allocating joint costs so that the gross-margin percentage is the same for every product.

    1) This method

        a) Determines the overall gross-margin percentage.

        b) Subtracts the appropriate gross margin from the final sales value of each product to calculate total costs for that product.

        c) Subtracts the separable costs to arrive at the joint cost amount.

EXAMPLE 14-23   **Constant-Gross-Margin % NRV Method**

The refinery from Example 14-20 uses the same calculation of expected final sales price as under the estimated NRV method:

Asphalt	300 barrels @ US $ 70/barrel	=	US $ 21,000
Fuel oil	300 barrels @ US $200/barrel	=	60,000
Diesel fuel	200 barrels @ US $180/barrel	=	36,000
Kerosene	100 barrels @ US $ 90/barrel	=	9,000
Gasoline	100 barrels @ US $190/barrel	=	19,000
	Total of final sales prices		US $145,000

-- Continued on next page --

EXAMPLE 14-23 -- Continued

The final sales value for the entire production run is US $145,000. From this total, the joint costs and total separable costs are subtracted to determine a total gross margin for all products:

$$US \$145,000 - \$100,000 - \$7,000 = US \$38,000$$

The gross margin percentage then can be derived:

$$US \$38,000 \div \$145,000 = 26.21\%$$

Gross margin is subtracted from each product to determine cost of goods sold:

Asphalt	US $21,000 – ($21,000 × 26.21%) =	US $15,497
Fuel oil	US $60,000 – ($60,000 × 26.21%) =	44,276
Diesel fuel	US $36,000 – ($36,000 × 26.21%) =	26,565
Kerosene	US $ 9,000 – ($ 9,000 × 26.21%) =	6,641
Gasoline	US $19,000 – ($19,000 × 26.21%) =	14,021

The separable costs from each product are subtracted to determine the allocated joint costs:

Asphalt	US $15,497 – $1,000 =	US $ 14,497
Fuel oil	US $44,276 – $1,000 =	43,276
Diesel fuel	US $26,565 – $1,000 =	25,565
Kerosene	US $ 6,641 – $2,000 =	4,641
Gasoline	US $14,021 – $2,000 =	12,021
Joint costs allocated		US $100,000

EXAMPLE 14-24   Sell vs. Process Further at Split-Off

A joint process yields two products, X and Y. Each product can be sold at its split-off point or processed further. All additional processing costs are variable and can be traced to each product. Joint production costs are US $25,000. Other sales and cost data are as follows:

	Product X	Product Y
Sales value at split-off point	US $55,000	US $30,000
Final sales value if processed further	75,000	45,000
Additional costs beyond split-off	12,000	17,000

Whether the profit is higher to sell at the split-off point or to process further is determined as follows:

	Product X	Product Y
Sales value	US $ 75,000	US $ 45,000
Allocated joint costs	(16,176)*	(8,824)**
Further processing costs	(12,000)	(17,000)
Profit	US $ 46,824	US $ 19,176

	Split Off X	Split Off Y
Sales value	US $ 55,000	US $ 30,000
Allocated joint costs	16,176*	(8,824)**
Profit	US $ 38,824	US $ 21,176

$$* \left[\left(\frac{US \$55,000}{\$55,000 + \$30,000}\right) \times \$25,000\right]$$

$$** \left[\left(\frac{US \$30,000}{\$55,000 + \$30,000}\right) \times \$25,000\right]$$

The profit is higher for Product X after further processing and higher for Y at the split-off point. Accordingly, Product X should be processed further and Product Y should be used at the split-off point.

9. **Disinvestment Decisions**

   a. Disinvestment decisions are the opposite of capital budgeting decisions, that is, to terminate an operation, product or product line, business segment, branch, or major customer rather than start one.

      1) In general, if the marginal cost of a project exceeds the marginal revenue, the firm should disinvest.

   b. An entity making a disinvestment decision should

      1) Identify fixed costs that will be eliminated by the disinvestment decision (e.g., insurance on equipment used).

      2) Determine the revenue needed to justify continuing operations. In the short run, this amount should at least equal the variable cost of production or continued service.

      3) Establish the opportunity cost of funds that will be received upon disinvestment (e.g., salvage value).

      4) Determine whether the carrying amount of the assets is equal to their economic value. If not, reevaluate the decision using current fair value rather than the carrying amount.

   c. When a firm disinvests, excess capacity exists unless another project uses this capacity immediately. The cost of idle capacity should not be treated as a relevant cost. However, the additional costs incurred for using idle capacity should be treated as a relevant cost.

EXAMPLE 14-25   Disinvestment Decision

A firm needs to decide whether to discontinue unprofitable segments. Abbreviated income statements of the two possible unprofitable segments are shown below. The other segments, not shown, are profitable with income over US $200,000.

	Department A	Department B
Sales	US $275,000	US $115,000
Cost of goods sold	160,000	55,000
Other variable costs	130,000	50,000
Allocated corporate costs	70,000	30,000
Income (loss)	(85,000)	(20,000)

Only relevant costs should be considered in making this decision. Because the allocated corporate costs will be incurred if the segment is discontinued, they should be ignored. Accordingly, the income (loss) for each segment is calculated as follows:

	Department A	Department B
Sales	US $ 275,000	US $115,000
Cost of goods sold	(160,000)	(55,000)
Other variable costs	(130,000)	(50,000)
Income (loss)	US $ (15,000)	US $ 10,000

The amount of US $15,000 will be saved if Department A discontinued. Thus, it should be discontinued. But, discontinuing Department B loses a profit of US $10,000, so it should continue.

STOP & REVIEW

You have completed the outline for this subunit.
Study multiple-choice questions 16 through 20 beginning on page 501.

SU 14: Managerial Accounting: Costing Systems and Decision Making

QUESTIONS

14.1 Cost Behavior and Relevant Range

1. An assembly plant accumulates its variable and fixed manufacturing overhead costs in a single cost pool, which is then applied to work in process using a single application base. The assembly plant management wants to estimate the magnitude of the total manufacturing overhead costs for different volume levels of the application activity base using a flexible budget formula. If there is an increase in the application activity base that is within the relevant range of activity for the assembly plant, which one of the following relationships regarding variable and fixed costs is true?

A. The variable cost per unit is constant, and the total fixed costs decrease.

B. The variable cost per unit is constant, and the total fixed costs increase.

C. The variable cost per unit and the total fixed costs remain constant.

D. The variable cost per unit increases, and the total fixed costs remain constant.

Answer (C) is correct.
REQUIRED: The effect on variable and fixed costs of a change in activity within the relevant range.
DISCUSSION: Total variable cost changes when changes in the activity level occur within the relevant range. The cost per unit for a variable cost is constant for all activity levels within the relevant range. Thus, if the activity volume increases within the relevant range, total variable costs will increase. A fixed cost does not change when volume changes occur in the activity level within the relevant range. If the activity volume increases within the relevant range, total fixed costs will remain unchanged.
Answer (A) is incorrect. The variable cost per unit and the total fixed costs are constant if the activity level increases within the relevant range. **Answer (B) is incorrect.** The variable cost per unit and the total fixed costs are constant if the activity level increases within the relevant range. **Answer (D) is incorrect.** The variable cost per unit and the total fixed costs are constant if the activity level increases within the relevant range.

14.2 Activity-Based Costing

2. Cost allocation is the process of assigning indirect costs to a cost object. The indirect costs are grouped in cost pools and then allocated by a common allocation base to the cost object. The base that is employed to allocate a homogeneous cost pool should

A. Have a cause-and-effect relationship with the cost items in the cost pool.

B. Assign the costs in the pool uniformly to cost objects even if the cost objects use resources in a nonuniform way.

C. Be a nonfinancial measure (e.g., number of setups) because a nonfinancial measure is more objective.

D. Have a high correlation with the cost items in the cost pool as the sole criterion for selection.

Answer (A) is correct.
REQUIRED: The characteristic of a base used to allocate a homogeneous cost pool.
DISCUSSION: A cost allocation base is the common denominator for systematically correlating indirect costs and a cost object. The cost driver of the indirect costs is ordinarily the allocation base. In a homogeneous cost pool, all costs should have the same or a similar cause-and-effect relationship with the cost allocation base.
Answer (B) is incorrect. If an allocation base uniformly assigns costs to cost objects when the cost objects use resources in a nonuniform way, the base is smoothing or spreading the costs. Smoothing can result in undercosting or overcosting of products, with adverse effects on product pricing, cost management and control, and decision making. **Answer (C) is incorrect.** Financial measures (e.g., sales dollars and direct labor costs) and nonfinancial measures (e.g., setups and units shipped) can be used as allocation bases. **Answer (D) is incorrect.** High correlation between the cost items in a pool and the allocation base does not necessarily mean that a cause-and-effect relationship exists. Two variables may move together without such a relationship. The perceived relationship between the cost driver (allocation base) and the indirect costs should have economic plausibility and high correlation.

3. Which of the following is true about activity-based costing?

A. It should not be used with process or job costing.
B. It can be used only with process costing.
C. It can be used only with job costing.
D. It can be used with either process or job costing.

Answer (D) is correct.
REQUIRED: The true statement about ABC.
DISCUSSION: Activity-based costing may be used by manufacturing, service, or retailing entities and in job-order or process costing systems.

4. A company with three products classifies its costs as belonging to five functions: design, production, marketing, distribution, and customer services. For pricing purposes, all company costs are assigned to the three products. The direct costs of each of the five functions are traced directly to the three products. The indirect costs of each of the five business functions are collected into five separate cost pools and then assigned to the three products using appropriate allocation bases. The allocation base that will most likely be the best for allocating the indirect costs of the distribution function is

A. Number of customer phone calls.
B. Number of shipments.
C. Number of sales persons.
D. Dollar sales volume.

Answer (B) is correct.
REQUIRED: The best allocation base for allocating the indirect costs of the distribution function.
DISCUSSION: The number of shipments is an appropriate cost driver. A cause-and-effect relationship may exist between the number of shipments and distribution costs.
Answer (A) is incorrect. The number of customer phone calls has little relation to distribution. It is probably more closely related to customer service. **Answer (C) is incorrect.** The number of sales persons is not related to distribution. It is more closely related to marketing. **Answer (D) is incorrect.** The dollar sales volume is not necessarily related to distribution. It is more likely related to marketing.

5. Which of the following statements about activity-based costing (ABC) is **false**?

A. Activity-based costing is useful for allocating marketing and distribution costs.
B. Activity-based costing is more likely to result in major differences from traditional costing systems if the firm manufactures only one product rather than multiple products.
C. In activity-based costing, cost drivers are what cause costs to be incurred.
D. Activity-based costing differs from traditional costing systems in that products are not cross-subsidized.

Answer (B) is correct.
REQUIRED: The false statement about activity-based costing (ABC).
DISCUSSION: ABC determines the activities that will serve as cost objects and then accumulates a cost pool for each activity using the appropriate activity base (cost driver). It is a system that may be employed with job order or process costing methods. Thus, when there is only one product, the allocation of costs to the product is trivial. All of the cost is assigned to the one product; the particular method used to allocate the costs does not matter.
Answer (A) is incorrect. Marketing and distribution costs should be allocated to specific products.
Answer (C) is incorrect. ABC determines the activities that will serve as cost objects and then accumulates a cost pool for each activity using the appropriate activity base (cost driver). **Answer (D) is incorrect.** Under ABC, a product is allocated only those costs that pertain to its production; that is, products are not cross-subsidized.

14.3 Process Costing

6. A new advertising agency serves a wide range of clients including manufacturers, restaurants, service businesses, department stores, and other retail establishments. The accounting system the advertising agency has most likely adopted for its recordkeeping in accumulating costs is

A. Job-order costing.
B. Operation costing.
C. Relevant costing.
D. Process costing.

Answer (A) is correct.
  REQUIRED: The most likely accounting system adopted by a company with a wide range of clients.
  DISCUSSION: Job-order costing is used by organizations whose products or services are readily identified by individual units or batches. The advertising agency accumulates its costs by client. Job-order costing is the most appropriate system for this type of nonmanufacturing firm.
  Answer (B) is incorrect. Operation costing would most likely be employed by a manufacturer producing goods that have common characteristics plus some individual characteristics. This would not be an appropriate system for an advertising agency with such a diverse client base. **Answer (C) is incorrect.** Relevant costing refers to expected future costs that are considered in decision making. **Answer (D) is incorrect.** Process costing is employed when a company mass produces a homogeneous product in a continuous fashion through a series of production steps.

7. A company employs a process cost system using the first-in, first-out (FIFO) method. The product passes through both Department 1 and Department 2 in order to be completed. Units enter Department 2 upon completion in Department 1. Additional direct materials are added in Department 2 when the units have reached the 25% stage of completion with respect to conversion costs. Conversion costs are added proportionally in Department 2. The production activity in Department 2 for the current month was as follows:

Beginning work-in-process inventory (40% complete with respect to conversion costs)	15,000
Units transferred in from Department 1	80,000
Units to account for	95,000
Units completed and transferred to finished goods	85,000
Ending work-in-process inventory (20% complete with respect to conversion costs)	10,000
Units accounted for	95,000

How many equivalent units for direct materials were added in Department 2 for the current month?

A. 70,000 units.
B. 80,000 units.
C. 85,000 units.
D. 95,000 units.

Answer (A) is correct.
  REQUIRED: The equivalent units for direct materials added in Department 2 for the current month.
  DISCUSSION: Beginning inventory is 40% complete. Thus, direct materials have already been added. Ending inventory has not reached the 25% stage of completion, so direct materials have not yet been added to these units. Thus, the equivalent units for direct materials calculated on a FIFO basis are equal to the units started and completed in the current period (85,000 units completed − 15,000 units in BWIP = 70,000 units started and completed).
  Answer (B) is incorrect. The number of units transferred in from Department 1 was 80,000.
  Answer (C) is incorrect. Improperly using the weighted-average method to calculate equivalent units results in 85,000. **Answer (D) is incorrect.** The total of the units to be accounted for is 95,000.

8. Companies characterized by the production of basically homogeneous products will most likely use which of the following methods for the purpose of averaging costs and providing management with unit-cost data?

A. Job-order costing.
B. Direct costing.
C. Absorption costing.
D. Process costing.

Answer (D) is correct.
REQUIRED: The method of averaging costs and providing management with unit cost data used by companies with homogeneous products.
DISCUSSION: Like products that are mass produced should be accounted for using process costing methods to assign costs to products. Costs are accumulated by departments or cost centers rather than by jobs, work-in-process is stated in terms of equivalent units, and unit costs are established on a departmental basis. Process costing is an averaging process that calculates the average cost of all units.
Answer (A) is incorrect. Job-order costing is employed when manufacturing involves different (heterogeneous) products. Answer (B) is incorrect. Direct costing includes only variable manufacturing costs in unit cost. It may be used whether products are homogeneous or heterogeneous and with either process or job-order costing. Answer (C) is incorrect. Absorption costing includes all manufacturing costs as part of the cost of a finished product. It may be used whether products are homogeneous or heterogeneous and with either process or job-order costing.

9. The units transferred in from the first department to the second department should be included in the computation of the equivalent units for the second department under which of the following methods of process costing?

	FIFO	Weighted-Average
A.	Yes	Yes
B.	Yes	No
C.	No	Yes
D.	No	No

Answer (A) is correct.
REQUIRED: The cost flow method(s) that include(s) transferred-in costs in EUP calculations.
DISCUSSION: The units transferred from the first to the second department should be included in the computation of equivalent units for the second department regardless of the cost flow assumption used. The transferred-in units are considered raw materials added at the beginning of the period.
Answer (B) is incorrect. Units transferred in also should be included in the EUP computation under the weighted-average method. Answer (C) is incorrect. Units transferred in also should be included in the EUP computation under the FIFO method. Answer (D) is incorrect. Units transferred in should be included in the EUP computation under both methods.

10. In a process-costing system, the cost of abnormal spoilage should be

A. Prorated between units transferred out and ending inventory.
B. Included in the cost of units transferred out.
C. Treated as a loss in the period incurred.
D. Ignored.

Answer (C) is correct.
REQUIRED: The best accounting treatment for abnormal spoilage.
DISCUSSION: Abnormal spoilage is spoilage that is not expected to occur under normal, efficient operating conditions. Because of its unusual nature, abnormal spoilage is typically treated as a loss in the period in which it is incurred.
Answer (A) is incorrect. Abnormal spoilage costs are not considered a component of the cost of good units produced. Answer (B) is incorrect. Abnormal spoilage costs are not considered a component of the cost of good units produced. Answer (D) is incorrect. Abnormal spoilage costs must be taken out of the manufacturing account.

14.4 Absorption (Full) vs. Variable (Direct) Costing

11. In an income statement prepared using the variable-costing method, fixed manufacturing overhead would

A. Not be used.
B. Be used in the computation of operating income but not in the computation of the contribution margin.
C. Be used in the computation of the contribution margin.
D. Be treated the same as variable manufacturing overhead.

Answer (B) is correct.
REQUIRED: The treatment of fixed manufacturing overhead in an income statement based on variable costing.
DISCUSSION: Under the variable-costing method, the contribution margin equals sales minus variable expenses. Fixed selling and administrative costs and fixed manufacturing overhead are subtracted from the contribution margin to arrive at operating income. Thus, fixed costs are included only in the computation of operating income.
Answer (A) is incorrect. Fixed manufacturing overhead is deducted from the contribution margin to determine operating income. Answer (C) is incorrect. Only variable expenses are used in the computation of the contribution margin. Answer (D) is incorrect. Variable manufacturing overhead is included in the computation of contribution margin and fixed manufacturing overhead is not.

12. During its first year of operations, a company produced 275,000 units and sold 250,000 units. The following costs were incurred during the year:

Variable costs per unit:
  Direct materials   US $15.00
  Direct labor   10.00
  Manufacturing overhead   12.50
  Selling and administrative   2.50

Total fixed costs:
  Manufacturing overhead US $2,200,000
  Selling and administrative US $1,375,000

The difference between operating profit calculated on the absorption-costing basis and on the variable-costing basis is that absorption-costing operating profit is

A. US $200,000 greater.
B. US $220,000 greater.
C. US $325,000 greater.
D. US $62,500 less.

Answer (A) is correct.
REQUIRED: The difference between absorption-costing and variable-costing operating profit.
DISCUSSION: Absorption-costing operating profit exceeds variable-costing operating income because production exceeds sales, resulting in a deferral of fixed manufacturing overhead in the inventory calculated using the absorption method. The difference of US $200,000 is equal to the fixed manufacturing overhead per unit (US $2,200,000 ÷ 275,000 = US $8.00) times the difference between production and sales (275,000 – 250,000 = 25,000, which is the inventory change in units).
Answer (B) is incorrect. Units produced, not units sold, should be used as the denominator to calculate the fixed manufacturing cost per unit. Answer (C) is incorrect. Fixed selling and administrative costs are not properly inventoriable under absorption costing. Answer (D) is incorrect. Variable selling and administrative costs are period costs under both variable- and absorption-cost systems in the determination of operating profit.

13. Using the variable costing method, which of the following costs are assigned to inventory?

	Variable Selling and Administrative Costs	Variable Factory Overhead Costs
A.	Yes	Yes
B.	Yes	No
C.	No	No
D.	No	Yes

Answer (D) is correct.
REQUIRED: The costs assigned to inventory.
DISCUSSION: Under variable costing, only variable manufacturing costs (not variable selling, general, and administrative costs) are assigned to inventory. Variable manufacturing overhead is a variable manufacturing cost. Thus, it is assigned to inventory.

14. In a company, products pass through some or all of the production departments during manufacturing, depending upon the product being manufactured. Direct material and direct labor costs are traced directly to the products as they flow through each production department. Manufacturing overhead is assigned in each department using separate departmental manufacturing overhead rates. The inventory costing method that the manufacturing company is using in this situation is

A. Absorption costing.
B. Activity-based costing.
C. Backflush costing.
D. Variable costing.

Answer (A) is correct.
REQUIRED: The appropriate inventory costing method.
DISCUSSION: Under absorption costing, inventories include all direct manufacturing costs and both variable and fixed manufacturing overhead (indirect) costs.
Answer (B) is incorrect. Activity-based costing develops cost pools for activities and then allocates those costs to cost objects based on the drivers of the activities.
Answer (C) is incorrect. A backflush costing system applies costs based on output. Answer (D) is incorrect. Variable costing excludes fixed manufacturing overhead costs from inventoriable costs and treats them as period costs.

15. When comparing absorption costing with variable costing, which of the following statements is **false**?

A. Absorption costing enables managers to increase operating profits in the short run by increasing inventories.
B. When sales volume is more than production volume, variable costing will result in higher operating profit.
C. A manager who is evaluated based on variable costing operating profit would be tempted to increase production at the end of a period in order to get a more favorable review.
D. Under absorption costing, operating profit is a function of both sales volume and production volume.

Answer (C) is correct.
REQUIRED: The false statement comparing absorption costing and variable costing.
DISCUSSION: Absorption (full) costing is the accounting method that considers all manufacturing costs as product costs. These costs include variable and fixed manufacturing costs whether direct or indirect. Variable (direct) costing considers only variable manufacturing costs to be product costs, i.e., inventoriable. Fixed manufacturing costs are considered period costs and are expensed as incurred. If production is increased without increasing sales, inventories will rise. However, all fixed costs associated with production will be an expense of the period under variable costing. Thus, this action will not artificially increase profits and improve the manager's review.
Answer (A) is incorrect. Increasing inventories increases absorption costing profit as a result of capitalizing fixed manufacturing overhead. Answer (B) is incorrect. When sales volume exceeds production, inventories decline. Thus, fixed manufacturing overhead expensed will be greater under absorption costing. Answer (D) is incorrect. Under variable costing, operating profit is a function of sales. Under absorption costing, it is a function of sales and production.

14.5 Relevant Costs and Decision Making

Questions 16 through 18 are based on the following information. The segmented income statement for a retail company with three product lines is presented below:

	Total Company	Product Line 1	Product Line 2	Product Line 3
Volume (in units)		20,000	28,000	50,000
Sales revenue	US $2,000,000	US $800,000	US $700,000	US $500,000
Costs & expenses:				
Variable costs	1,020,000	376,000	434,000	210,000
Fixed costs	810,000	294,000	316,000	200,000
Total costs & expenses	US $1,830,000	US $670,000	US $750,000	US $410,000
Operating income (loss)	US $ 170,000	US $130,000	US $ (50,000)	US $ 90,000

16. One company executive has expressed concern about the operating loss that has occurred in Product Line 2 and has suggested that Product Line 2 be discontinued. If Product Line 2 were to be dropped, the operating income of the company would

A. Increase by US $50,000.
B. Decrease by US $384,000.
C. Decrease by US $266,000.
D. Decrease by US $424,000.

Answer (C) is correct.
REQUIRED: The operating income effect of dropping a product line.
DISCUSSION: The operating income will decrease. Product Line 2 income will be lost, but only the variable costs will be avoided. Accordingly, the decrease will be US $266,000 [($700,000) + $434,000]. The other shared costs will have to be absorbed by the two remaining product lines.
Answer (A) is incorrect. An increase of US $50,000 assumes the revenue will be lost and all of its costs will be avoided. Answer (B) is incorrect. A decrease of US $384,000 assumes the revenue will be lost and fixed costs will be avoided. Answer (D) is incorrect. If Product Line 1 were to be dropped, the operating income of the company would decrease by US $424,000.

17. A customer, operating in an isolated foreign market, has approached the head salesperson for Product Line 1 and offered to purchase 4,000 units of a special-order product over the next 12 months. This product would be sold in the same manner as Product Line 1's other products except that the customer is hoping for a price break. Product Line 1 has excess capacity, meaning that the rate or amount of the remaining operating costs would not change as a consequence of the purchase and sale of this special-order product. The minimum selling price for this special-order product would be

A. US $18.80
B. US $33.50
C. US $12.25
D. US $14.70

Answer (A) is correct.
REQUIRED: The minimum selling price for a special-order product.
DISCUSSION: Product Line 1 needs to cover its variable out-of-pocket costs as a minimum on this special-order product; therefore, any selling price greater than the variable cost will contribute towards profits. Thus, the minimum selling price of the special-order product is US $18.80 ($376,000 ÷ 20,000 units).
Answer (B) is incorrect. US $33.50 is calculated based on a full cost approach. Answer (C) is incorrect. Dividing total fixed costs by 24,000 units results in US $12.25. Answer (D) is incorrect. Dividing total fixed costs by 20,000 units results in US $14.70.

18. Refer to the information on the preceding page. The company has an opportunity to promote one of its product lines by making a one-time US $7,000 expenditure. The company can choose only one of the three product lines to promote. The incremental sales revenue that would be realized from this US $7,000 promotion expenditure in each of the product lines is estimated as follows:

	Increase in Sales Revenue
Product Line 1	US $15,000
Product Line 2	20,000
Product Line 3	14,000

In order to maximize profits, the promotion expenditure should be spent on <List A>, resulting in an increase in operating income of <List B>.

	List A	List B
A.	Product Line 2	US $13,000
B.	Product Line 2	US $5,000
C.	Product Line 3	US $1,400
D.	Product Line 3	US $1,120

Answer (D) is correct.
REQUIRED: The product line to be promoted by a one-time advertising expenditure and the resulting income increase.
DISCUSSION: Fixed costs, being irrelevant, are ignored. The first step is to determine the contribution margin ratio for each product line.

	Product Line 1	Product Line 2	Product Line 3
Sales revenue	US $800,000	US $700,000	US $500,000
Total variable costs	376,000	434,000	210,000
Contribution margin	US $424,000	US $266,000	US $290,000
Divided by: Sales	÷ 800,000	÷ 700,000	÷ 500,000
CM ratio	53%	38%	58%

The incremental promotion cost (US $7,000) is subtracted from the incremental revenue to determine the marginal benefit of promoting each product line.

Incremental revenue	US $15,000	US $20,000	US $14,000
Times: CM ratio	× .53	× .38	× .58
Incremental contribution margin	US $ 7,950	US $ 7,600	US $ 8,120
Minus: Promotion cost	(7,000)	(7,000)	(7,000)
Incremental profits	US $ 950	US $ 600	US $ 1,120

The promotion expense should be spent on Product Line 3, resulting in an increase in operating income of US $1,120.

Answer (A) is incorrect. Product Line 2 has an increased profit of US $600. **Answer (B) is incorrect.** Product Line 2 has an increased profit of US $600. **Answer (C) is incorrect.** US $1,400 omits the commissions from the calculation.

SU 14: Managerial Accounting: Costing Systems and Decision Making

Questions 19 and 20 are based on the following information. A company manufactures and sells a single product. It takes 2 machine hours to produce one unit. Annual sales are expected to be 75,000 units. Annual production capacity is 200,000 machine hours. Expected selling price is US $10 per unit. Cost data for manufacturing and selling the product are as follows:

Variable costs (per unit)	
Direct materials	US $3.00
Direct labor	1.00
Variable manufacturing overhead	0.80
Variable selling	2.00
Fixed costs (per year)	
Fixed manufacturing overhead	US $90,000
Fixed selling	60,000

19. The company receives a special order for 10,000 units at US $7.60. Variable selling cost for each of these 10,000 units will be US $1.20 instead of the normal US $2.00. This special order will not affect regular sales of 75,000 units. If the company accepts this special order, its profit will

A. Increase by US $8,000.
B. Increase by US $16,000.
C. Decrease by US $4,000.
D. Decrease by US $12,000.

Answer (B) is correct.
  REQUIRED: The change in profit resulting from a special order.
  DISCUSSION: If the company accepts the special order, its revenue will increase by US $76,000 (10,000 units × $7.60). However, its incremental cost will include only the variable costs because fixed manufacturing and selling costs will be unchanged. The increase in cost from accepting the special order is US $60,000 [10,000 units × ($3.00 + $1.00 + $0.80 + $1.20)]. Thus, acceptance of the special order will increase profits by US $16,000 ($76,000 – $60,000).

20. The company estimates that by reducing its selling price to US $9.30 per unit, it can increase sales to 90,000 units annually. Fixed costs per year and unit variable costs will remain unchanged. If the company reduces its selling price to US $9.30 per unit, its profit will

A. Decrease by US $5,000.
B. Decrease by US $15,000.
C. Decrease by US $45,000.
D. Increase by US $15,000.

Answer (B) is correct.
  REQUIRED: The effect on profit if selling price is reduced.
  DISCUSSION: Because total fixed costs are unaffected, the change in profit is the change in the contribution margin. The contribution margin at the current selling price is US $240,000 [75,000 units × ($10 – $3 – $1 – $0.80 – $2)]. The contribution margin at the US $9.30 selling price is US $225,000 [90,000 units × ($9.30 – $3 – $1 – $0.80 – $2)]. Hence, profit will be reduced by US $15,000 ($240,000 – $225,000) if the selling price is lowered to US $9.30.

GLEIM
GO TO ONLINE COURSE

Access the **Gleim CIA Premium Review System** featuring our SmartAdapt technology from your Gleim Personal Classroom to continue your studies. You will experience a personalized study environment with exam-emulating multiple-choice questions.

GLEIM CIA REVIEW
#1 CIA EXAM PREP

Featuring our innovative **SmartAdapt™** technology so you'll know what to study, know when you're ready, and be prepared to pass with confidence.

- One-of-a-kind, no-hassle Access Until You Pass® guarantee
- Personalized support from our team of exam experts
- Comprehensive test bank of exam-quality questions

GLEIMCIA.COM | 800.874.5346 | accountingteam@gleim.com

APPENDIX A
THE IIA CIA EXAM SYLLABUS AND CROSS-REFERENCES

For your convenience, we have reproduced verbatim The IIA's CIA Exam Syllabus for Part 3 of the CIA exam. Note that the "basic" cognitive level means the candidate must retrieve relevant knowledge from memory and/or demonstrate basic comprehension of concepts or processes. Those levels labeled "proficient" mean the candidate must apply concepts, processes, or procedures; analyze, evaluate, and make judgments based on criteria; and/or put elements or material together to formulate conclusions and recommendations.

We also have provided cross-references to the study units and subunits in this book that correspond to The IIA's more detailed coverage. Please visit The IIA's website for updates and more information about the exam. Rely on the Gleim materials to help you pass each part of the exam. We have researched and studied The IIA's CIA Exam Syllabus as well as questions from prior exams to provide you with an excellent review program.

PART 3 – BUSINESS KNOWLEDGE FOR INTERNAL AUDITING

		Domain	Cognitive Level	Gleim Study Unit(s) or Subunit(s)
Business Acumen (35%)			
1. Organizational Objectives, Behavior, and Performance			
	A	Describe the strategic planning process and key activities (objective setting, globalization and competitive considerations, alignment to the organization's mission and values, etc.)	Basic	SU 1
	B	Examine common performance measures (financial, operational, qualitative vs. quantitative, productivity, quality, efficiency, effectiveness, etc.)	Proficient	2.5-2.6
	C	Explain organizational behavior (individuals in organizations, groups, and how organizations behave, etc.) and different performance management techniques (traits, organizational politics, motivation, job design, rewards, work schedules, etc.)	Basic	2.1-2.4
	D	Describe management's effectiveness to lead, mentor, guide people, build organizational commitment, and demonstrate entrepreneurial ability	Basic	3.1
2. Organizational Structure and Business Processes			
I	A	Appraise the risk and control implications of different organizational configuration structures (centralized vs. decentralized, flat structure vs. traditional, etc.)	Basic	3.2
	B	Examine the risk and control implications of common business processes (human resources, procurement, product development, sales, marketing, logistics, management of outsourced processes, etc.)	Proficient	3.3-3.5
	C	Identify project management techniques (project plan and scope, time/team/resources/cost management, change management, etc.)	Basic	4.1-4.3
	D	Recognize the various forms and elements of contracts (formality, consideration, unilateral, bilateral, etc.)	Basic	4.4-4.5
3. Data Analytics			
	A	Describe data analytics, data types, data governance, and the value of using data analytics in internal auditing	Basic	7.4
	B	Explain the data analytics process (define questions, obtain relevant data, clean/normalize data, analyze data, communicate results)	Basic	7.4
	C	Recognize the application of data analytics methods in internal auditing (anomaly detection, diagnostic analysis, predictive analysis, network analysis, text analysis, etc.)	Basic	7.4

		Domain	Cognitive Level	Gleim Study Unit(s) or Subunit(s)
II	**Information Security (25%)**			
	1. Information Security			
	A	Differentiate types of common physical security controls (cards, keys, biometrics, etc.)	Basic	8.1
	B	Differentiate the various forms of user authentication and authorization controls (password, two-level authentication, biometrics, digital signatures, etc.) and identify potential risks	Basic	8.1-8.2
	C	Explain the purpose and use of various information security controls (encryption, firewalls, antivirus, etc.)	Basic	8.1-8.3
	D	Recognize data privacy laws and their potential impact on data security policies and practices	Basic	8.3
	E	Recognize emerging technology practices and their impact on security (bring your own device [BYOD], smart devices, internet of things [IoT], etc.)	Basic	8.3
	F	Recognize existing and emerging cybersecurity risks (hacking, piracy, tampering, ransomware attacks, phishing attacks, etc.)	Basic	8.3
	G	Describe cybersecurity and information security-related policies	Basic	8.1, 8.3
III	**Information Technology (20%)**			
	1. Application and System Software			
	A	Recognize core activities in the systems development lifecycle and delivery (requirements definition, design, developing, testing, debugging, deployment, maintenance, etc.) and the importance of change controls throughout the process	Basic	5.2
	B	Explain basic database terms (data, database, record, object, field, schema, etc.) and internet terms (HTML, HTTP, URL, domain name, browser, click-through, electronic data interchange [EDI], cookies, etc.)	Basic	5.1, 6.2
	C	Identify key characteristics of software systems (customer relationship management [CRM] systems; enterprise resource planning [ERP] systems; and governance, risk, and compliance [GRC] systems; etc.)	Basic	5.1, 6.4
	2. IT Infrastructure and IT Control Frameworks			
	A	Explain basic IT infrastructure and network concepts (server, mainframe, client-server configuration, gateways, routers, LAN, WAN, VPN, etc.) and identify potential risks	Basic	6.1-6.3
	B	Define the operational roles of a network administrator, database administrator, and help desk	Basic	5.1, 6.1
	C	Recognize the purpose and applications of IT control frameworks (COBIT, ISO 27000, ITIL, etc.) and basic IT controls	Basic	7.1-7.3
	3. Disaster Recovery			
	A	Explain disaster recovery planning site concepts (hot, warm, cold, etc.)	Basic	8.4
	B	Explain the purpose of systems and data backup	Basic	8.4
	C	Explain the purpose of systems and data recovery procedures	Basic	8.4

	Domain		Cognitive Level	Gleim Study Unit(s) or Subunit(s)
IV	**Financial Management (20%)**			
	1. Financial Accounting and Finance			
	A	Identify concepts and underlying principles of financial accounting (types of financial statements and terminologies such as bonds, leases, pensions, intangible assets, research and development, etc.)	Basic	SU 9
	B	Recognize advanced and emerging financial accounting concepts (consolidation, investments, fair value, partnerships, foreign currency transactions, etc.)	Basic	10.1-10.5
	C	Interpret financial analysis (horizontal and vertical analysis and ratios related to activity, profitability, liquidity, leverage, etc.)	Proficient	10.6-10.10
	D	Describe revenue cycle, current asset management activities and accounting, and supply chain management (including inventory valuation and accounts payable)	Basic	3.4, 9.1, 9.5, 9.7, SU 11
	E	Describe capital budgeting, capital structure, basic taxation, and transfer pricing	Basic	SU 12
	2. Managerial Accounting			
	A	Explain general concepts of managerial accounting (cost-volume-profit analysis, budgeting, expense allocation, cost-benefit analysis, etc.)	Basic	SU 13
	B	Differentiate costing systems (absorption, variable, fixed, activity-based, standard, etc.)	Basic	14.1-14.4
	C	Distinguish various costs (relevant and irrelevant costs, incremental costs, etc.) and their use in decision making	Basic	14.5

APPENDIX B
THE IIA EXAMINATION BIBLIOGRAPHY

The Institute has prepared a listing of references for Part 3 of the revised version of the CIA exam. These publications have been chosen by the Professional Certifications Department as reasonably representative of the common body of knowledge for internal auditors. However, all of the information in these texts will not be tested. When possible, questions will be written based on the information contained in the suggested reference list. This bibliography is provided to give you an overview of the scope of the exam.

The IIA bibliography is for your information only. The texts you need to prepare for the CIA exam depend on many factors, including

1. Innate ability
2. Length of time out of school
3. Thoroughness of your undergraduate education
4. Familiarity with internal auditing due to relevant experience

CIA EXAM REFERENCES

Title/URL	Author	Year Published	Publisher
International Professional Practices Framework (IPPF), including • Mission • Definition of Internal Auditing • Core Principles • Code of Ethics • *Standards* • Implementation Guides • Practice Guides • Global Technology Audit Guides (GTAGs) URL: *http://bit.ly/1AilTOC*	The Institute of Internal Auditors, Inc.	Updated continually	The Institute of Internal Auditors, Inc.
Internal Auditing: Assurance & Advisory Services, 4th Edition URL: *https://bookstore.theiia.org/Internal-Auditing-Assurance-Advisory-Services-fourth-edition-2*	Urton L. Anderson, Michael J. Head, Sridhar Ramamoorti, Cris Riddle, Mark Salamasick, Paul J. Sobel	2017	The Internal Audit Foundation
Sawyer's Internal Auditing, 5th, 6th, and 7th Editions URL: *https://bookstore.theiia.org/sawyers-internal-auditing-enhancing-and-protecting-organizational-value-7th-edition*	L.B. Sawyer	2003, 2012, 2019	The Institute of Internal Auditors Research Foundation
Enterprise Risk Management – Integrating with Strategy and Performance URL: *https://www.coso.org/Pages/ERM-Framework-Purchase.aspx*	Committee of Sponsoring Organizations of the Treadway Commission (COSO)	2017	COSO
COSO – Internal Control – Integrated Framework: 2013 (Framework) URL: *https://www.coso.org/Pages/ic.aspx*	Committee of Sponsoring Organizations of the Treadway Commission (COSO)	2013	American Institute of Certified Public Accountants (AICPA)
Understanding Management, 11th Edition URL: *https://www.cengage.com/c/mindtap-for-understanding-management-11e-daft*	Richard L. Daft and Dorothy Marcic	2020	Cengage Learning

-- Continued on next page --

CIA EXAM REFERENCES – Continued

A Guide to the Project Management Body of Knowledge (PMBOK® GUIDE), 6th Edition URL: https://www.pmi.org/pmbok-guide-standards/foundational/pmbok	Project Management Institute	2017	Project Management Institute
Performance Auditing: Measuring Inputs, Outputs, and Outcomes, 3rd Edition	Ronell B. Raaum, Stephen L. Morgan, and Colleen G. Waring	2016	The Internal Audit Foundation
Auditing Human Resources, 2nd Edition	Kelli W. Vito	2010	The Institute of Internal Auditors
Auditing the Procurement Function, 2nd Edition	David J. O'Regan	2017	The Institute of Internal Auditors
Contract and Commercial Management: The Operational Guide URL: https://www.iaccm.com/store/?vp=34	International Association for Contract and Commercial Management	2011	Van Haren Publishing
Data Analytics: Elevating Internal Audit's Value	Warren W. Stippich, Jr., and Bradley J. Preber	2016	The Institute of Internal Auditors
Implementing the NIST Cybersecurity Framework URL: https://www.isaca.org/Knowledge-Center/Research/ResearchDeliverables/Pages/Implementing-the-NIST-Cybersecurity-Framework.aspx	Information Systems Audit and Control Association	2014	Information Systems Audit and Control Association
Information Technology Control and Audit, 4th Edition	Sandra Senft, Frederick Gallegos, and Aleksandra Davis	2016	Auerbach Publications
IT Auditing Using Controls to Protect Information Assets, 2nd Edition	Chris Davis, Mike Schiller, and Kevin Wheeler	2011	McGraw-Hill Education
Principles of Information Security, 6th Edition URL: https://www.cengage.com/c/principles-of-information-security-6e-whitman	Michael E. Whitman and Herbert J. Mattord	2018	Cengage Learning
Accounting Principles, 13th Edition URL: https://www.wiley.com/en-us/Accounting+Principles%2C+13th+Edition-p-97811194110176	Jerry J. Weygandt, Paul D. Kimmel, and Donald E. Kieso	2018	Wiley

AVAILABILITY OF PUBLICATIONS

The listing above and on the previous page presents only some of the current technical literature available, and The IIA does not carry all of the reference books. Quantity discounts are provided by The IIA. Visit bookstore.theiia.org or contact The IIA at bookstore@theiia.org or +1-407-937-1470.

Contact the publisher directly if you cannot obtain the desired texts from The IIA, online, or your local bookstore. Begin your study program with the Gleim CIA Review, which most candidates find sufficient. If you need additional reference material, borrow books mentioned in The IIA's bibliography from colleagues, professors, or a library.

APPENDIX C
SAMPLE FINANCIAL STATEMENTS

We have annotated these audited financial statements to show how the various elements interrelate. For instance, (a) is the year-end balance of cash and equivalents; this annotation is found on both the balance sheet and the statement of cash flows.

MAVERICK MOTOR COMPANY AND SUBSIDIARIES
CONSOLIDATED INCOME STATEMENT
(in millions, except per share amounts)

	For the years ended December 31,		
	20Y0	20X9	20X8
Revenues			
Automotive	US $126,567	US $128,168	US $119,280
Financial Services	7,685	8,096	9,674
Total revenues	134,252	136,264	128,954
Costs and expenses			
Automotive cost of sales	112,578	113,345	104,451
Selling, administrative and other expenses	12,182	11,578	11,909
Financial Services interest expense	3,115	3,614	4,345
Financial Services provision for credit and insurance losses	86	(33)	(216)
Total costs and expenses	127,961	128,504	120,489
Automotive interest expense	713	817	1,807
Automotive interest income and other non-operating income/(expense), net	1,185	825	(362)
Financial Services other income/(loss), net	369	413	315
Equity in net income/(loss) of affiliated companies	588	500	538
Income before income taxes	7,720	8,681	7,149
Provision for/(Benefit from) income taxes	2,056	(11,541)	592
Net income	5,664 (a)	20,222 (b)	6,557 (c)
Minus: Income/(Loss) attributable to noncontrolling interests	(1)	9	(4)
Net income/(loss) attributable to Maverick Motor Company	US $ 5,665	US $ 20,213	US $ 6,561

AMOUNTS PER SHARE ATTRIBUTABLE TO MAVERICK MOTOR COMPANY COMMON AND CLASS B STOCK

Basic income	US $ 1.48	US $ 5.33	US $ 1.90
Diluted income	US $ 1.42	US $ 4.94	US $ 1.66
Cash dividends declared	US $ 0.15	US $ 0.05	US $ —

CONSOLIDATED STATEMENT OF COMPREHENSIVE INCOME
(in millions)

	For the years ended December 31,		
	20Y0	20X9	20X8
Net income	US $ 5,664	US $ 20,222	US $ 6,557
Other comprehensive income/(loss), net of tax			
Foreign currency translation	142	(720)	(2,234)
Derivative instruments	6	(152)	(24)
Pension and other postretirement benefits	(4,268)	(3,553)	(1,190)
Net holding gain/(loss)	–	2	(2)
Total other comprehensive income/(loss), net of tax	(4,120) (d)	(4,423) (e)	(3,450) (f)
Comprehensive income	1,544	15,799	3,107
Minus: Comprehensive income/(loss) attributable to noncontrolling interests	(1)	9	(4)
Comprehensive income attributable to Maverick Motor Company	US $ 1,545	US $ 15,790	US $ 3,111

MAVERICK MOTOR COMPANY AND SUBSIDIARIES
CONSOLIDATED BALANCE SHEET
(in millions)

	December 31, 20Y0	December 31, 20X9
ASSETS		
Cash and cash equivalents	US $ 15,659 (g)	US $ 17,148 (h)
Marketable securities	20,284	18,618
Finance receivables, net	71,510	69,976
Other receivables, net	10,828	8,565
Net investment in operating leases	16,451	12,838
Inventories	7,362	5,901
Equity in net assets of affiliated companies	3,246	2,936
Net property	24,942	22,371
Deferred income taxes	15,185	15,125
Net intangible assets	87	100
Other assets	5,000	4,770
Total assets	US $190,554	US $178,348
LIABILITIES		
Payables	US $ 19,308	US $ 17,724
Accrued liabilities and deferred revenue	49,407	45,369
Debt	105,058	99,488
Deferred income taxes	470	696
Total liabilities	US $174,243	US $163,277
Redeemable noncontrolling interest	322	–
EQUITY		
Capital stock		
Common Stock, par value US $0.01 per share (3,745 million shares issued)	US $ 39 (i)	US $ 37 (j)
Class B Stock, par value US $0.01 per share (71 million shares issued)	1 (i)	1 (j)
Capital in excess of par value of stock	20,976 (k)	20,905 (l)
Retained earnings	18,077 (m)	12,985 (n)
Accumulated other comprehensive income/(loss)	(22,854) (o)	(18,734) (p)
Treasury stock	(292) (q)	(166) (r)
Total equity attributable to Maverick Motor Company	US $ 15,947 (s)	US $ 15,028 (t)
Equity attributable to noncontrolling interests	42	43
Total equity	US $ 15,989	US $ 15,071
Total liabilities and equity	US $190,554	US $178,348

MAVERICK MOTOR COMPANY AND SUBSIDIARIES
CONDENSED CONSOLIDATED STATEMENT OF CASH FLOWS
(in millions)

	For the years ended December 31,		
	20Y0	20X9	20X8
Cash flows from operating activities of continuing operations			
Net cash provided by/(used in) operating activities	US $ 9,045	US $ 9,784	US $ 11,477
Cash flows from investing activities of continuing operations			
Capital expenditures	(5,488)	(4,293)	(4,092)
Acquisitions of retail and other finance receivables and operating leases	(39,208)	(35,866)	(28,873)
Collections of retail and other finance receivables and operating leases	32,333	33,964	37,757
Purchases of securities	(95,135)	(68,723)	(100,150)
Sales and maturities of securities	93,749	70,795	101,077
Cash change due to initial consolidation of businesses	191	–	94
Proceeds from sale of business	66	333	1,318
Settlements of derivatives	(737)	353	(37)
Elimination of cash balances upon disposition of discontinued/held-for-sale operations	–	(69)	(456)
Other	(61)	465	270
Net cash provided by/(used in)investing activities	(14,290)	(3,041)	6,908
Cash flows from financing activities of continuing operations			
Cash dividends	(763)	–	–
Purchases of Common Stock	(125)	–	–
Sales of Common Stock	–	–	1,339
Changes in short-term debt	1,208	2,841	(1,754)
Proceeds from issuance of other debt	32,436	35,921	30,821
Principle payments on other debt	(29,210)	(43,095)	(47,625)
Payments on notes/transfer of cash equivalents to the UAW Voluntary Employee Benefit Association ("VEBA") Trust	–	–	(7,302)
Other	159	92	100
Net cash provided by/(used in) financing activities	3,705	(4,241)	(24,421)
Effect of exchange rate changes on cash and cash equivalents	51	(159)	(53)
Net increase/(decrease) in cash and cash equivalents	US $ (1,489)	US $ 2,343	US $ (6,089)
Cash and cash equivalents at January 1	US $ 17,148	US $ 14,805	US $ 20,894
Net increase/(decrease) in cash and cash equivalents	(1,489)	2,343	(6,089)
Cash and cash equivalents at December 31	US $ 15,659 (g)	US $ 17,148 (h)	US $ 14,805

MAVERICK MOTOR COMPANY AND SUBSIDIARIES
CONSOLIDATED STATEMENT OF EQUITY
(in millions)

	Equity/(Deficit) Attributable to Maverick Motor Company						Equity/(Deficit) Attributable to Non-controlling Interests	Total Equity/(Deficit)
	Capital Stock	Cap. in Excess of Par Value of Stock	Retained Earnings/ (Accumulated Deficit)	Accumulated Other Comprehensive Income/(Loss)	Treasury Stock	Total		
Balance at December 31, 20X7	US $34	US $16,786	US $(13,599)	US $(10,864)	US $(177)	US $ (7,820)	US $ 38	US $(7,782)
Net income	–	–	6,561	–	–	6,561	(4)	6,557 (c)
Other comprehensive income/(loss), net of tax	–	–	–	(3,449)	–	(3,449)	(1)	(3,450) (f)
Common stock issued (including share-based compensation impacts)	4	4,017	–	–	–	4,021	–	4,021
Treasury stock/other	–	–	–	–	14	14	–	14
Cash dividends declared	–	–	–	–	–	–	(2)	(2)
Balance at December 31, 20X8	**US $38**	**US $20,803**	**US $ (7,038)**	**US $(14,313)**	**US $(163)**	**US $ (673)**	**US $ 31**	**US $ (642)**
Balance at December 31, 20X8	US $38	US $20,803	US $ (7,038)	US $(14,313)	US $(163)	US $ (673)	US $ 31	US $ (642)
Net income	–	–	20,213	–	–	20,213	9	20,222 (b)
Other comprehensive income/(loss), net of tax	–	–	–	(4,421)	–	(4,421)	(2)	(4,423) (e)
Common stock issued (including share-based compensation impacts)	–	102	–	–	–	102	–	102
Treasury stock/other	–	–	–	–	(3)	(3)	5	2
Cash dividends declared	–	–	(190)	–	–	(190)	–	(190)
Balance at December 31, 20X9	**US $38 (j)**	**US $20,905 (l)**	**US $ 12,985 (n)**	**US $(18,734) (p)**	**US $(166) (r)**	**US $15,028 (t)**	**US $ 43**	**US $15,071**
Balance at December 31, 20X9	US $38	US $20,905	US $12,985	US $(18,734)	US $(166)	US $15,028	US $ 43	US $15,071
Net income	–	–	5,665	–	–	5,665	(1)	5,664 (a)
Other compensation income/(loss), net of tax	–	–	–	(4,120)	–	(4,120)	–	(4,120) (d)
Common stock issued (including share-based compensation impacts)	2	71	–	–	–	73	–	73
Treasury stock/other	–	–	–	–	(126)	(126)	–	(126)
Cash dividends declared	–	–	(573)	–	–	(573)	–	(573)
Balance at December 31, 20Y0	US $40 (i)	US $20,976 (k)	US $ 18,077 (m)	US $(22,854) (o)	US $(292) (q)	US $15,947 (s)	US $ 42	US $15,989

APPENDIX D
GLOSSARY OF ACCOUNTING TERMS
U.S. TO BRITISH VS. BRITISH TO U.S.

U.S. TO BRITISH

U.S.	British
Accounts payable	Trade creditors
Accounts receivable	Trade debtors
Accrual	Provision (for liability or charge)
Accumulated depreciation	Aggregate depreciation
Additional paid-in capital	Share premium account
Allowance	Provision (for diminution in value)
Allowance for credit losses	Provision for bad debt
Annual Stockholders' Meeting	Annual General Meeting
Authorized capital stock	Authorized share capital
Bellweather stock	Barometer stock
Bond	Loan finance
Business combination	Merger accounting
Bylaws	Articles of Association
Certificate of Incorporation	Memorandum of Association
Checking account	Current account
Common stock	Ordinary shares
Consumer price index	Retail price index
Corporation	Company
Cost of goods sold	Cost of sales
Credit Memorandum	Credit note
Equity	Reserves
Equity interest	Ownership interest
Financial statements	Accounts
Income statement	Profit and loss account
Income taxes	Taxation
Inventories	Stocks
Investment bank	Merchant bank
Labor union	Trade union
Land	Freehold
Lease not for a short term	Long leasehold
Liabilities	Creditors
Listed company	Quoted company
Long-term investments	Fixed asset investments
Merchandise trade	Visible trade
Mutual funds	Unit trusts
Net income	Net profit
Note payable	Bill payable
Note receivable	Bill receivable
Paid-in surplus	Share premium
Par value	Nominal value
Preferred stock	Preference share
Prime rate	Base rate
Property, plant, and equipment	Tangible fixed assets
Provision for credit losses	Charge
Purchase method	Acquisition accounting
Purchase on account	Purchase on credit
Retained earnings	Profit and loss account
Real estate	Property
Revenue	Income
Reversal of accrual	Release of provision
Sales on account	Sales on credit
Sales/revenue	Turnover
Savings and loan association	Building society
Shareholders' equity	Shareholders' funds
Stock	Inventory
Stock dividend	Bonus share
Stockholder	Shareholder
Stockholders' equity	Share capital and reserves or Shareholders' funds
Taxable income	Taxable profit
Treasury bonds	Gilt-edged stock (gilts)

BRITISH TO U.S.

British	U.S.
Accounts	Financial statements
Acquisition accounting	Purchase method
Aggregate depreciation	Accumulated depreciation
Annual General Meeting	Annual Stockholders' Meeting
Articles of Association	Bylaws
Authorized share capital	Authorized capital stock
Barometer stock	Bellweather stock
Base rate	Prime rate
Bill payable	Note payable
Bill receivable	Note receivable
Bonus share	Stock dividend
Building society	Savings and loan association
Charge	Provision for credit losses
Company	Corporation
Cost of sales	Cost of goods sold
Credit note	Credit Memorandum
Creditors	Liabilities
Current account	Checking account
Fixed asset investments	Long-term investments
Freehold	Land
Gilt-edged stock (gilts)	Treasury bonds
Income	Revenue
Inventory	Stock
Loan finance	Bond
Long leasehold	Lease not for a short term
Memorandum of Association	Certificate of Incorporation
Merchant bank	Investment bank
Merger accounting	Business combination
Net profit	Net income
Nominal value	Par value
Ordinary shares	Common stock
Ownership interest	Equity interest
Preference share	Preferred stock
Profit and loss account	Income statement
Profit and loss account	Retained earnings
Property	Real estate
Provision for bad debt	Allowance for credit losses
Provision (for diminution in value)	Allowance
Provision (for liability or charge)	Accrual
Purchase on credit	Purchase on account
Quoted company	Listed company
Release of provision	Reversal of accrual
Reserves	Equity
Retail price index	Consumer price index
Sales on credit	Sales on account
Share capital and reserves or Shareholders' funds	Stockholders' equity
Shareholder	Stockholder
Shareholders' funds	Shareholders' equity
Share premium	Paid-in surplus
Share premium account	Additional paid-in capital
Stocks	Inventories
Tangible fixed assets	Property, plant, and equipment
Taxable profit	Taxable income
Taxation	Income taxes
Trade creditors	Accounts payable
Trade debtors	Accounts receivable
Trade union	Labor union
Turnover	Sales/revenue
Unit trusts	Mutual funds
Visible trade	Merchandise trade

INDEX

ABC. 471
   Inventory management. 380
Ability to pay. 418
Abraham Maslow. 45
Absorption costing. 483
Acceptance
   Needs. 45
   Of
      Authority. 83
      Offer. 135
      Testing. 166
      Theory. 83
Access control matrices. 249
Accountability. 83
Accounting
   Assumptions. 280
   Cycle. 294
   Equation. 283
   Information System (AIS). 197
   Principles. 281
   Rate of return. 412
   System. 293
Accounts
   Chart of. 293
   Payable. 106, 305
      Turnover. 352
   Permanent (real). 293
   Receivable. 297, 375
      Turnover ratio. 350
   Temporary (nominal). 293
Accrual basis. 290
Accrued expenses. 306
Achievement-oriented style. 77
Acid-test ratio. 348
Active follower. 80
Activities. 130
   Definition. 123
   Sequencing. 123
Activity
   Analysis. 440, 474
   -Based
      Budgeting. 446
      Costing (ABC). 471
      System. 473
   Cost driver. 473
   Drivers. 476
   Ratios. 349
Adaptive organizations. 43
Adhocracy. 81
Adjusting entries. 294
Advanced Encryption Standard (AES). 254
Advisory authority. 86
Agent. 104
Aging
   Accounts receivable. 376
   Schedule. 298
Agreement. 135
AIS. 197
Alarmed systems resources. 261
Alienated follower. 80
Allocation. 291

Allowance method. 297
Alternate processing facility. 267
American National Standards Institute (ANSI). . . . 119
Amortization of discount/premium. 312
Analyze data. 231
Annual interest expense. 312
Annuity, ordinary/due. 310
Anomaly detection. 231
Anti-malware software. 264
Applicant testing. 96
Application
   Authentication. 252
   Controls. 226, 227
   Development. 163
   Gateway. 250
Appraisal costs. 57
Arithmetic controls. 229
Array. 230
Ask-the-network distributed database. 159
Assertiveness. 25
Assets. 283
Assumption
   Economic-entity. 280
   Going-concern. 280
   Monetary-unit (unit-of-money). 280
   Periodicity (time period). 280
ATM (asynchronous transfer mode). 193
Attacks. 254, 258
   Password. 258
Attribute listing. 56
Audit trail. 223
Auditor's responsibility. 105
Authentic leadership. 79
Authentication. 251, 253, 264
   Information. 252
   Two-level. 252
Authoritarian managers. 72
Authority. 71, 83
   Acceptance. 83
   Advisory. 86
   -Compliance management. 74
   Functional. 87
   Hierarchy. 40
   Informal. 86
   Line. 87
Automatic log-off. 249
Average
   Collection period. 350, 377
   Payables period. 353
   Tax rate. 419
Avoidable costs. 487
Avoidance learning. 49

Back-office functions. 199
Backflush costing. 482
Backup. 265
Backward placement. 105
Balance sheet. 283
Balanced scorecard. 58
Bank reconciliation. 296

518 Index

Bankers' acceptances. 416
Bargaining power. 18
Barriers entry. 18
Batch
    Input controls. 227
    -Level activities. 474
    Processing. 224
Bearer bonds. 399
Behavior. 72
    -Based detection. 261
    Political, positive and negative. 51
Behavioral sciences. 43
Behaviorally anchored rating scales (BARS). 99
Benefits management plan. 120
Berners-Lee, Tim. 186
Best practices. 58
Beta coefficient. 331
Big data. 232, 234
Bilateral contracts. 138
Bill of materials (BOM). 382
Binary. 149
Biometric technologies. 248
Bit. 149
Black-box testing. 166
Blake and Mouton. 74
Bluetooth. 194
Board of directors. 438
Bond
    Discount. 312
    Effective-interest. 312
    Premium. 312
Bonds. 311, 398, 399
    Carrying amount. 312
    Issuance. 312
    Ratings. 400
    Sold at
        Discount. 312
        Premium. 312
Book value per share. 359
Boolean. 230
Bottom
    Of the pyramid (BOP). 21
    -Up (participative) budgeting. 438
Brainstorming. 56
Brand
    Elements. 28
    Equity. 28
    Global. 28
Branding partnerships. 28
Breach. 134
Breakeven
    Analysis. 101, 449
    Point. 449, 451
Bridge 184
Bring your own device (BYOD). 263
Broker. 104
Browser. 186
Brute-force attack. 258

Budget. 437
    Calendar. 441
    Committee. 438
    Direct
        Labor. 443
        Materials. 443
    Manufacturing overhead. 444
    Nonmanufacturing. 445
    Participation. 438
    Purchases. 442
    Sales, order of preparation. 442
    Static (master). 448
    Systems. 441
Budgetary slack. 439
Build
    Or buy. 164
    Strategy. 16
Bullwhip effect. 102
Bureaucracy. 42
Bus network. 194
Business
    Case. 120
    Combination. 340
    Continuity. 265
        Management (BCM). 268
    Documents. 121
    Global development. 22
    Growth rate (BGR). 16
    Impact analysis (BIA). 269
    Process
        Design. 163, 164
        Level. 225
        Reengineering. 163
    Recovery. 269
    Risk. 332
    Software Alliance (BSA). 196
Buyer bargaining power. 18
Byte. 150

Call option. 333
Callable bonds. 399
Capacity. 136
Capital
    Additional paid-in. 344
    Asset pricing model (CAPM). 331
    Budgeting. 408
    Structure. 354
Card reader controls. 248
Cardinality. 159
CASE. 171

Cash
    Balances. 296
    Budget. 373
    Conversion cycle. 352
    Cows. 16
    Disbursements. 106
    Flow. 373
    Flows from
        Financing activities. 288
        Investing activities. 288
    Inflows. 288
    Management. 372
    Outflows. 288
    Payments. 373
    Receipts. 373
Cell phone. 195
Central index. 159
Centralization. 88, 456
Chain
    Of command. 83
    Scalar. 83
Change
    Agents. 133
    Cultural. 133
    Management. 133, 168
        Process. 169
    Product. 133
    Resistance. 133
    Structural. 133
Channel conflict. 104
Characteristics model, job. 50
Charismatic leader. 78
Charter. 121
Charts, Gantt. 128
Check
    Digits. 228
    -The-box. 99
Checksums. 251
China. 20
CIA exam. 1
    Nondisclosure policy. 2
    Syllabus. 2, 505
Circuit
    -Level gateway. 250
    Switching. 192
Classification of controls. 225
Clean/normalize data. 231
Client devices. 189
Closed-loop verification. 228
Closing processes. 125
Cloud computing. 187, 251
Cluster organizations. 82
Coalition tactics. 70
COBIT. 211, 225
    5. . . . . 211, 212, 214
    2019. 216
    Framework. 211
    Performance Management (CPM). 217
Coefficient of correlation. 332
Coercive power. 71
Cognitive element. 20
Cohesive groups. 54, 55
Cold site. 267
Collaboration. 92
Collecting requirements. 122
Commercial paper. 416

Commodity-backed bonds. 399
Common
    Costs. 437, 457
    Stock. 283, 400
        Valuation. 401
Communication. 25
    Offer. 135
    Processes. 122
    Testing. 270
Comparability. 281
Compatibility tests. 249
Compensating
    Balance. 373, 416
    Controls. 106
Competitive
    Forces. 17, 18
    Pricing. 101
    Scope. 13
    Strategies. 13
Competitor-centered firms. 19
Complacency, management. 41
Completeness. 228
    Checks. 228
Compliance risks. 264
Component assembly. 22
Comprehensive income. 286
Computer
    -Aided
        Design (CAD). 383
        Manufacturing (CAM). 383
        Software engineering (CASE). 171
    -Integrated manufacturing (CIM). 383
    Tampering. 259
    Viruses. 250
Conformance costs. 57
Conformist. 80
Conformity. 55
Consideration. 134, 136
Consignment. 104, 300
Consolidated
    Financial statements. 342
    Procedures. 342
Constant
    Gross-margin percentage NRV method. 492
    Growth model. 401
Consultation. 70
Contingencies. 319
Contingency
    Planning. 265
    Theory of leadership. 75
Contingent
    Asset. 319
    Liability. 319
Continuing professional
    Education. 3
Continuous
    Budget (rolling). 447
    Process production. 94
Contract. 134
    Executory and executed. 138
    Express and implied. 138
    Law. 134
    Liability. 291, 308
    Oral. 137
    Unilateral and bilateral. 138
    Valid, unenforceable, voidable, void. 139

Contributed capital. 344
Contribution margin. 450, 484
Control
    EUC. 171, 172
    Framework. 209
    Inventory. 106
    Malicious software. 256
    Objectives for Information and
        Related Technology (COBIT). . . . 211, 212, 225
    Of rewards. 71
    Point. 121
    Quality. 381
Controllability. 457
Controlled disposal of documents. 249
Controls. 108, 188
    Corrective. 219
    Detective. 219
    Preventive. 218
Convenience goods. 105
Conversion
    Cost. 436, 478
    Cutover. 167
    Phased. 167
    Pilot. 167
Convertibility. 402
Convertible bonds. 399
Cookies. 187
Copyright software. 196
Core competencies. 13
Corporate-level strategy. 152
Corporations
    Foreign. 421
    Income tax. 419
    Multinational. 420
Corrective controls. 170, 219
COSO. 210
    Framework. 210

Cost. 435
    Avoidable. 487
    Behavior. 471
    -Benefit analysis. 454
    Center. 456, 457
    Conversion. 436, 478
    Current (replacement). 282
    Drivers. 435
    Fixed. 449
    Focus. 15
    Historical. 282
    Incremental. 488
    Joint (common). 490
    Leadership. 14
    Objects. 435, 476
    Of
        Capital. 404
        Goods sold. 384, 444
            Manufacturer. 385
            Retailer. 384
        Long-term debt. 404
        Preferred stock. 404
        Retained earnings. 405
    -Oriented pricing. 101
    -Plus
        -Award-fee. 137
        -Fixed fee. 137
        Price. 422
        Pricing. 101
    Pools. 437, 474, 476
    Processes. 122
    Standards. 439
    Strategy. 12
    Synergy. 12
    Variable. 449
    -Volume-profit (CVP). 449, 452
Costing
    Absorption. 483
    Activity-based (ABC). 471
    Job-order. 482
    Variable. 483
Costs
    Carrying. 378
    Currently attainable (practical) standards. 440
    Ideal (theoretical) standards. 440
    Joint (common). 457
    Manufacturing. 436
    Ordering. 378
    Resource. 475
    Underwriting. 401
Counteroffer. 135
Country club management. 74
Covering the enterprise end-to-end. 214
Crashing a project. 131
Creative leap. 56
Credit
    Default risk. 332
    Terms. 377
Crisis
    Management. 268
    Planning. 11
    Preparation. 11
    Prevention. 11
Critical
    Path method (CPM). 130, 131
    Success factors (CSFs). 58

Cross-
    Functional team. 90
    Subsidization. 471
Cultural
    Change. 133
    Intelligence (CQ). 25
Cultures, organizational. 51
Currency, functional. 337
Current
    Assets. 284, 346, 371
    Liabilities. 284, 305, 347, 371
    Ratio. 348
Currently attainable (practical) standards. 440
Custody of assets. 106
Customer
    -Centered firms. 19
    Relationship management (CRM). 153
    Service. 59
Cutover conversion. 167
Cybersecurity. 246
Cyphertext. 252

Data
    Analytics. 230
        Methods. 231
    Cleansing. 162
    Command interpreter languages. 161
    Control language. 161
    -Definition language. 161
    Dictionary. 161
    Encryption Standard (DES). 254
    Governance. 152
    Integrity. 247
    Item. 150
    Management. 234
    Manipulation language. 155
    Mart. 162
    Mining. 162, 234
    Security. 264
    Storage. 251
    Type. 230
    Warehouse. 162
Database. 154, 155
    Administrator (DBA). 161, 182, 251
    Distributed. 159
    Hypermedia. 162
    Management system (DBMS). 154, 251
    Mapping facility. 161
    Non-relational. 160
    Object-oriented. 161
    View. 155
Days' sales
    In
        Inventory. 351
        Receivables. 350
    Outstanding. 350
        In receivables. 377
De
    Facto standards. 247
    Jure standards. 247
Deadly embrace. 160
Deadweight loss. 419
Debentures. 399
Debit-credit. 293

Debt
    Financing. 397
    Securities. 313
Decentralization. 88, 456
    Of information processing. 185
Decision-making, group-aided. 55
Decisions
    Make-or-buy. 489
    Sell-or-process. 490
Deep-discount bonds. 399
Default risk. 376
Deferrals. 291
Deferred revenue. 291
Defining scope. 122
Delegation. 83
Deliverable. 120
Delivery strategy. 12
Demand-oriented pricing. 101
Democratic leadership. 72
Denial of service (DoS). 255, 259
Departmentation. 89
Deposits. 308
Depreciable base. 302
Depreciation methods. 302
Derivatives. 333
Descriptive analysis. 231
Desk check. 270
Detection. 261
Detective controls. 170, 219
Determining the budget. 123
Developing a schedule. 123
Development. 304
Device authorization table. 249
Diagnostic analysis. 231
Dialogue approach. 228
Differentiation. 13, 14
Digital certificate. 253
Direct
    -Access storage device. 155
    Costs. 437
    Financing lease. 318
    Investment. 22
    Labor. 436, 440
        Budget. 443
    Materials. 436, 440
        Budget. 443
    Method. 287
    Requests. 70
    Taxes. 419
Directive style. 77
Disaster recovery. 265
    Plan (DRP). 266
Discontinued operation. 285
Discount trade. 414
Discounted loans. 415
Disinvestment decisions. 494
Dissatisfiers. 46
Distributed
    Network. 191
    Processing. 185
Distribution channel. 103
Distributions to owners (dividends paid). 286
Diversification. 332
Divest strategy. 17

Dividend
   Payout ratio. 360
   Yield ratio. 360
Division of labor. 40
Divisional structure. 81
Document disposal, controlled. 249
Dogs. 16
Domain names. 187
Double-entry convention. 293
Downsizing. 41
Draft. 374
Dual logging. 156, 251
Dumb terminals. 184
DuPont model. 357
Duties, segregation of. 226
Dynamic
   Host configuration protocol (DHCP). 193
   Testing. 166

Earned revenue. 281
Earnings
   Coverage. 355
   Per share (EPS). 358
Economic
   Integration. 26
   Order quantity (EOQ). 379
   Profit. 413
   Value added (EVA). 413
Economists, supply-side. 420
Edisonian approach. 56
Edit routine. 228
Effective
   Follower. 80
   Rate. 415
   Tax rate. 419
Effectiveness. 40
Efficiency. 40
   Internal. 10
Efficient markets hypothesis. 333
Electronic
   Data interchange (EDI). 151, 382
   Funds transfer (EFT). 151
   Software distribution (ESD). 196
   Systems Assurance and Control (eSAC). 210
Eligibility extension. 3
Emotional intelligence. 70
Employee. 95
   Appraisals. 99
   -Centered. 73
   Empowerment. 71
   Evaluation. 98
   Selection. 96
Enabling a holistic approach. 215
Encryption. 249, 252, 264
End
   -To-end testing. 270
   User. 183
      Computing (EUC). 171
Enterprise
   Environmental factors (EEFs). 126
   Resource planning (ERP). 198
Entry barriers. 18
Environment. 43

Environmental
   Controls. 248
   Management system (EMS). 221
   Quality. 221
   (State) uncertainty. 43
EOQ model. 379
Equity. 283
   Method. 340
   Theory. 44
Equivalent units of production (EUP). 480
ERG theory. 46
ERP. 198
   Software. 199
   System. 198, 199
Error listings. 229
Esteem. 45
Estimated
   Net realizable value (NRV) method. 492
   Useful life. 302
Estimating
   Activity
      Durations. 123
      Resources. 123
   Costs. 123
Ethernet. 192
Ethnocentric. 21, 24
EUP. 480
   FIFO. 480
   Weighted average. 480
European Union (EU). 26
Evaluation, employee. 98
Events. 130
Exchange
   Rate. 337
   Risk. 332
   Tactics. 70
Excise tax. 418
Executed contracts. 138
Executing processes. 124
Executive management level. 225
Executory contracts. 138
Exercise price. 334
Expansion. 22
Expectancy. 48
   Theory. 48
Expectations, society. 40
Expected duration. 131
Expenses. 285
   Accrued. 306
   Administrative. 436
Expert power. 71
Exporting. 22
Express contracts. 138
External
   Effectiveness. 10
   Failure costs. 57
   Stakeholders. 121
Extinction. 49
Extranet. 187
Extrinsic
   Motivation. 45
   Rewards. 44

Facilitating intermediaries. 104

Index

Facility-sustaining activities. 474
Factoring. 377, 417
Fair value. 340
    Option. 340
Faithful representation. 281
Fault-tolerant computer systems. 268
Fiedler, Fred E. 75
Field. 150, 158
    (Edit)/format checks. 228
FIFO method. 387, 480, 482
File. 151, 158
    Attributes. 249
Finance lease. 318
Financial
    Budget. 441
    Leverage. 356
    Performance. 58
    Position, statement of. 283
    Reporting, general-purpose. 280
    Statement
        Notes to. 289
        Relationships. 289
    Statements. 283, 293
        Common-size. 360
    Totals. 227
Financing
    Long-term. 372, 398
    Secured. 417
    Short-term. 372, 414
Firewall. 248, 250
Firm-fixed-price. 137
Firms
    Competitor-centered. 19
    Customer-centered. 19
    Market-centered. 19
    Product-centered. 19
First-in, first-out (FIFO) method. 387, 480, 482
Five competitive forces. 17, 18
Fixed
    Cost. 468
    Overhead. 444
Flat
    Files. 156
    Organizational structures. 84
Flexibility strategy. 12
Flexible budgeting. 448
Float. 230
Flowchart, purchases-payables-cash disbursements 106
FOB, destination/shipping point. 300
Focus area. 218
Focused differentiation. 15
Follower styles. 80
Foreign
    Affiliate. 23
    Corporations. 421
    Currency transactions. 337
    Markets. 21
Formal groups. 52
Formalization. 93
Forward
    Contracts. 335
    Placement. 105
Fragmentation. 159
Frame relay. 193
Free association. 56
Front-office functions. 199

Functional
    Authority. 87
    -Level strategy. 152
Future
    Orientation. 25
    Value (FV) of an amount. 310
Futures contracts. 335
Future value (FV) of annuities. 311

Gains. 285
Gantt charts. 128
Gateway. 184, 250
Geert Hofstede. 24
Gender differentiation. 25
General
    Controls. 226
    Ledger. 106
Generic competitive strategies. 17
Geocentric. 21
Global
    Branding. 28
    Business development. 22
    Environment. 23
    Firms. 27
    Integration. 27
    Marketing organization, strategies. 26
    Mindset. 20
    Strategy. 27
    Technology Audit Guide (GTAG). 218
Globalization. 19
Glocal strategy. 27
Goal
    Congruence. 457
    -Setting theory. 48
Goodwill. 341
Governance. 120
Grapevine. 53
Graphical user interface. 189
Gray-box testing. 166
GRC systems. 153
Greenfield venture. 23
Gross
    Method payables. 305
    Profit. 483
        Margin. 388
Group
    Aided decision. 55
    Attractiveness. 54
    Cohesiveness. 54, 55
    Commitment. 54
    Decision making. 55
    Dynamics. 52
    Formal. 52
    Informal. 53
Groupshift. 56
Groupthink. 55
Growth-share matrix. 15

Hacking. 259
Hadoop. 235
Hard power. 71
Hardware controls. 227
Harvest strategy. 16

Hash totals.	227
Header signature.	260
Hedging.	336
Help desks.	183
Herzberg, Frederick.	46
Hierarchical structure.	157

Hierarchy of
Authority.	40
Needs, Maslow's.	45

High-
Context culture.	25
Low method.	470
Hoaxes.	256
Hold strategy.	16
Holder.	333

Horizontal
Common-size analysis.	360
Coordination.	92
Distribution systems.	104
Host.	257
IDS.	260
Hot site.	267
Hotspot.	194
Hourglass organizations.	82
HTML.	186
HTTP.	186
HTTPS (Hypertext Transfer Protocol Secure).	253

Human
Relations.	43
Resources.	43, 95
Humane orientation.	25
Humanistic perspective.	43
Hygiene factors.	46
Hypermedia database.	162

Hypertext
Markup language (HTML).	186
Transfer protocol (HTTP).	186
Secure (HTTPS).	253

ID numbers.	248
Ideal (theoretical) standards.	440
Identifying risks.	123
Idle cash.	375
Implied contracts.	138
Impoverished management.	74
Impression management.	51
In-memory analytics.	235
Incidence of taxation.	419

Income
Bonds.	399
Equation.	285
Statement.	285
Approach.	298

Tax
Corporate.	419
Optimal.	420
Worldwide.	421

Incremental
Budgeting.	447
Costs.	488
India.	20

Indirect
Costs.	437
Export strategy.	22
Labor.	436
Materials.	436
Method.	288
Taxes.	419
Individualism-collectivism.	24
Industry.	17
Inflation risk.	332
Influence.	70

Informal
Authority.	86
Organization.	53

Information
Criteria.	212
Integrity.	262
Resources management (IRM).	197
Security.	246
Officers.	183
Technology (IT).	223
Operations.	182
Infrastructure-as-a-service.	187
Ingratiating tactics.	70
Initiating processes.	122
Inspirational appeals.	70
Intangible assets.	301
Amortization.	304
Definition.	303
Integer.	230
Integrated systems.	197

Integration
Global.	27
Processes.	122
Testing.	166
Integrity controls.	229
Interactive leadership.	79
Interest.	309
Intermediaries.	104

Internal
Business processes.	59
Control system.	210
Efficiency.	10
Failure costs.	57
Rate of return (IRR).	411
Stakeholders.	121

International
Organization for Standardization (ISO).	220
Strategy.	27
Tax considerations.	420
Internationalization process.	21
Internet.	184, 193
Backbones.	184
Of things (IoT).	263
Relay chat.	259
Security.	250
Service providers (ISPs).	184
Telephony.	195
Interviewing.	96
Intraentity transactions.	343
Intranet.	187

Intrinsic
Motivation.	45
Rewards.	44
Value.	334

Intrusion
    Detection System (IDS). 260
    Responses. 261
Inventory. 299
    Accounting system
        Periodic. 387
        Perpetual. 387
    Control. 106, 378
    Conversion period. 351
    Cost. 299
        Valuation methods. 385
    Ending. 384
    Errors. 388
    Estimation. 388
    Levels. 380
    Management. 378
    Periodic. 384, 386
    Perpetual. 384
    Placement. 105
    Systems. 384
    Turnover. 351
Investment
    Center. 456, 457
    Direct. 22
    In equity securities. 340
    Risk. 332
    Securities. 330
    Tax credits. 419
IP addressing. 193
IRR. 411
ISO
    9000. 220
    10012:2003. 222
    14000. 221
    14050:2009. 222
    14063:2006. 222
    19011:2018. 221
    Certification. 220
    QMS. 220
IT
    Business assurance objectives. 254
    Environment walk-through. 270
    Risk. 213
    Steering committee. 164, 225

JIT systems. 381
Job
    Analysis. 95
    -Centered leaders. 73
    Characteristics model. 50
    Content. 46
    Descriptions. 95
    Design. 50
    Enlargement. 50
    Enrichment. 50
    Specifications. 95
Joining. 158
Joint
    (Common) costs. 490
    Products, allocation of. 491
    Ventures. 22
Journal entries. 294

Just-in-
    Case method. 380
    Time (JIT). 380

Kaizen. 447
Key
    Integrity. 229
    Performance indicators (KPI). 230
Keypad devices. 248
Killer application. 164
Knowledge-based detection. 261

Labor, division of. 40
Laffer curve. 420
Lagging indicators. 58
Laissez-faire leadership. 72
LAN. 190
Last-in, first-out (LIFO) method. 387
Lateral thinking. 56
Leader
    Behavior. 72
    Charismatic. 78
    -Member relations. 75
    Traits. 70
    Transactional. 78
    Transformational. 78
Leadership. 69
    Authentic. 79
    Grid. 74
    Interactive. 79
    Path-goal. 77
    Servant. 79
    Situational. 76
        Theories. 75
Leading indicators. 58
Learning and growth. 59
Lease. 316
    Direct financing. 318
    Finance. 316, 318
    Operating. 318
    Sales-type. 316, 318
Ledger, general. 293, 294
Legal
    Benefit. 136
    Detriment. 136
    Sufficiency. 136
Legality. 136
Legitimate power. 71
Lessee. 318
Lessor. 318
Leverage. 355
Liabilities. 283, 306
    Contract. 308
    Current. 305
Licensing. 22
LIFO method. 387
Limit (reasonableness) and range checks. 228
Line
    And staff. 85
    Of credit. 414
Linux. 188
Liquidity. 346
    Risk. 332

Loading, vertical. 50
Loan. 414
Local area network (LAN). 190
Lockbox system. 374
Logic bomb. 255
Logical
    Data model. 155
    Log-on procedures. 249
    Security controls. 248
Long
    Position. 336
    -Term
        Financing. 372, 398
        Orientation. 25
Loss
    Contingency. 319
    Deadweight. 419
Losses. 285
Low-context culture. 25

Machine bureaucracy. 81
Magazine subscriptions. 308
Mainframe. 184
Make-or-buy decisions. 489
Malicious software (malware). 255
Malware. 255
Man-in-the-middle attack. 258
Management. 69
    Authority-compliance. 74
    By
        Means (MBM). 11
        Objectives (MBO). 11, 99
    Change. 133
    Complacency. 41
    Functions of. 42
    Human resources. 95
    Impoverished. 74
    Impression. 51
    Information System (MIS). 197
    Inventory. 378
    Middle-of-the-road. 74
    Release. 227
    Scientific school. 41
    Span of. 84
    Synergy. 12
    System, measurement. 222
    Team. 74
    Trails. 229
Management's responsibility. 105
Manager motivation. 456
Managerial effort. 422
Manufacturing
    Cycle time. 381
    Overhead. 436
        Budget. 442
    Philosophy. 381
    Resource planning (MRP-II). 383
Margin
    Of safety. 452
    Requirements. 335
Marginal
    Cost of capital. 407
    Tax rate. 419
Mark to market. 335

Market
    -Based instruments. 416
    -Centered firms. 19
    Definition
        Strategic. 9
        Target. 9
    Global. 22
    Pricing. 422
    Risk. 332
        Premium. 331
    Share. 16
    Synergy. 12
Marketing
    Communications. 28
    Global organization, strategies. 26
    Infrastructure. 28
Masculinity versus femininity. 24
Maslow's hierarchy of needs. 45
Mass production. 94
Master
    (Comprehensive) budget. 441
    Production schedule (MPS). 383
Materials
    Purchases. 442
    Requirements planning (MRP). 382
Matrix
    Boss. 90
    Structure. 90
Maturity
    Date. 313
    Matching. 372
    Model. 212
    Risk. 332
Maximal flow algorithm. 132
Measurement. 282
    Attributes. 282
    Management system (MMS). 222
    Principle. 341
Mechanistic structure. 92
Meeting stakeholder needs. 214
Mentoring. 78
Merchant middlemen. 104
Mesh network. 194
Method
    Acquisition. 341
    Average. 386
    Depreciation. 302
    FIFO (First-in, first-out). 387, 480, 482
    Gross profit. 388
    Inventory cost valuation. 385
    LIFO (Last-in, first-out). 387
    Moving-average. 386
    Specific identification. 385
    Units-of-production. 302
    Weighted-average. 386
Metropolitan area network (MAN). 191
Middle-of-the-road management. 74
Minimal spanning tree algorithm. 132
Minimum transfer price. 424
Mintzberg, Henry. 81
Mission statement. 9
Mixed (semivariable) costs. 469
Monitoring and controlling processes. 125
Mortgage bonds. 399
Motivation. 44, 45, 77
Multichannel system. 104

Multidivisional structure. 89
Multilocal or multidomestic strategy. 27
Multinational
   Corporations. 20, 420, 421
   Strategy. 26
Mutual assent. 134

Needs, Maslow's hierarchy of. 45
Negative political behaviors. 51
Negotiated pricing. 422
Net
   Income. 286, 288
   Method payables. 305
   Present value (NPV). 410, 411
   Realizable value (NRV). 297
Network. 184
   Administrator. 183
   Analysis. 231
   Distributed. 191
   Equipment. 189
   IDS. 260
   Infrastructure. 260
   Interface card (NIC). 189
   Local area. 190
   Models. 132
   Of relationships. 71
   Organizations. 82
   Peer-to-peer. 190
   Structure. 157
   Technicians. 183
   Topology. 194
   Types of. 190
   Virtual. 91
Networks
   Client-server. 190
   Switched. 192
   Wireless. 194
Nonaccrual. 307
Nonconformance costs. 57
Noncontrolling interest. 341
Nonmanufacturing costs. 436
Nonprice competition. 101
Non-relational database. 160
Normalization. 158
Norms. 54
   Enforcement. 54
   Functions. 54
North American Free Trade Agreement (NAFTA). . . 26

Object-oriented database. 161
Obligation, mutuality. 136
Offeree. 135
Ohio State University leadership model. 72
Online
   Analytical processing (OLAP). 162
   Input controls. 228

Operating
   Activities. 287
   Budget. 441
   Cycle. 352
   Income. 483
   Lease. 318
   Leverage. 355
   System. 188
Operational planning and execution. 11
Operations
   Parallel. 167
   Risk. 332
   Strategies. 12
Operators. 183
Optimal
   Capital structure. 406
   Income tax rate. 420
   Level of cash. 373
Option valuing. 334
Options. 333
Oral contract. 137
Ordering costs. 378
Organic
   Organizations. 87
   Structure. 93
Organization-wide network security policy. 247
Organizational
   Charts. 41
   Culture. 51
   Decline. 41
   Development (OD). 43, 134
   Needs assessment. 163
   Planning. 11
   Politics. 51, 52
   Process assets (OPAs). 126
   Structures. 40
   Theory. 40
Organizations
   Adaptive. 43
   Cluster. 82
   Hourglass. 82
   Informal. 53
   Network. 82
   Organic. 87
   Service-oriented. 94
   Virtual. 82
Organizing
   Global marketing. 26
   Process. 40
Orientation. 270
Other manufacturing costs. 436
Output controls. 229
Outsourcing
   Advantages. 100
   Business process. 99
   Disadvantages. 100

Packet
   Filtering system. 250
   Switching. 192
PAN. 194
Par value. 344, 402
Parallel operation. 167
Parent. 340

528 Index

Participation. 402
Participative. 72
   Style. 77
Partitioning. 159
Partnership
   Formation. 345
   Income or loss. 345
   Liquidation. 346
Passive follower. 80
Passwords. 248
   Attacks. 258
   Optimal. 258
Path-goal leadership theory. 77
Payable through draft (PTD). 374
Payables, turnover in days. 353
Payback. 412
   Method. 412
   Period. 412
Payment float. 374
Peanut-butter costing. 471
Pearson VUE. 1
Peer-to-peer network. 190
Penetration pricing. 101
Pension
   Asset. 315
   Liability. 315
   Plan. 314
      Defined
         Benefit. 314
         Contribution. 314
      Projected benefit obligation. 315
People-centered human resource strategy. 95
Percentage-of
   Receivables. 297
   Sales. 297
Performance
   Appraisal, 360°. 99
   Measurement. 153, 213
   Measures. 456
   Orientation. 25
Period costs. 436
Permanent team. 91
Perpetual inventory accounting system. 386
Personal
   Area network. 194
   Communications services (PCS). 195
   Effort. 71
PERT network. 130
Phase. 120
Phased conversion. 167
Phishing. 258
Physical
   Access controls. 248
   Security risks. 264
Physiological needs. 45
Pilot conversion. 167
Plaintext. 252

Planning. 9
   Communication management. 123
   Cost management. 123
   Processes. 122
   Procurement management. 123
   Quality management. 123
   Resource management. 123
   Risk
      Management. 123
      Responses. 123
   Schedule management. 123
   Scope. 122
   Stakeholder engagement. 123
Platform-as-a-service. 187
Pledging. 377
Pointer. 157
Political
   Behaviors. 51
   Risk. 24, 332
   Tactics. 52
Polycentric. 21
Port. 260
Porter, Michael E. 13, 17
   Five competitive forces. 17, 18
Portfolio. 120
   Return. 332
   Risk. 332
Positive
   Political behaviors. 51
   Reinforcement. 49
Power. 70, 71
   Bargaining. 18
   Coercive. 71
   Distance. 24
   Expert. 71
   Failures. 267
   Hard. 71
   Legitimate. 71
   Position. 75
   Referent. 71
   Soft. 71
PPE. 301
   Depreciation. 302
   Disposal. 303
   Initial measurement. 301
   Measurement subsequent to initial recognition. . 301
   Subsequent expenditures. 301
Pragmatic survivor. 80
Predictive
   Analysis. 231
   Analytics. 235
Preferred stock. 283, 344, 402
Preformatting. 228
Prepaid expense. 291
Prescriptive analysis. 231
Present value. 309
   Of
      An amount. 309
      Annuities. 310
Pressure tactics. 70
Prevention costs. 57
Preventive controls. 170, 218
Price
   -Earnings (P/E) ratio. 359
   Elasticity of demand. 101

Pricing. 101
   Cost
      -Oriented. 101
      -Plus. 101
   Demand-oriented. 101
   Objectives. 101
   Value-based. 101
Prime costs. 436
Principle
   Full-disclosure. 281
   Historical cost. 281
   Matching. 282
   Revenue recognition. 281
Privacy. 262
   Risks. 264
Private
   Branch exchange (PBX). 191
   Information systems. 172
   -Key encryption. 254
Privileged software. 189
Pro forma income statement. 445
Process. 119
   Costing. 477
Processing
   Batch. 224
   Controls. 228
   Real-time. 224
Procurement processes. 122
Product
   -Centered firms. 19
   Change. 133
   -Cost cross-subsidization. 471
   Costs. 436
   Realization. 221
   -Sustaining activities. 474
Production
   Budgets. 442
   Continuous process. 94
   Mass. 94
   Single-unit. 94
   Small-batch. 94
Productivity. 40
Professional bureaucracy. 81
Profit center. 456, 457
Profitability
   Gross profit margin. 358
   Ratios. 358
Program. 120
   Development. 171
   Evaluation and review technique (PERT). 129
Programmers. 182
Progressive tax-rate structures. 418
Project. 119
   Budget. 446
   Documents. 127
   Life cycle. 121
   Management. 119
      Plan. 122, 127
      Software. 128
      Triangle. 128
   Manager. 92, 121
Projecting. 158
Property, plant, and equipment (PPE). 301
Proportional tax-rate structures. 418
Protocol. 192
Prototyping. 171

Proxy server. 250
Psychic proximity. 21
Psychological
   Element. 20
   States. 50
Public
   Key
      Encryption. 253
         Infrastructure. 253
   -Switched networks. 191
Pull system. 381
Punishment. 49
Purchasing agent. 106
Push system. 382
Put option. 333

Qualitative
   Characteristics. 281
   Risk analysis. 123
Quality
   Control. 381
   Environmental. 221
   Management system (QMS). 220
   Processes. 122
   Strategy. 12
Quantitative risk analysis. 123
Question marks. 16
Quick (acid-test) ratio. 348

Radio-frequency identification (RFID). 194
Ransomware. 255
Rate
   Of return. 330
   Tax. 418
Ratio
   Accounts receivable turnover. 350
   Activity. 349
   Current. 348
   Debt to total assets. 354
   Inventory. 351
   Quick (acid-test). 348
   Times interest earned. 355
   Total debt to equity capital. 355
Rational persuasion. 70
Realizable revenue. 281
Realized revenue. 281
Real-time processing. 224
Receivables. 375
   Factoring. 377, 417
   Formulas. 350, 377
   Pledging. 377, 417
Receiving report. 106
Record. 150, 158
   Counts. 227, 229
Recovery
   Center. 267
   Point objective. 269
   Time objective. 269
Redundant array of inexpensive discs (RAID). . . . 268
Referent power. 71
Referential integrity. 159
Registered bonds. 399
Regression (scattergraph) method. 470

Regressive tax-rate structures. 418
Reinforcement. 49
Reinvestment rate. 411
Rejection. 135
Relational
    Coordination. 92
    Data structure. 159
    Structure. 158
Relationship-motivated style. 75
Relevance. 281
Relevant
    Cash flows. 408
    Data. 231
    Range. 471
    Revenues and costs. 487
Remote wipe. 264
Replication. 159
Required rate of return. 401
Research and development. 304
Residual income. 330
Resistance to change. 133
Resource
    Cost driver. 473
    Costs. 475
    Drivers. 475
    Management. 153, 213
    Processes. 122
Responsibility. 83
    Centers. 456
Retained
    Dividends. 345
    Earnings. 283, 345
Return. 330
    On
        Assets (ROA). 356
        Equity (ROE). 357
        Investment (ROI). 356
    Rate of. 330
Revenue
    Bonds. 399
    Center. 456, 457
    Cycle. 282
Revenues. 285
Revocation. 135
Right-of-use asset. 318
Ring network. 194
Risk. 330
    And return. 330
    Assessment. 172, 266
    Diversifiable. 332
    Financial. 332
    -Free rate. 331
    Interest rate. 332
    Investment. 332
    Management. 153, 213
        Processes. 122
    Systematic. 332
    Undiversifiable. 332
    Unsystematic. 332
Risks and controls. 170
Rivalry among established firms. 18
Role
    Conflict. 54
    Models. 54
    Playing. 54
Routers. 193

Row. 158
RSA. 253
Run-to-run control totals. 229

Safe computing. 246
Safety
    Needs. 45
    Stock. 378
Sales-type lease. 318
Sales value at split-off method. 491
Salvage value. 302
Satisfiers. 46
Scalar chain. 83
Scheduling processes. 122
Schema. 161
Scientific
    Method. 56
    School of management. 41
Scope processes. 122
SDLC. 165
Sector. 17
Securitization. 417
Security
    Awareness. 254
    Card. 248
    Internet. 250
    Personnel. 249
    Problems. 156
    Risk premium. 331
    System. 247
Segment, market. 17
Segregation of
    Duties. 170, 182, 226
    Functions. 223
Selecting. 158
Self-
    Actualization. 45
    Assessment. 97
Selling (marketing) costs. 436
Semi-structured data. 232
Separating governance from management. 215
Sequence checks. 228, 229
Serial bond. 399
Servant leadership. 79
Server. 184, 185, 190, 260
    File. 185
    Web. 185
Service
    -Oriented organizations. 94
    Strategy. 12
Shareware. 196
Sheep dip. 257
Short
    Position. 336
    -Term orientation. 25
Shortest-route algorithm. 132
Signature. 260
Simple
    Interest loan. 414
    Structure. 81
Single-unit production. 94
Situational theories. 75
Skimming. 101
Slack time. 130

Index

Small-batch production... 94
Smart machines... 263
SmartAdapt... 4
Snapshot... 159
Sniffing... 258
Social
    Capital... 52
    Element... 20
    Learning theory... 49
Society's expectations... 40
Soft power... 71
Software
    -As-a-service... 187
    Licensing agreement... 196
    Piracy... 196, 259
Solvency... 354
Span of management... 84
Special orders... 488
Split-off point... 490
Spoilage... 482
Sponsor... 120
Spontaneous financing... 372
Spoofing... 258
SSL (Secure Sockets Layer)... 253
Stakeholder processes... 122
Stakeholders... 119, 121
Standard costs... 439, 448
Star network... 194
Stars... 16
Stateful inspection... 250
Statement of
    Cash flows... 287
    Changes in equity... 286
    Comprehensive income... 286
Static testing... 166
Stock
    Authorized... 400
    Common... 344
    Dividends... 345
    Issued... 400
    Outstanding... 400
    Preferred... 344
    Safety... 378
    Splits... 345
    Treasury... 344
Storage, data... 251
Stovepipe systems... 197
Straight-line (S-L) depreciation... 302
Strategic
    Alignment... 153, 213
    Business units (SBUs)... 17, 88, 456
    Controls... 10
    Drivers... 153
    Management... 9, 12
    Market definition... 9
    Pricing... 101
Strategies
    Competitive... 13
        Generic... 17
    Global... 27
    Glocal... 27
    Human resource... 95
    Multinational... 26
    Operations... 12

Strategy... 9
    Business-level... 152
    Corporate-level... 152
    Focus... 15
    Functional-level... 152
    International... 27
    Penetration pricing... 101
    Regional... 27
    Skimming... 101
Stretch goals... 11
String... 230
    Signatures... 260
Structural
    Analysis... 17
    Change... 133
    Determinants... 92
Structure
    Matrix... 90
    Mechanistic... 92
    Multidivisional... 89
    Organic... 93
    Task... 75
    Team-based... 91
    Work breakdown... 123
Structured
    Data... 232
    Query language (SQL)... 233
Stuck in the middle... 17
Subordinated debentures... 399
Subschema... 161
Subsidiary... 340
Substitute... 76
Substitutes... 18
Suppliers bargaining power... 18
Supply
    Chain... 102, 199
    -Side economists... 420
Supportive style... 77
Switches... 192
SWOT analysis... 13
Syllabus, CIA exam... 2, 505
Synergy... 12
    Cost... 12
    Management... 12
    Technological... 12
System
    Access log... 249
    Administrator... 183
    Controls... 226
    Design, SDLC... 165
    Security... 247
    Testing... 166
    Theory... 88
Systematic risk... 332
Systems
    Analysts... 182
    Client-server... 190
    Control... 171
    Development life cycle... 165
    Private information... 172
    Software... 188

Tables... 158
Tabletop exercise... 270

Tactics pressure. 70
Tall organizational structures. 84
Target
    Income. 453
    Market. 9
    Rate of return. 101
Task
    Force. 92
    -Motivated style. 75
Tax
    Direct. 419
    Income, corporate. 419
    Indirect. 419
    International considerations. 420
    Rate structures. 418
    Value-added. 421
    Windfall profits. 419
Taxation
    Incidence. 419
    Methods. 418
Team. 90
    -Based structure. 91
    Cross-functional. 90
    Management. 74
    Permanent. 91
Technical support unit. 183
Technology. 93
Teleconferencing. 195
Term
    Bond. 399
    Loan. 414
Text
    Analysis. 231
    Mining. 235
The IIA's requirements. 3
Theories of organizing. 41
Theory
    Contingency. 75
    Situational. 75
    X. 47
    Y. 47
Thin clients. 189
Threat of substitutes. 18
Time
    -And-materials. 137
    -Cost-quality triangle. 128
    Manufacturing cycle. 381
    Premium. 334
    Value of money. 309
Timeliness. 281
TLS (Transport Layer Security). 253
Top
    -Down (authoritative) budgeting. 438
    Leader. 90
Total direct labor cost. 443
Trade discount. 414
Training. 97
    -Needs assessment. 97
Transaction
    Logs. 229
    Trails. 223
Transactional leader. 78
Transfer prices. 422, 424
Transferred-in costs. 480
Transformational leader. 78
Transition information. 3

Transmission Control Protocol/Internet Protocol
    (TCP/IP). 193
Transnational firms. 26
Treasury bonds. 417
Treaties. 420
Trial balance. 294
Trojan horse. 255, 257
Turnover
    Fixed assets. 353
    Total assets. 353
Two-
    Factor theory of motivation. 46
    Phase commit. 160

Uncertainty
    Avoidance. 25
    Environmental (state). 43
Underlying. 333
Understandability. 281
Underwriting costs. 401
Unenforceable contracts. 139
Uniform
    Processing of transactions. 223
    Resource locator (URL). 187
Unilateral contracts. 138
Unit-level activities. 474
Unit testing. 166
Unity of command. 83, 85
Unix. 188
Unstructured data. 232
Unsystematic risk. 332
Upward appeals. 70
User
    Account management. 250
    Authentication. 248
Utility programs. 189

Valid contracts. 139
Validation. 228
Validity checks. 228
Value
    -Added
        Networks (VANs). 191
        Tax (VAT). 421
    -Based pricing. 101
    Chain. 102
    Delivery. 153, 213
    Fair. 282
    Net realizable. 282
    Present. 282
Variable
    Costing. 483
    Costs. 468
    (Or floating) rate bonds. 399
    Overhead. 444
Variety. 233
    -Based value. 234
Velocity. 233
    -Based value. 234
Vendor assistance. 183
Ventures, multiple or joint. 22
Veracity. 233
    -Based value. 234

Verifiability. 281
Vertical
    Common-size analysis. 360
    Distribution systems. 104
Vertically loading. 50
Vicarious (observational) learning. 49
Videoconferencing. 195
Virtual
    Network. 91
    Organizations. 82
    Private networks (VPNs). 191
Viruses, computer. 250, 255, 267
Voice
    Communications channels. 195
    Mail. 195
    Output device. 195
    -Over IP (VoIP). 195
    Recognition. 195
Void contracts. 139
Voidable contracts. 139
Volume. 233
    -Based
        Systems. 473
        Value. 234

Warehouse
    Data. 162
    Receipt. 417
Warm site. 267
Warranties. 319
Webmaster. 182
Weighted-average
    Cost of capital (WACC). 405
    Method. 480, 482
Whiplash effect. 102
Whistleblowing. 51
White-box testing. 166
Wide area network (WAN). 191
Wi-Fi. 194
Willingness. 76
WiMax. 194
Windfall profits taxes. 419
Work
    Breakdown structure. 123
    -In-process. 477
    Specialization. 83
Working capital. 347, 371
    Policy. 372
    Ratio. 348
Workstations. 149
World
    Trade Organization. 26
    Wide Web (Web). 186
Worldwide income. 421
Worm. 255
Writer. 333

XBRL. 186
XML. 186

Yield. 398

Zero
    Balance
        Account (ZBA). 374
        Checks. 228
    -Based budgeting (ZBB). 447
    -Coupon bonds. 399
    Defects. 381

GLEIM® CIA REVIEW

GLEIM
L♡VES
STUDENTS

SAVE 20% WITH OUR STUDENT DISCOUNT!

800.874.5346 | gleim.com/**students**